D0178101

Books are to be returned on or before
the last date below.

423 CoR 0609963

15905

NOT TO BE
TAKEN AWAY

LIBREX

060963
YCFHE LIBRARY

The Oxford Children's Visual DICTIONARY

lily

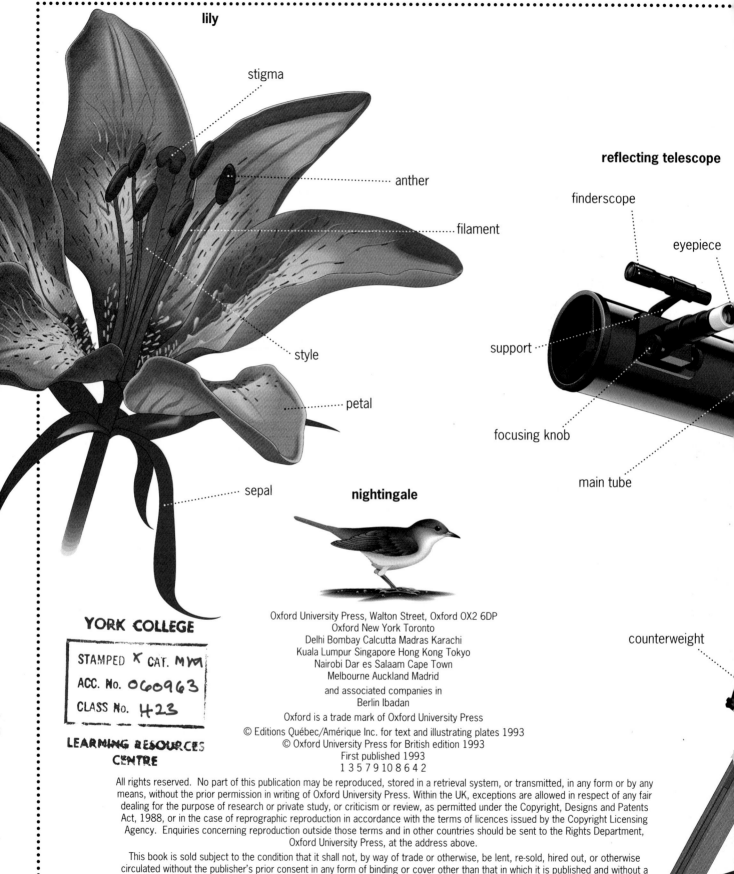

stigma
anther
filament
style
petal
sepal

reflecting telescope

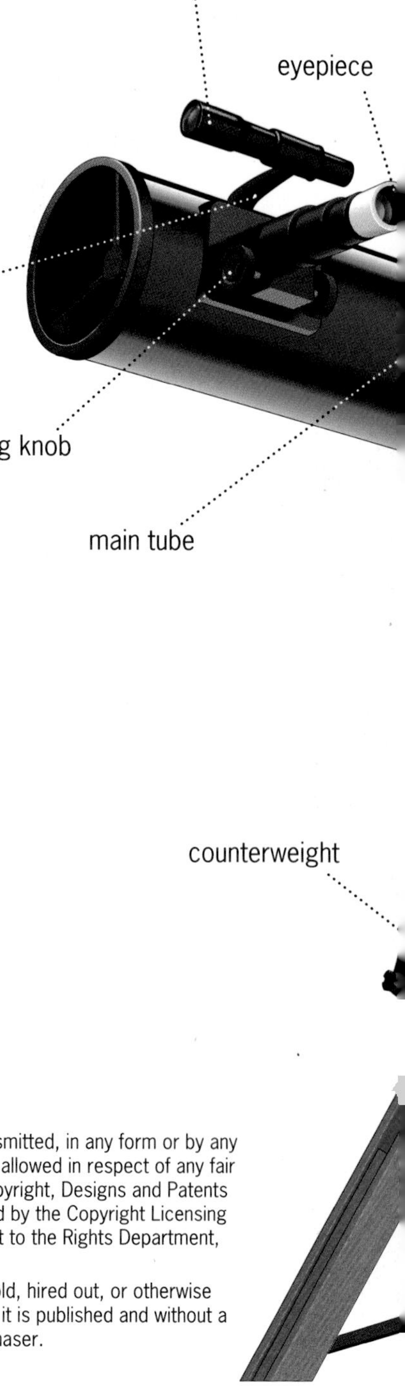
finderscope
eyepiece
support
focusing knob
main tube
counterweight

nightingale

YORK COLLEGE
STAMPED X CAT. MW
ACC. No. 060963
CLASS No. 423
LEARNING RESOURCES CENTRE

Oxford University Press, Walton Street, Oxford OX2 6DP
Oxford New York Toronto
Delhi Bombay Calcutta Madras Karachi
Kuala Lumpur Singapore Hong Kong Tokyo
Nairobi Dar es Salaam Cape Town
Melbourne Auckland Madrid
and associated companies in
Berlin Ibadan

Oxford is a trade mark of Oxford University Press

© Editions Québec/Amérique Inc. for text and illustrating plates 1993
© Oxford University Press for British edition 1993

First published 1993
1 3 5 7 9 10 8 6 4 2

All rights reserved. No part of this publication may be reproduced, stored in a retrieval system, or transmitted, in any form or by any means, without the prior permission in writing of Oxford University Press. Within the UK, exceptions are allowed in respect of any fair dealing for the purpose of research or private study, or criticism or review, as permitted under the Copyright, Designs and Patents Act, 1988, or in the case of reprographic reproduction in accordance with the terms of licences issued by the Copyright Licensing Agency. Enquiries concerning reproduction outside those terms and in other countries should be sent to the Rights Department, Oxford University Press, at the address above.

This book is sold subject to the condition that it shall not, by way of trade or otherwise, be lent, re-sold, hired out, or otherwise circulated without the publisher's prior consent in any form of binding or cover other than that in which it is published and without a similar condition including this condition being imposed on the subsequent purchaser.

British Library Cataloguing in Publication Data
Data available

ISBN 019 910302 X (net hardback)

Printed in Canada

The Oxford Children's Visual DICTIONARY

Authors
Jean-Claude Corbeil
Ariane Archambault

Director of Computer Graphics
François Fortin

Art Directors
Jean-Louis Martin
François Fortin

Graphic Designer
Anne Tremblay

Computer Graphics Designers
Marc Lalumière
Jean-Yves Ahern
Rielle Lévesque
Anne Tremblay

Jacques Perrault
Jocelyn Gardner
Christiane Beauregard
Michel Blais
Stéphane Roy
Alice Comtois
Benoît Bourdeau

Computer Programming
Yves Ferland

Data Capture
Serge D'Amico

Page Make-up
Lucie Mc Brearty
Pascal Goyette

Technical Support
Gilles Archambault

Production
Tony O'Riley

Anglicized Text
Alexandra Clayton

OXFORD UNIVERSITY PRESS

SKY

EARTH

VEGETABLE KINGDOM

FRUITS AND VEGETABLES

GARDENING

ANIMAL KINGDOM

HUMAN BODY

ARCHITECTURE

HOUSE

DO-IT-YOURSELF

CLOTHING

PERSONAL ARTICLES

COMMUNICATIONS

ROAD TRANSPORT

RAIL TRANSPORT

MARITIME TRANSPORT

AIR TRANSPORT

SPACE TRANSPORT

SCHOOL

MUSIC

TEAM GAMES

WATER SPORTS

WINTER SPORTS

ATHLETICS

CAMPING

INDOOR GAMES

MEASURING DEVICES

ENERGY

HEAVY MACHINERY

SYMBOLS

SOLAR SYSTEM

planets and moons

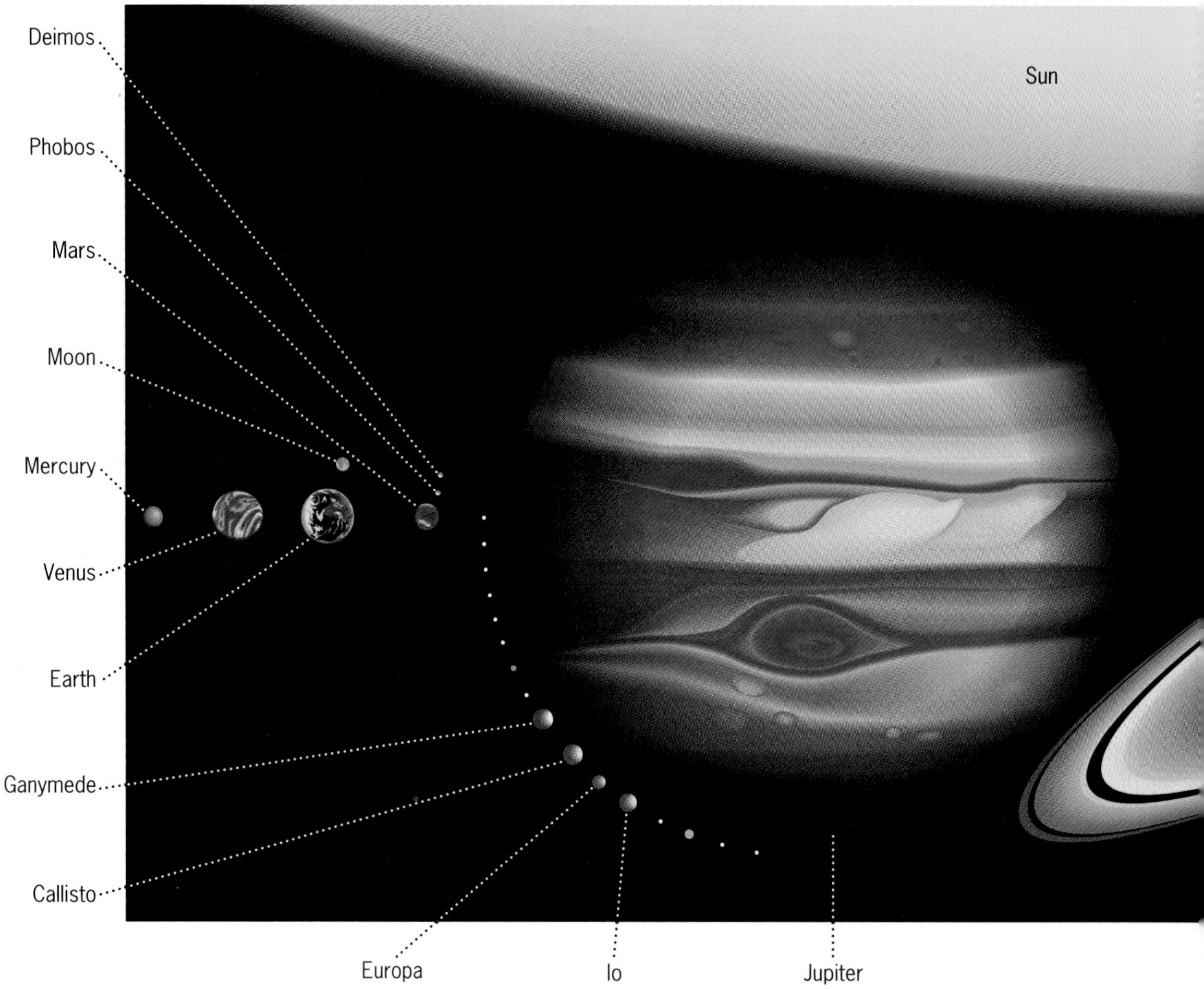
Deimos
Phobos
Mars
Moon
Mercury
Venus
Earth
Ganymede
Callisto
Sun
Europa
Io
Jupiter

orbits of the planets

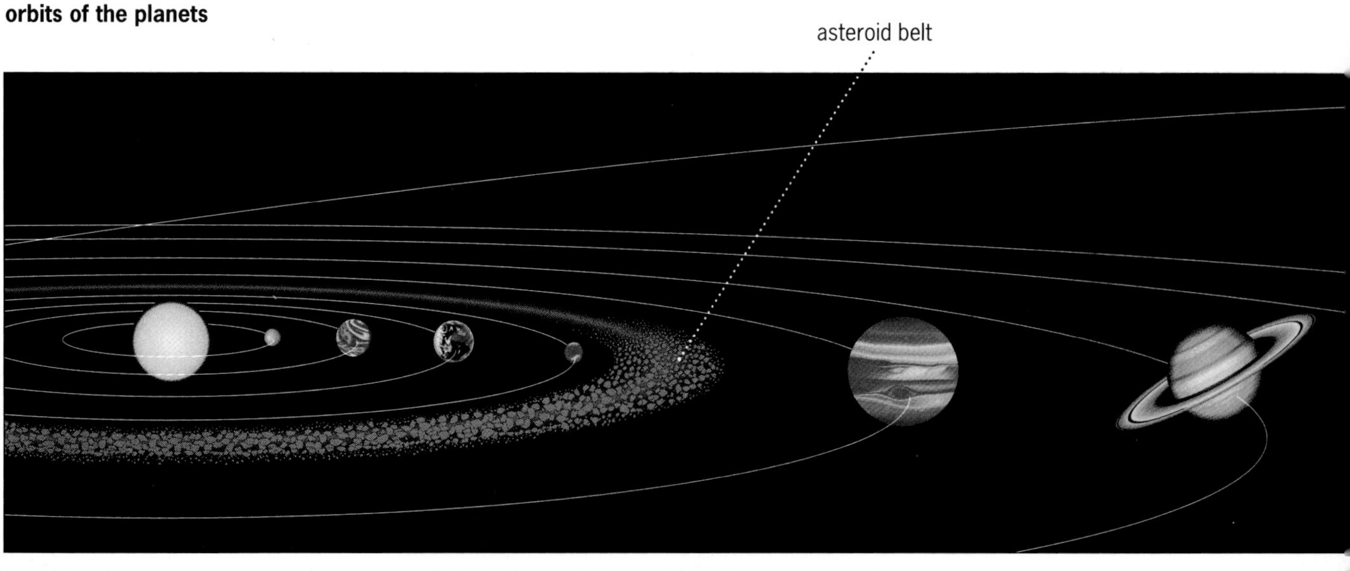
asteroid belt

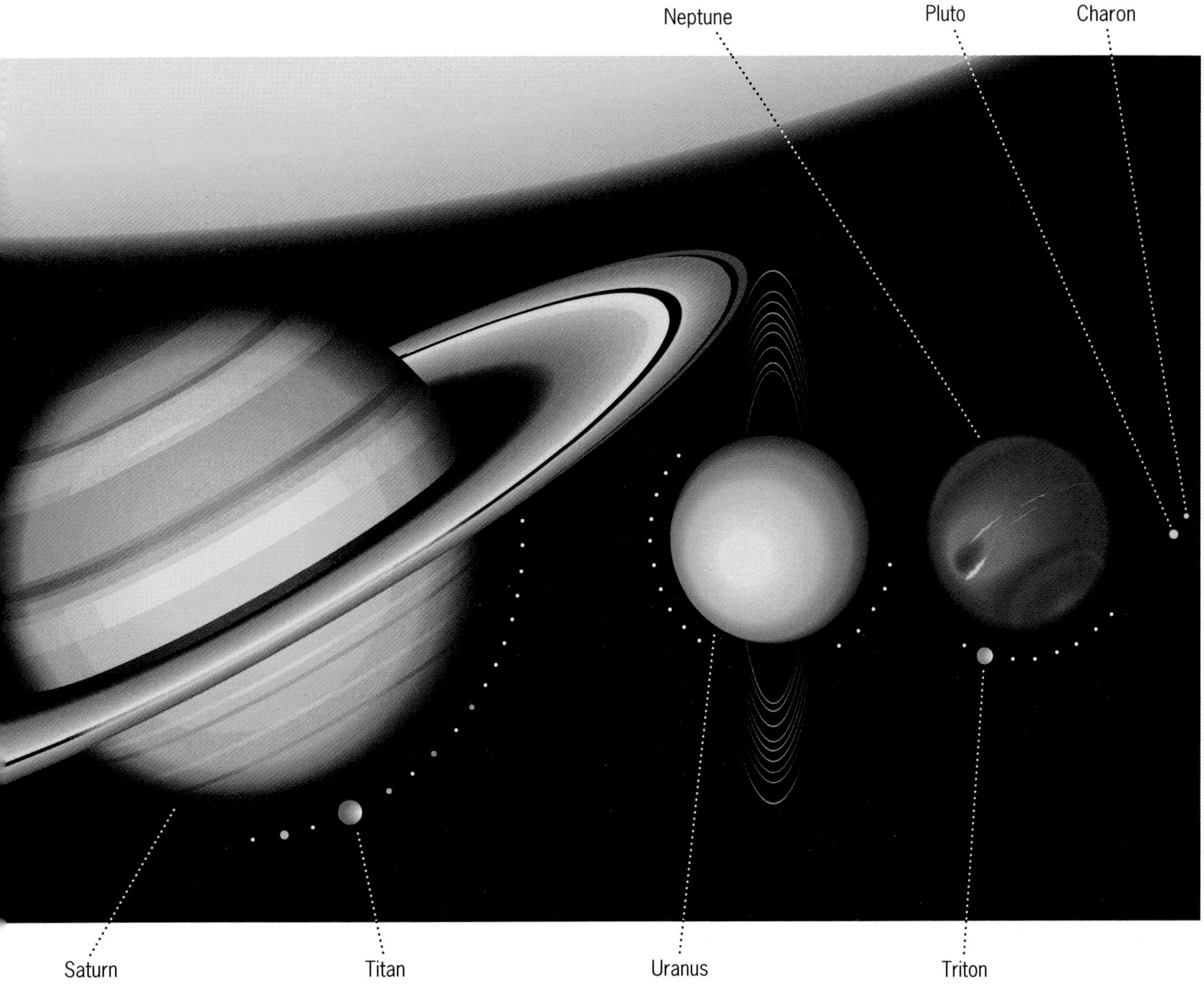
Neptune
Pluto
Charon
Saturn
Titan
Uranus
Triton

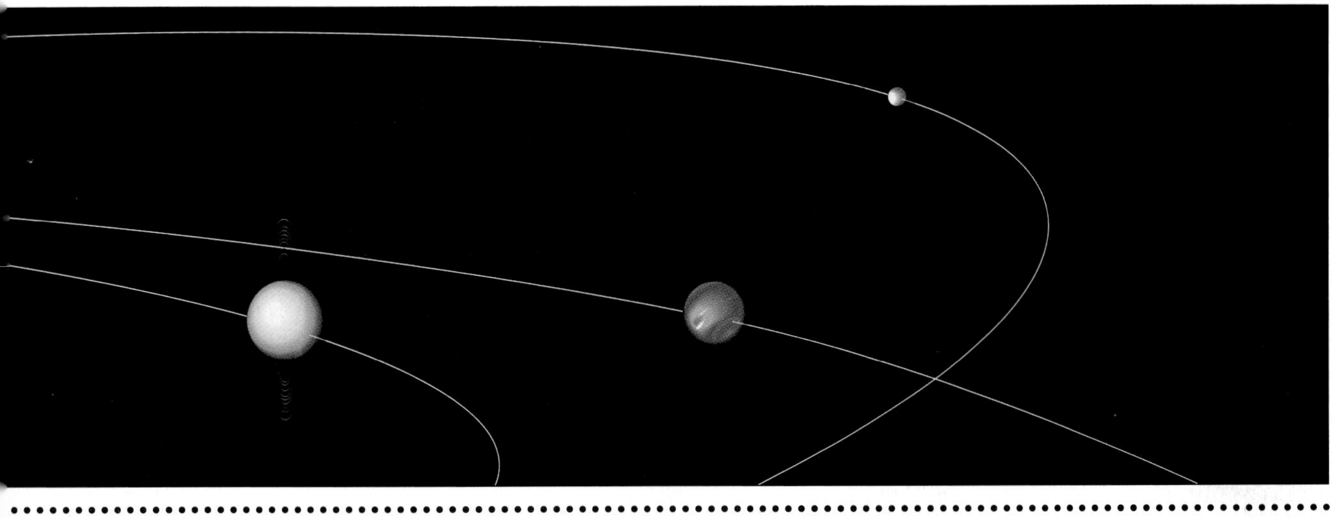

SUN

structure of the Sun

radiation zone
convection zone
Sun's surface
corona
prominence
sunspot
core
flare

MOON

lunar features

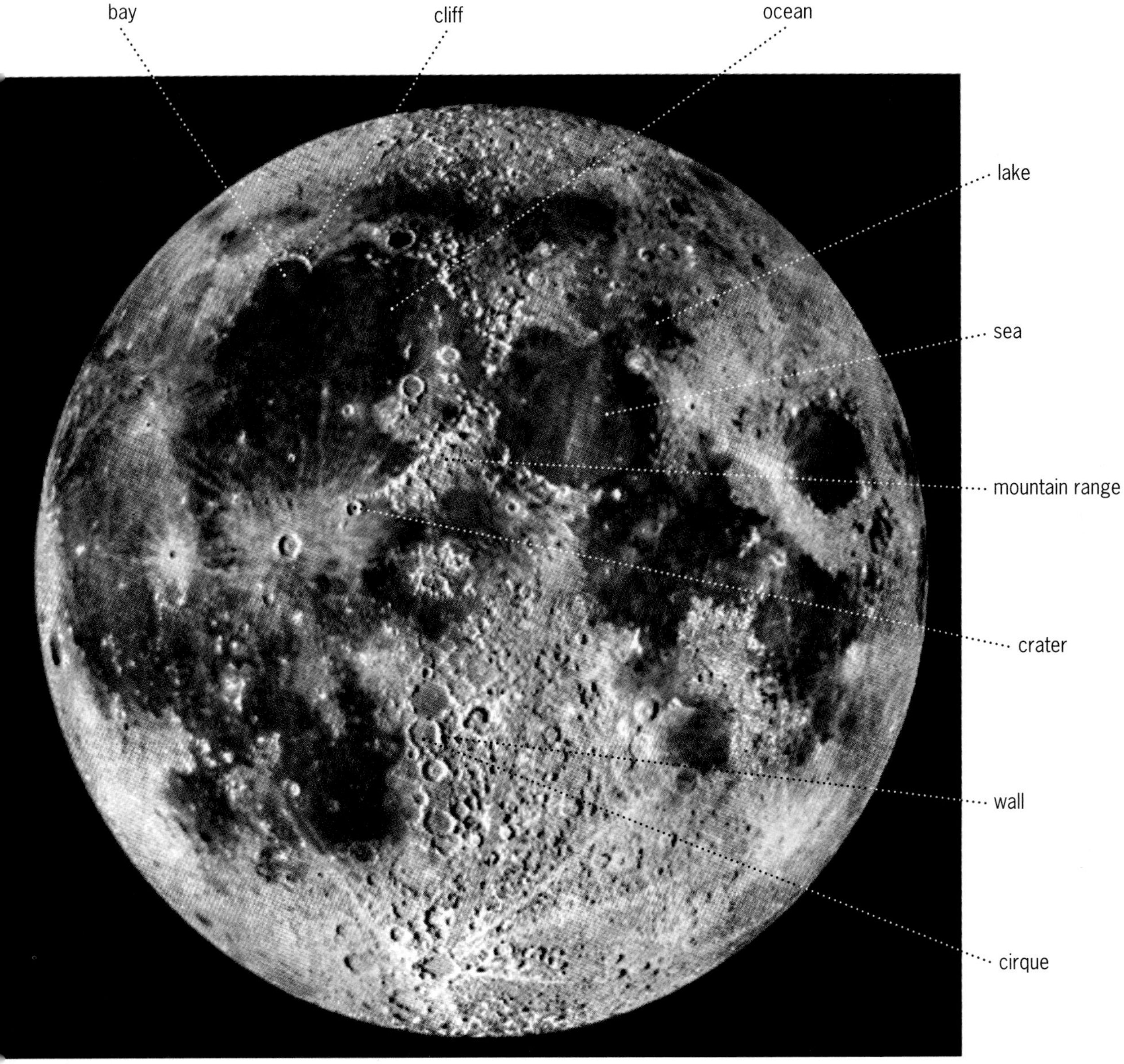
bay
cliff
ocean
lake
sea
mountain range
crater
wall
cirque

PHASES OF THE MOON

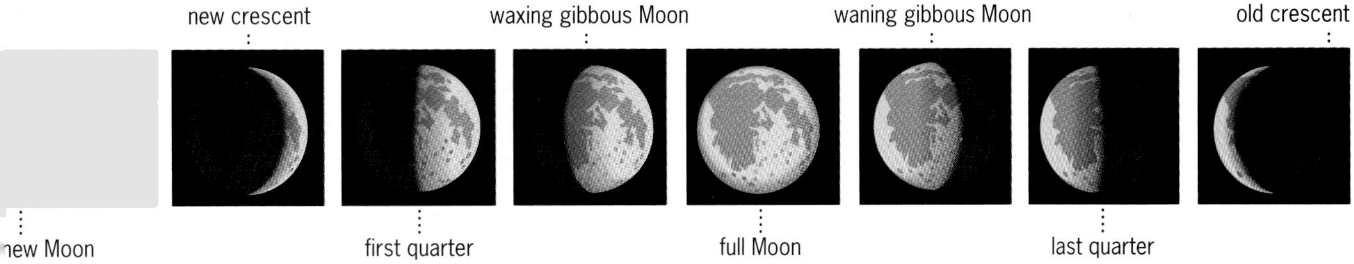
new crescent
waxing gibbous Moon
waning gibbous Moon
old crescent
new Moon
first quarter
full Moon
last quarter

COMET

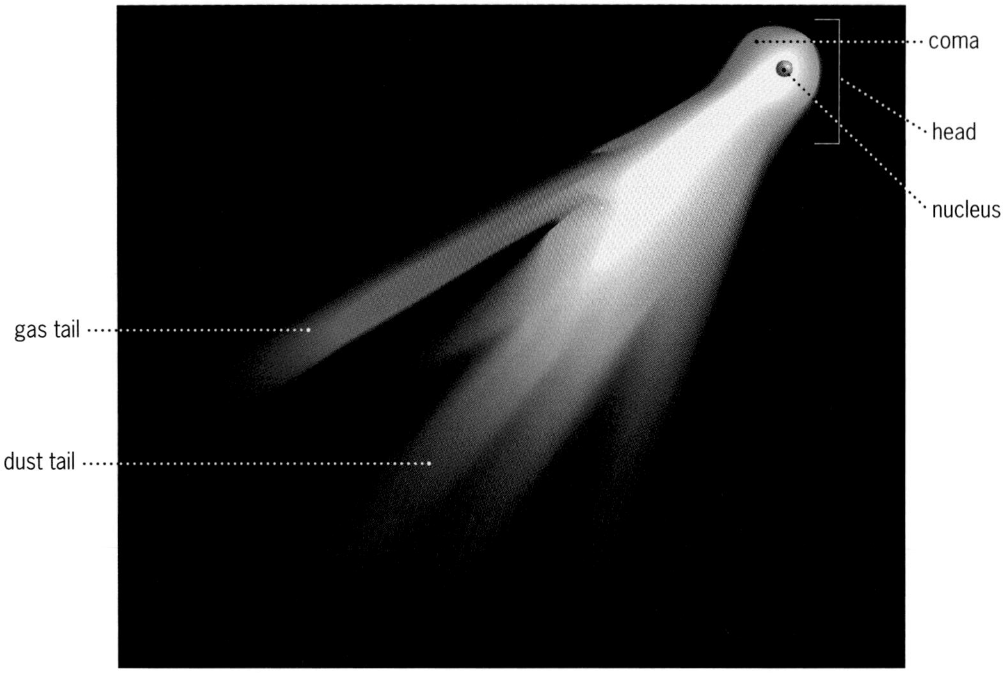
coma
head
nucleus
gas tail
dust tail

SOLAR ECLIPSE

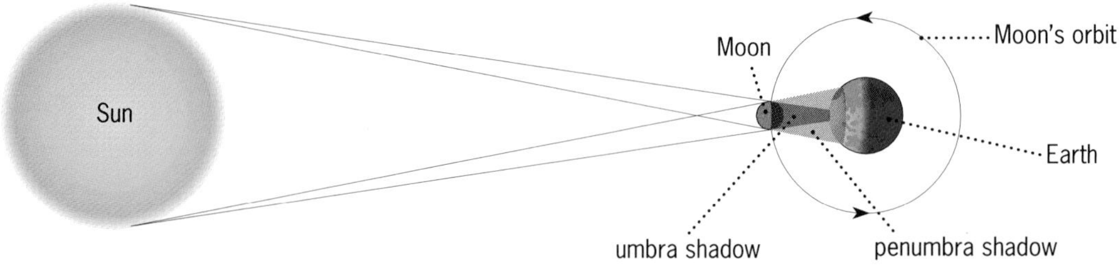
Sun
Moon
Moon's orbit
Earth
umbra shadow
penumbra shadow

TYPES OF SOLAR ECLIPSES

total eclipse

annular eclipse

partial eclipse

LUNAR ECLIPSE

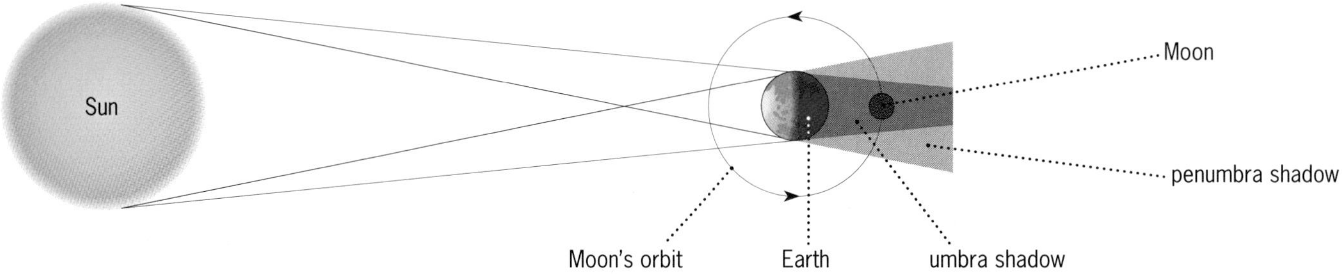
Sun
Moon
penumbra shadow
Moon's orbit
Earth
umbra shadow

TYPES OF LUNAR ECLIPSES

partial eclipse

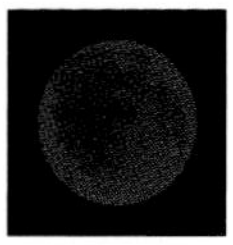

total eclipse

REFLECTING TELESCOPE

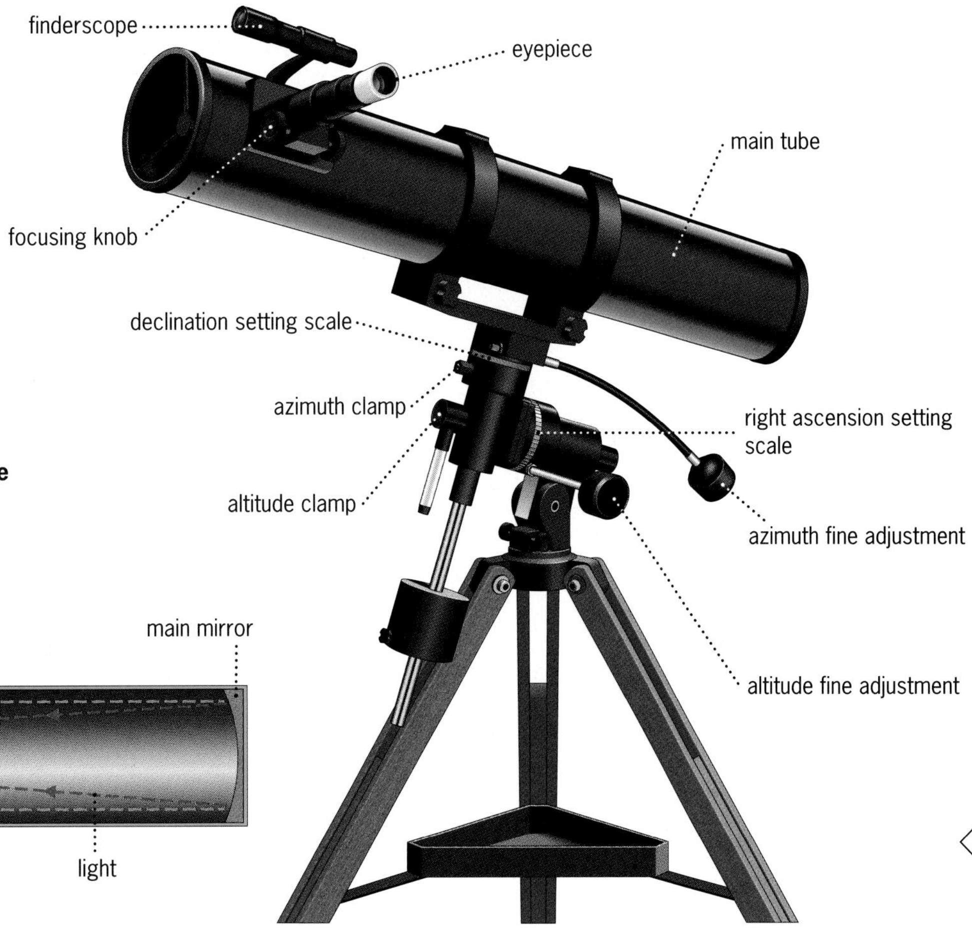
finderscope
eyepiece
main tube
focusing knob
declination setting scale
azimuth clamp
right ascension setting scale
altitude clamp
azimuth fine adjustment
altitude fine adjustment

cross section of a reflecting telescope

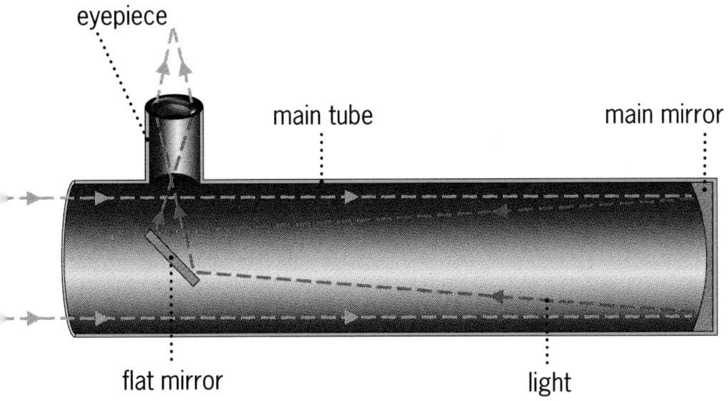
eyepiece
main tube
main mirror
flat mirror
light

REFRACTING TELESCOPE

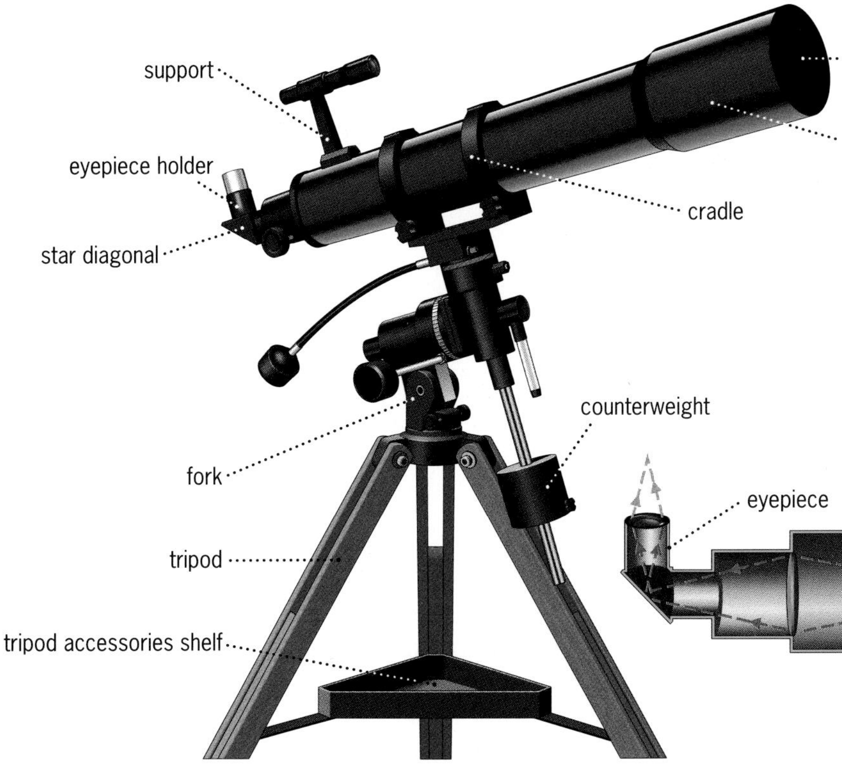
support
objective lens
dew shield
eyepiece holder
cradle
star diagonal
counterweight
fork
tripod
tripod accessories shelf

cross section of a refracting telescope

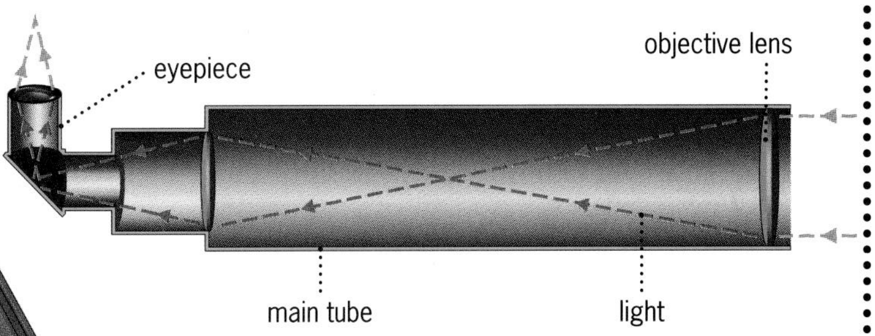
eyepiece
objective lens
main tube
light

EARTH COORDINATE SYSTEM

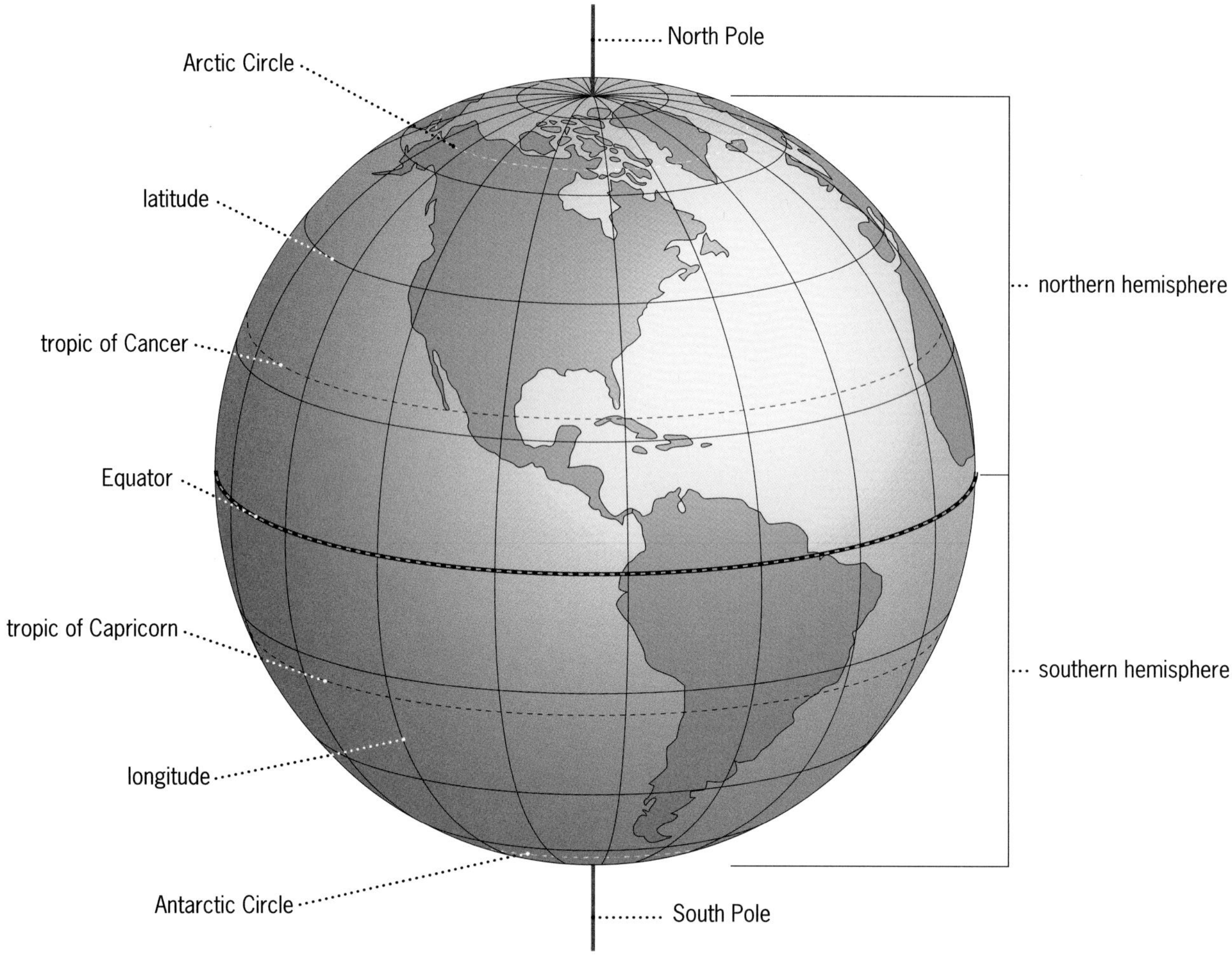
North Pole
Arctic Circle
latitude
northern hemisphere
tropic of Cancer
Equator
tropic of Capricorn
southern hemisphere
longitude
Antarctic Circle
South Pole

STRUCTURE OF THE EARTH

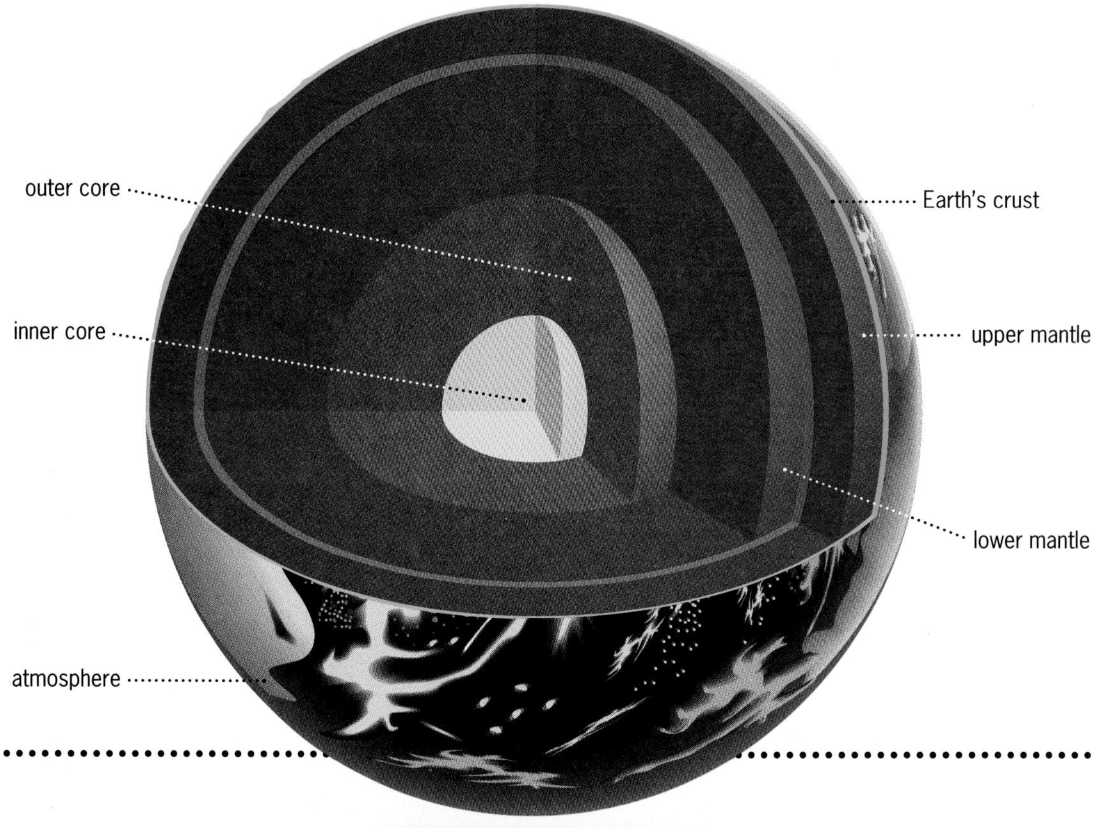
outer core
Earth's crust
inner core
upper mantle
lower mantle
atmosphere

EARTHQUAKE

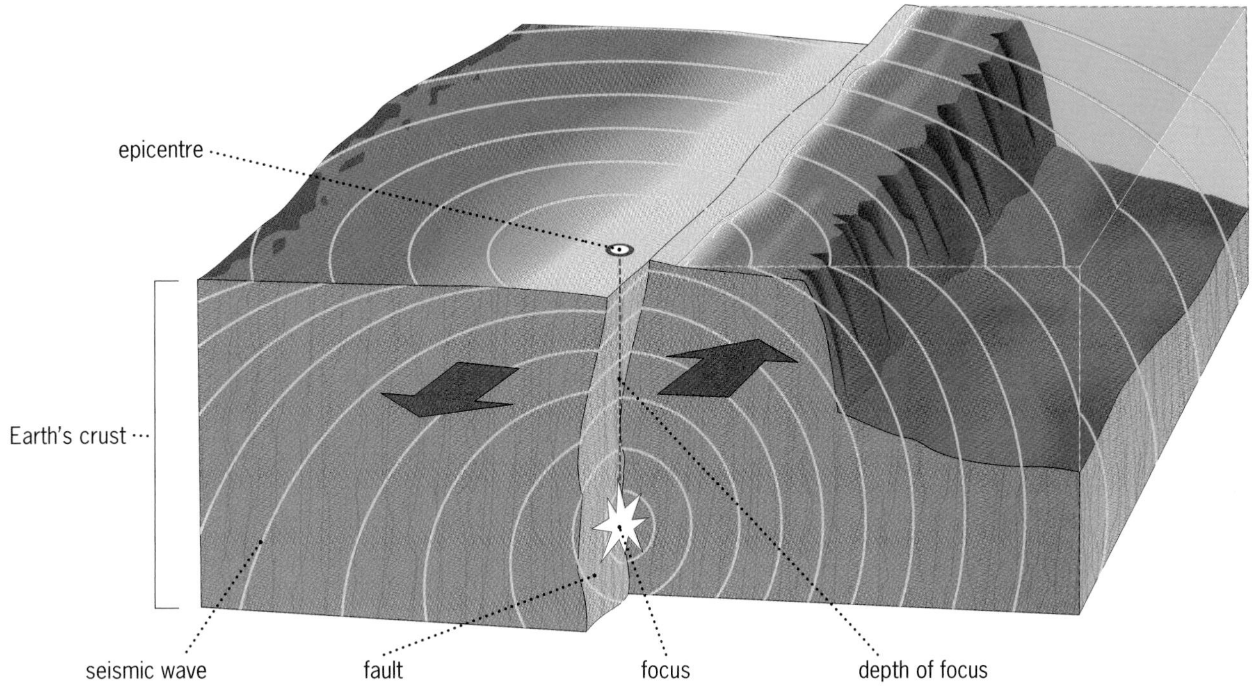
epicentre
Earth's crust
seismic wave
fault
focus
depth of focus

CAVE

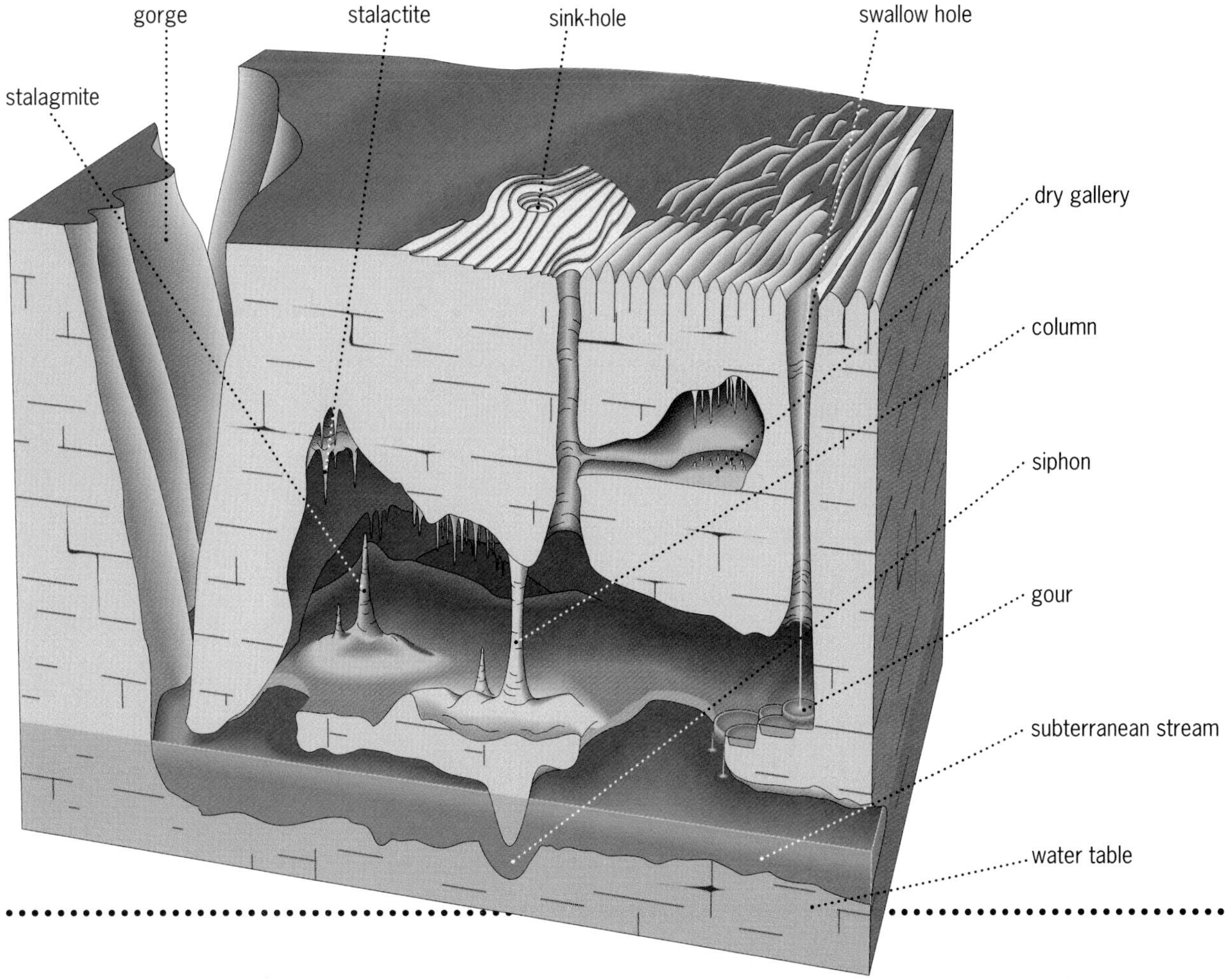
gorge
stalactite
sink-hole
swallow hole
stalagmite
dry gallery
column
siphon
gour
subterranean stream
water table

COASTAL FEATURES

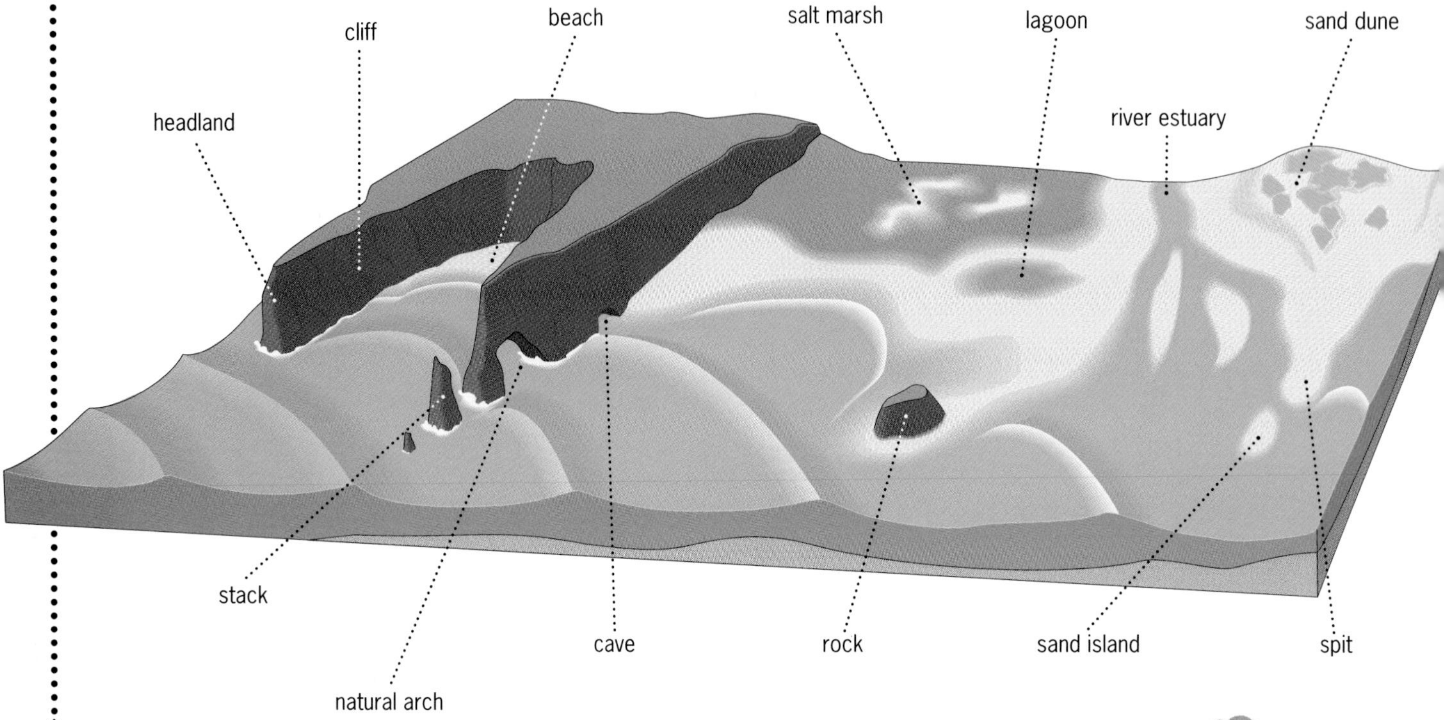
cliff
beach
salt marsh
lagoon
sand dune
headland
river estuary
stack
natural arch
cave
rock
sand island
spit

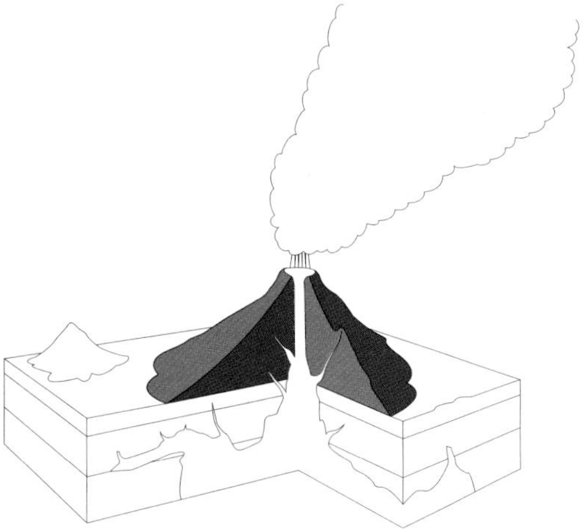

cone

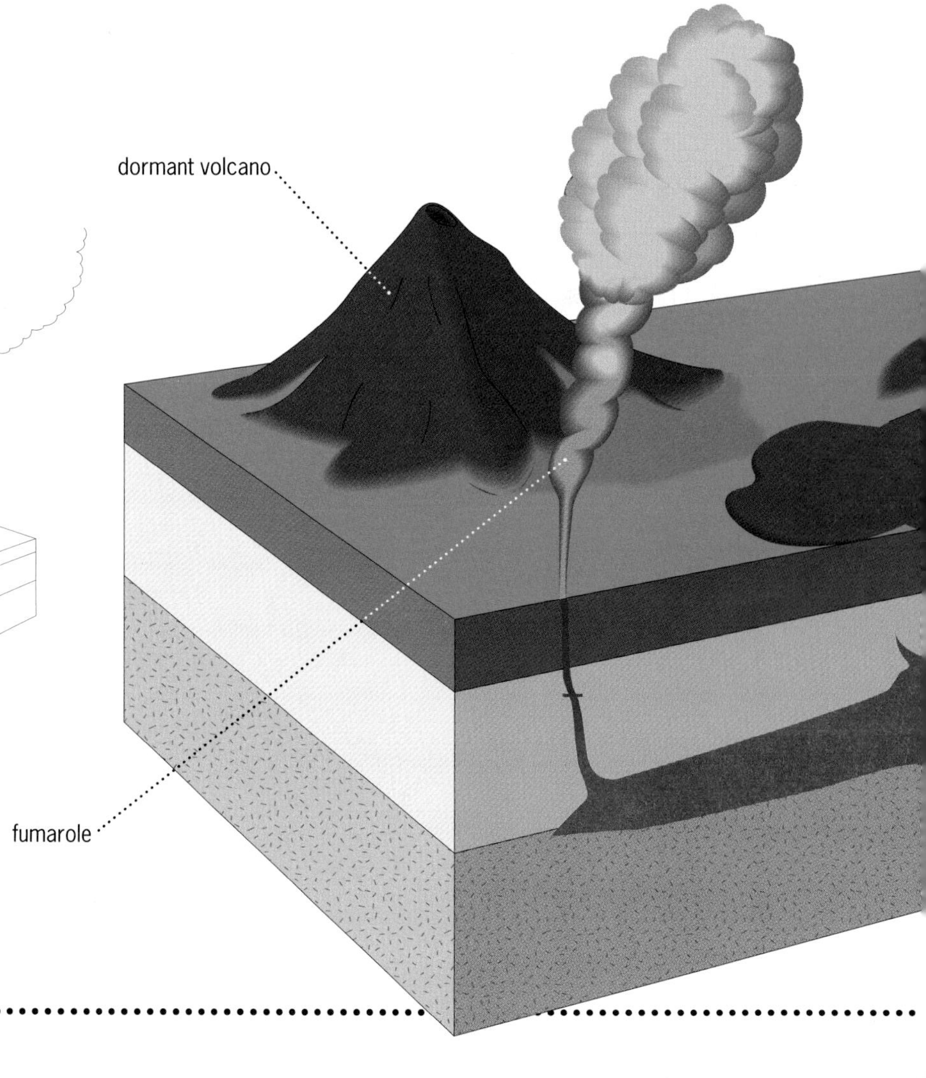
dormant volcano
fumarole

VOLCANO

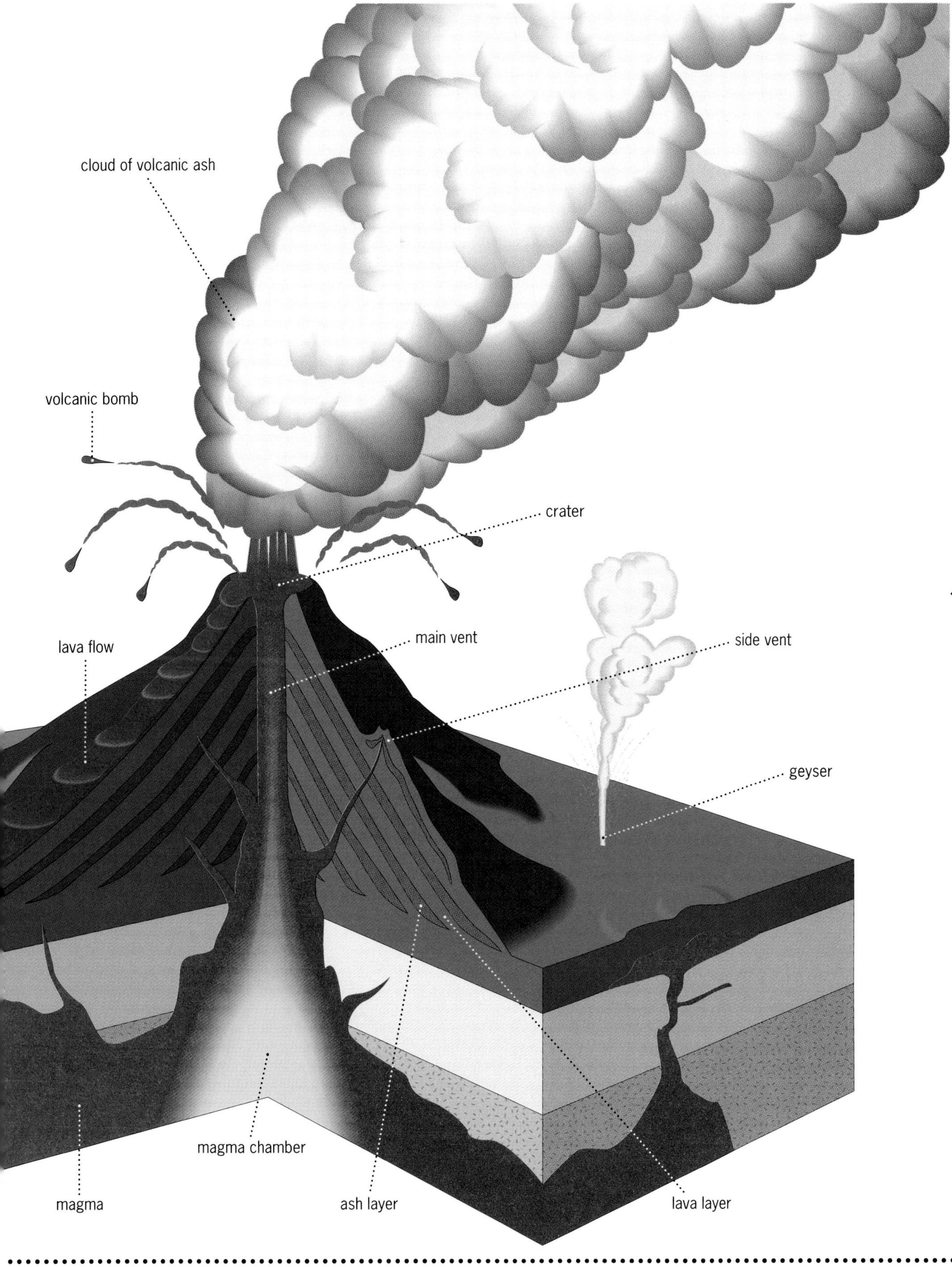
cloud of volcanic ash
volcanic bomb
crater
lava flow
main vent
side vent
geyser
magma chamber
magma
ash layer
lava layer

GLACIER

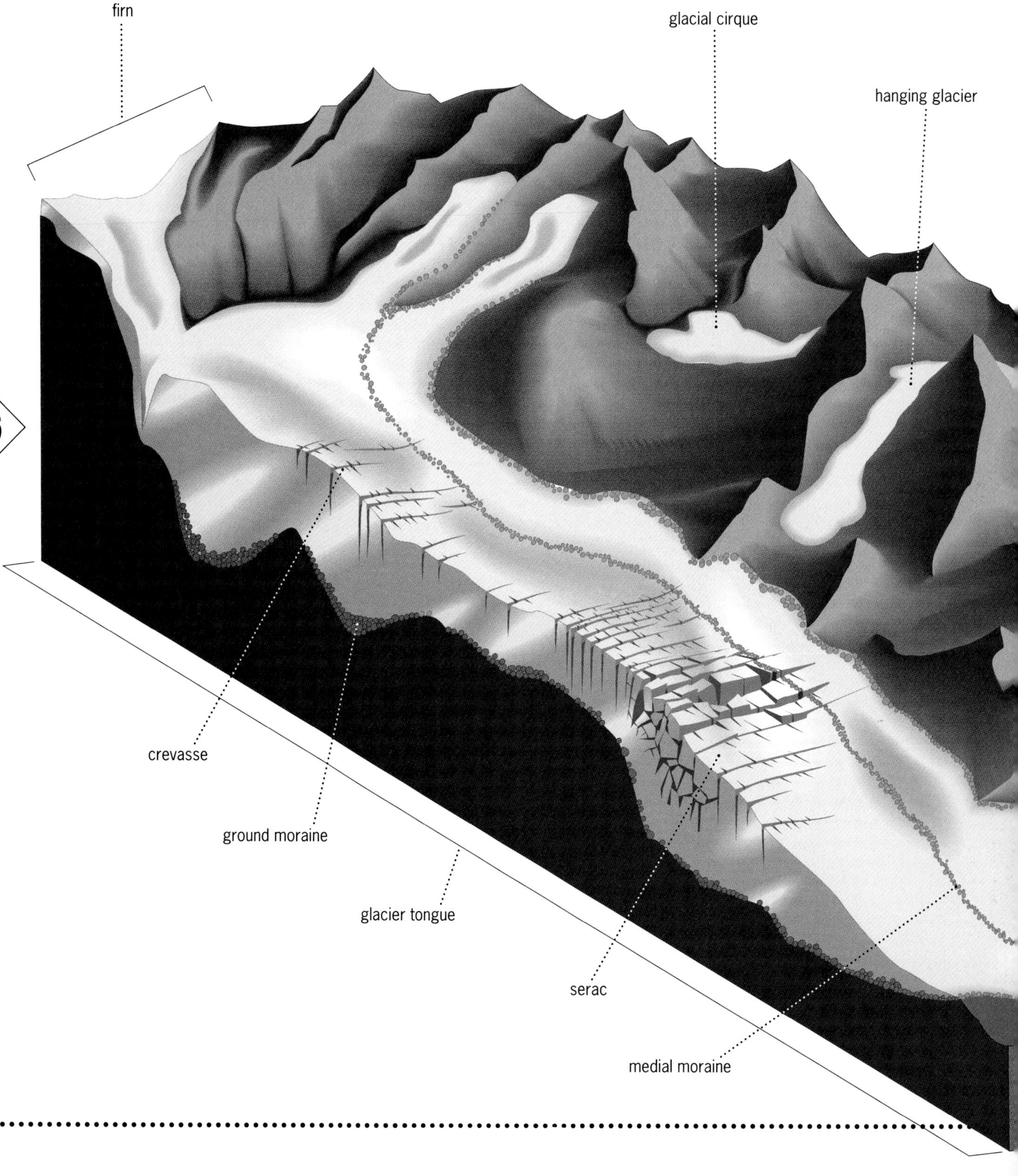
firn
glacial cirque
hanging glacier
crevasse
ground moraine
glacier tongue
serac
medial moraine

MOUNTAIN

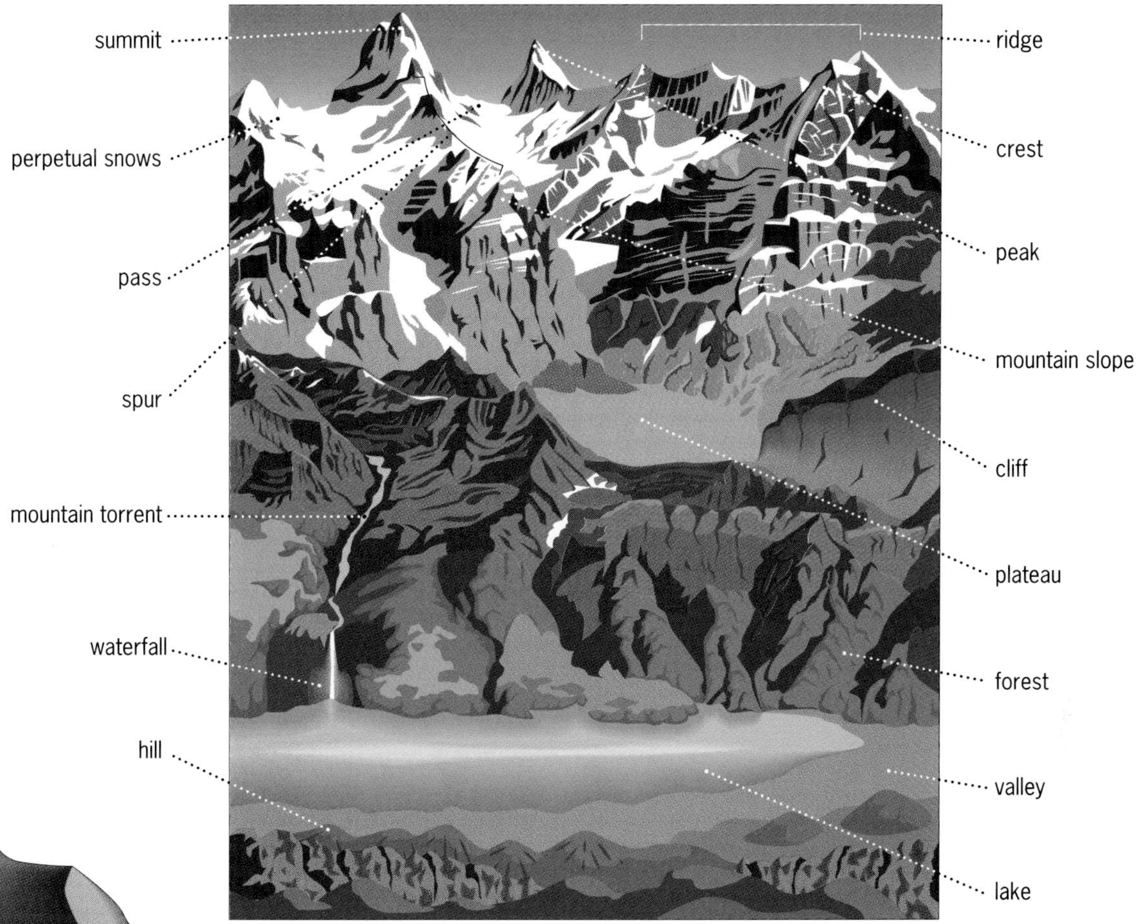
summit
perpetual snows
pass
spur
mountain torrent
waterfall
hill
ridge
crest
peak
mountain slope
cliff
plateau
forest
valley
lake

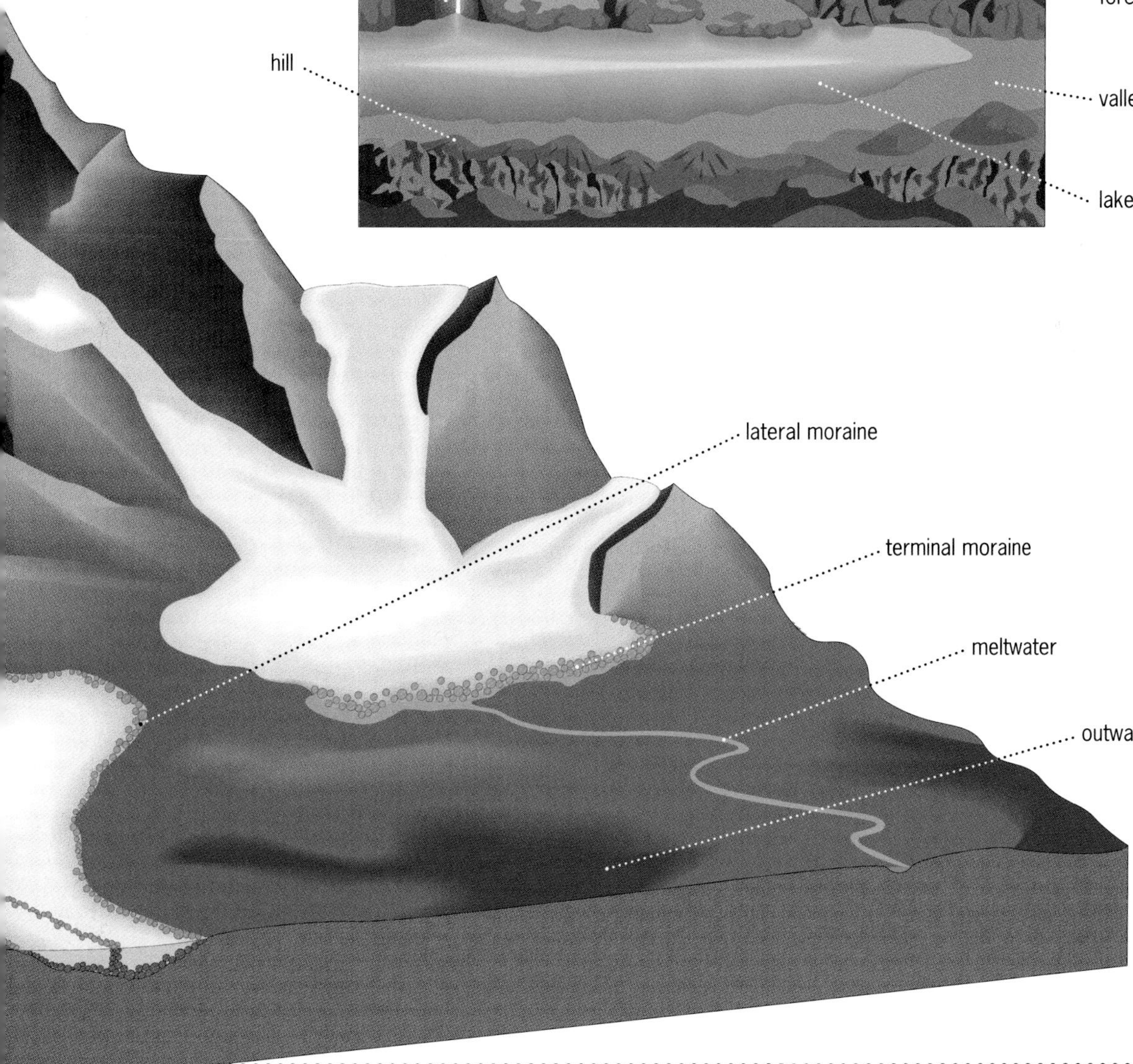
lateral moraine
terminal moraine
meltwater
outwash plain

CONFIGURATION OF THE CONTINENTS

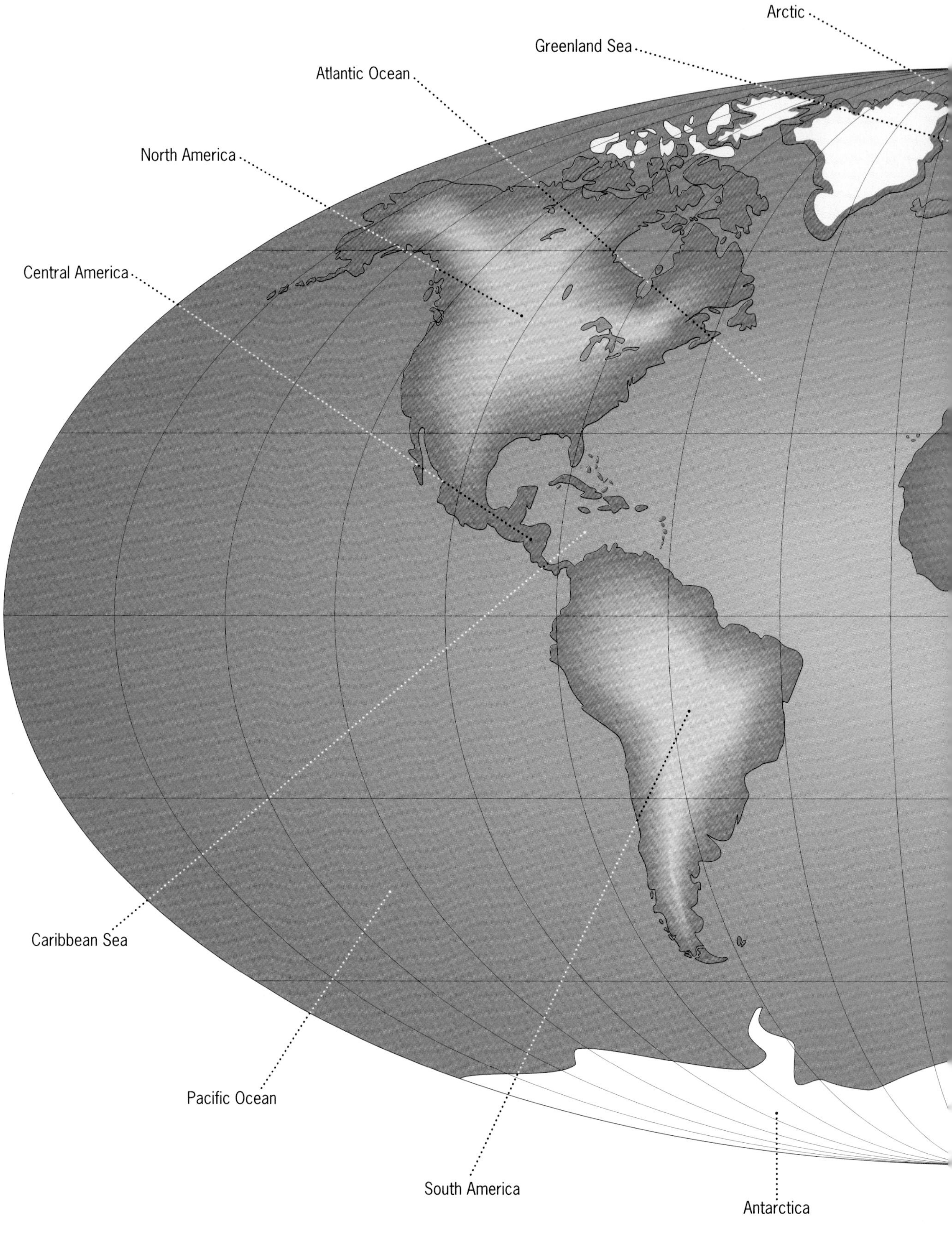
Arctic
Greenland Sea
Atlantic Ocean
North America
Central America
Caribbean Sea
Pacific Ocean
South America
Antarctica

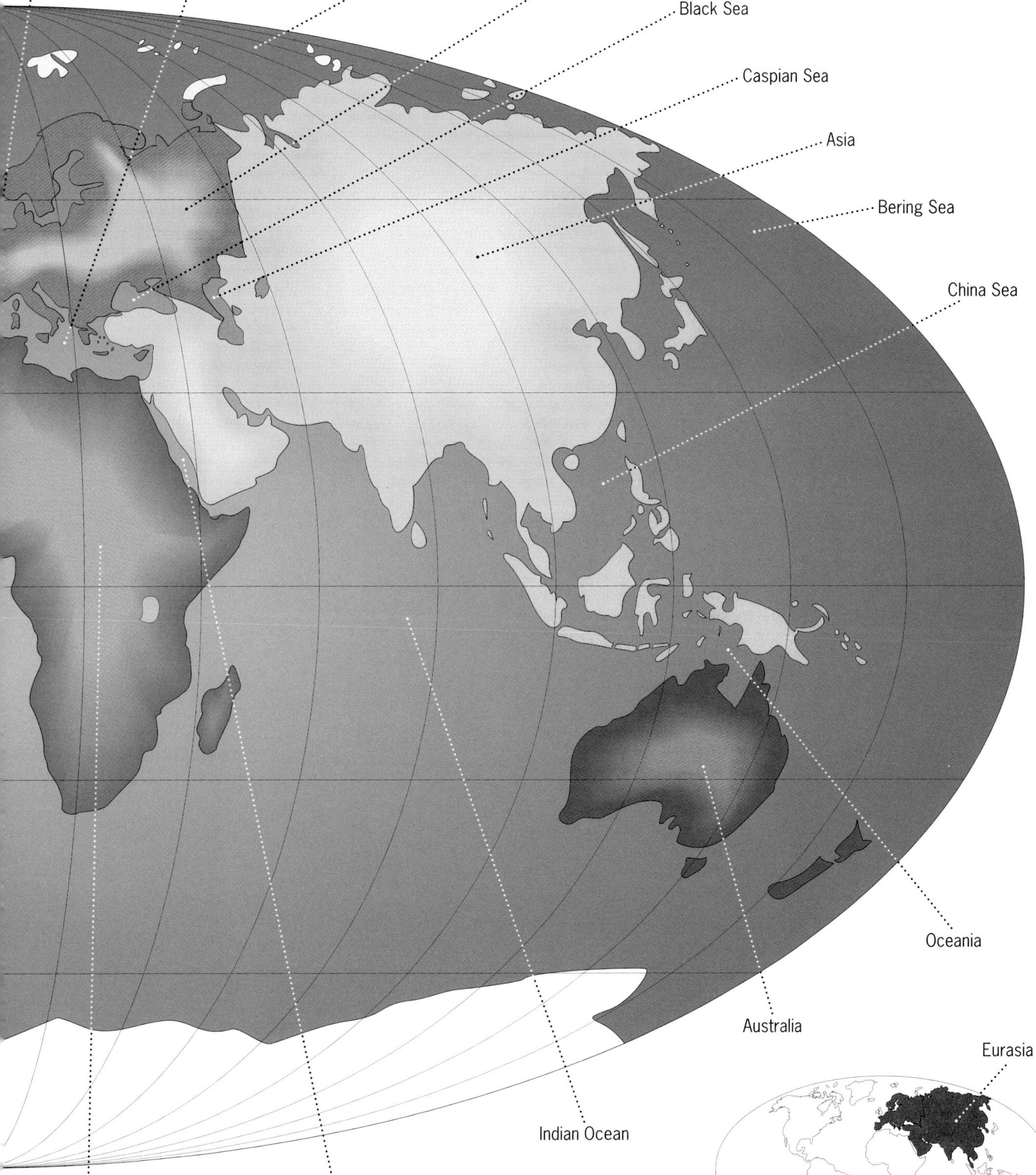
North Sea
Mediterranean Sea
Arctic Ocean
Europe
Black Sea
Caspian Sea
Asia
Bering Sea
China Sea
Oceania
Australia
Indian Ocean
Red Sea
Africa

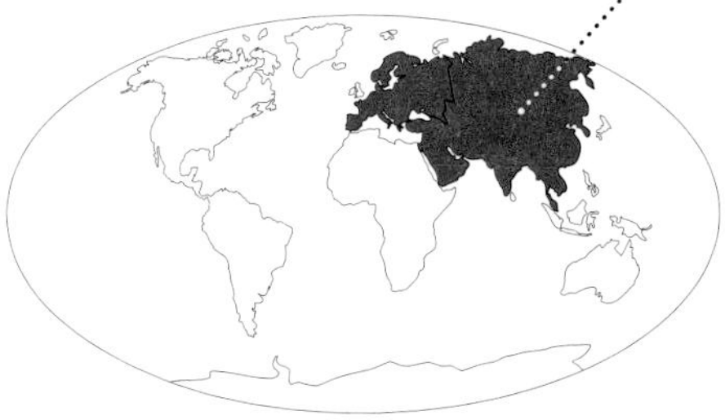
Eurasia

SEASONS OF THE YEAR

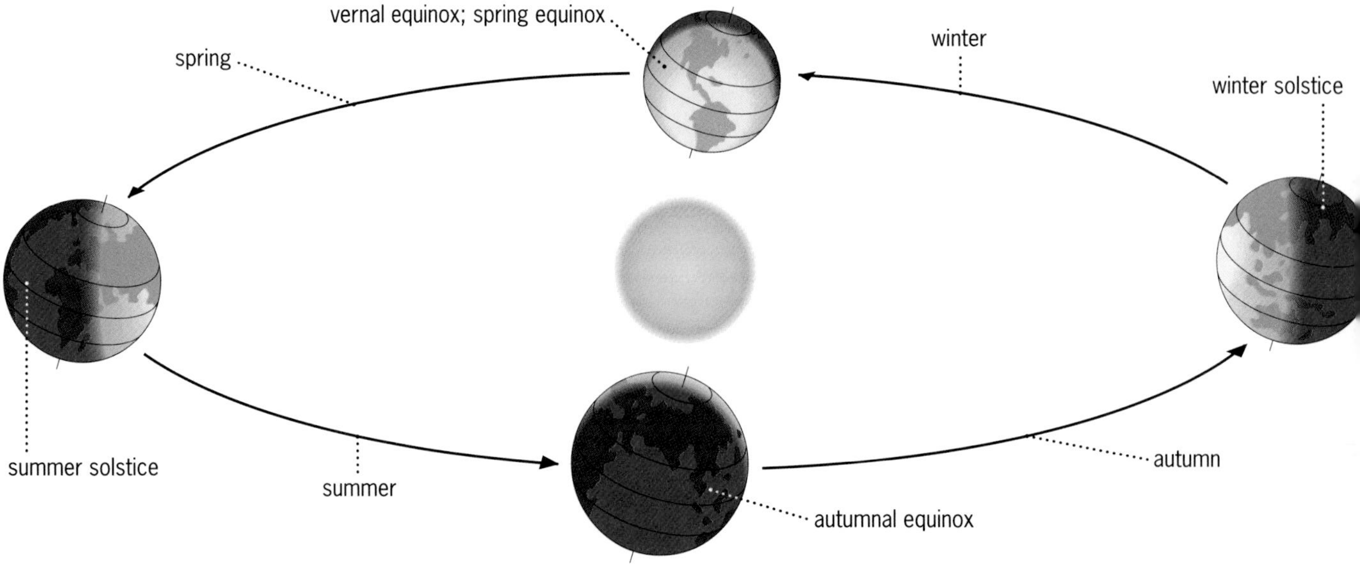
vernal equinox; spring equinox
spring
winter
winter solstice
summer solstice
summer
autumn
autumnal equinox

STRUCTURE OF THE BIOSPHERE

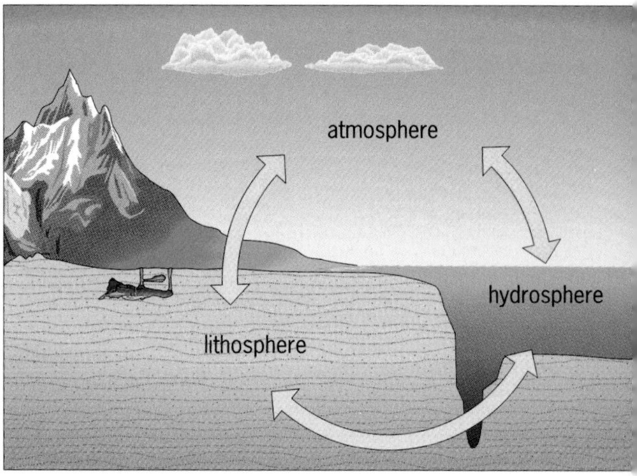
atmosphere
hydrosphere
lithosphere

ELEVATION ZONES AND VEGETATION

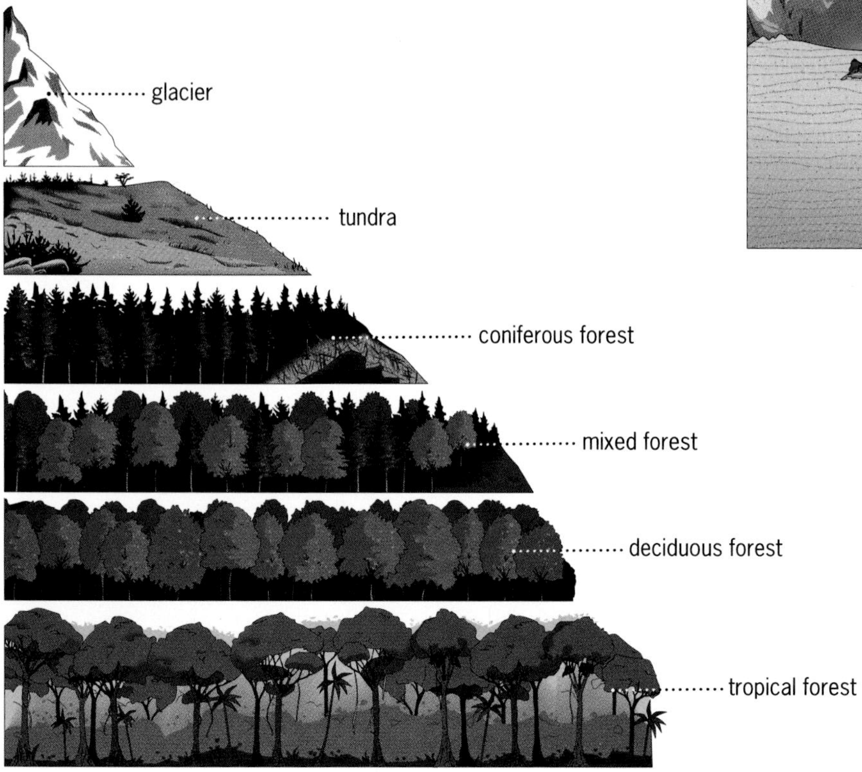
glacier
tundra
coniferous forest
mixed forest
deciduous forest
tropical forest

CLIMATES OF THE WORLD

tropical climates

- tropical rain forest
- tropical savanna
- steppe
- desert

temperate climates

- humid - long summer
- humid - short summer
- marine

polar climates

- polar tundra
- polar ice cap

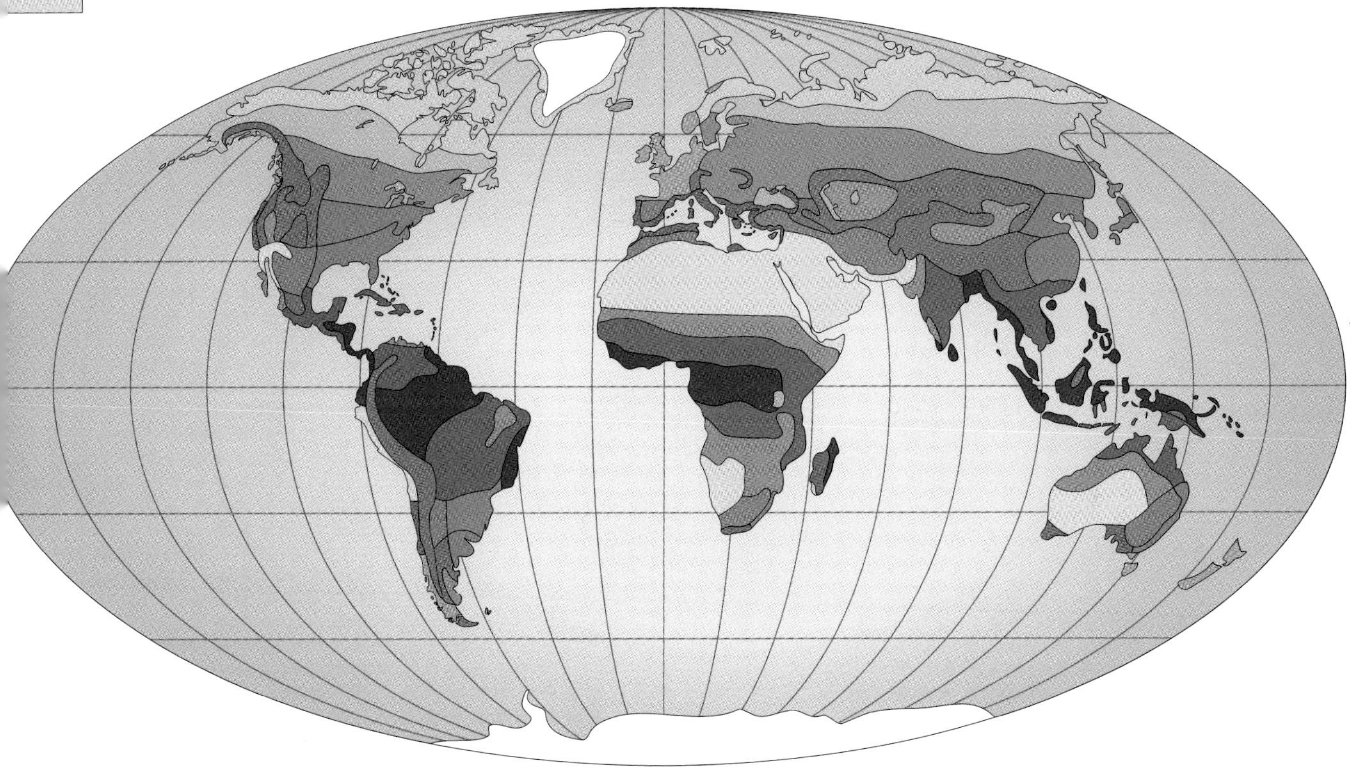

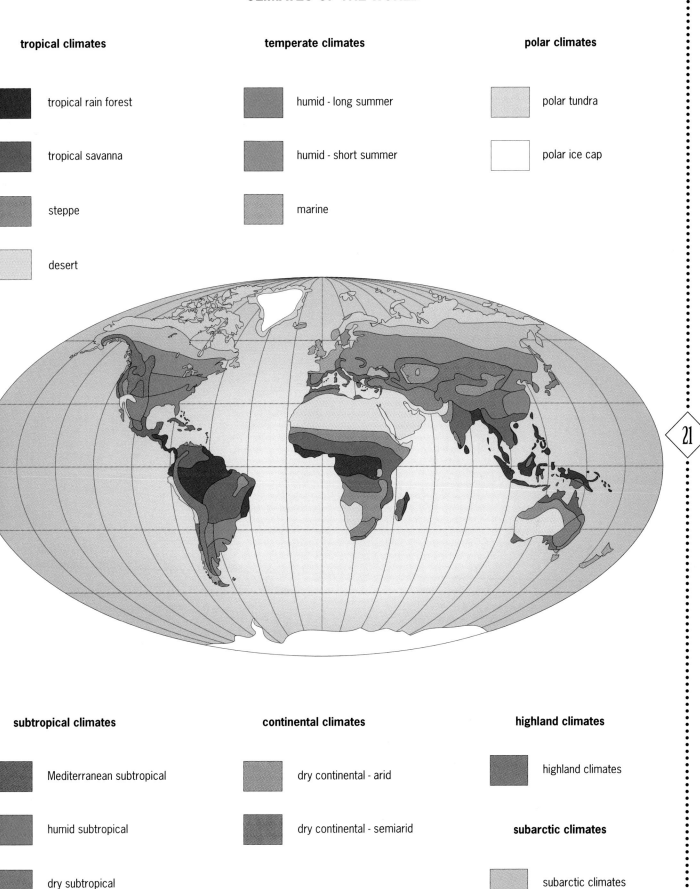

subtropical climates

- Mediterranean subtropical
- humid subtropical
- dry subtropical

continental climates

- dry continental - arid
- dry continental - semiarid

highland climates

- highland climates

subarctic climates

- subarctic climates

WEATHER

mist

fog

dew

glazed frost

stormy sky

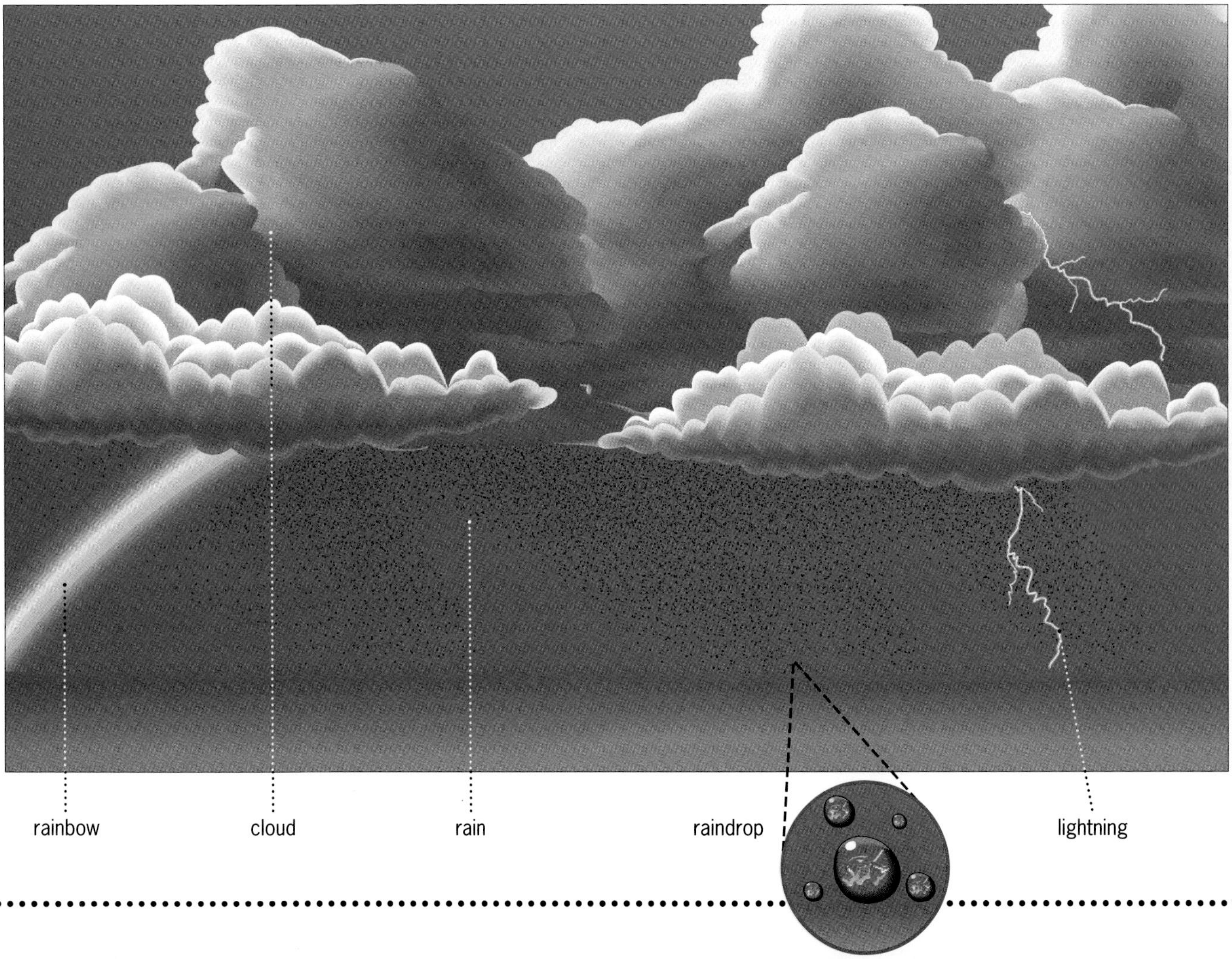
rainbow
cloud
rain
raindrop
lightning

METEOROLOGICAL MEASURING INSTRUMENTS

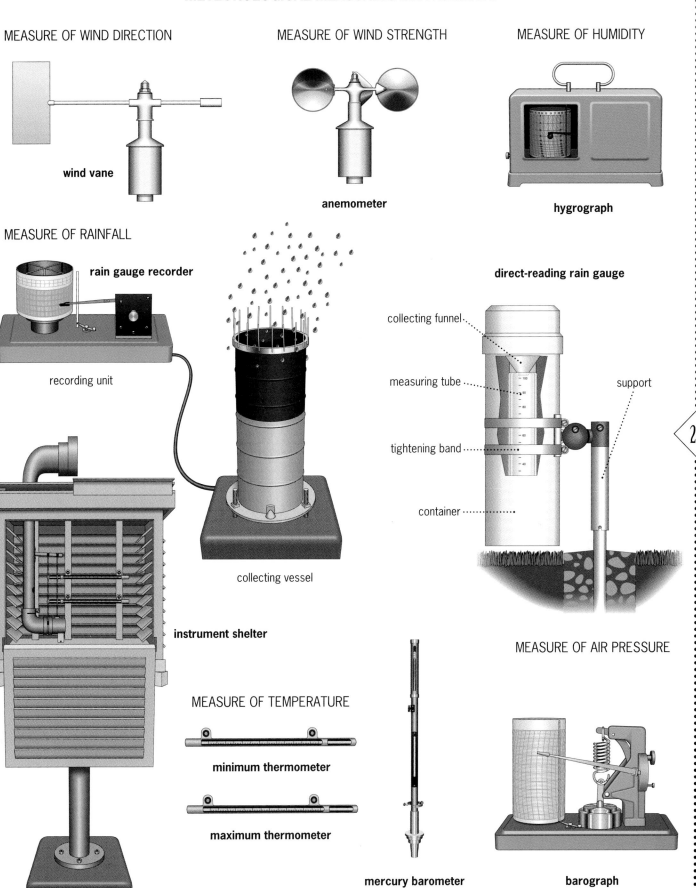

MEASURE OF WIND DIRECTION

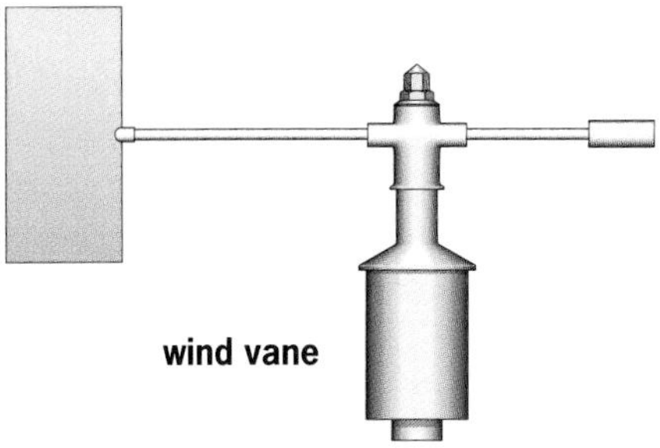

wind vane

MEASURE OF WIND STRENGTH

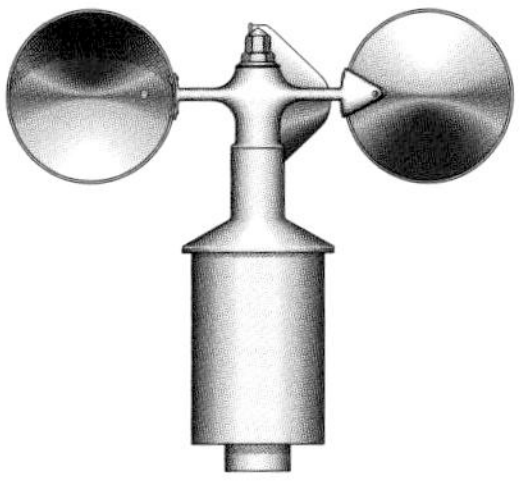

anemometer

MEASURE OF HUMIDITY

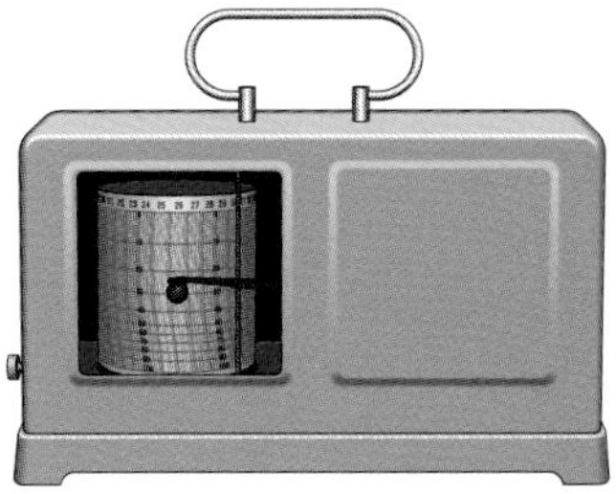

hygrograph

MEASURE OF RAINFALL

rain gauge recorder

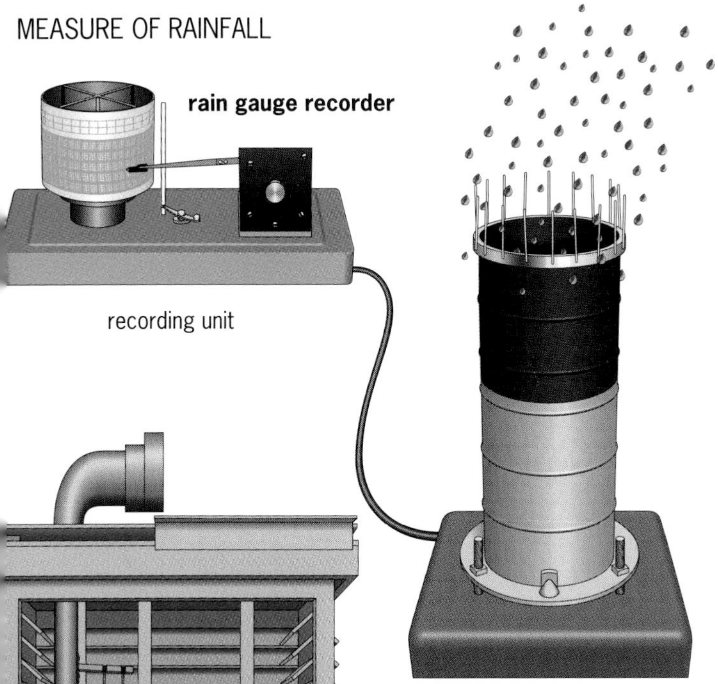

recording unit

collecting vessel

direct-reading rain gauge

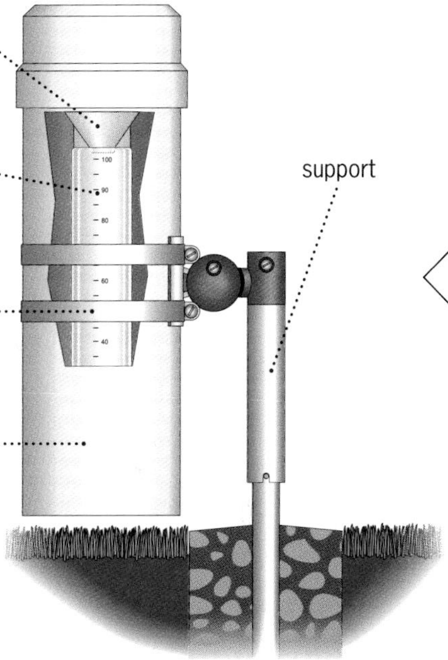
collecting funnel
measuring tube
support
tightening band
container

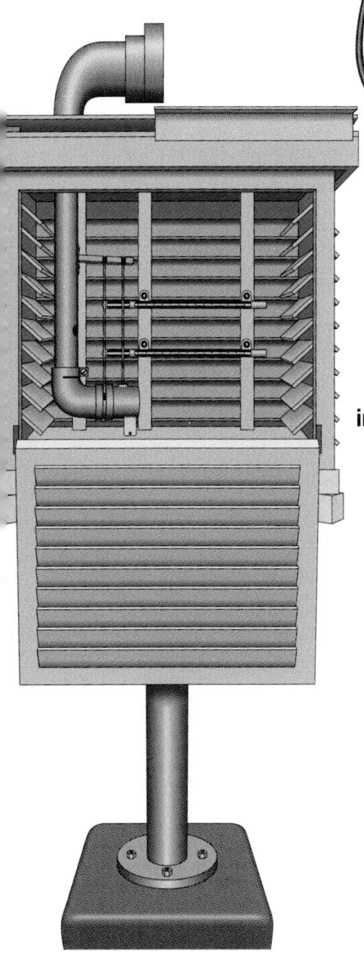

instrument shelter

MEASURE OF TEMPERATURE

minimum thermometer

maximum thermometer

mercury barometer

MEASURE OF AIR PRESSURE

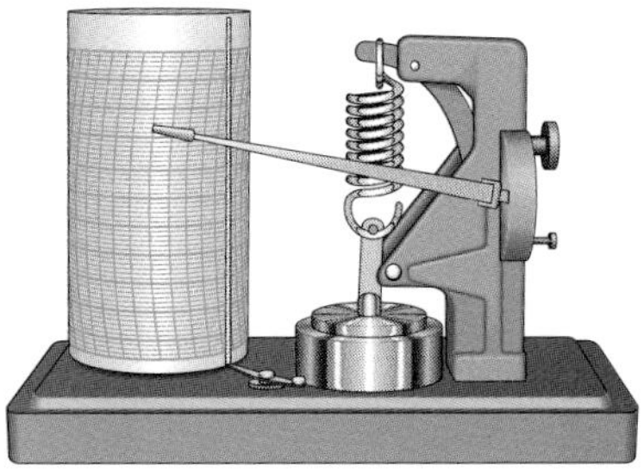

barograph

CARTOGRAPHY

hemispheres

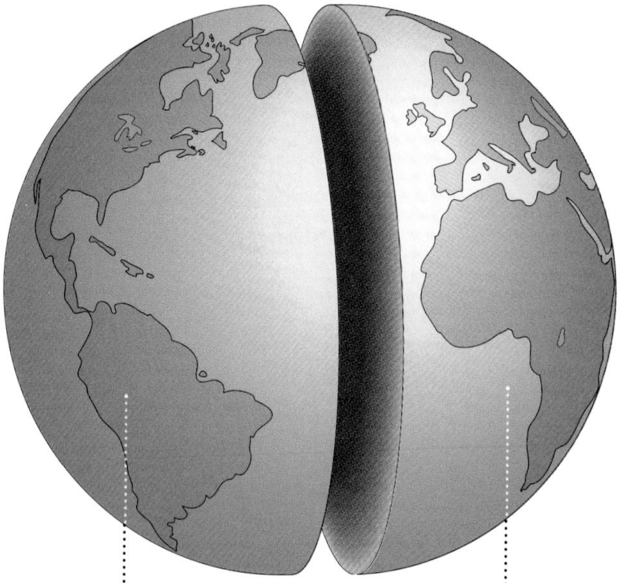
western hemisphere
eastern hemisphere

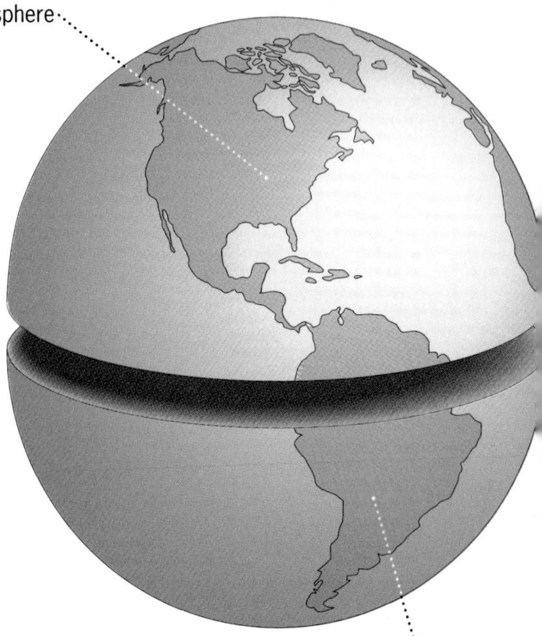
northern hemisphere
southern hemisphere

GRID SYSTEM

lines of latitude

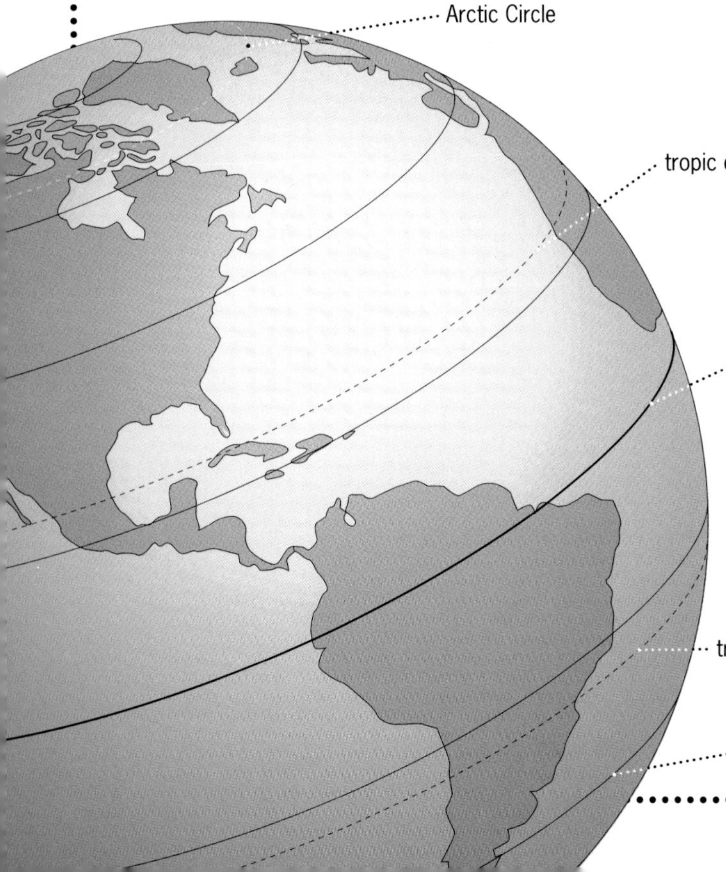
Arctic Circle
tropic of Cancer
equator
tropic of Capricorn
parallel

lines of longitude

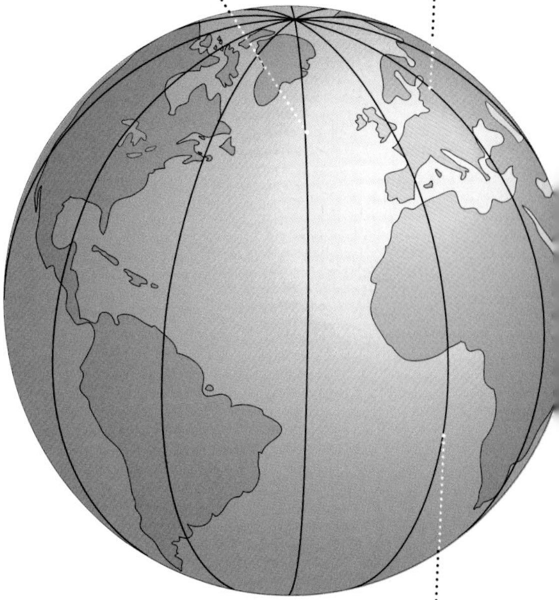
western meridian
eastern meridian
prime meridian

MAP PROJECTIONS

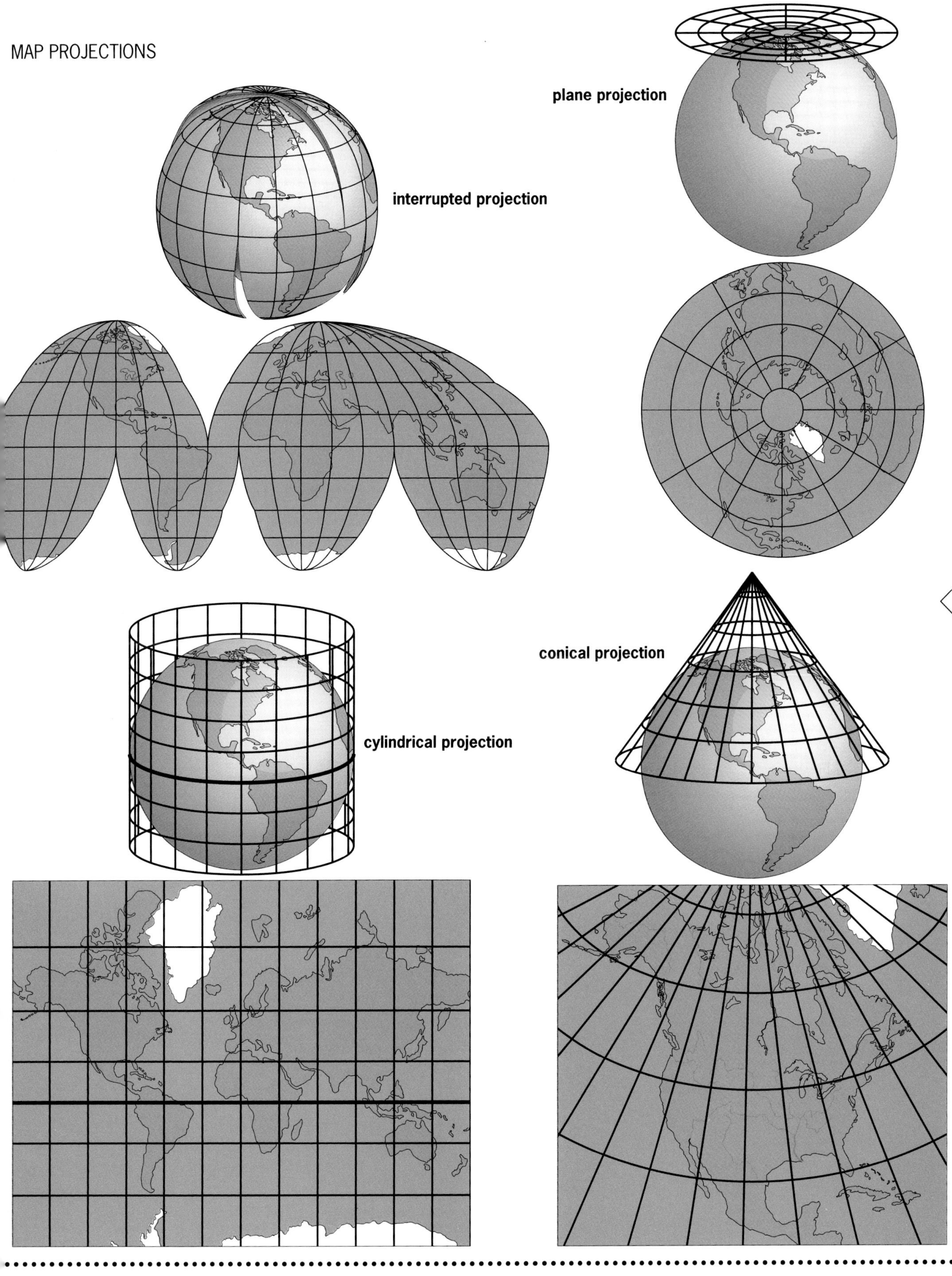
plane projection
interrupted projection
conical projection
cylindrical projection

CARTOGRAPHY

political map

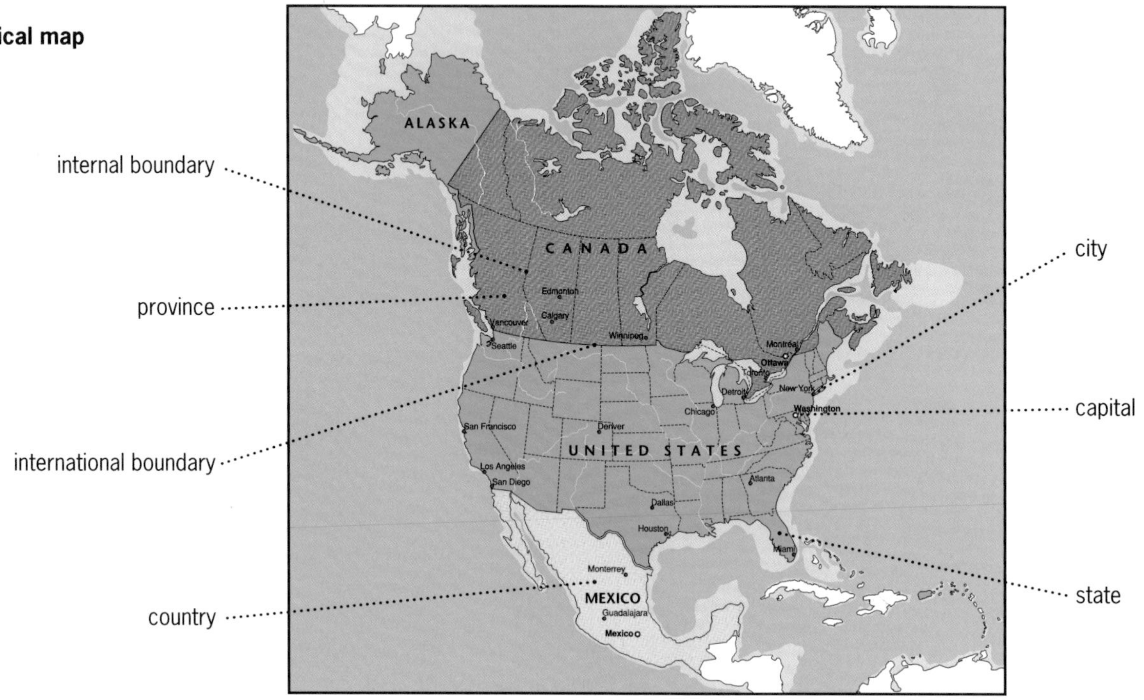
internal boundary
province
international boundary
country
city
capital
state
ALASKA
CANADA
UNITED STATES
MEXICO
Edmonton
Calgary
Vancouver
Seattle
Winnipeg
Montréal
Ottawa
Toronto
Detroit
New York
Washington
Chicago
Denver
San Francisco
Los Angeles
San Diego
Atlanta
Dallas
Houston
Miami
Monterrey
Guadalajara
Mexico

physical map

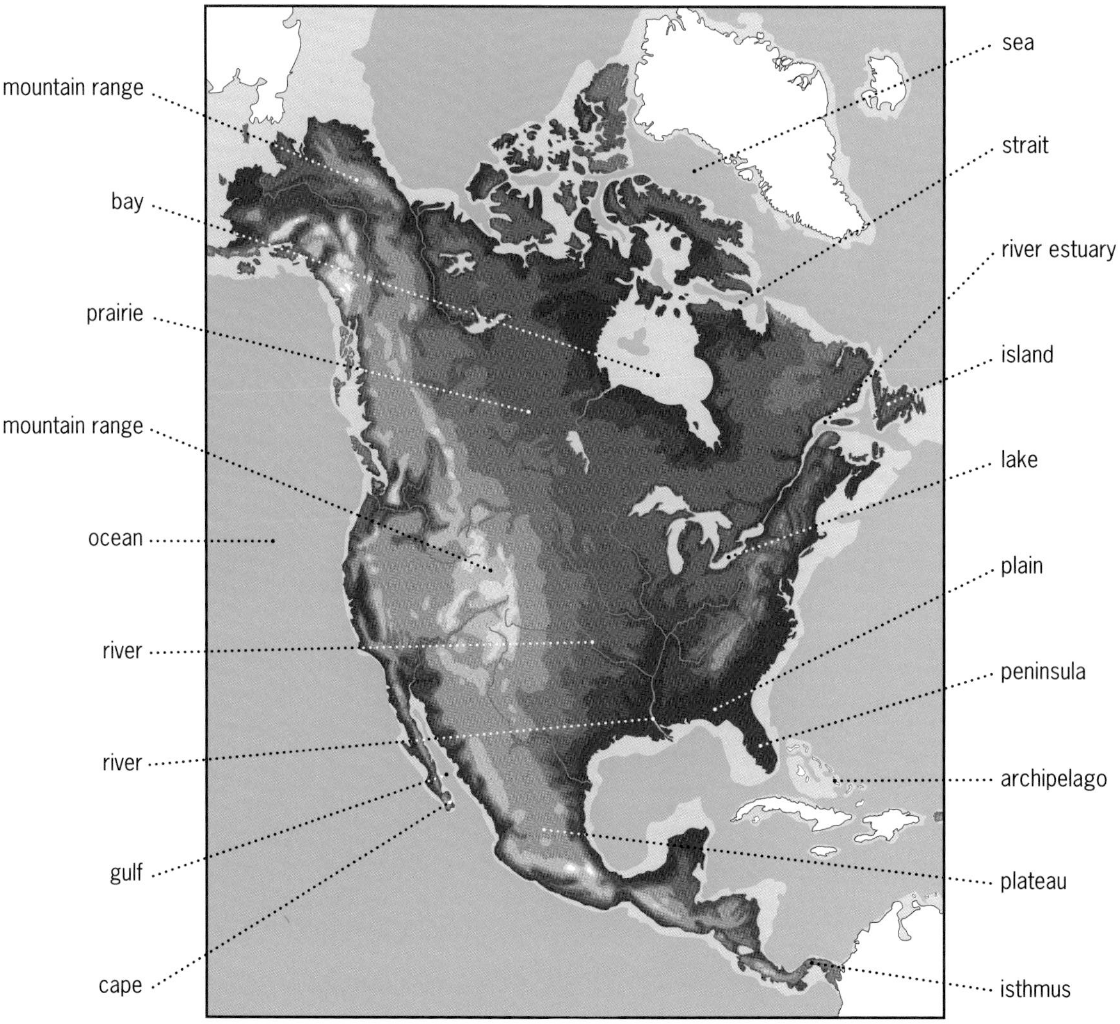
mountain range
bay
prairie
mountain range
ocean
river
river
gulf
cape
sea
strait
river estuary
island
lake
plain
peninsula
archipelago
plateau
isthmus

road map

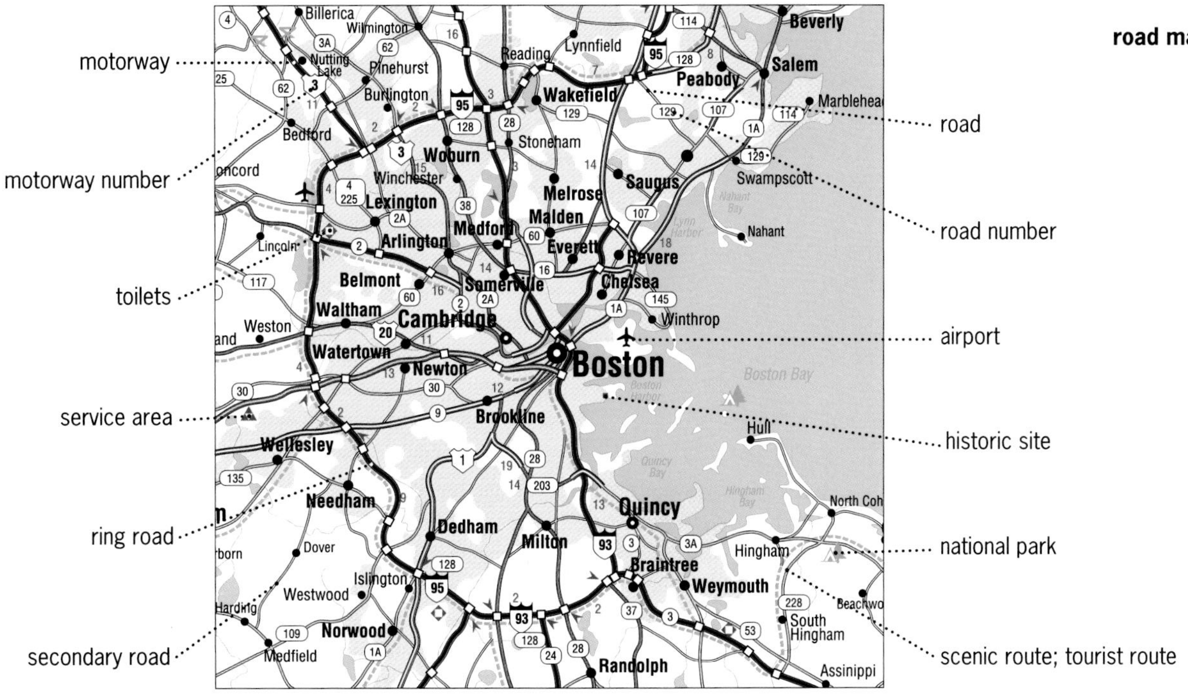

motorway
motorway number
toilets
service area
ring road
secondary road
road
road number
airport
historic site
national park
scenic route; tourist route
Boston

COMPASS CARD

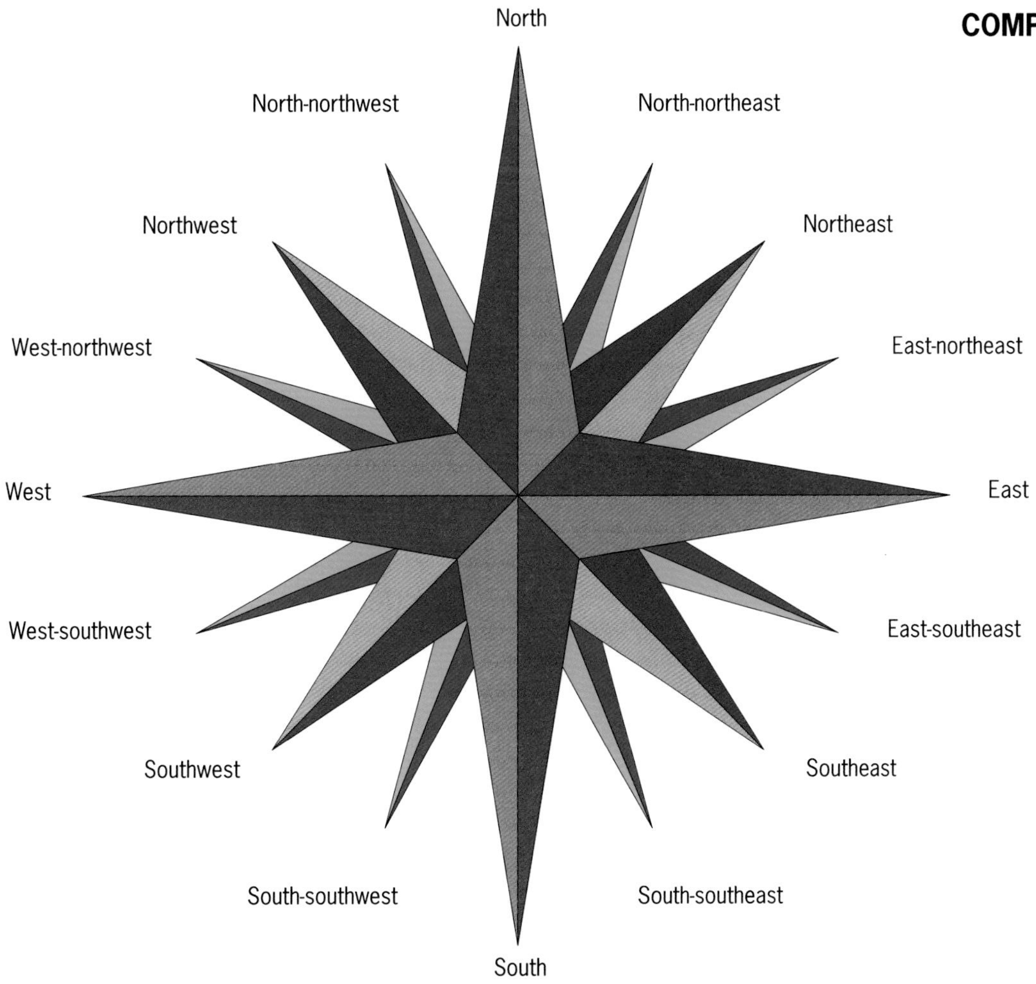

North
North-northeast
Northeast
East-northeast
East
East-southeast
Southeast
South-southeast
South
South-southwest
Southwest
West-southwest
West
West-northwest
Northwest
North-northwest

ECOLOGY

greenhouse effect

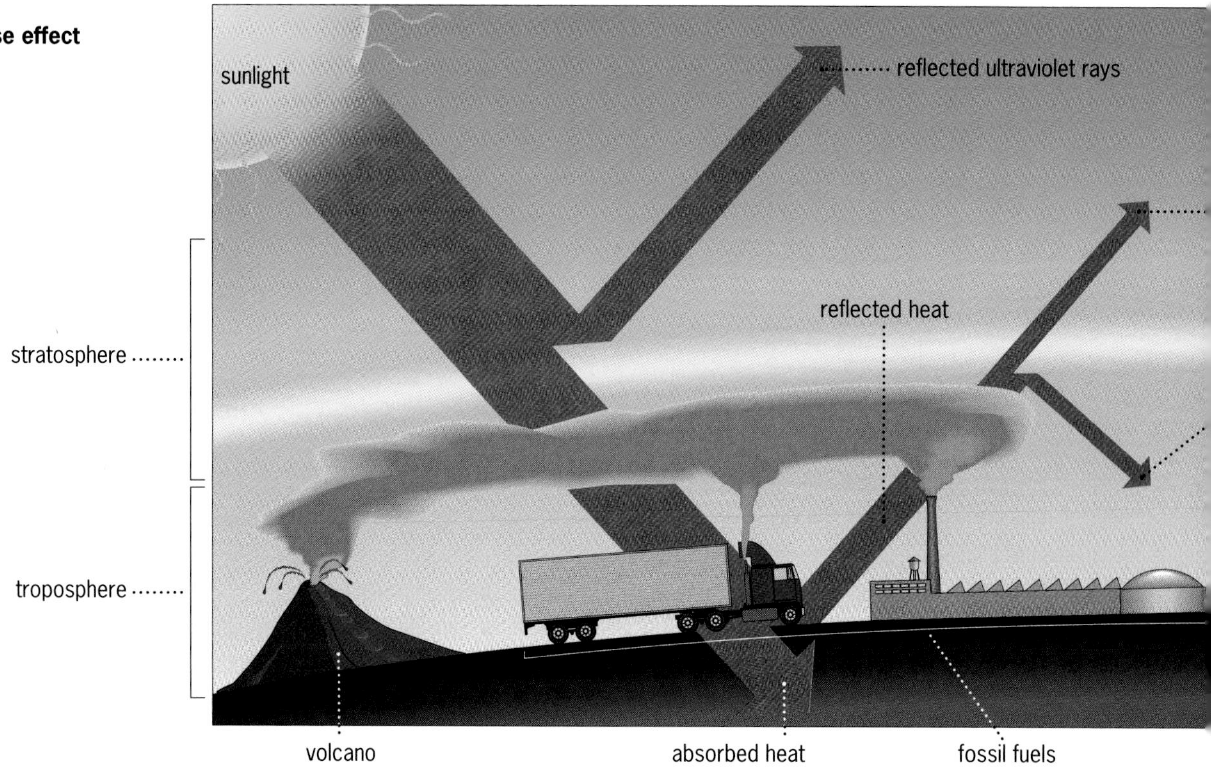
sunlight
reflected ultraviolet rays
reflected heat
stratosphere
troposphere
volcano
absorbed heat
fossil fuels

food chain

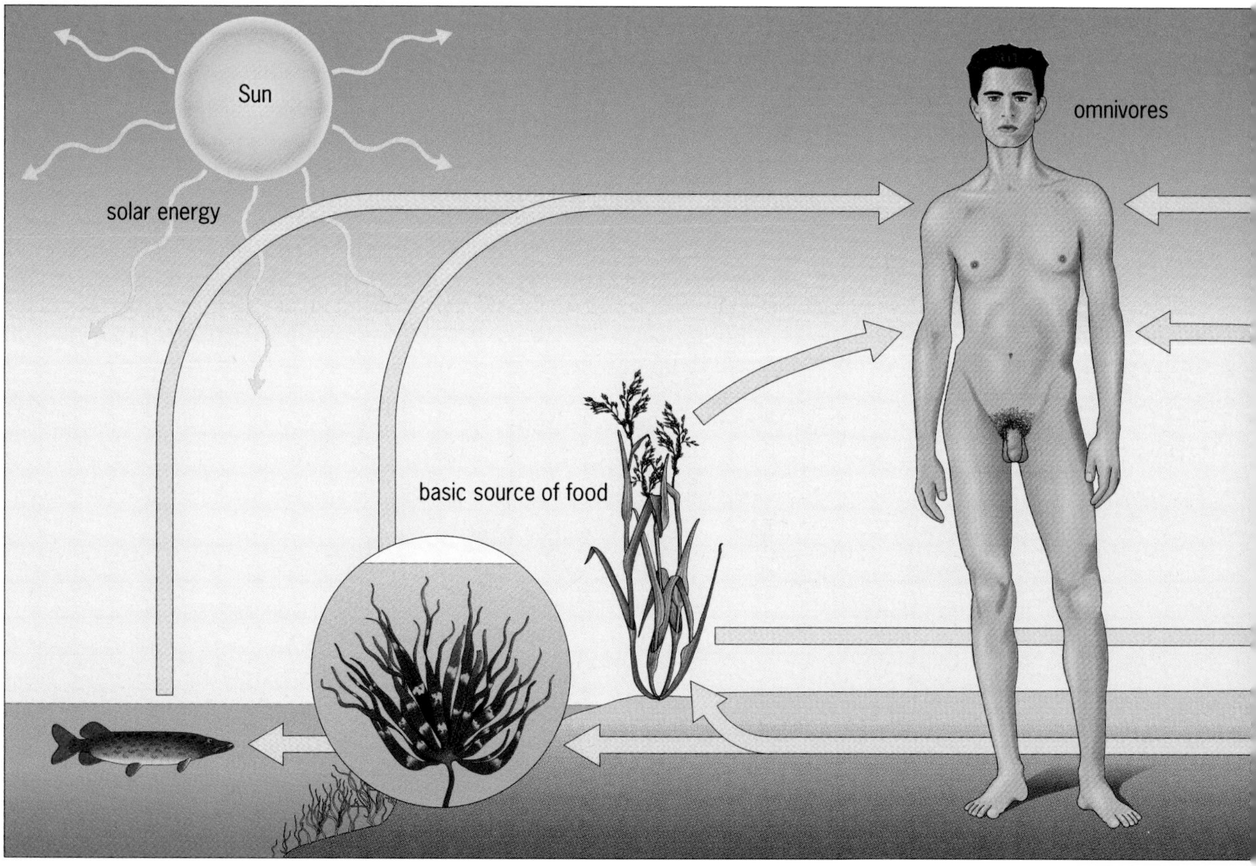
Sun
solar energy
omnivores
basic source of food

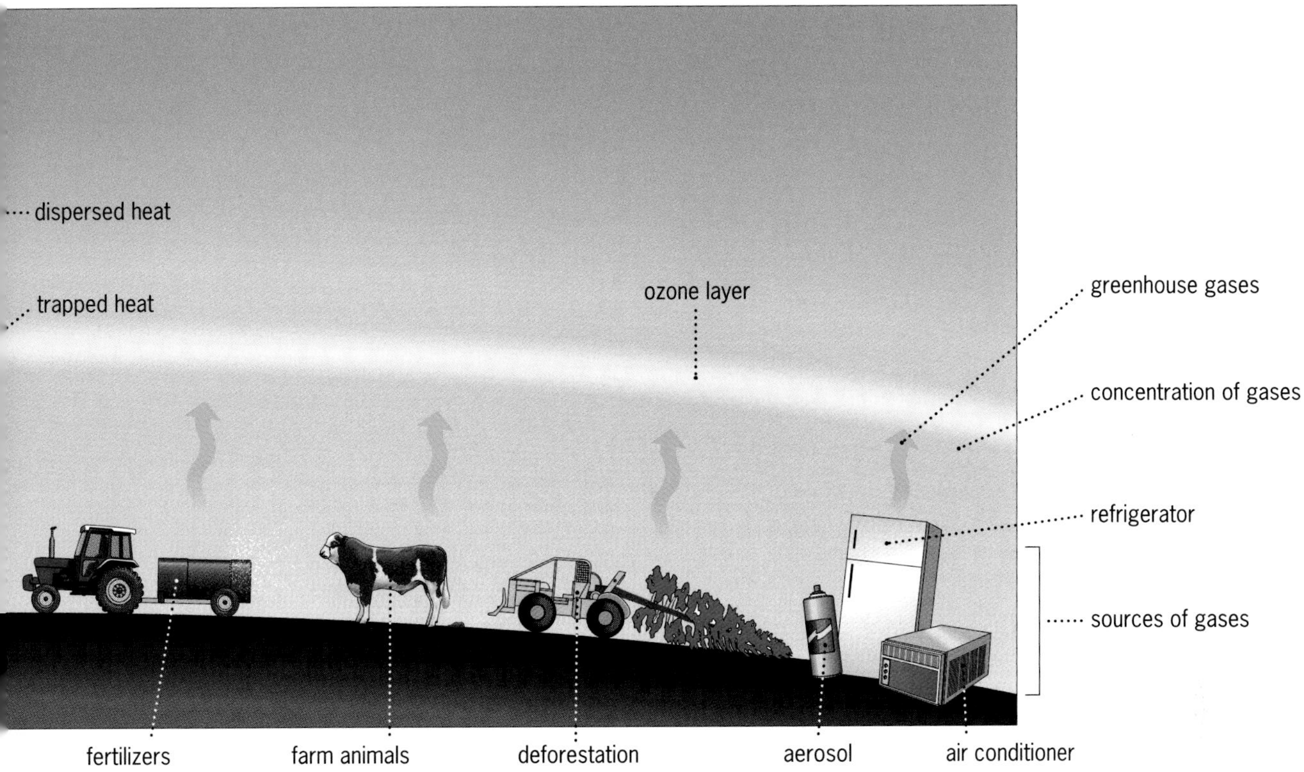
dispersed heat
trapped heat
ozone layer
greenhouse gases
concentration of gases
refrigerator
sources of gases
fertilizers
farm animals
deforestation
aerosol
air conditioner

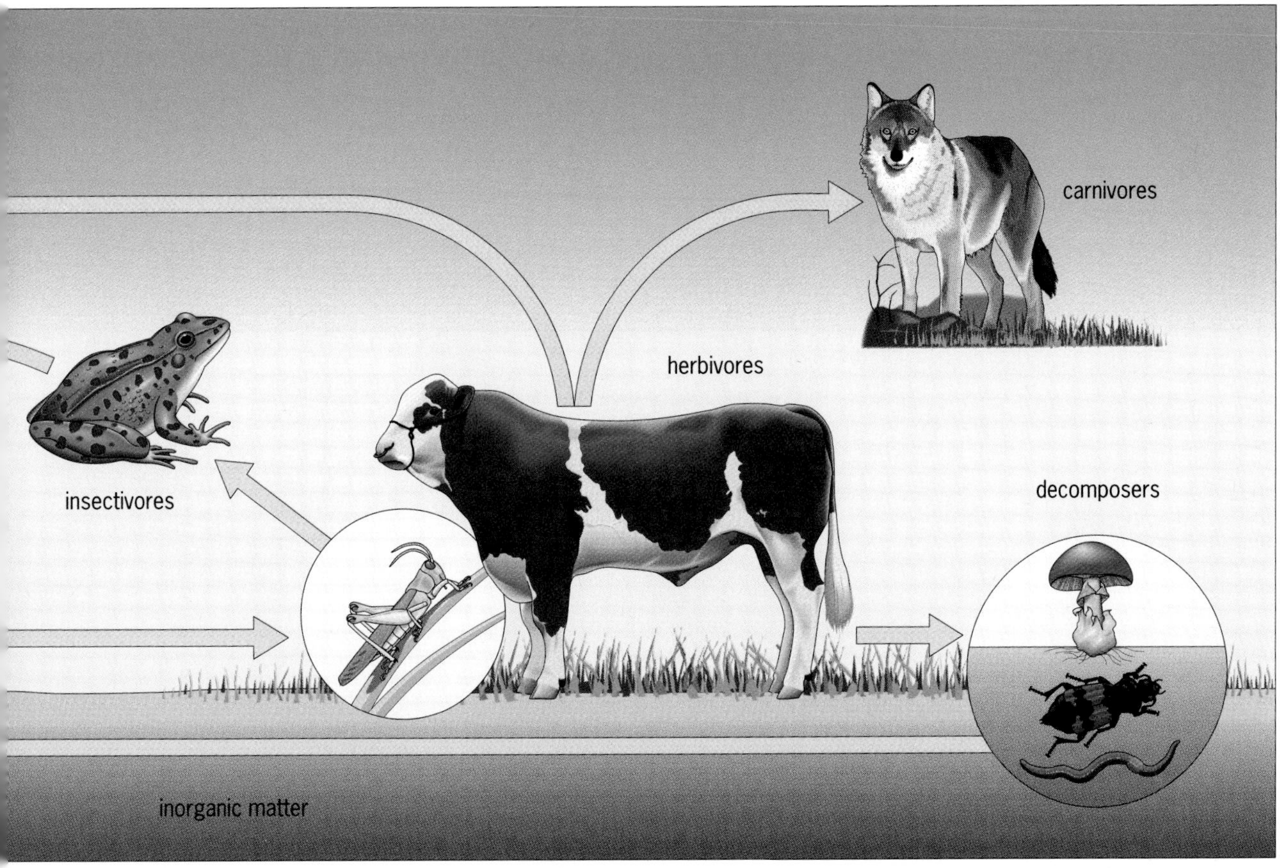
carnivores
herbivores
insectivores
decomposers
inorganic matter

ECOLOGY

atmospheric pollution

moisture in the air
gas
dust
sources of pollution

hydrological cycle

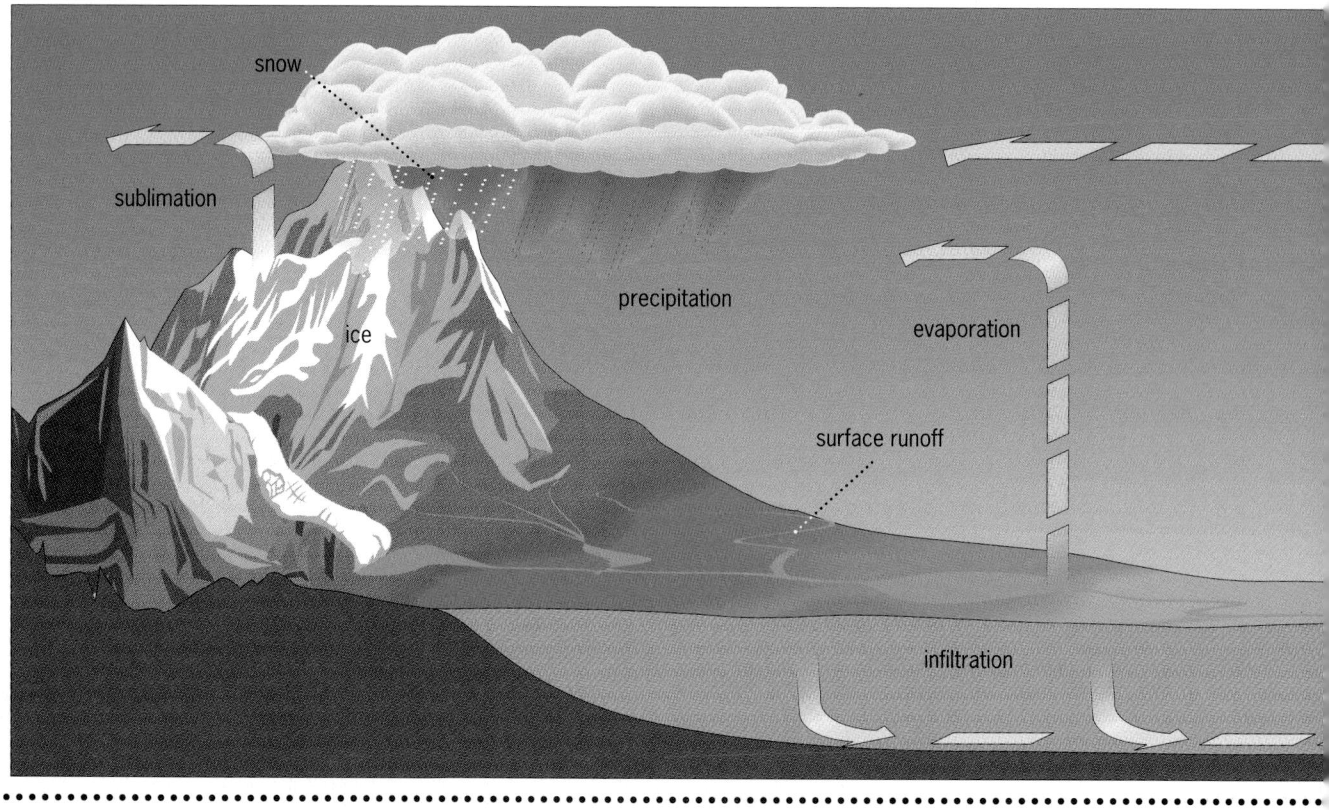
snow
sublimation
ice
precipitation
evaporation
surface runoff
infiltration

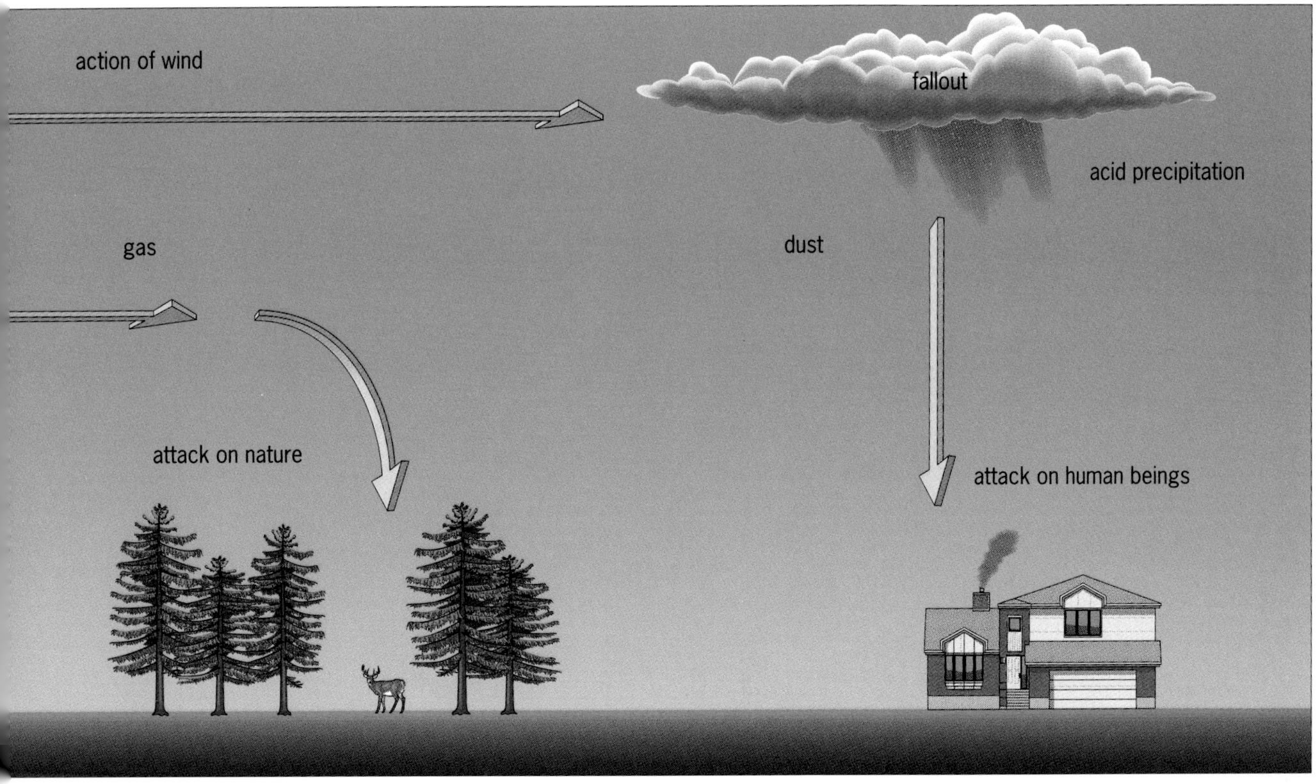
action of wind
fallout
acid precipitation
gas
dust
attack on nature
attack on human beings

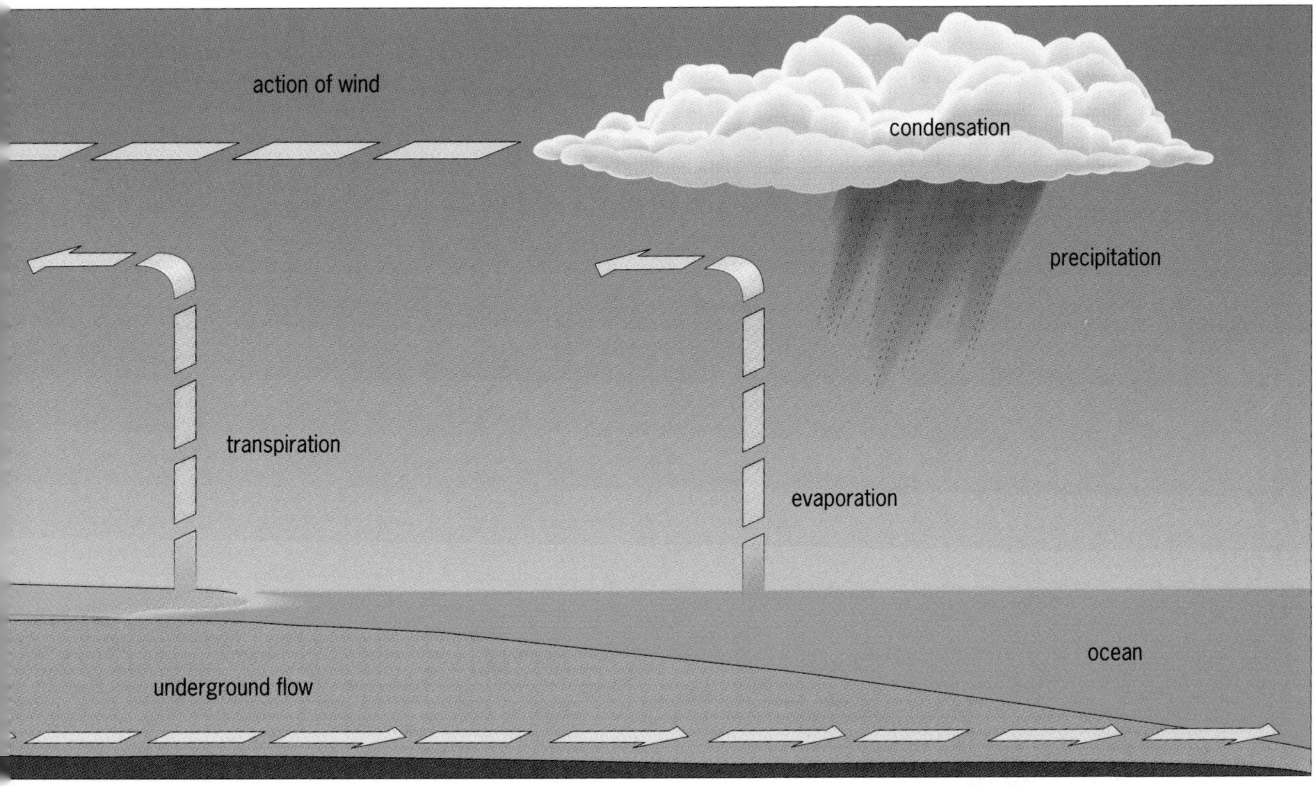
action of wind
condensation
precipitation
transpiration
evaporation
ocean
underground flow

ECOLOGY

food pollution on ground

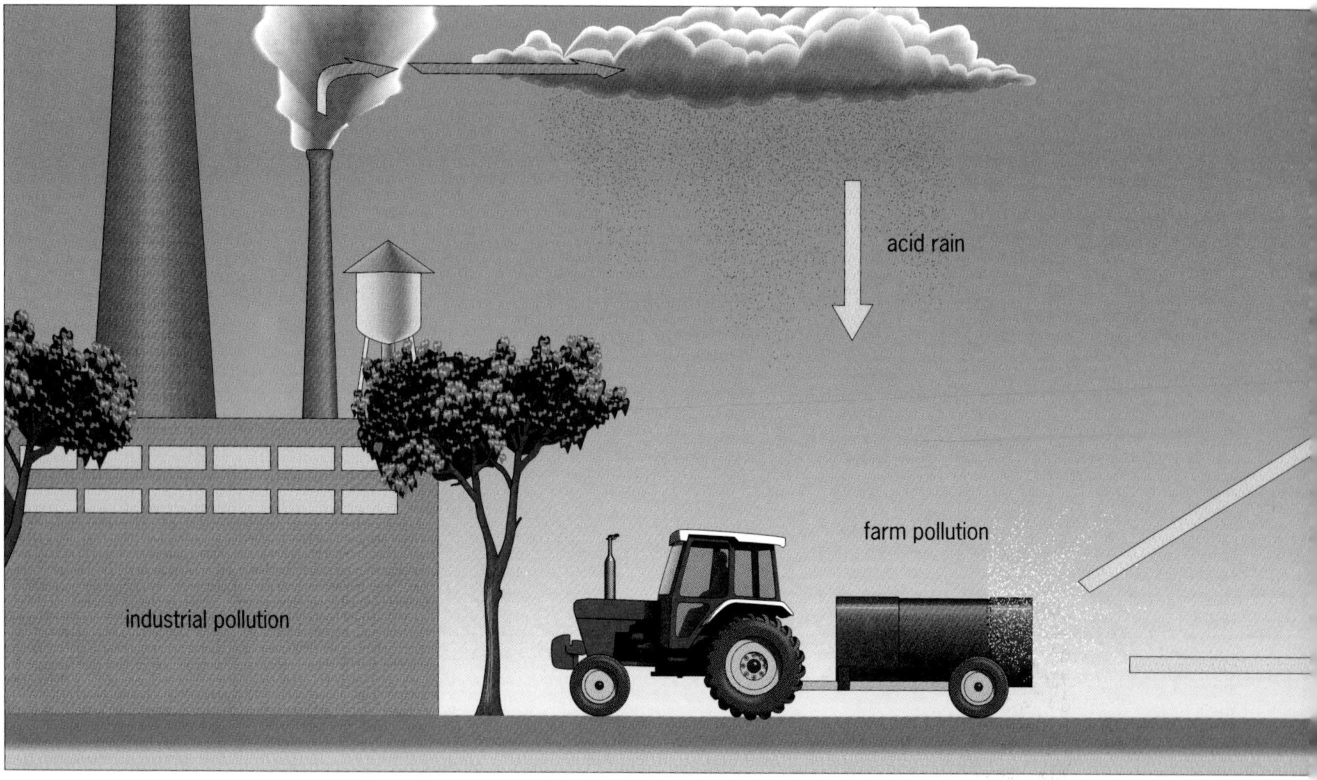
acid rain
farm pollution
industrial pollution

food pollution in water

fertilizers
pesticides
surface runoff
farm pollution
underground flow

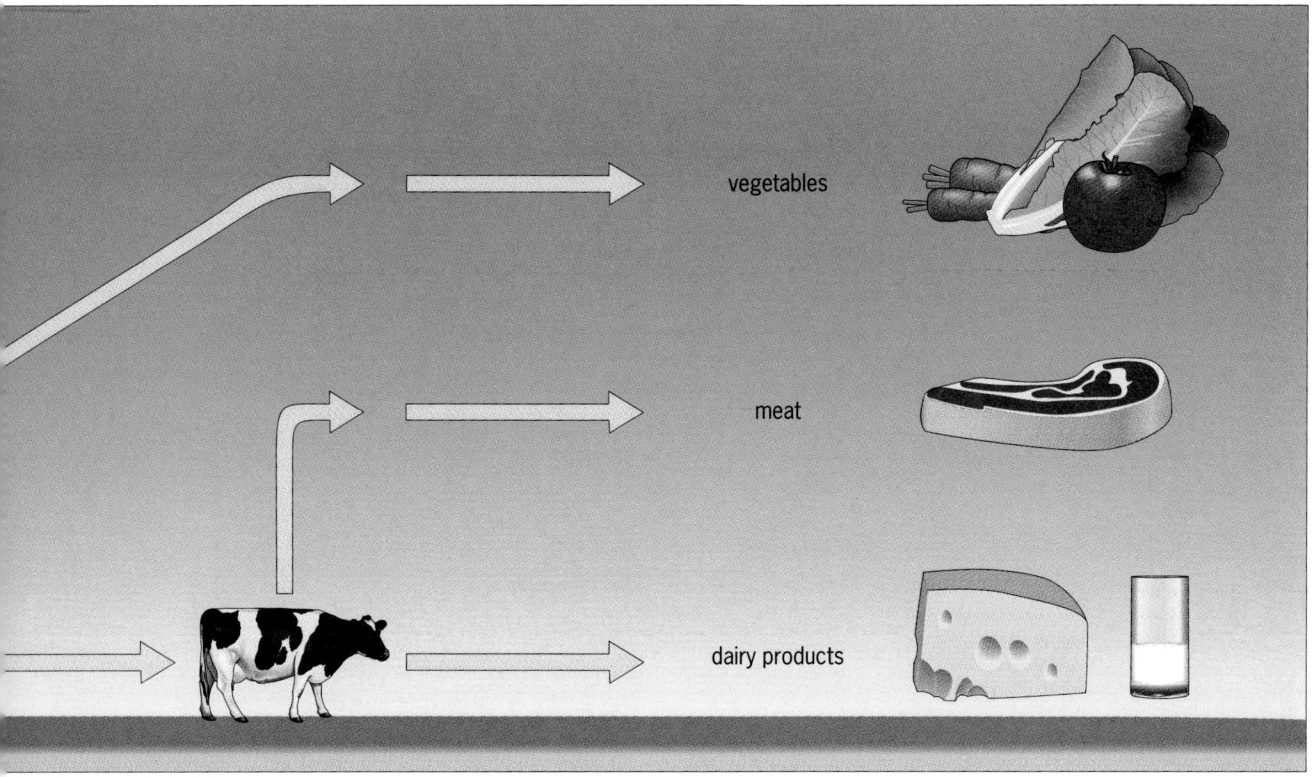
vegetables
meat
dairy products

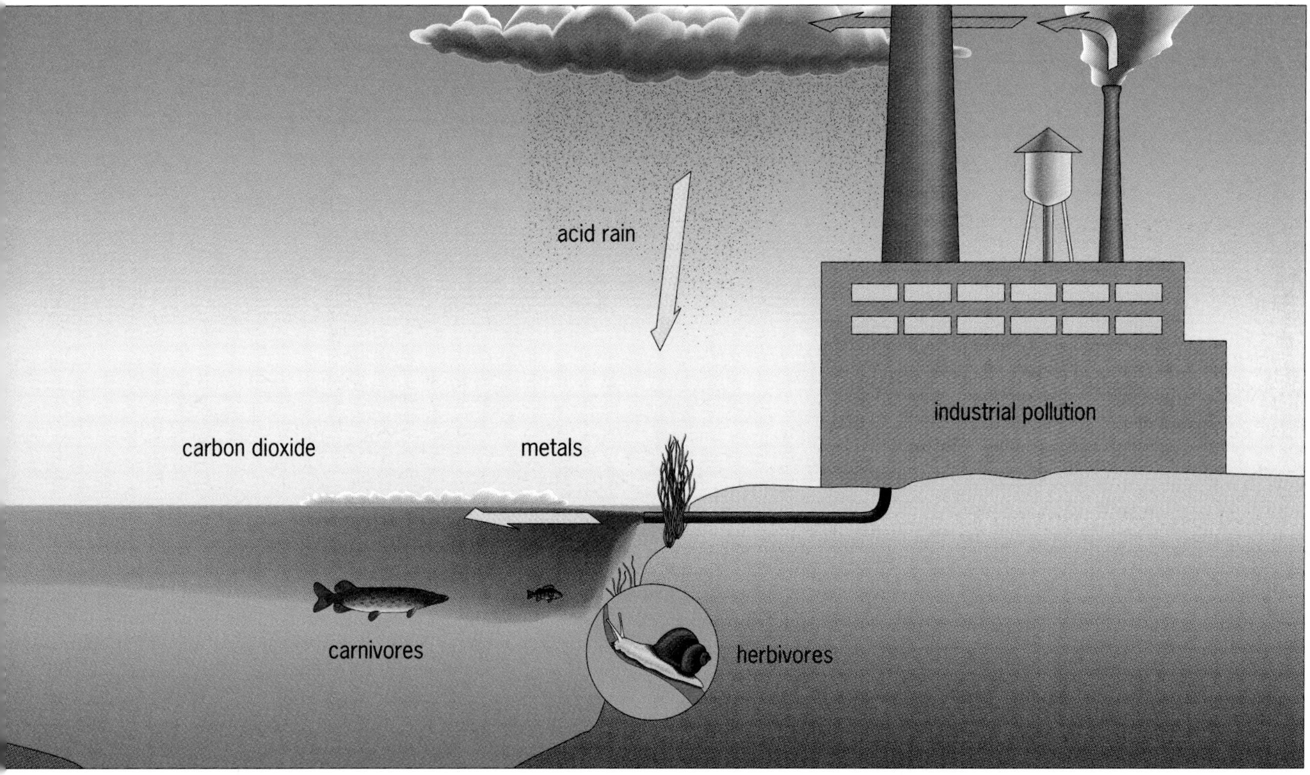
acid rain
industrial pollution
carbon dioxide
metals
carnivores
herbivores

PLANT AND SOIL

SOIL PROFILE

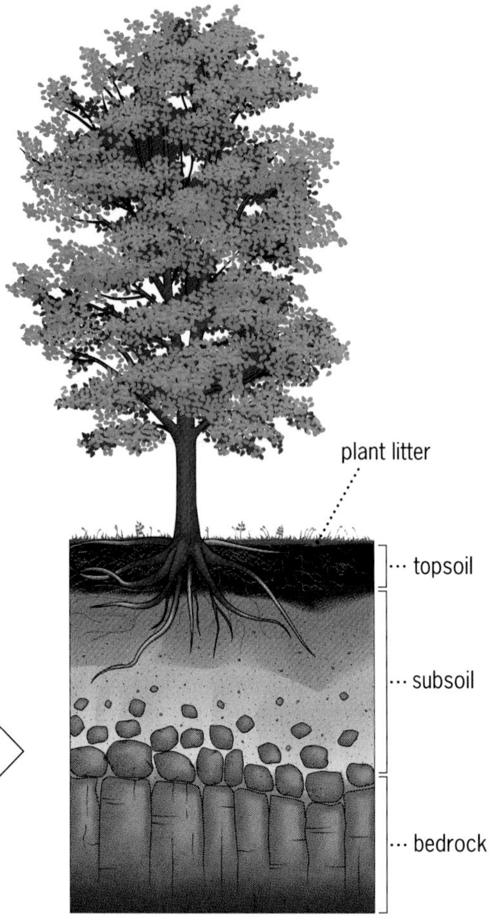
plant litter
topsoil
subsoil
bedrock

GERMINATION

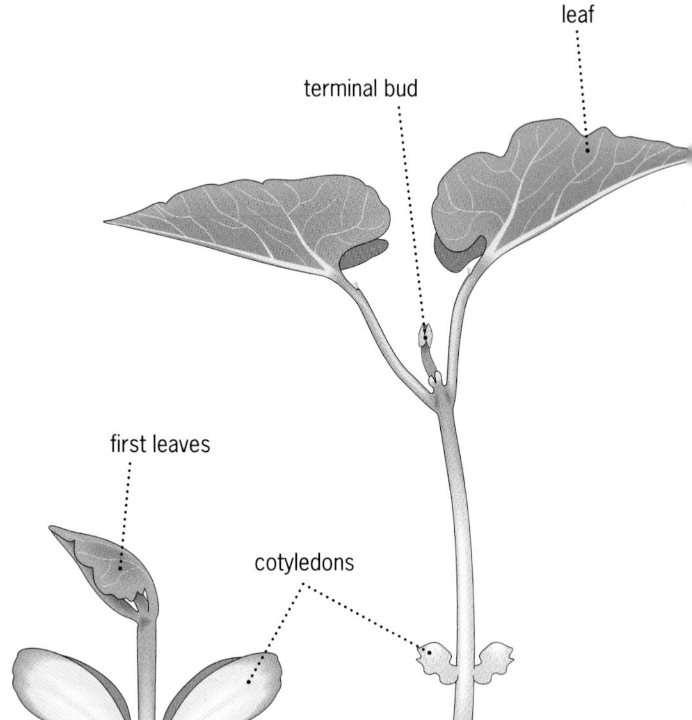
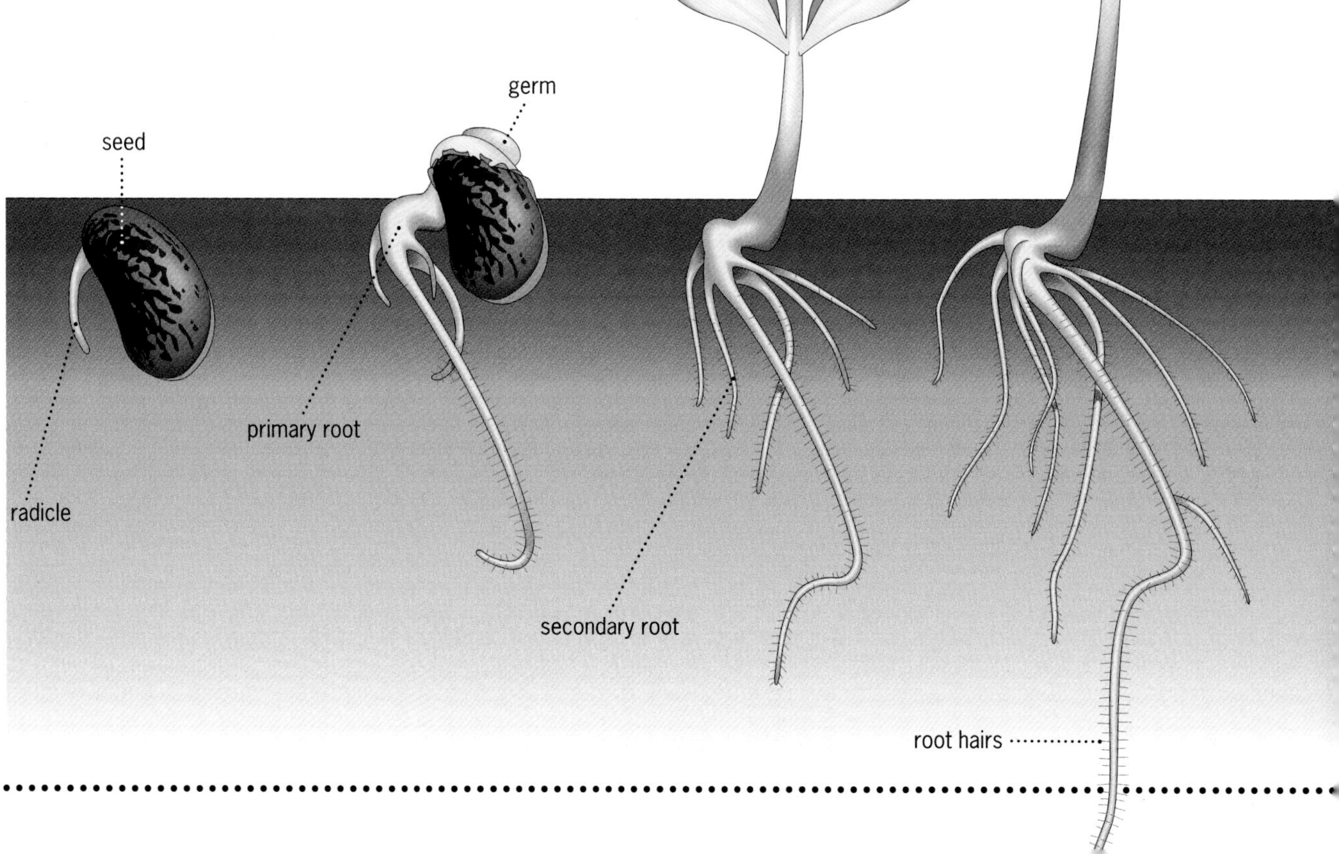
leaf
terminal bud
first leaves
cotyledons
germ
seed
primary root
radicle
secondary root
root hairs

MUSHROOM

structure of a mushroom

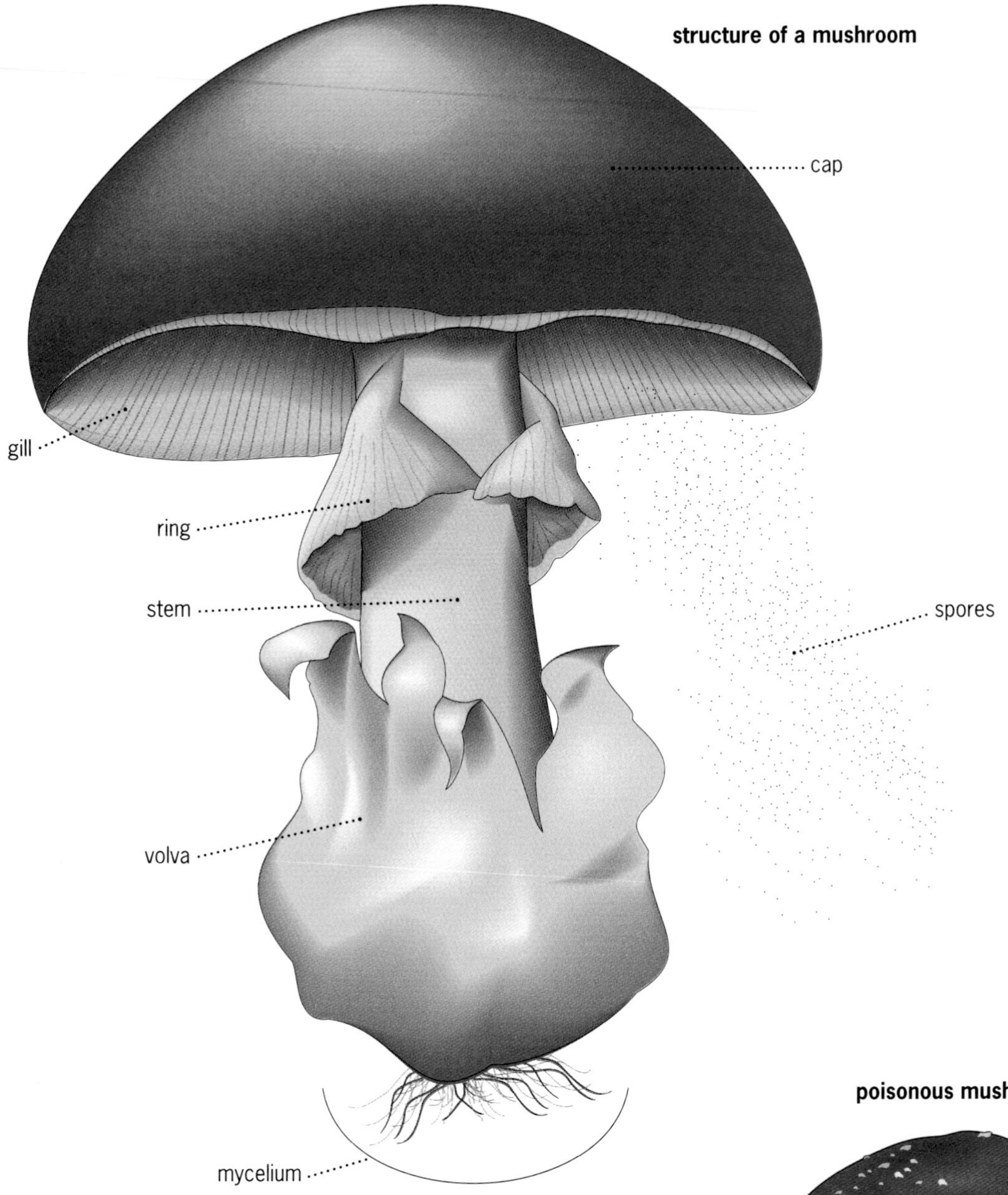
cap
gill
ring
stem
spores
volva
mycelium

edible mushroom

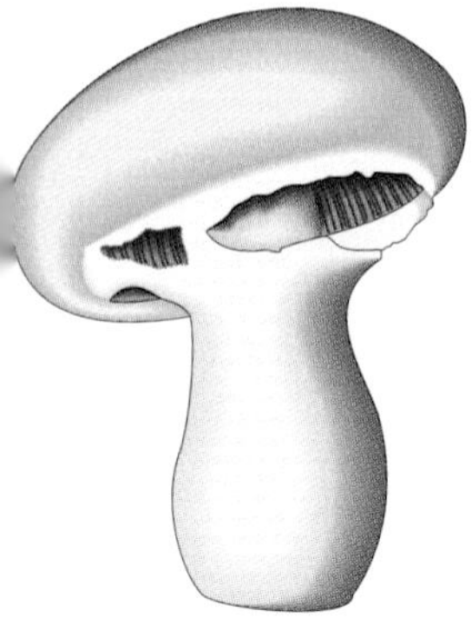

cultivated mushroom

deadly mushroom

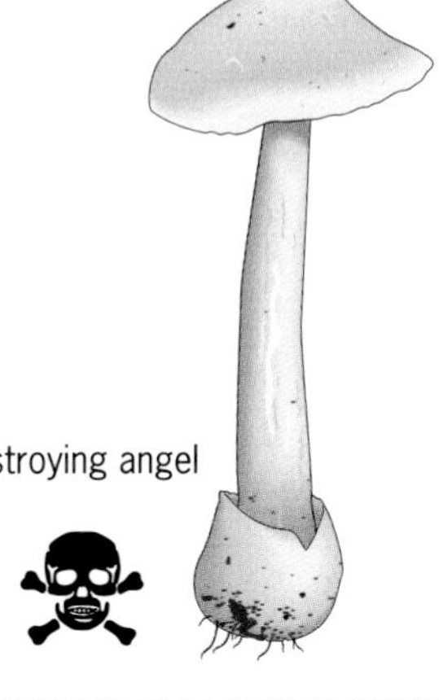
destroying angel

poisonous mushroom

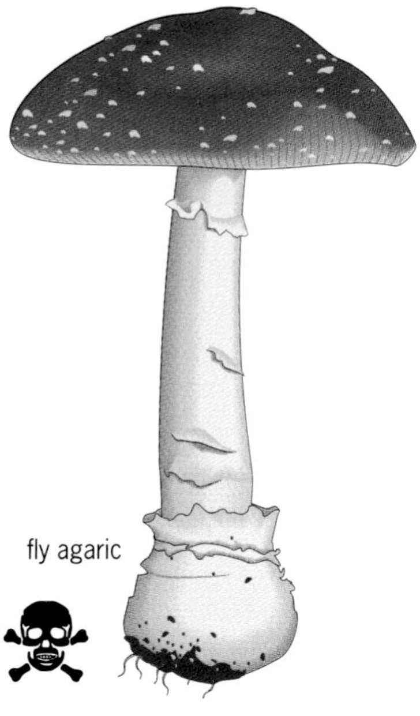
fly agaric

STRUCTURE OF A PLANT

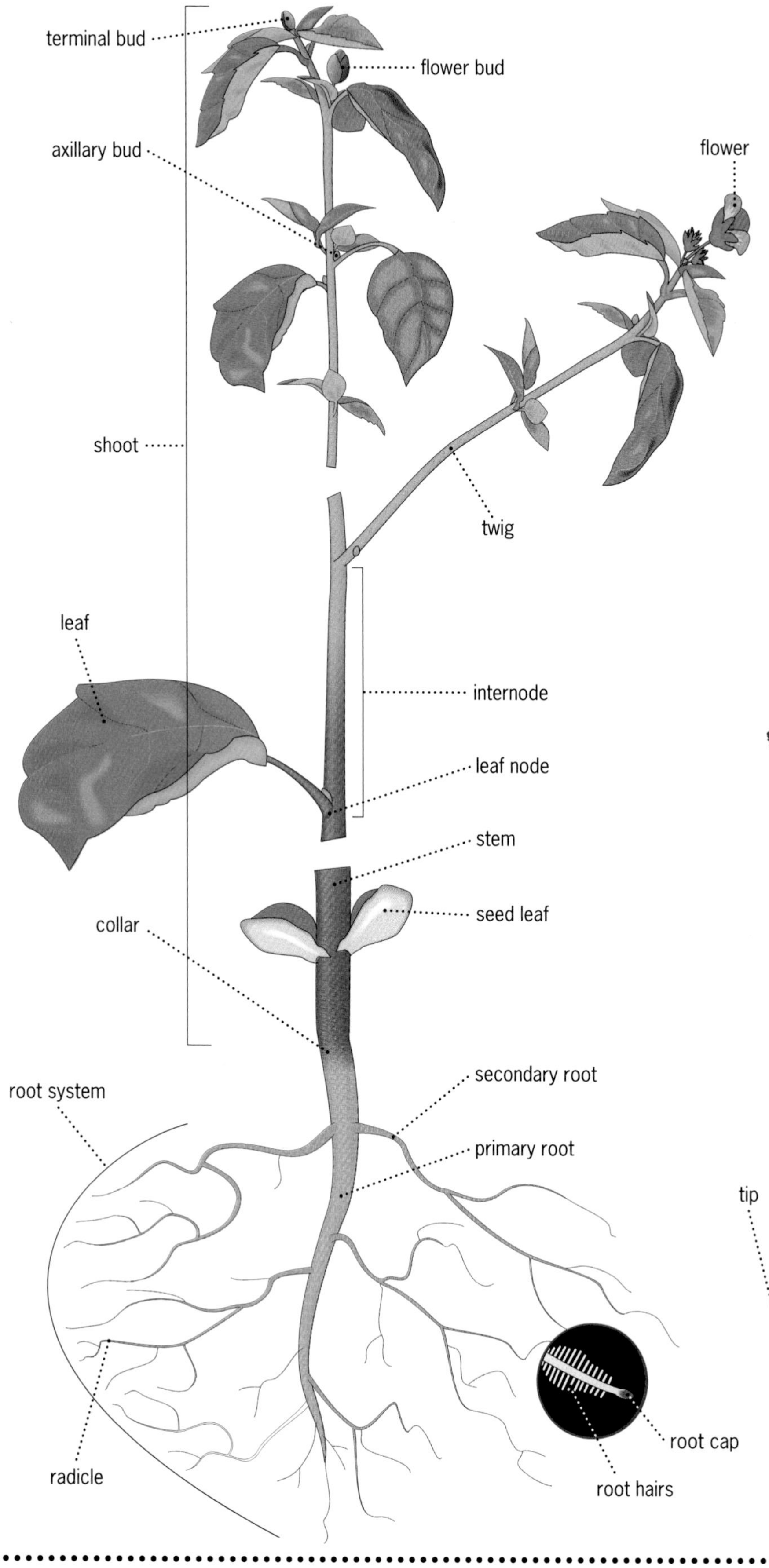
terminal bud
flower bud
axillary bud
flower
shoot
twig
leaf
internode
leaf node
stem
seed leaf
collar
secondary root
root system
primary root
radicle
root cap
root hairs

COMPOUND LEAVES

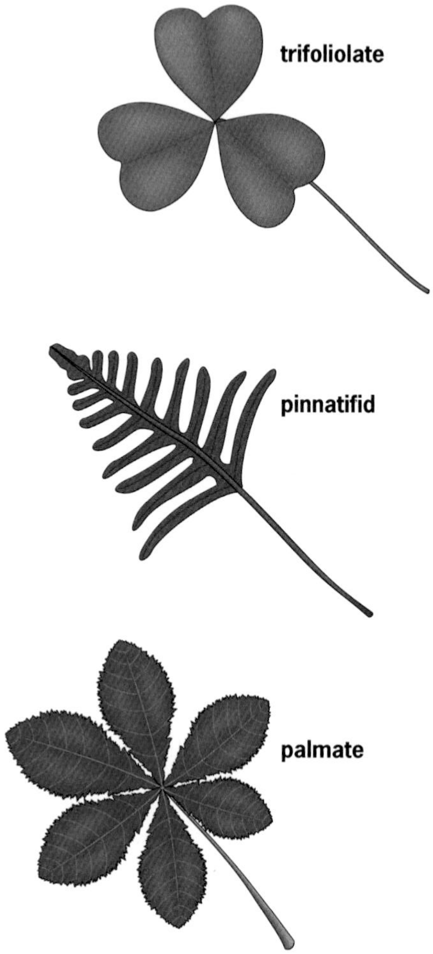
trifoliolate
pinnatifid
palmate

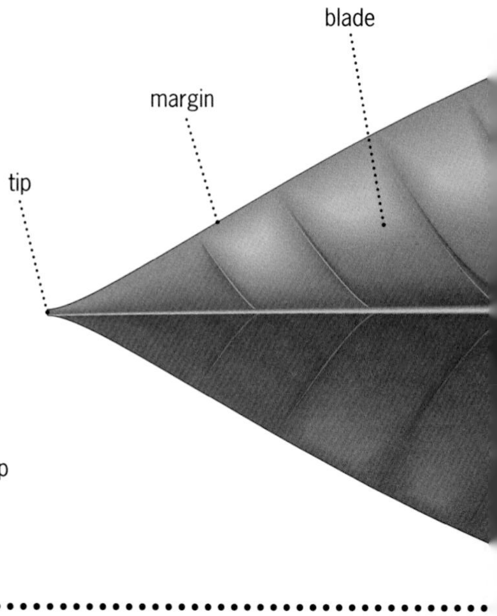
blade
margin
tip

SIMPLE LEAVES

LEAF MARGINS

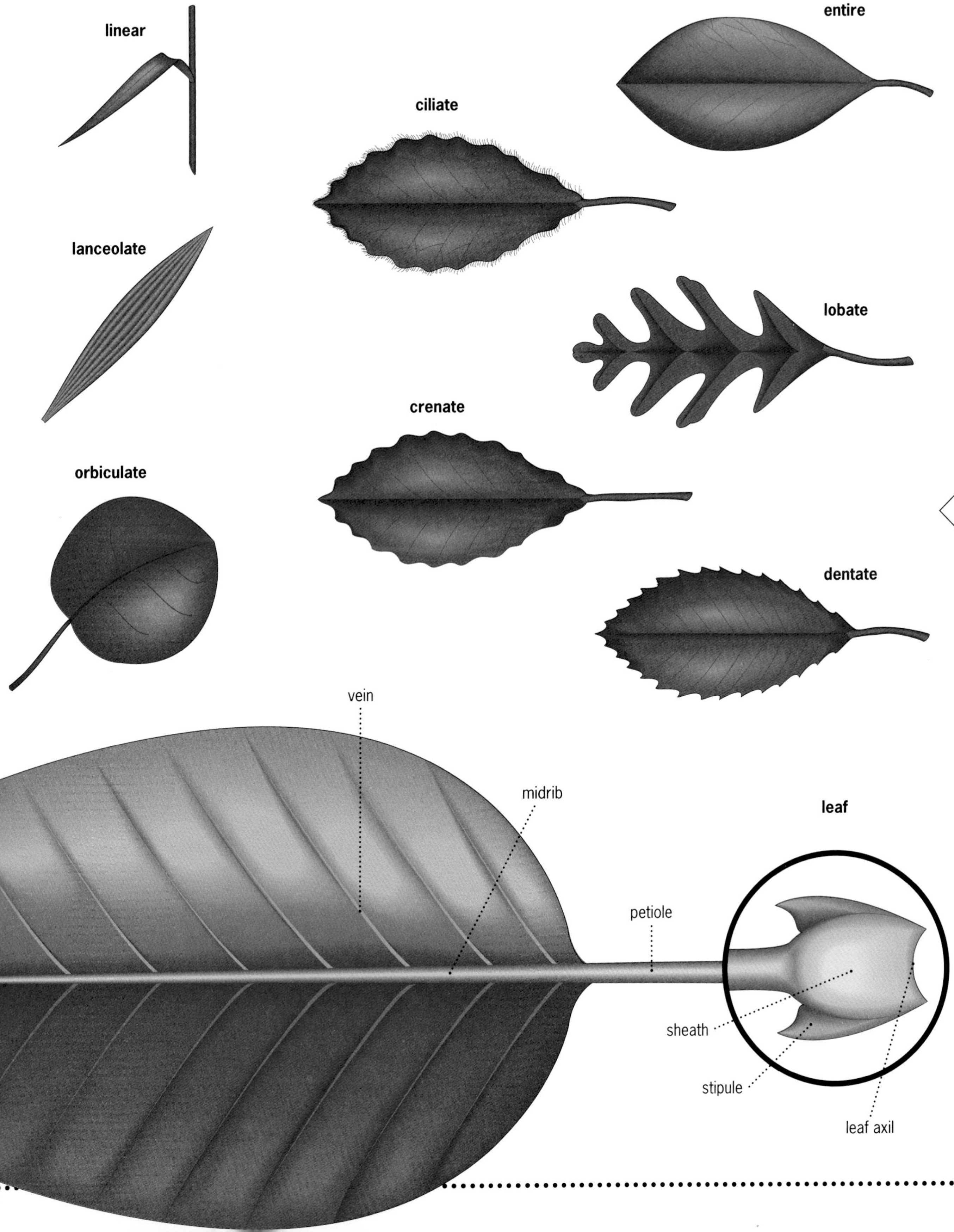
linear
lanceolate
orbiculate
ciliate
crenate
entire
lobate
dentate
vein
midrib
petiole
leaf
sheath
stipule
leaf axil

FLOWERS

structure of a flower

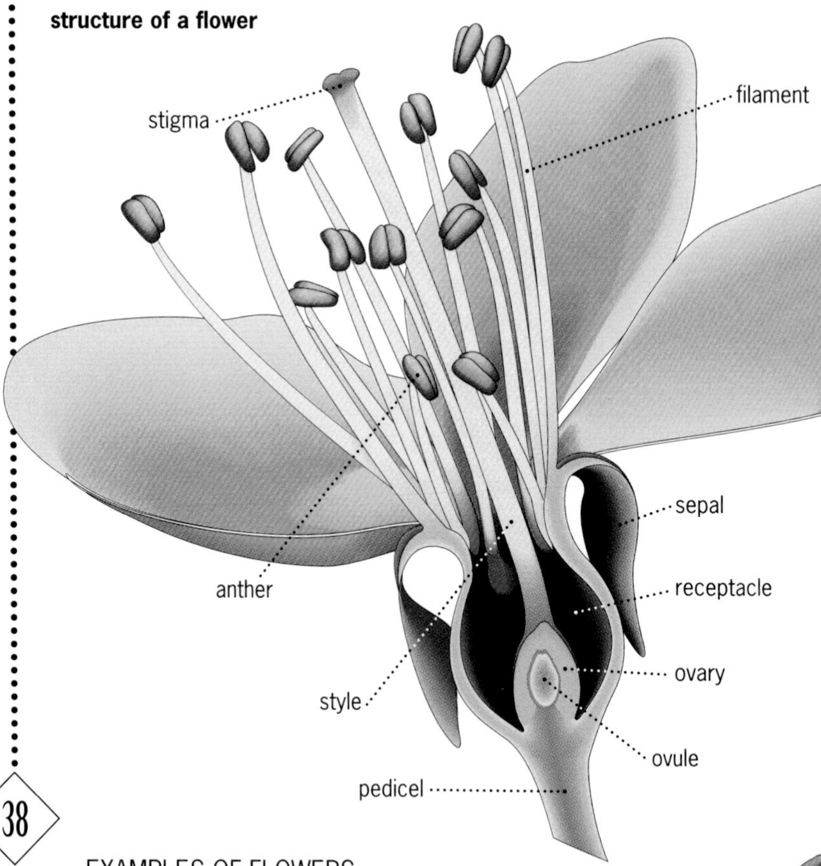
stigma
filament
petal
sepal
anther
receptacle
ovary
style
ovule
pedicel

corolla

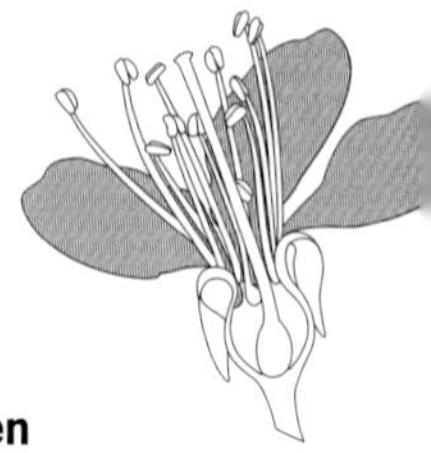

stamen

pistil

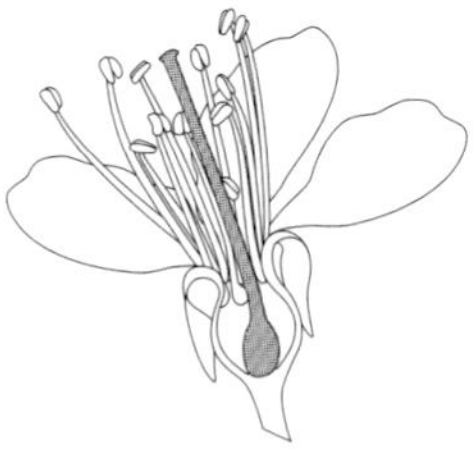

calyx

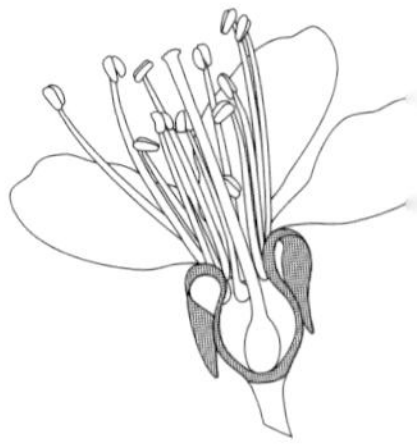

EXAMPLES OF FLOWERS

orchid

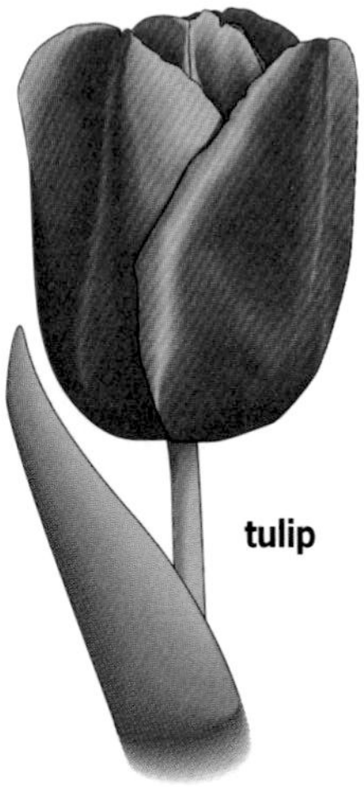

tulip

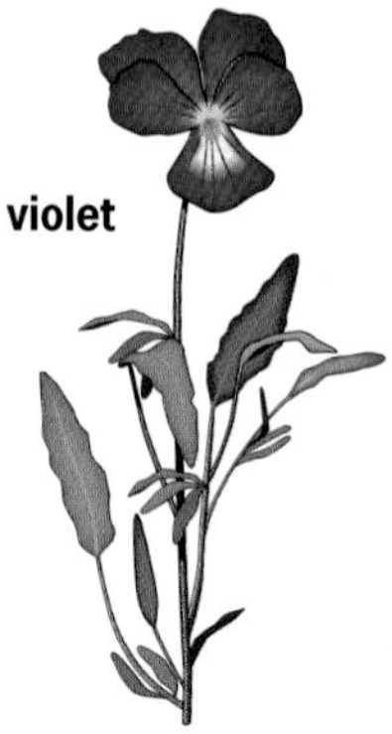

violet

begonia

poppy

rose

sunflower

lily

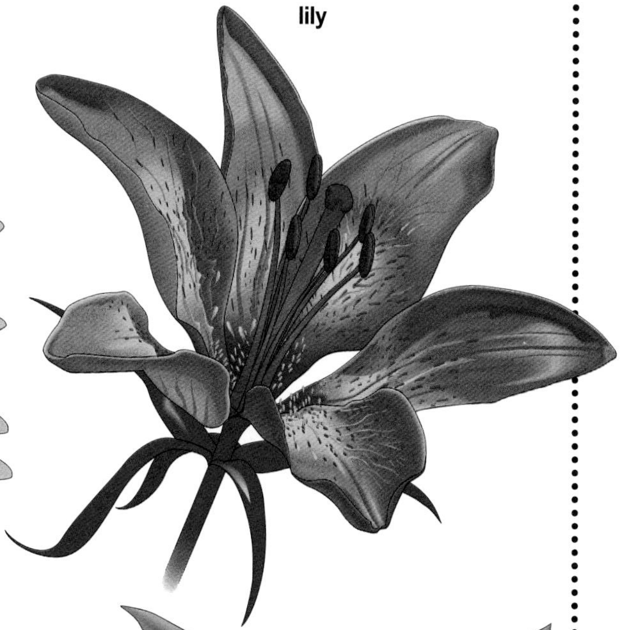

lily of the valley

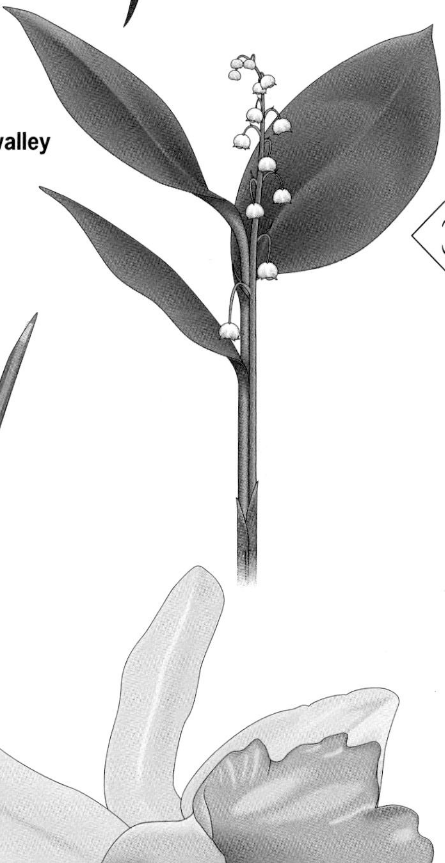

crocus

carnation

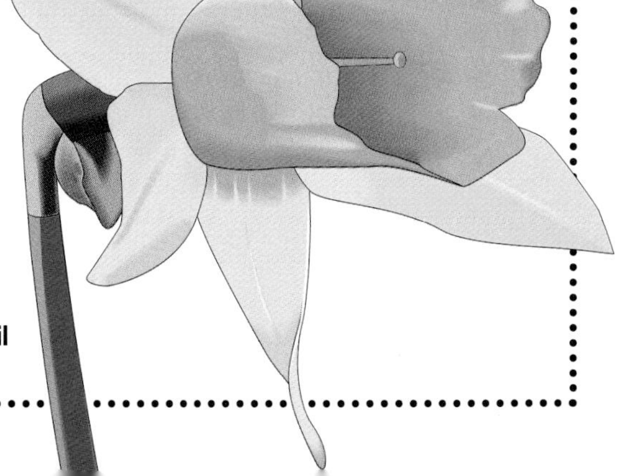

daffodil

TREE

structure of a tree

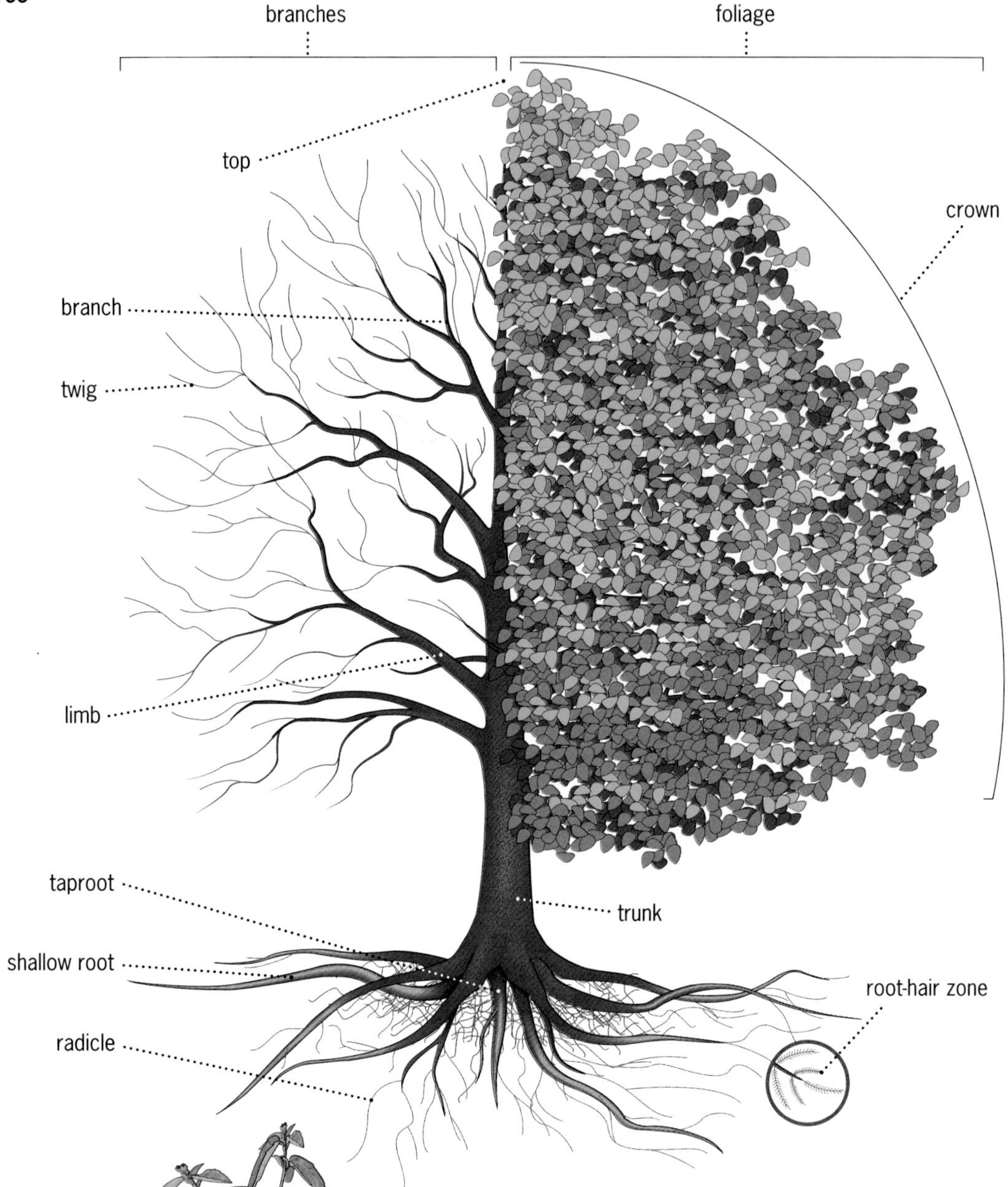
branches
foliage
top
crown
branch
twig
limb
taproot
trunk
shallow root
root-hair zone
radicle

stump

shoot

cross section of a trunk

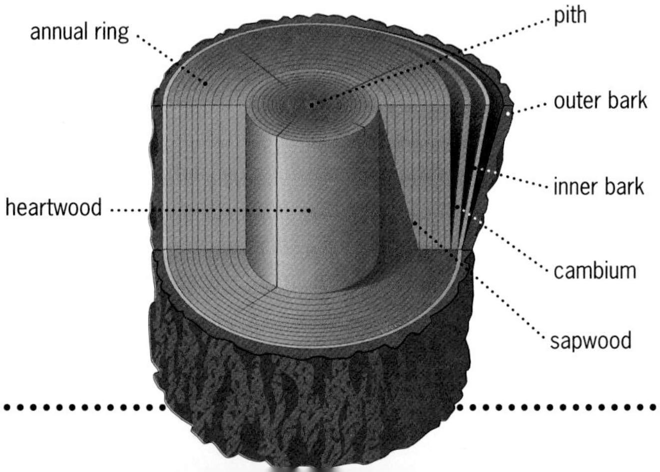
annual ring
pith
outer bark
inner bark
heartwood
cambium
sapwood

EXAMPLES OF TREES

poplar
oak
maple

palm tree

weeping willow

birch

CONIFER

larch

umbrella pine

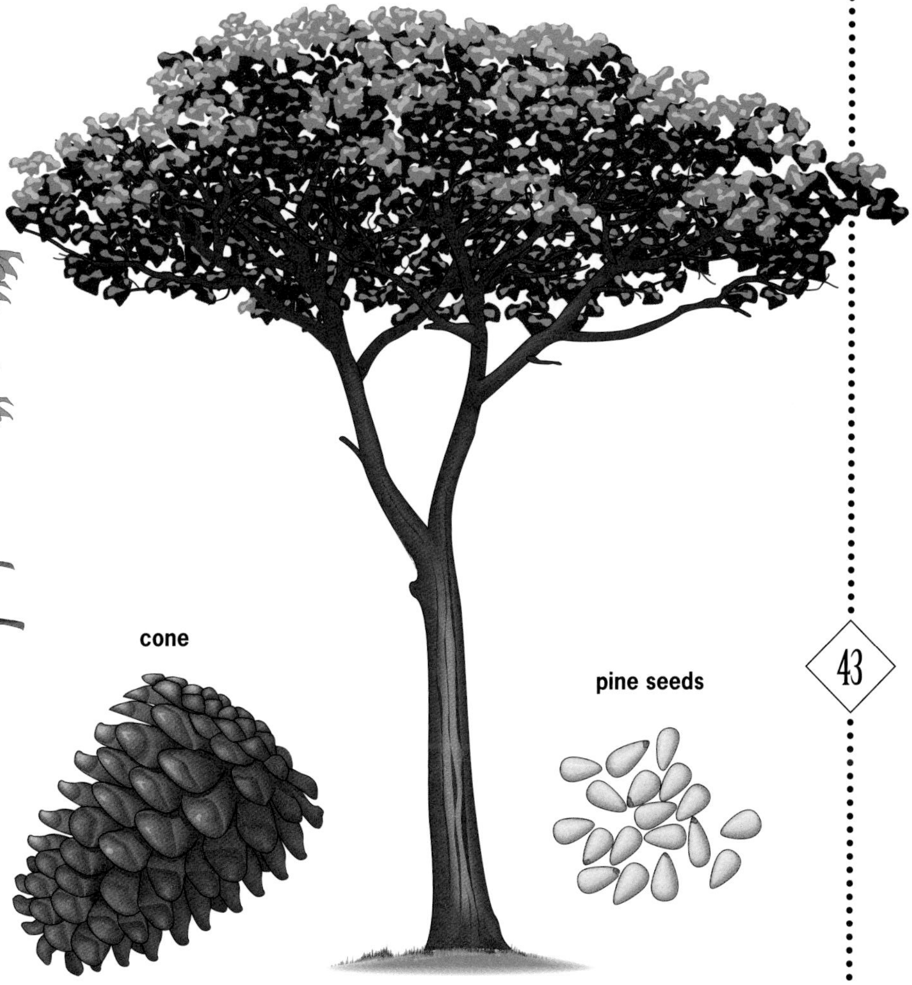

cone

pine seeds

TYPES OF LEAVES

fir needles

cypress scalelike leaves

pine needles

branch

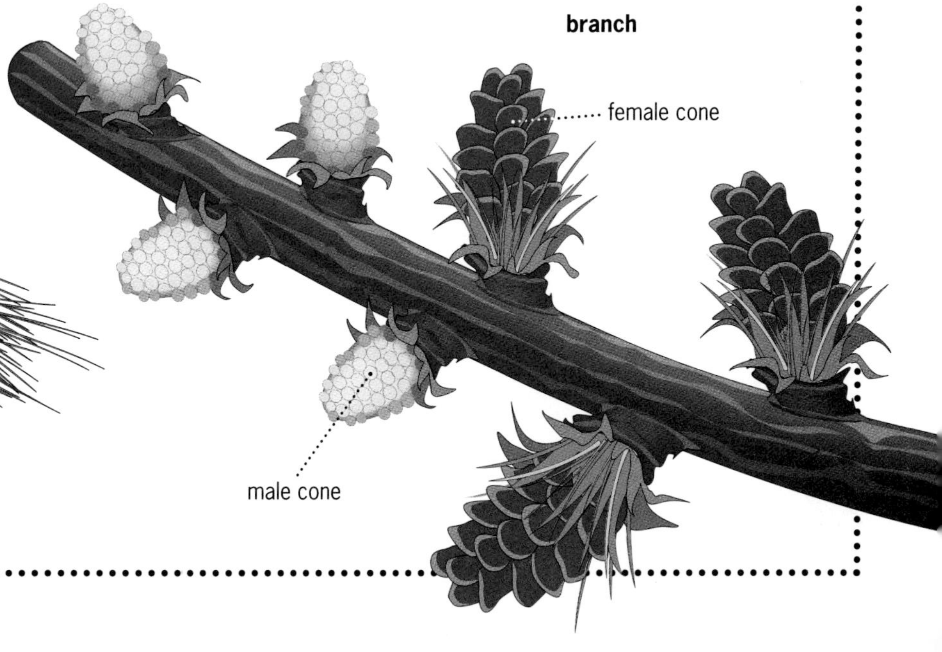
female cone
male cone

FLESHY FRUITS: BERRY FRUITS

section of a berry

grape

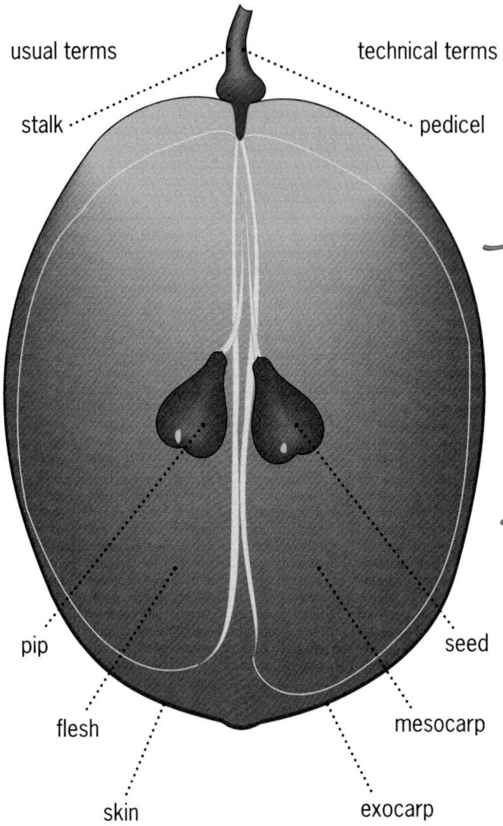
usual terms
technical terms
stalk
pedicel
pip
seed
flesh
mesocarp
skin
exocarp

MAJOR TYPES OF BERRIES

cranberry

blueberry

redcurrant

grape

blackcurrant

gooseberry

huckleberry

section of a strawberry

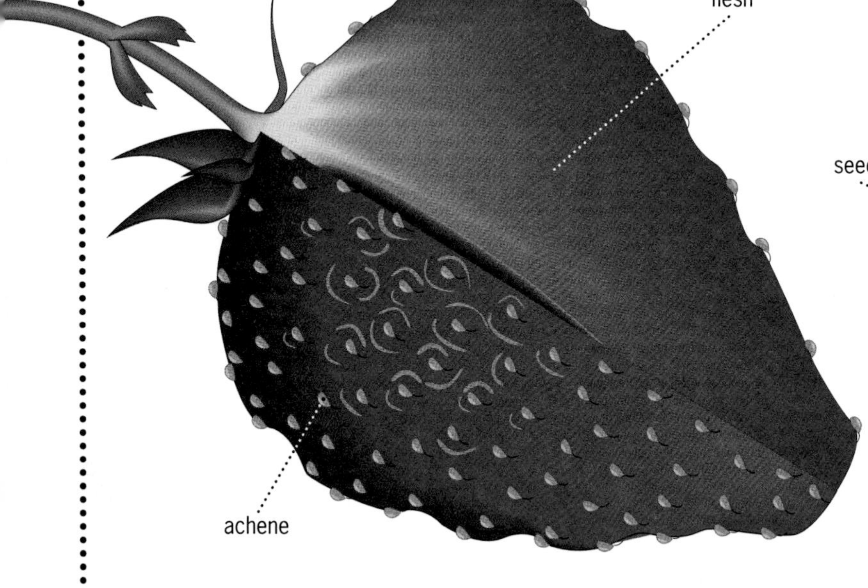
flesh
achene

section of a raspberry

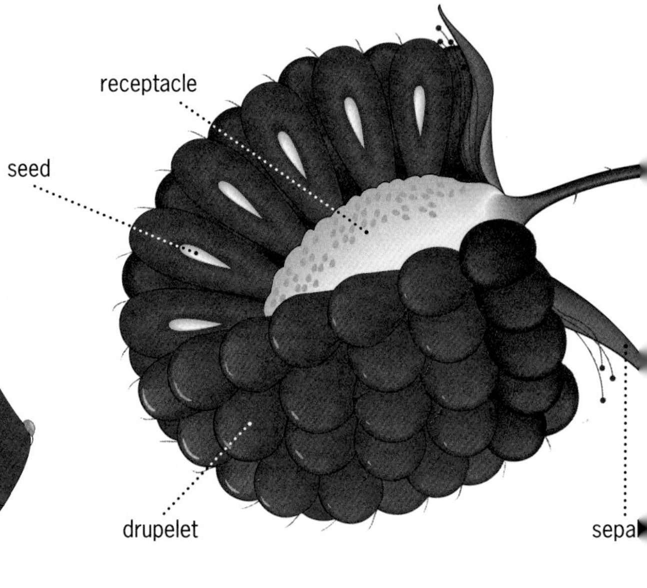
receptacle
seed
drupelet
sepa

FLESHY STONE FRUITS

section of a stone fruit

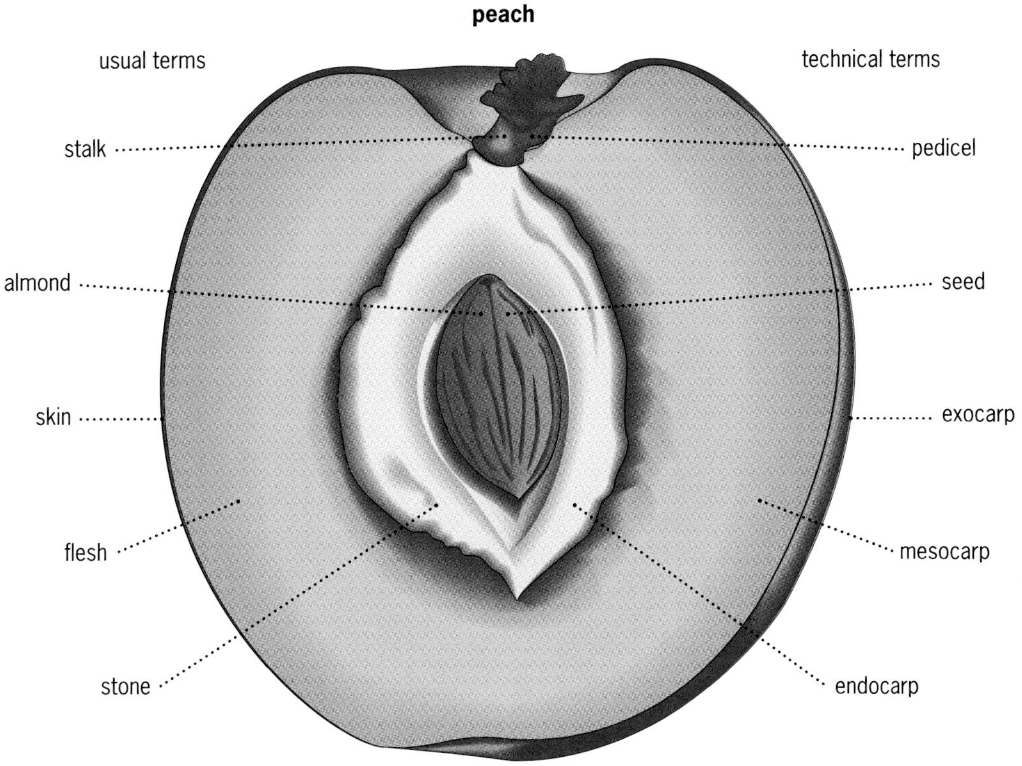
peach
usual terms
technical terms
stalk
pedicel
almond
seed
skin
exocarp
flesh
mesocarp
stone
endocarp

MAJOR TYPES OF STONE FRUITS

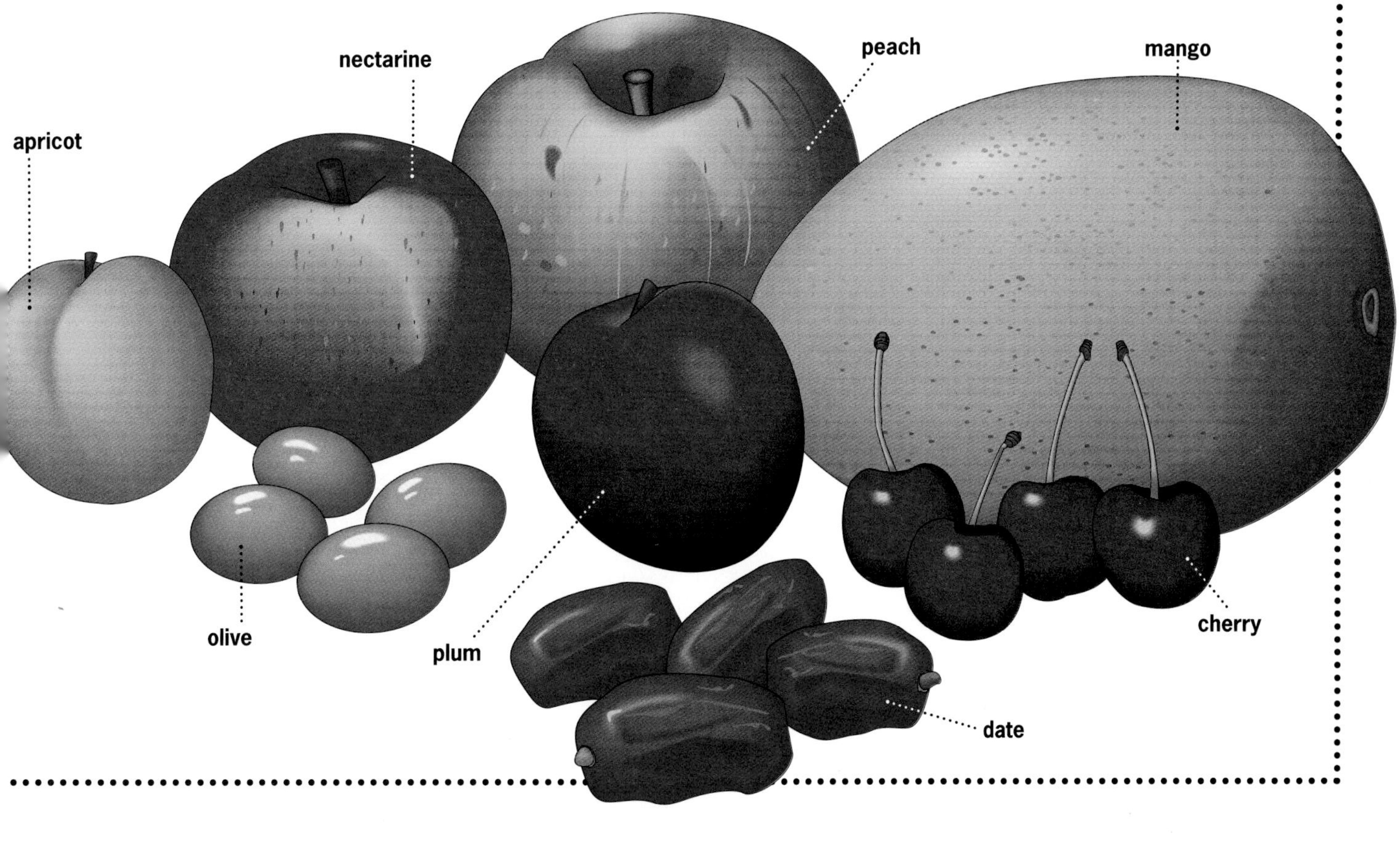
nectarine
peach
mango
apricot
olive
plum
cherry
date

FLESHY POME FRUITS

section of a pome fruit

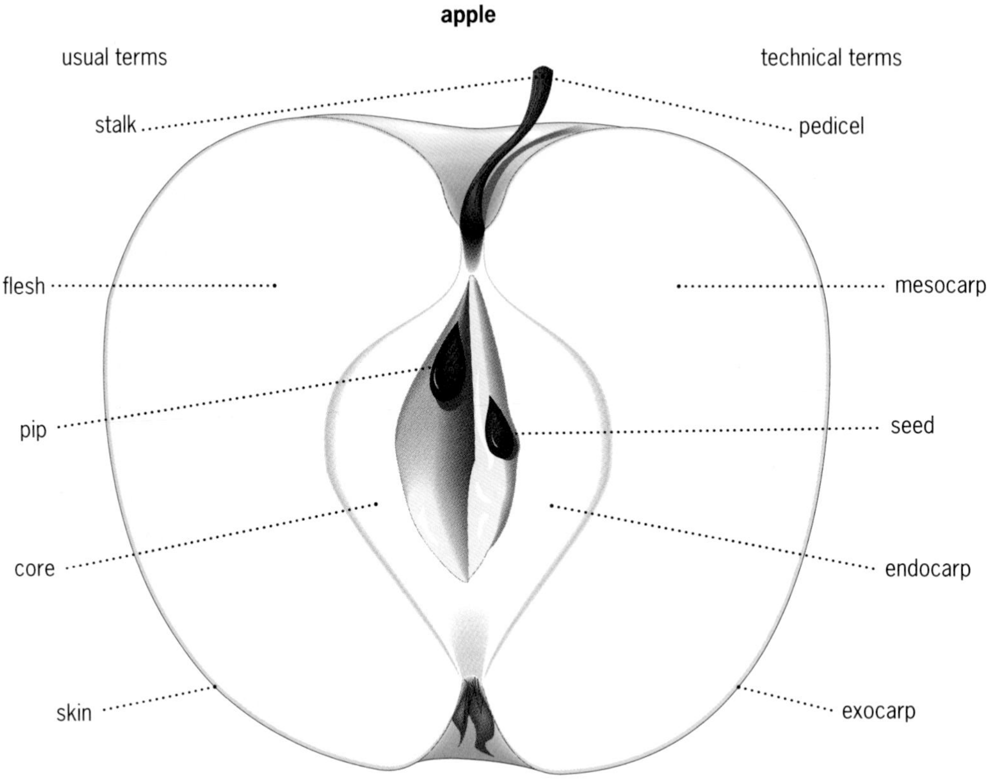
apple
usual terms
technical terms
stalk
pedicel
flesh
mesocarp
pip
seed
core
endocarp
skin
exocarp

MAJOR TYPES OF POME FRUITS

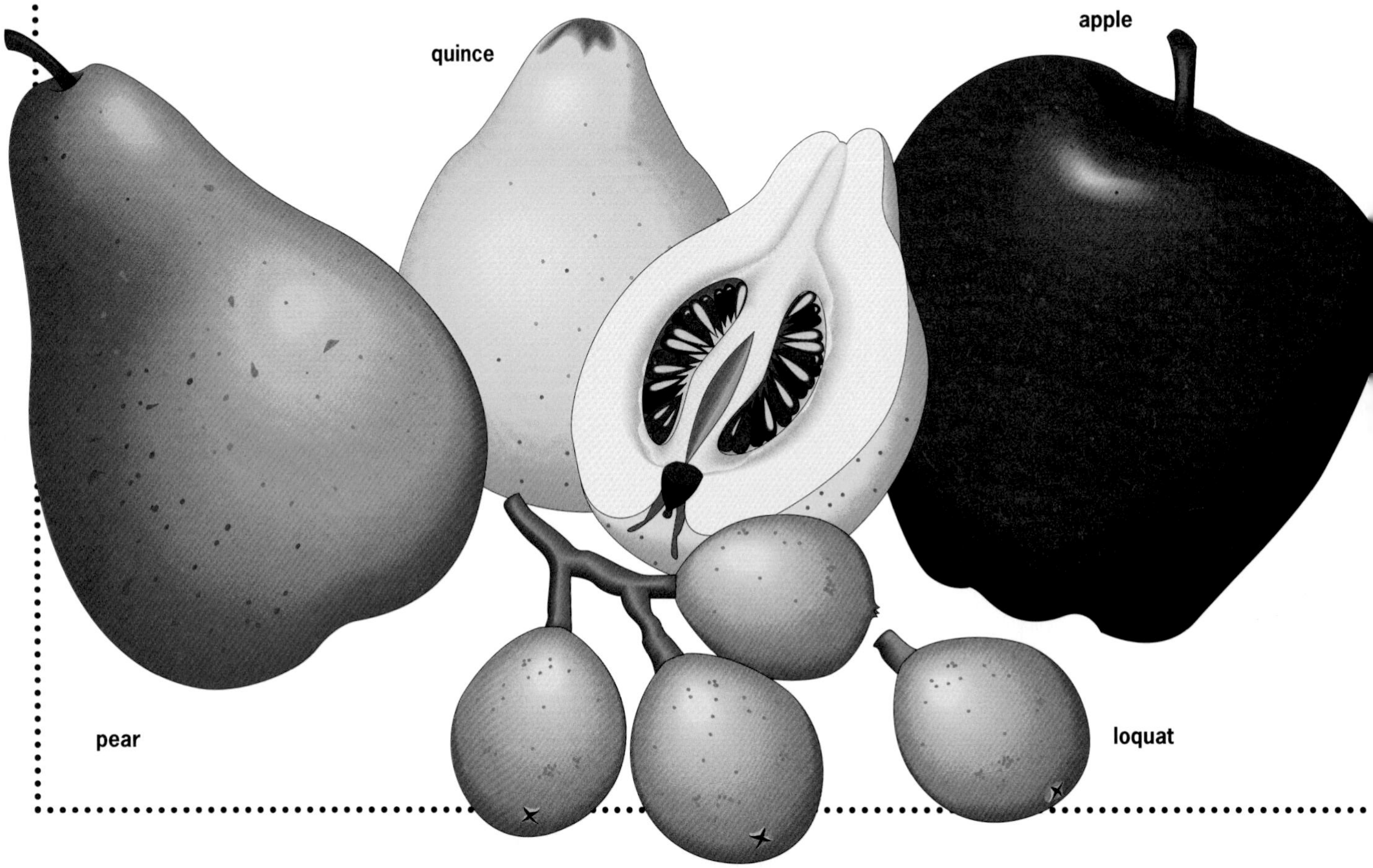
quince
apple
pear
loquat

FLESHY FRUITS: CITRUS FRUITS

section of a citrus fruit

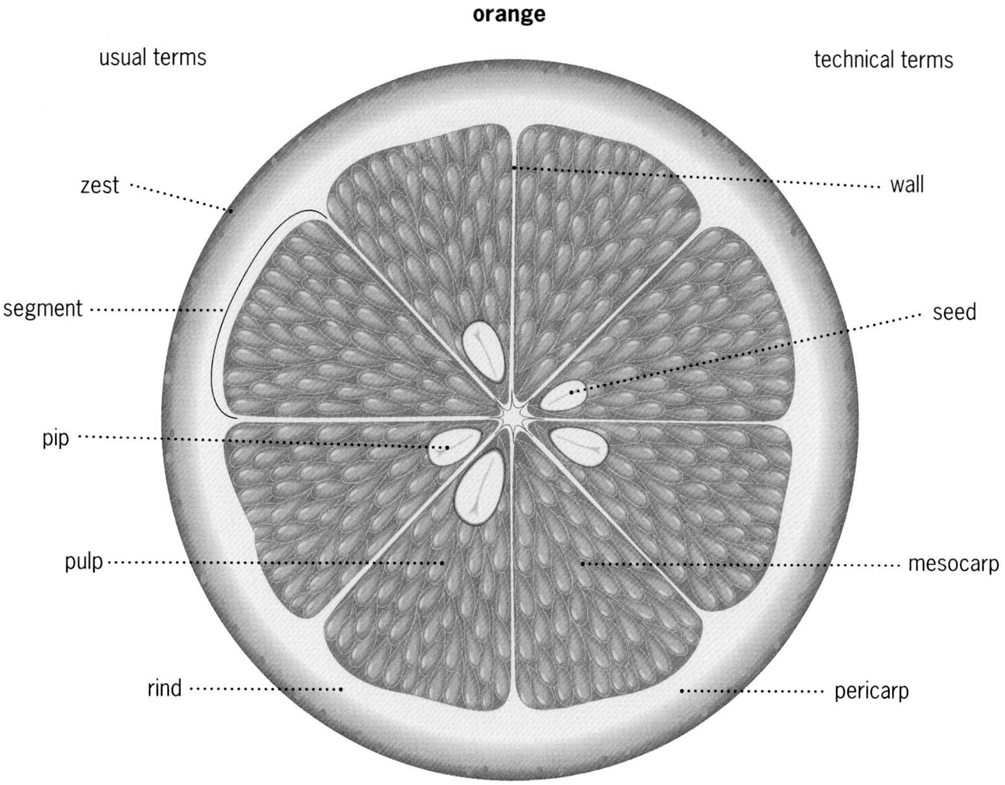
orange
usual terms
technical terms
zest
wall
segment
seed
pip
pulp
mesocarp
rind
pericarp

MAJOR TYPES OF CITRUS FRUITS

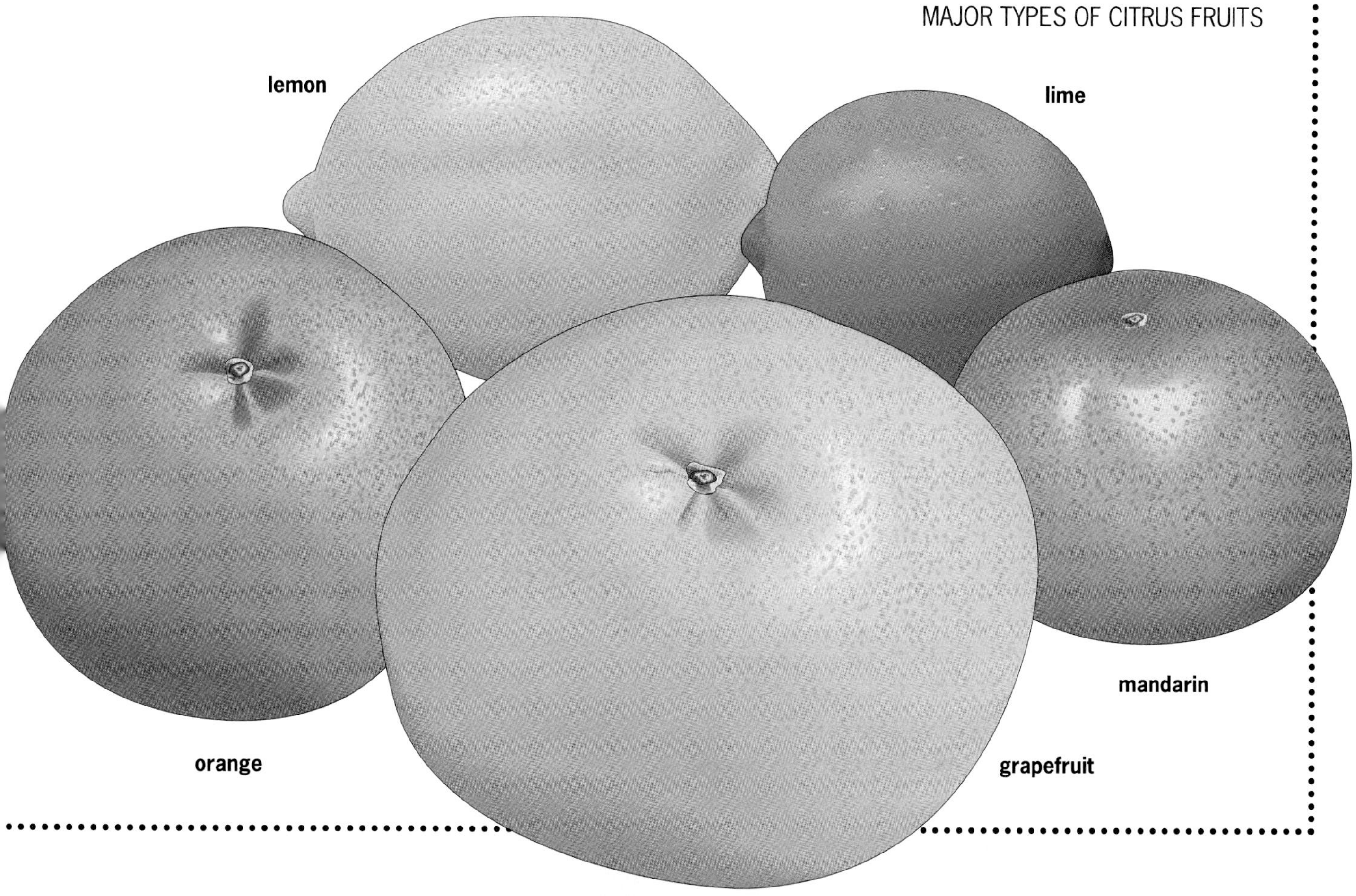
lemon
lime
mandarin
orange
grapefruit

TROPICAL FRUITS

MAJOR TYPES OF TROPICAL FRUITS

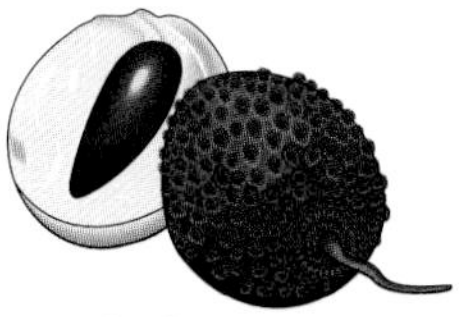

lychee

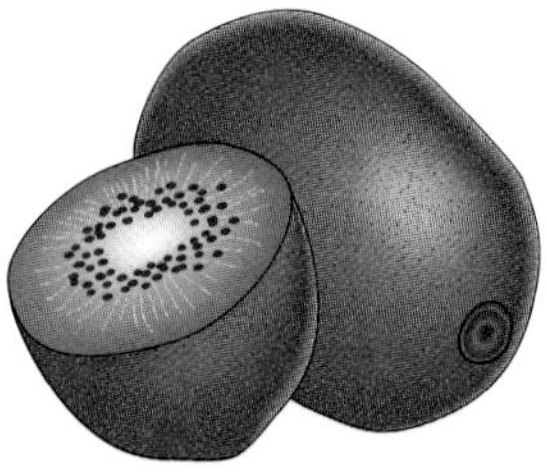

kiwi fruit

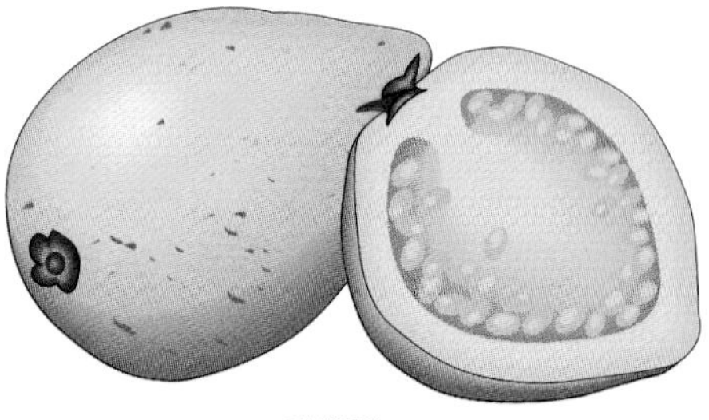

guava

persimmon

prickly pear

cherimoya

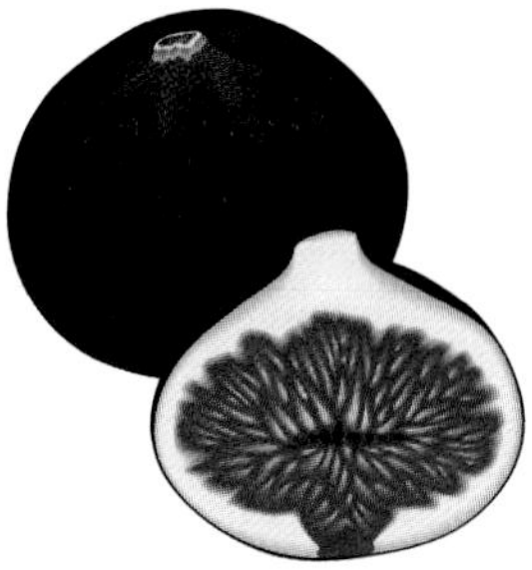

fig

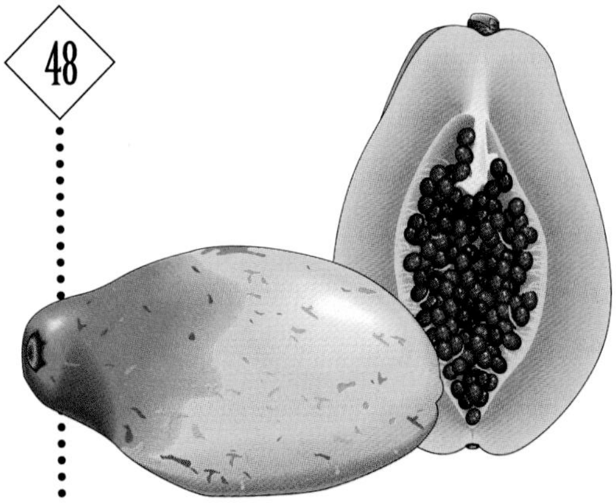

papaya

pomegranate

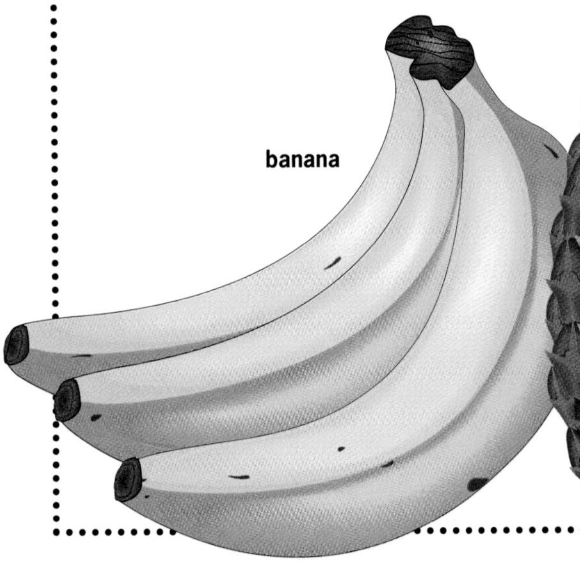

banana

pineapple

avocado

VEGETABLES

INFLORESCENT VEGETABLES

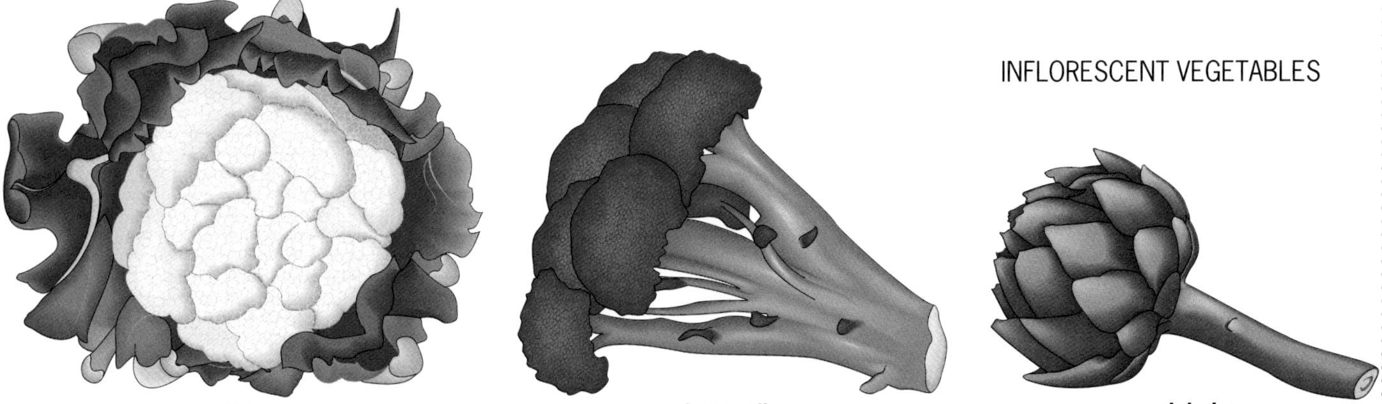
cauliflower
broccoli
artichoke

FRUIT VEGETABLES

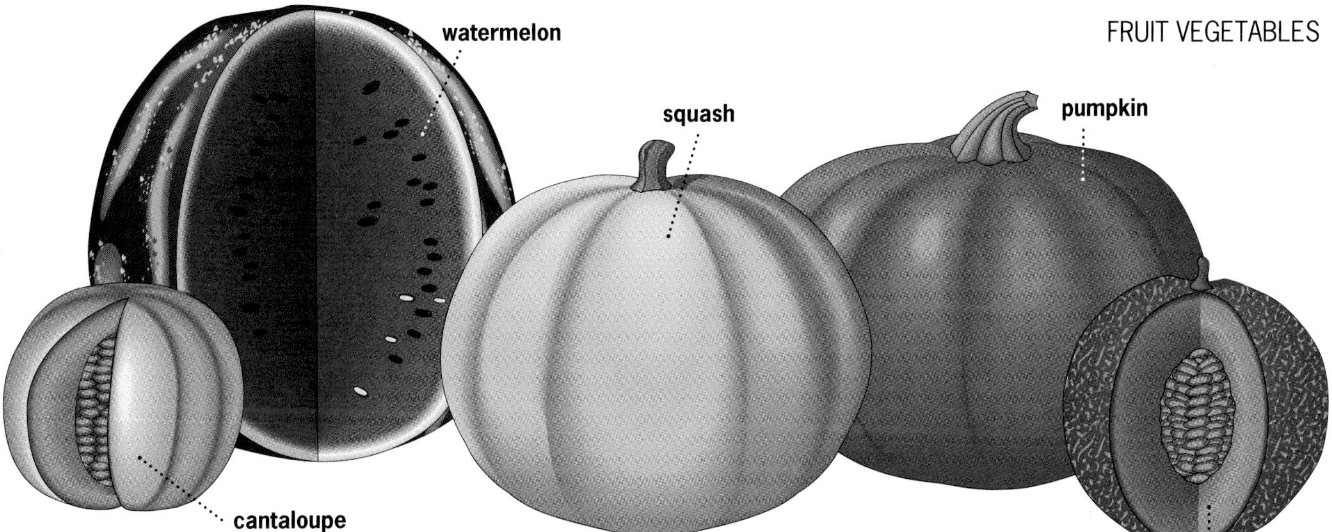
watermelon
squash
pumpkin
cantaloupe
musk melon

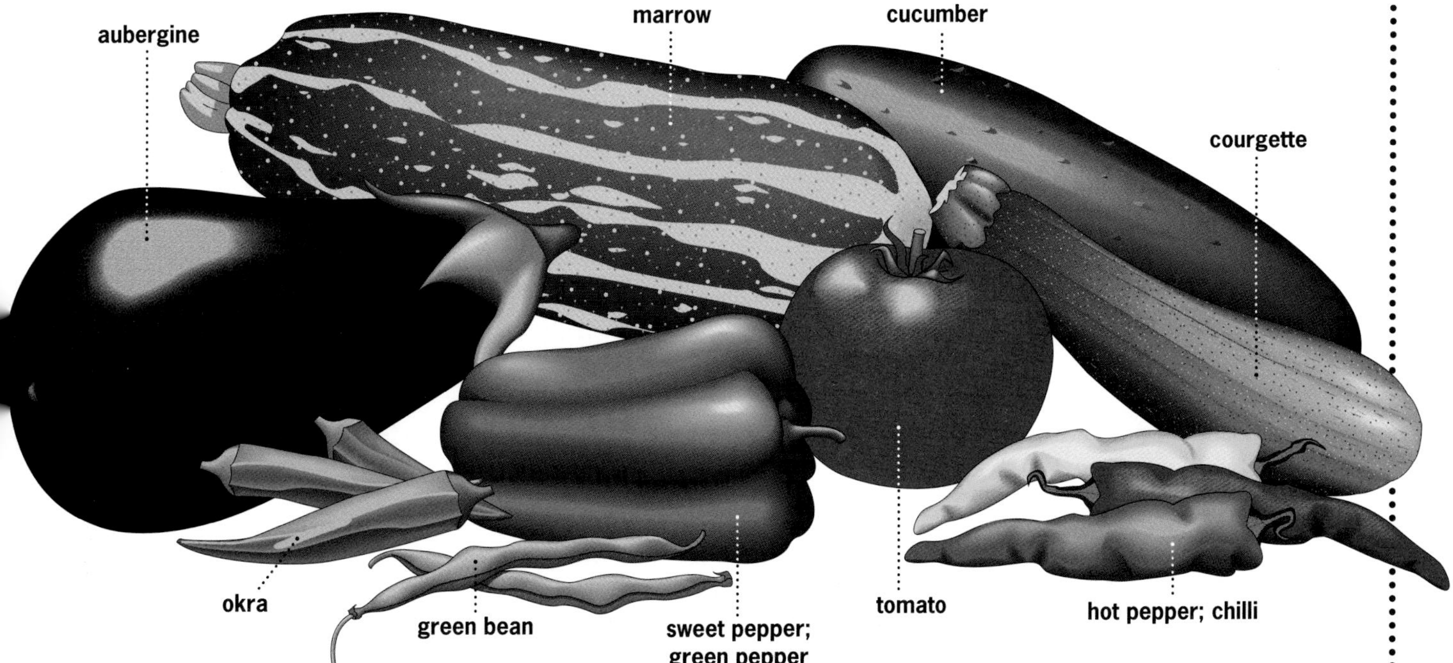
aubergine
marrow
cucumber
courgette
okra
green bean
sweet pepper; green pepper
tomato
hot pepper; chilli

VEGETABLES

section of a bulb

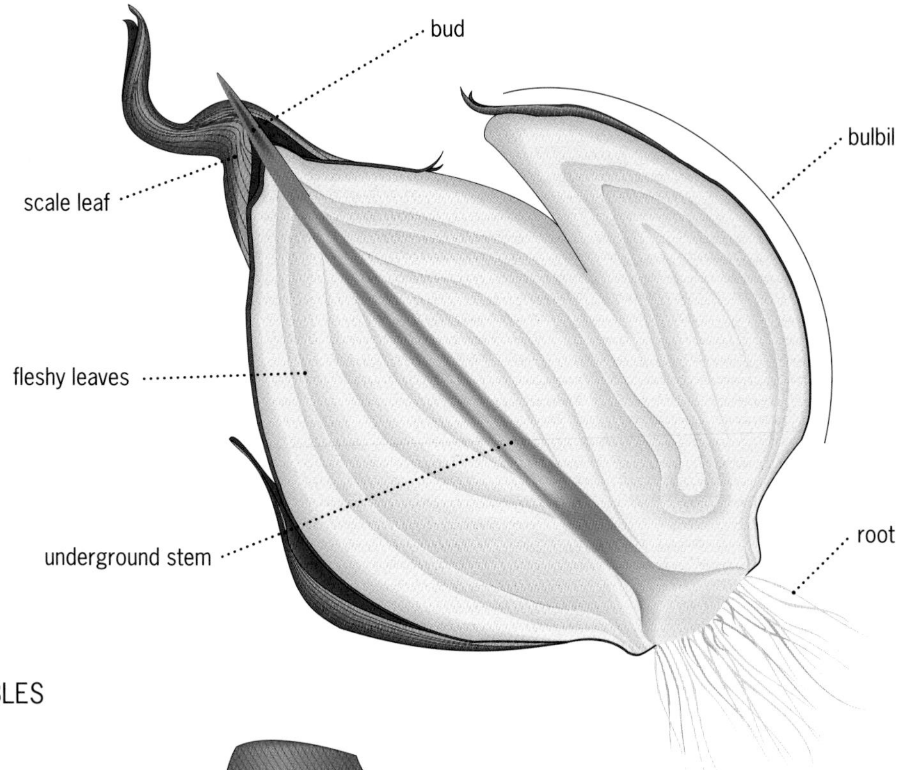
bud
bulbil
scale leaf
fleshy leaves
underground stem
root

BULB VEGETABLES

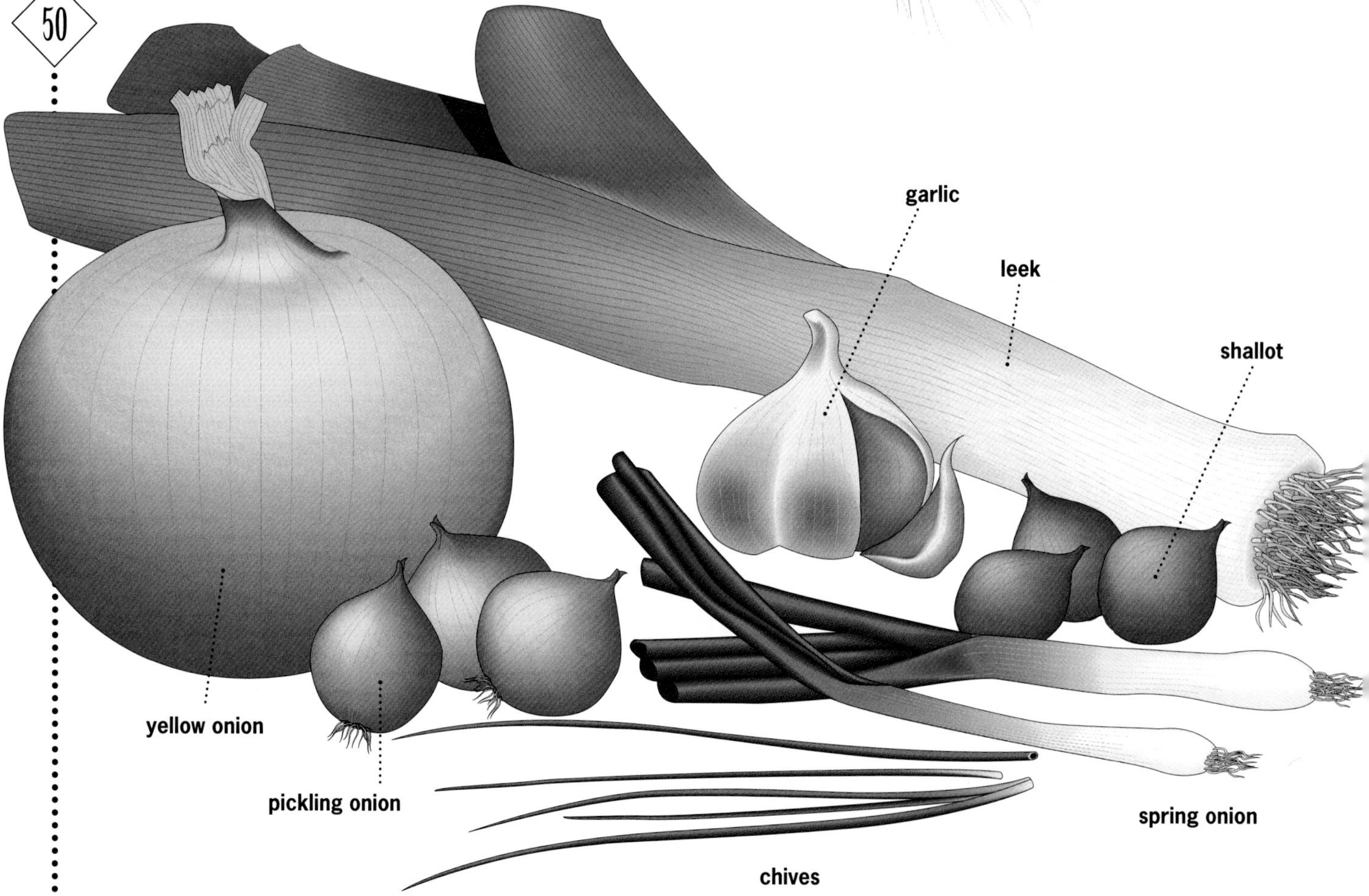
garlic
leek
shallot
yellow onion
pickling onion
spring onion
chives

TUBER VEGETABLES

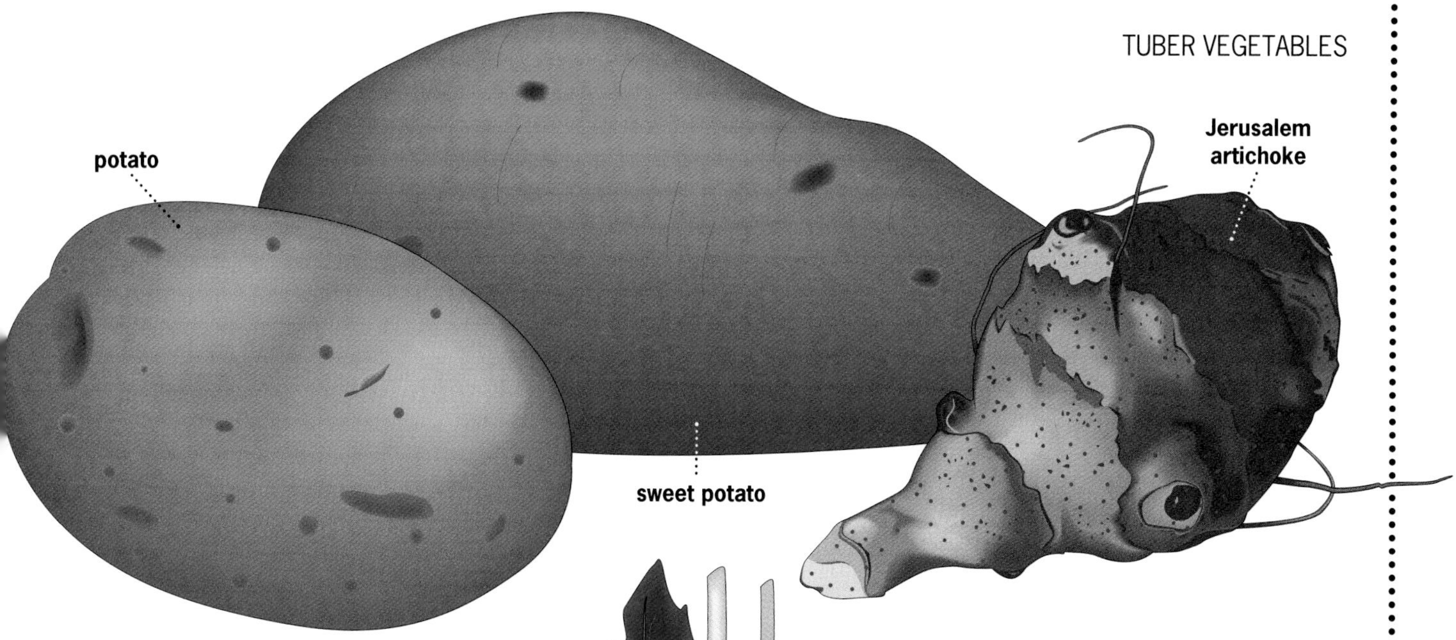
potato
sweet potato
Jerusalem artichoke

ROOT VEGETABLES

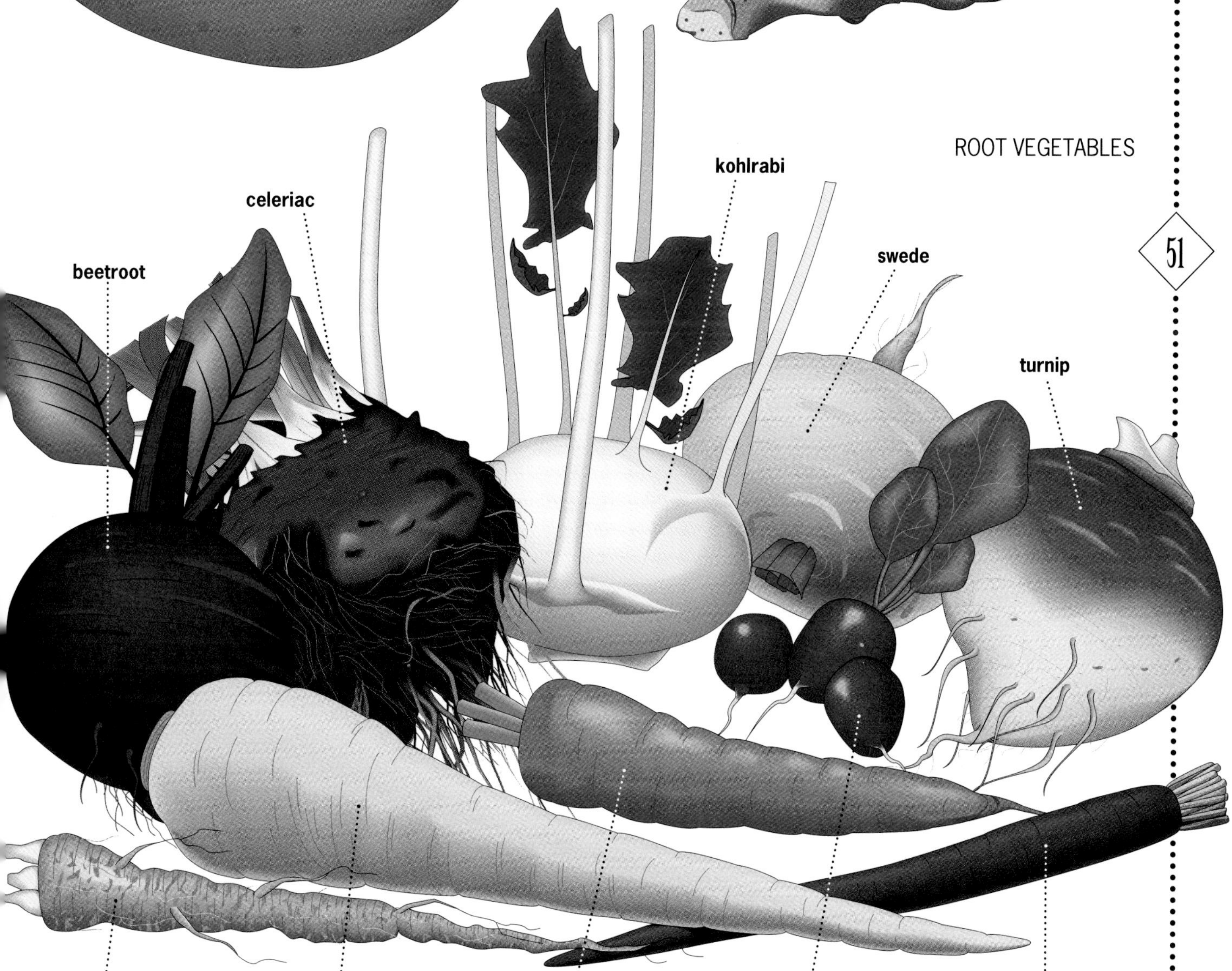
beetroot
celeriac
kohlrabi
swede
turnip
horseradish
parsnip
carrot
radish
salsify

VEGETABLES

STALK VEGETABLES

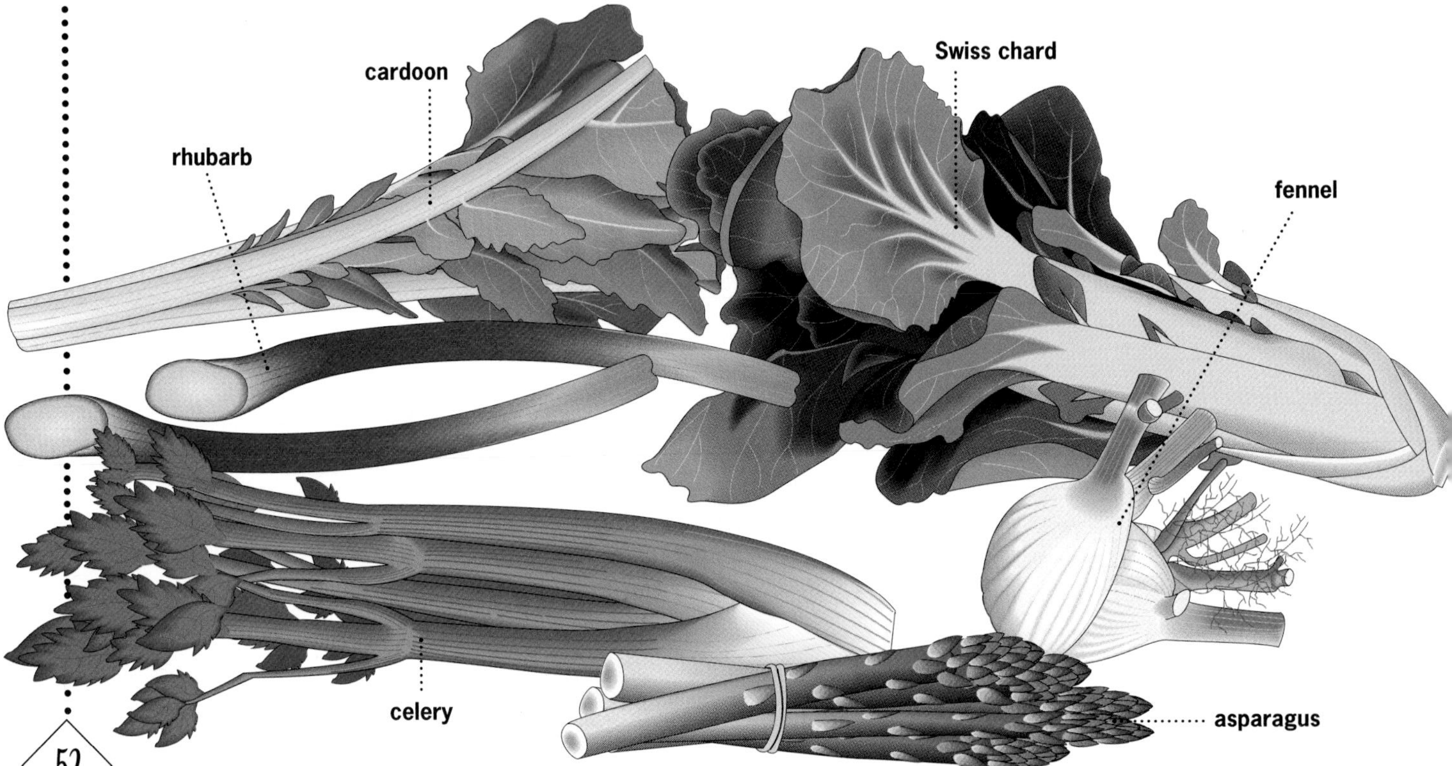
cardoon
Swiss chard
rhubarb
fennel
celery
asparagus

SEED VEGETABLES

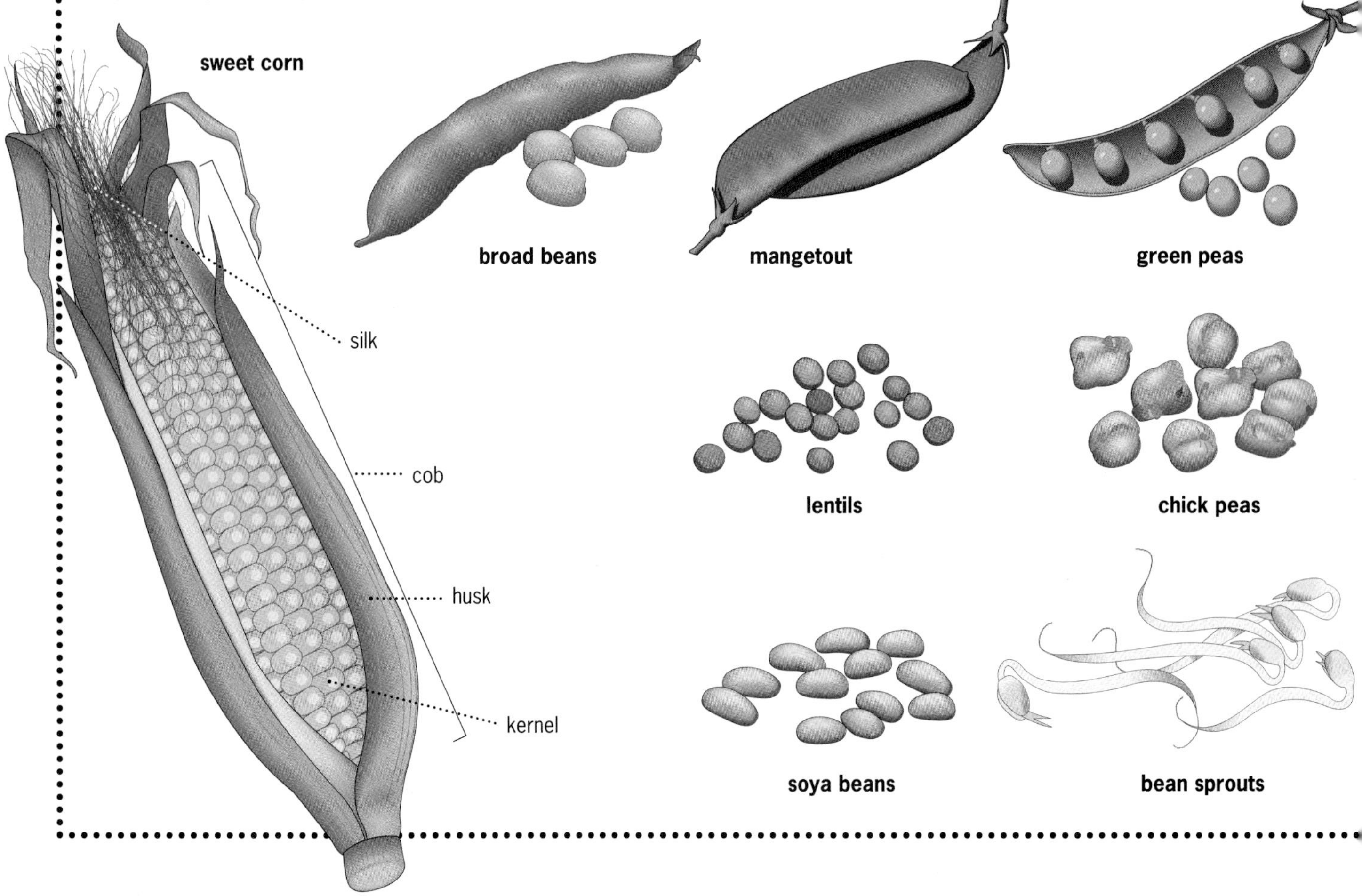
sweet corn
silk
cob
husk
kernel
broad beans
mangetout
green peas
lentils
chick peas
soya beans
bean sprouts

LEAF VEGETABLES

green cabbage
round lettuce
curly endive
spinach
white cabbage
cos lettuce
chicory
broad-leaved endive
Chinese leaf
dandelion
curly kale
Brussels sprouts
garden sorrel
watercress
lamb's lettuce
vine leaf

GARDENING

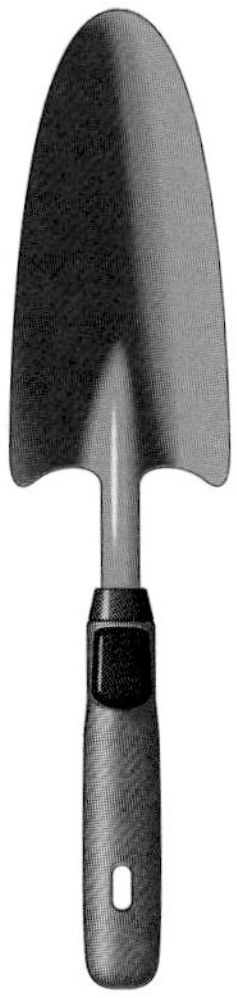
trowel

hand fork

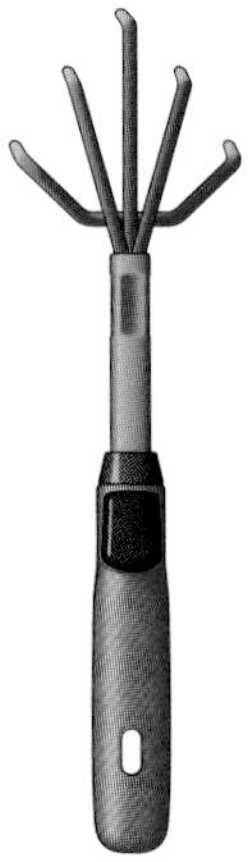
hand cultivator

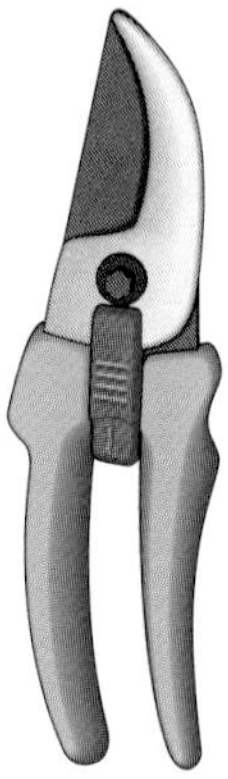
secateurs

lawnmower

speed control
ignition key
handle
safety handle
grassbox
starter
motor
deflector
casing

watering can

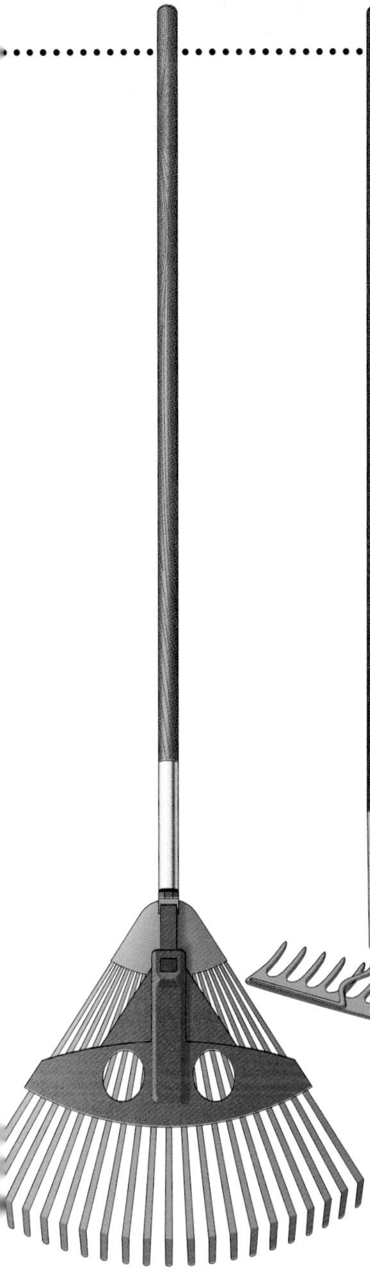

lawn rake

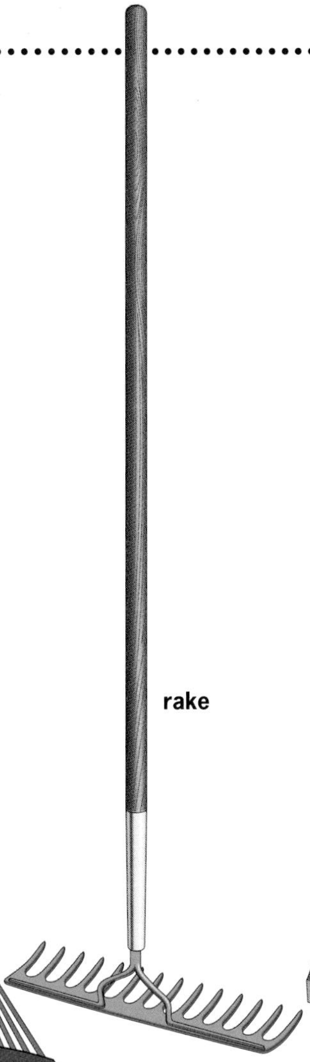

rake

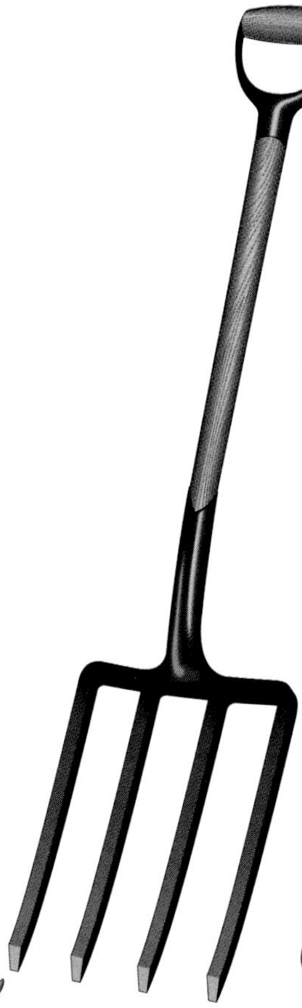

fork

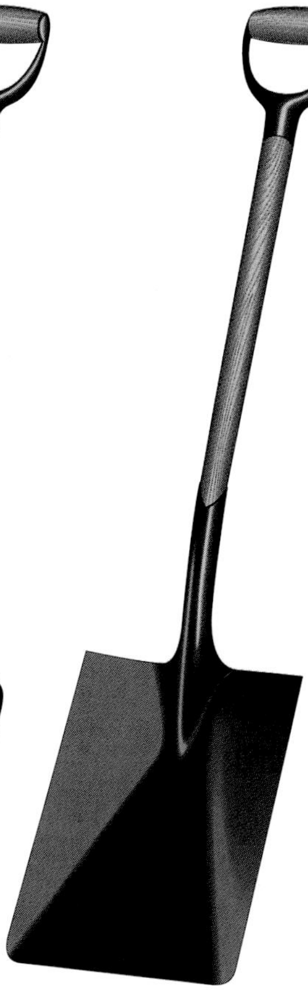

spade

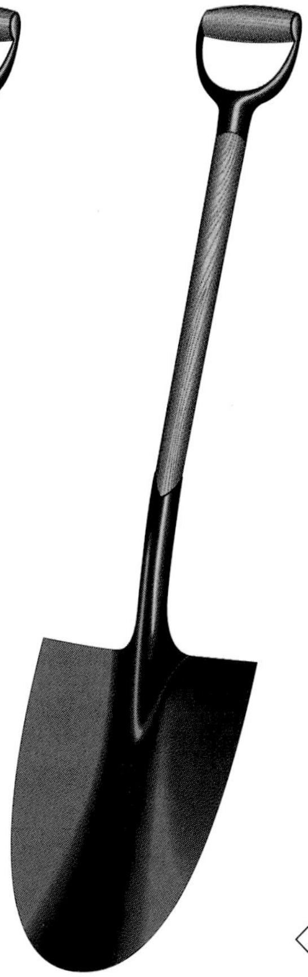

shovel

wheelbarrow

compost bin

INSECTS AND SPIDER

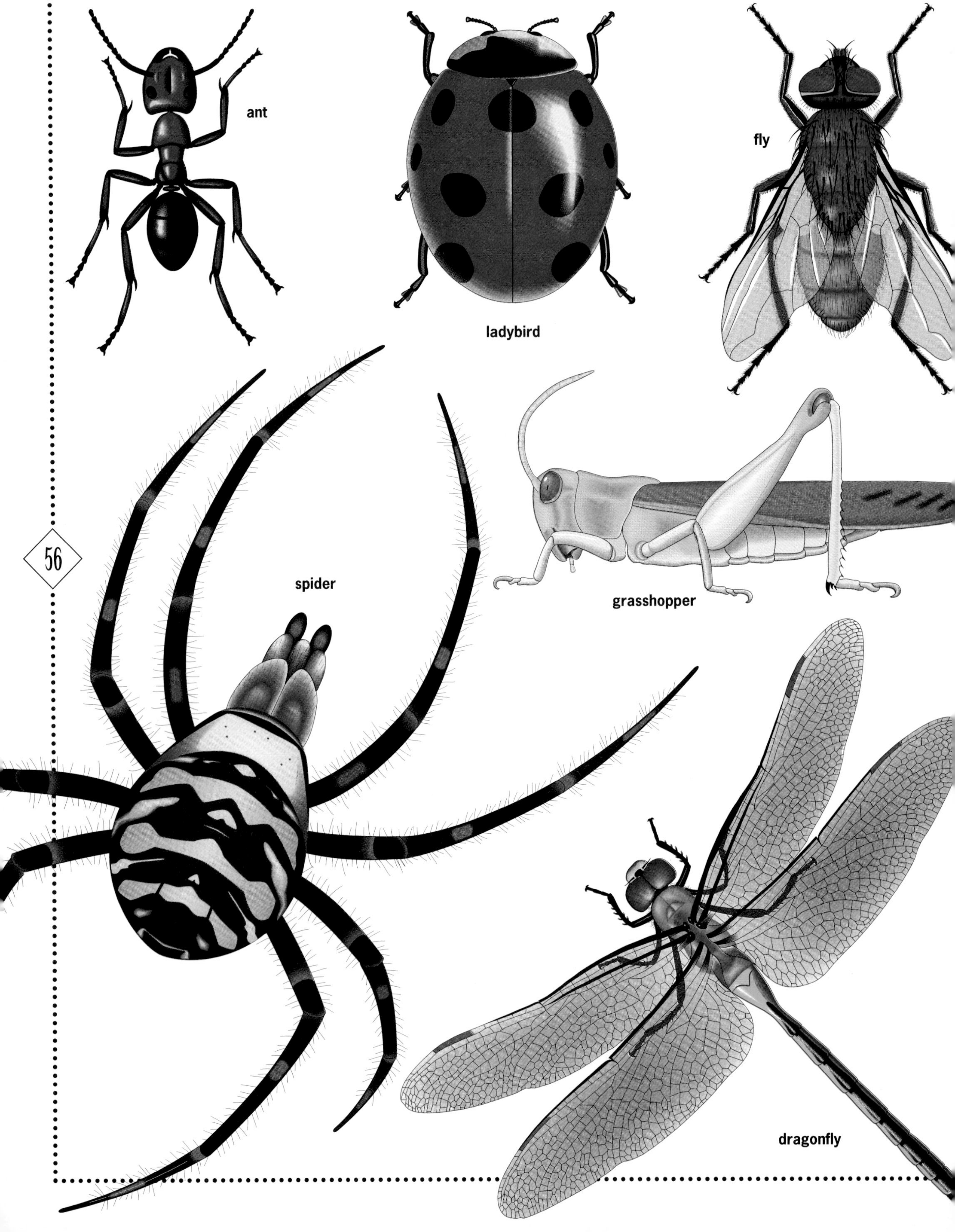
ant
ladybird
fly
spider
grasshopper
dragonfly

BUTTERFLY

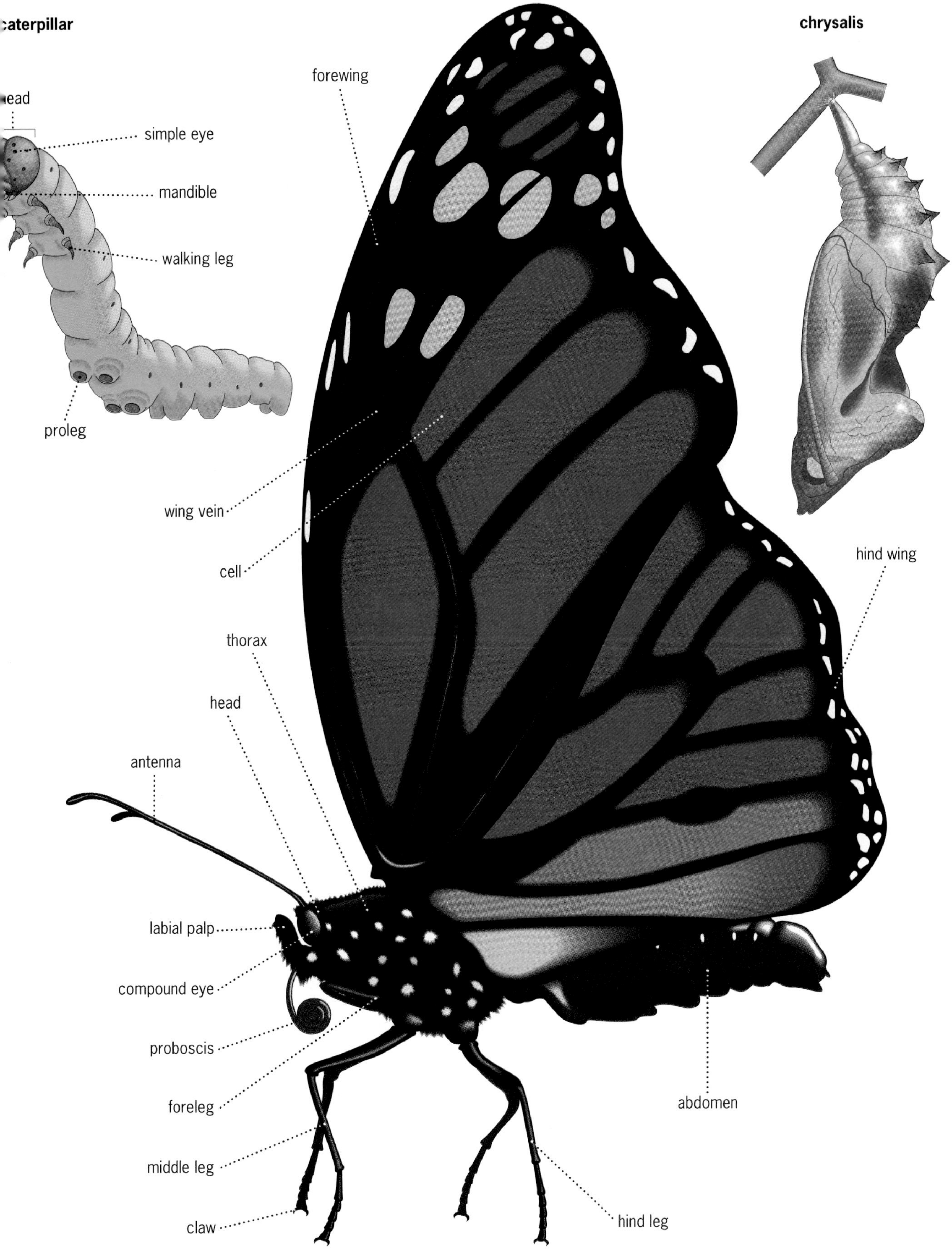
caterpillar
head
simple eye
mandible
walking leg
proleg
chrysalis
forewing
wing vein
cell
hind wing
thorax
head
antenna
labial palp
compound eye
proboscis
foreleg
middle leg
claw
hind leg
abdomen

HONEY-BEE

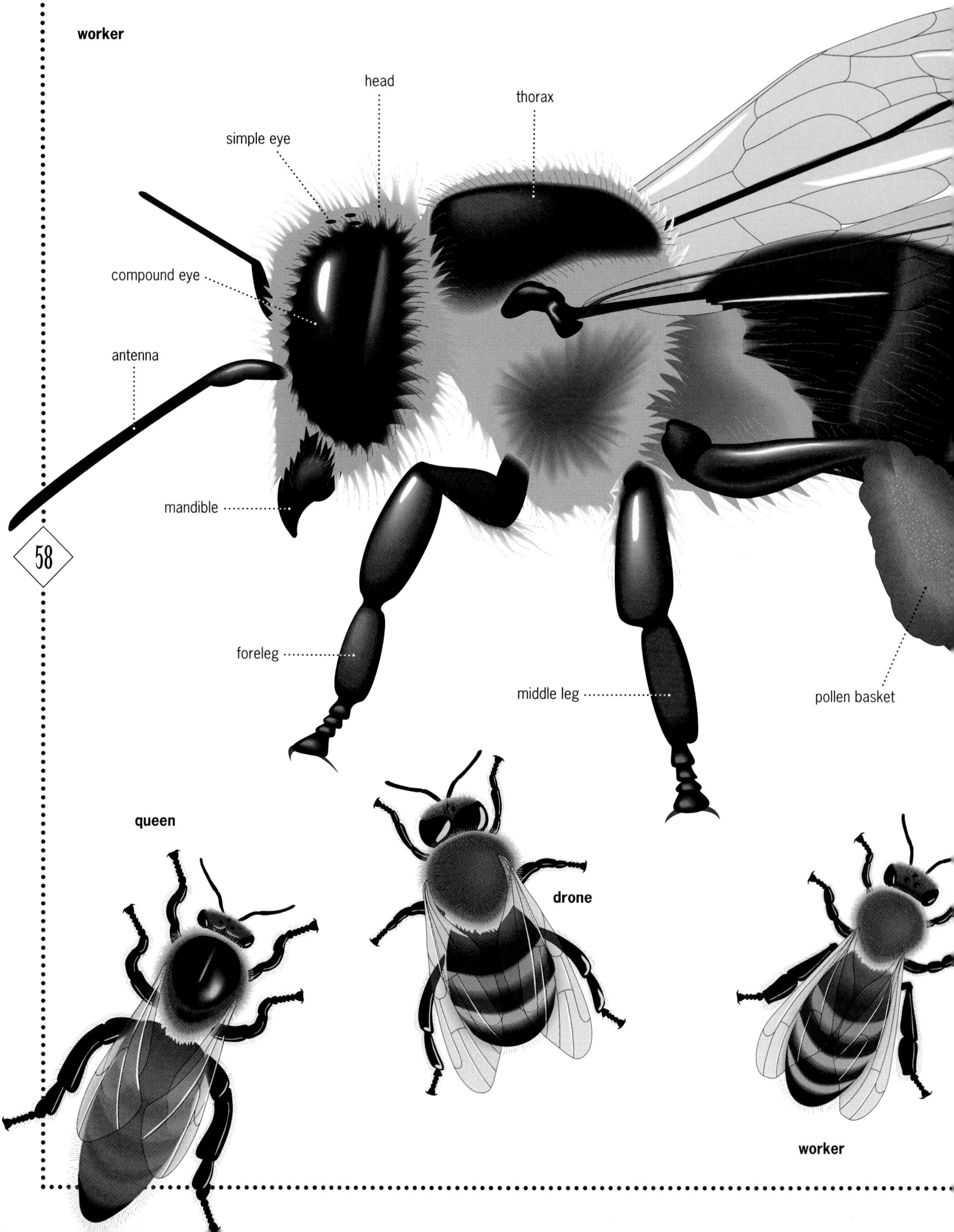
worker
head
thorax
simple eye
compound eye
antenna
mandible
foreleg
middle leg
pollen basket
queen
drone
worker

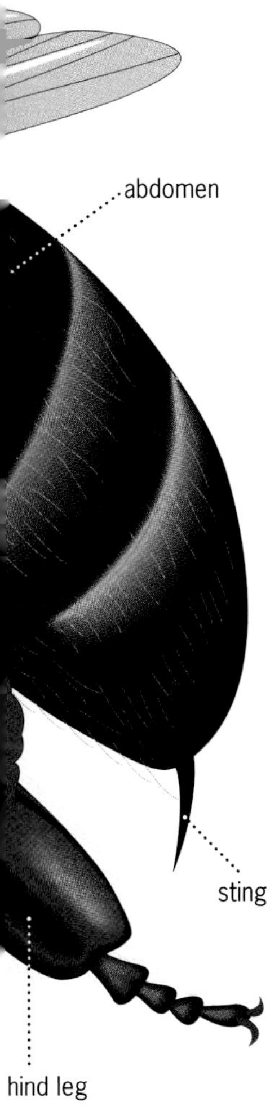
abdomen
sting
hind leg

hive

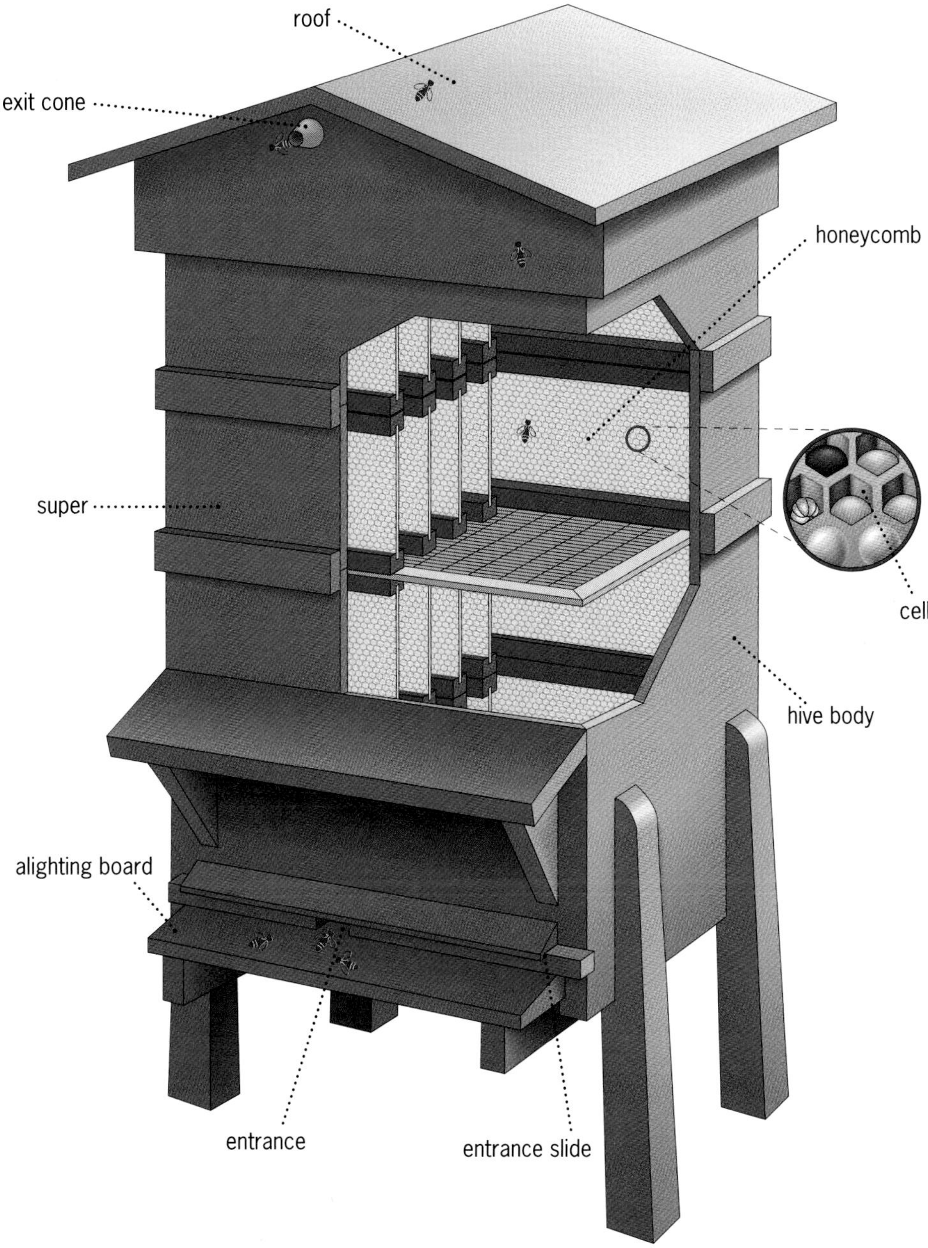
roof
exit cone
honeycomb
super
cell
hive body
alighting board
entrance
entrance slide

honeycomb section

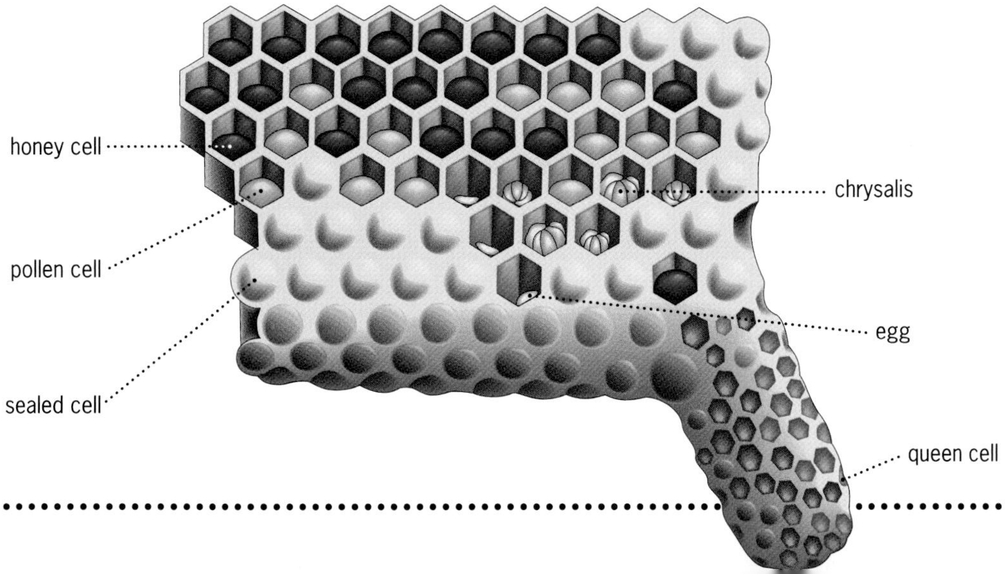
honey cell
chrysalis
pollen cell
egg
sealed cell
queen cell

AMPHIBIANS

frog

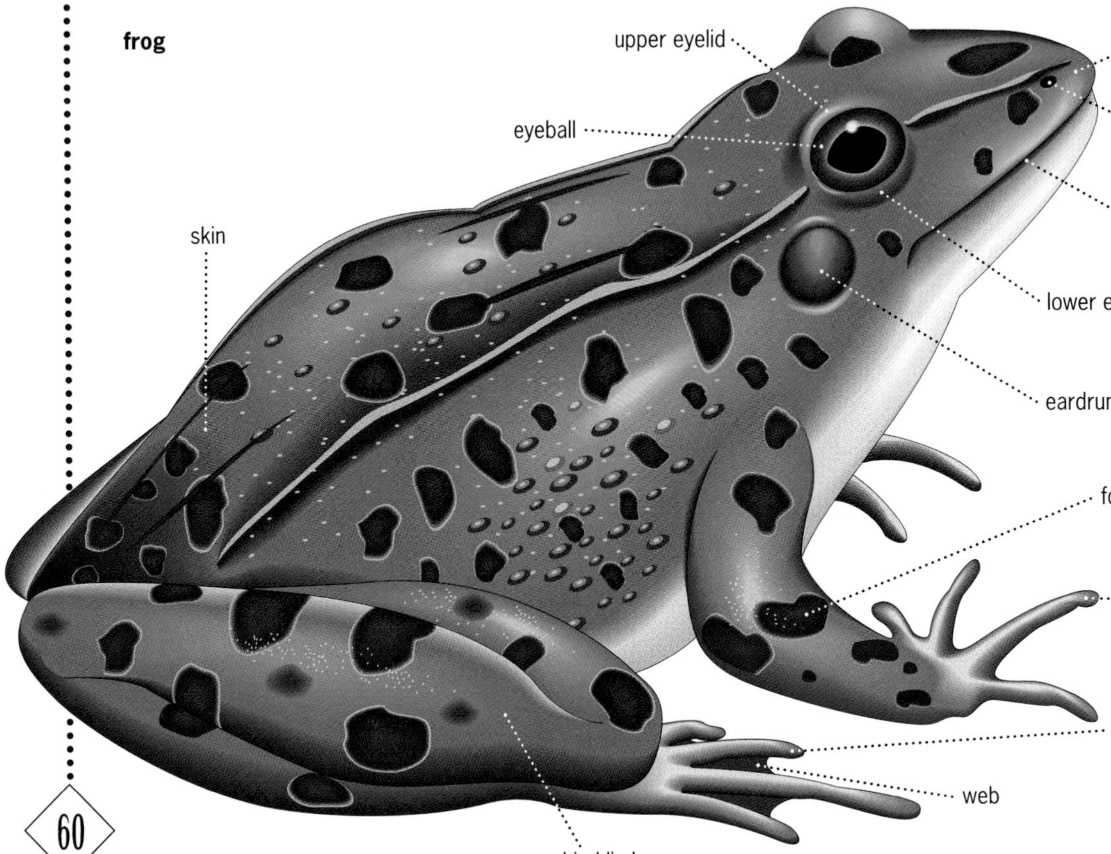
upper eyelid
snout
eyeball
nostril
mouth
skin
lower eyelid
eardrum
forelimb
digit
webbed foot
web
hind limb

LIFE CYCLE OF THE FROG

eggs

tadpole

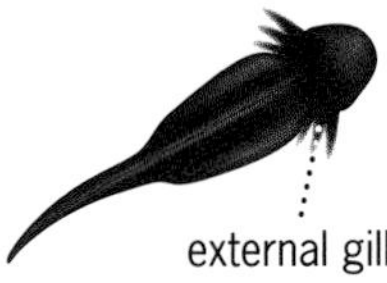
external gills

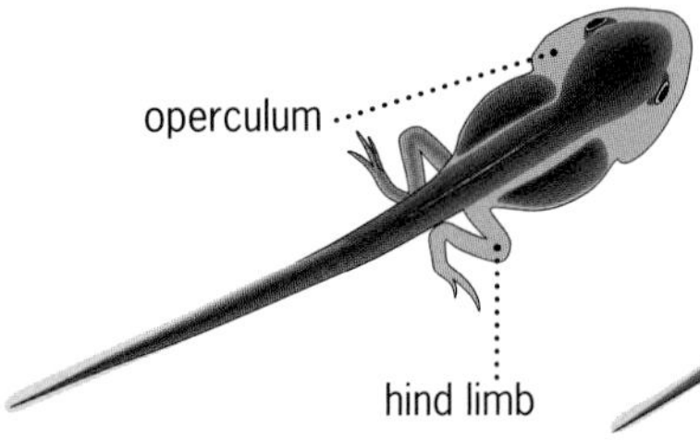
operculum
hind limb

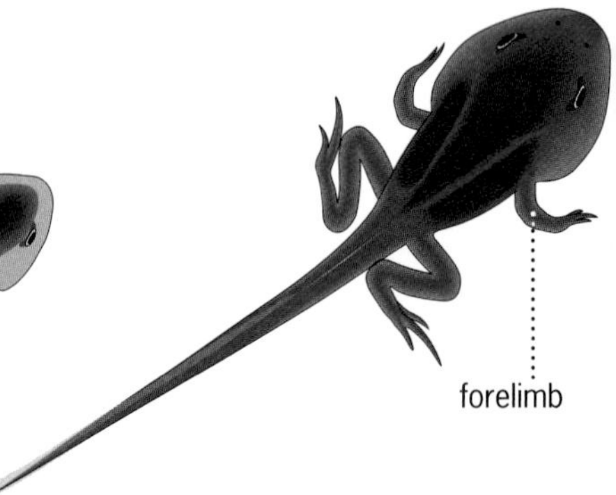
forelimb

MAJOR AMPHIBIANS

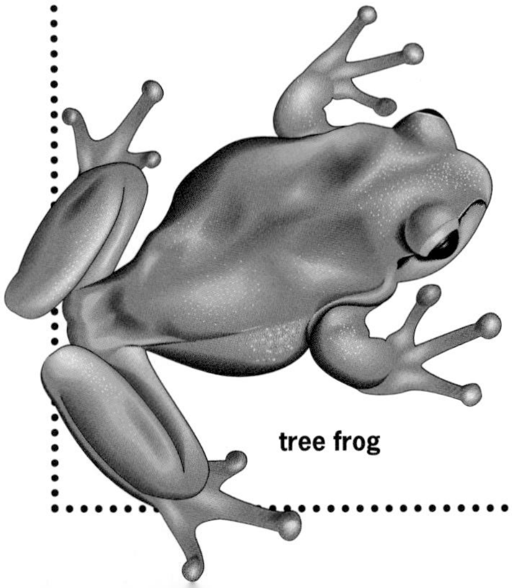

tree frog

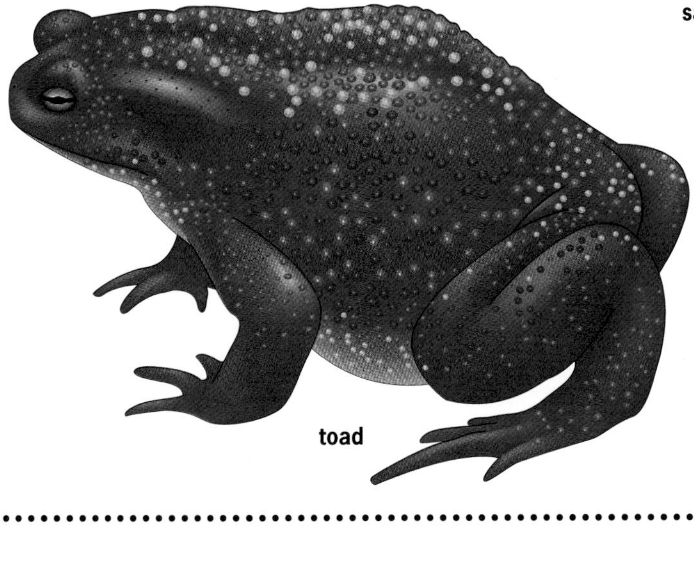

toad

salamander

CRUSTACEANS

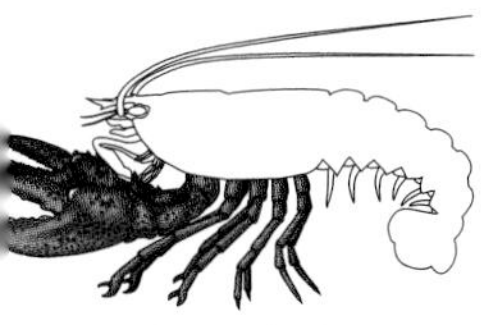

thoracic legs

lobster

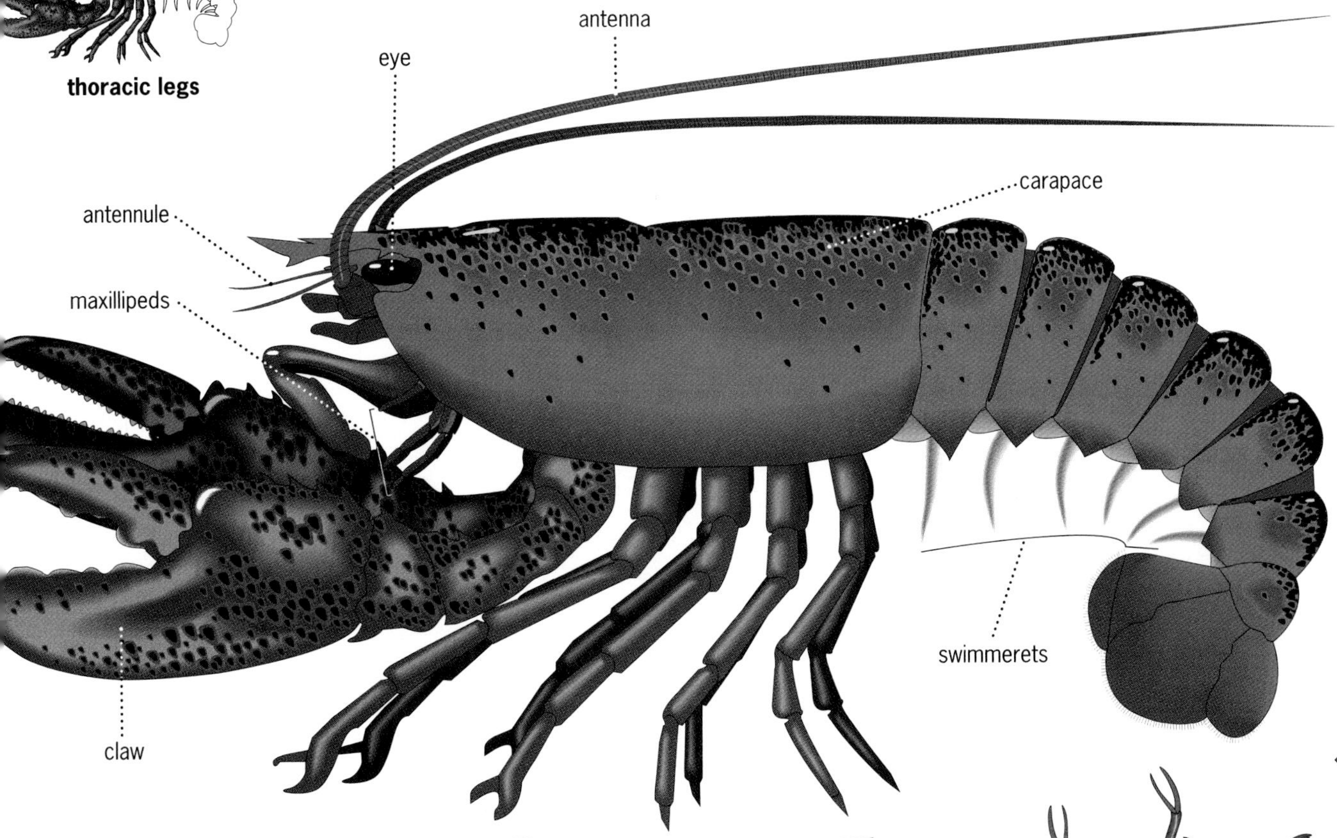
antenna
eye
carapace
antennule
maxillipeds
swimmerets
claw

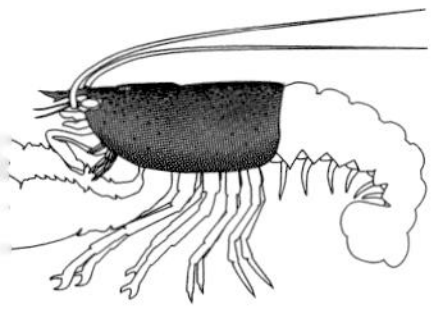

cephalothorax

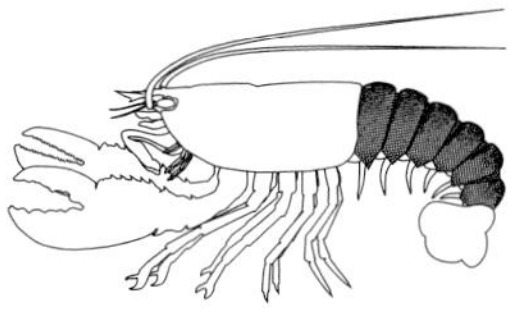

abdomen

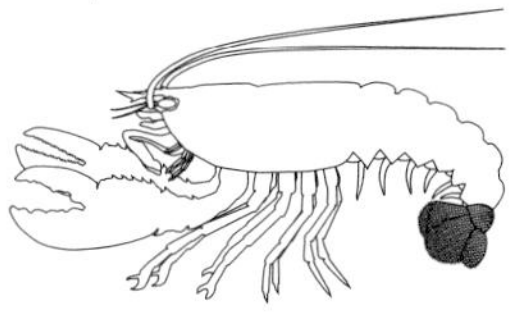

tail

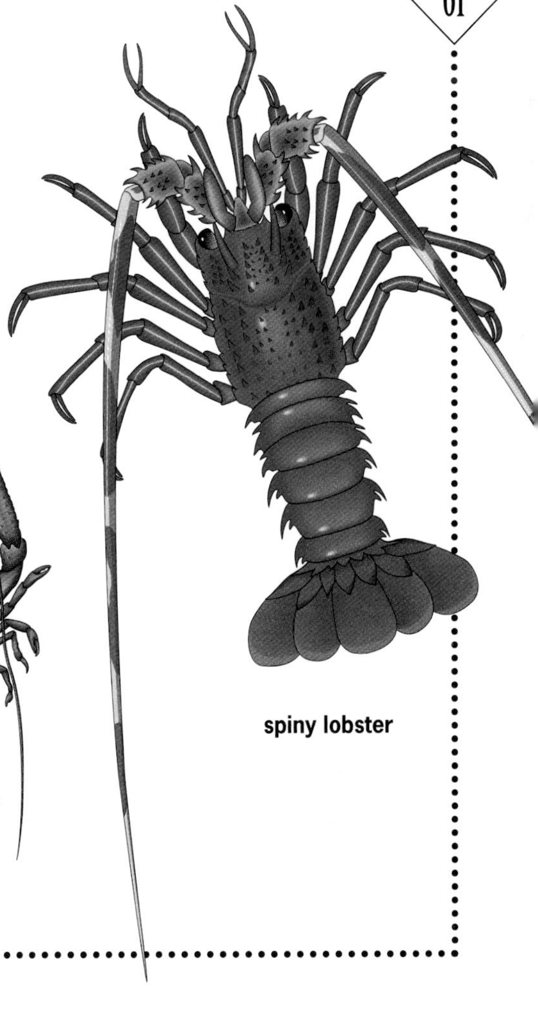

spiny lobster

MAJOR EDIBLE CRUSTACEANS

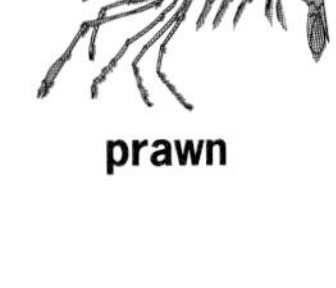

prawn

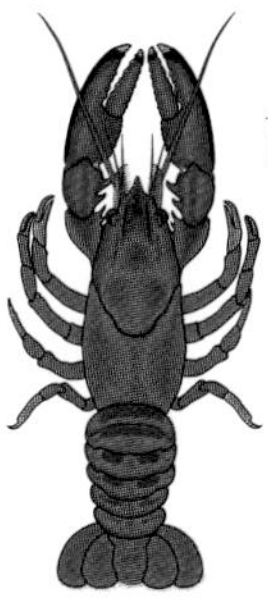

crayfish

crab

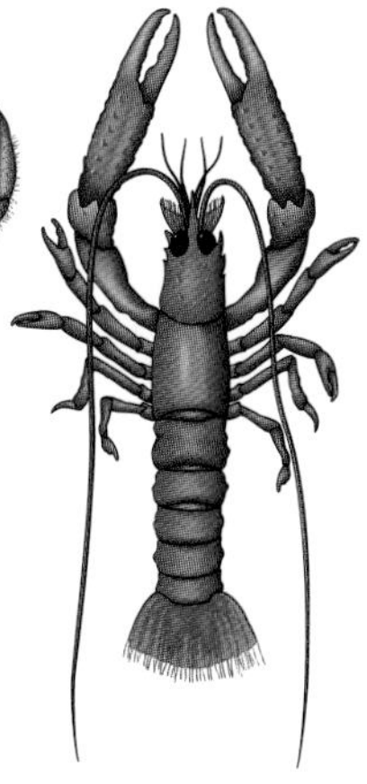

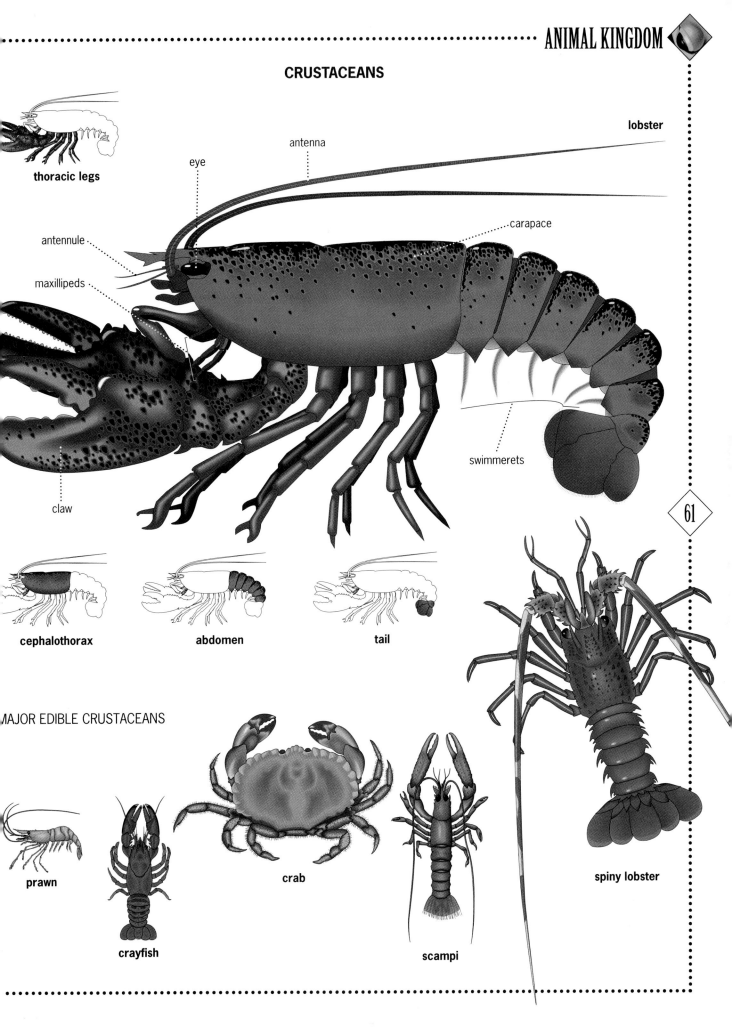

scampi

FISHES

MORPHOLOGY

gills

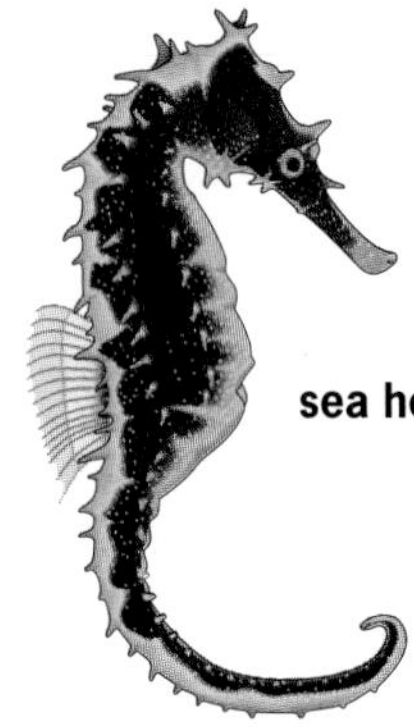

sea horse

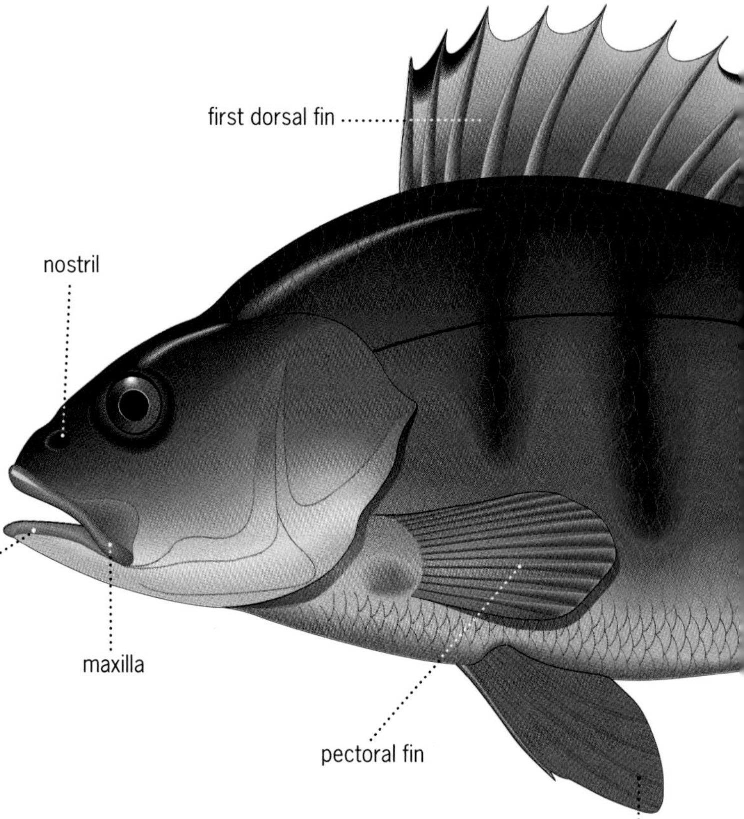
first dorsal fin
nostril
mandible
maxilla
pectoral fin
pelvic fin

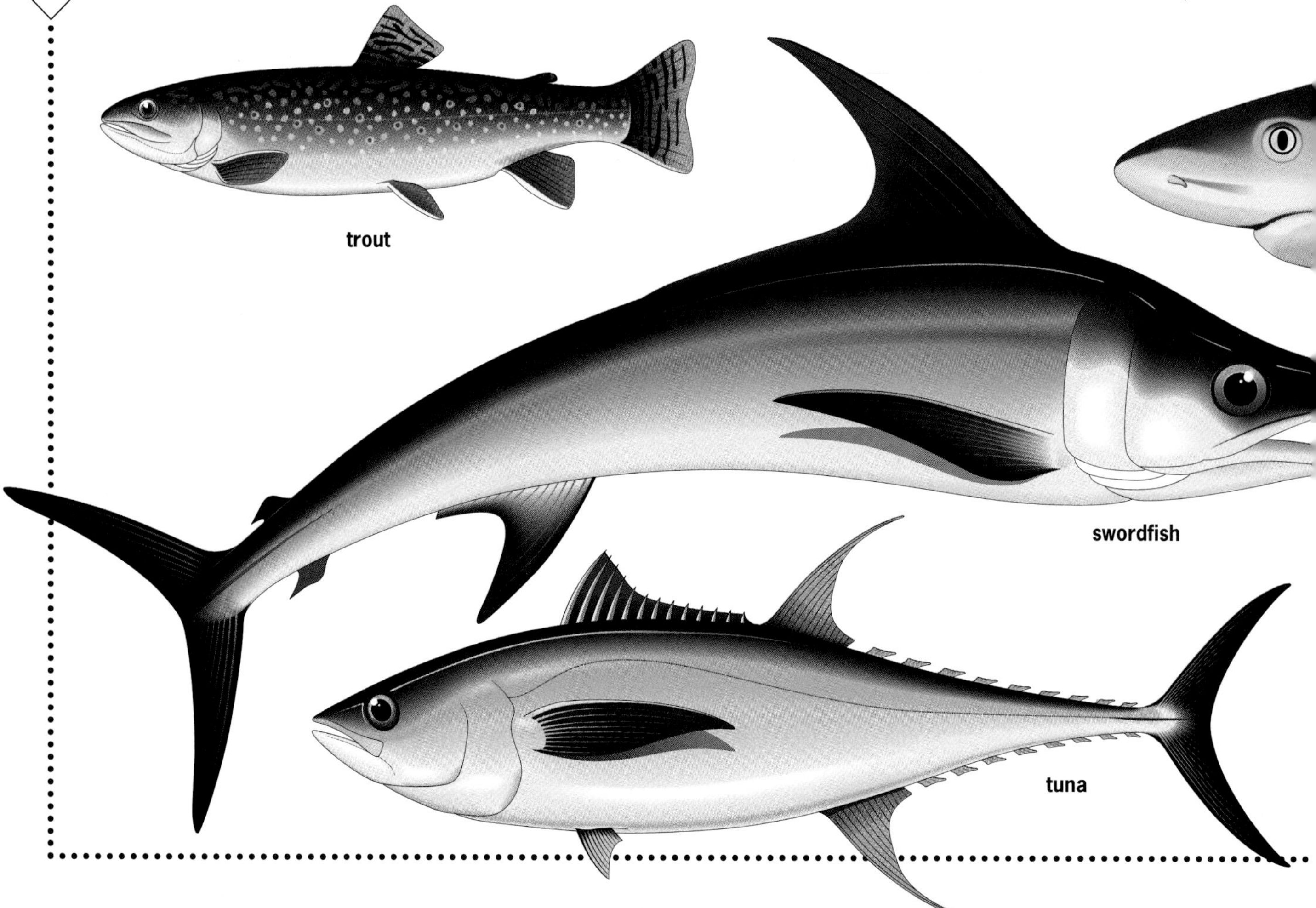

trout

swordfish

tuna

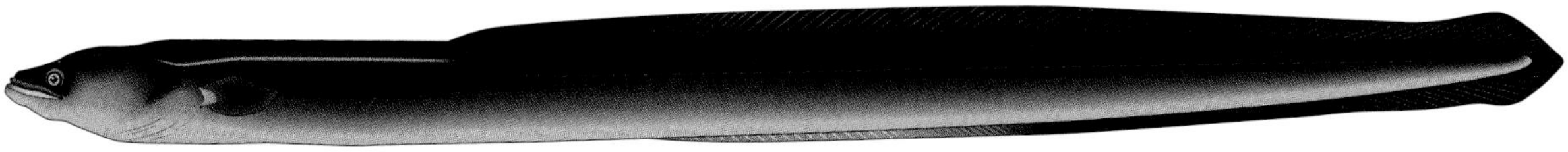

eel

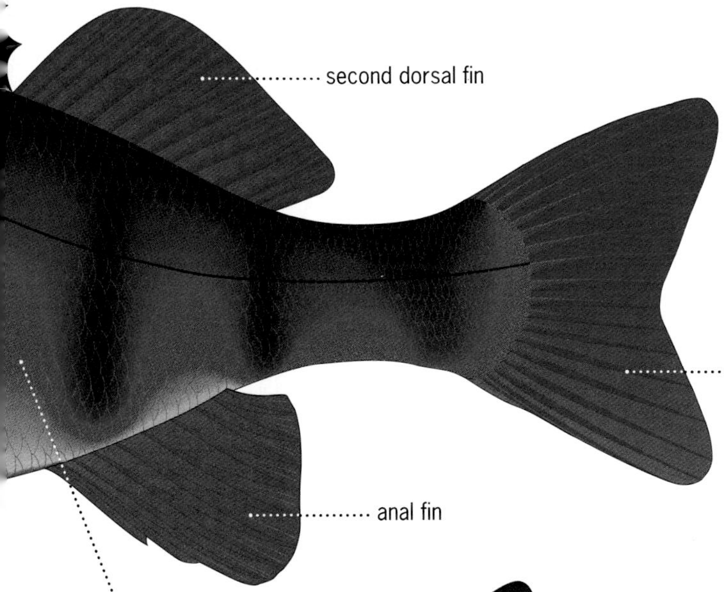
second dorsal fin
caudal fin
anal fin
scale

black bass

plaice

shark

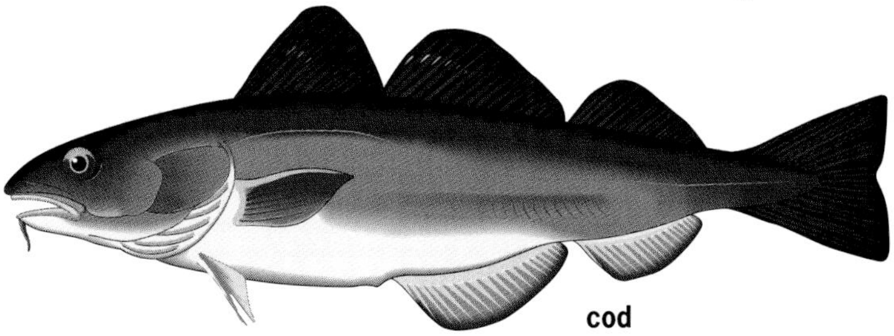

cod

pike

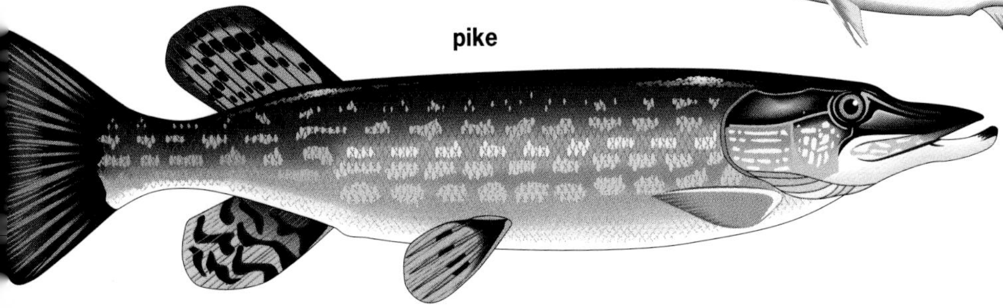

REPTILES

turtle

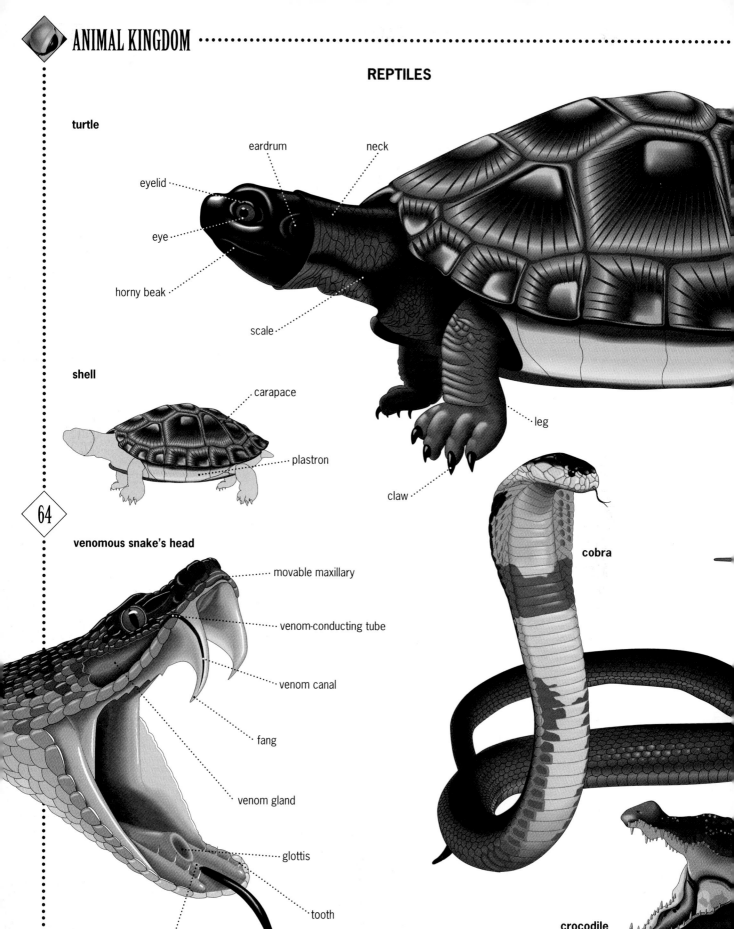

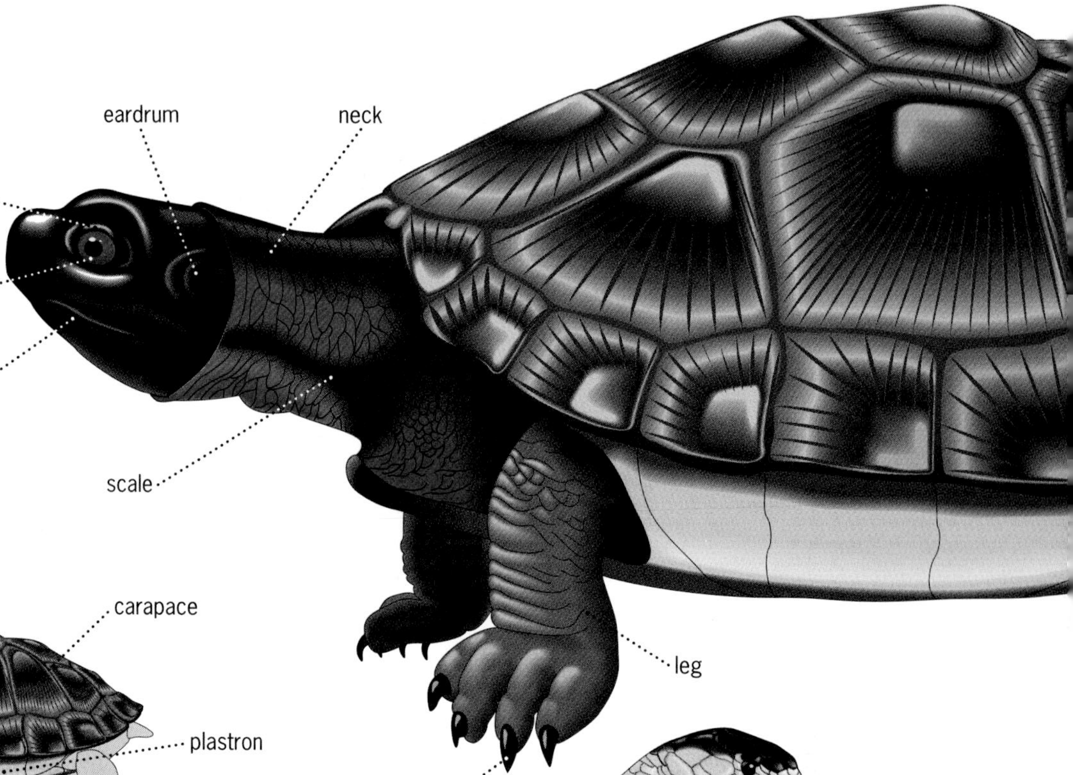
eardrum
neck
eyelid
eye
horny beak
scale
leg
claw

shell

carapace
plastron

venomous snake's head

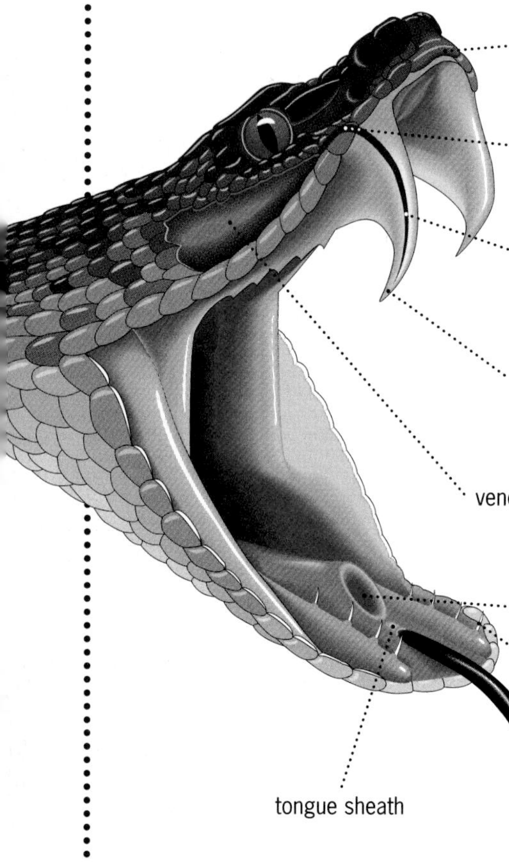
movable maxillary
venom-conducting tube
venom canal
fang
venom gland
glottis
tooth
tongue sheath
forked tongue

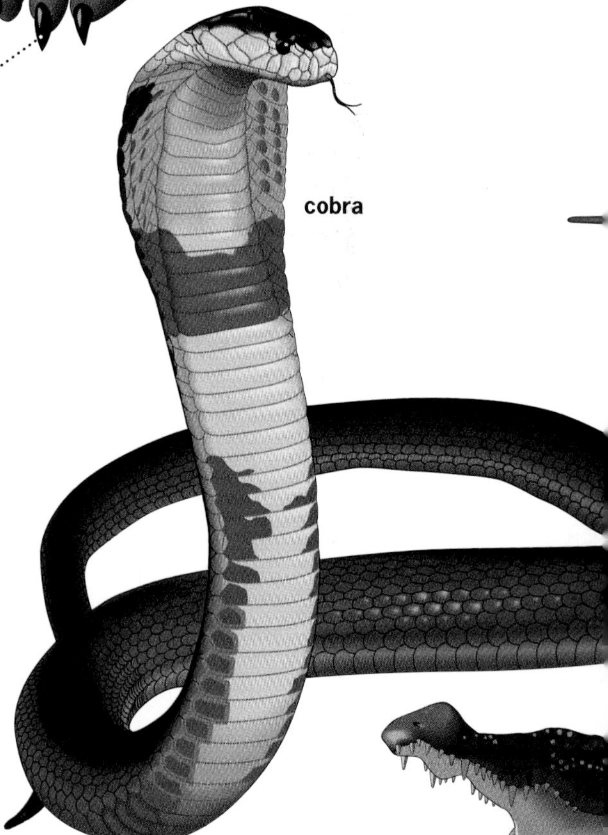

cobra

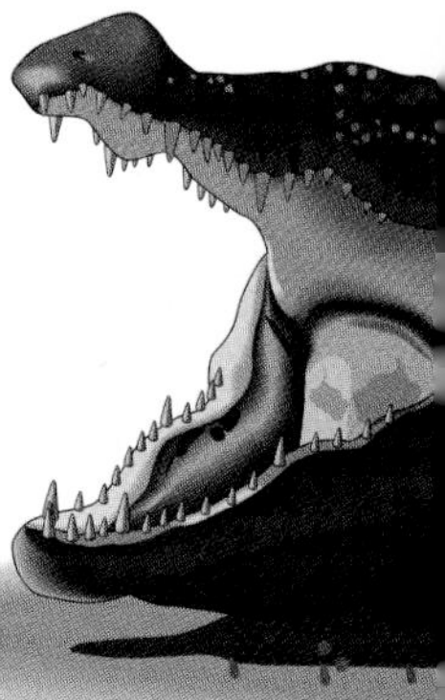

crocodile

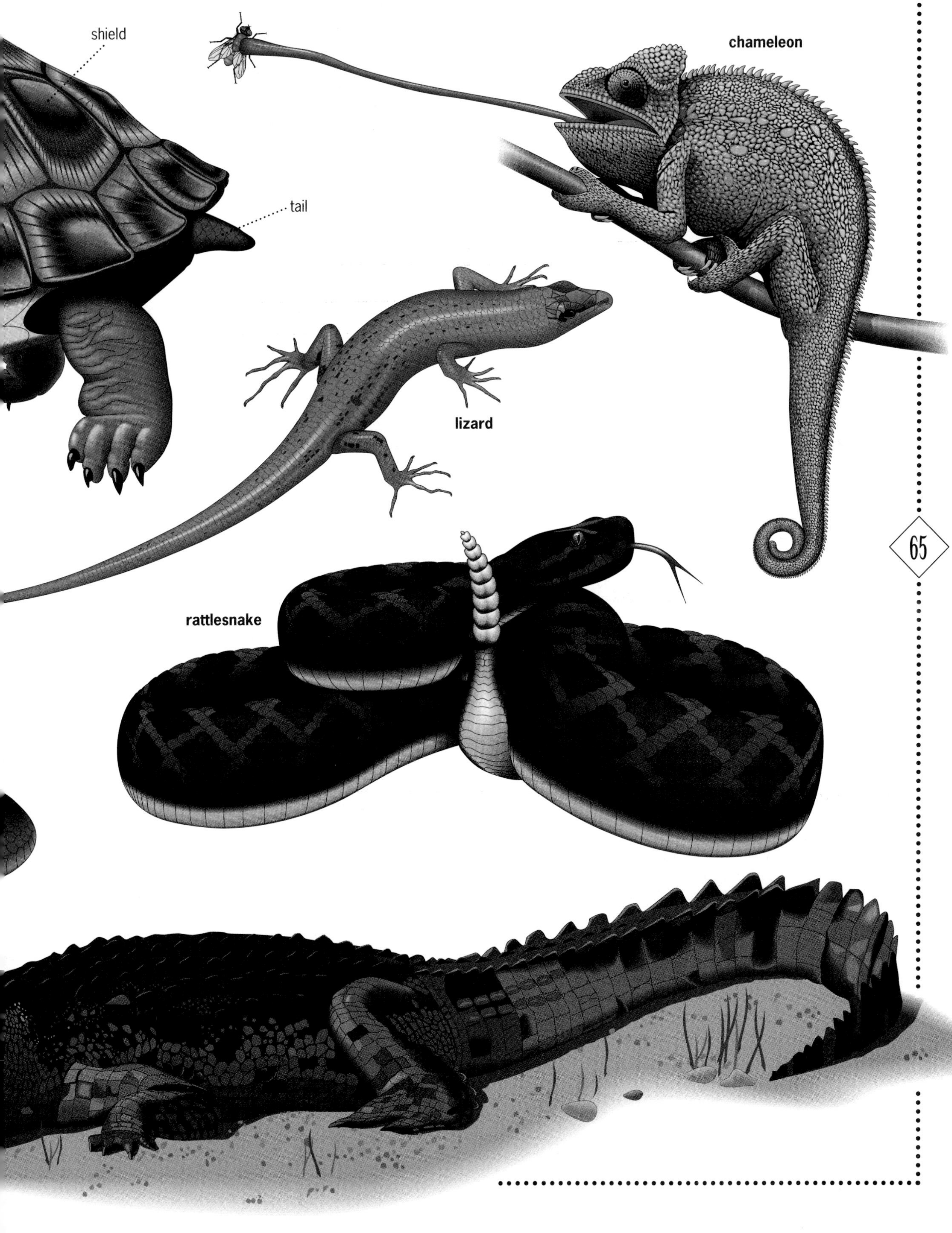
shield
tail
chameleon
lizard
rattlesnake

CAT

whiskers
upper eyelid
lower eyelid
nictitating membrane
whiskers
lip
eyelashes
pupil
nose leather
muzzle

DOG

MORPHOLOGY

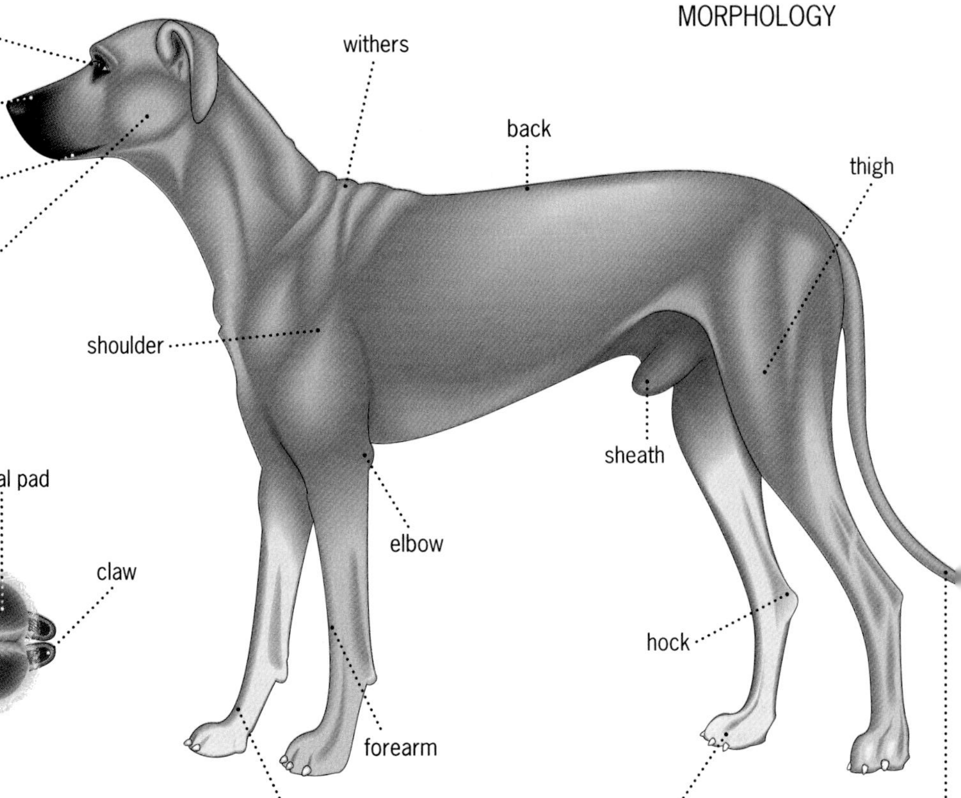
stop
muzzle
flews
cheek
withers
back
thigh
shoulder
sheath
elbow
hock
forearm
wrist
toe

dog's forepaw

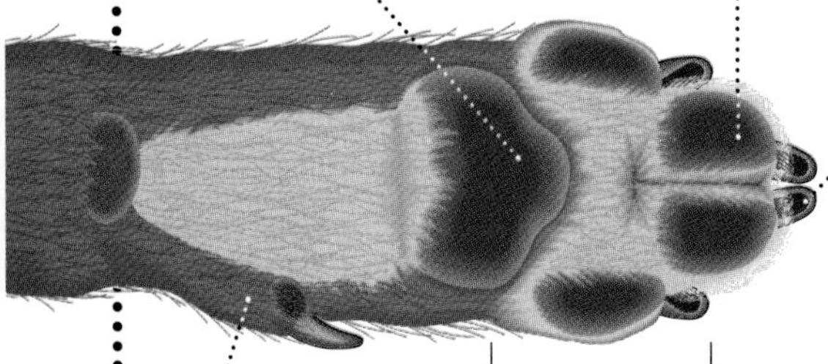
palmar pad
digital pad
claw
dewclaw
toe

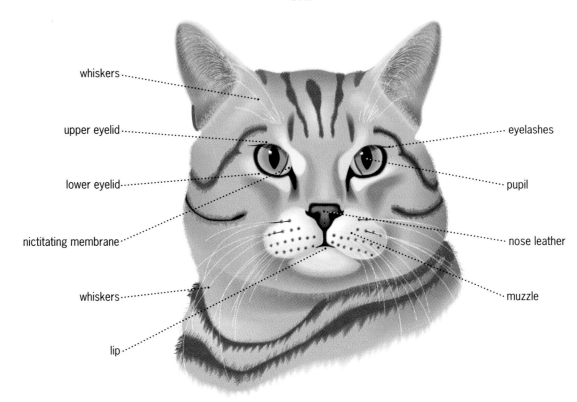

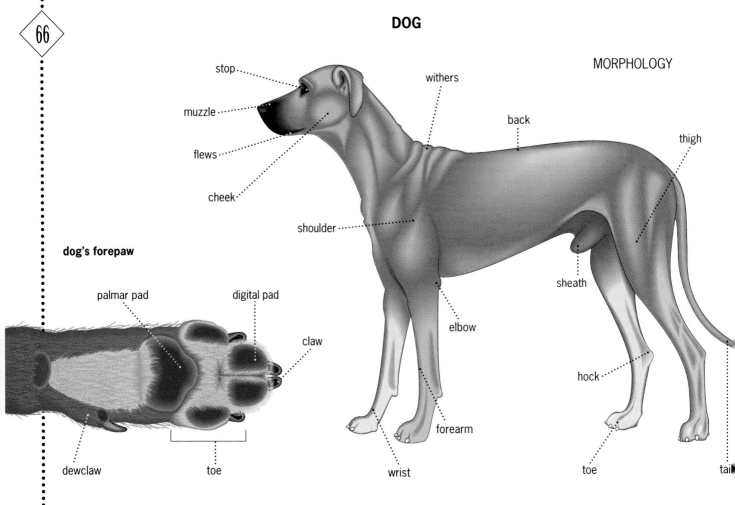

HORSE

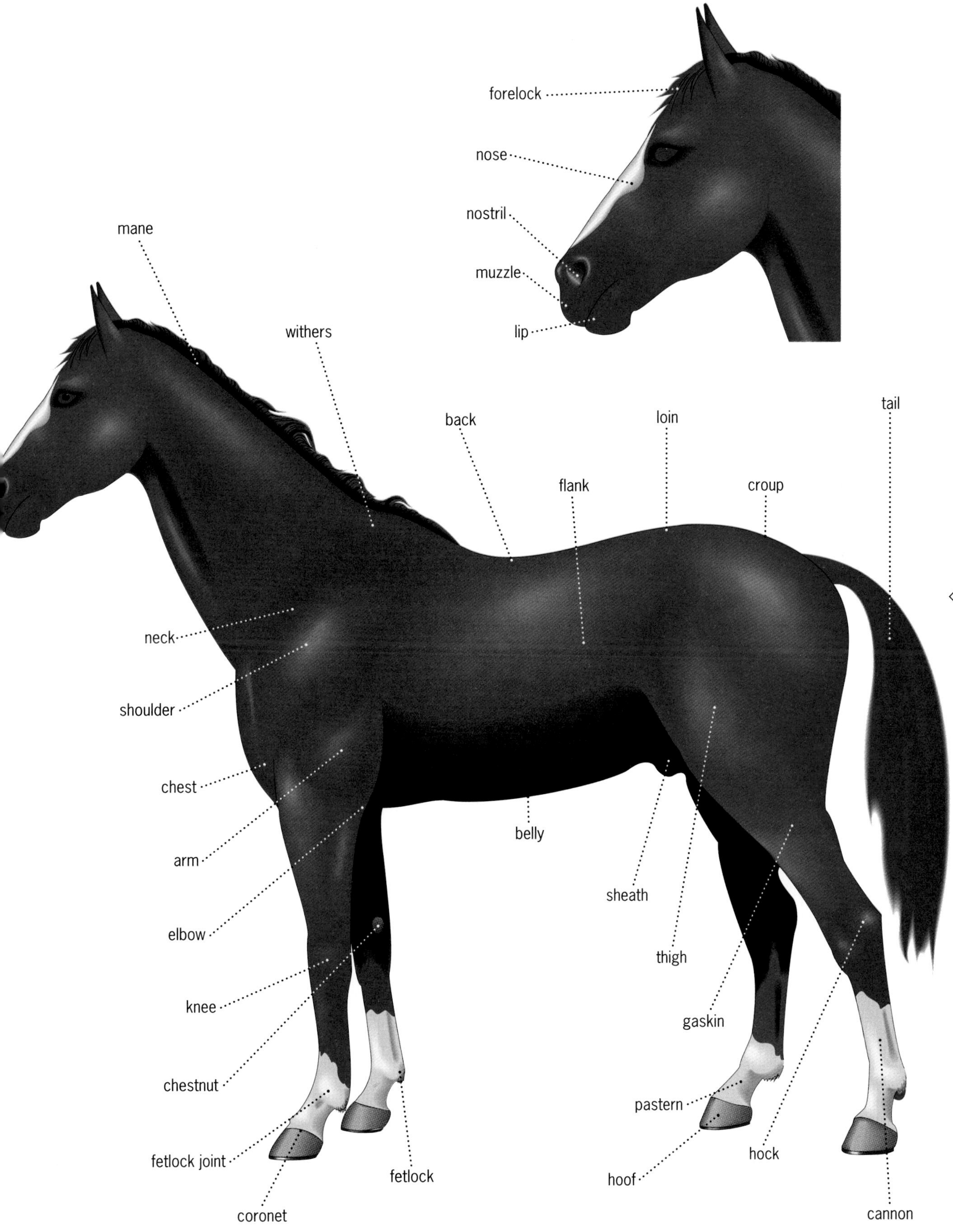
forelock
nose
nostril
muzzle
lip
mane
withers
back
loin
tail
flank
croup
neck
shoulder
chest
arm
belly
elbow
sheath
thigh
knee
gaskin
chestnut
pastern
fetlock joint
hock
hoof
fetlock
coronet
cannon

FARM ANIMALS

hen

chick

rooster; cock

goose

duck

turkey

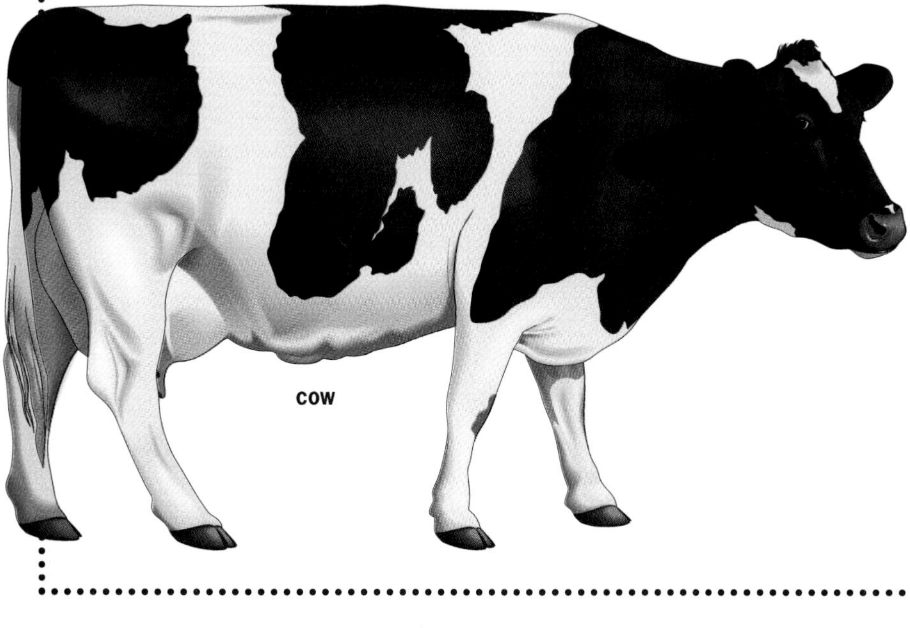

cow

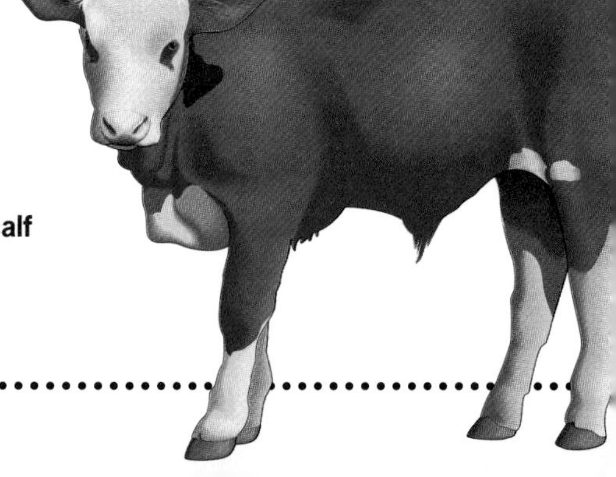

calf

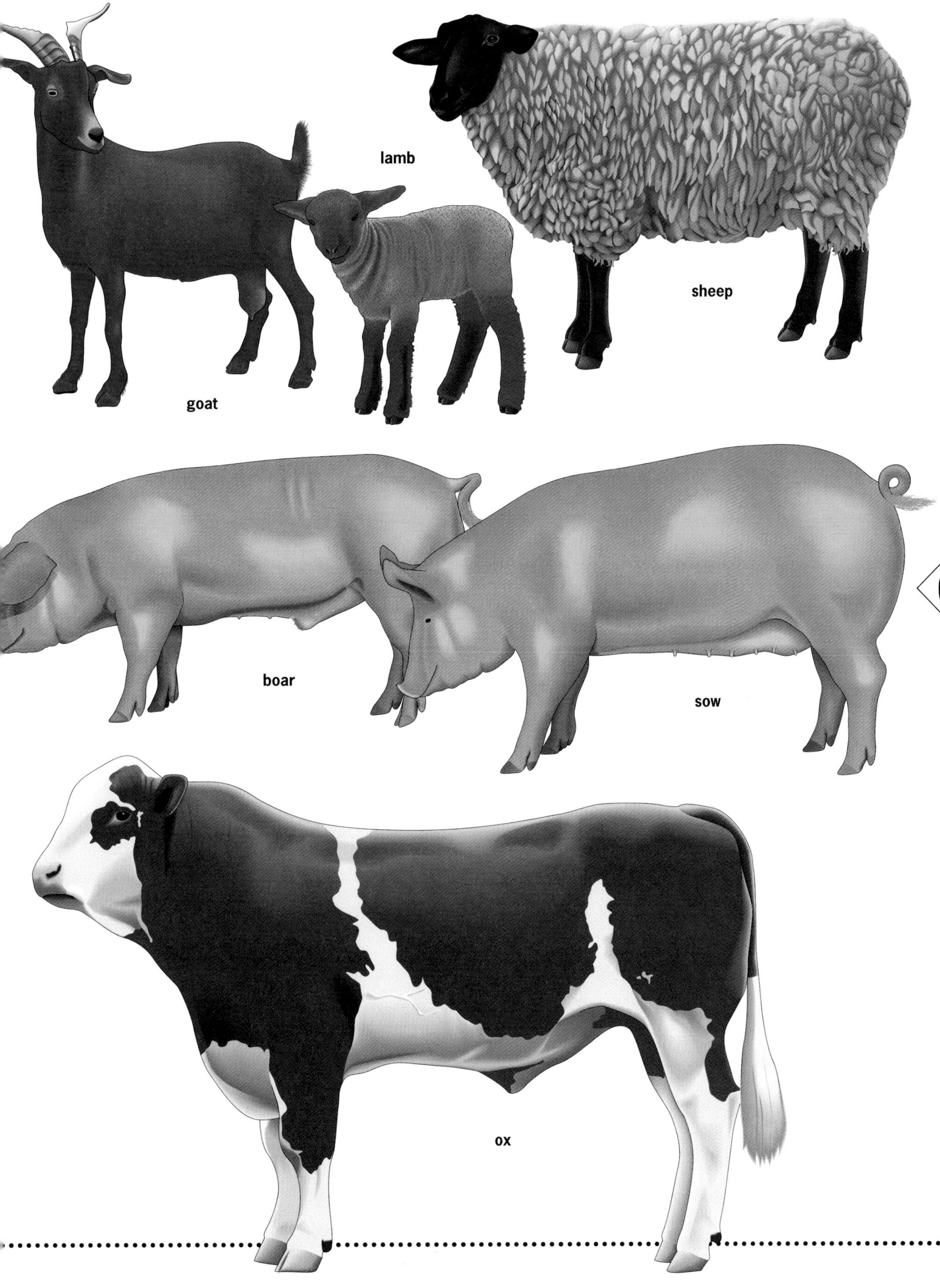
lamb
sheep
goat
boar
sow
ox

TYPES OF JAWS

rodent's jaw

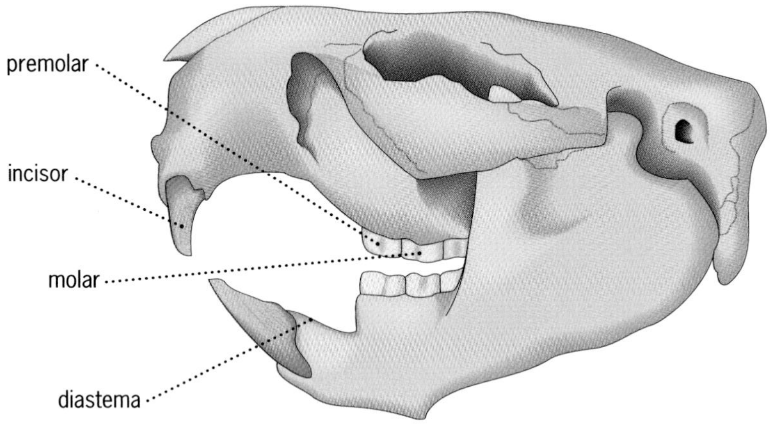
premolar
incisor
molar
diastema

beaver

carnivore's jaw

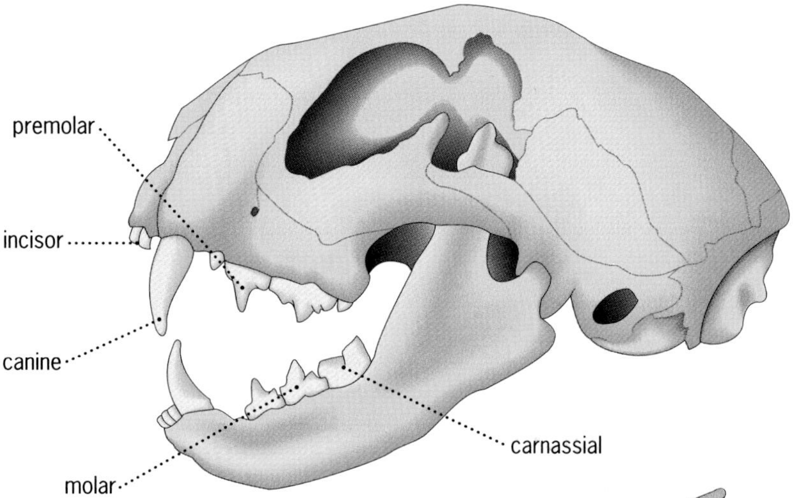
premolar
incisor
canine
carnassial
molar

lion

herbivore's jaw

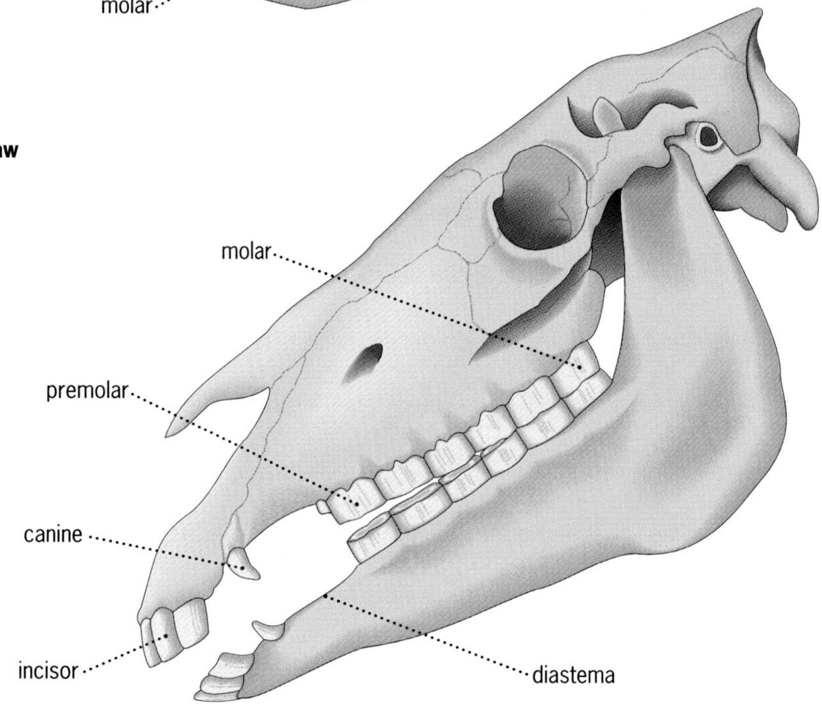
molar
premolar
canine
incisor
diastema

horse

MAJOR TYPES OF HORNS

horns of mouflon

horns of giraffe

horns of rhinoceros

MAJOR TYPES OF TUSKS

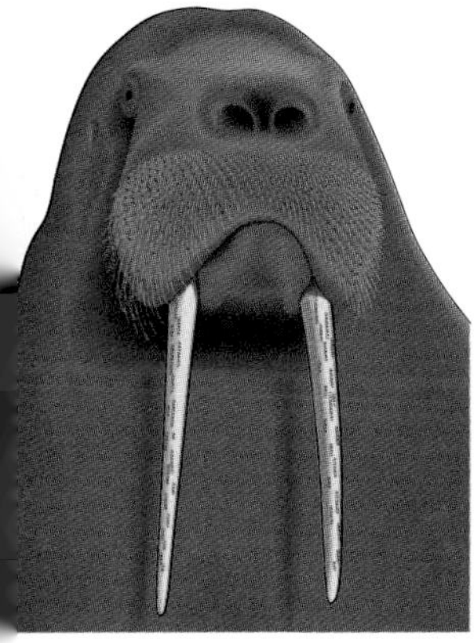

tusks of walrus

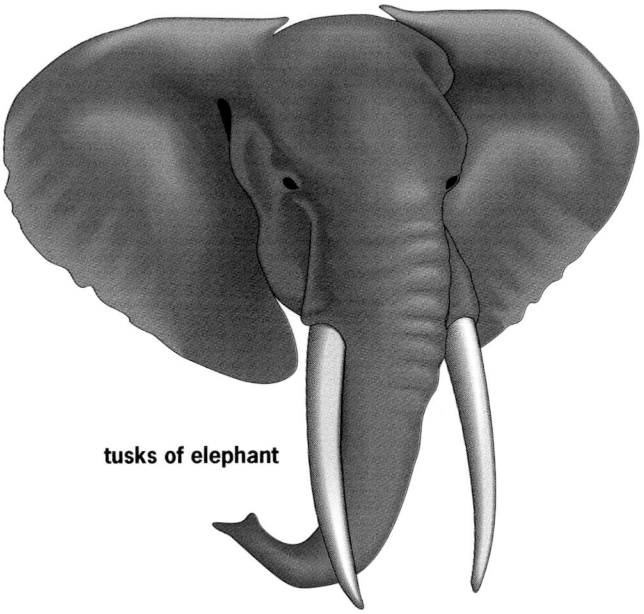

tusks of elephant

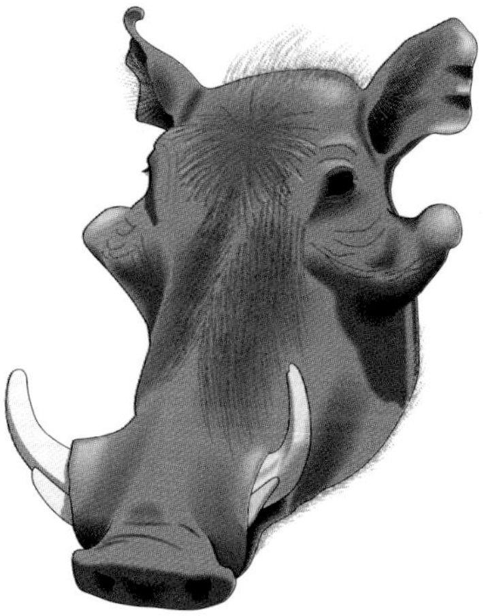

tusks of wart hog

TYPES OF HOOFS

one-toe hoof

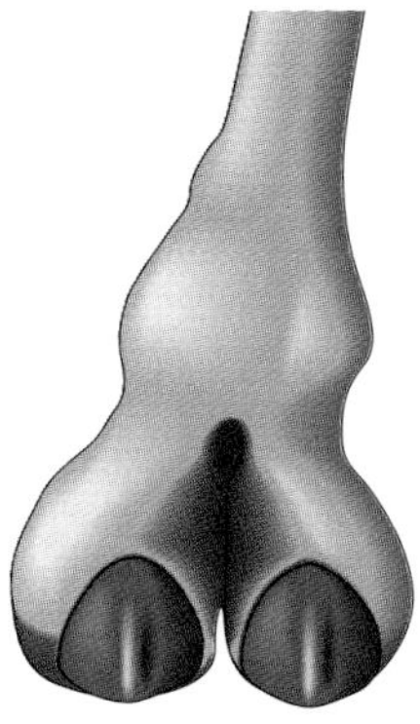

two-toed hoof

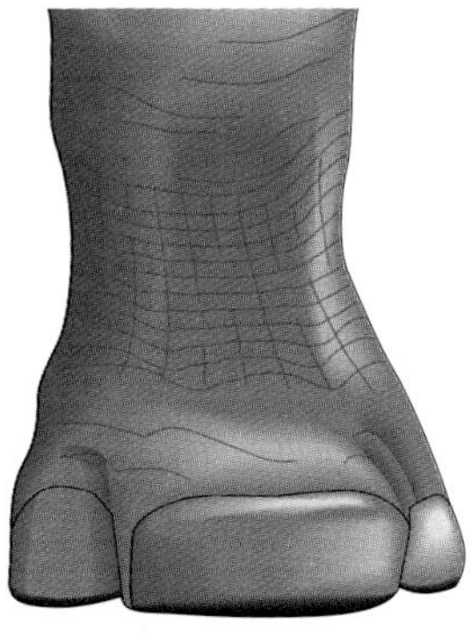

three-toed hoof

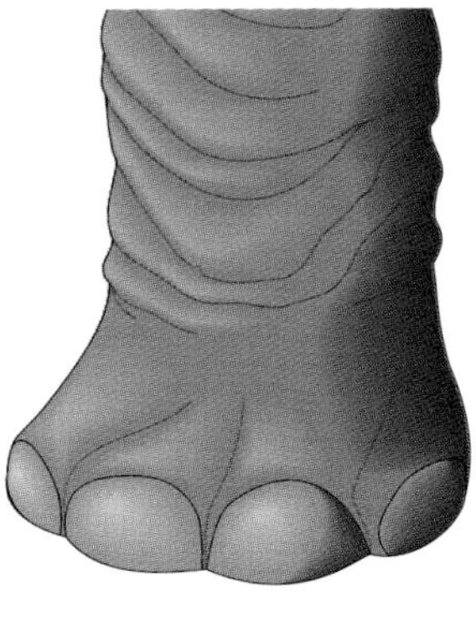

four-toed hoof

WILD ANIMALS

polar bear

giraffe

monkey

lion

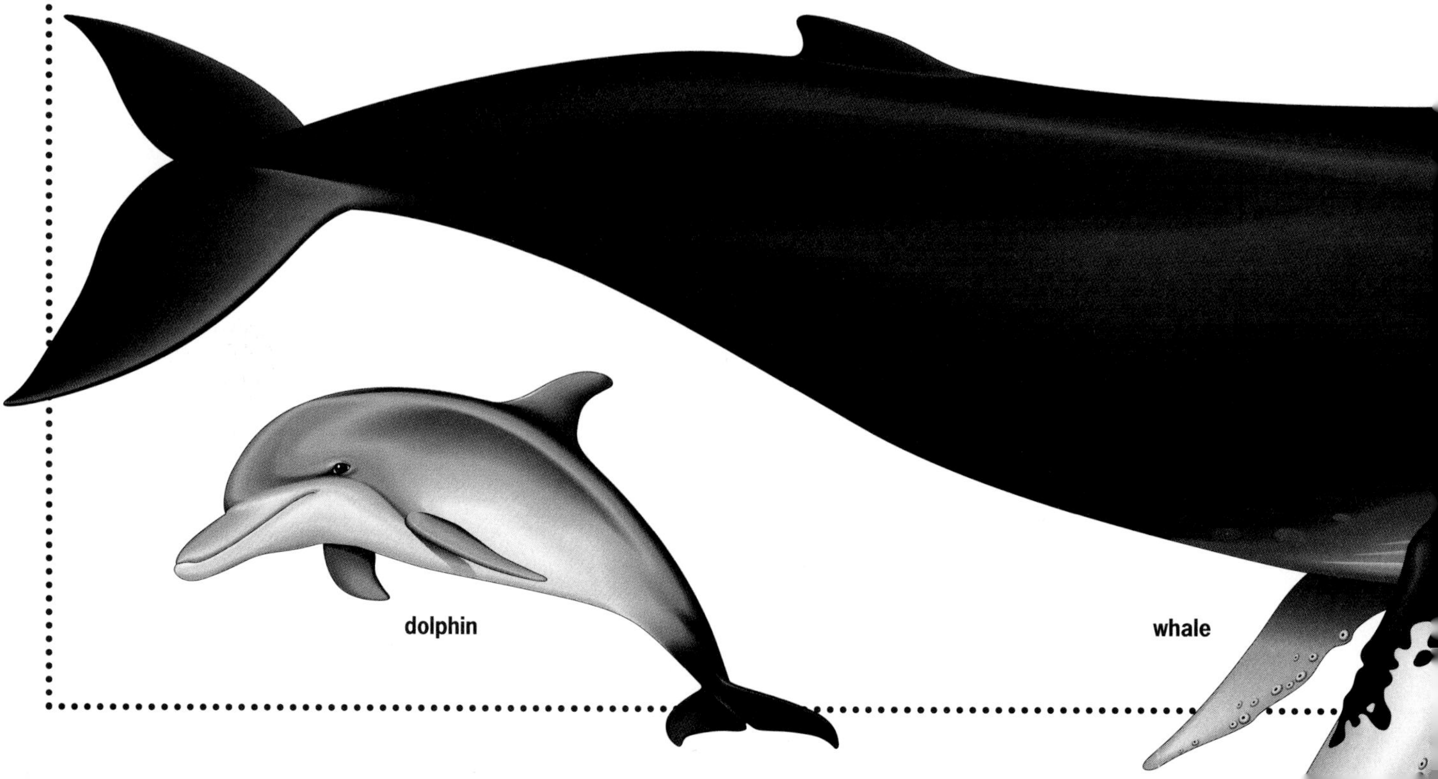

dolphin

whale

kangaroo

elephant

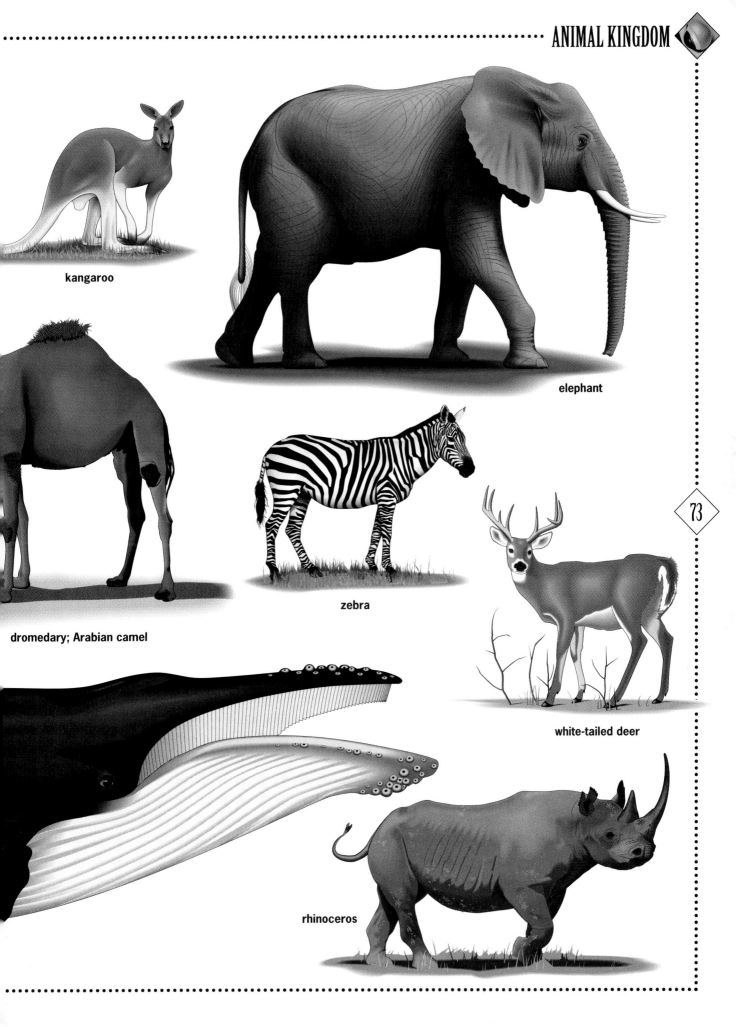

dromedary; Arabian camel

zebra

white-tailed deer

rhinoceros

BIRD

PRINCIPAL TYPES OF BILLS

aquatic bird

insectivorous bird

wading bird

granivorous bird

bird of prey

PRINCIPAL TYPES OF FEET

bird of prey

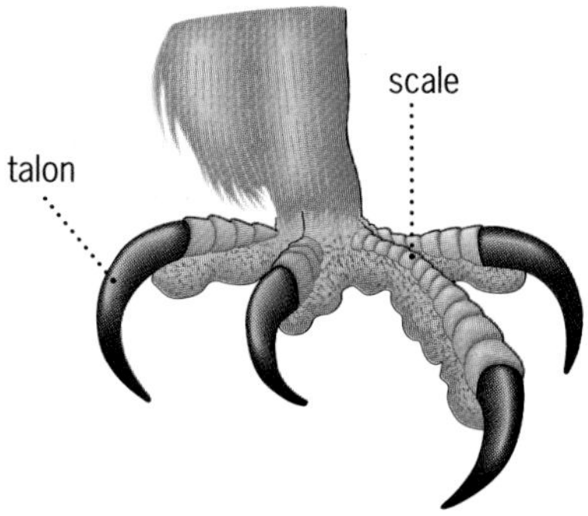
scale
talon

aquatic bird

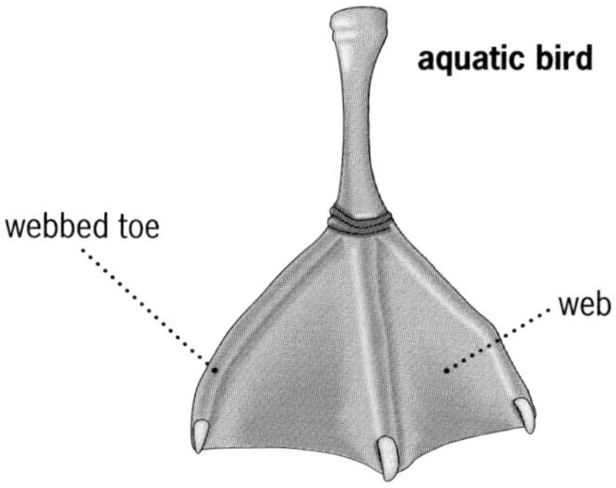
webbed toe
web

aquatic bird

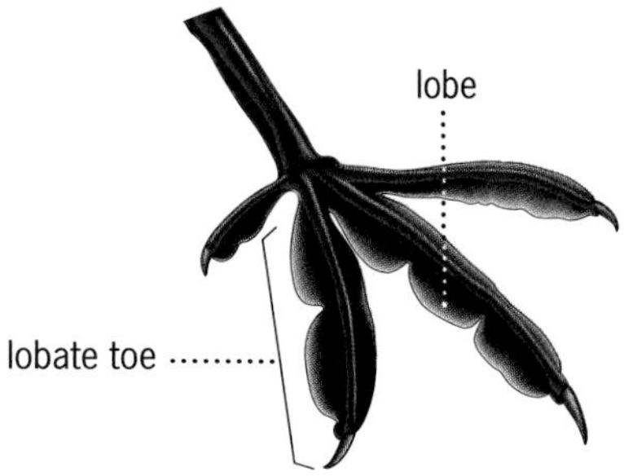
lobe
lobate toe

perching bird

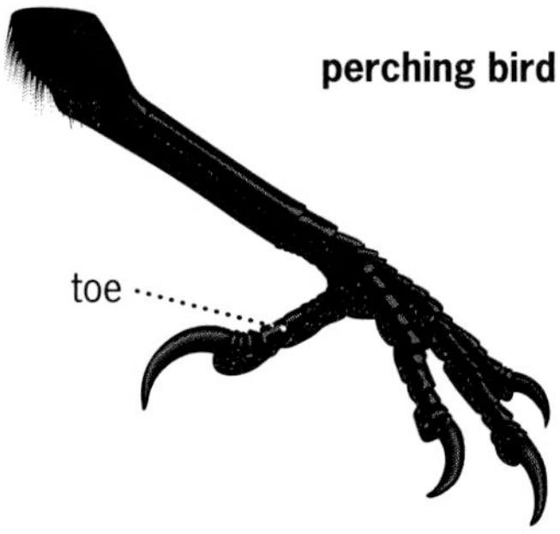
toe

MORPHOLOGY

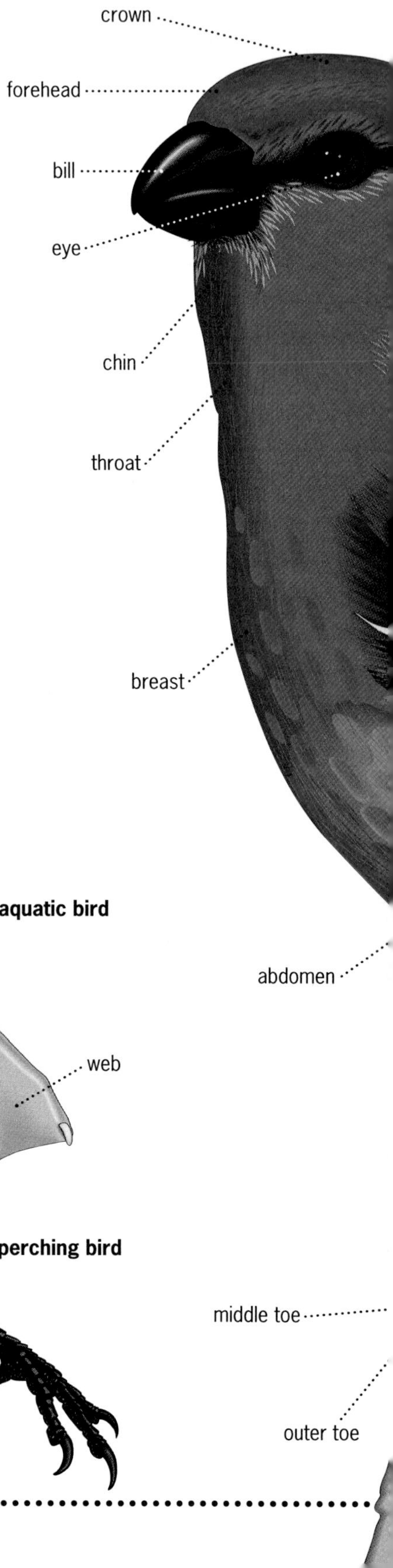
crown
forehead
bill
eye
chin
throat
breast
abdomen
middle toe
outer toe

bird's nest

birdhouse

bird feeder

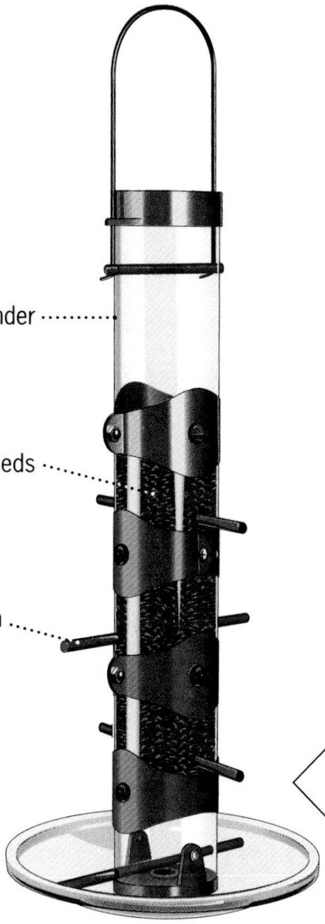
cylinder
seeds
perch

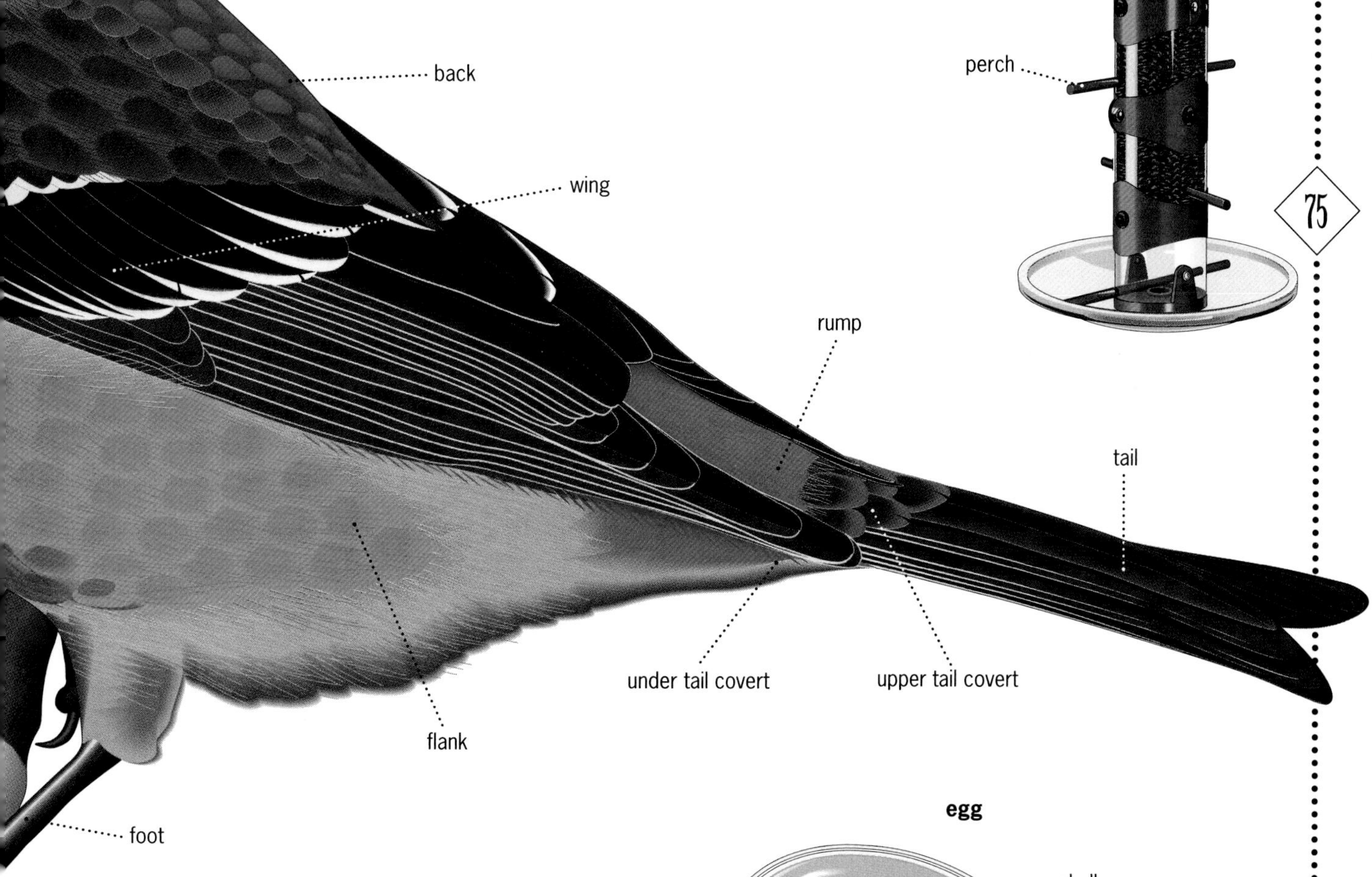
nape
back
wing
rump
tail
under tail covert
upper tail covert
flank
foot
hind toe
claw

egg

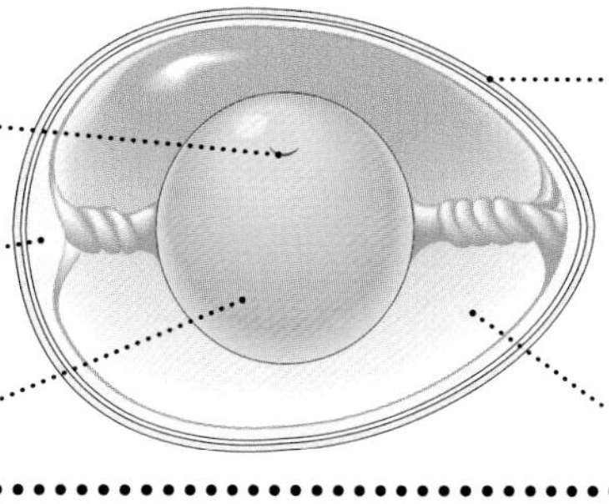
shell
blastodisc
air space
yolk
albumen

EXAMPLES OF BIRDS

crow
parrot
stork
swallow
flamingo
ostrich

robin

jay

hummingbird

nightingale

owl

peacock

HUMAN BODY, ANTERIOR VIEW

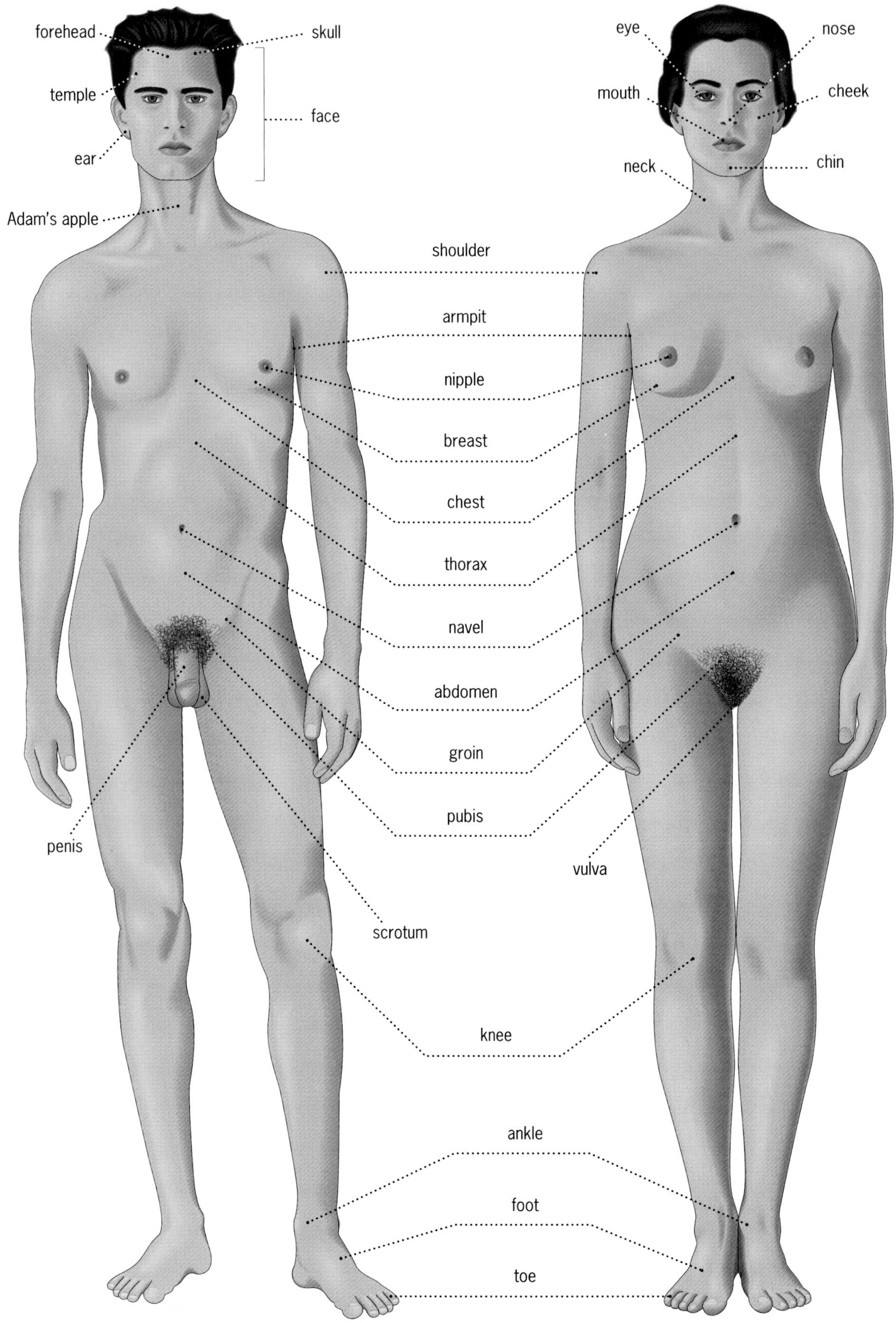
forehead
skull
temple
face
ear
Adam's apple
eye
nose
mouth
cheek
neck
chin
shoulder
armpit
nipple
breast
chest
thorax
navel
abdomen
groin
pubis
penis
vulva
scrotum
knee
ankle
foot
toe

HUMAN BODY, POSTERIOR VIEW

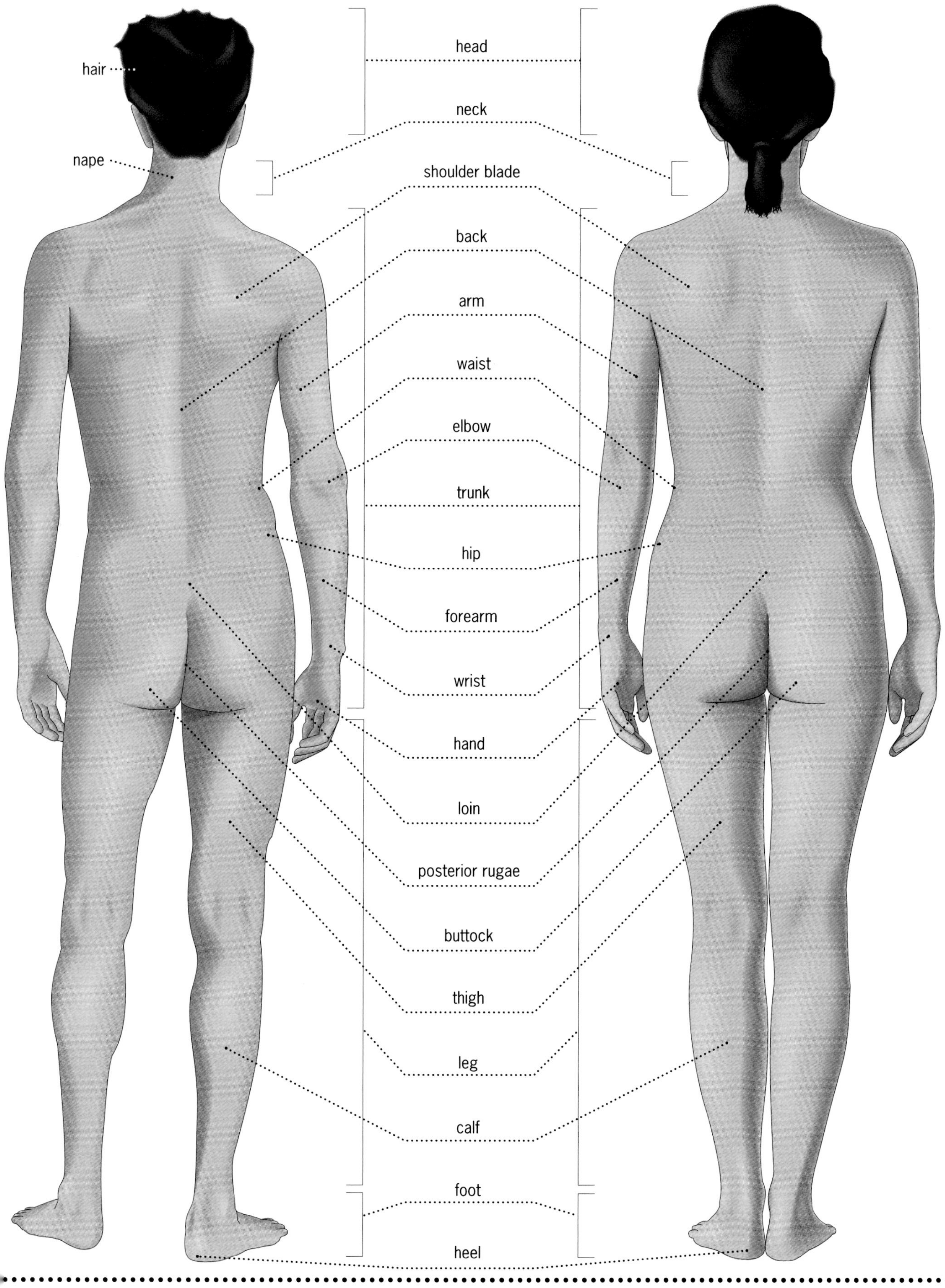

hair
nape
head
neck
shoulder blade
back
arm
waist
elbow
trunk
hip
forearm
wrist
hand
loin
posterior rugae
buttock
thigh
leg
calf
foot
heel

SKELETON

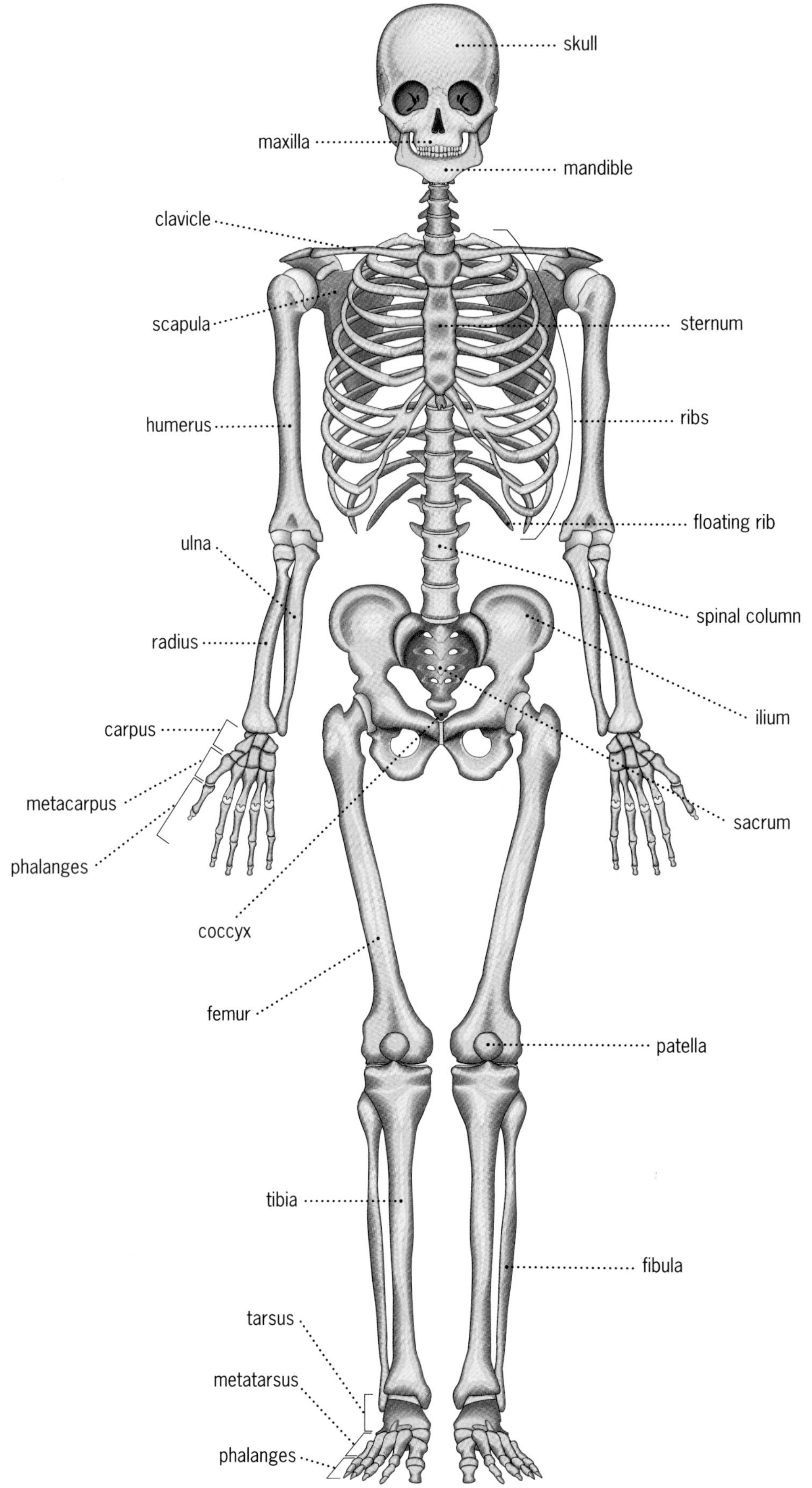

skull
maxilla
mandible
clavicle
scapula
sternum
humerus
ribs
floating rib
ulna
spinal column
radius
ilium
carpus
metacarpus
sacrum
phalanges
coccyx
femur
patella
tibia
fibula
tarsus
metatarsus
phalanges

HUMAN ANATOMY

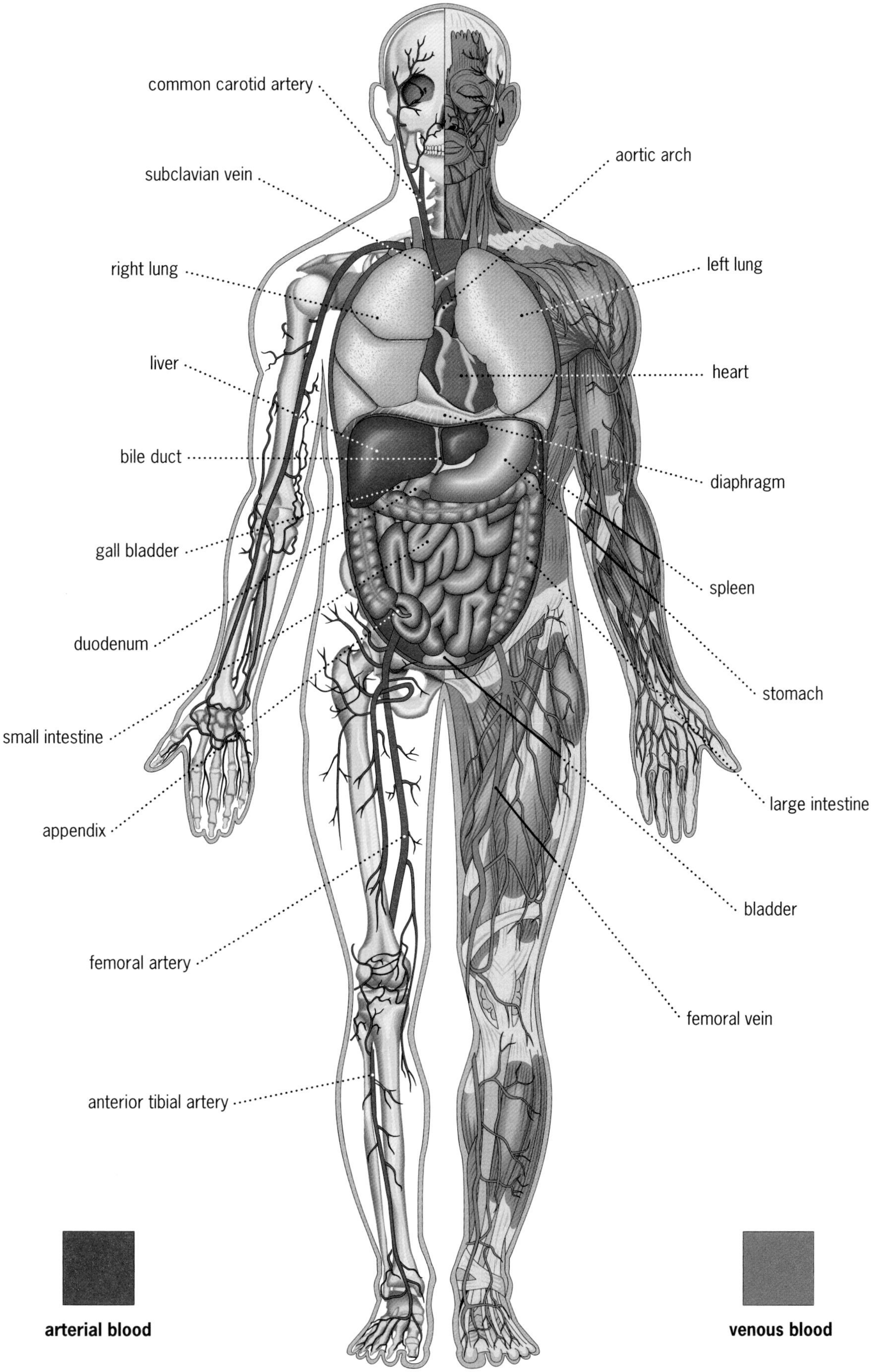
common carotid artery
subclavian vein
right lung
liver
bile duct
gall bladder
duodenum
small intestine
appendix
femoral artery
anterior tibial artery
aortic arch
left lung
heart
diaphragm
spleen
stomach
large intestine
bladder
femoral vein
arterial blood
venous blood

EYE: THE ORGAN OF SIGHT

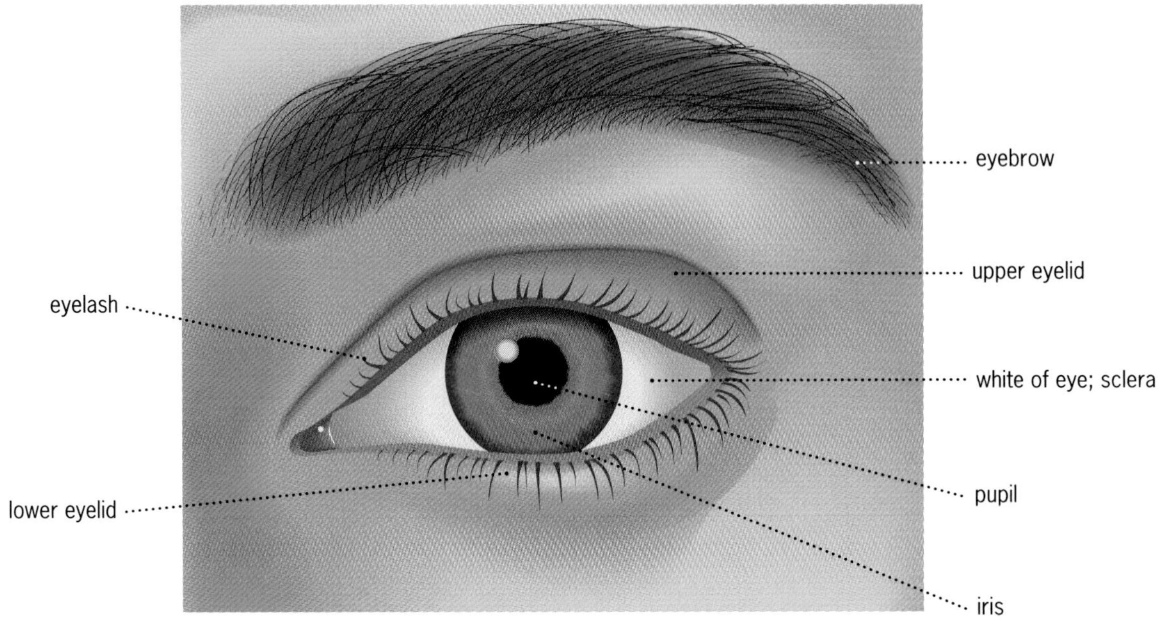
eyebrow
upper eyelid
eyelash
white of eye; sclera
pupil
lower eyelid
iris

HAND: THE ORGAN OF TOUCH

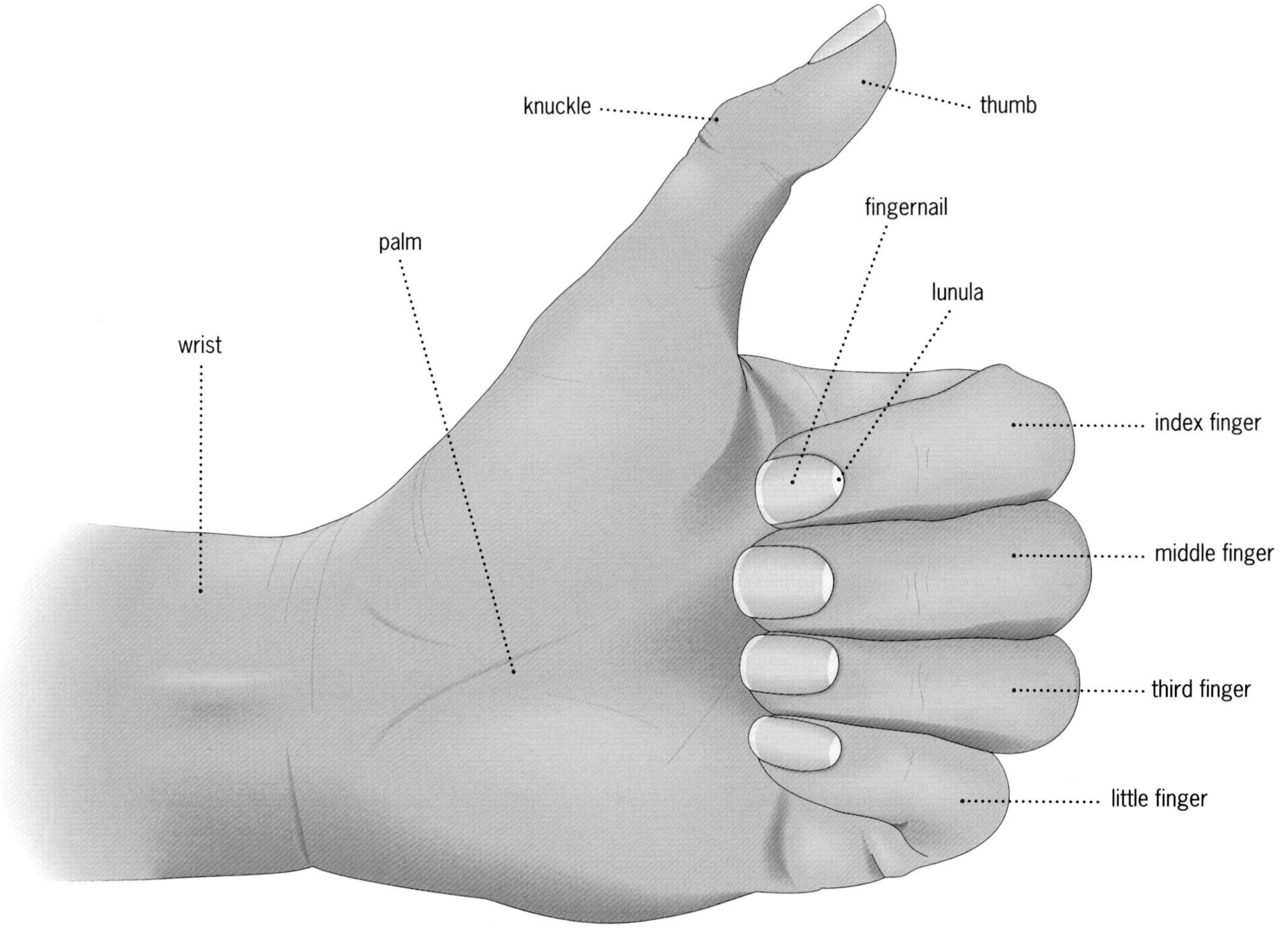
knuckle
thumb
fingernail
palm
lunula
wrist
index finger
middle finger
third finger
little finger

EAR: THE ORGAN OF HEARING

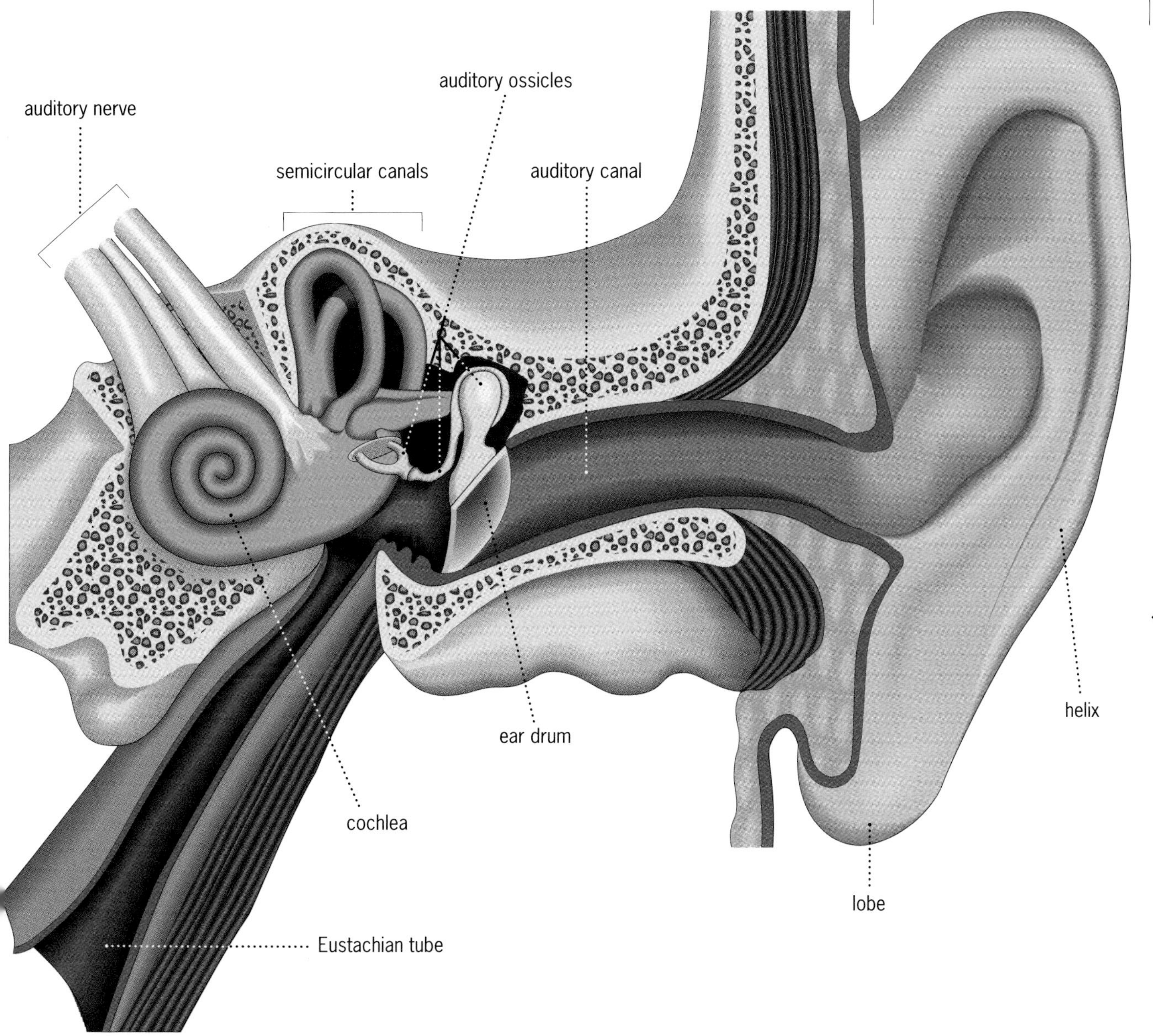
auricle
auditory ossicles
auditory nerve
semicircular canals
auditory canal
helix
ear drum
cochlea
lobe
Eustachian tube

PARTS OF THE EAR

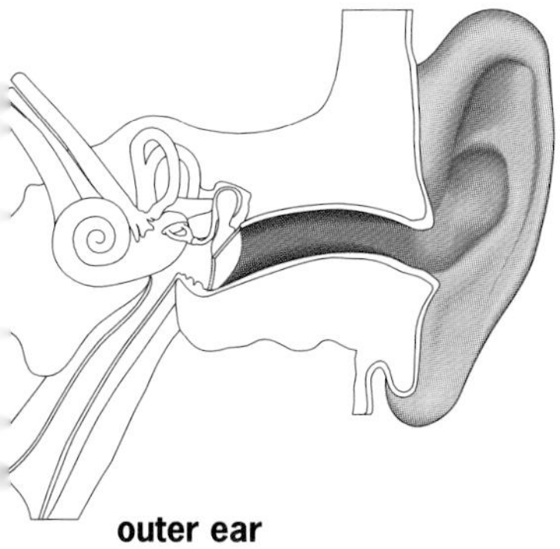

outer ear

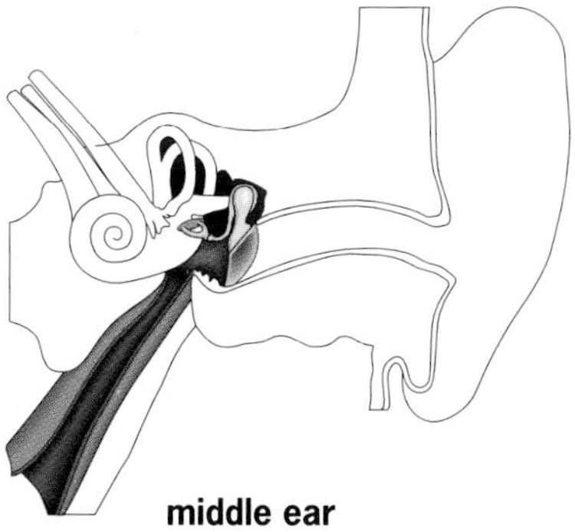

middle ear

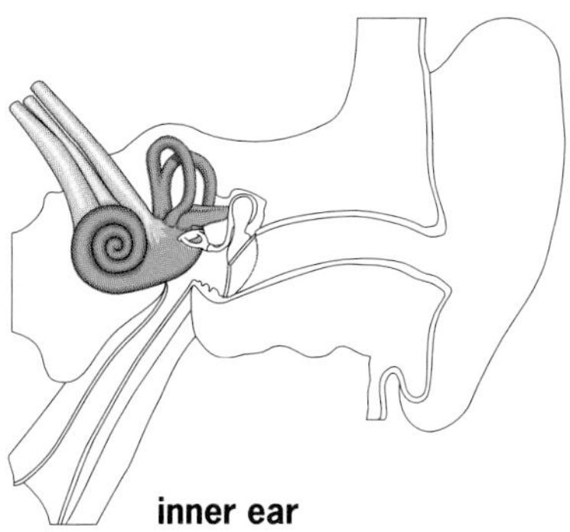

inner ear

NOSE: THE ORGAN OF SMELL

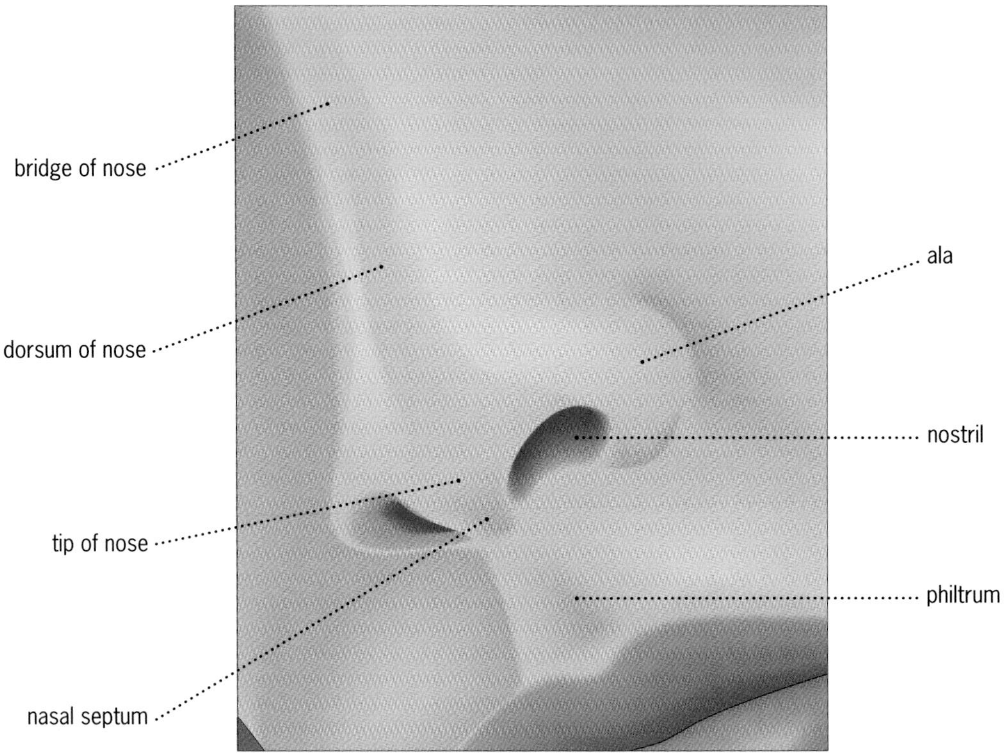
bridge of nose
dorsum of nose
tip of nose
nasal septum
ala
nostril
philtrum

MOUTH: THE ORGAN OF TASTE

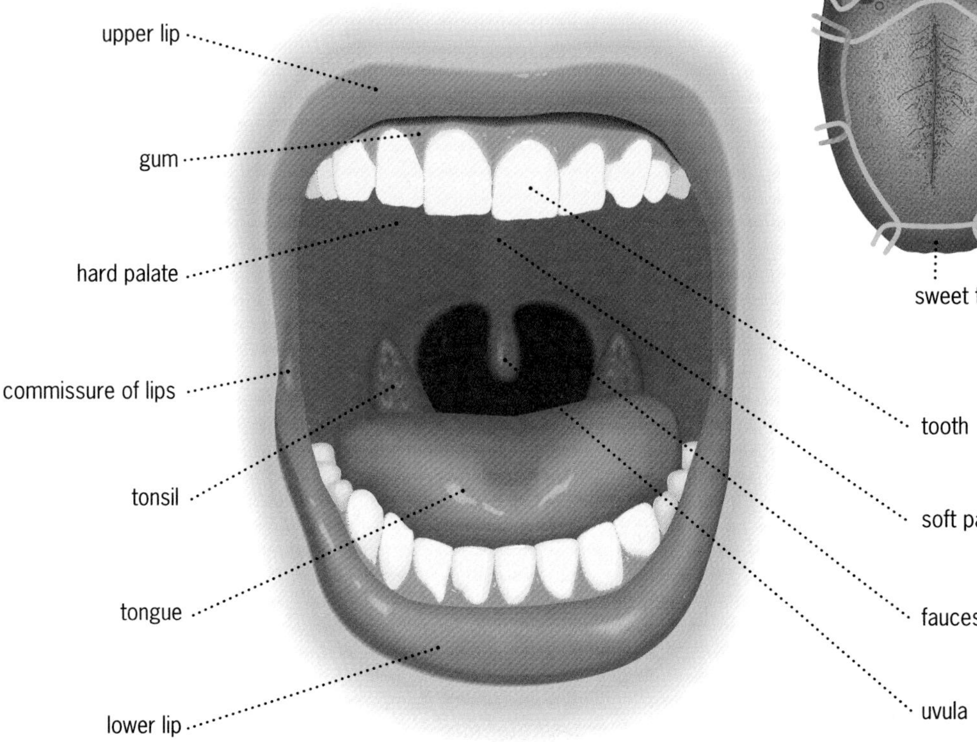
upper lip
gum
hard palate
commissure of lips
tonsil
tongue
lower lip
tooth
soft palate
fauces
uvula

taste sensations

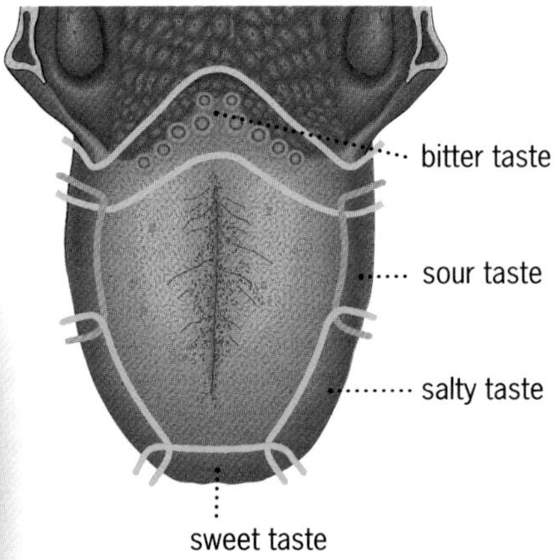
bitter taste
sour taste
salty taste
sweet taste

HUMAN DENTURE

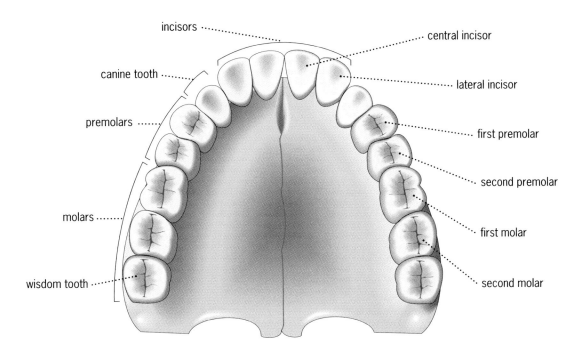

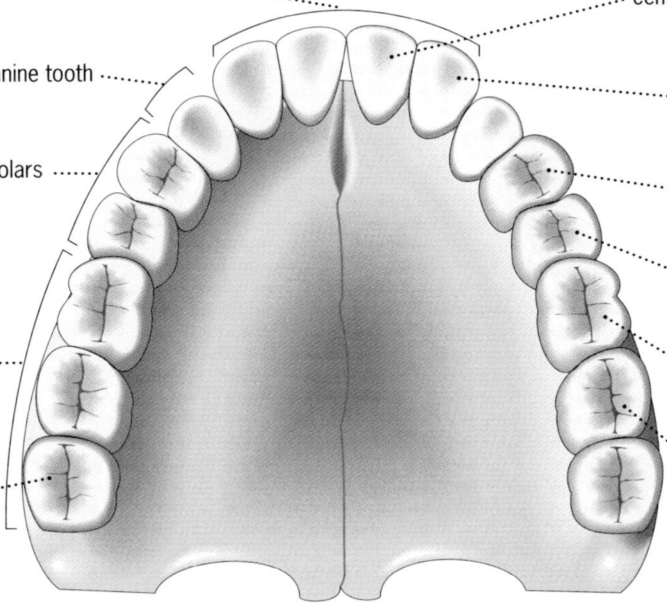
incisors
central incisor
canine tooth
lateral incisor
premolars
first premolar
second premolar
molars
first molar
wisdom tooth
second molar

cross section of a molar

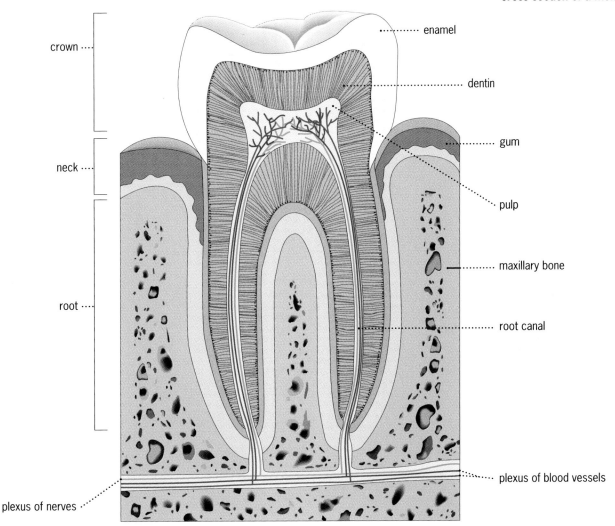

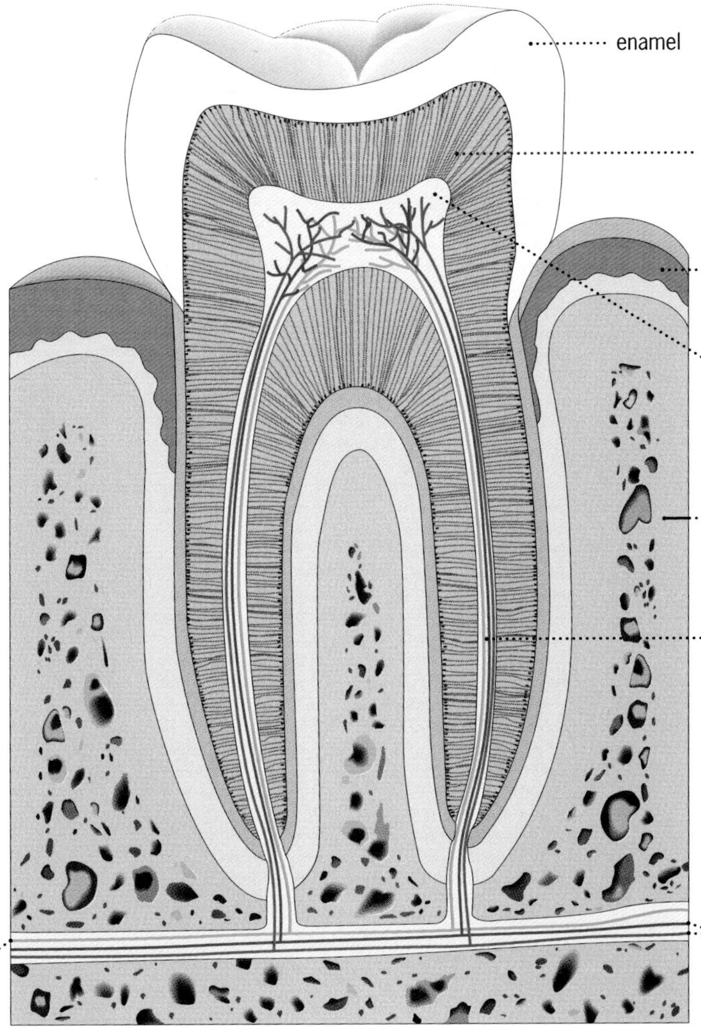
crown
enamel
dentin
neck
gum
pulp
root
maxillary bone
root canal
plexus of blood vessels
plexus of nerves

TRADITIONAL HOUSES

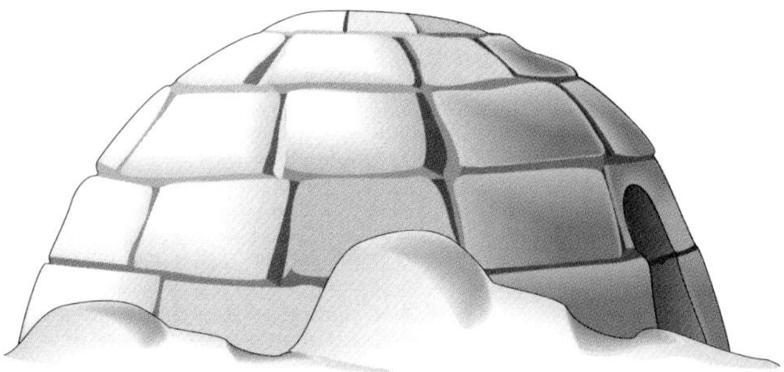

igloo

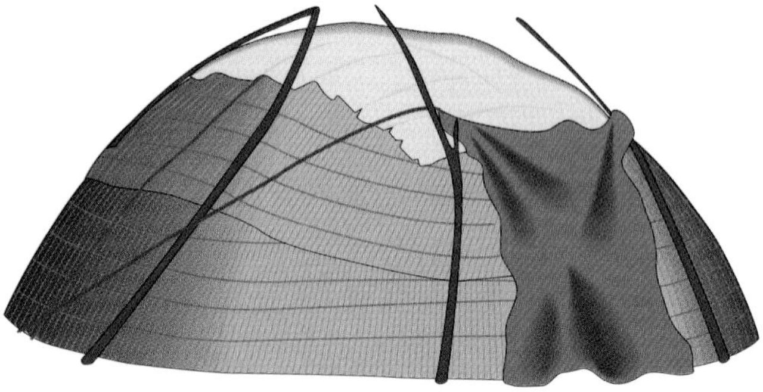

wigwam

log cabin

mud hut

house on stilts

tepee

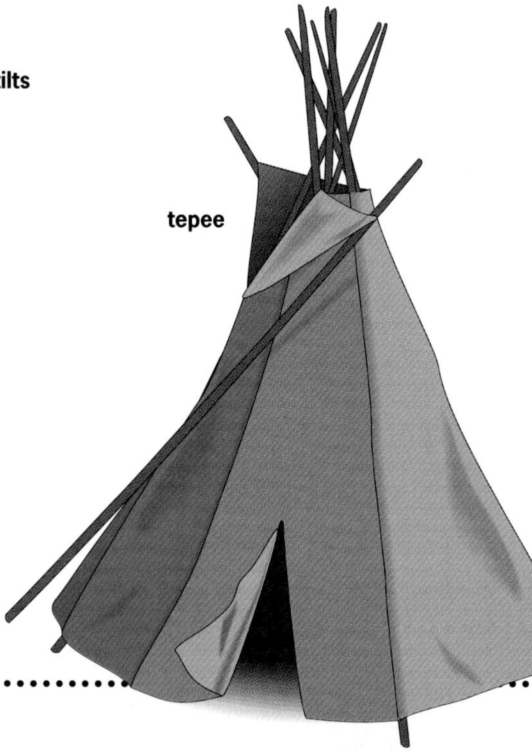

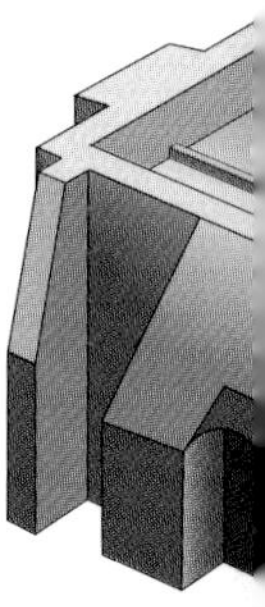

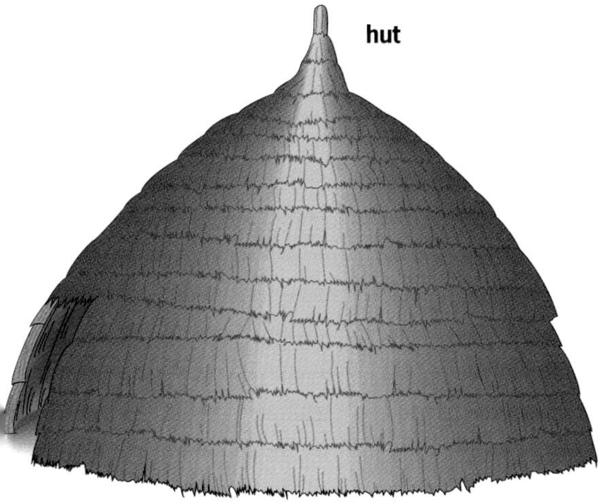
hut

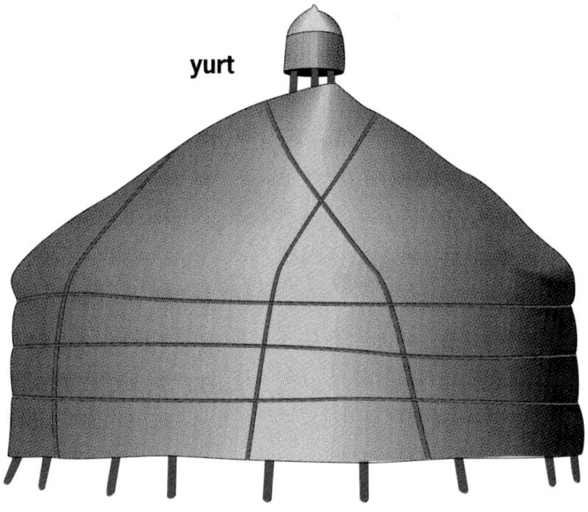
yurt

MOSQUE

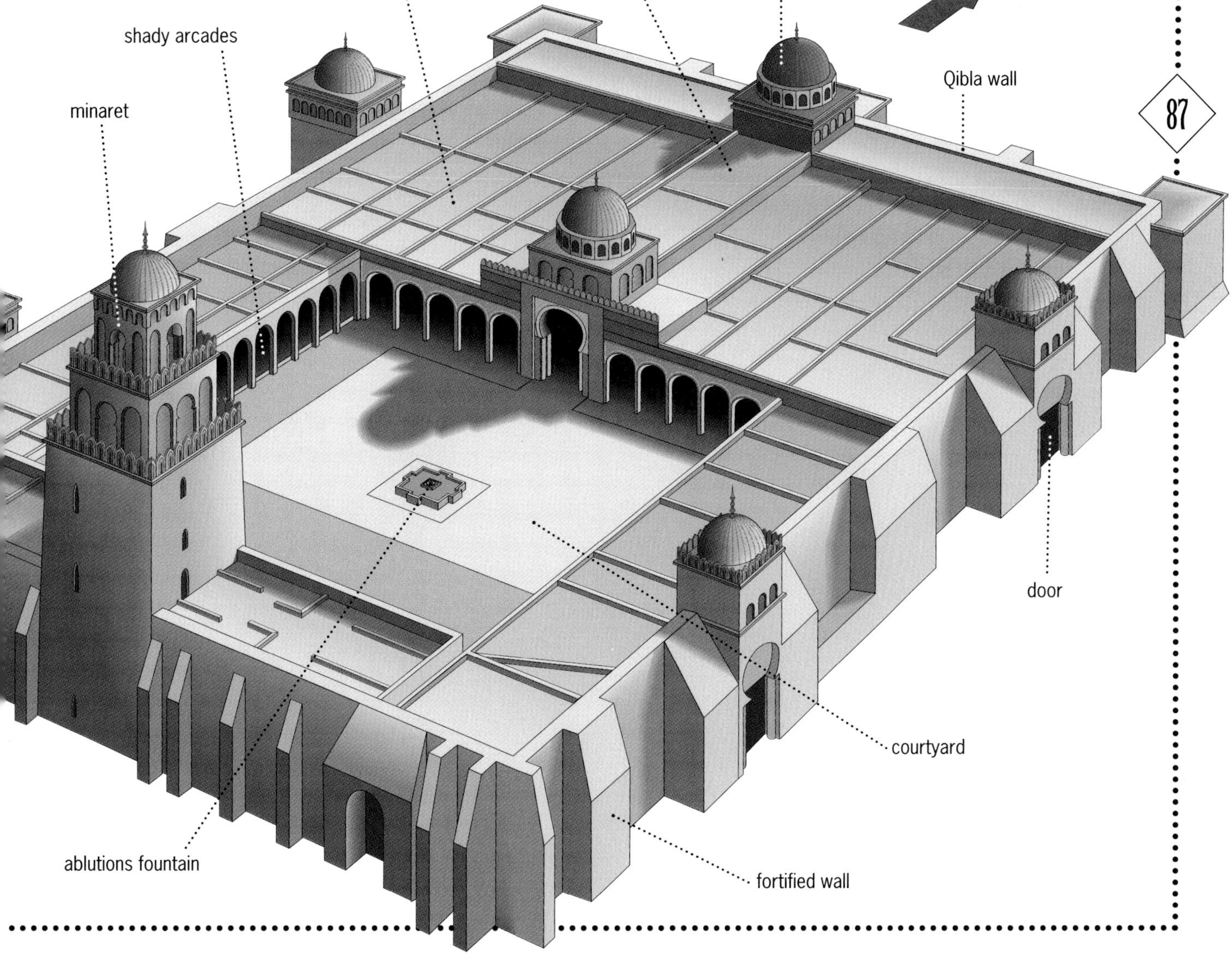
prayer hall
central nave
Mihrab dome
direction of Mecca
shady arcades
Qibla wall
minaret
door
courtyard
ablutions fountain
fortified wall

CASTLE

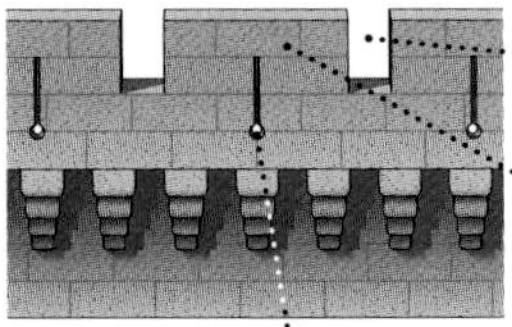
machicolation
crenel
merlon
loophole

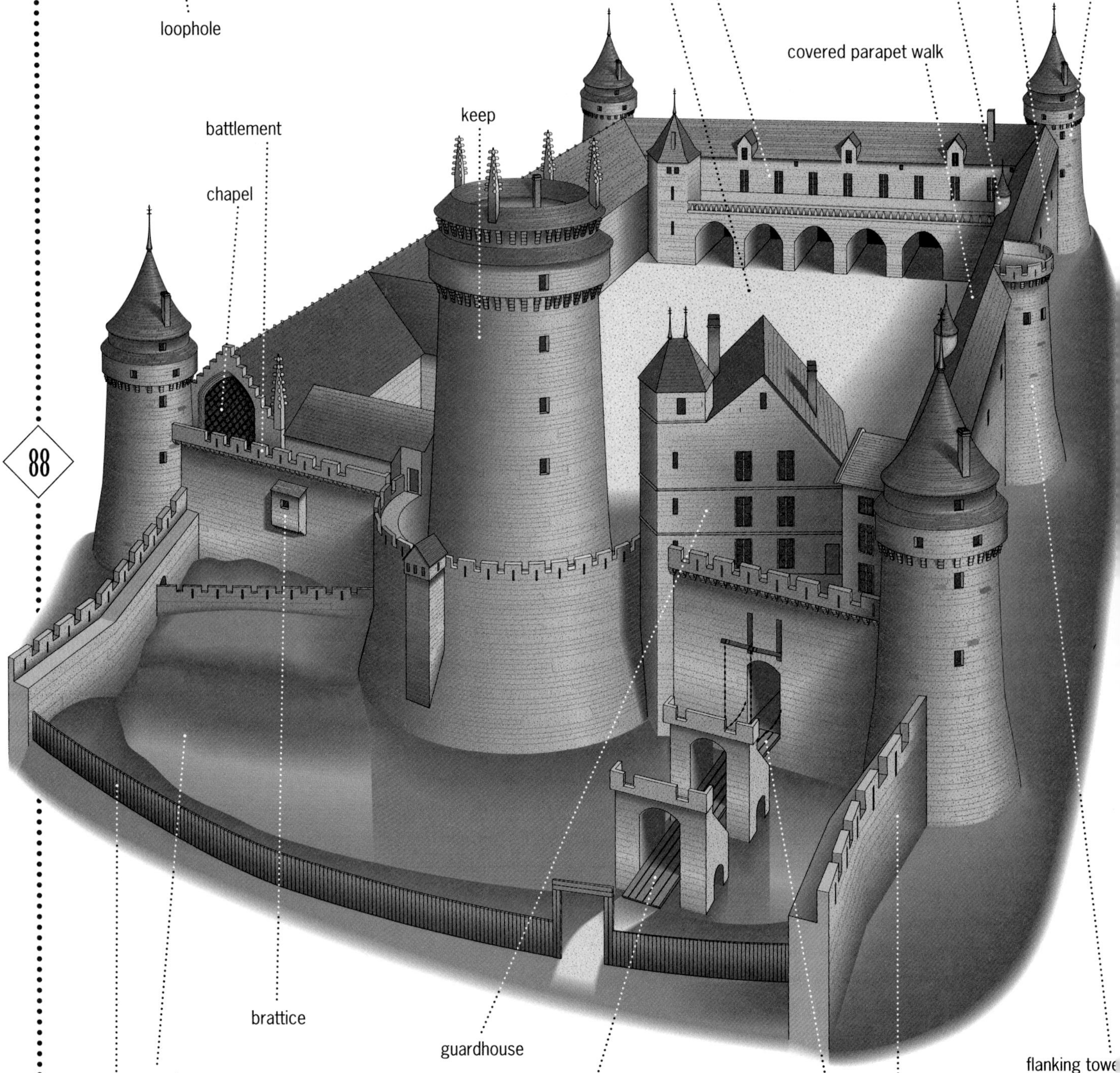
corner tow
castle
curtain wall
bailey
turret
covered parapet walk
keep
battlement
chapel
brattice
guardhouse
moat
footbridge
drawbridge
rampart
flanking towe
stockade

GOTHIC CATHEDRAL

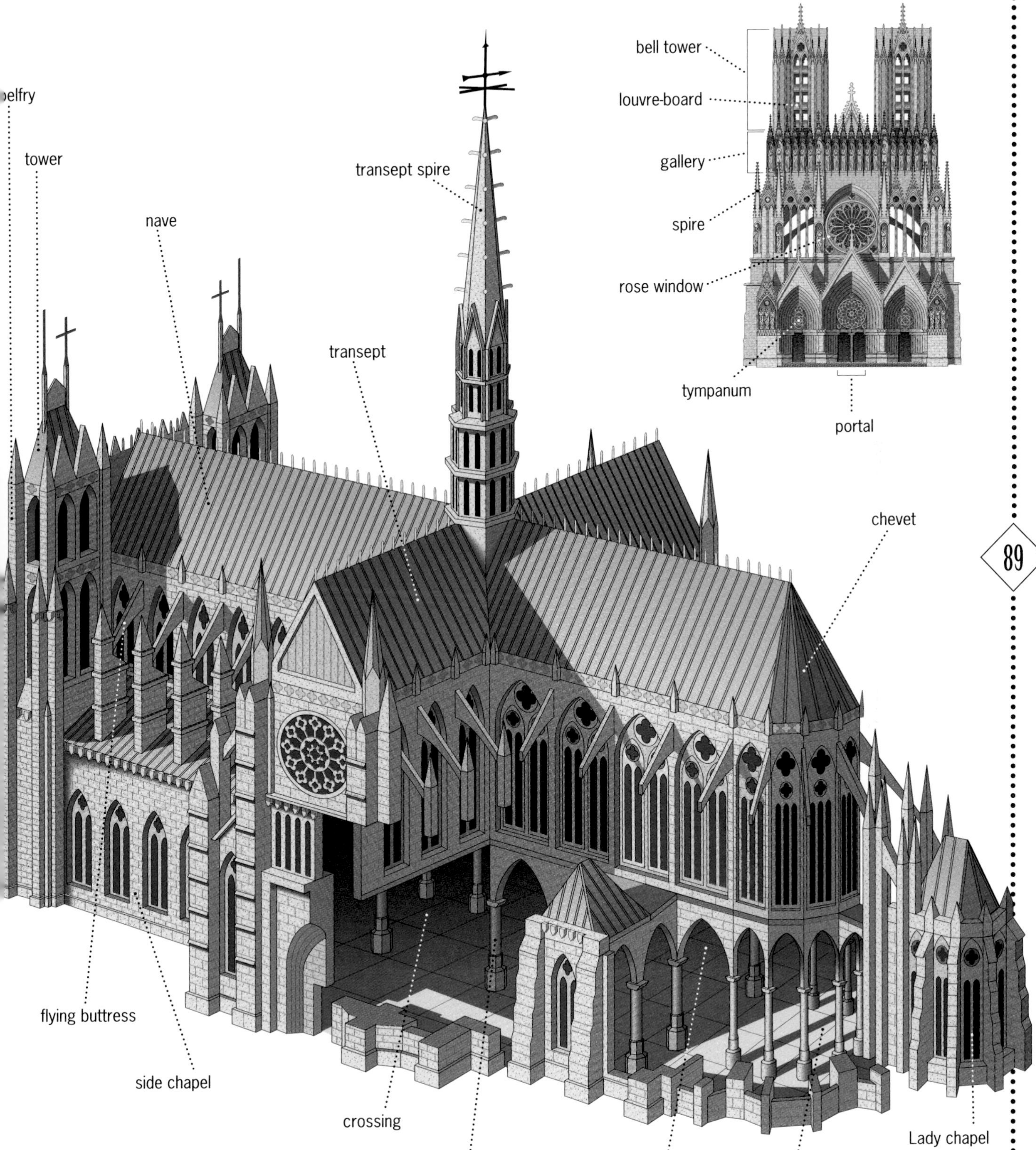
façade
bell tower
louvre-board
gallery
spire
rose window
tympanum
portal
elfry
tower
nave
transept spire
transept
chevet
flying buttress
side chapel
crossing
pillar
choir
ambulatory
Lady chapel

CITY CENTRE

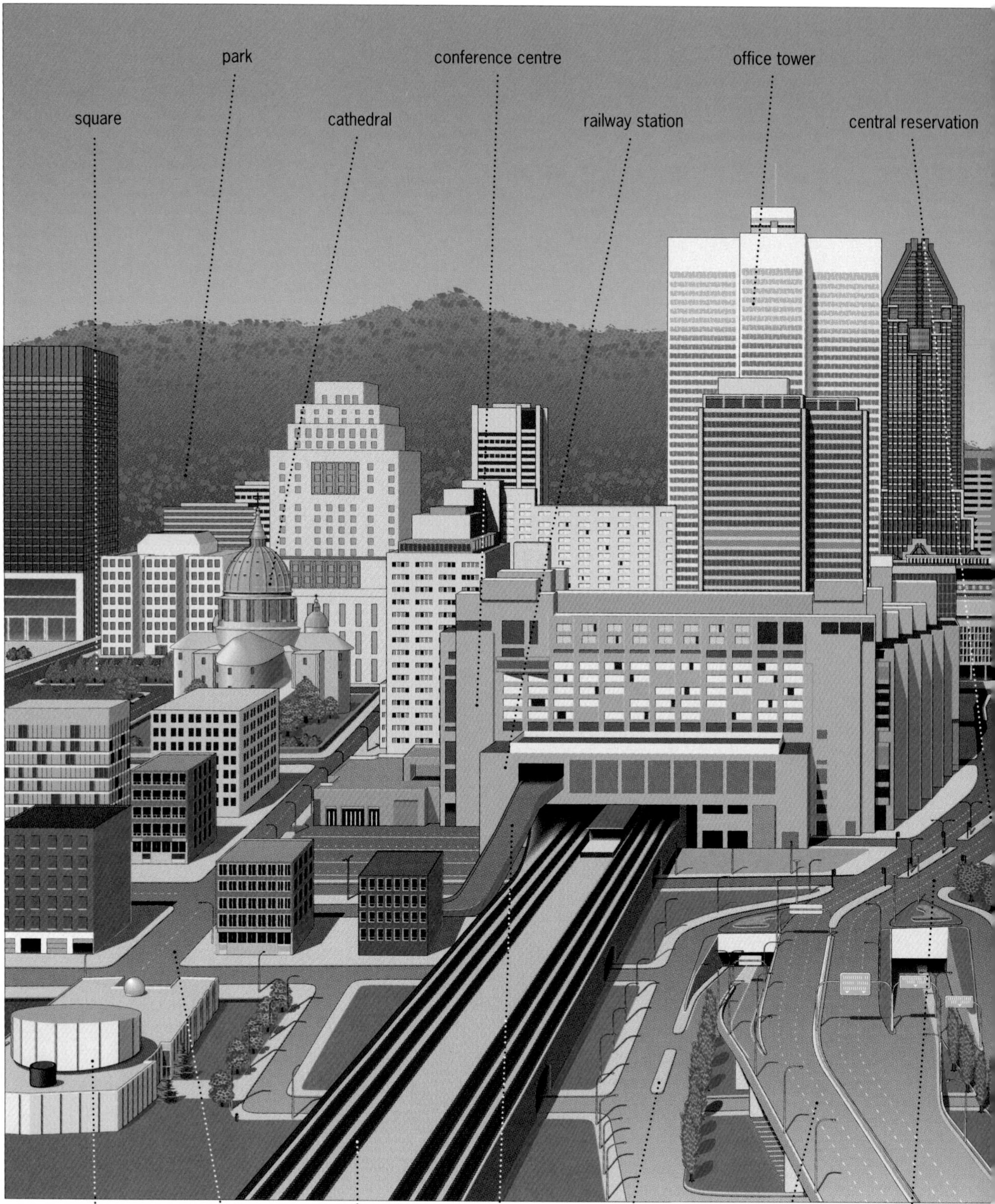
park
conference centre
office tower
square
cathedral
railway station
central reservation
planetarium
railway
traffic island
high street
street
delivery ramp
dual carriageway

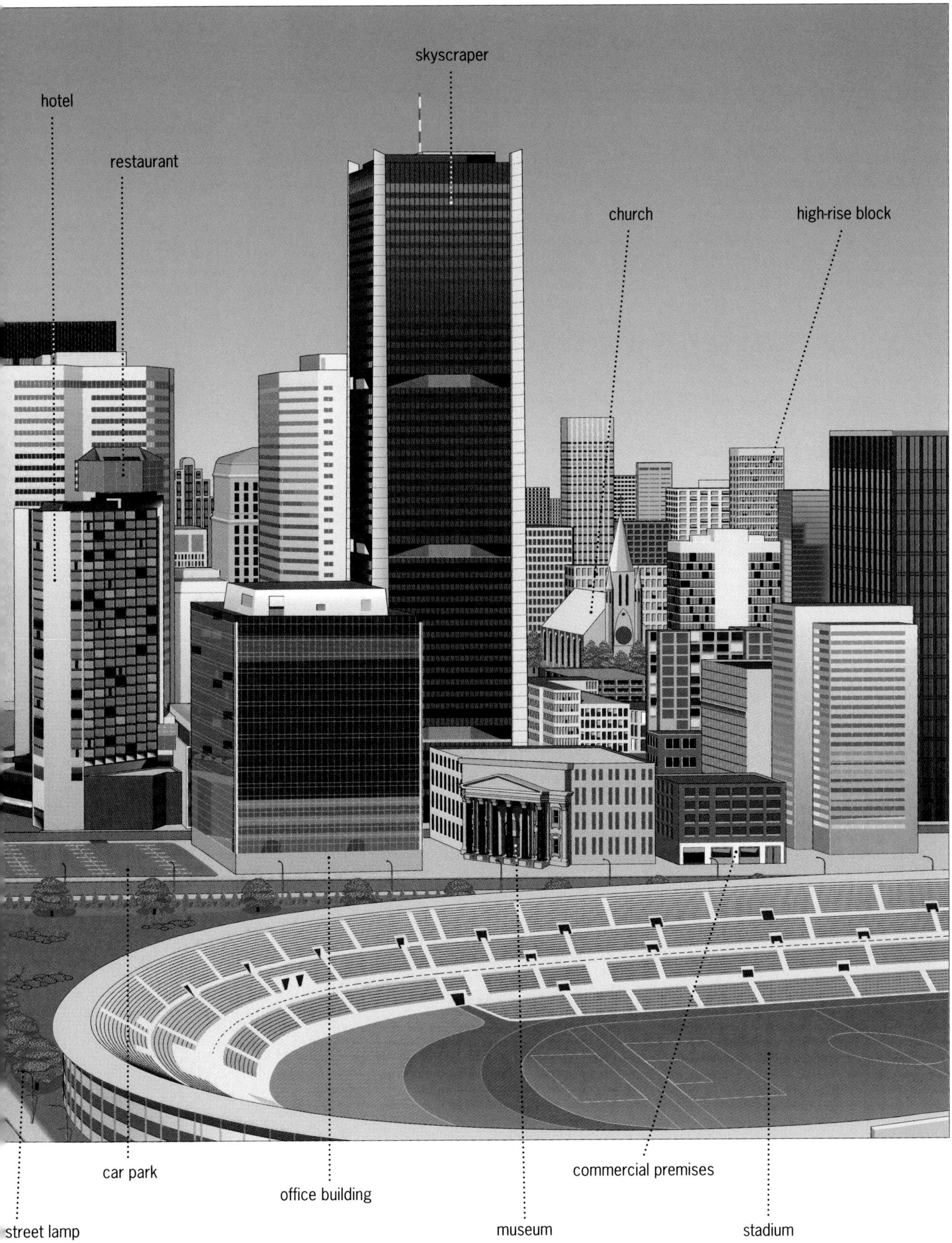
skyscraper
hotel
restaurant
church
high-rise block
car park
office building
street lamp
museum
commercial premises
stadium

HOUSE

exterior of a house

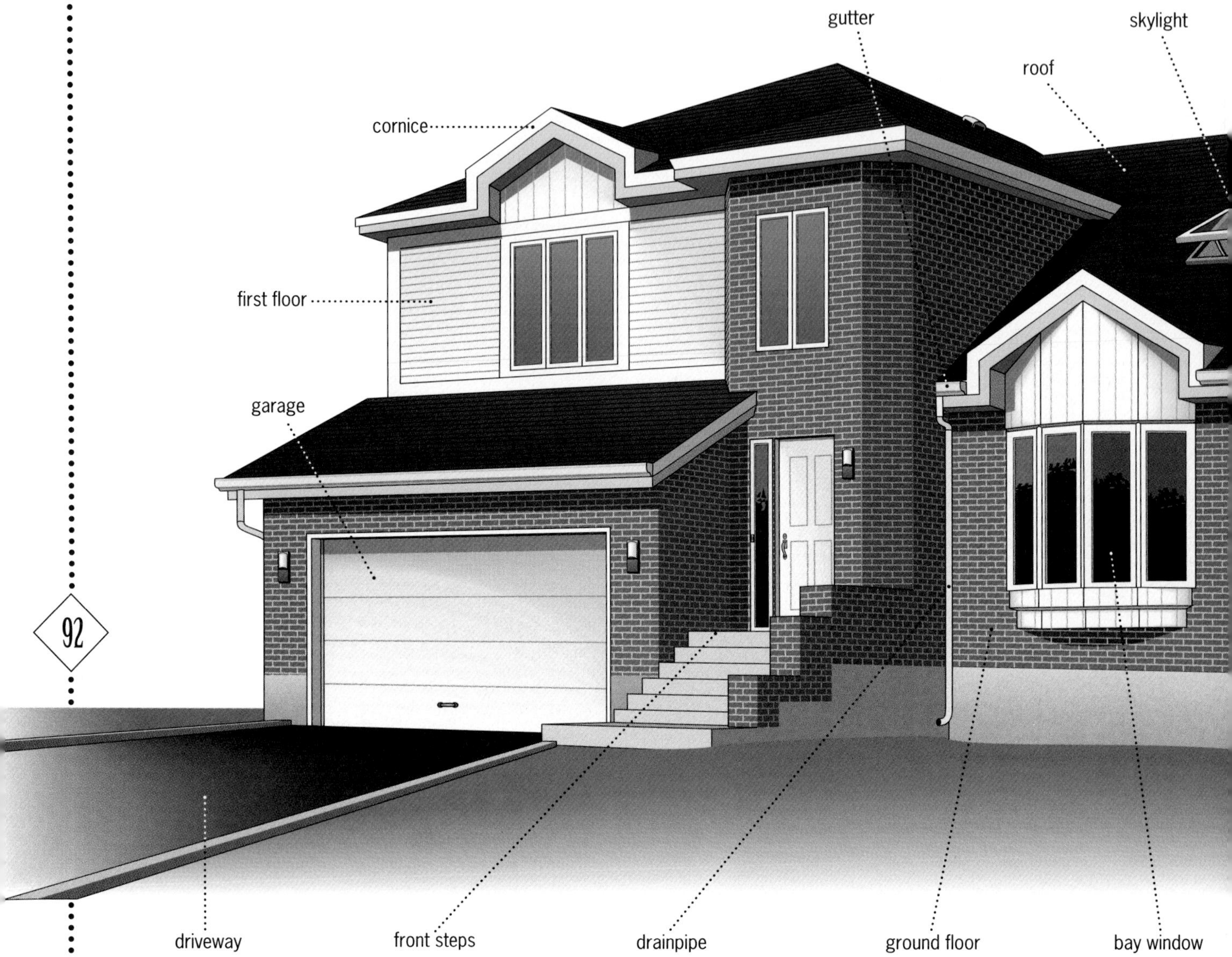
gutter
skylight
roof
cornice
first floor
garage
driveway
front steps
drainpipe
ground floor
bay window

TYPES OF DOORS

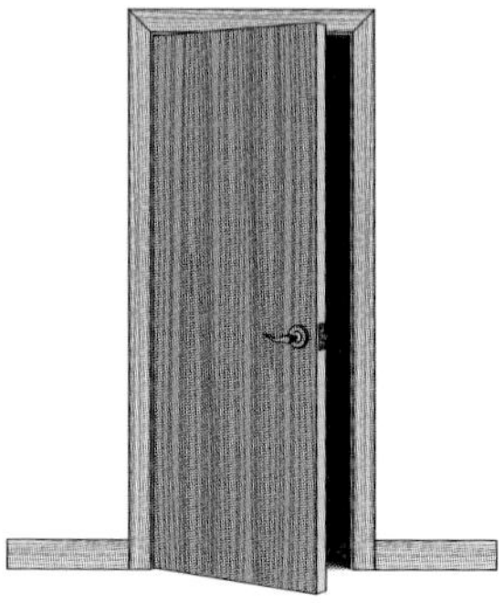
conventional door

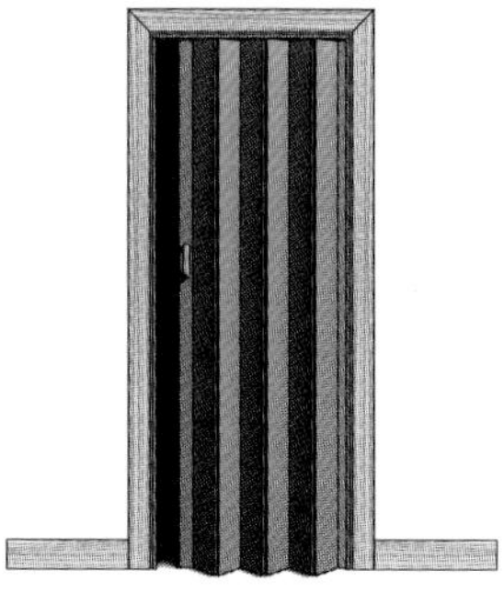
sliding folding door

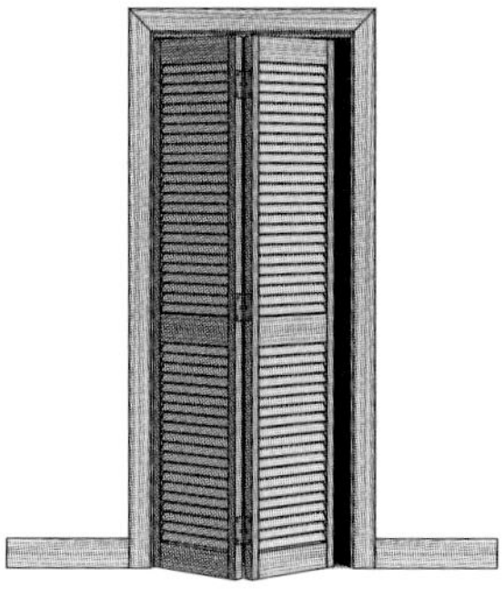
folding door

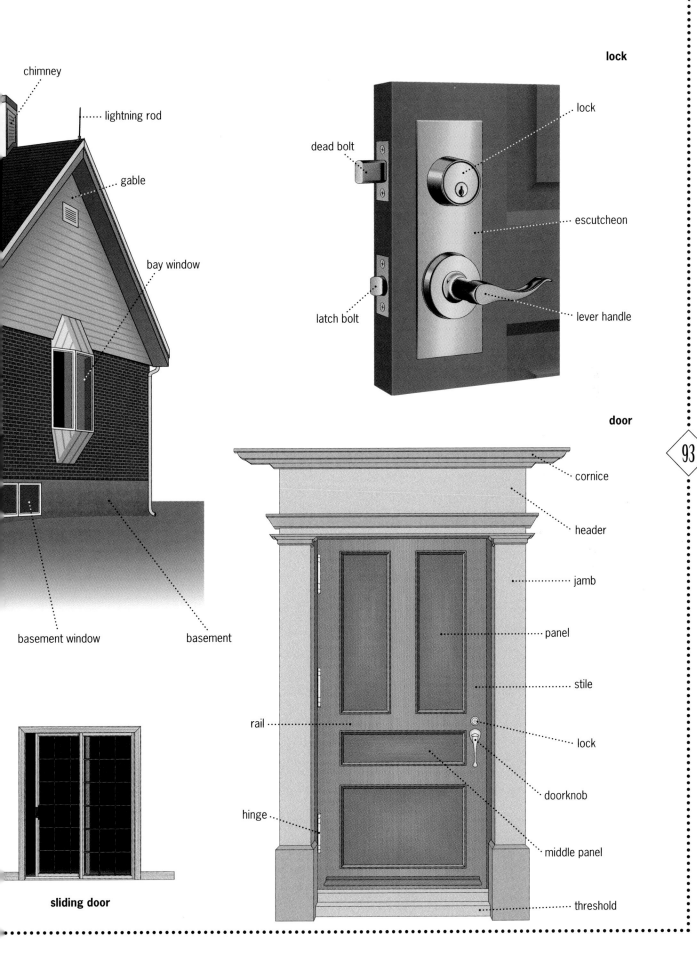

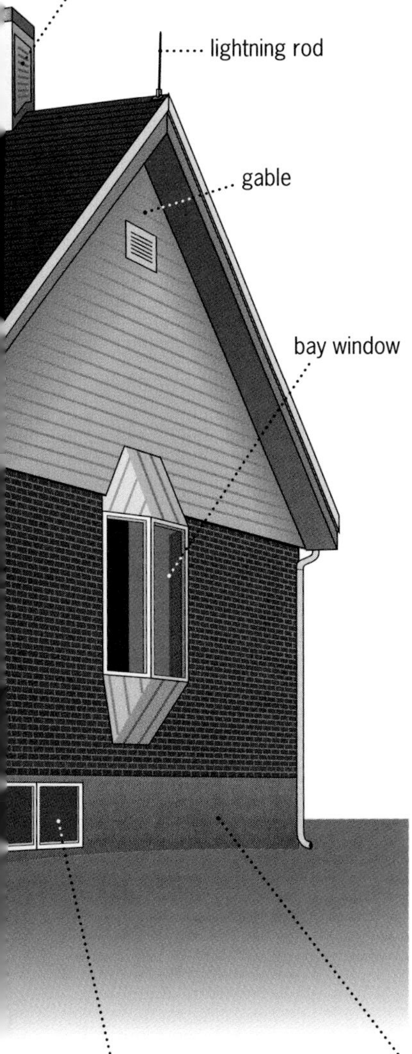
chimney
lightning rod
gable
bay window
basement window
basement

lock

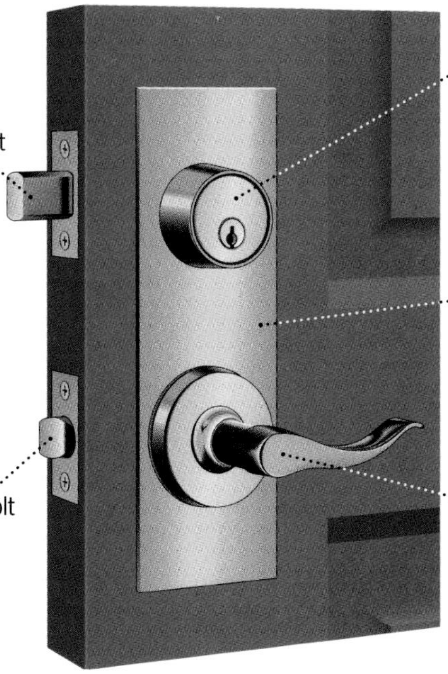
lock
dead bolt
escutcheon
latch bolt
lever handle

door

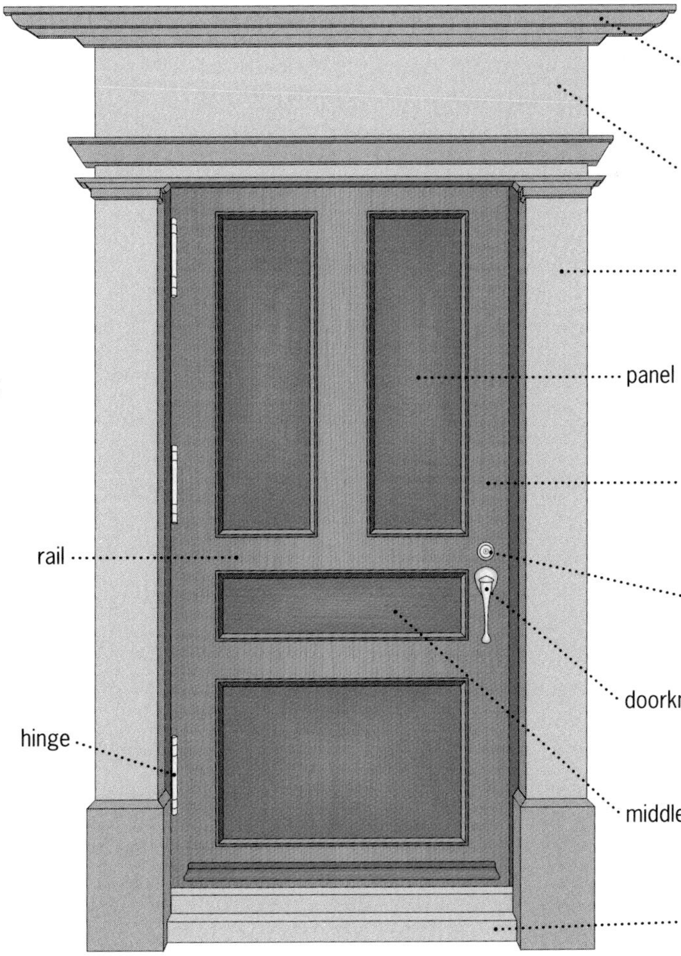
cornice
header
jamb
panel
stile
rail
lock
doorknob
hinge
middle panel
threshold

sliding door

WINDOW

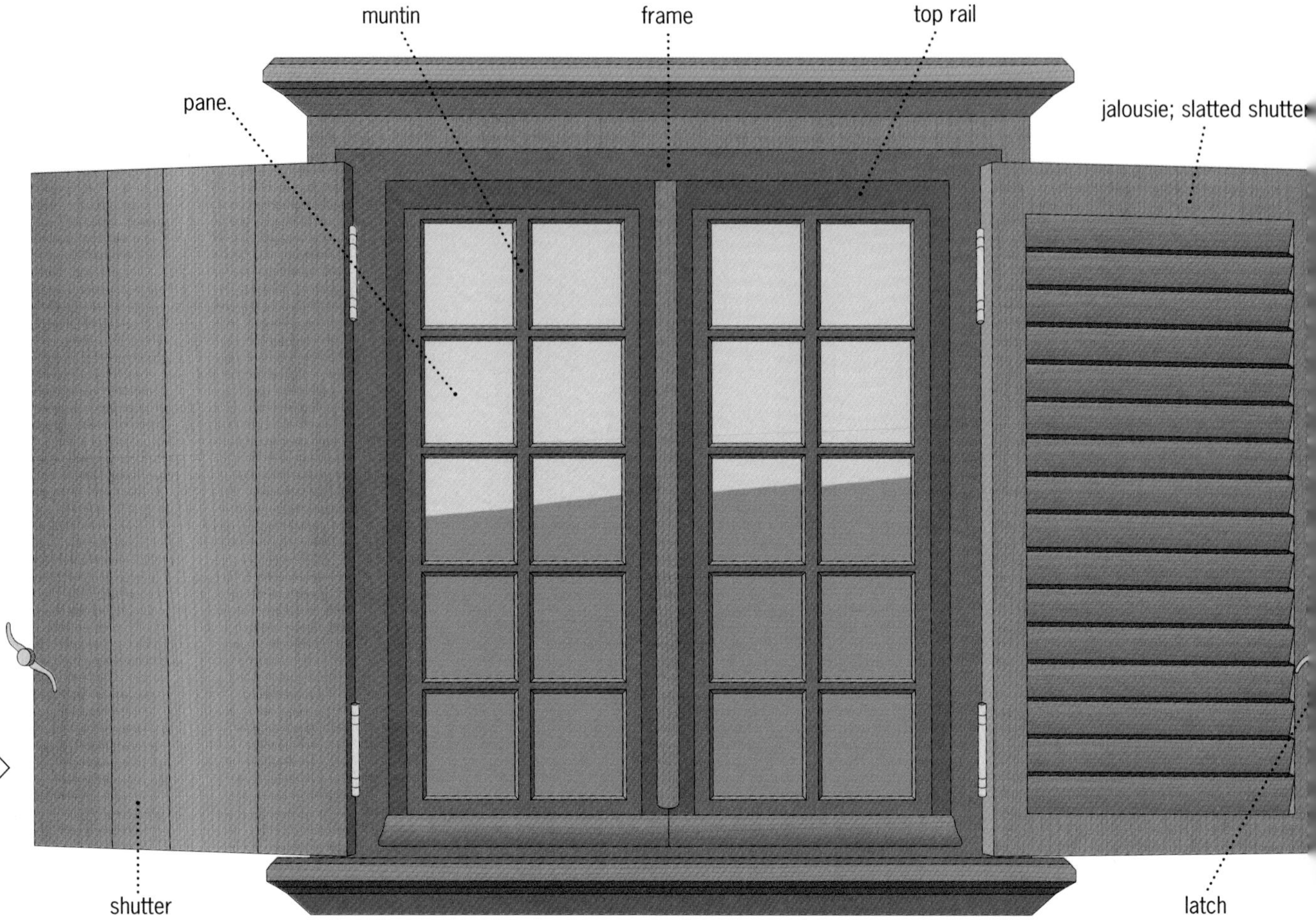
muntin
frame
top rail
pane
jalousie; slatted shutter
shutter
latch

TYPES OF WINDOWS

casement window (inward opening)

casement window (outward opening)

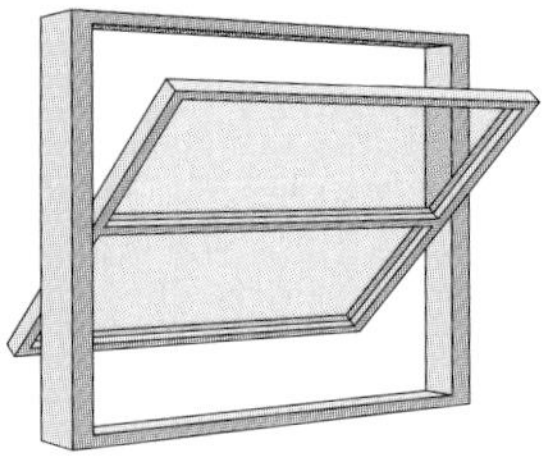
horizontal pivoting window

sliding window

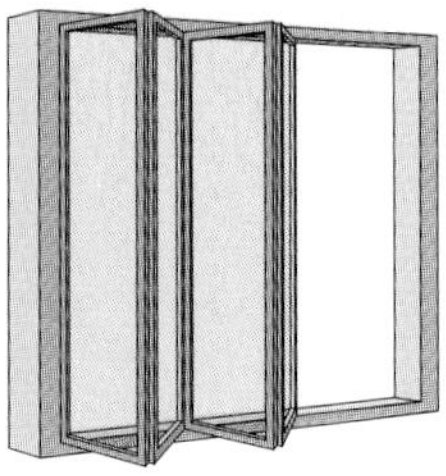
sliding folding window

vertical pivoting window

sash window

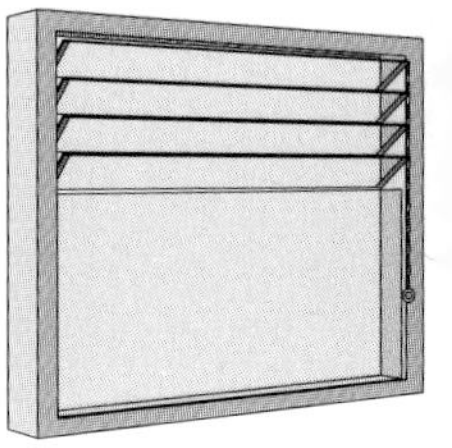
louvred window

BED

parts

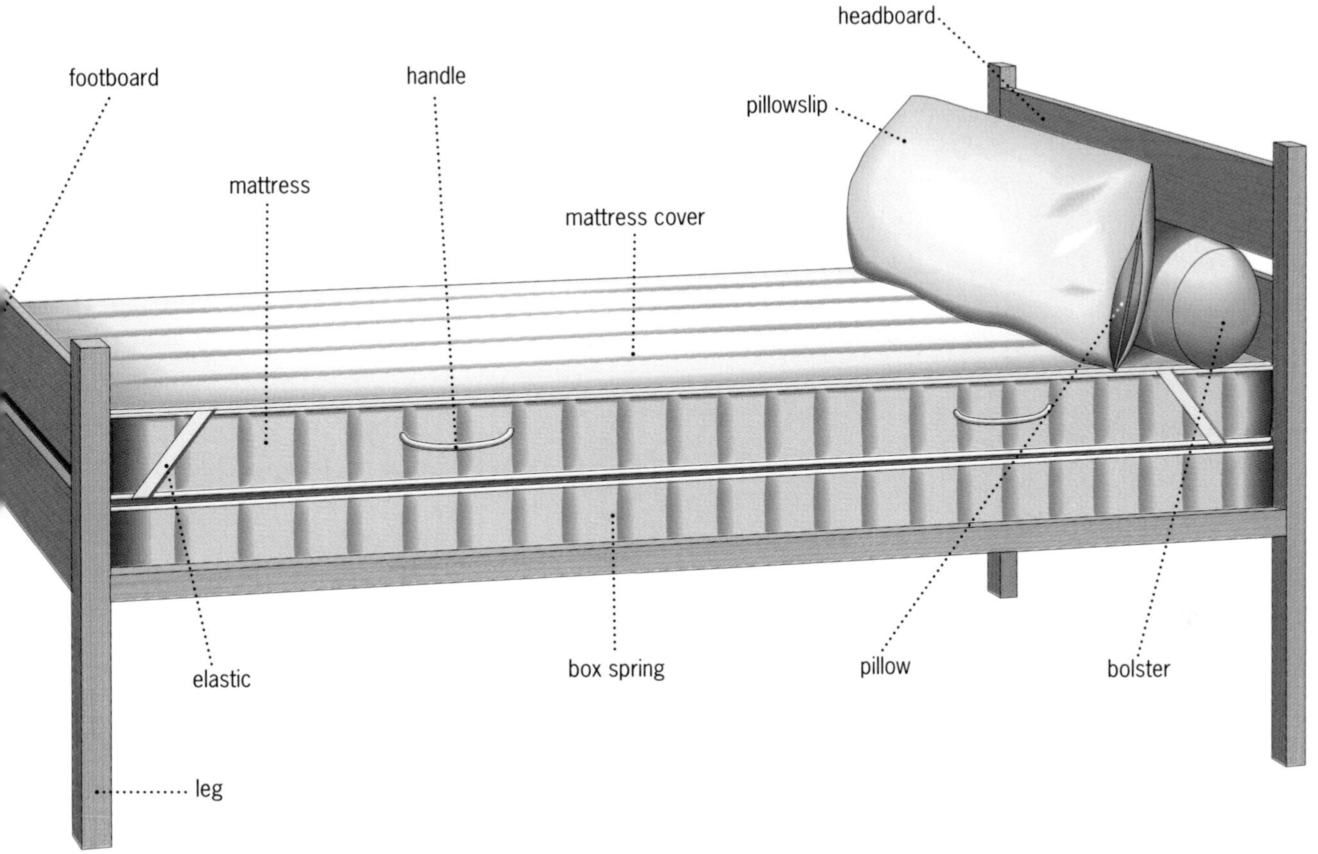
headboard
footboard
handle
pillowslip
mattress
mattress cover
elastic
box spring
pillow
bolster
leg

linen

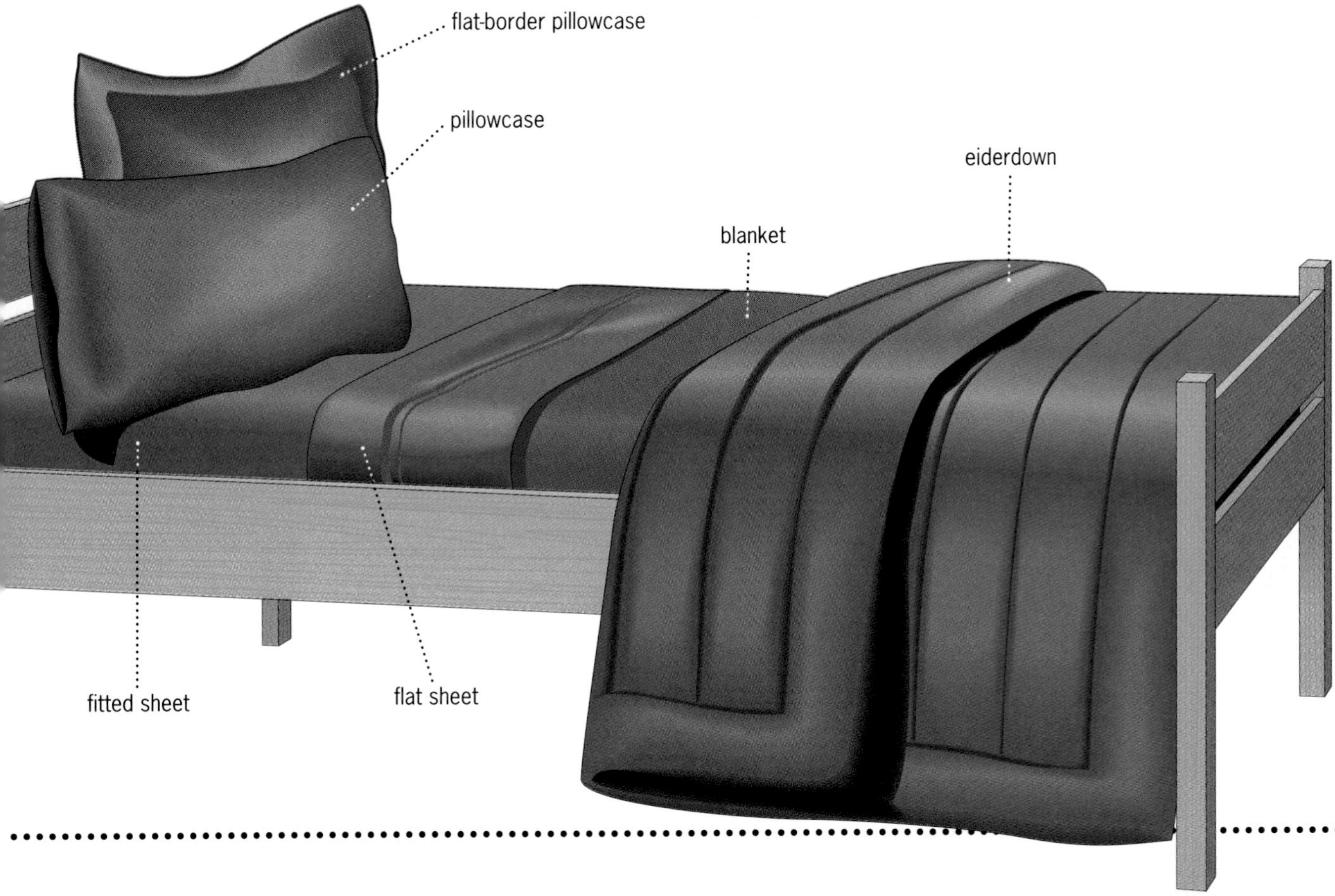
flat-border pillowcase
pillowcase
eiderdown
blanket
fitted sheet
flat sheet

SEATS

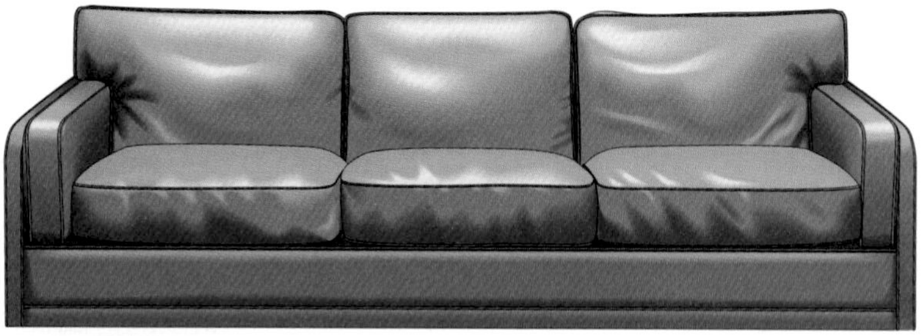

three–seater sofa or settee

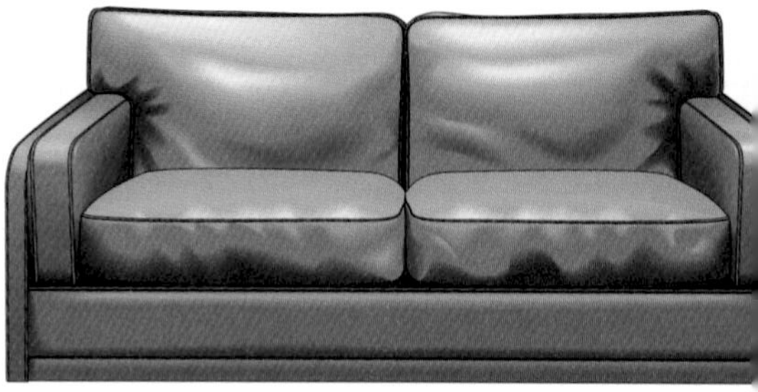

two-seater sofa or settee

armchair

footstool; pouffe

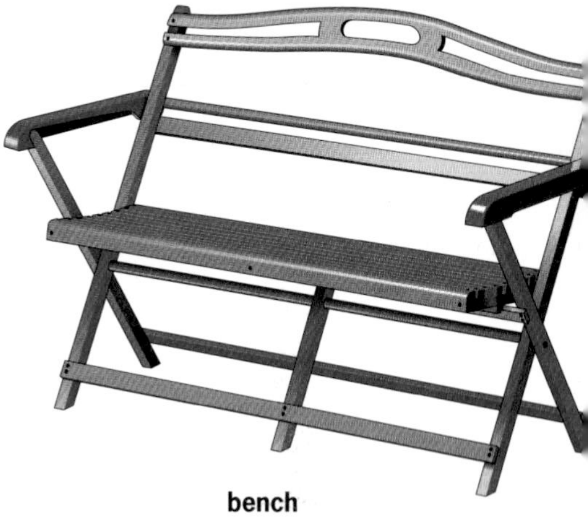

bench

bar stool

stool

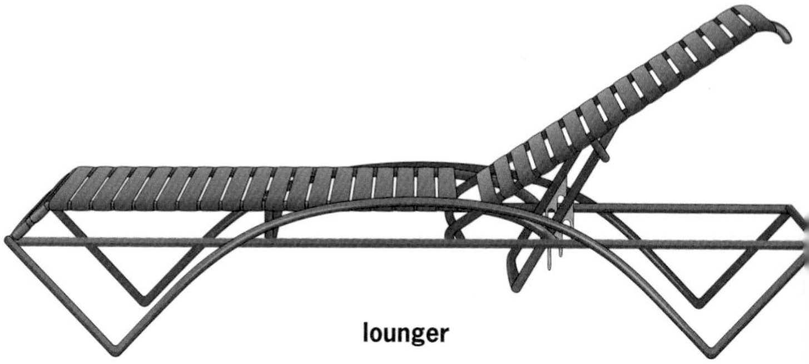

lounger

folding chair

rocking chair

stacking chairs

TABLE AND CHAIRS

side chair

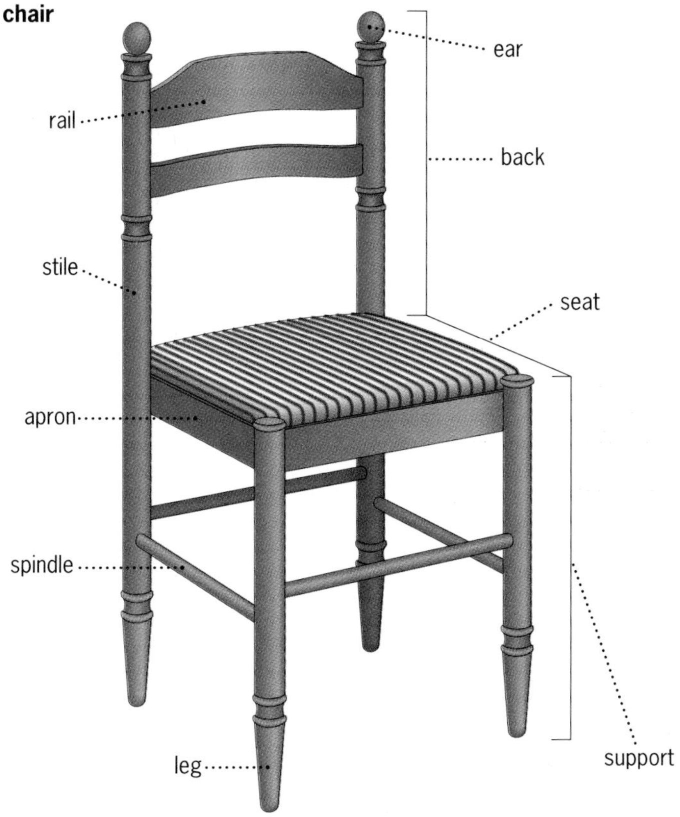
ear
rail
back
stile
seat
apron
spindle
support
leg

carver

arm

table

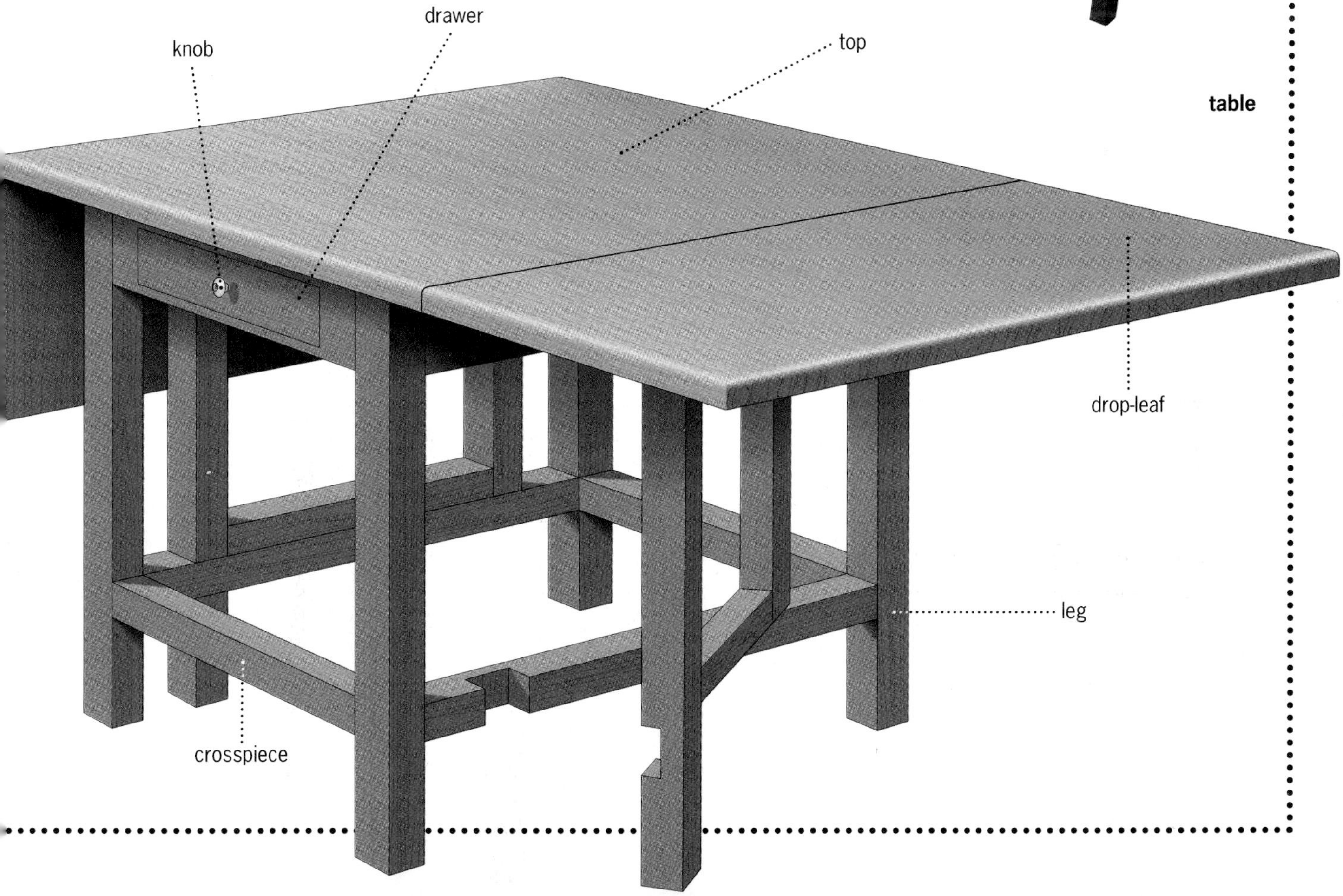
drawer
knob
top
drop-leaf
leg
crosspiece

LIGHTS

spotlight

track lighting
transformer

standard lamp

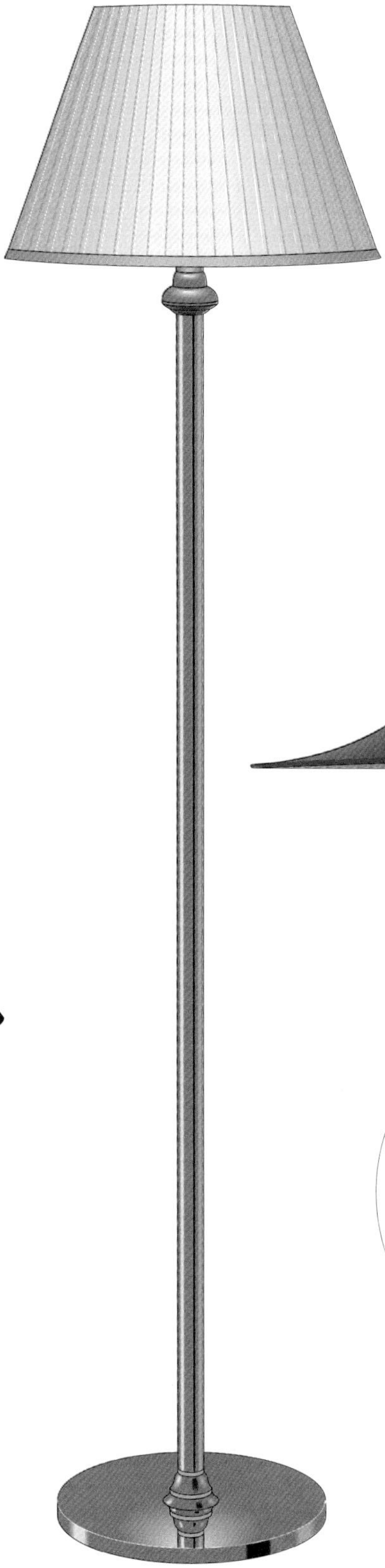

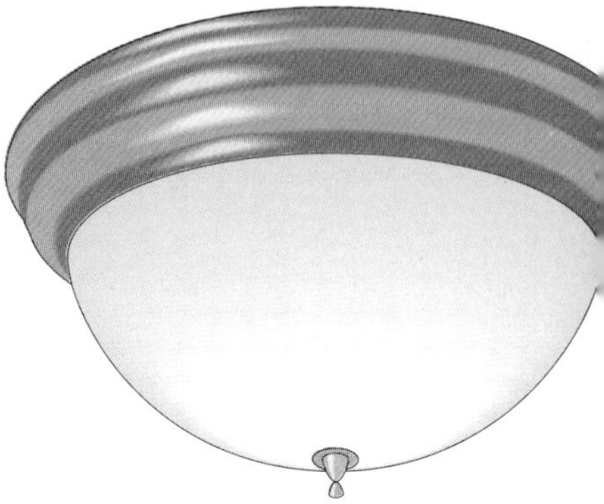

ceiling fitting

hanging pendant

table lamp

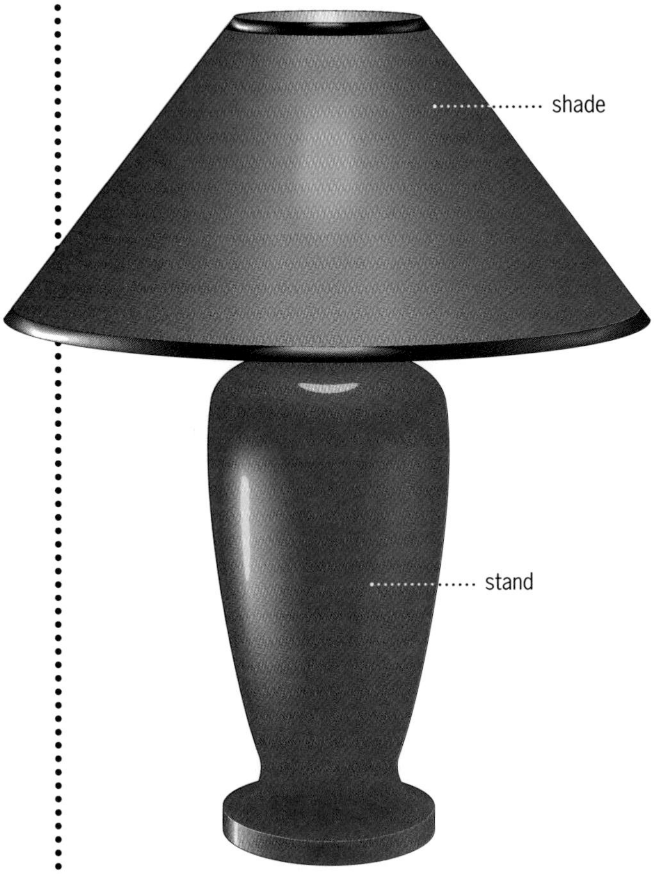
shade
stand

wall fitting

LIGHTING

incandescent lamp

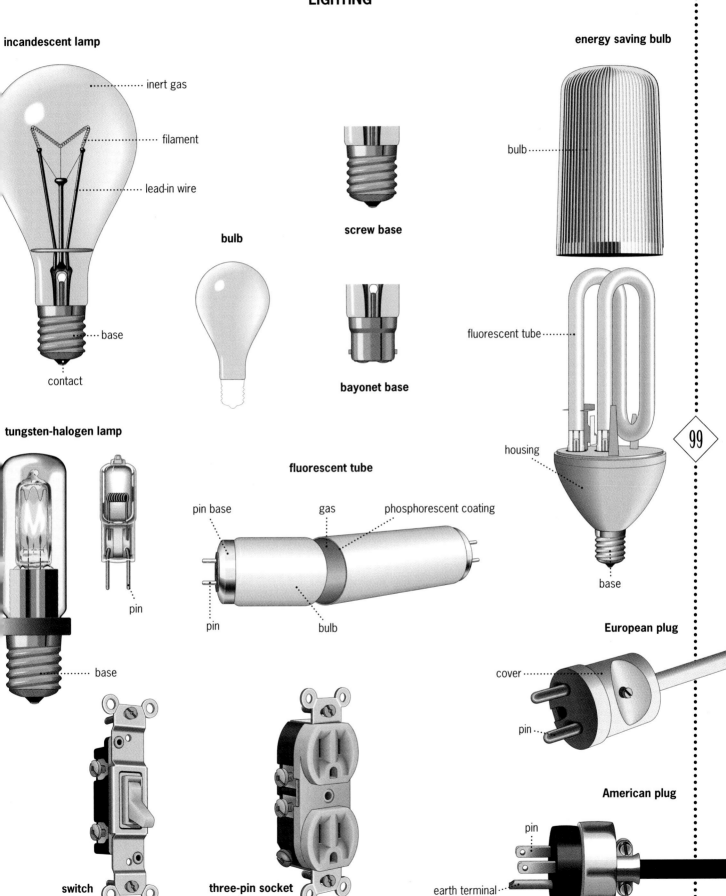

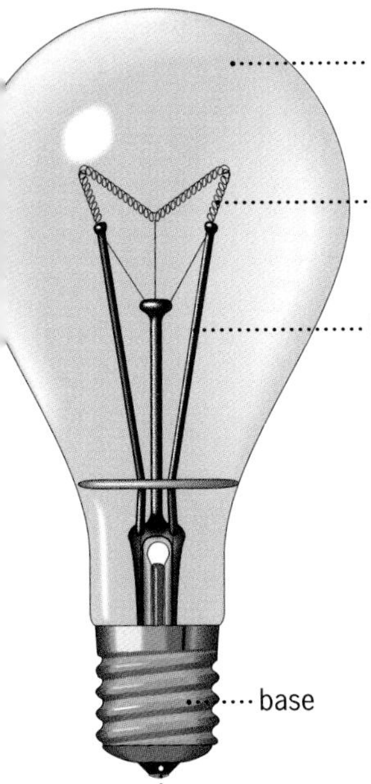
inert gas
filament
lead-in wire
base
contact

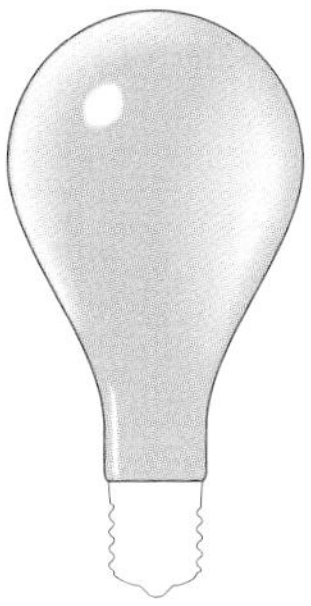

bulb

screw base

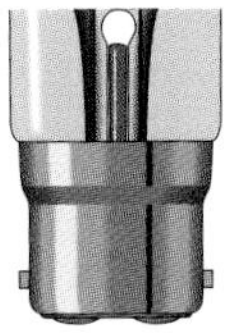

bayonet base

energy saving bulb

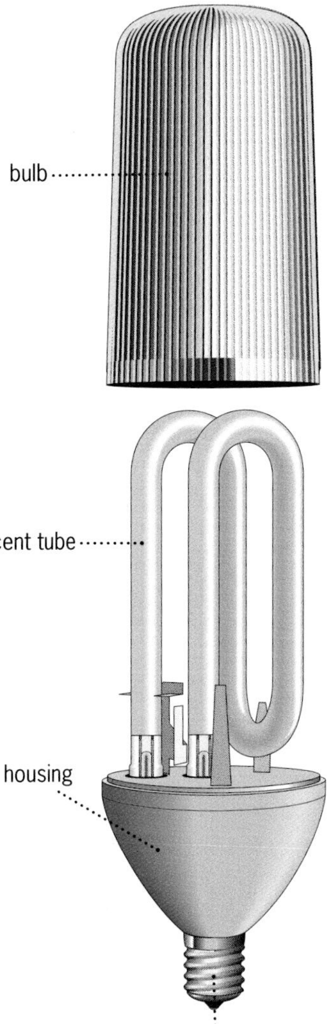
bulb
fluorescent tube
housing
base

tungsten-halogen lamp

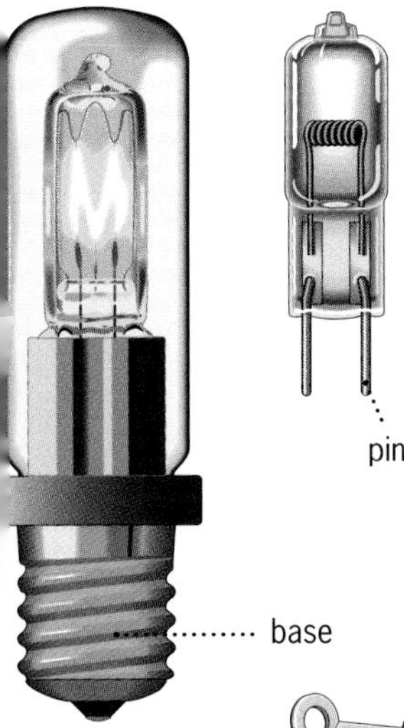
pin
base

fluorescent tube

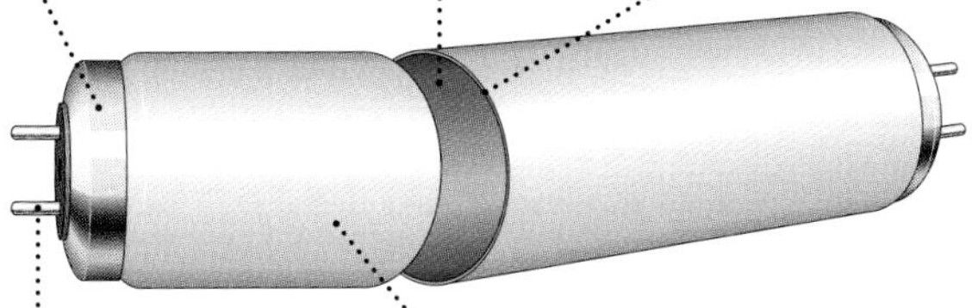
pin base
gas
phosphorescent coating
pin
bulb

European plug

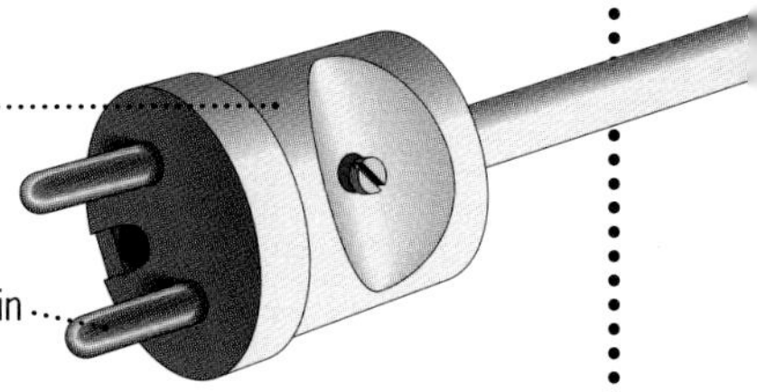
cover
pin

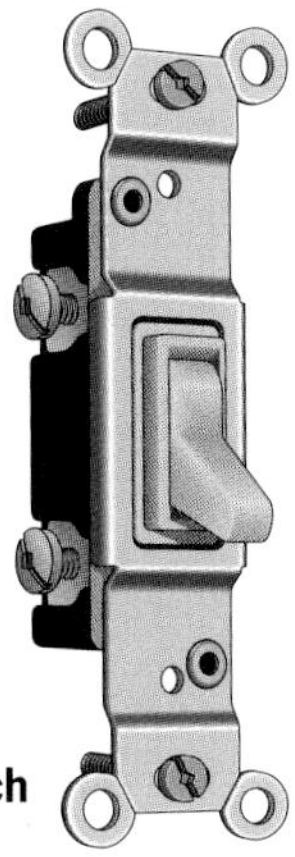

switch

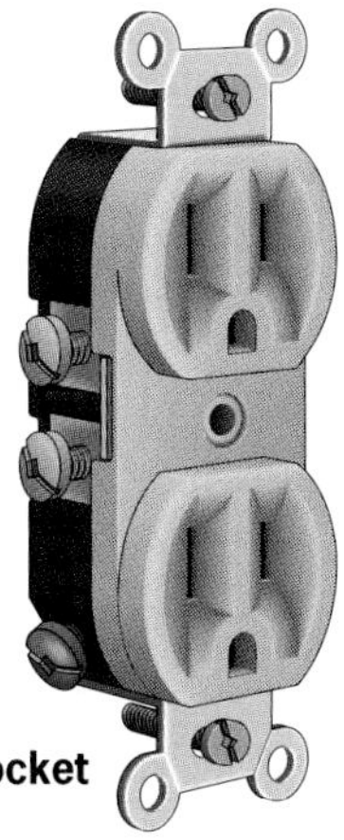

three-pin socket

American plug

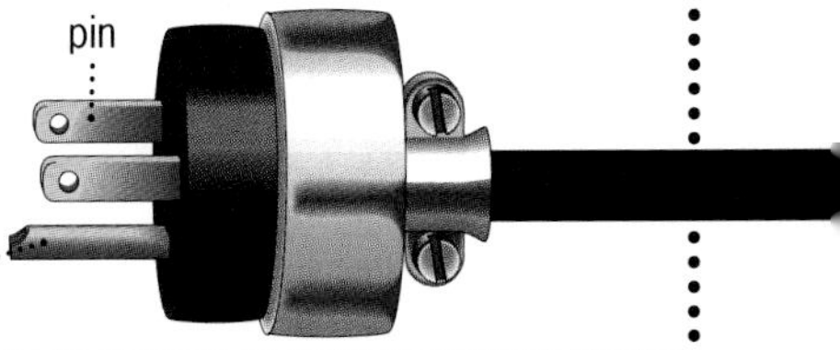
pin
earth terminal

GLASSWARE

champagne glass
white wine glass
red wine glass
champagne flute
tumbler; glass
beer mug
carafe
decanter

DINNERWARE

coffee cup
cup
mug
cream jug
sugar bowl
pepperpot
saltcellar
butter dish
cereal bowl
soup bowl
salad dish
dinner plate
salad plate
bread and butter plate; side plate
salad bowl
teapot
coffee plunger
soup tureen
water jug

CUTLERY

knife

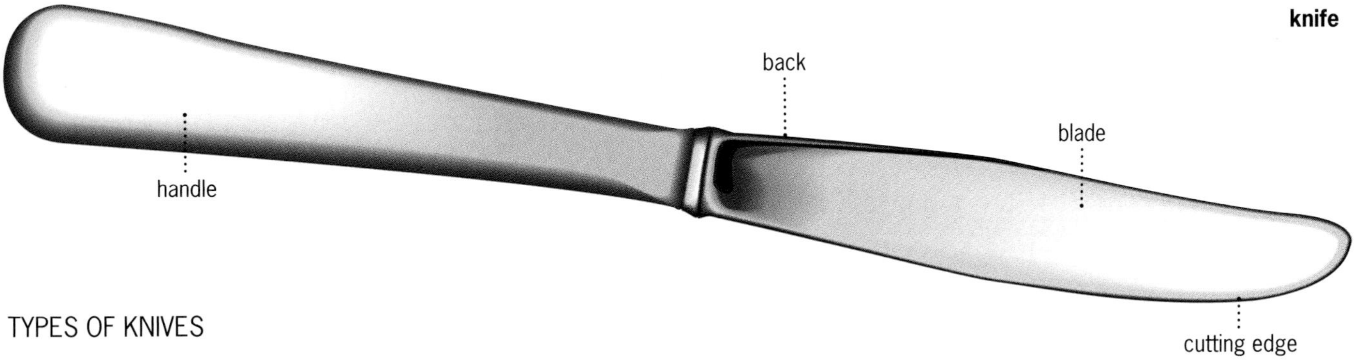
back
blade
handle
cutting edge

TYPES OF KNIVES

butter knife

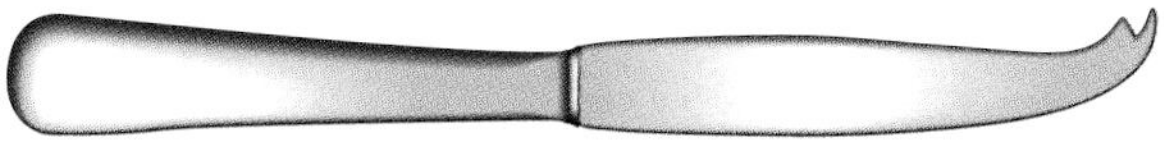

cheese knife

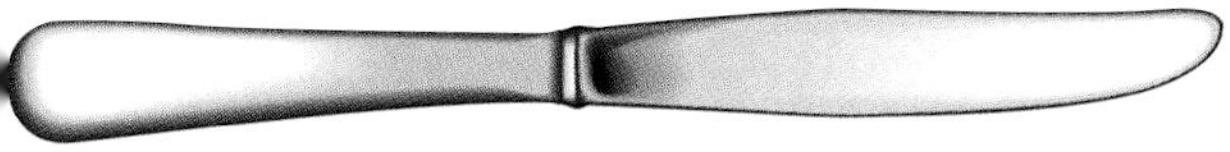

dinner knife

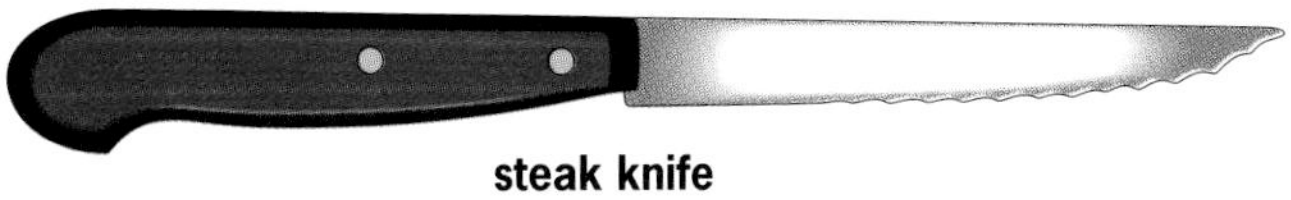

steak knife

fork

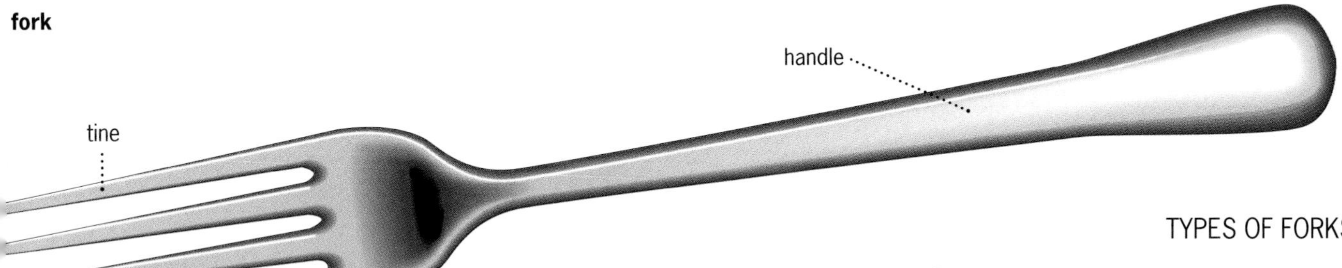
handle
tine
point

TYPES OF FORKS

dinner fork

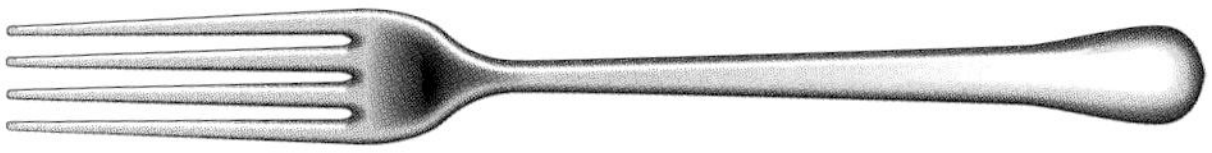

fondue fork

spoon

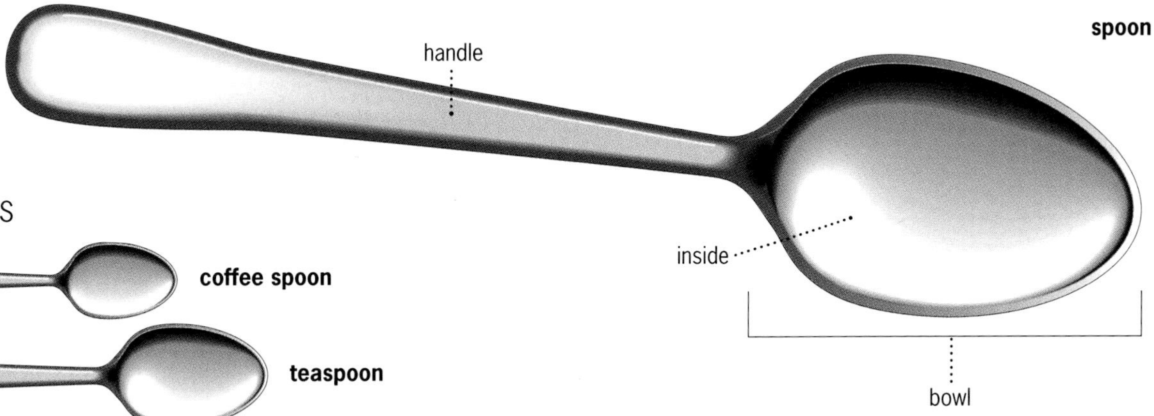
handle
inside
bowl

TYPES OF SPOONS

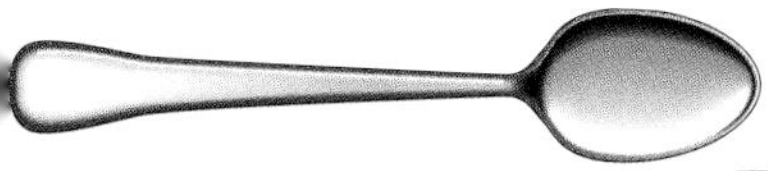

coffee spoon

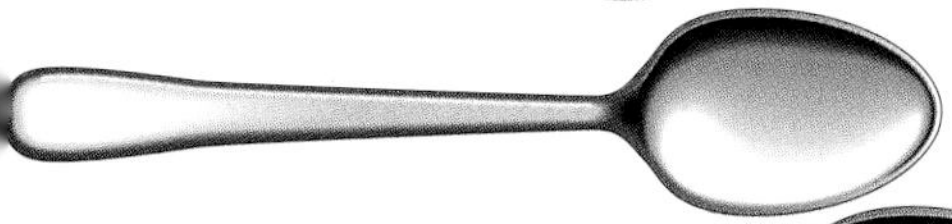

teaspoon

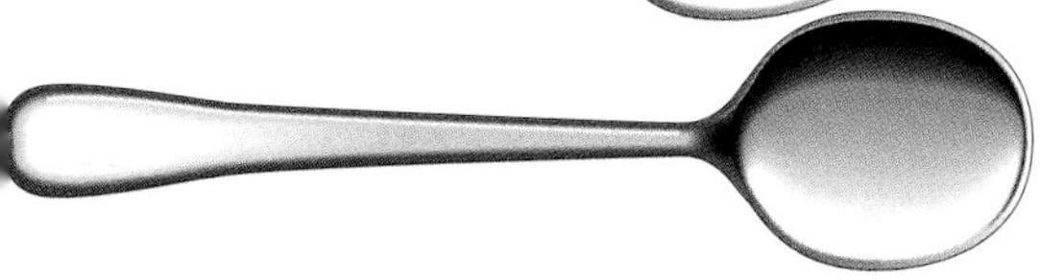

soup spoon

KITCHEN UTENSILS

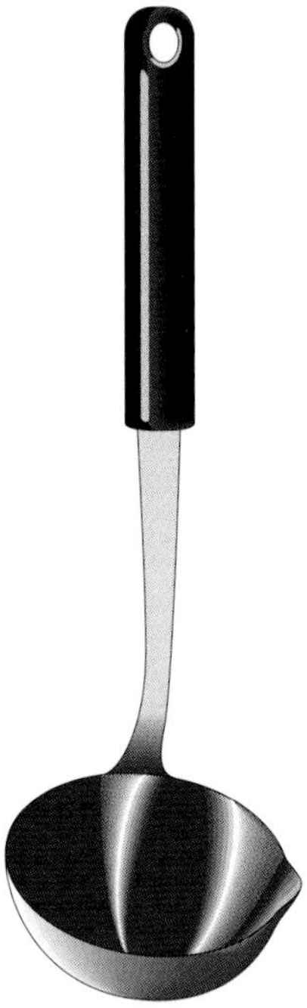
ladle

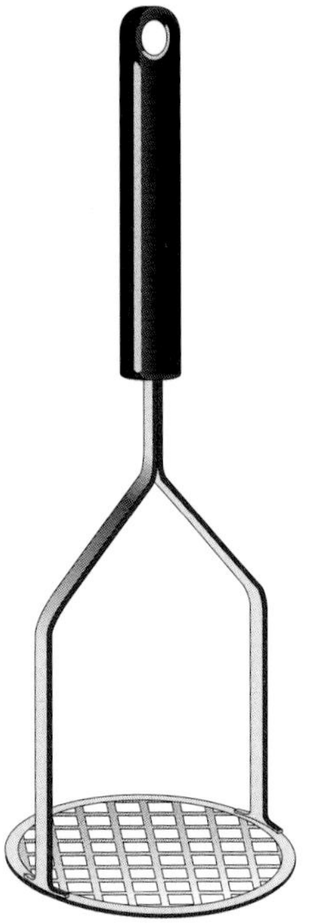
potato masher

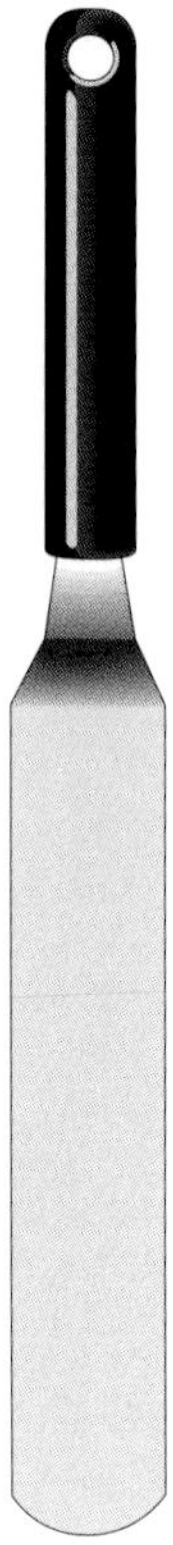
spatula

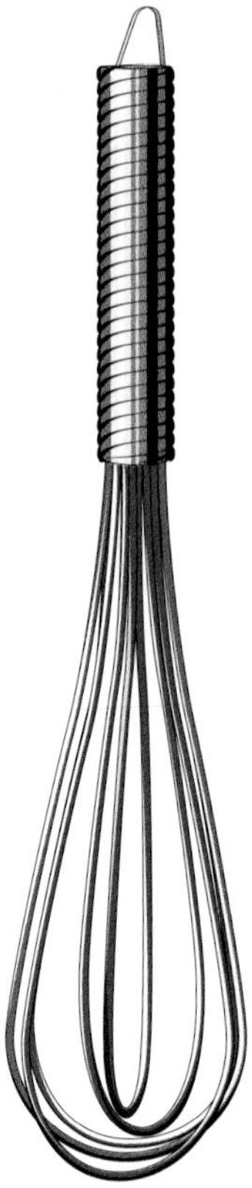
whisk

egg beater

measuring spoons

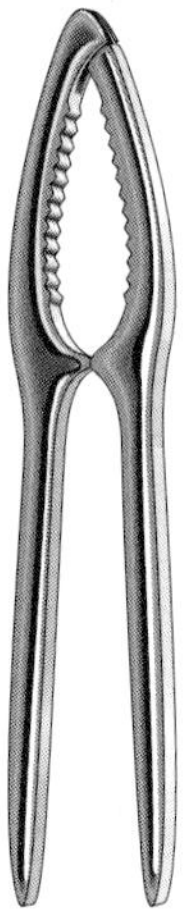
nutcracker

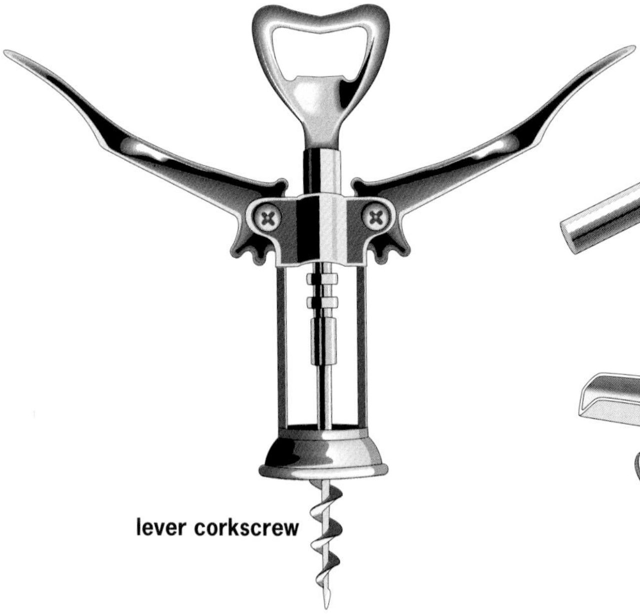
lever corkscrew

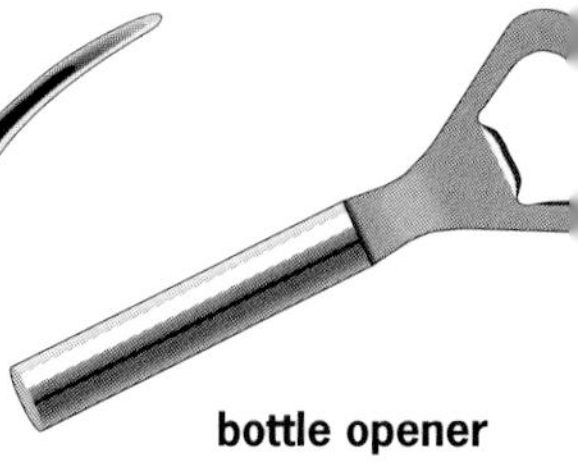
bottle opener

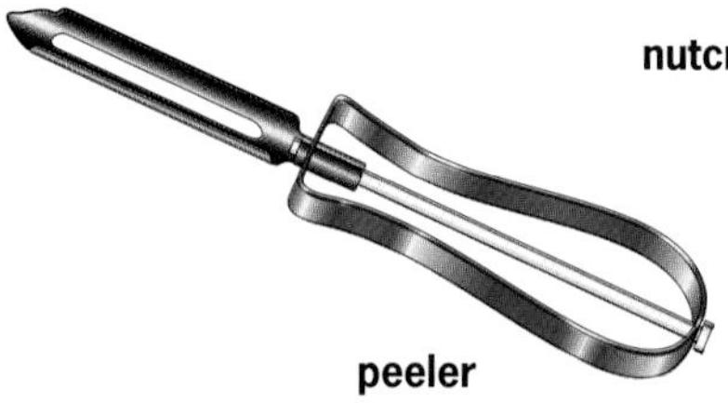
peeler

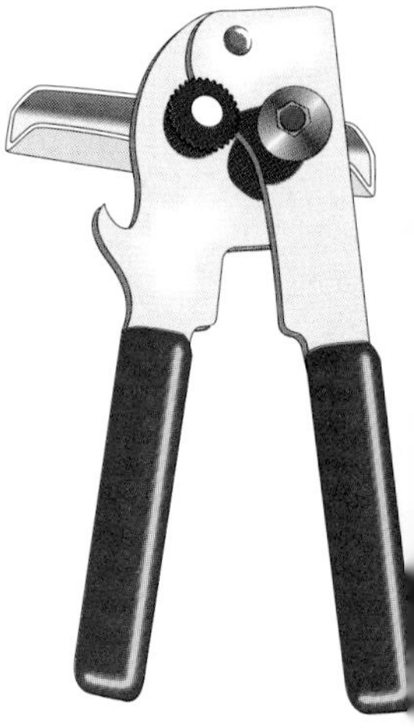
tin opener

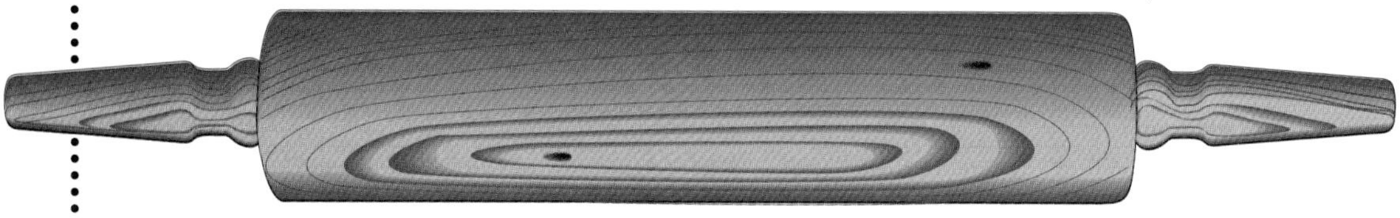
rolling pin

spaghetti tongs

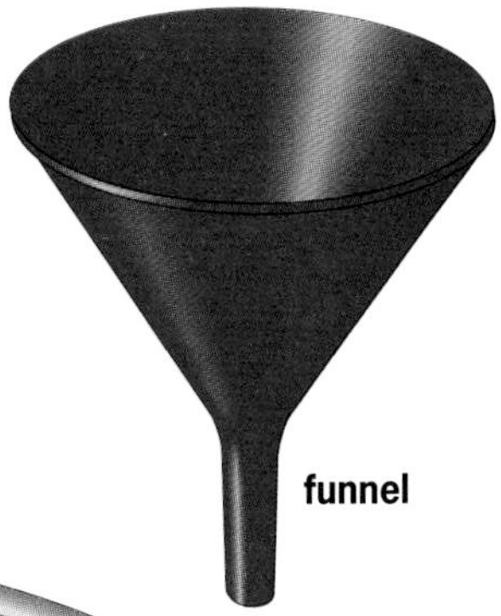

funnel

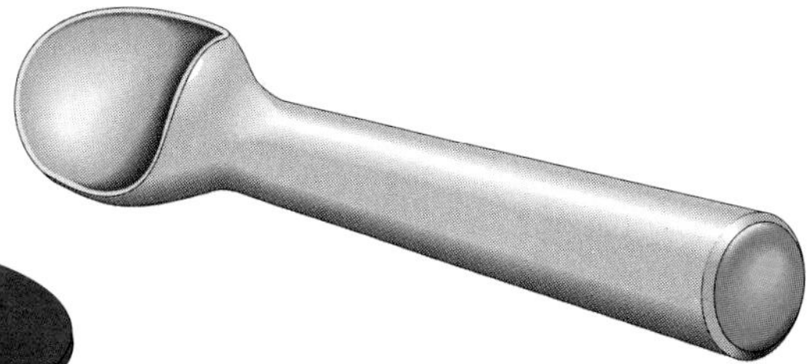

ice-cream scoop

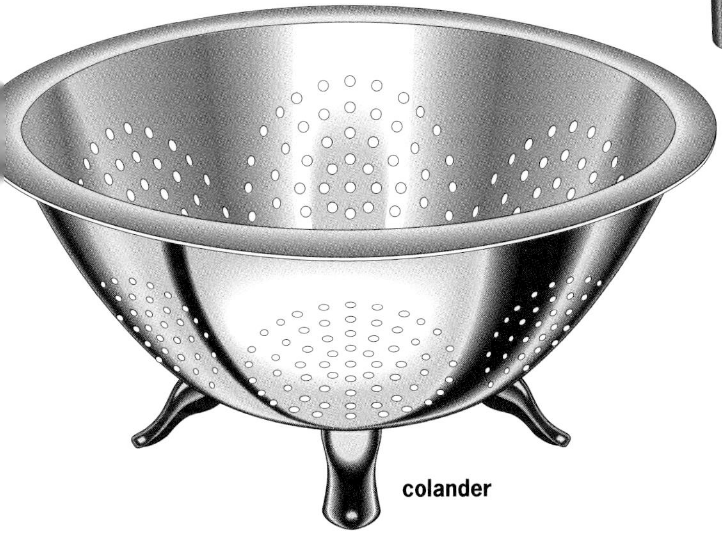

colander

lemon squeezer

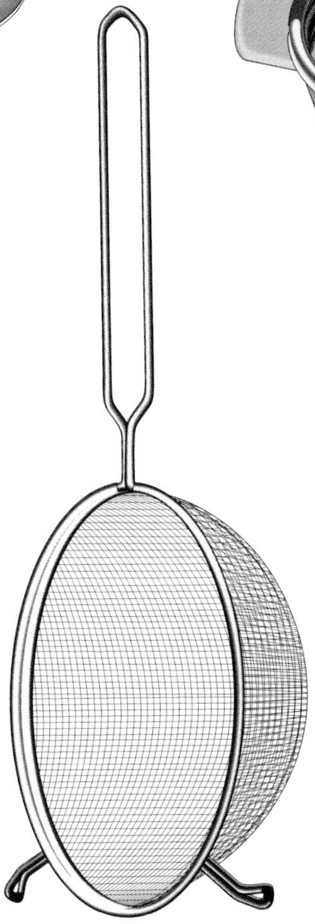

strainer

salad spinner

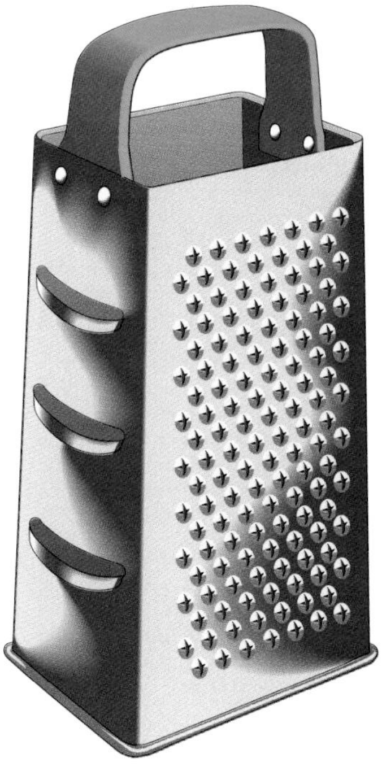

grater

COOKING UTENSILS

stockpot; casserole

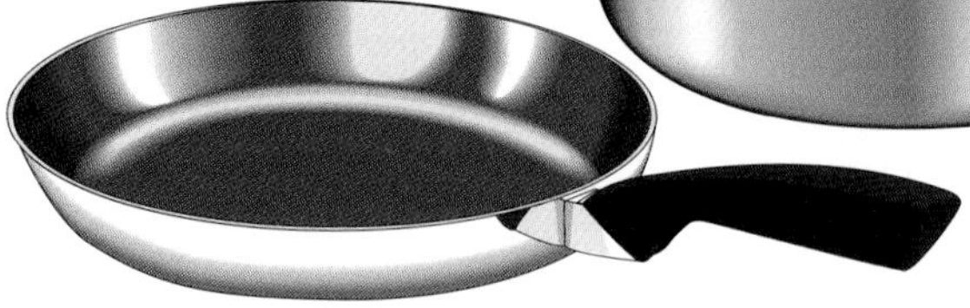
frying pan

sauté pan

wok

fondue set

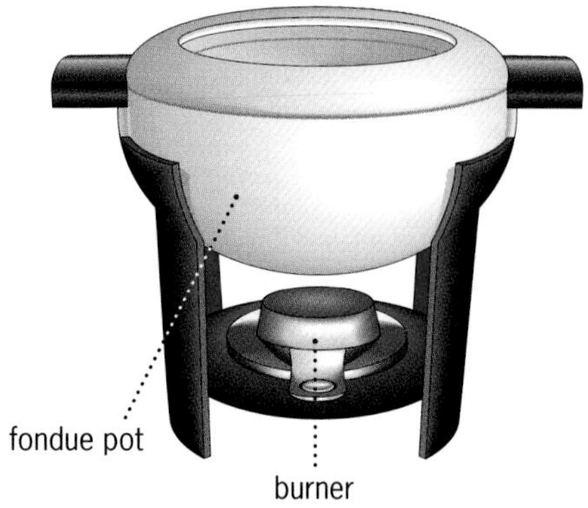
fondue pot
burner

double boiler

saucepan

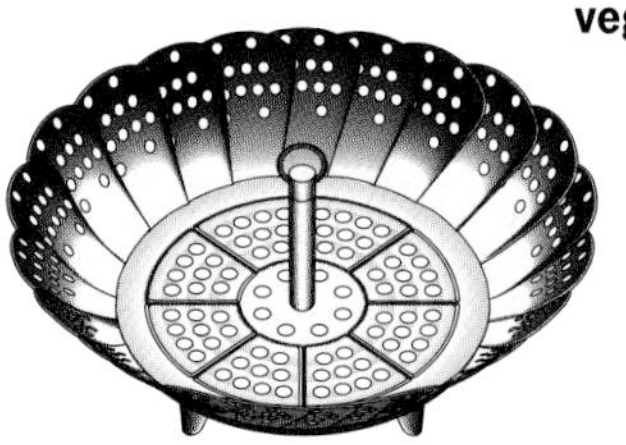
vegetable steamer

pressure cooker

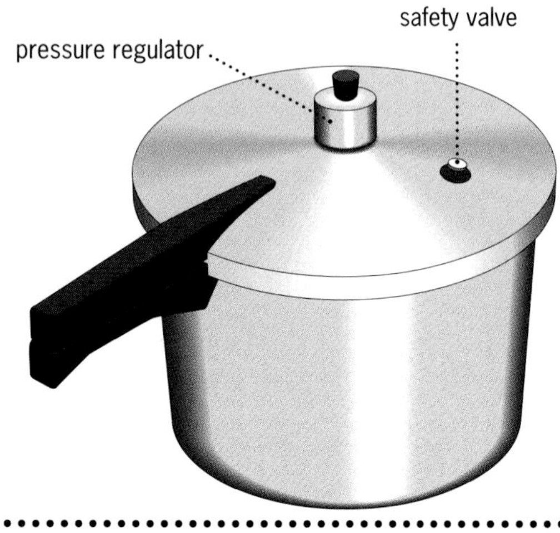
pressure regulator
safety valve

roasting pans

DOMESTIC APPLIANCES

automatic filter coffee maker

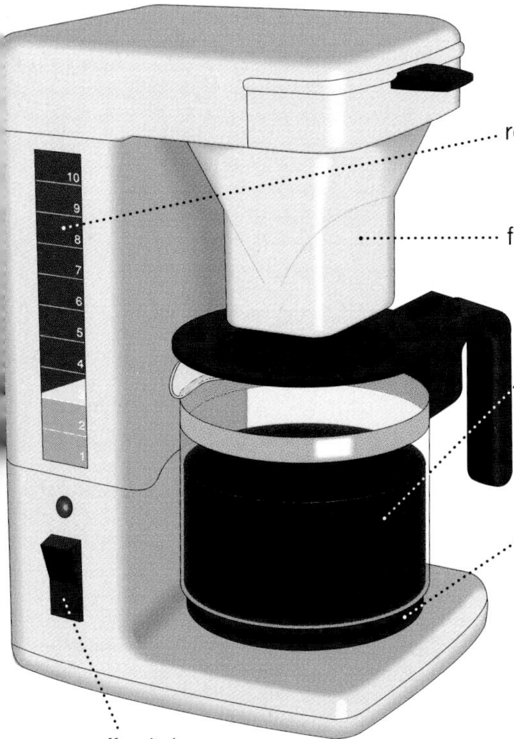
reservoir
filter holder
coffee jug
warming plate
on-off switch

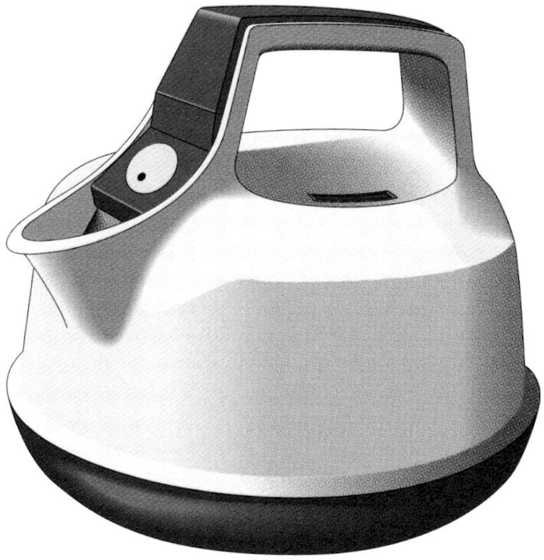

kettle

hand mixer

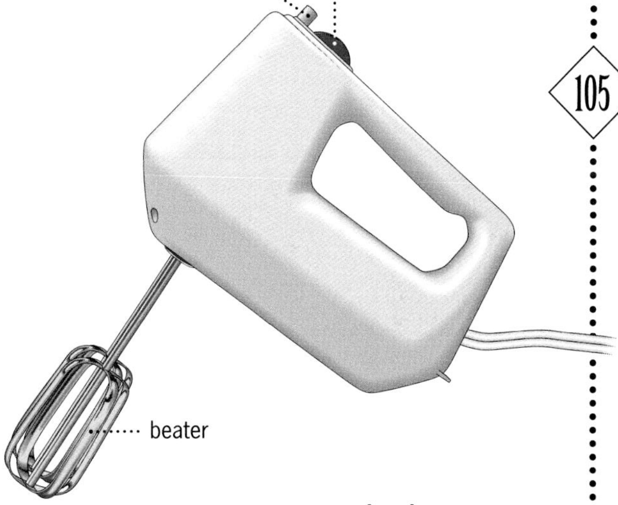
beater ejector
speed control
beater

hand blender

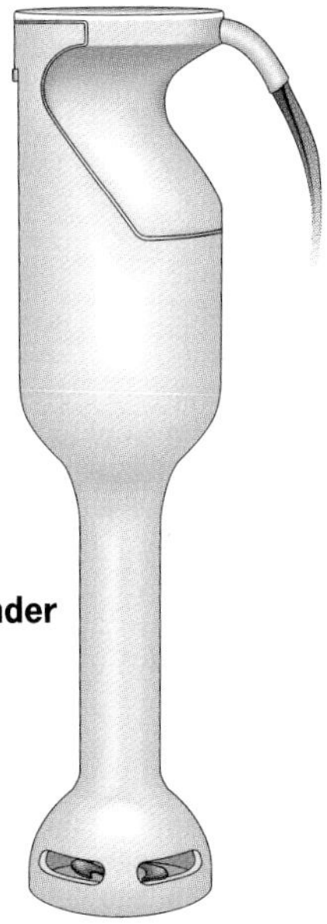

blender

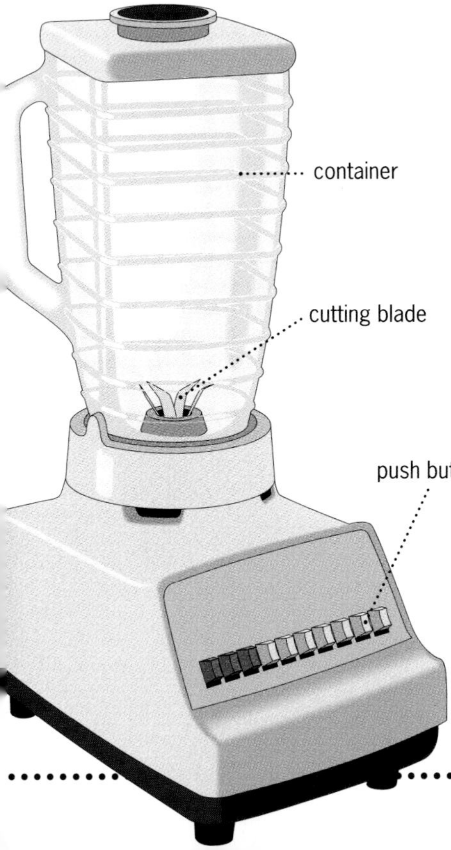
container
cutting blade
push button

toaster

slot
lever
thermostat

FRIDGE FREEZER

ice cube tray
egg tray
dairy compartment
freezer compartment
thermostat control
butter compartment
crisper
refrigerator compartment
guard rail
meat tray
glass cover
shelf
storage door

COOKING APPLIANCES

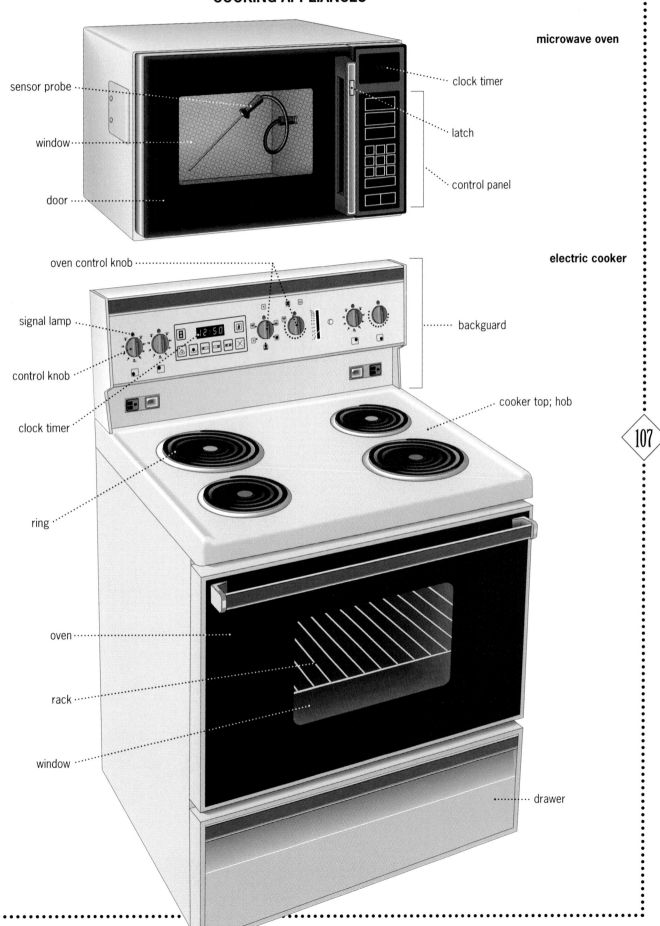

microwave oven

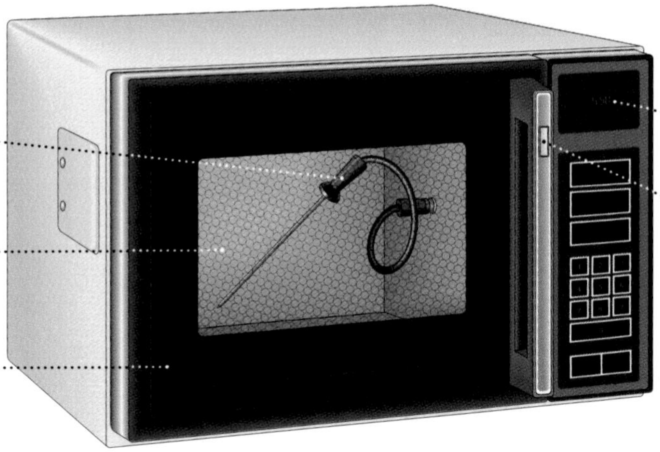
sensor probe
window
door
clock timer
latch
control panel

electric cooker

oven control knob
signal lamp
control knob
clock timer
ring
oven
rack
window
backguard
cooker top; hob
drawer

CARPENTRY TOOLS

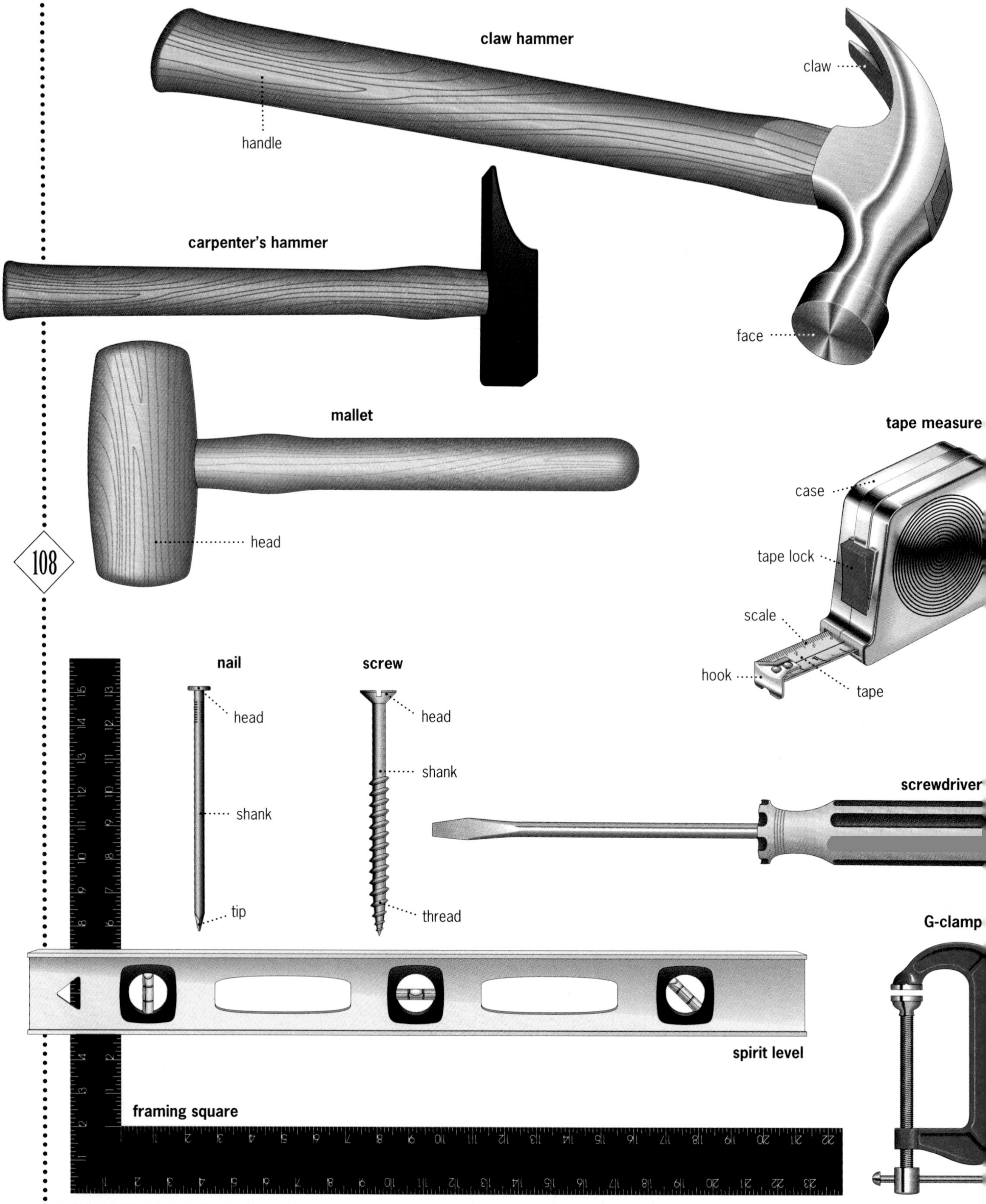
claw hammer
claw
handle
face
carpenter's hammer
mallet
head
tape measure
case
tape lock
scale
hook
tape
nail
head
shank
tip
screw
head
shank
thread
screwdriver
G-clamp
spirit level
framing square

handsaw

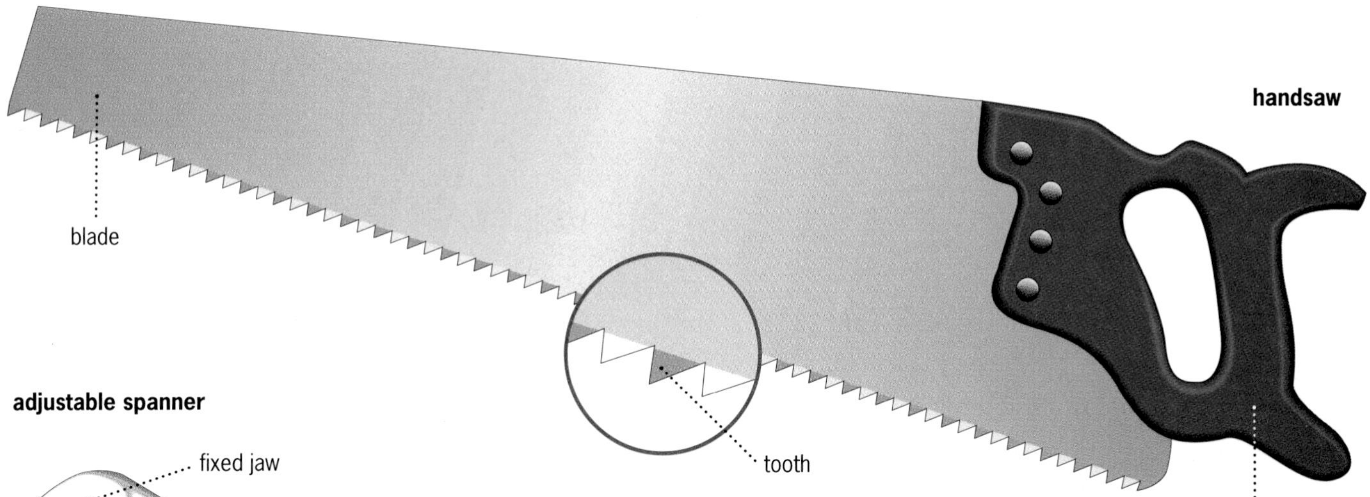
blade
tooth
handle

adjustable spanner

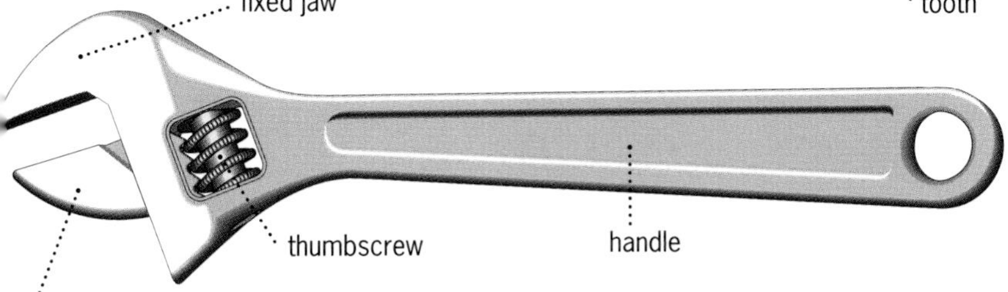
fixed jaw
thumbscrew
handle
movable jaw

adjustable pliers

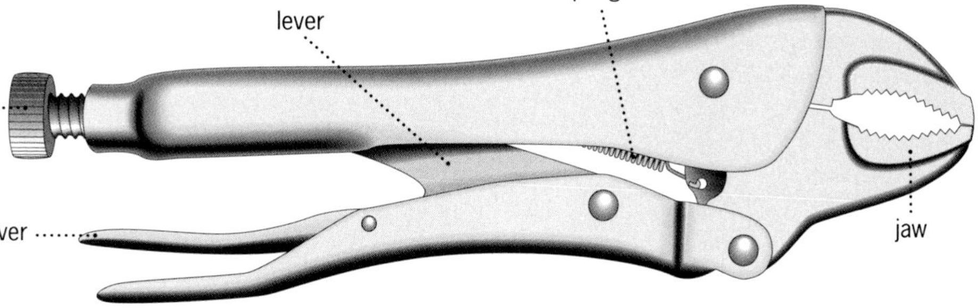
spring
lever
adjusting screw
release lever
jaw

rib joint pliers

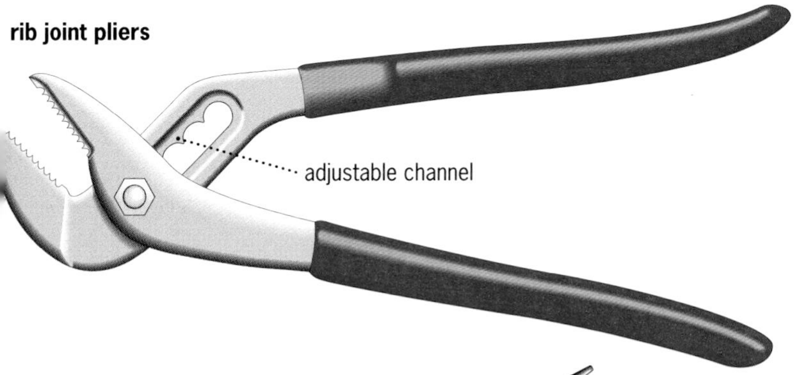
adjustable channel

bolt

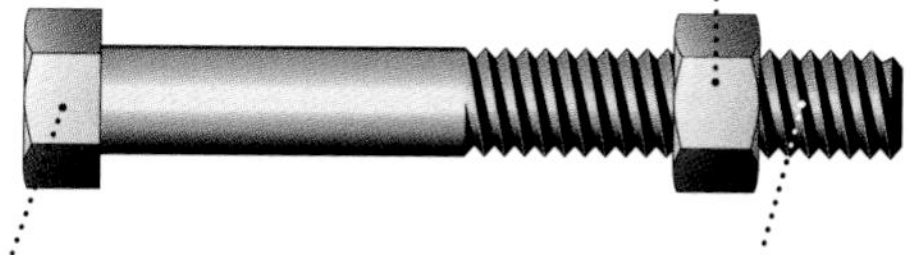
nut
head
threaded rod

long-nose pliers

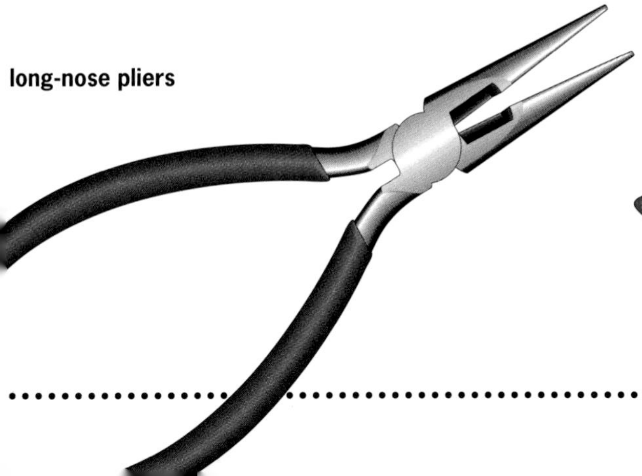

slip joint pliers

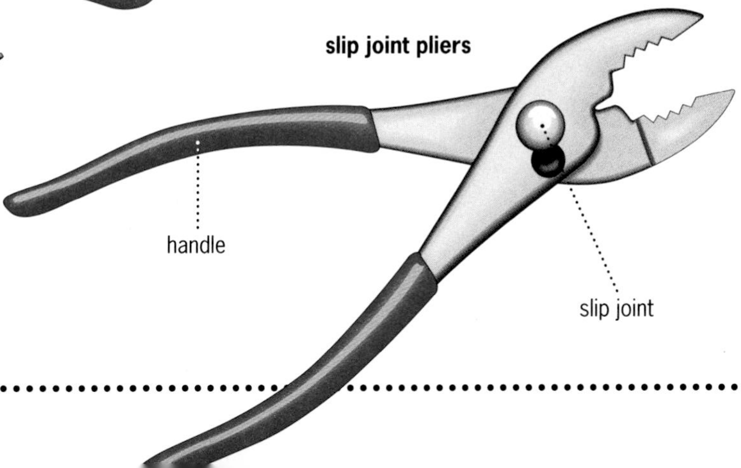
handle
slip joint

ELECTRIC TOOLS

electric drill

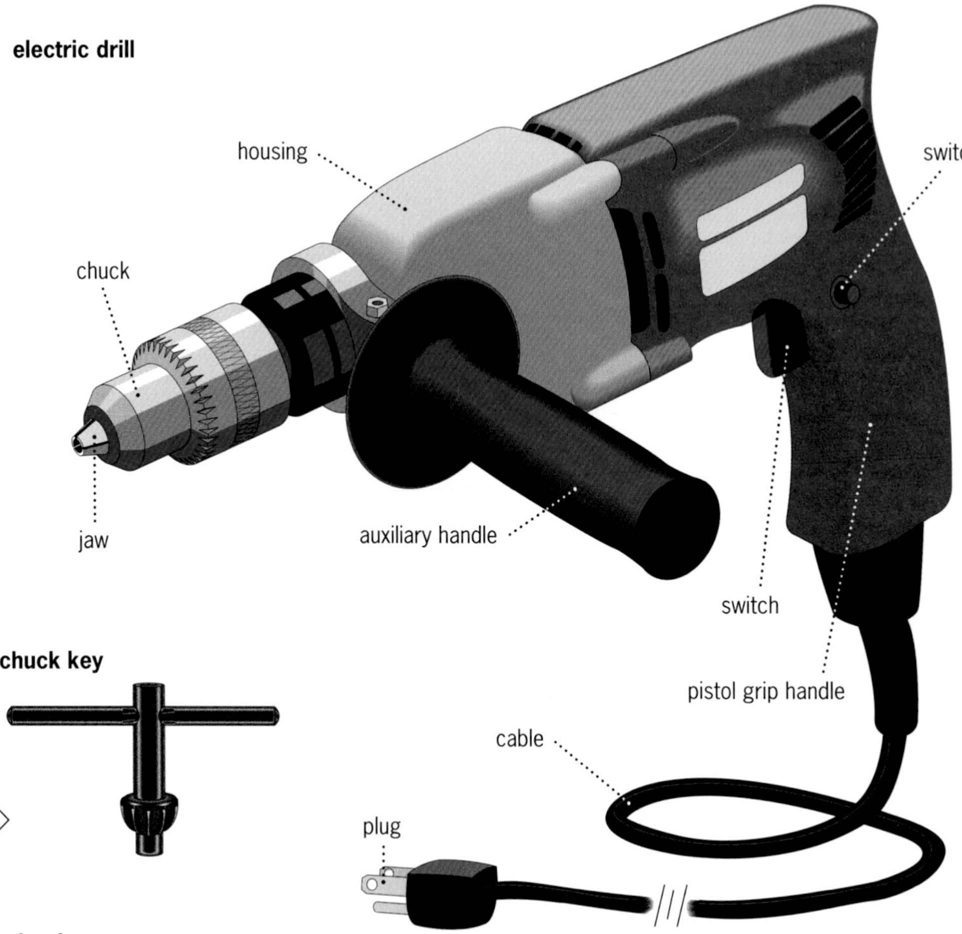
housing
switch lock
chuck
jaw
auxiliary handle
switch
pistol grip handle
cable
plug

chuck key

twist drill

auger bit

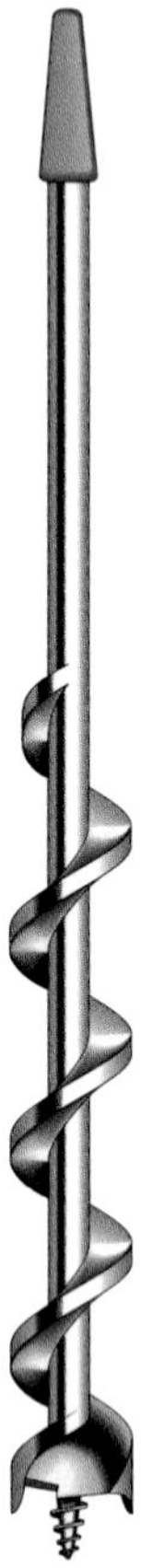

circular saw

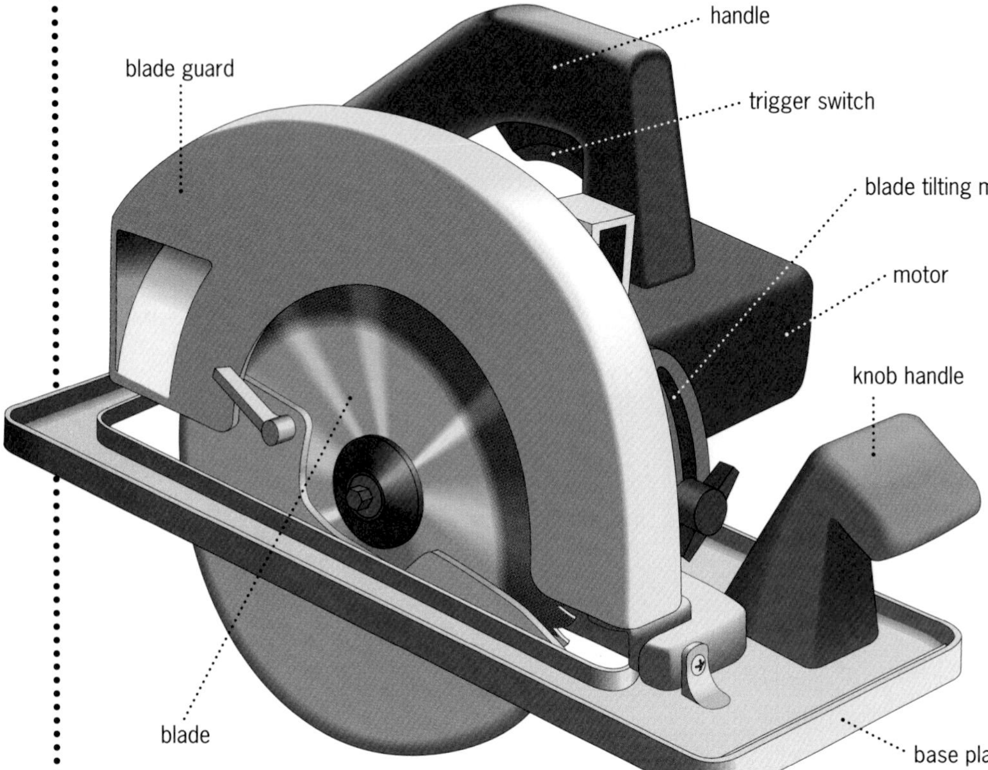
handle
blade guard
trigger switch
blade tilting mechanism
motor
knob handle
blade
base plate

circular saw blade

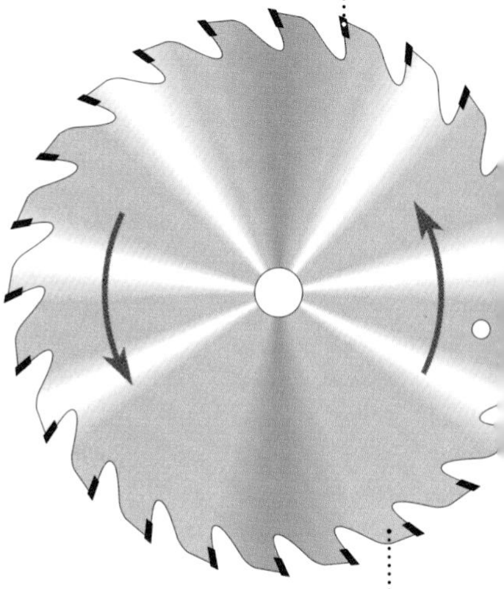
tip
tooth

PAINTING UPKEEP

paint roller

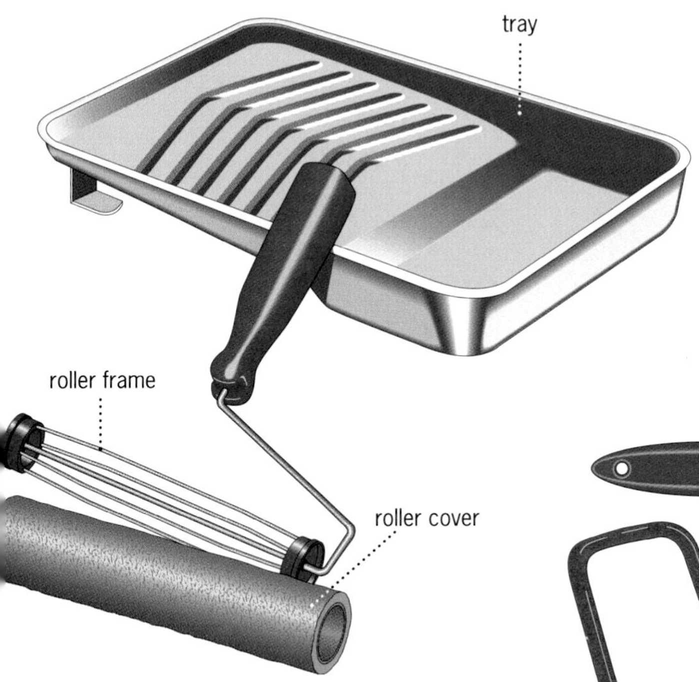
tray
roller frame
roller cover

scraper

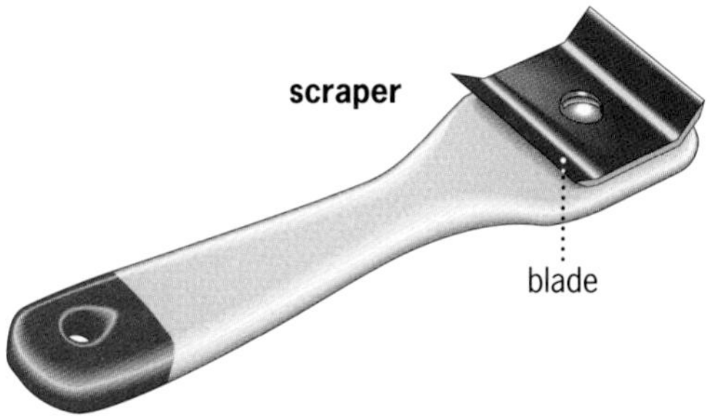
blade

brush

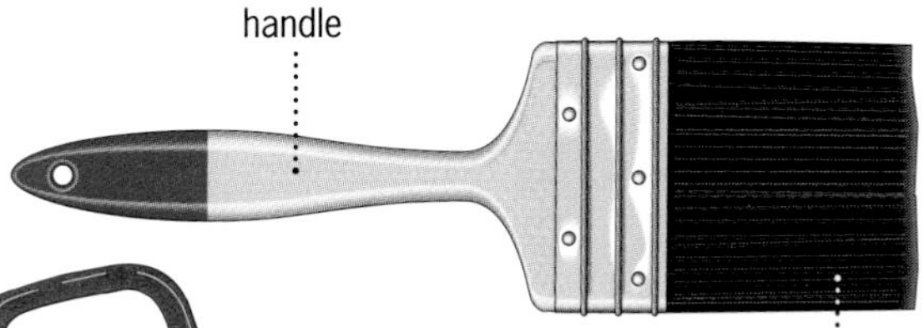
handle
bristles

extension ladder

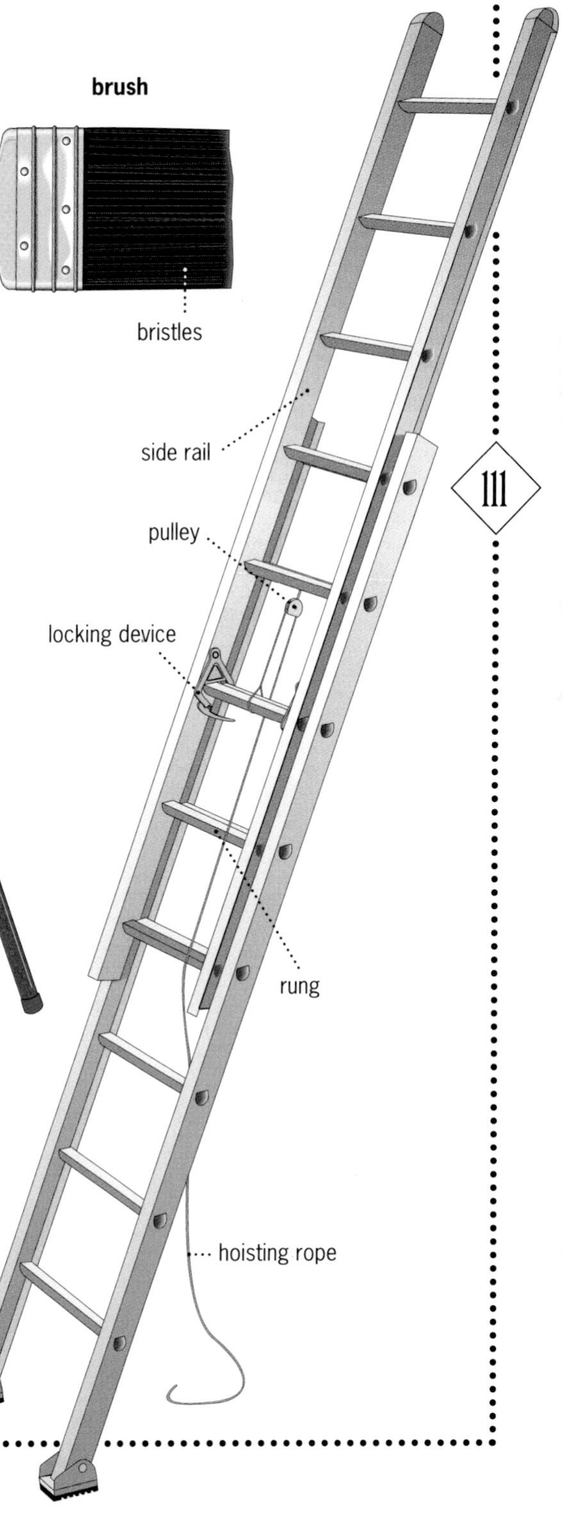
side rail
pulley
locking device
rung
hoisting rope
anti-slip shoe

stepladder

platform ladder

MEN'S CLOTHING

shirt

collar
collar point
placket
breast pocket
front
cuff
button
shirttail

braces

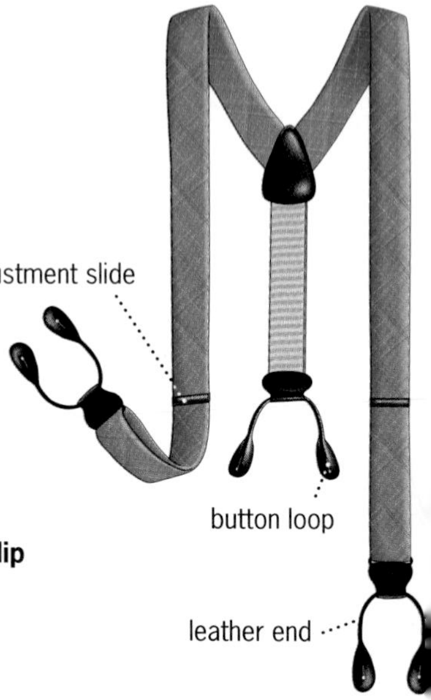
adjustment slide
button loop
leather end

brace clip

trousers

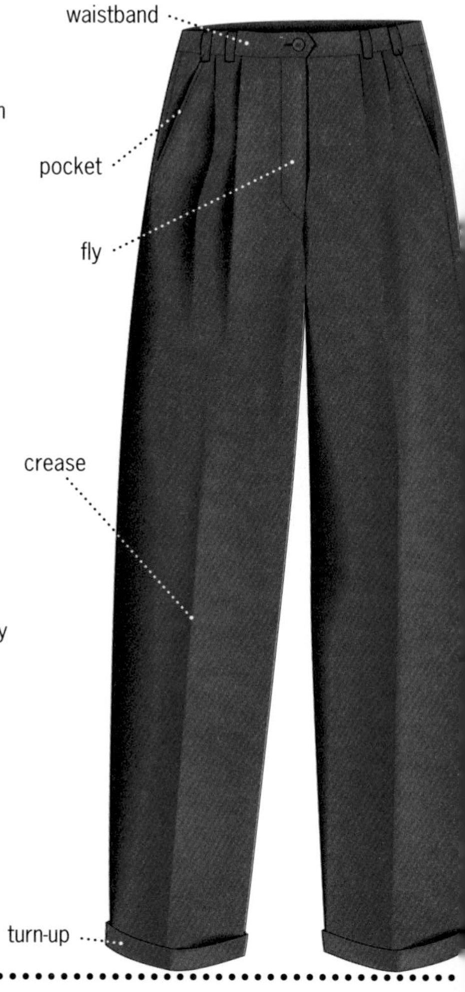
waistband
pocket
fly
crease
turn-up

tie

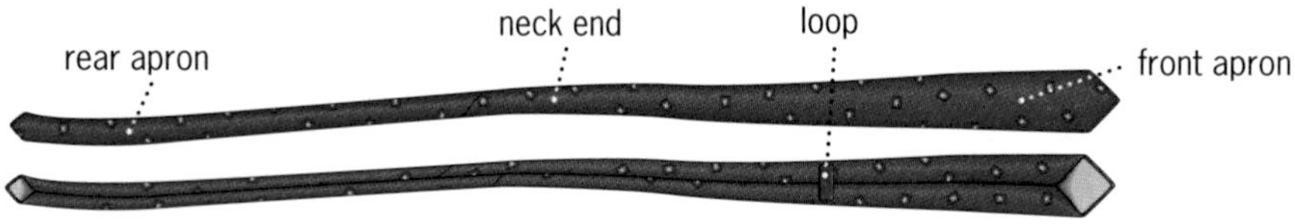
rear apron
neck end
loop
front apron

belt

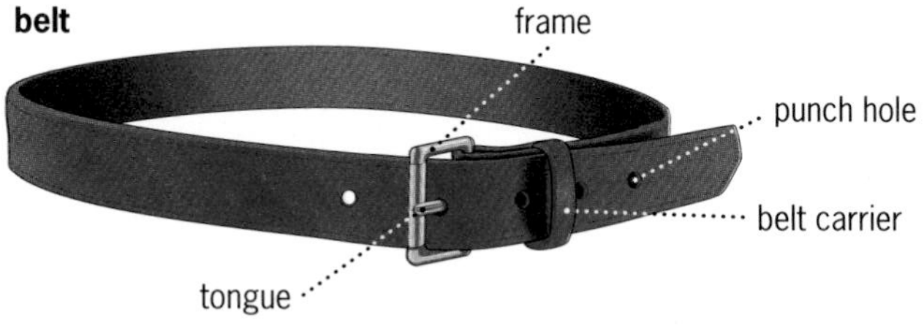
frame
punch hole
belt carrier
tongue

boxer shorts

vest

briefs

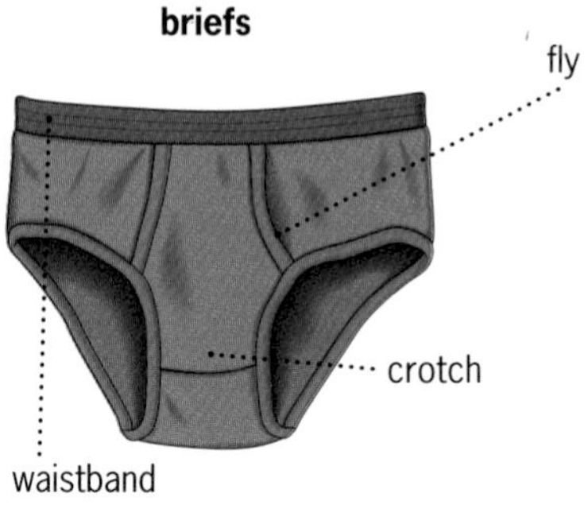
fly
crotch
waistband

double-breasted jacket

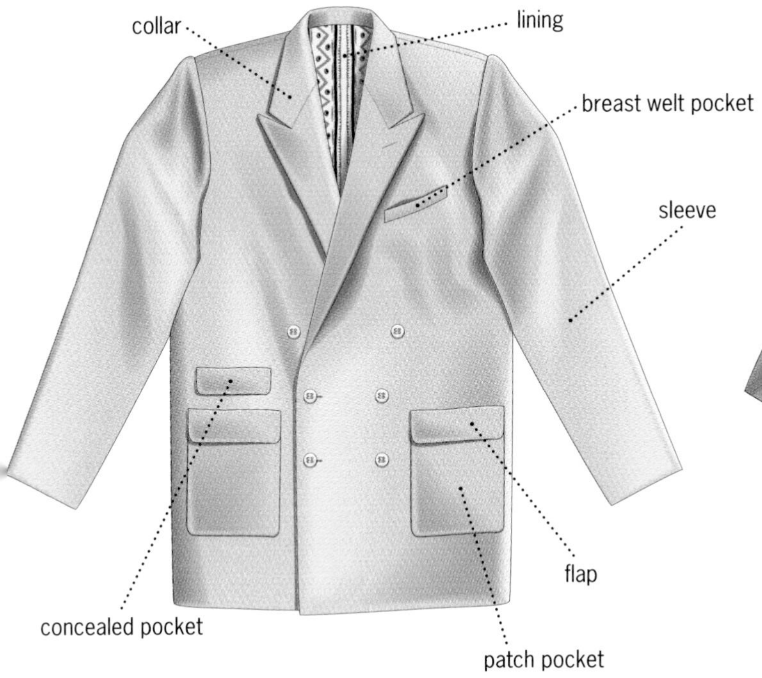
collar
lining
breast welt pocket
sleeve
flap
concealed pocket
patch pocket

duffle coat

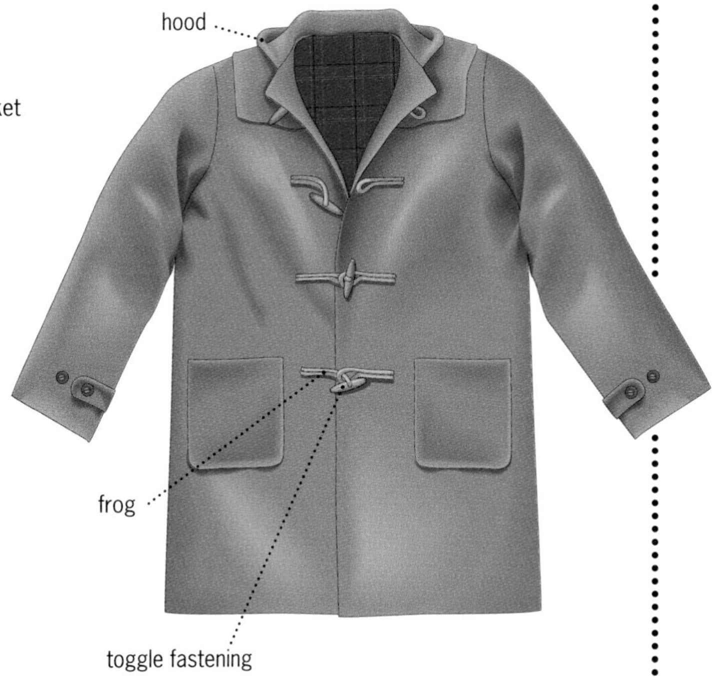
hood
frog
toggle fastening

cap

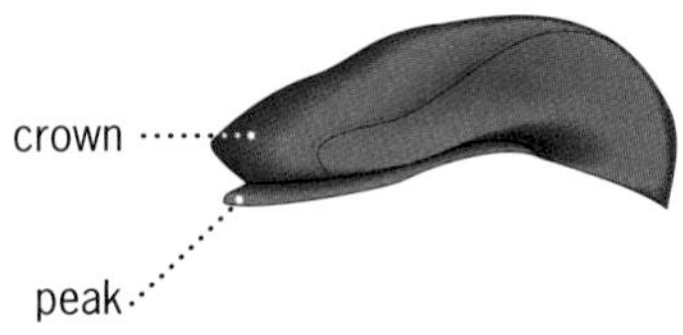
crown
peak

bobble hat

hunting cap

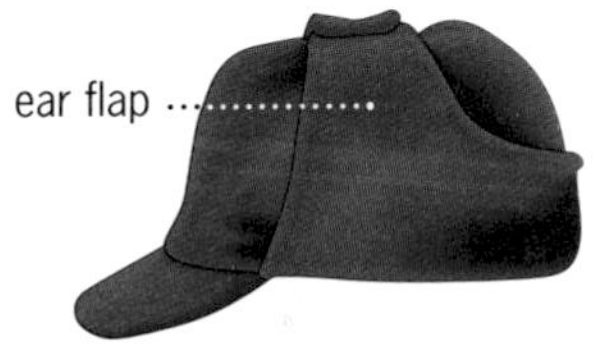
ear flap

bomber jacket

snap fastener
elastic waistband

windcheater

waistband
drawstring

WOMEN'S CLOTHING

toque

knitted hat

balaclava

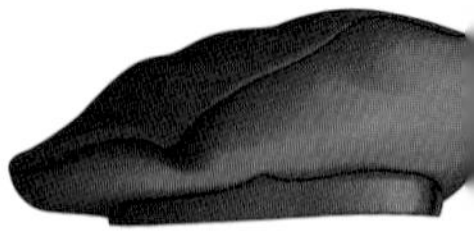

beret

suit

blouse

double-breasted jacket

overcoat

poncho

dress

jeans

ski pants

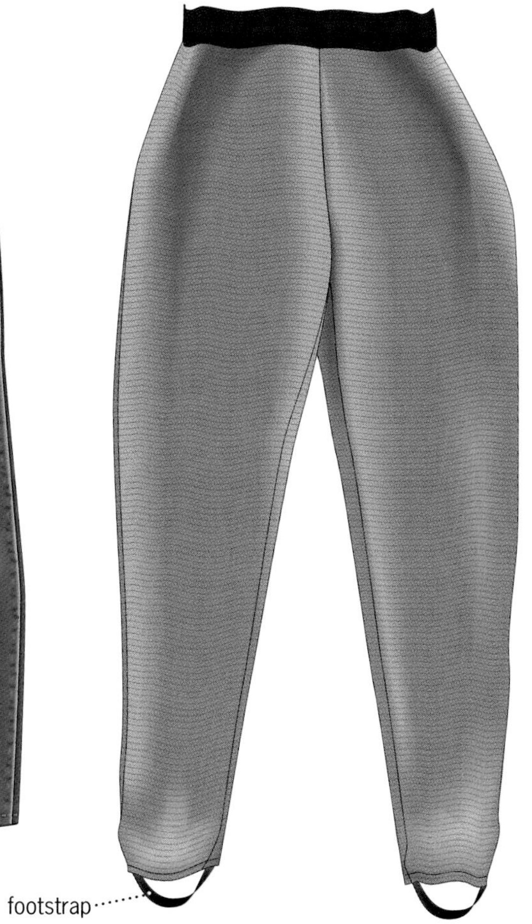

shorts

Bermuda shorts

straight skirt

culottes

pleated skirt

WOMEN'S CLOTHING

pyjamas

bra

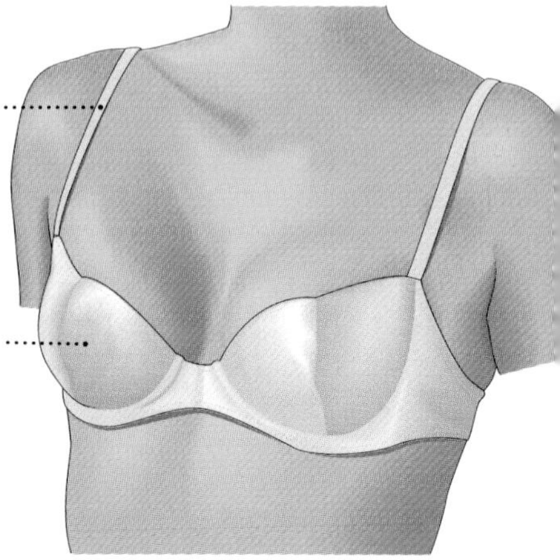
shoulder strap
cup

pants

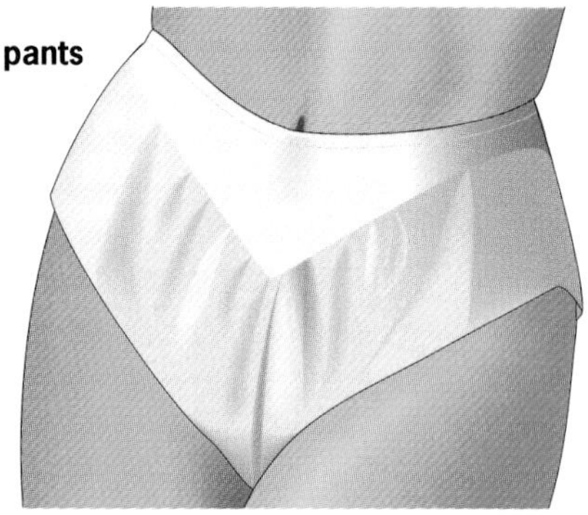

dressing gown

waist slip

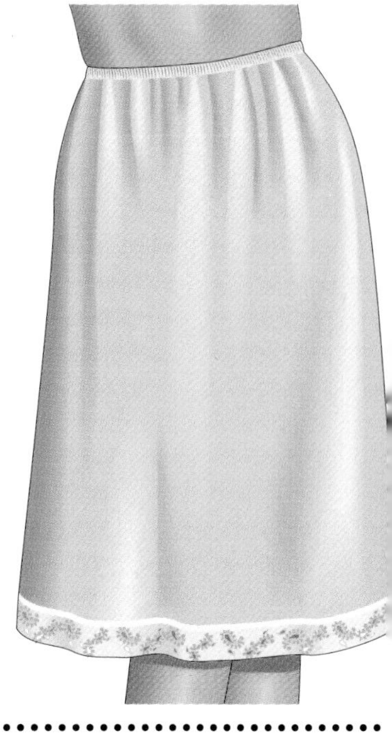

SWEATERS

cardigan

crew neck sweater

polo neck

polo shirt

slipover

V-neck cardigan

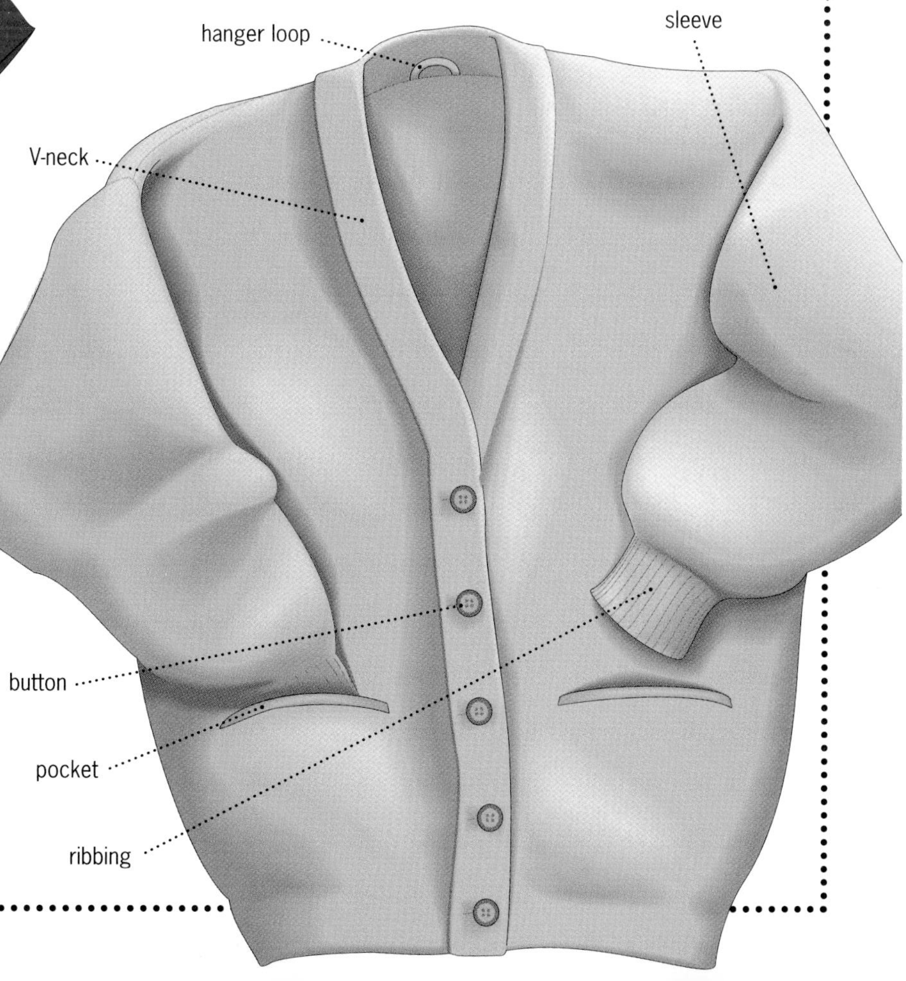
hanger loop
sleeve
V-neck
button
pocket
ribbing

GLOVES AND STOCKINGS

gloves

glove finger
thumb
palm
snap fastener
stitching

driving glove

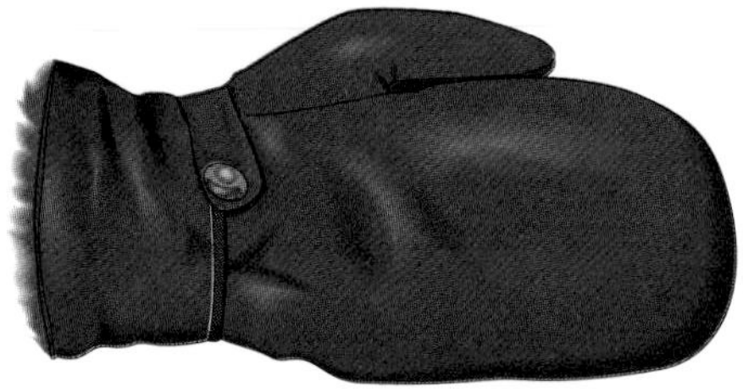

mitten

soc

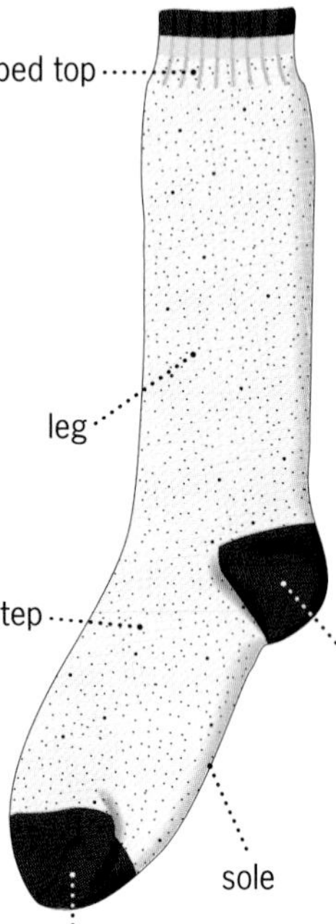
ribbed top
leg
instep
heel
sole
toe

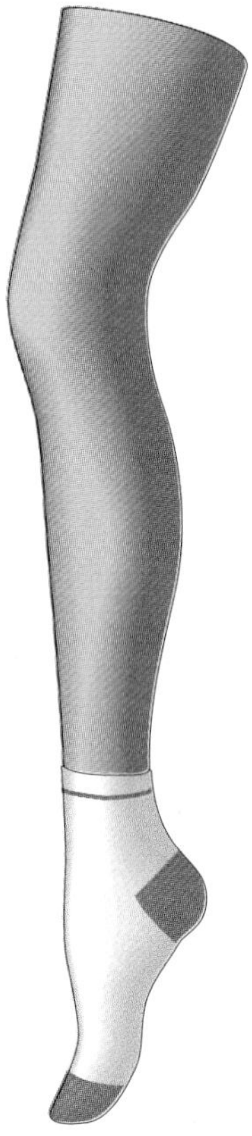

short sock

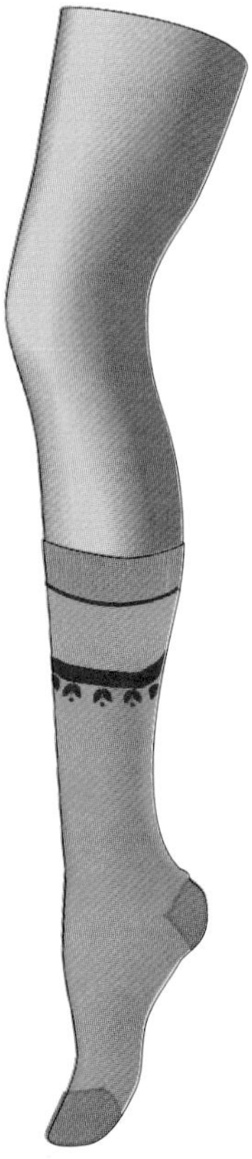

sock

knee-high sock

stocking

tights

SHOES

walking boot
slingback
pump
deck shoe
thigh-boot
court
espadrille
slip-on; loafer
moccasin
mule
boot
ankle boot

SPORTSWEAR

EXERCISE WEAR

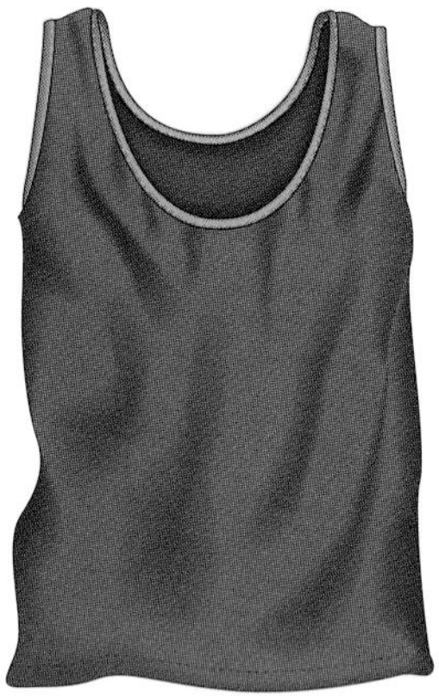

singlet

swimsuit

leotard

TRACK SUIT

sweatshirt

anorak

hooded sweatshirt

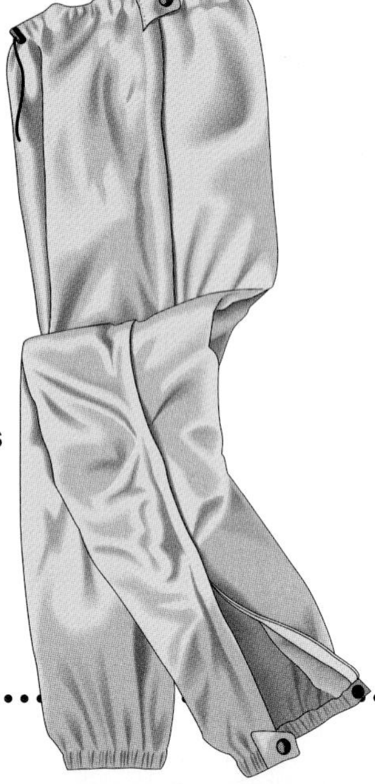

overtrousers

trousers

EXERCISE WEAR

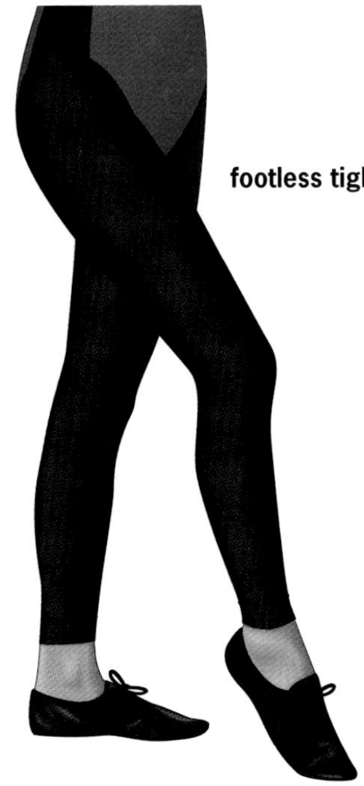

footless tights

leg-warmer

swimming trunks

boxer shorts

running shoe; trainer

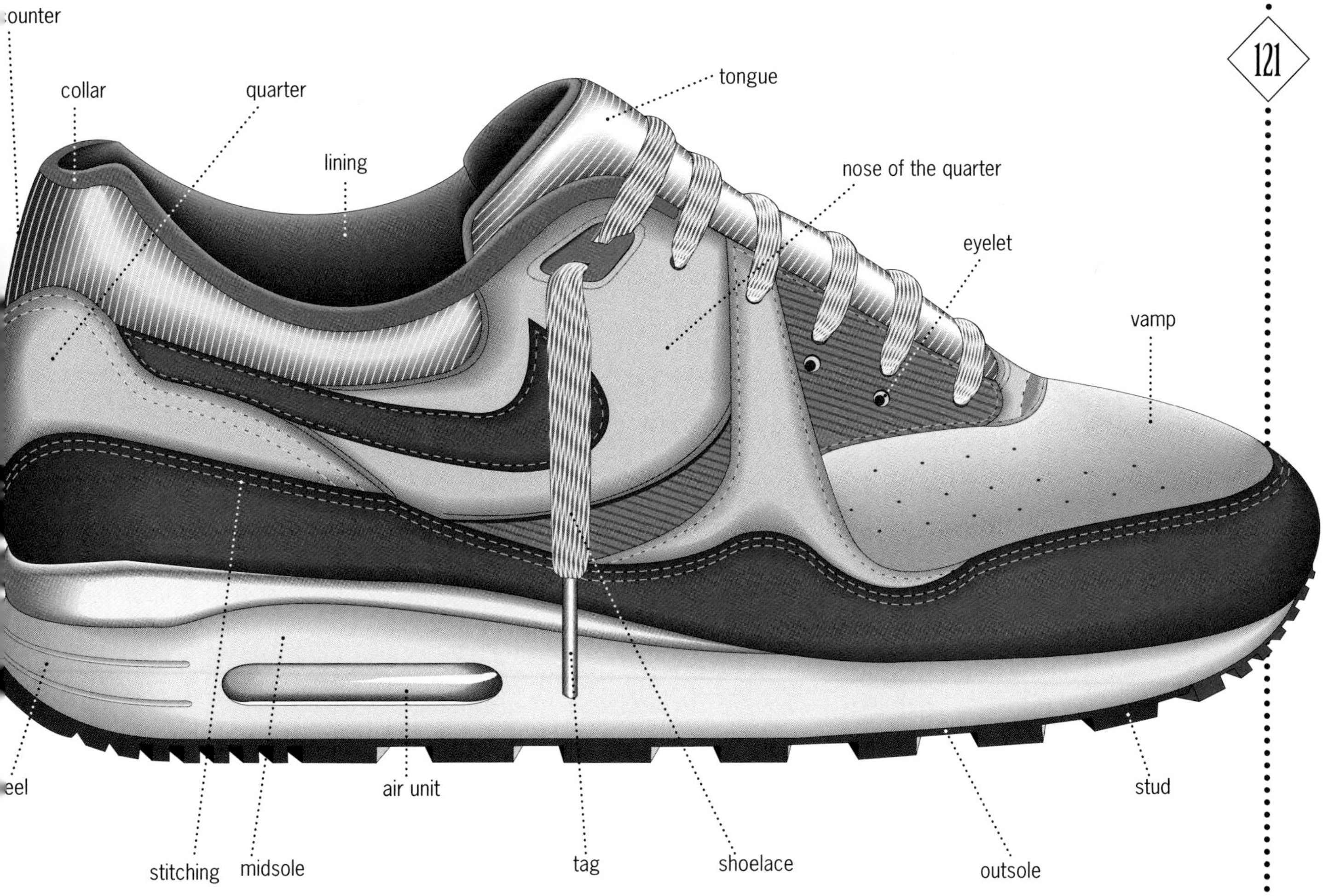
ounter
collar
quarter
lining
tongue
nose of the quarter
eyelet
vamp
eel
air unit
stud
stitching
midsole
tag
shoelace
outsole

DENTAL CARE

toothbrush

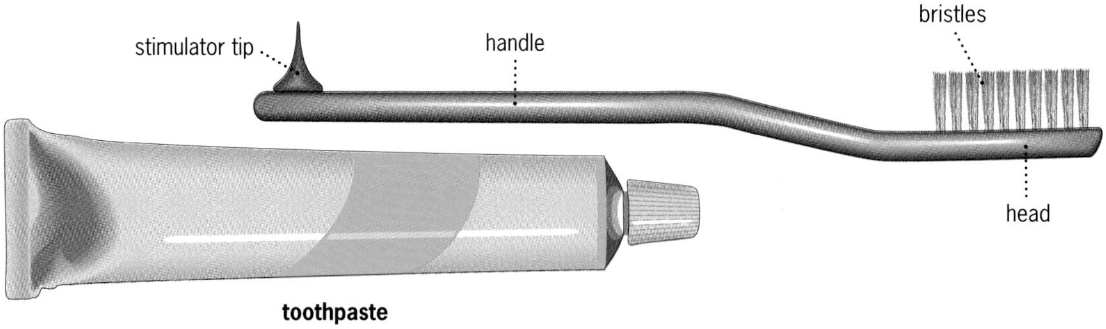
stimulator tip
handle
bristles
head

toothpaste

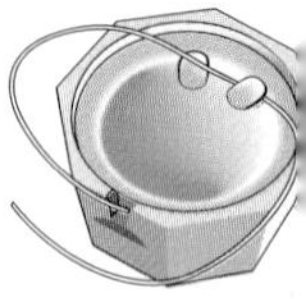

dental floss

HAIRDRESSING

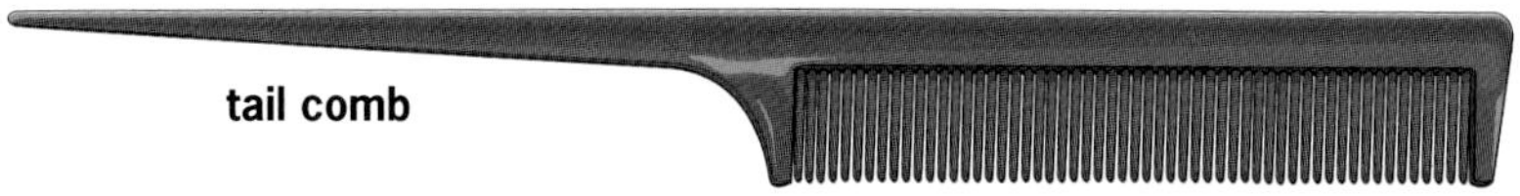

tail comb

rake comb

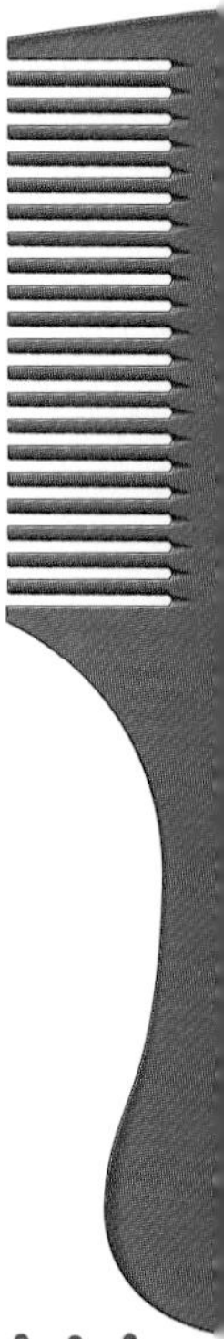

hair-dryer

fan
heat selector switch
barrel
heat
air
0
1
2
1
2
3
cha
air
speed selector switch
on-off switch
air-outlet grille
handle
air concentrator

hairbrush

Afro pick

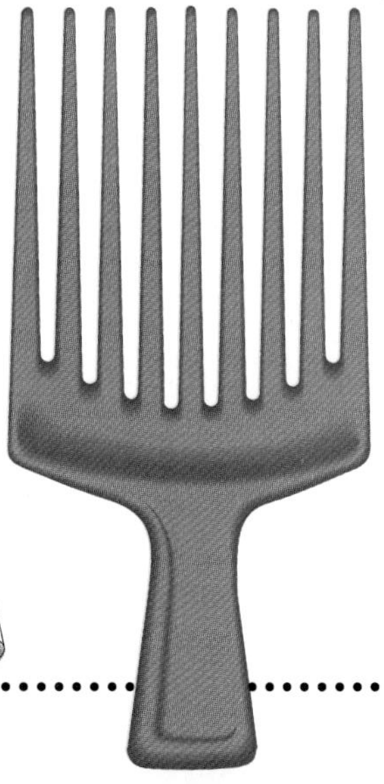

LEATHER GOODS

rawstring bag
rawstring
shoulder strap
front pocket

knapsack

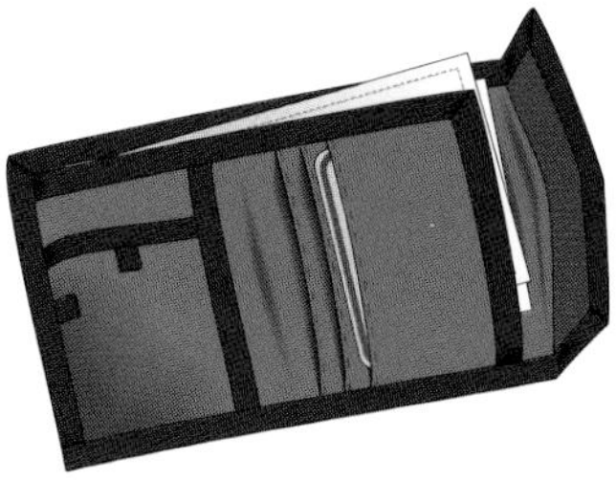
wallet

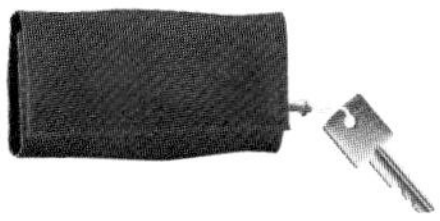
key case

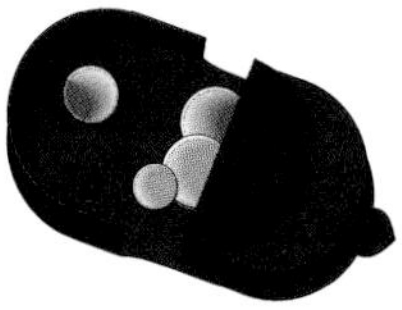
purse

GLASSES; SPECTACLES

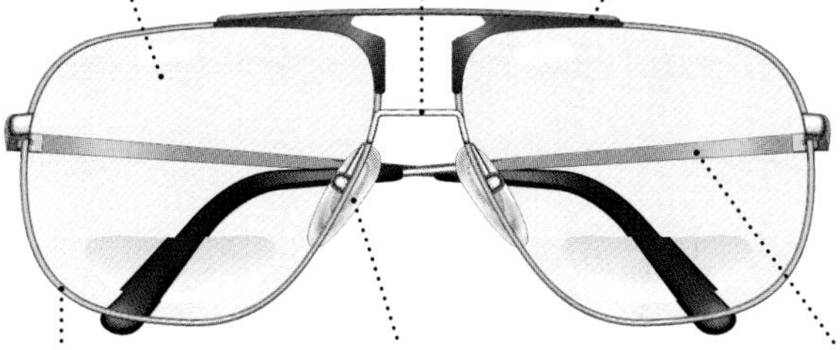
glass lens
bridge
bar
rim
nose pad
temple

UMBRELLA

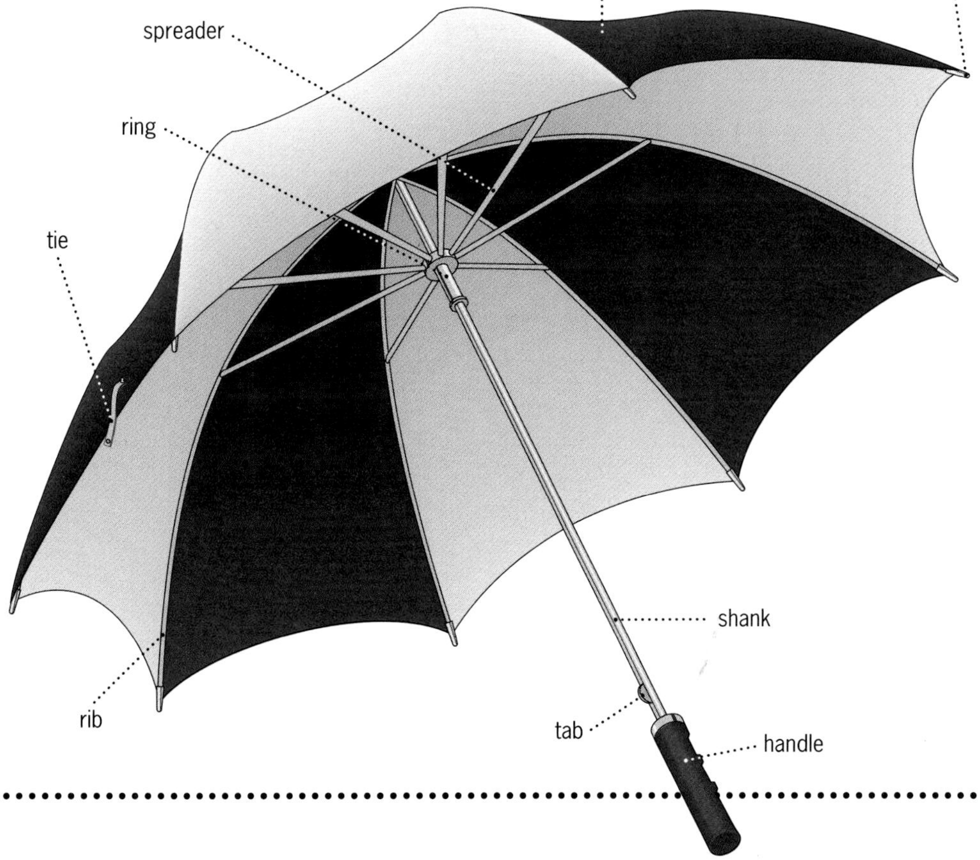
canopy
tip
spreader
ring
tie
shank
rib
tab
handle

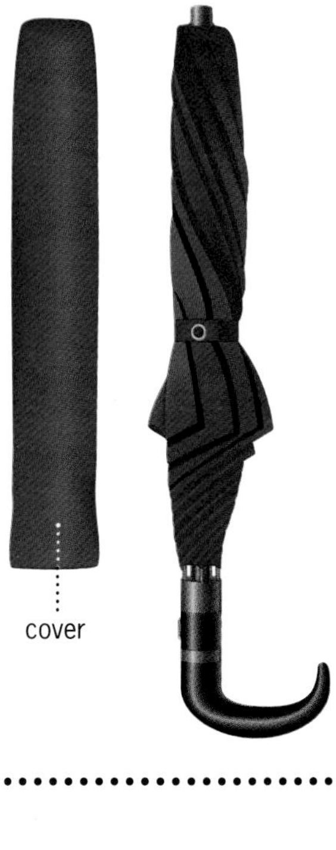
telescopic umbrella
cover

COMMUNICATION BY TELEPHONE

telephone set

handset
earpiece
display
mouthpiece
function selectors
automatic dialler
push buttons
handset flex
telephone index

telephone answering machi

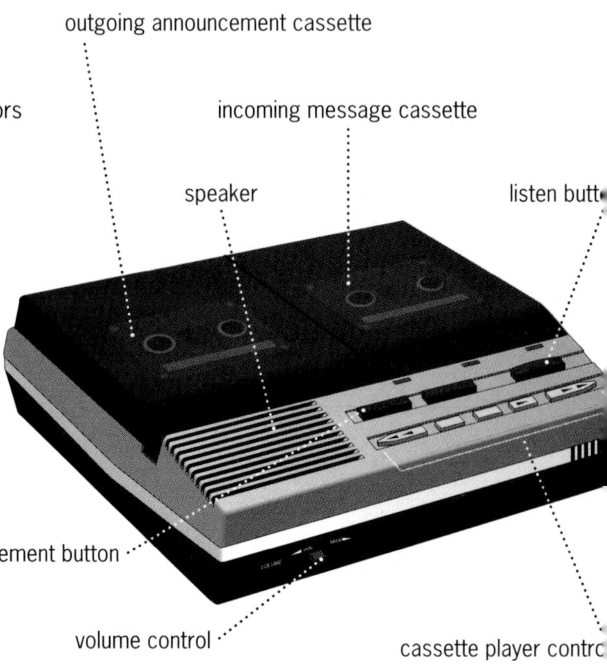
outgoing announcement cassette
incoming message cassette
speaker
listen butt
record announcement button
volume control
cassette player contr

pay phone

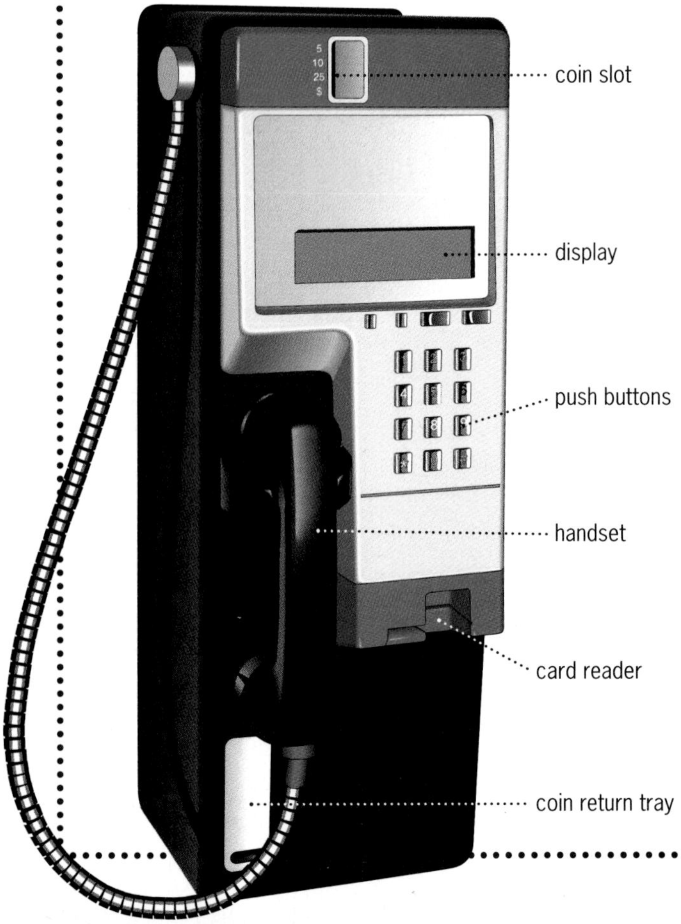
coin slot
display
push buttons
handset
card reader
coin return tray

push-button telephone

portable cellular telephone

cordless telephone

PHOTOGRAPHY

single lens reflex (slr) camera

accessory shoe
film rewind button
hot-shoe contact
film advance button
control dial
control panel
exposure button
film speed
remote control terminal
camera body
focus setting ring
shutter release button
objective lens

rangefinder; compact camera

electronic flash

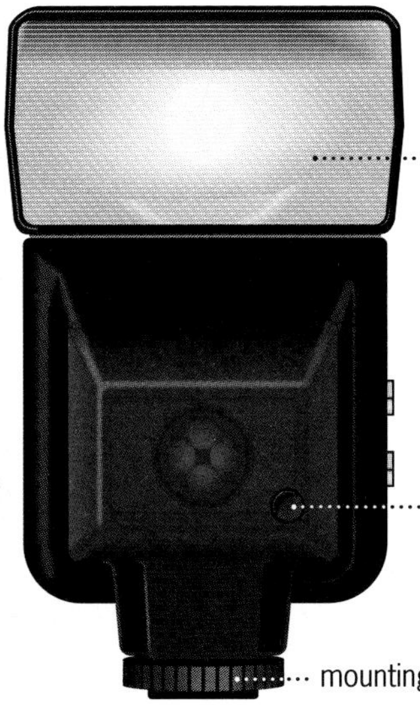
flashtube
photoelectric cell
mounting foot

cassette film

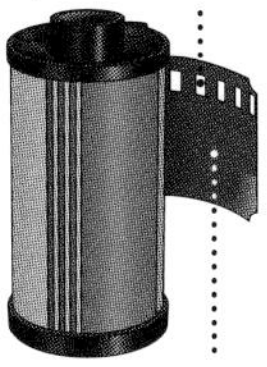
perforation
film leader

Polaroid® Land camera

ocket camera

cartridge film

film pack

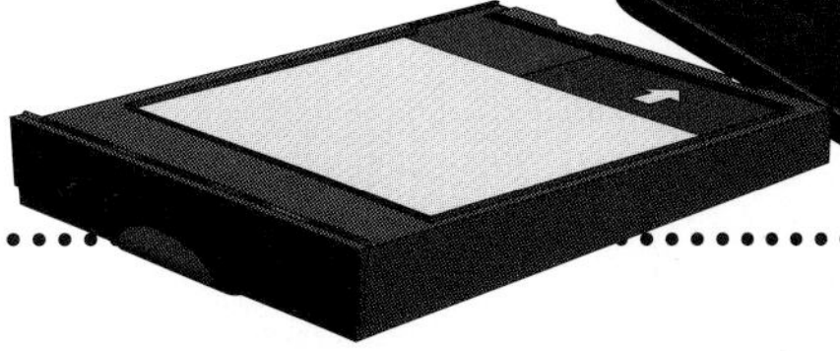

TELEVISION

television set

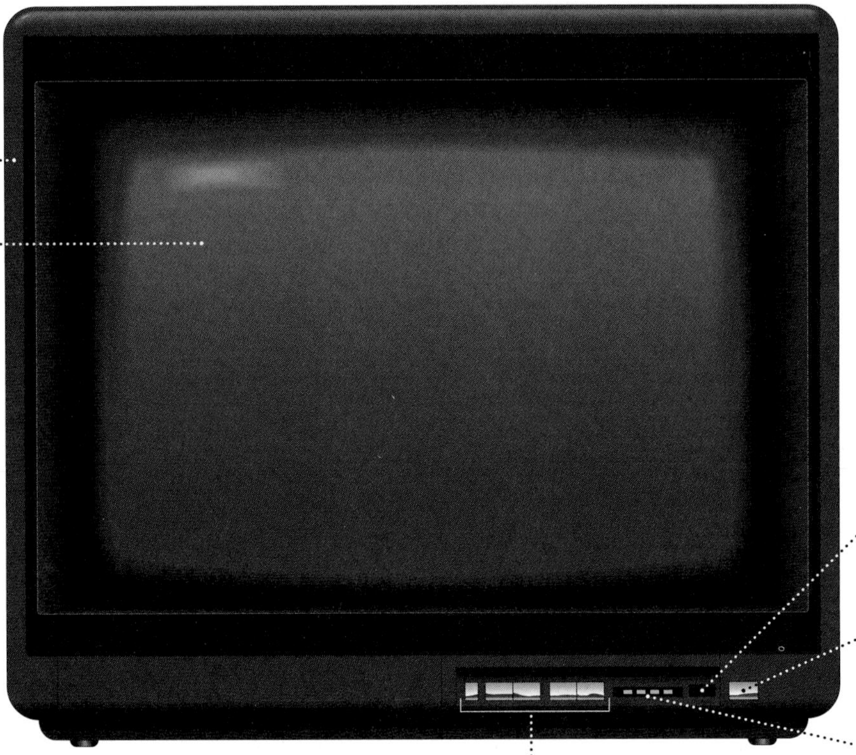
casing
screen
remote control sensor
on/off button
indicators
tuning controls

remote control

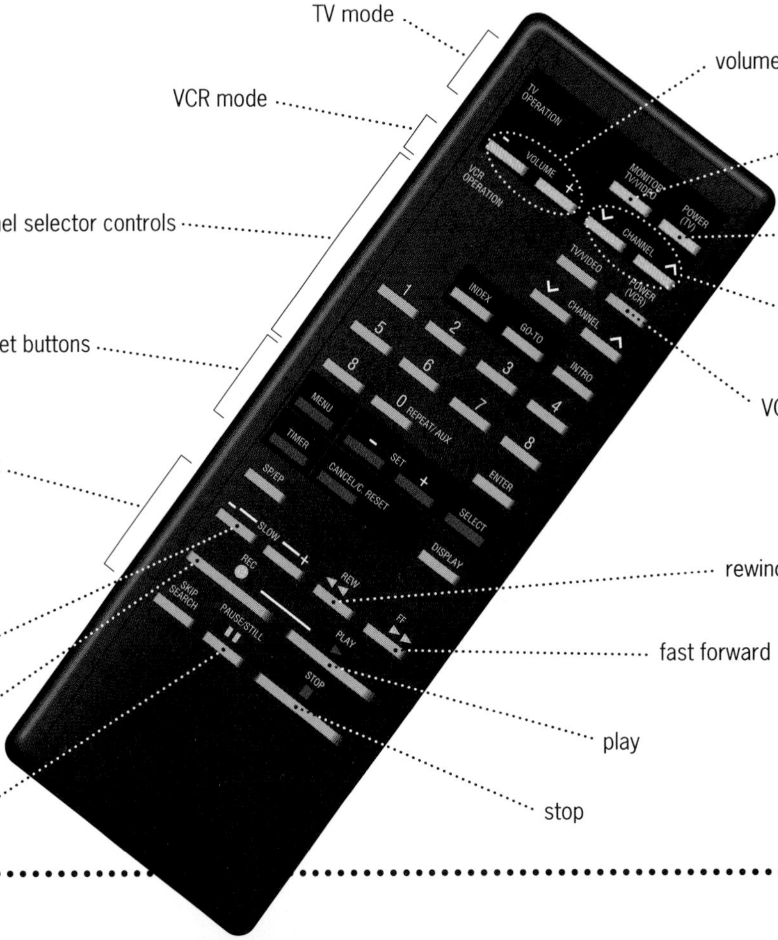
TV mode
VCR mode
channel selector controls
preset buttons
VCR controls
slow-motion
record
pause
volume control
TV/video button
TV on/off button
channel scan buttons
VCR on/off button
rewind
fast forward
play
stop

VIDEO

videocassette recorder

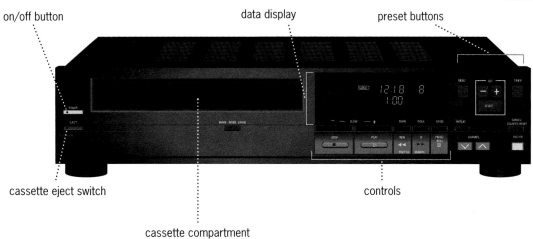

on/off button
data display
preset buttons
cassette eject switch
controls
cassette compartment

video camera

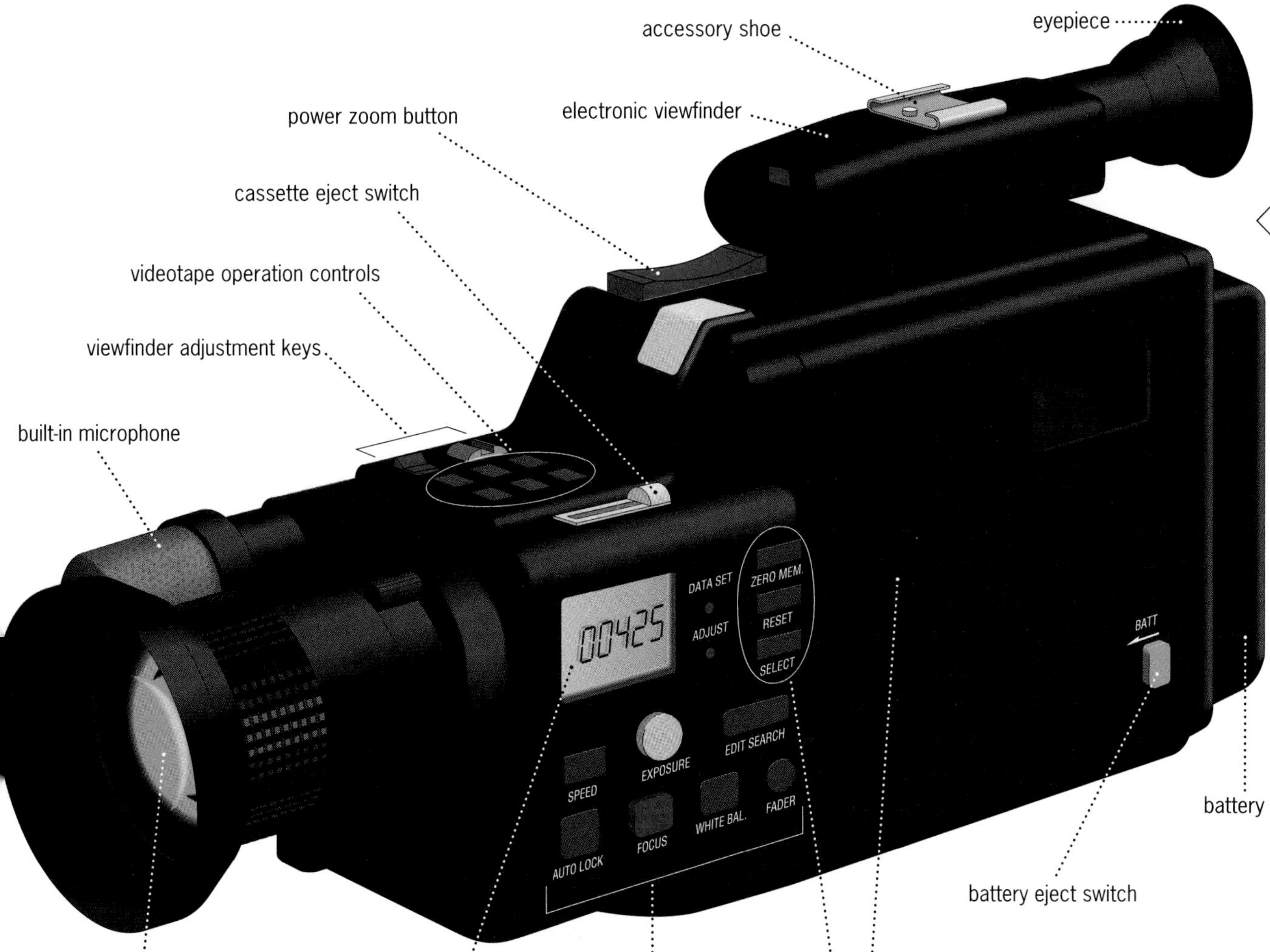
accessory shoe
eyepiece
power zoom button
electronic viewfinder
cassette eject switch
videotape operation controls
viewfinder adjustment keys
built-in microphone
DATA SET
ADJUST
ZERO MEM.
RESET
SELECT
00425
EXPOSURE
EDIT SEARCH
SPEED
FADER
WHITE BAL.
FOCUS
AUTO LOCK
BATT
battery
battery eject switch
zoom lens
shooting adjustment keys
cassette compartment
data display
edit/search buttons

HI-FI SYSTEM

SYSTEM COMPONENTS

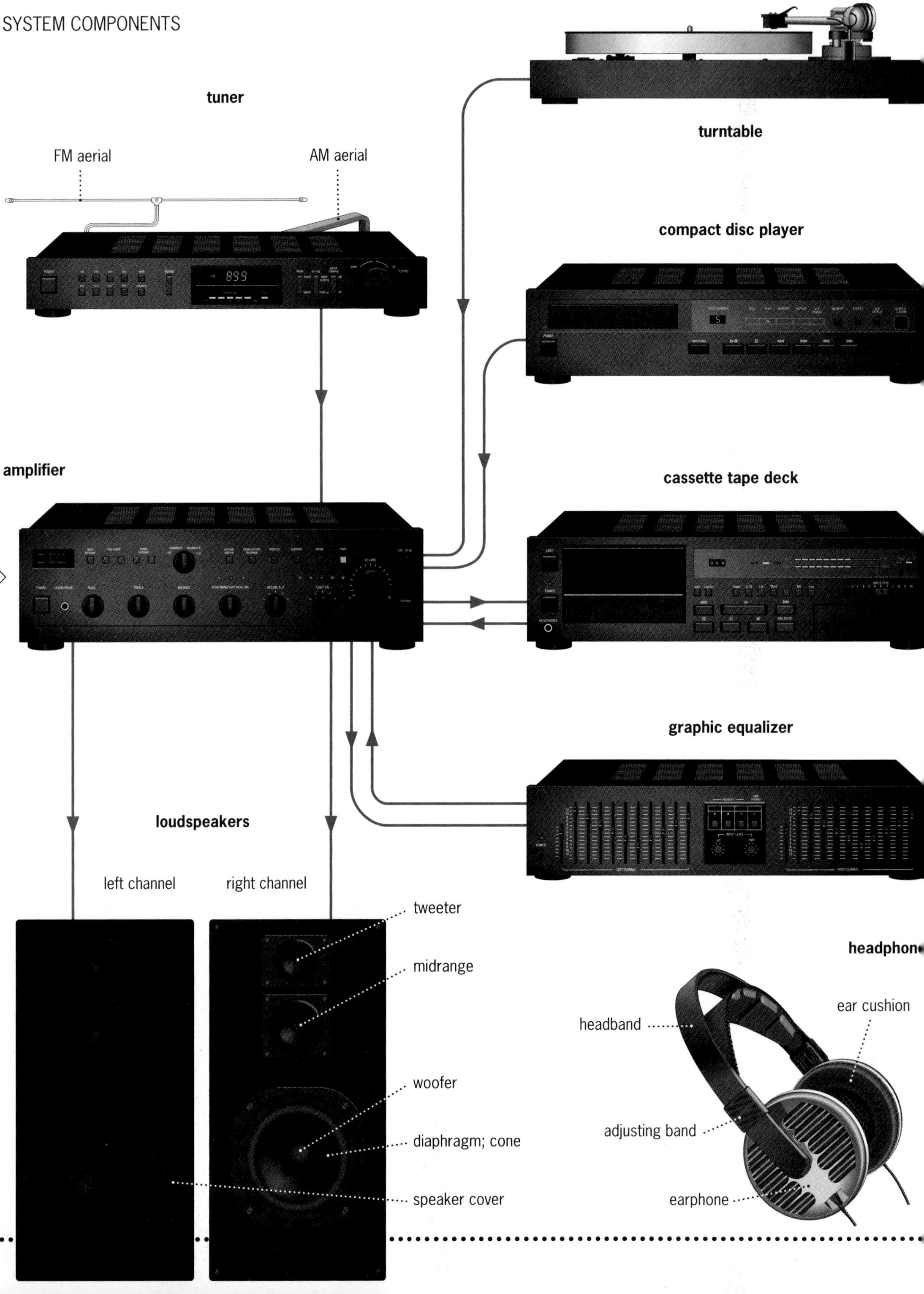
tuner
FM aerial
AM aerial
turntable
compact disc player
amplifier
cassette tape deck
graphic equalizer
loudspeakers
left channel
right channel
tweeter
midrange
woofer
diaphragm; cone
speaker cover
headphon
headband
ear cushion
adjusting band
earphone

PORTABLE SOUND SYSTEMS

portable CD radio cassette recorder

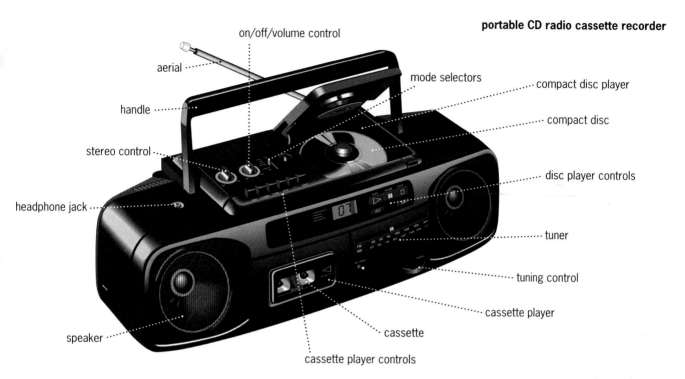

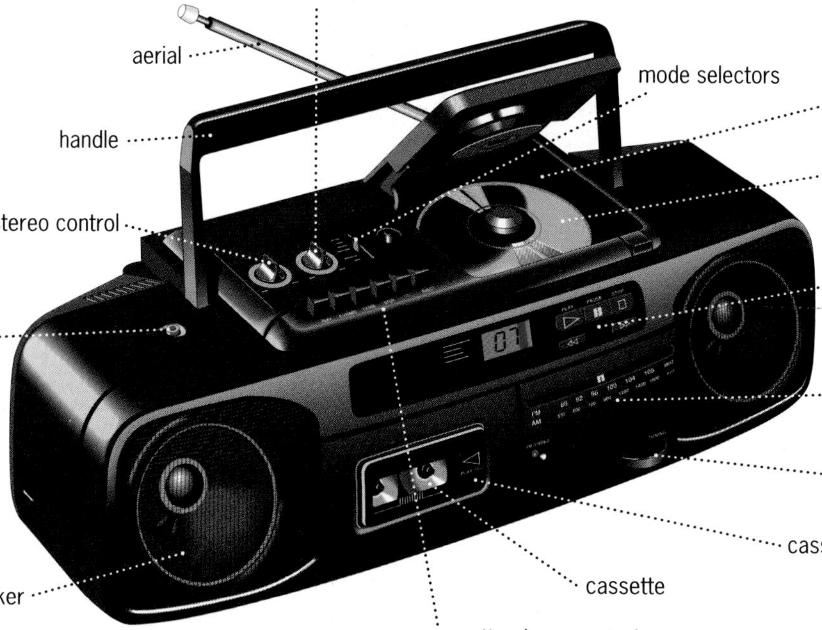
on/off/volume control
aerial
mode selectors
compact disc player
handle
compact disc
stereo control
disc player controls
headphone jack
tuner
tuning control
cassette player
speaker
cassette
cassette player controls

personal radio cassette player; Walkman®

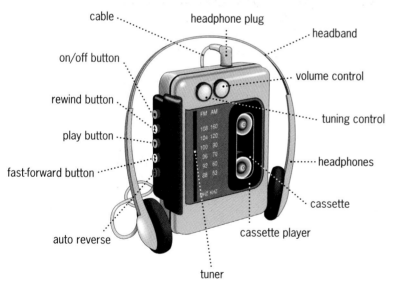

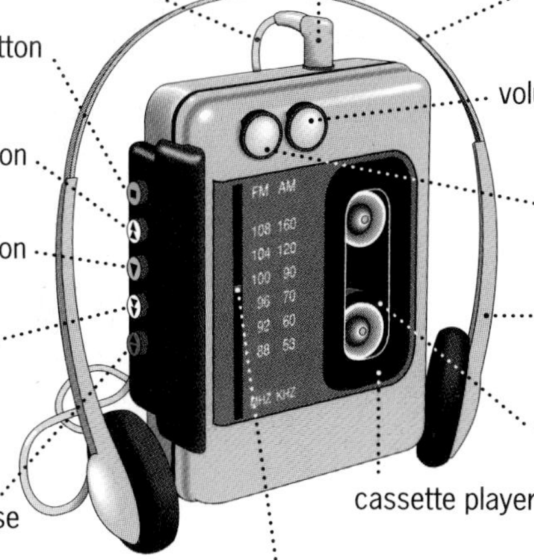
cable
headphone plug
headband
on/off button
volume control
rewind button
tuning control
play button
fast-forward button
headphones
cassette
cassette player
auto reverse
tuner

compact disc

pressed area
reading start
technical identification band

record

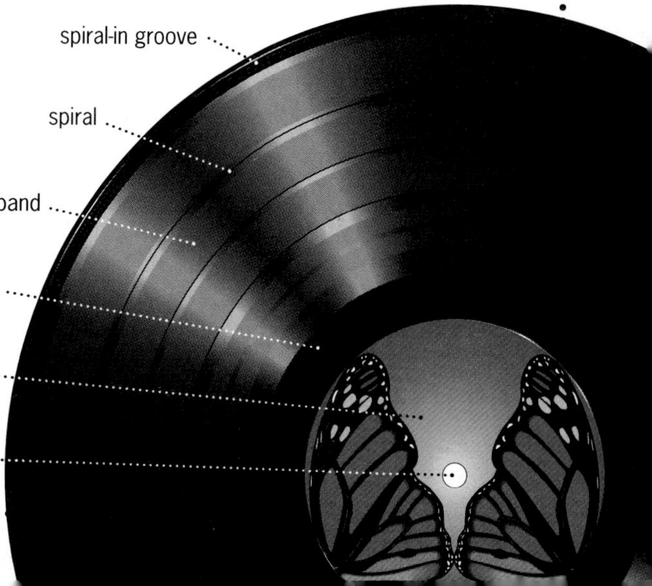
spiral-in groove
spiral
band
tail-out groove
label
centre hole

assette

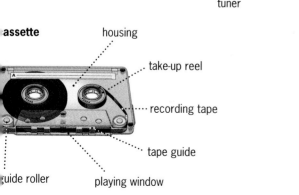

housing
take-up reel
recording tape
tape guide
uide roller
playing window

CAR

body

windscreen
windscreen wiper
wing mirror
washer nozzle
bonnet
headlight
grille
bumper
wing

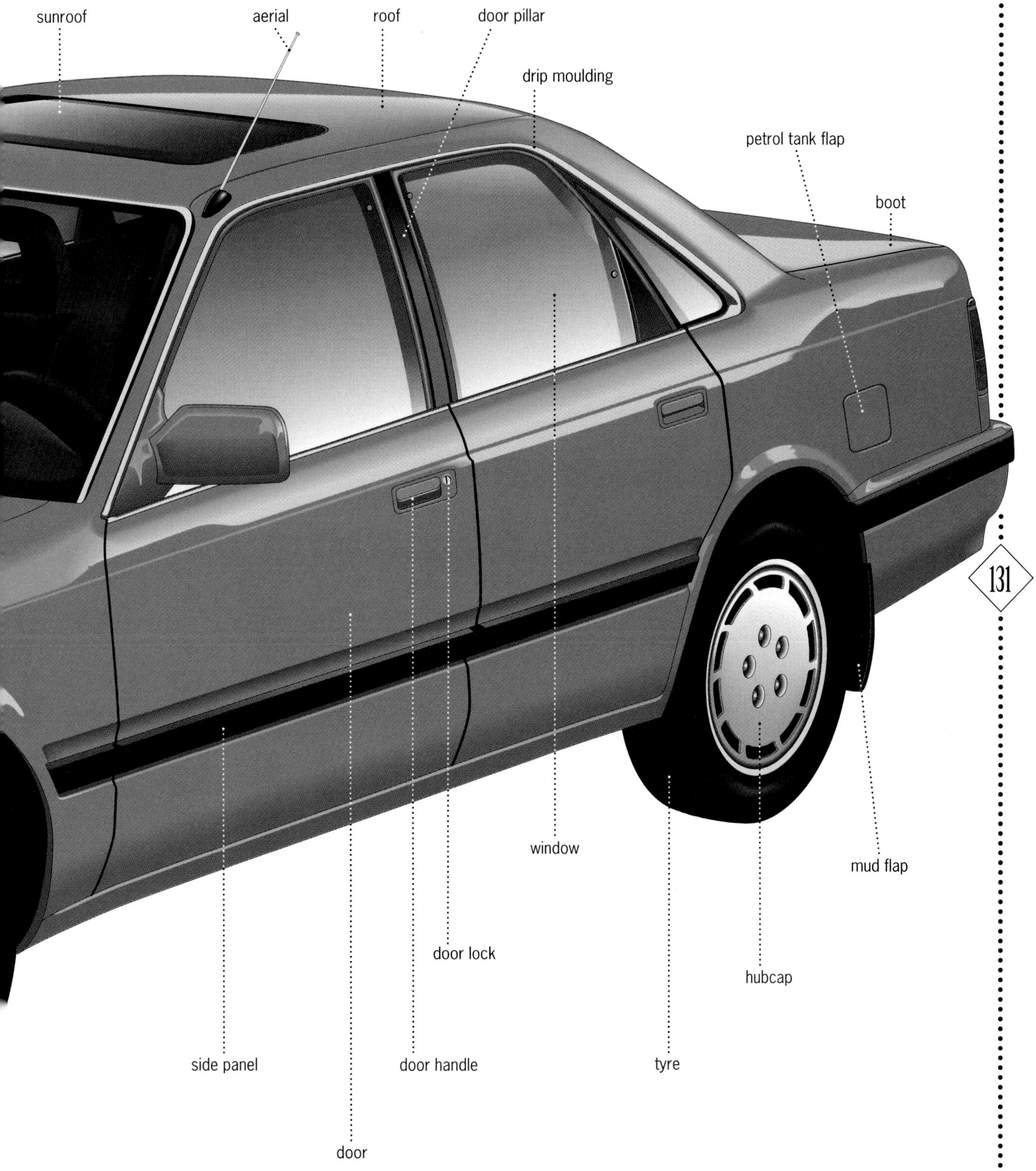
sunroof
aerial
roof
door pillar
drip moulding
petrol tank flap
boot
window
mud flap
door lock
hubcap
side panel
door handle
tyre
door

CAR

dashboard

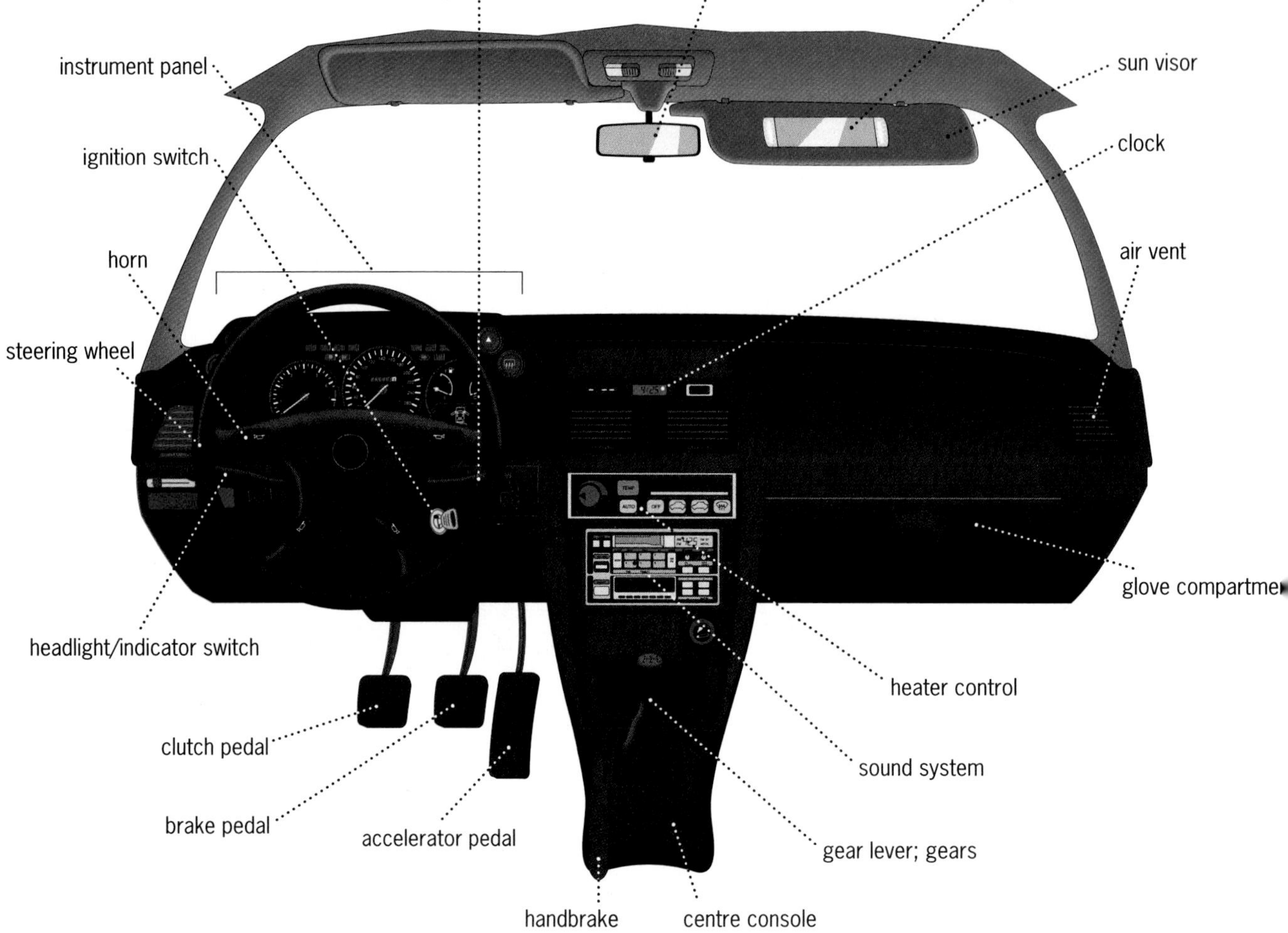
wiper switch
rearview mirror
vanity mirror
instrument panel
sun visor
ignition switch
clock
horn
air vent
steering wheel
glove compartme
headlight/indicator switch
heater control
clutch pedal
sound system
brake pedal
accelerator pedal
gear lever; gears
handbrake
centre console

instrument panel

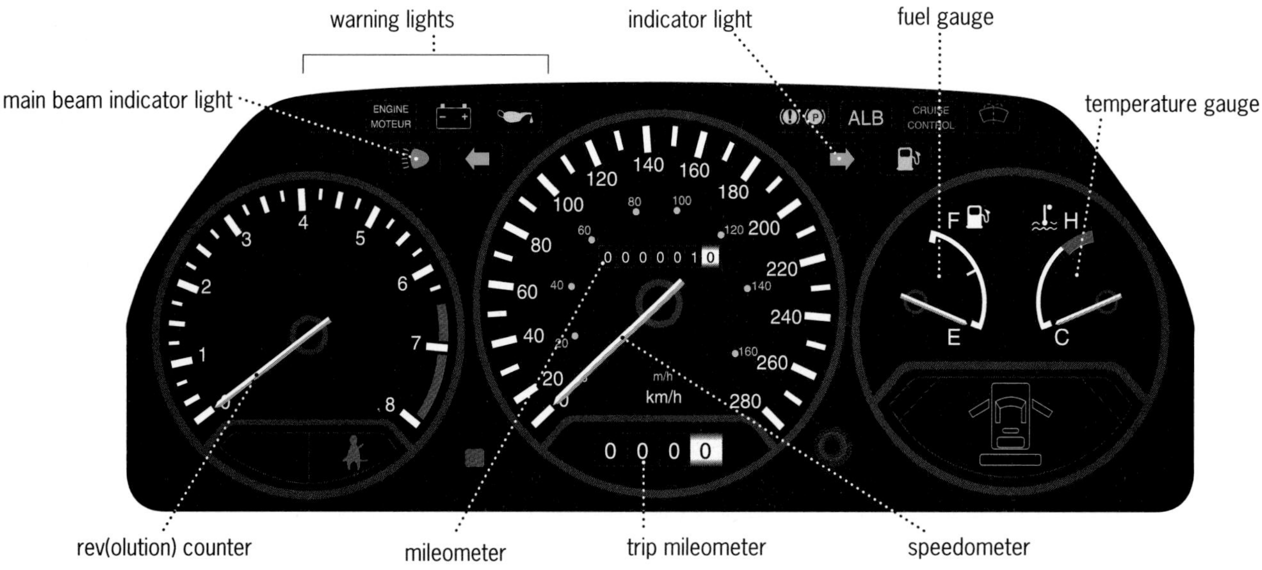
warning lights
indicator light
fuel gauge
main beam indicator light
temperature gauge
ENGINE
MOTEUR
ALB
CRUISE
CONTROL
F
H
E
C
km/h
m/h
rev(olution) counter
mileometer
trip mileometer
speedometer

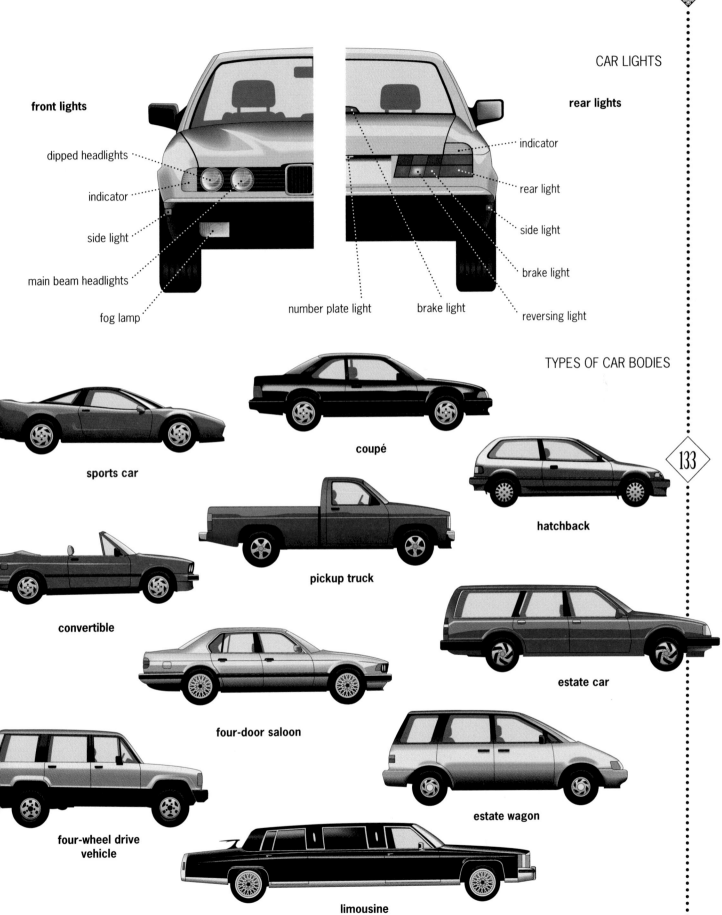

CAR LIGHTS

front lights

rear lights

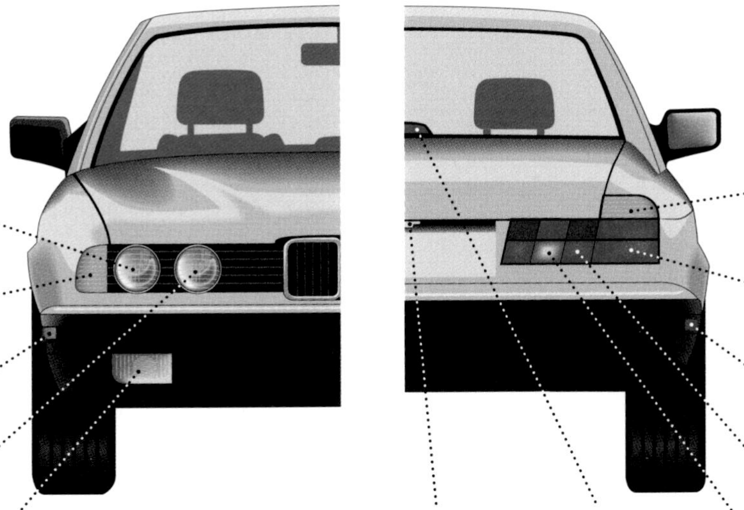
dipped headlights
indicator
side light
main beam headlights
fog lamp
number plate light
brake light
reversing light
brake light
side light
rear light
indicator

TYPES OF CAR BODIES

coupé

sports car

hatchback

pickup truck

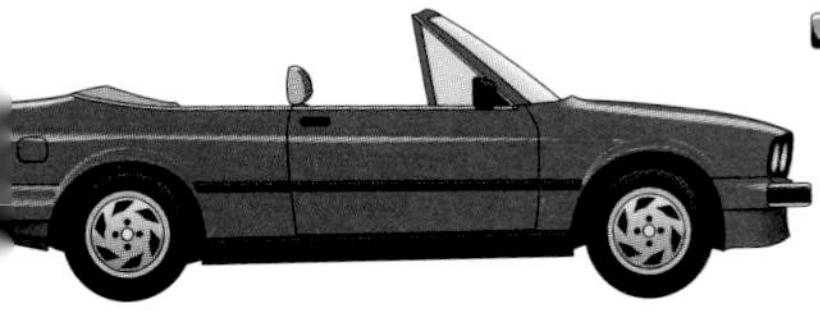

convertible

estate car

four-door saloon

estate wagon

four-wheel drive vehicle

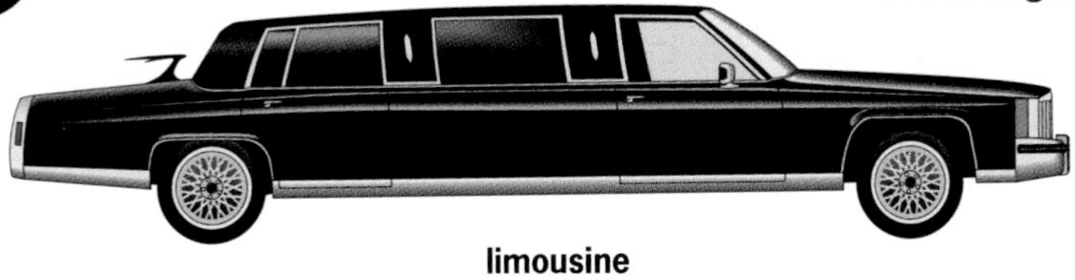

limousine

LORRY

tractor unit

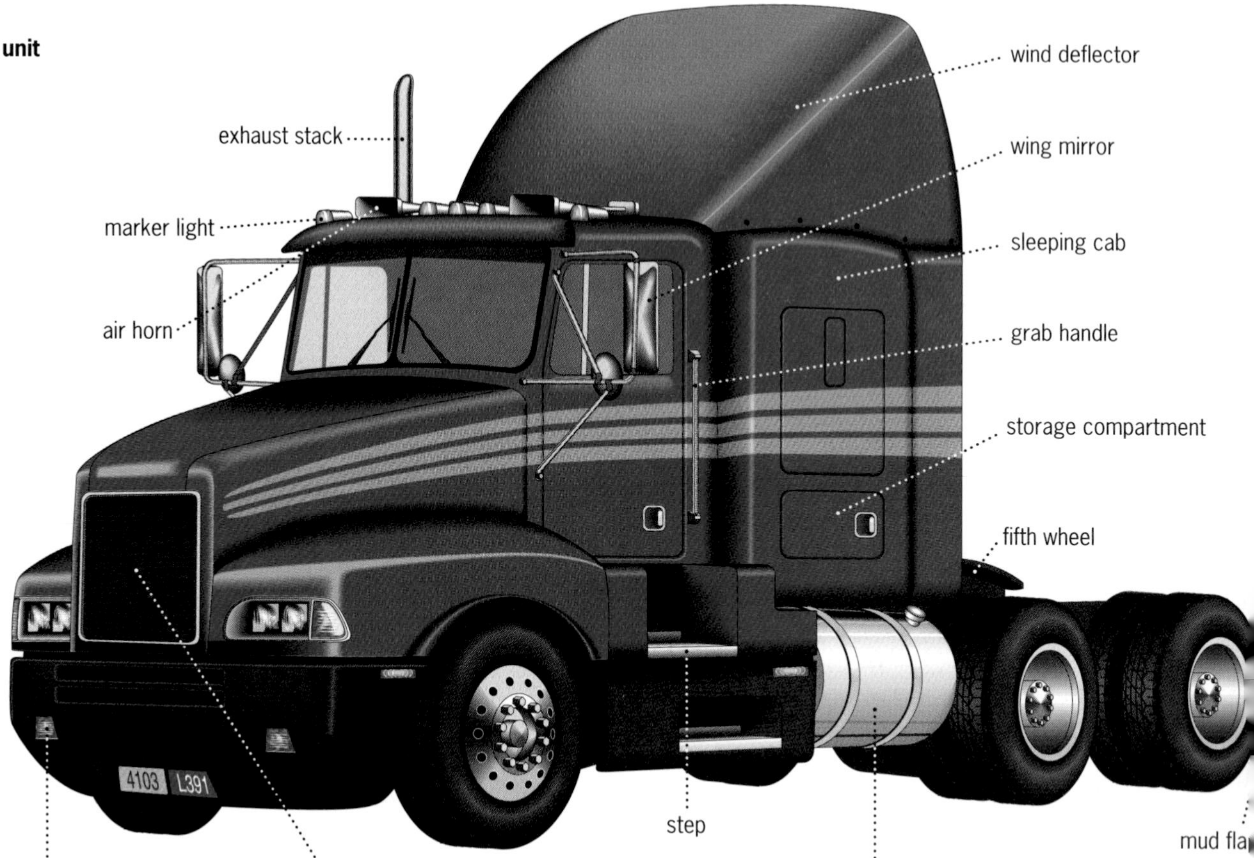
wind deflector
exhaust stack
wing mirror
marker light
sleeping cab
air horn
grab handle
storage compartment
fifth wheel
4103 L391
step
mud fla
fog light
radiator grille
fuel tank

petrol station

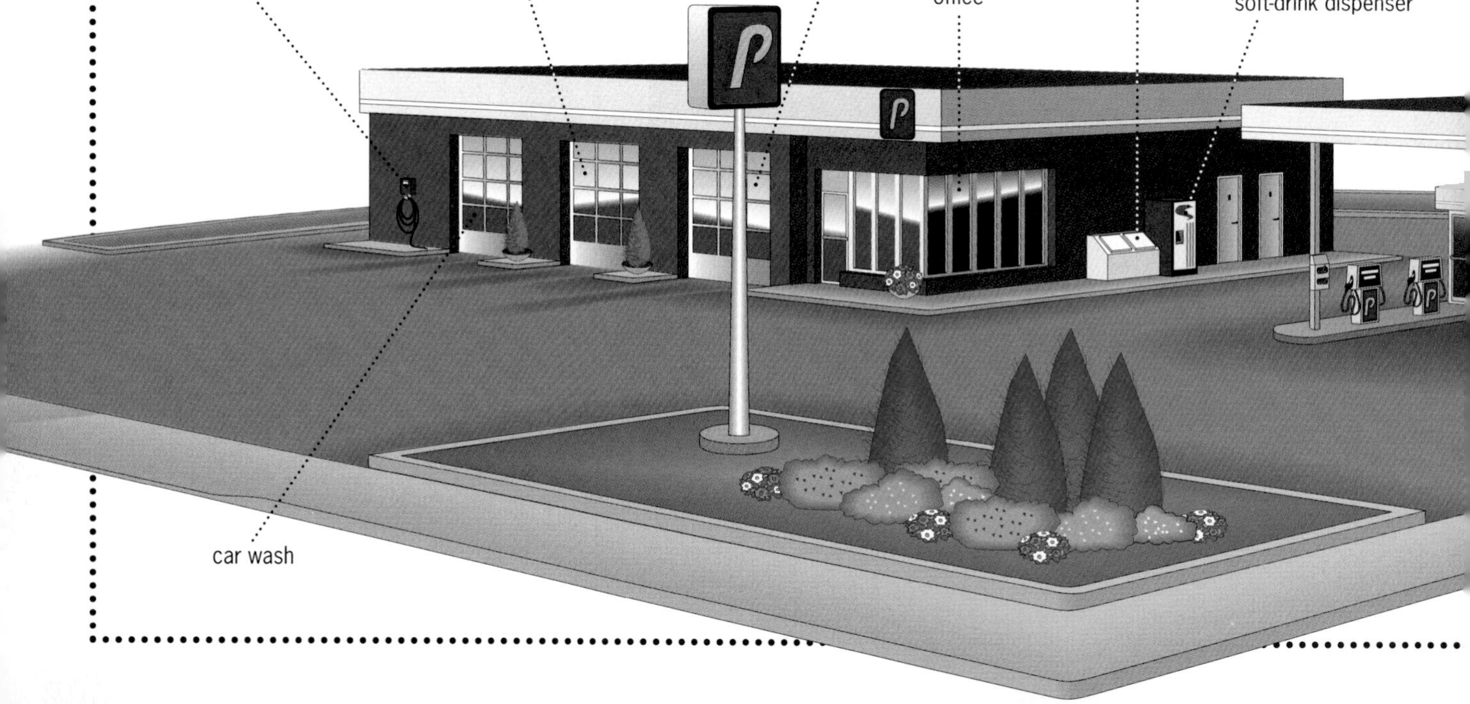
maintenance area
litter bin
air–pressure hose
repair shop
office
soft-drink dispenser
car wash

MOTORCYCLE

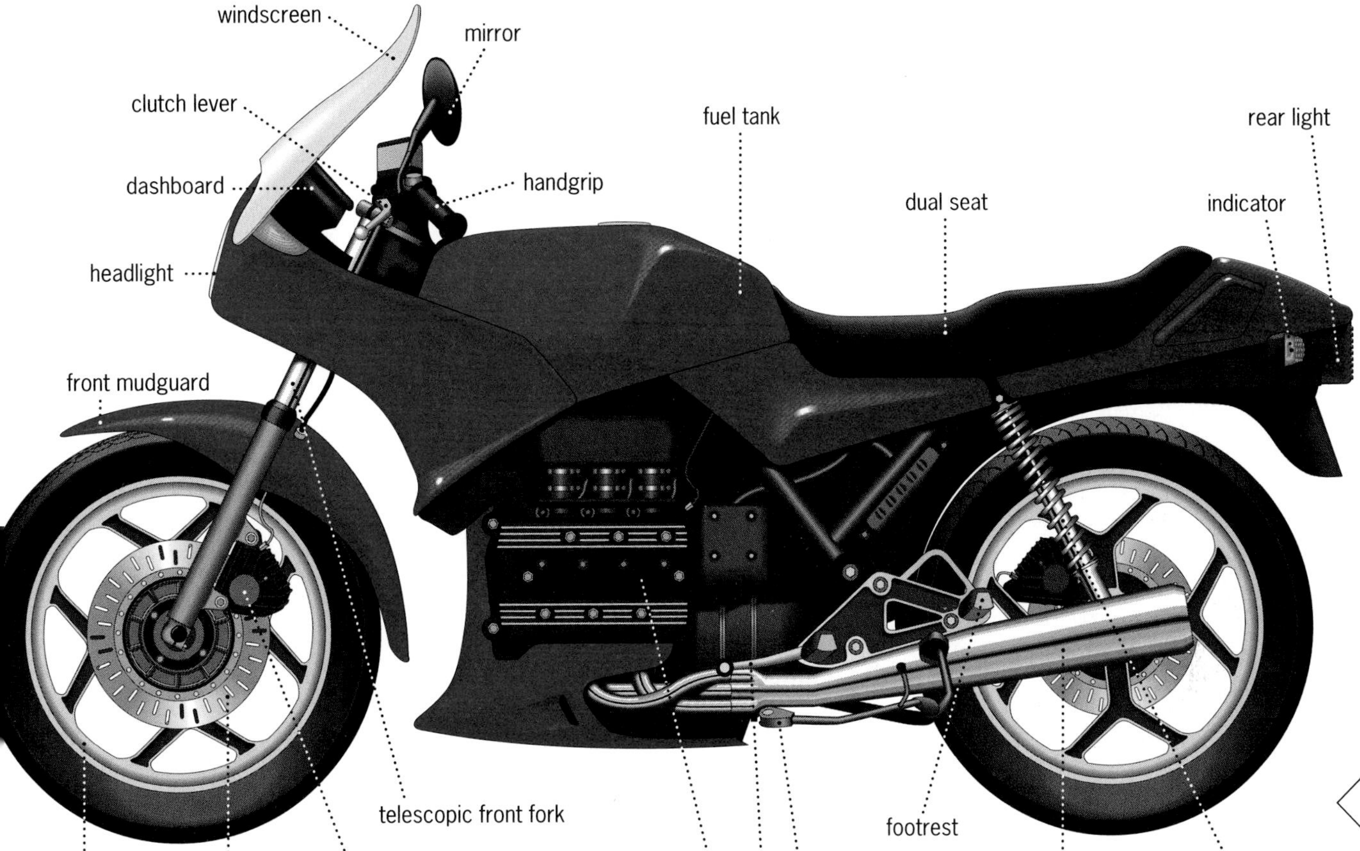
windscreen
mirror
clutch lever
fuel tank
rear light
dashboard
handgrip
dual seat
indicator
headlight
front mudguard
telescopic front fork
footrest
rear shock absorber
rim
brake caliper
engine
stand
disc brake
gearchange pedal
silencer

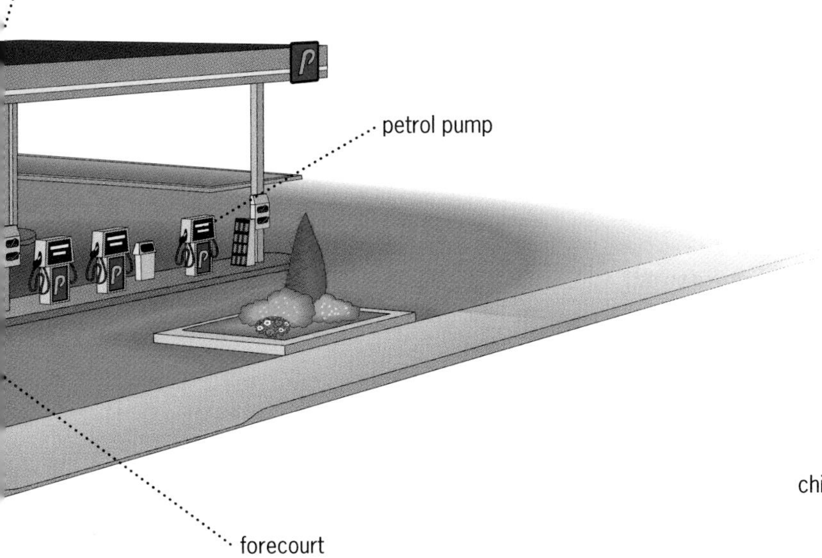
iosk
petrol pump
forecourt

protective helmet; crash helmet

bubble
visor
chin protector

BICYCLE

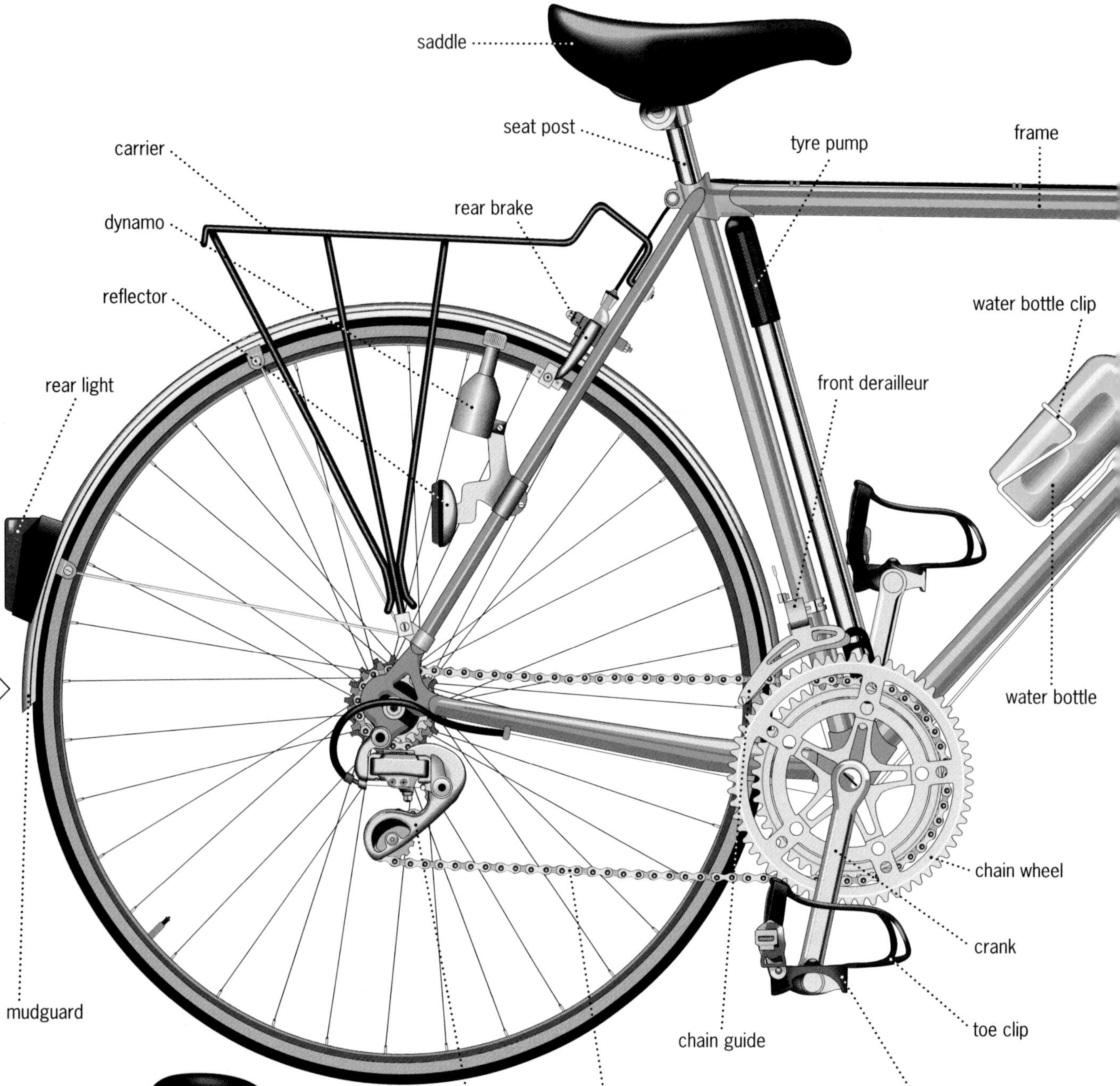
saddle
seat post
carrier
tyre pump
frame
rear brake
dynamo
reflector
water bottle clip
front derailleur
rear light
water bottle
chain wheel
crank
mudguard
toe clip
chain guide
pedal
rear derailleur
drive chain

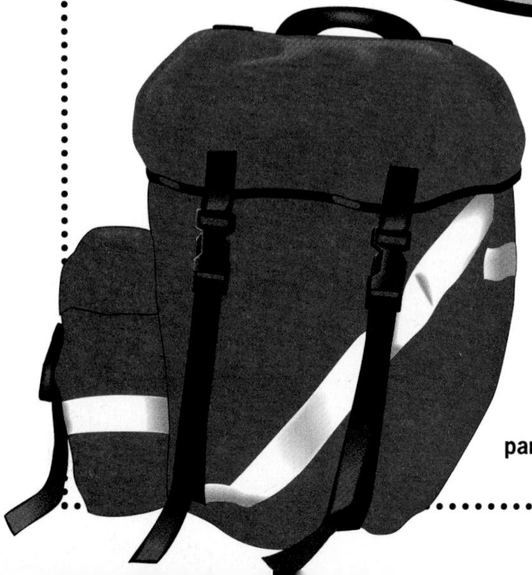

pannier bag

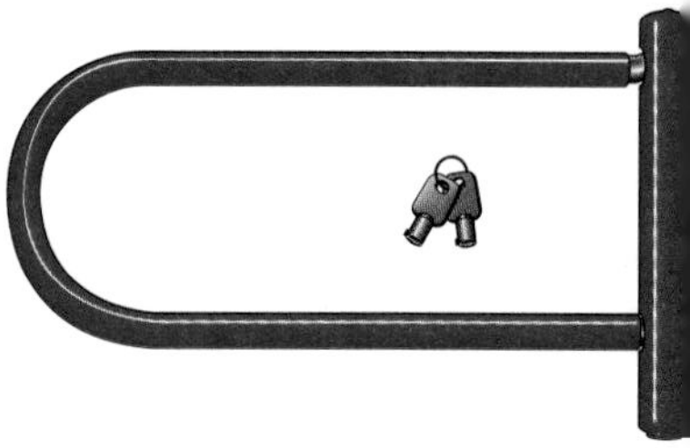

loc

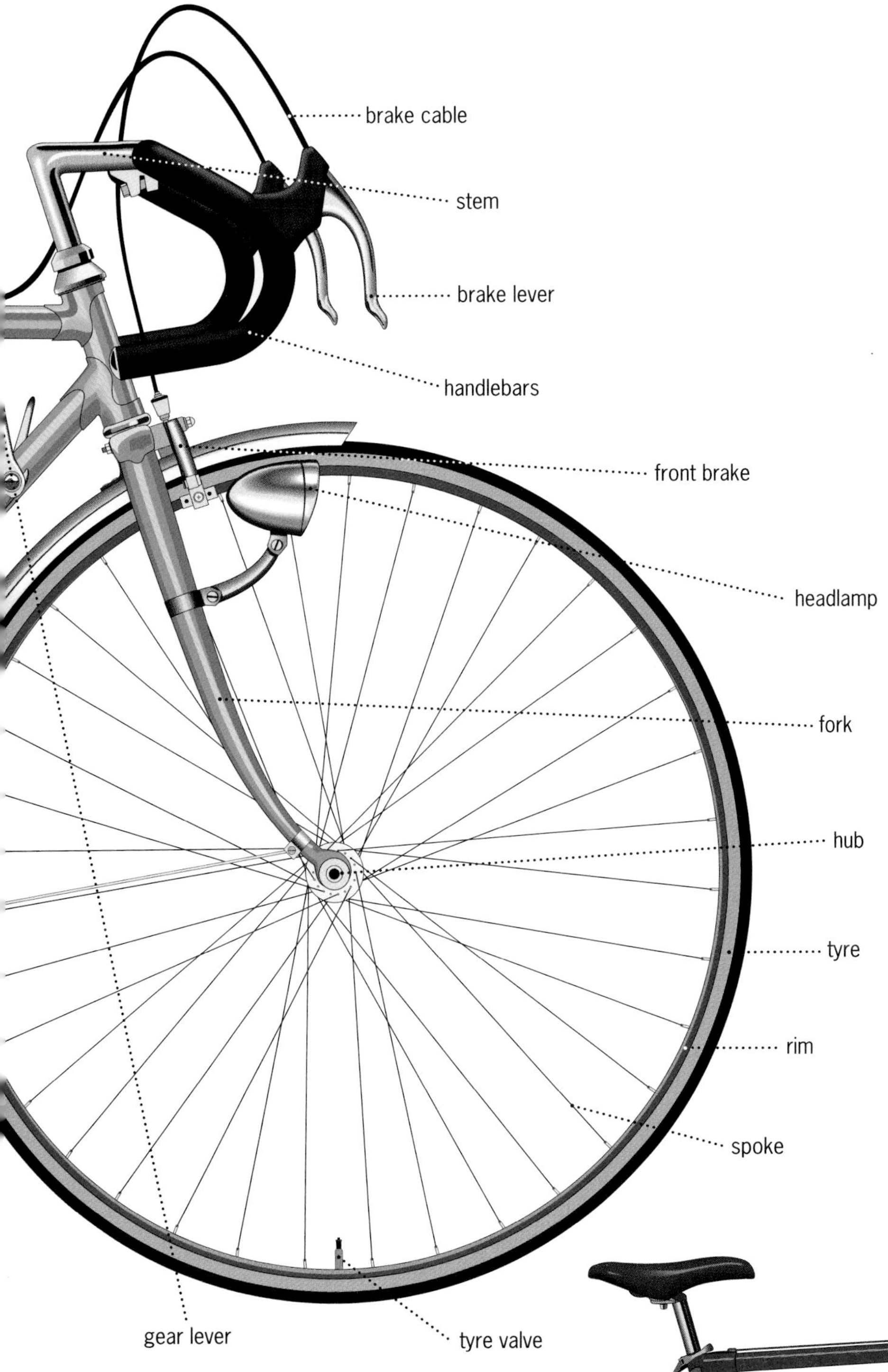
brake cable
stem
brake lever
handlebars
front brake
headlamp
fork
hub
tyre
rim
spoke
gear lever
tyre valve

protective helmet

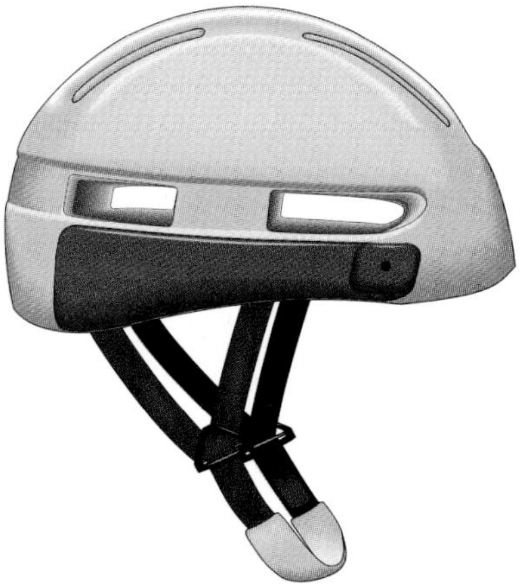

mountain bike

DIESEL-ELECTRIC LOCOMOTIVE

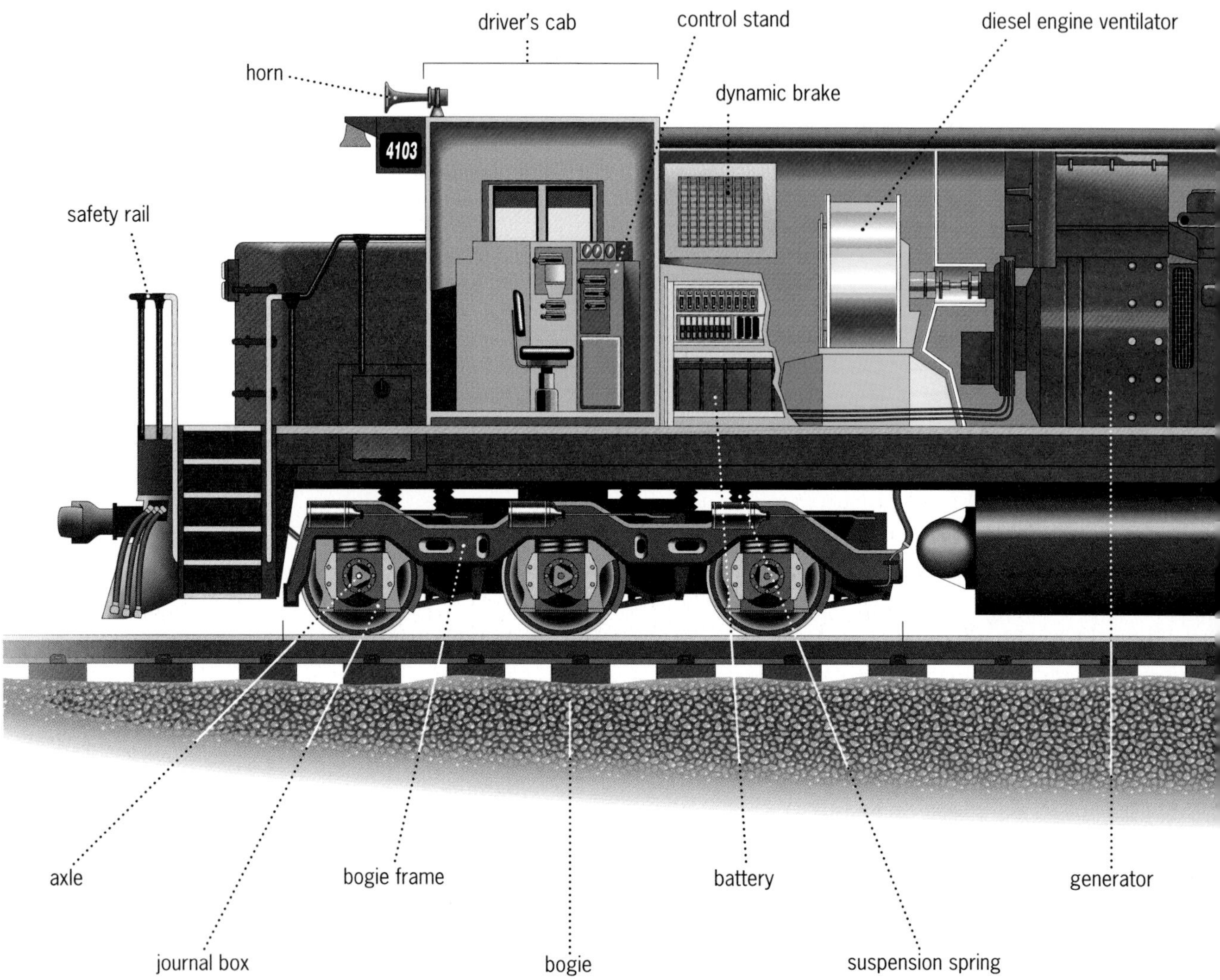
driver's cab
control stand
diesel engine ventilator
horn
dynamic brake
4103
safety rail
axle
bogie frame
battery
generator
journal box
bogie
suspension spring

TYPES OF FREIGHT WAGONS

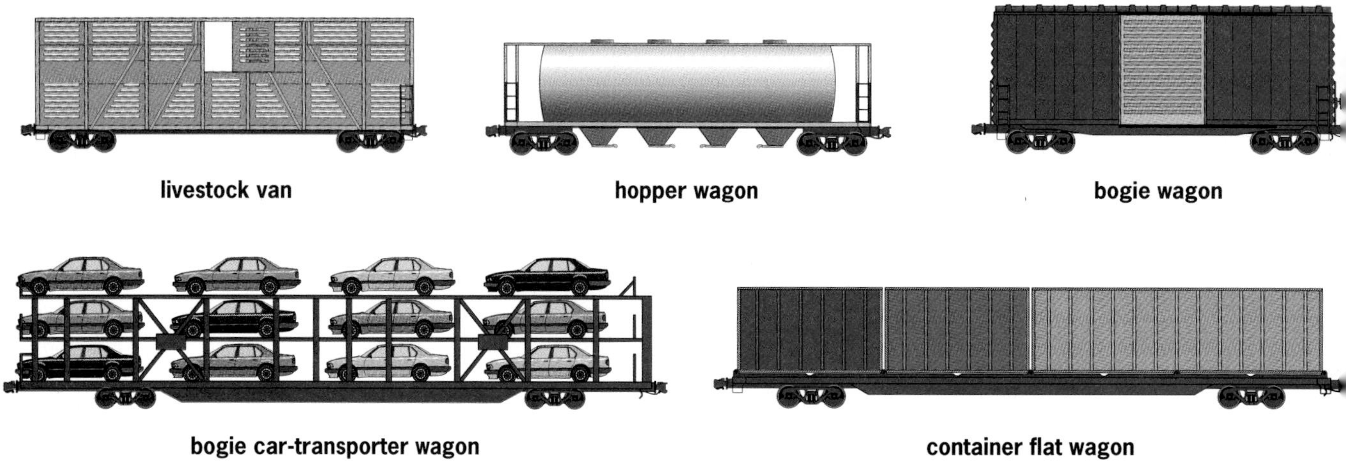
livestock van
hopper wagon
bogie wagon
bogie car-transporter wagon
container flat wagon

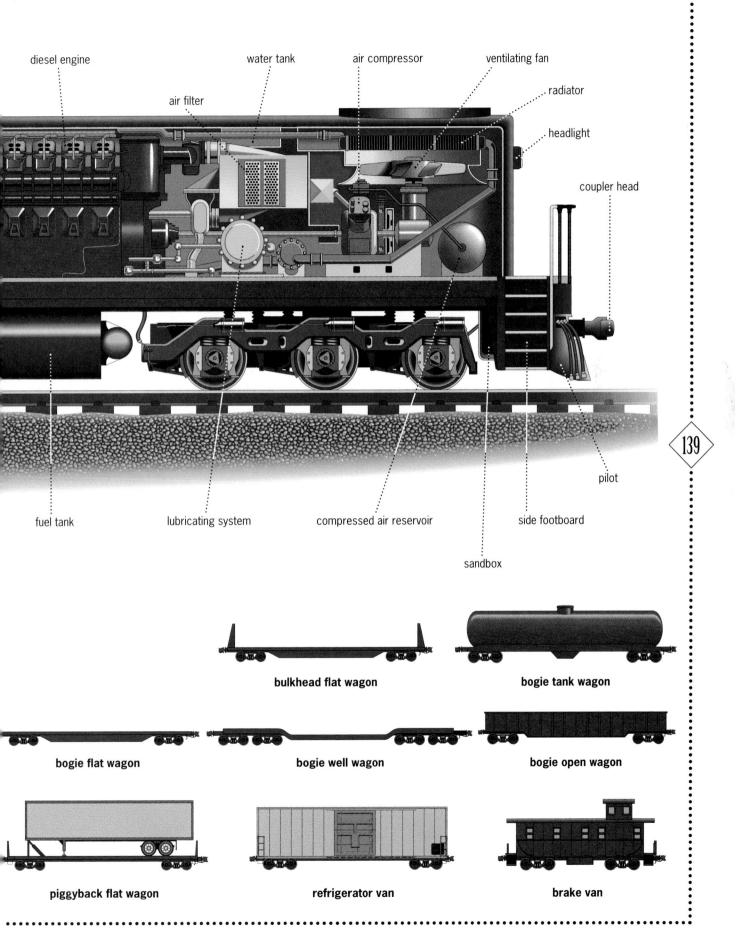

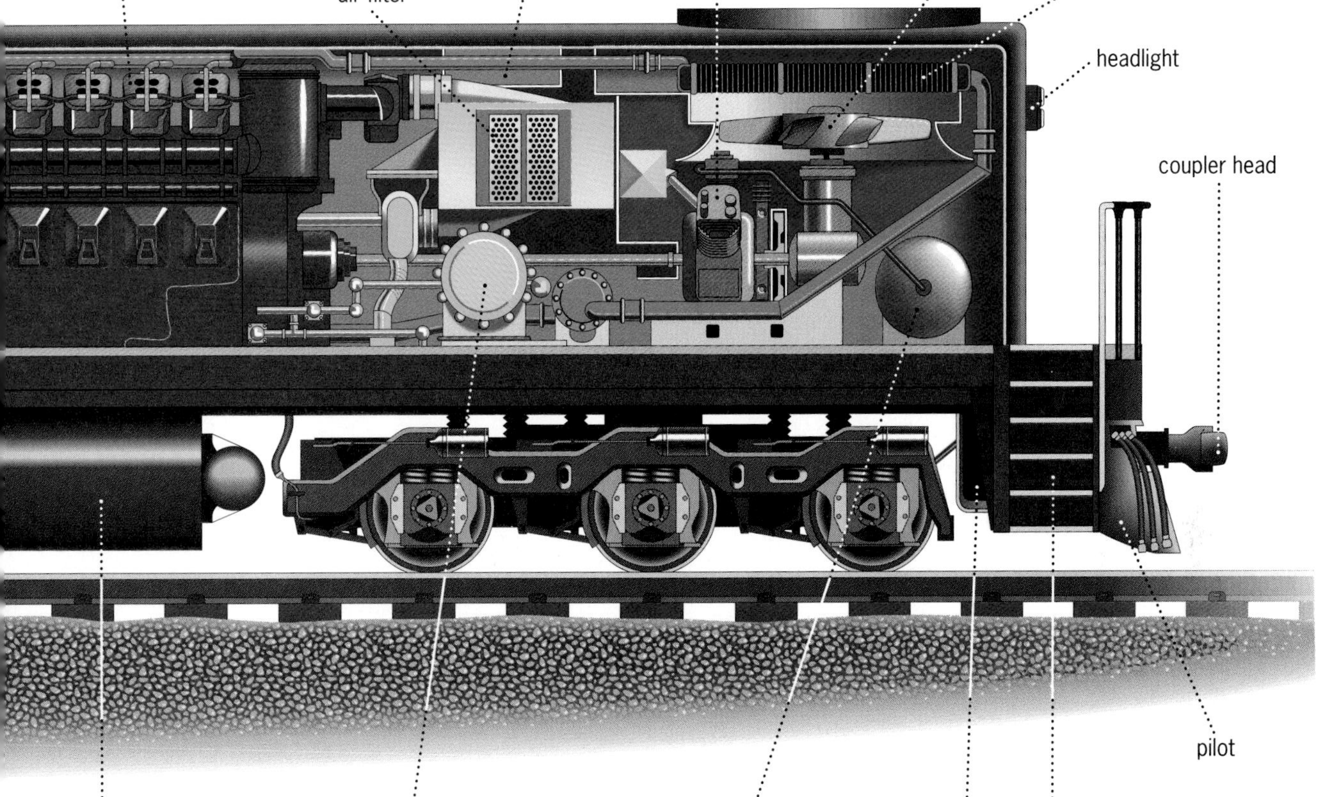
diesel engine
water tank
air compressor
ventilating fan
air filter
radiator
headlight
coupler head
pilot
fuel tank
lubricating system
compressed air reservoir
side footboard
sandbox

bulkhead flat wagon

bogie tank wagon

bogie flat wagon

bogie well wagon

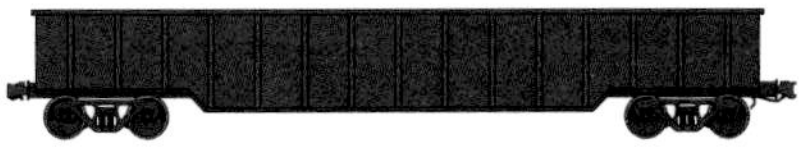

bogie open wagon

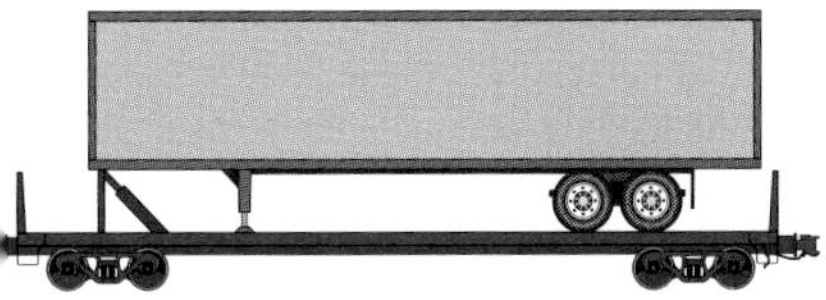

piggyback flat wagon

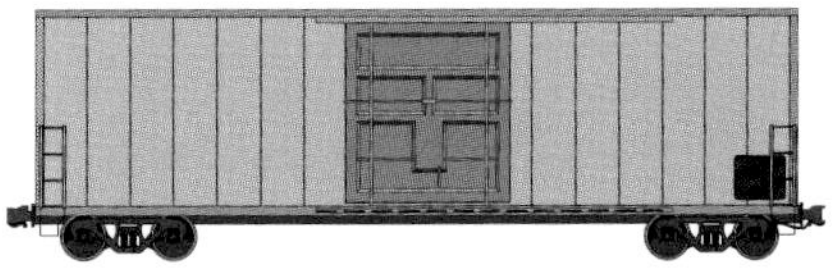

refrigerator van

brake van

LEVEL CROSSING

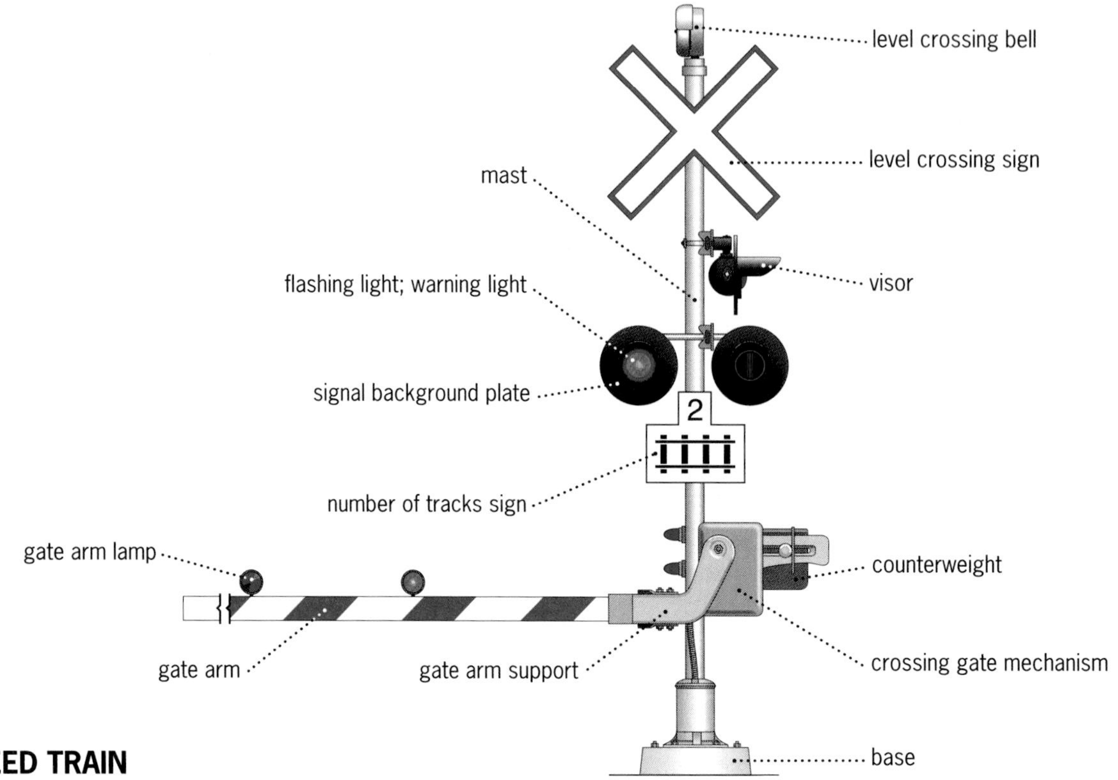
level crossing bell
level crossing sign
mast
visor
flashing light; warning light
signal background plate
2
number of tracks sign
gate arm lamp
counterweight
gate arm
gate arm support
crossing gate mechanism
base

HIGH-SPEED TRAIN

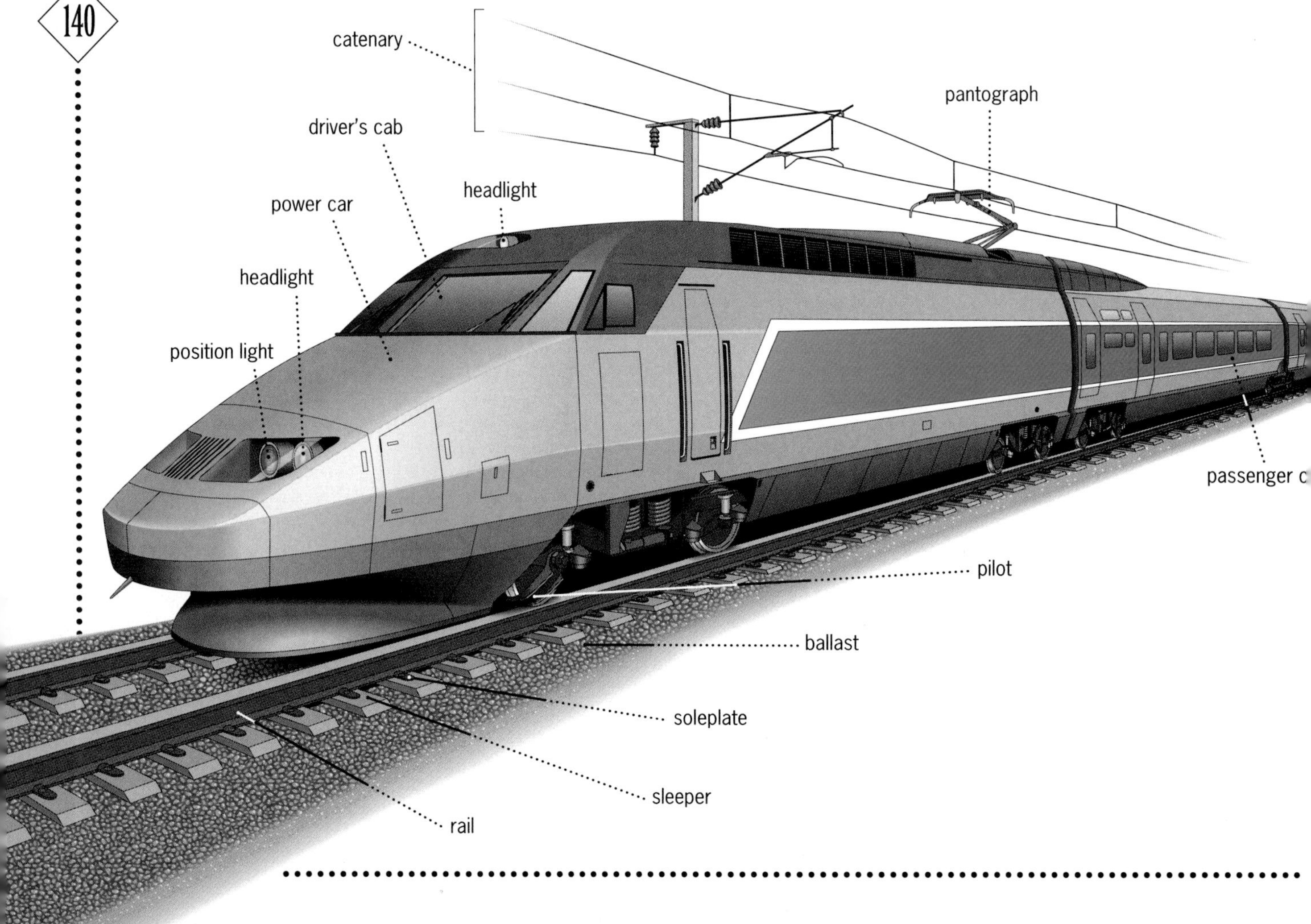
catenary
pantograph
driver's cab
power car
headlight
headlight
position light
passenger c
pilot
ballast
soleplate
sleeper
rail

FOUR-MASTED BARQUE

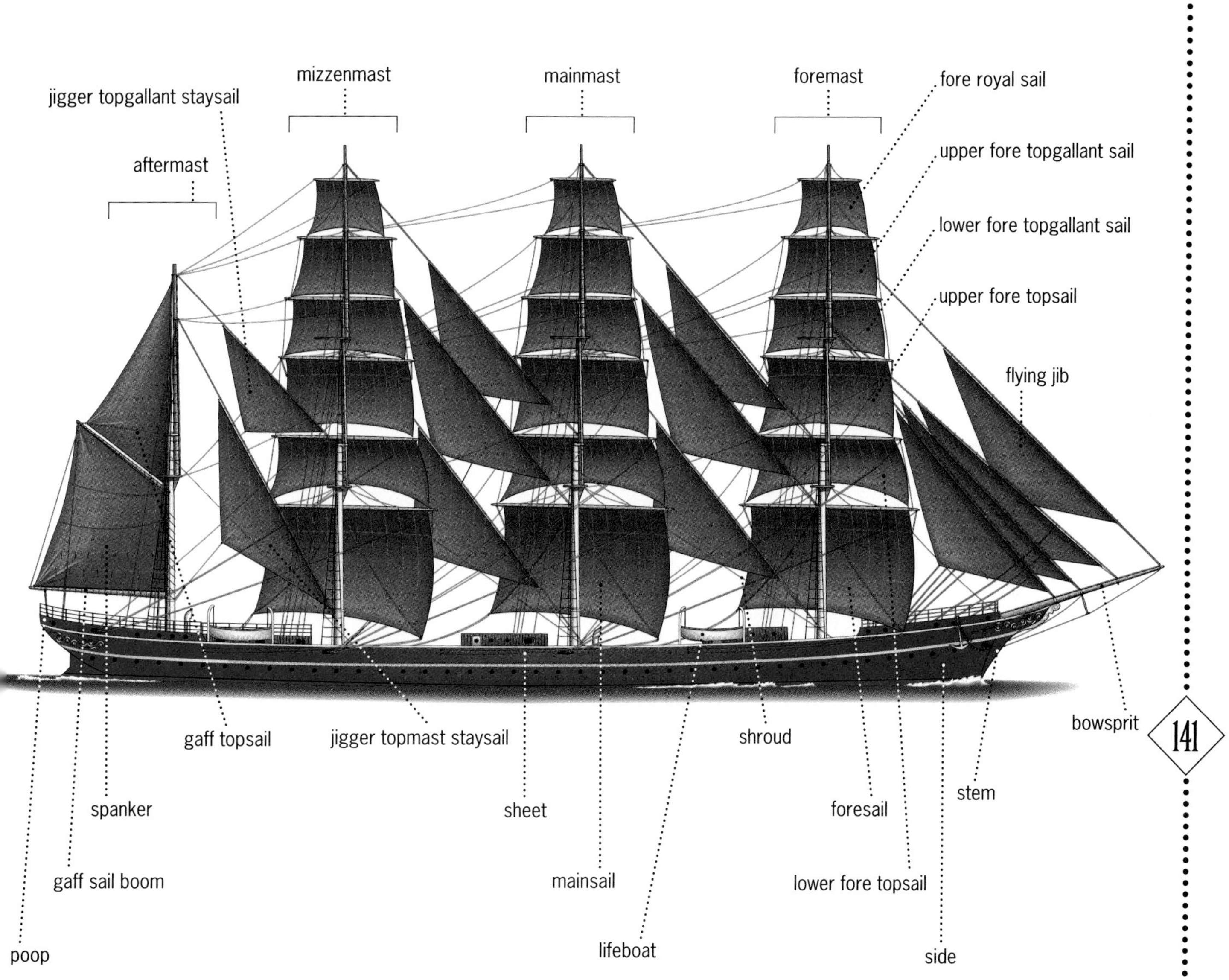
mizzenmast
mainmast
foremast
jigger topgallant staysail
aftermast
fore royal sail
upper fore topgallant sail
lower fore topgallant sail
upper fore topsail
flying jib
gaff topsail
jigger topmast staysail
shroud
bowsprit
spanker
sheet
foresail
stem
gaff sail boom
mainsail
lower fore topsail
poop
lifeboat
side

HOVERCRAFT

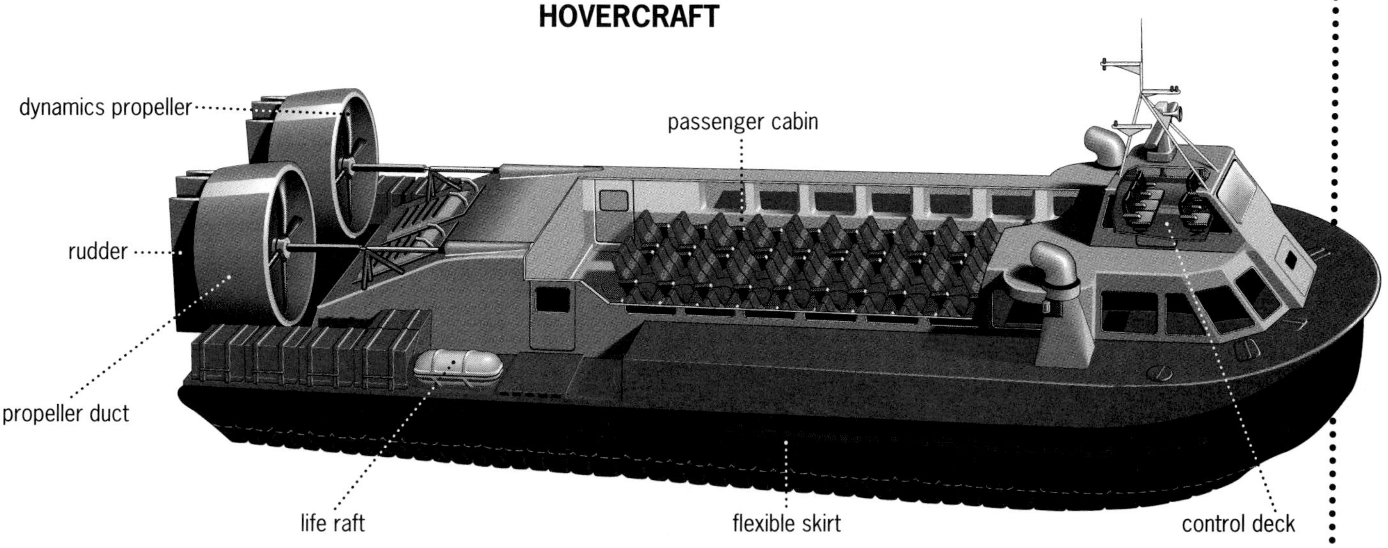
dynamics propeller
passenger cabin
rudder
propeller duct
life raft
flexible skirt
control deck

CRUISE LINER

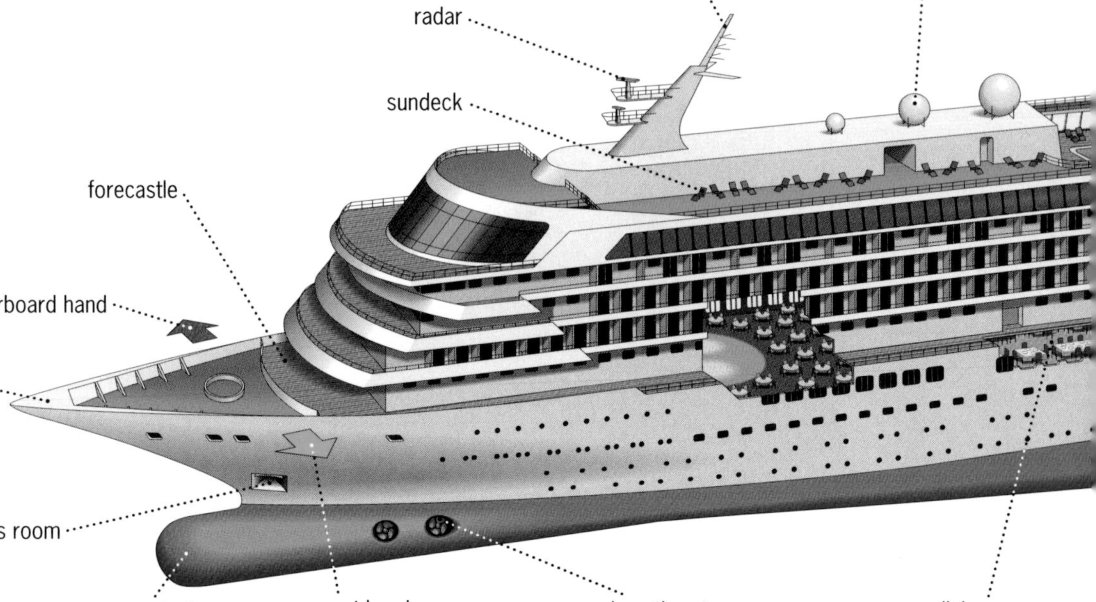
radio aerial
telecommunication aerial
radar
sundeck
forecastle
starboard hand
bow
anchor-windlass room
stem bulb
port hand
bow thruster
dining room

HARBOUR

bulk terminal
container-loading bridge
dry dock
quay
grain terminal
canal lock
silos
floating crane
container ship

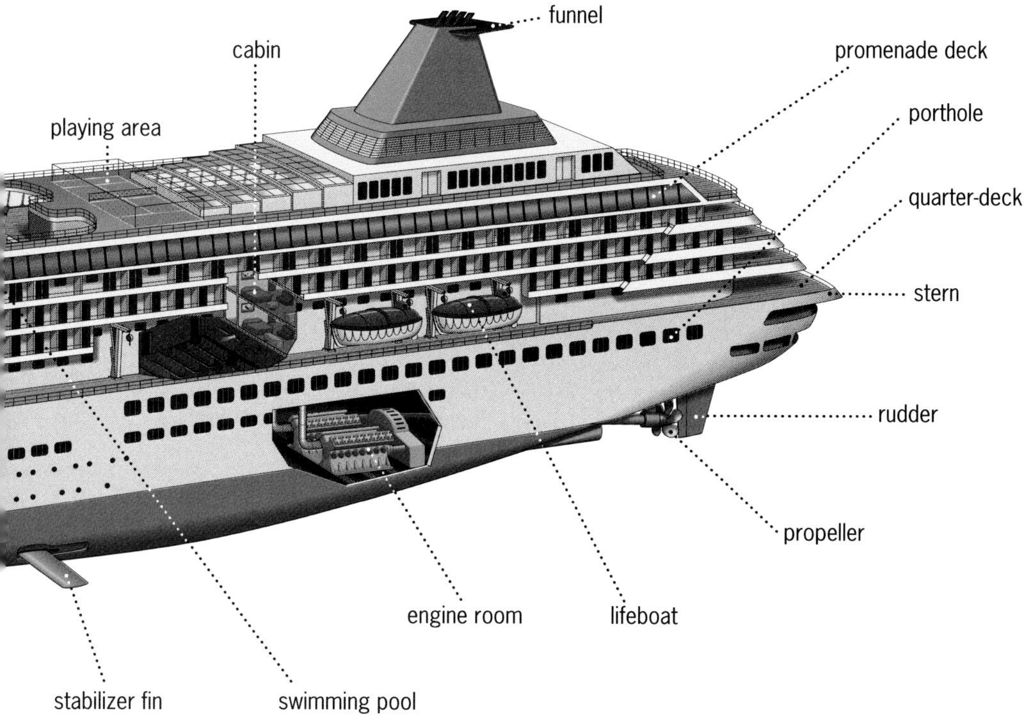
funnel
cabin
promenade deck
playing area
porthole
quarter-deck
stern
rudder
propeller
engine room
lifeboat
stabilizer fin
swimming pool

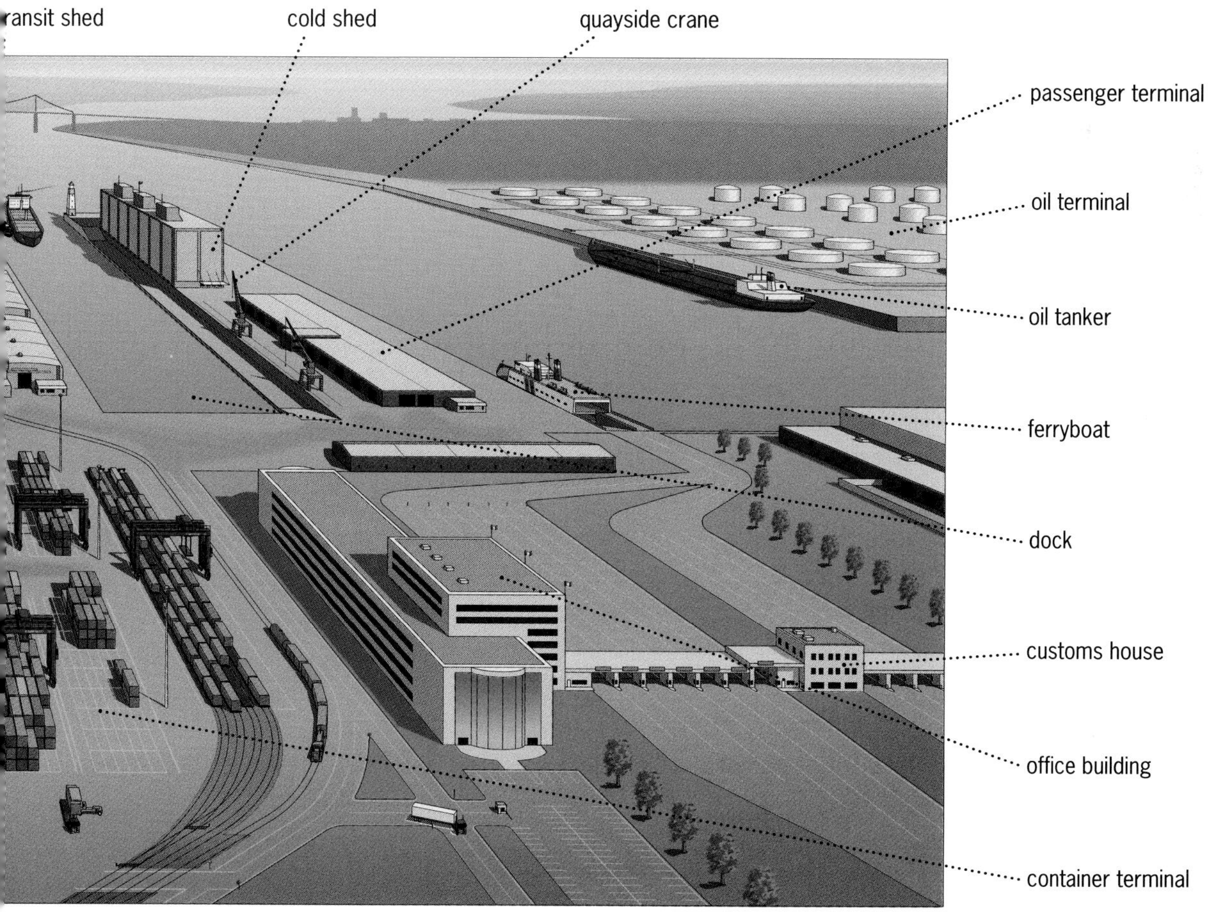
ransit shed
cold shed
quayside crane
passenger terminal
oil terminal
oil tanker
ferryboat
dock
customs house
office building
container terminal

PLANE

TYPES OF WING SHAPES

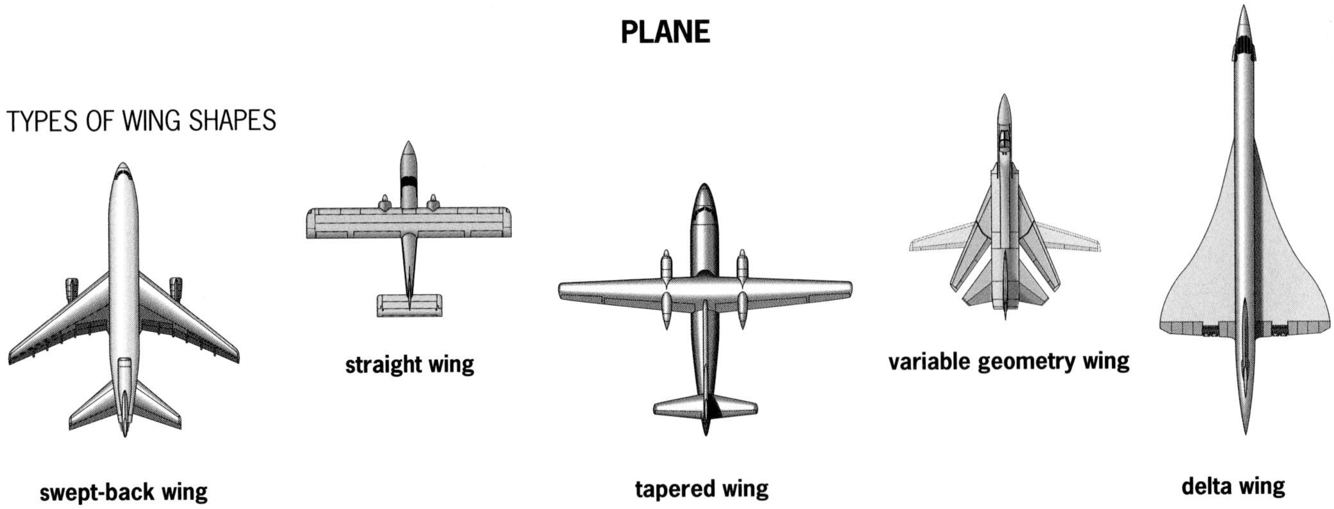
swept-back wing
straight wing
tapered wing
variable geometry wing
delta wing

long-range jet

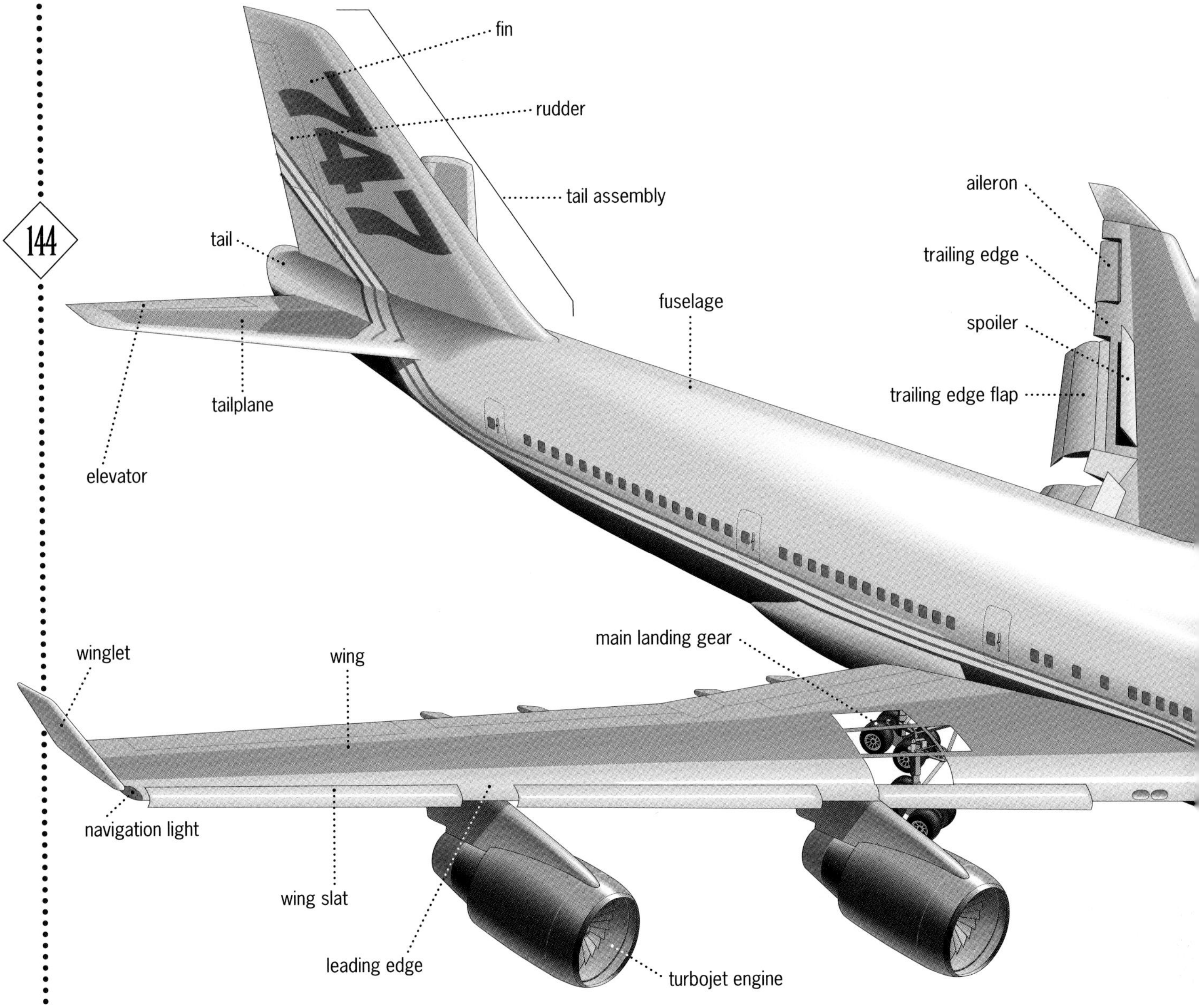
fin
rudder
tail assembly
tail
tailplane
elevator
fuselage
aileron
trailing edge
spoiler
trailing edge flap
winglet
wing
main landing gear
navigation light
wing slat
leading edge
turbojet engine

HELICOPTER

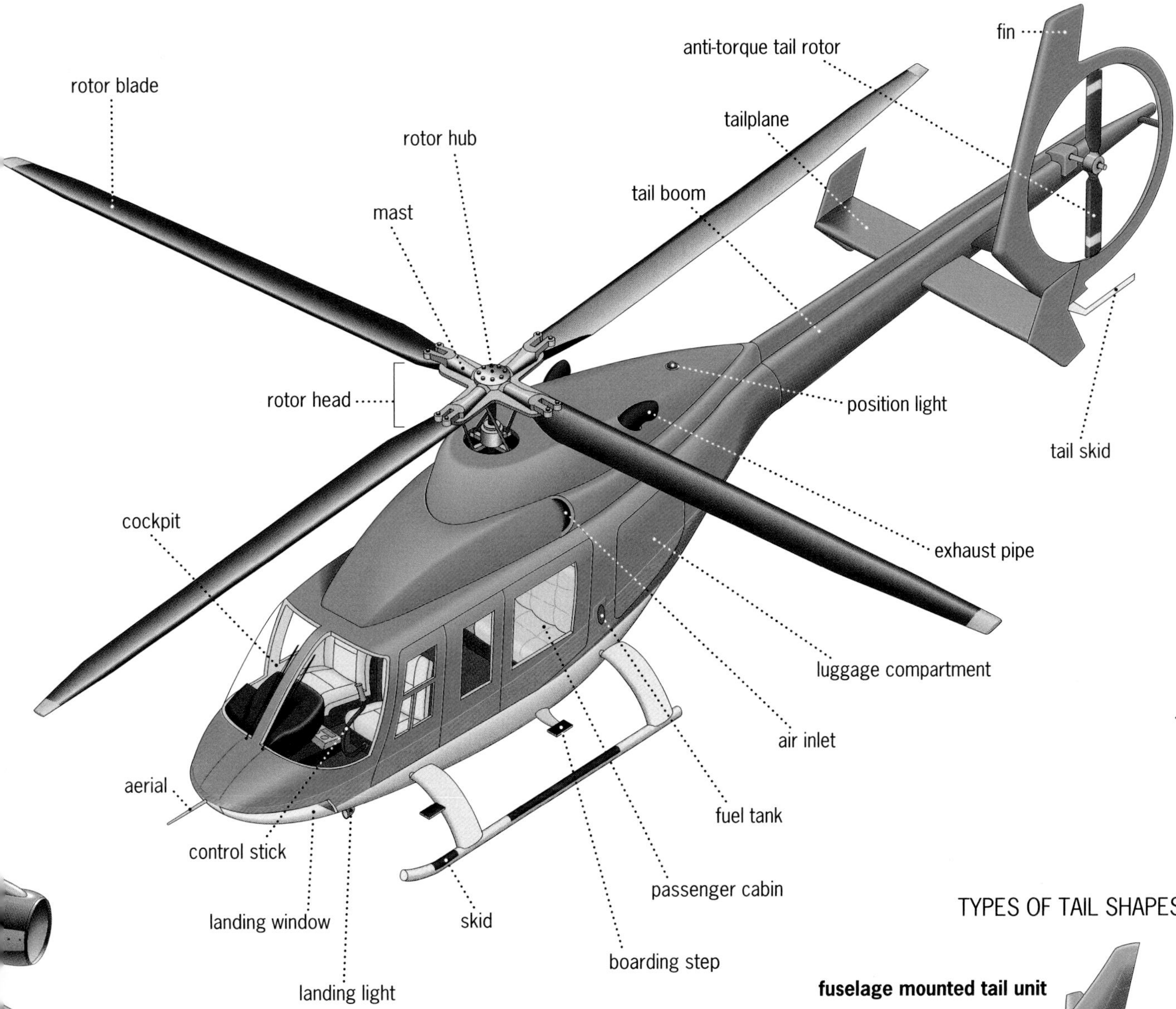
fin
anti-torque tail rotor
rotor blade
tailplane
rotor hub
tail boom
mast
rotor head
position light
tail skid
cockpit
exhaust pipe
luggage compartment
air inlet
aerial
fuel tank
control stick
passenger cabin
landing window
skid
boarding step
landing light

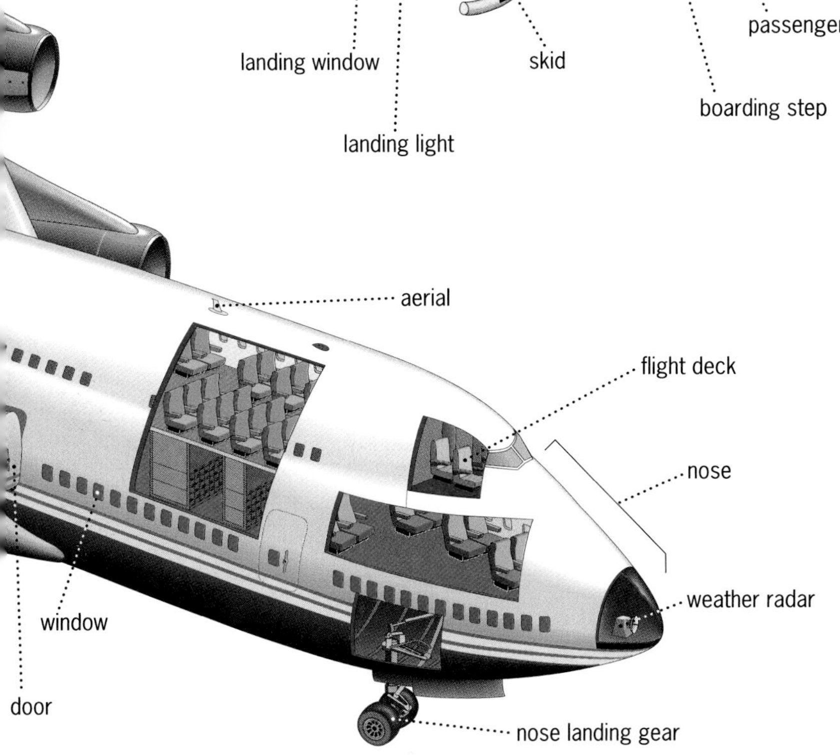
aerial
flight deck
nose
weather radar
window
door
nose landing gear

TYPES OF TAIL SHAPES

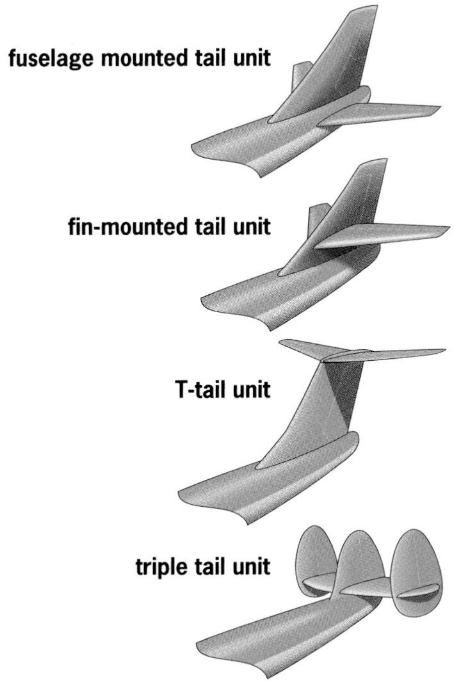
fuselage mounted tail unit
fin-mounted tail unit
T-tail unit
triple tail unit

AIRPORT

control tower
control tower cab
access road
high-speed exit runway
by-pass runway
apron
apron
service road
runway

AIRPORT GROUND EQUIPMENT

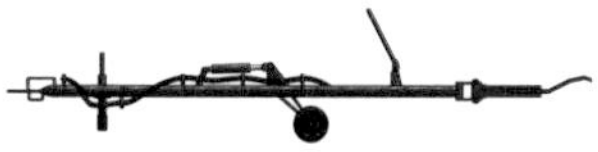

tow bar

tow lorry

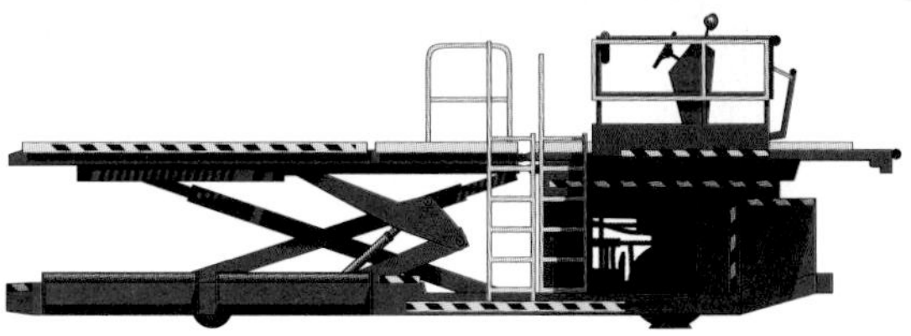

container/pallet loader

universal step

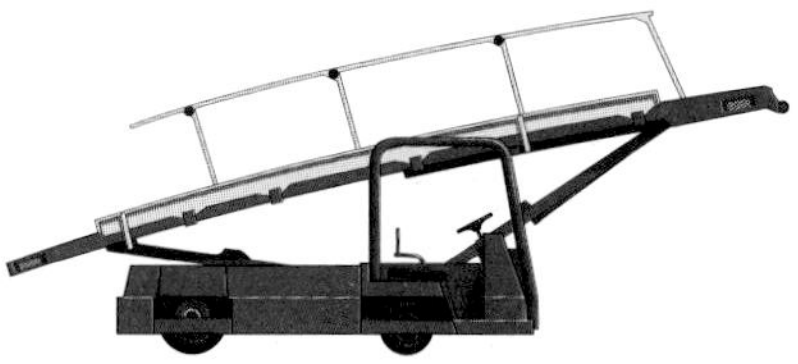

baggage transporter

wheel chock

127

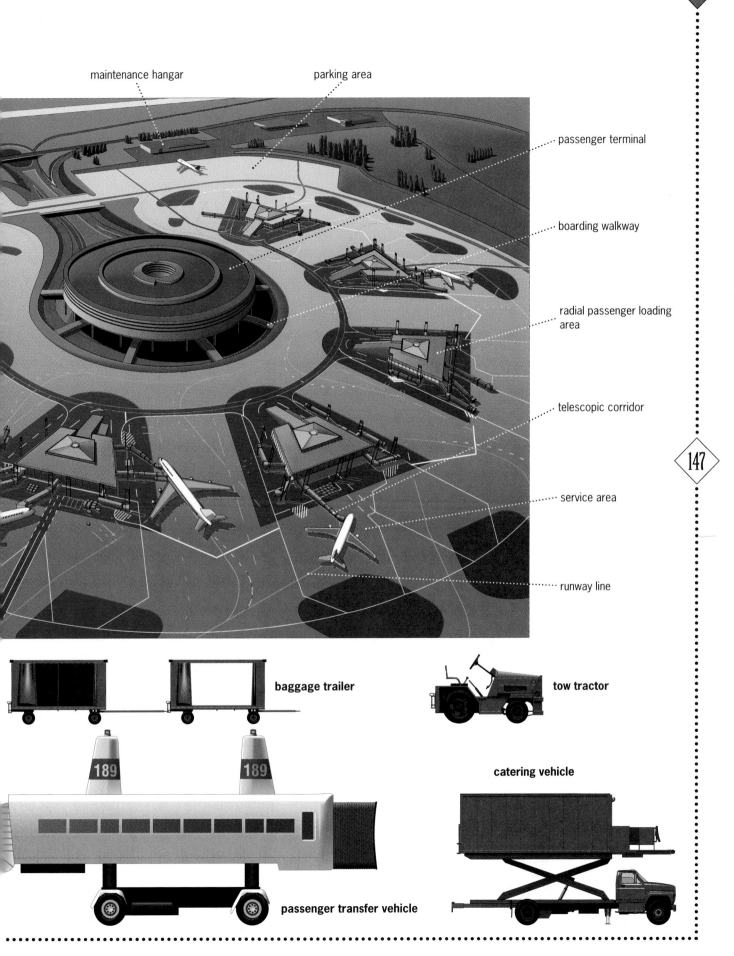

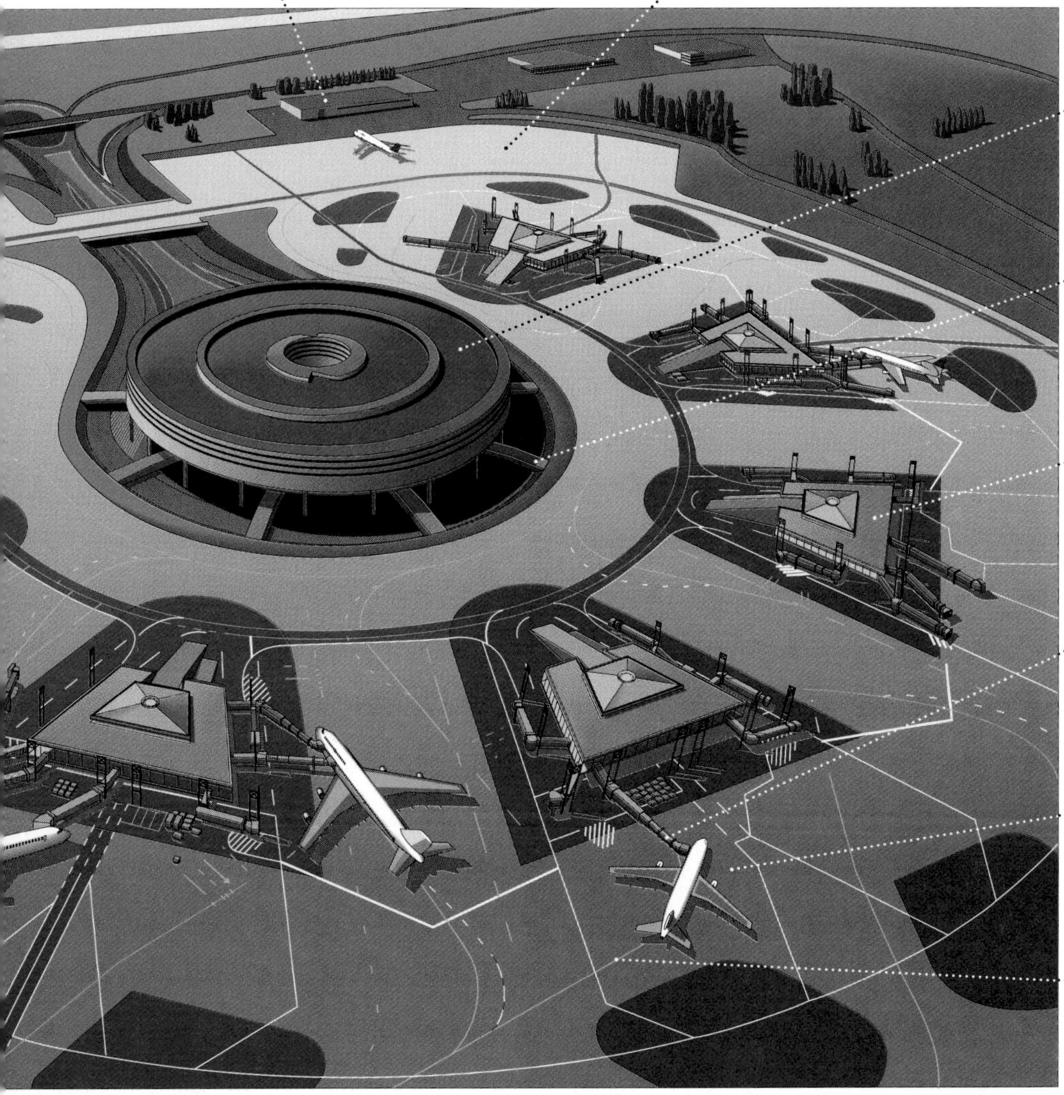
maintenance hangar
parking area
passenger terminal
boarding walkway
radial passenger loading area
telescopic corridor
service area
runway line

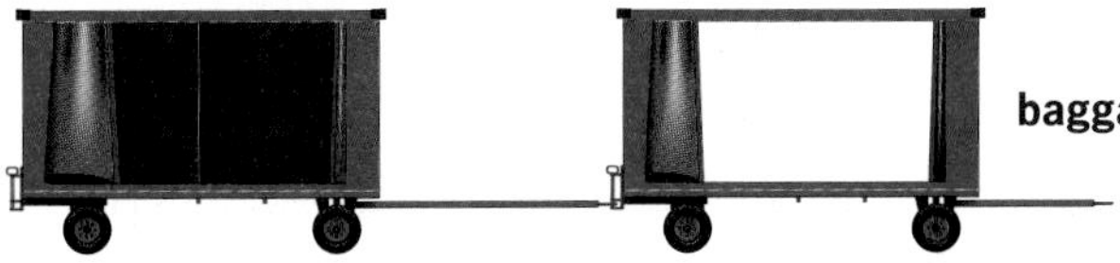
baggage trailer

tow tractor

189
189
passenger transfer vehicle

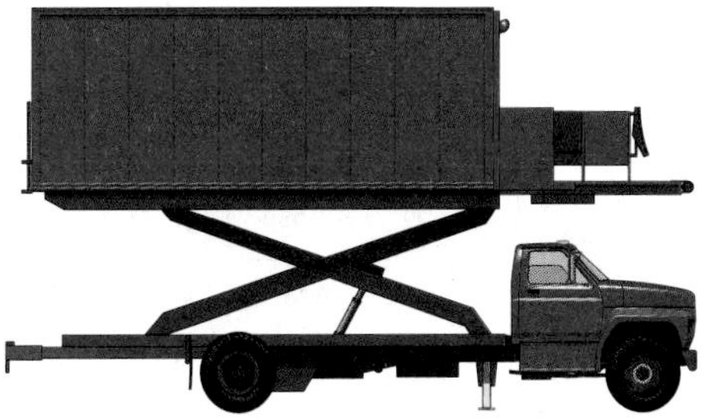
catering vehicle

SPACE SHUTTLE

space shuttle at takeoff

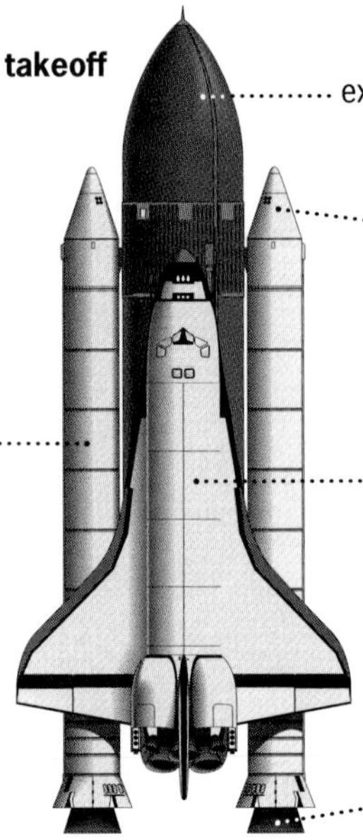
external tank
booster parachute
solid rocket booster
shuttle
nozzle

space shuttle in orbit

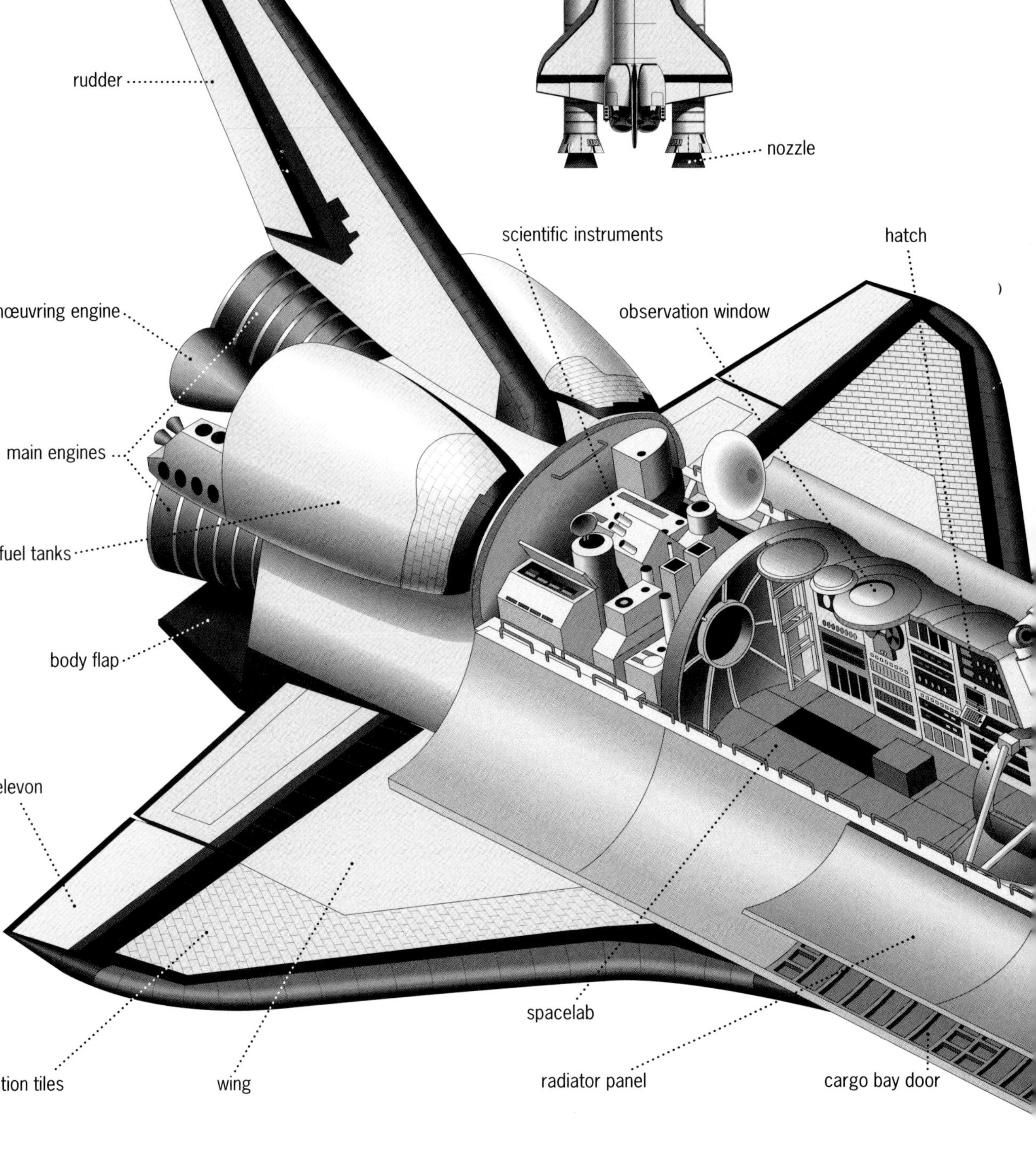
rudder
scientific instruments
hatch
observation window
manœuvring engine
main engines
fuel tanks
body flap
elevon
spacelab
insulation tiles
wing
radiator panel
cargo bay door

SPACESUIT

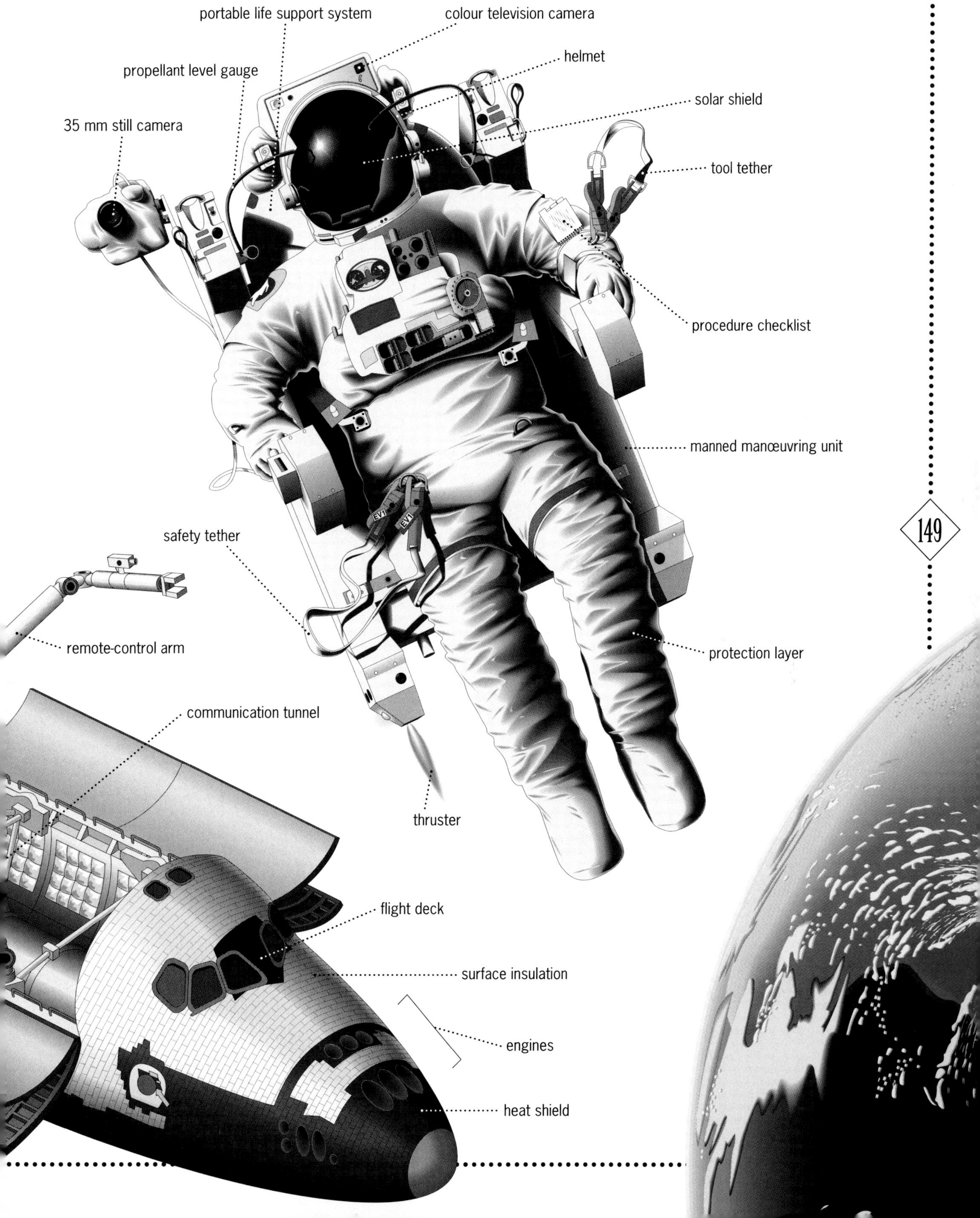
portable life support system
colour television camera
helmet
propellant level gauge
solar shield
35 mm still camera
tool tether
procedure checklist
manned manœuvring unit
safety tether
remote-control arm
protection layer
communication tunnel
thruster
flight deck
surface insulation
engines
heat shield

SCHOOL SUPPLIES

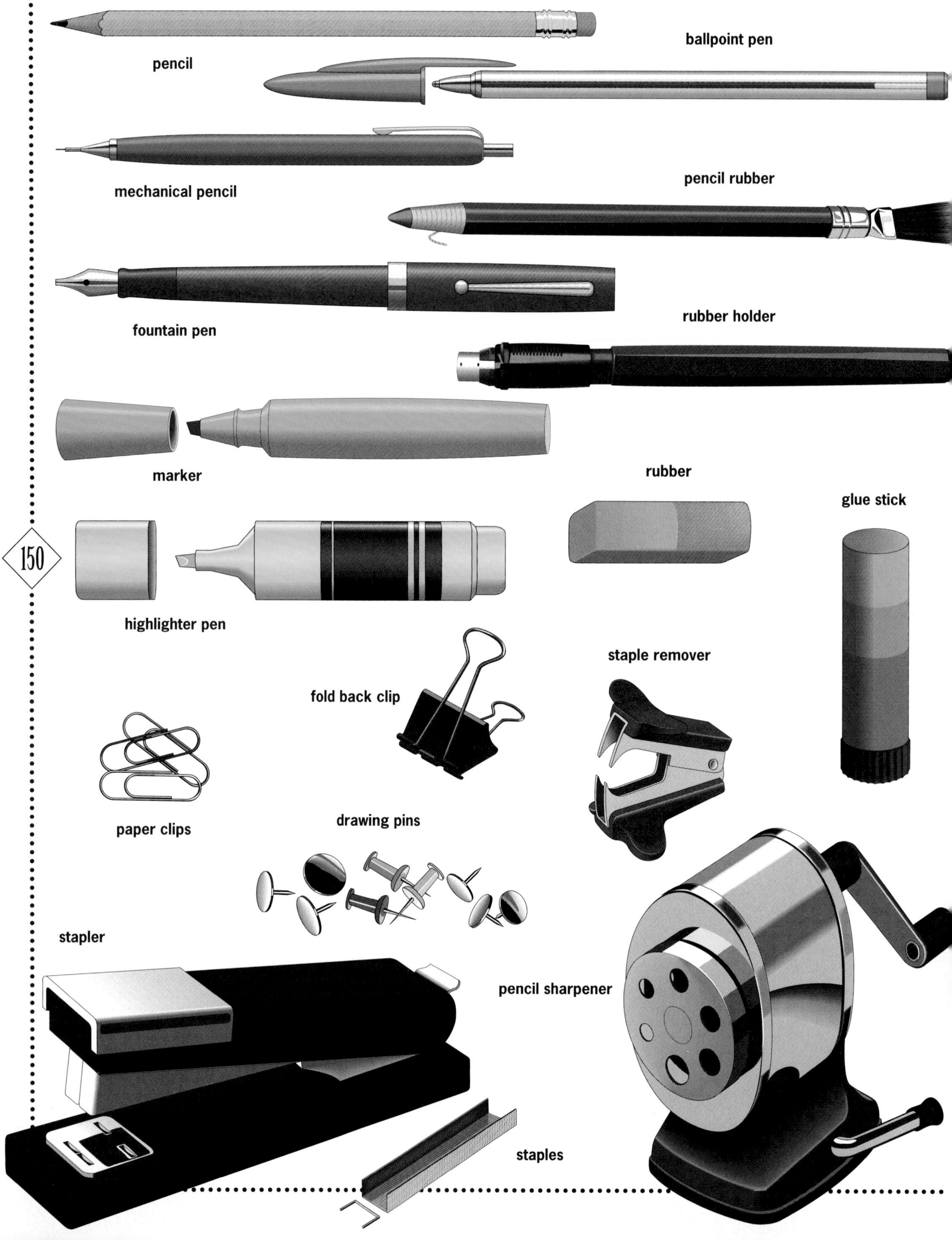
pencil
ballpoint pen
mechanical pencil
pencil rubber
fountain pen
rubber holder
marker
rubber
glue stick
highlighter pen
staple remover
fold back clip
paper clips
drawing pins
stapler
pencil sharpener
staples

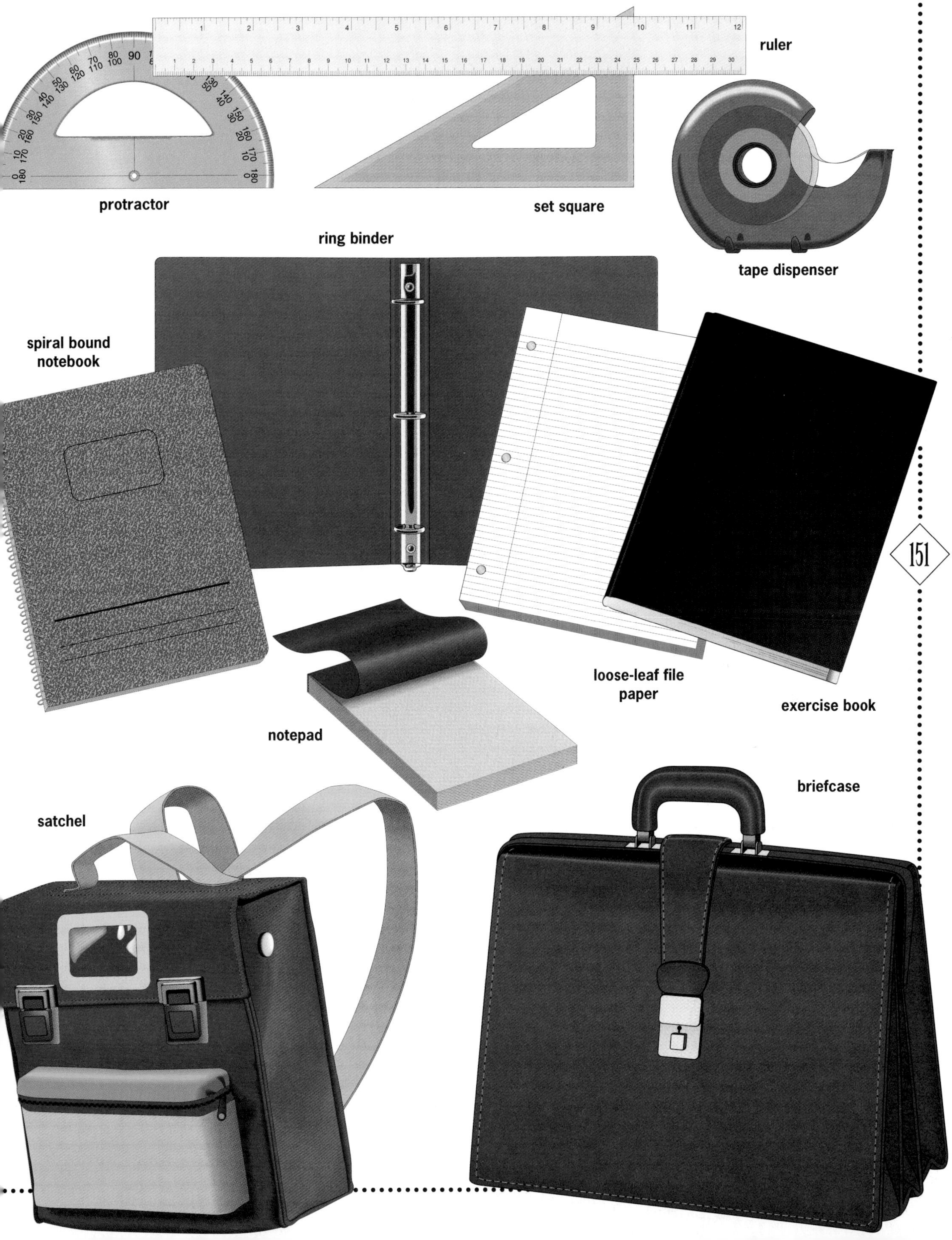
ruler
protractor
set square
tape dispenser
ring binder
spiral bound notebook
loose-leaf file paper
exercise book
notepad
briefcase
satchel

SCHOOL EQUIPMENT

blackboard

a b c
1 2 3

overhead projector

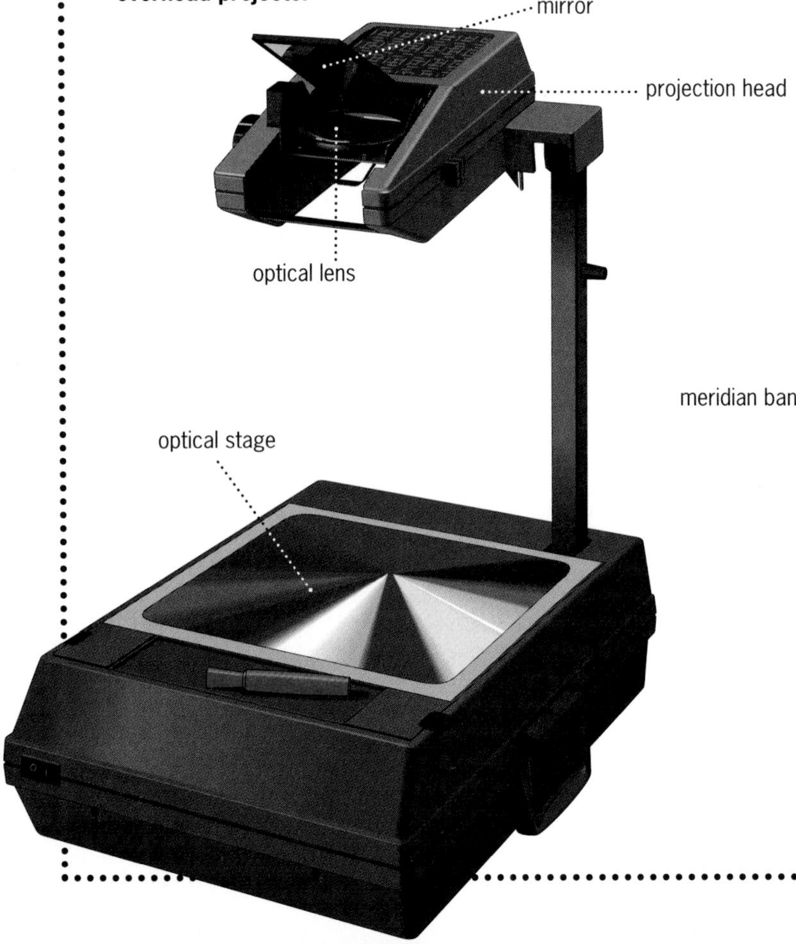
mirror
projection head
optical lens
optical stage

globe of Earth

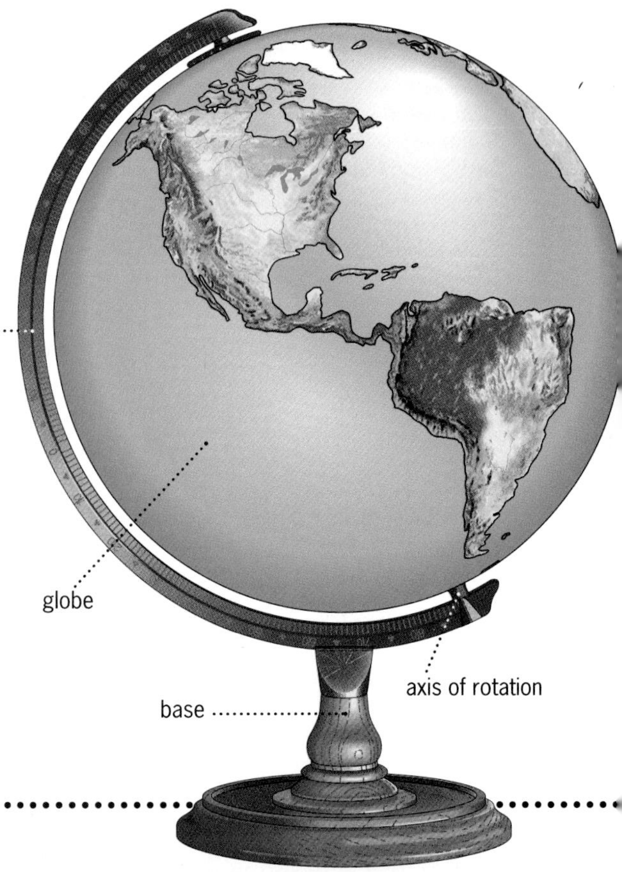
meridian band
globe
axis of rotation
base

slide projector

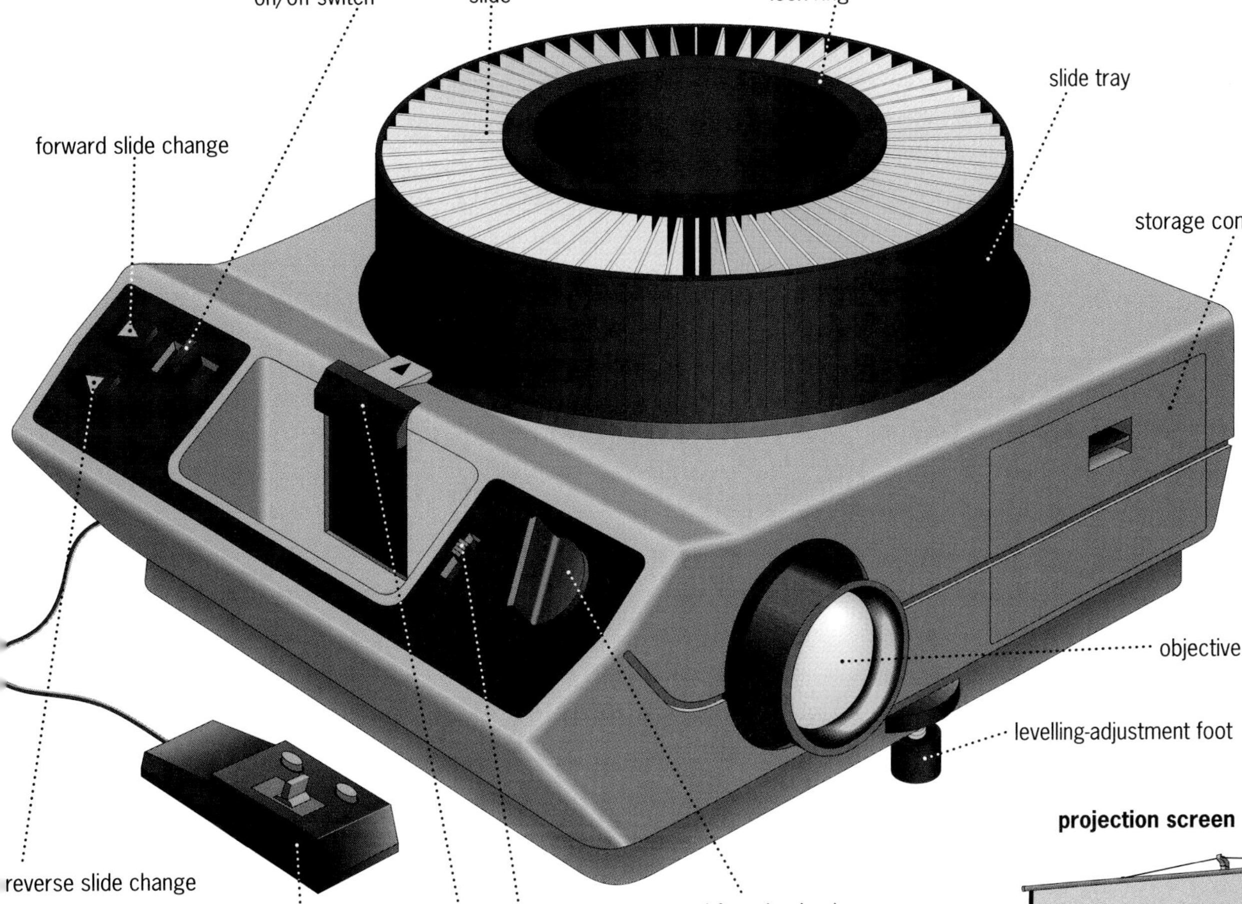
on/off switch
slide
lock ring
slide tray
forward slide change
storage compartment
objective lens
levelling-adjustment foot
reverse slide change
manual focusing knob
autofocus on/off switch
remote control
slide-select bar

projection screen

SLIDE

transparency

slide mount

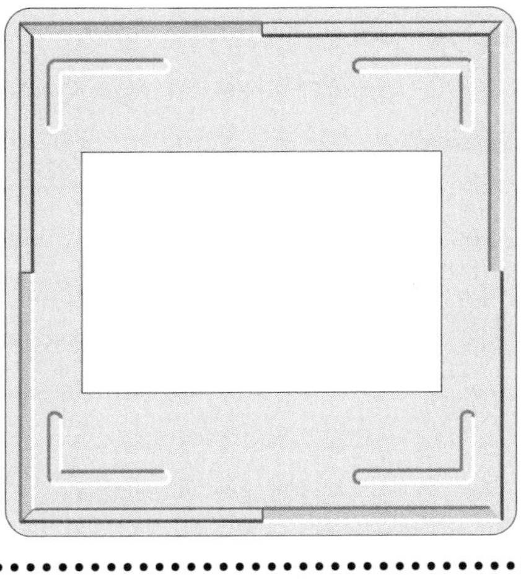

SCHOOL EQUIPMENT

pocket calculator

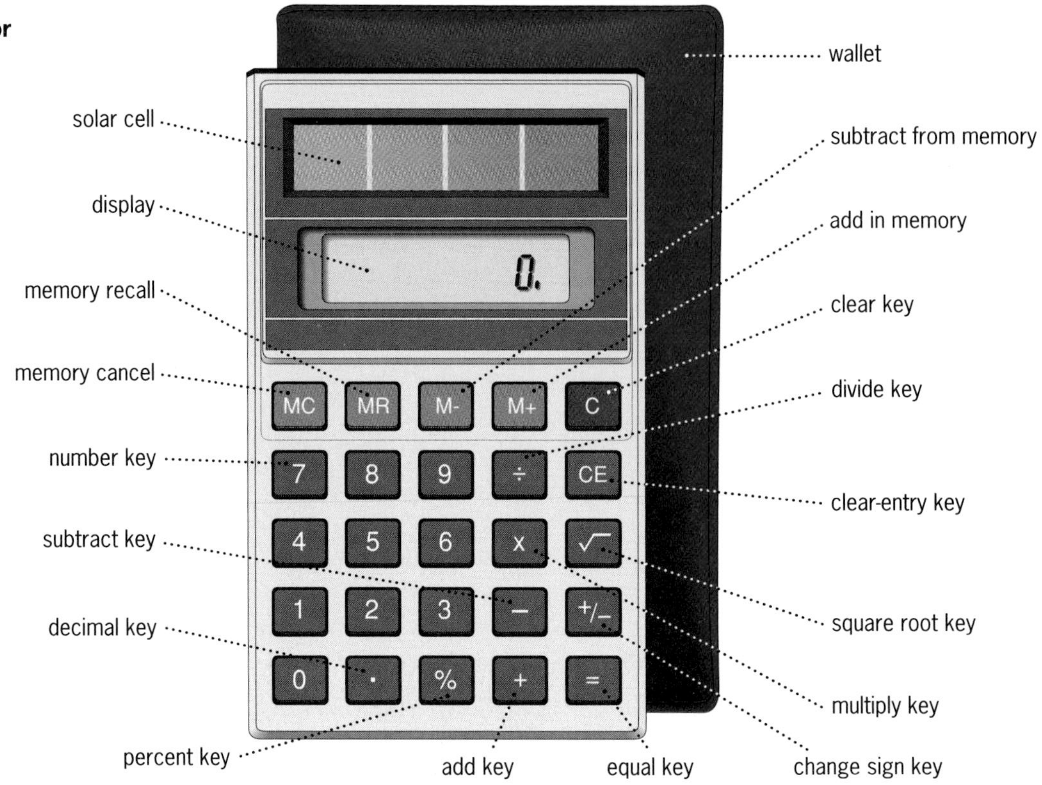
wallet
solar cell
subtract from memory
display
add in memory
0.
memory recall
clear key
memory cancel
divide key
MC
MR
M-
M+
C
number key
7
8
9
÷
CE
clear-entry key
subtract key
4
5
6
x
√
1
2
3
–
+/–
square root key
decimal key
0
.
%
+
=
multiply key
percent key
add key
equal key
change sign key

personal computer

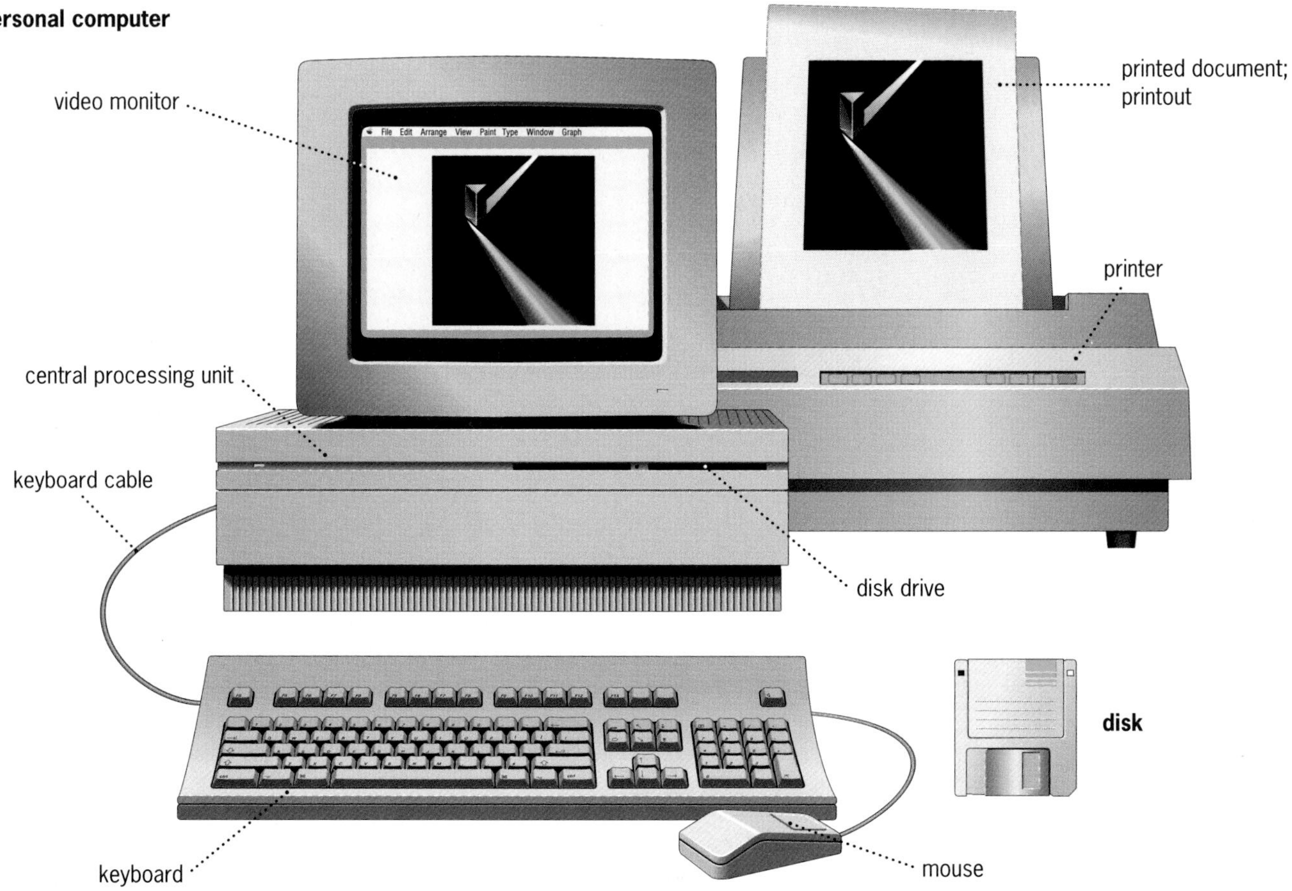
video monitor
printed document; printout
File Edit Arrange View Paint Type Window Graph
printer
central processing unit
keyboard cable
disk drive
disk
keyboard
mouse

magnifying glass

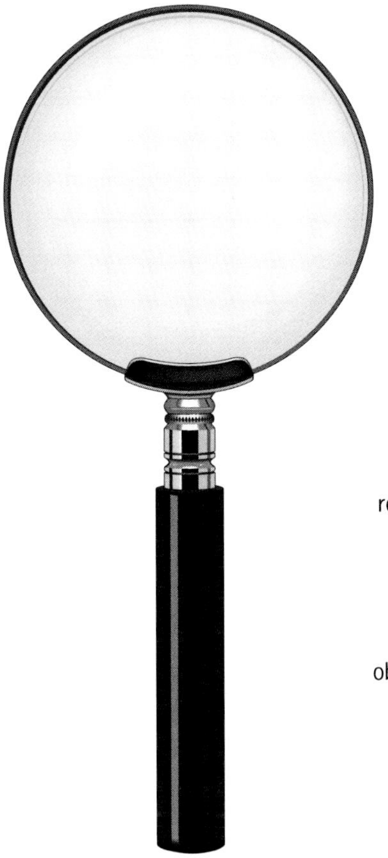

test tube

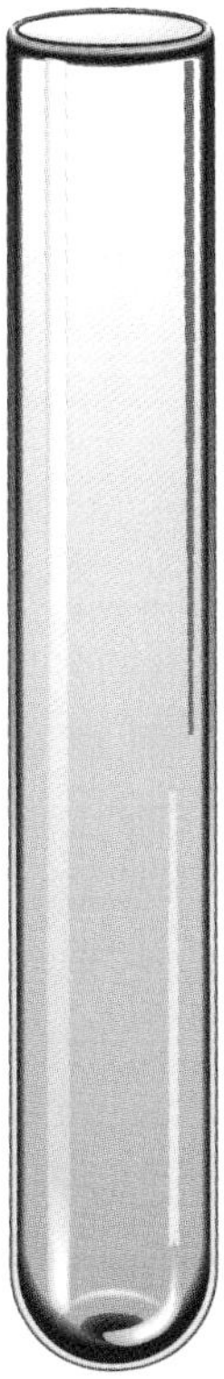

microscope

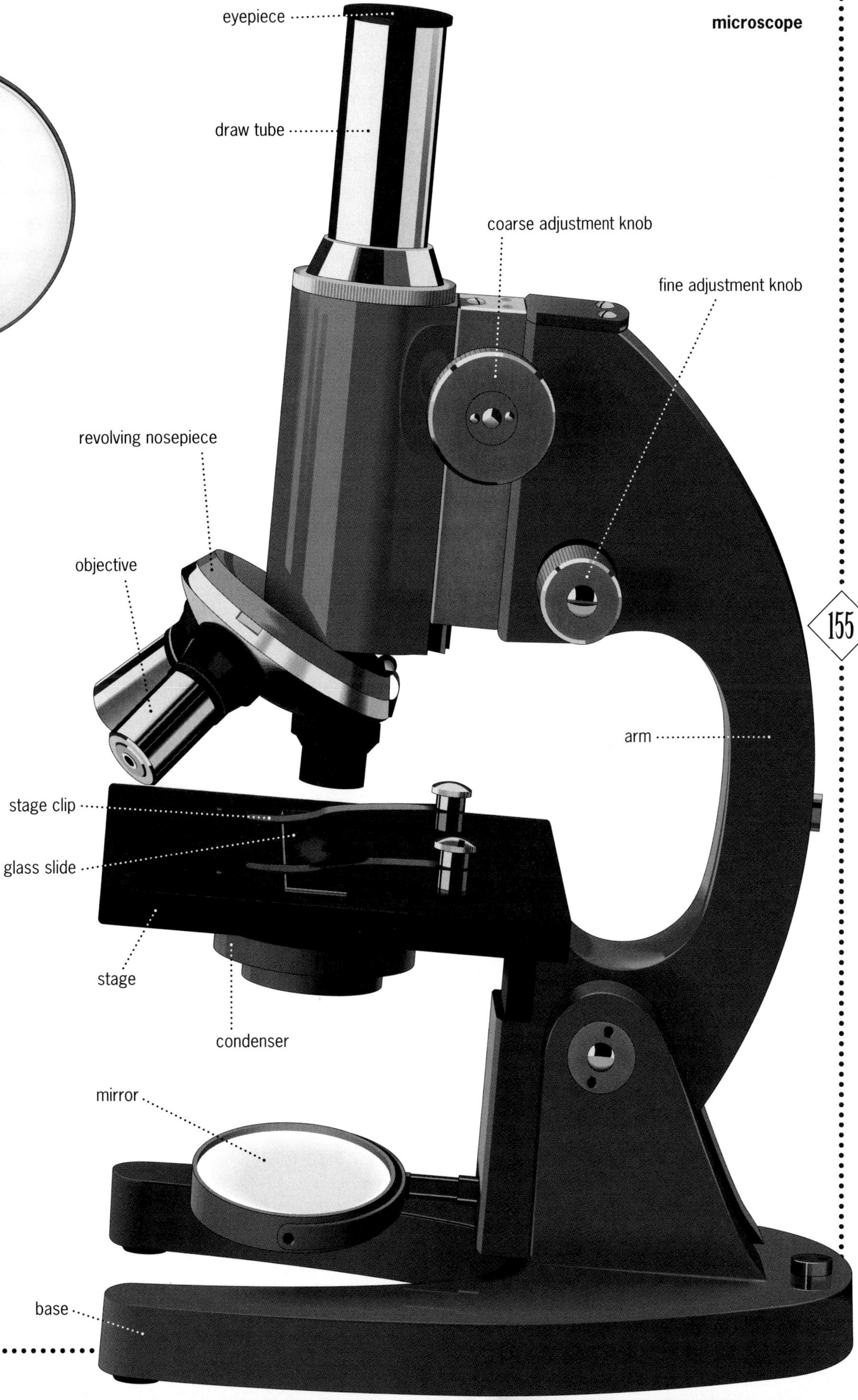
eyepiece
draw tube
coarse adjustment knob
fine adjustment knob
revolving nosepiece
objective
arm
stage clip
glass slide
stage
condenser
mirror
base

GEOMETRY

PLANE SURFACES

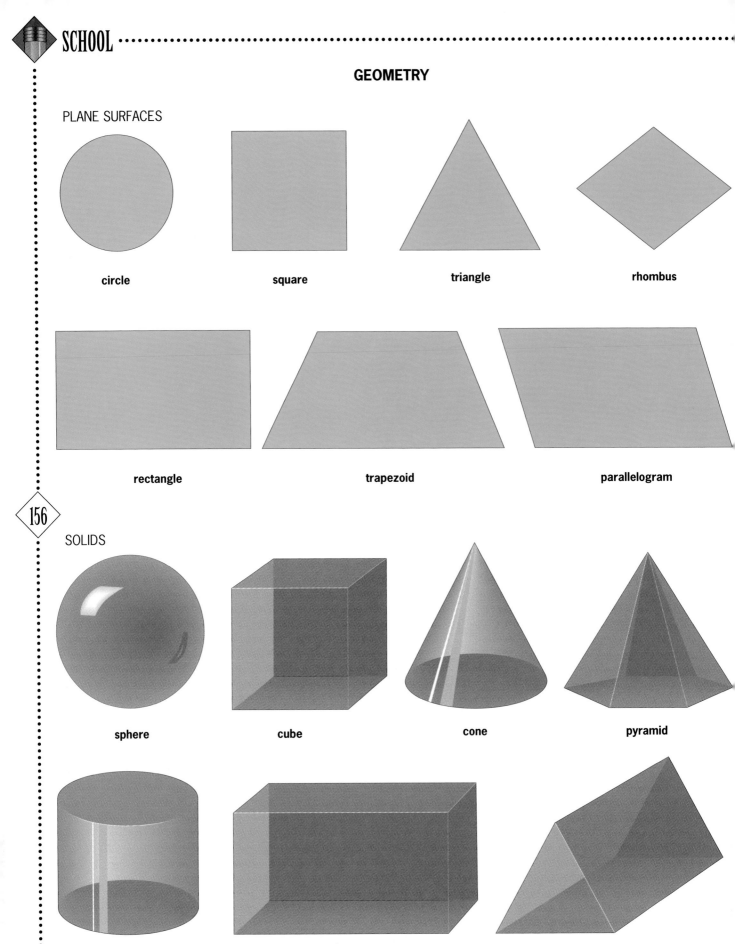

circle

square

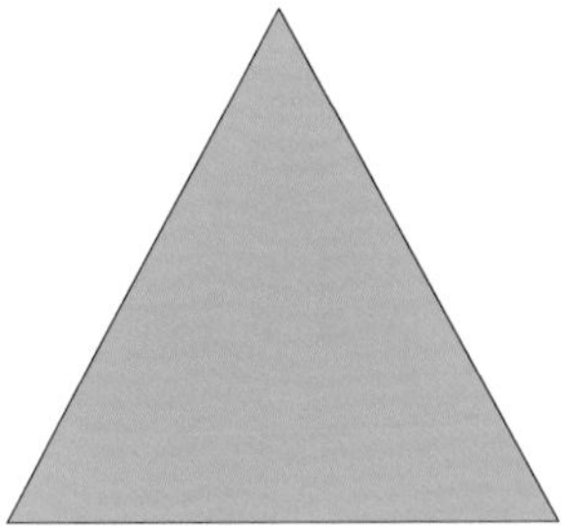

triangle

rhombus

rectangle

trapezoid

parallelogram

SOLIDS

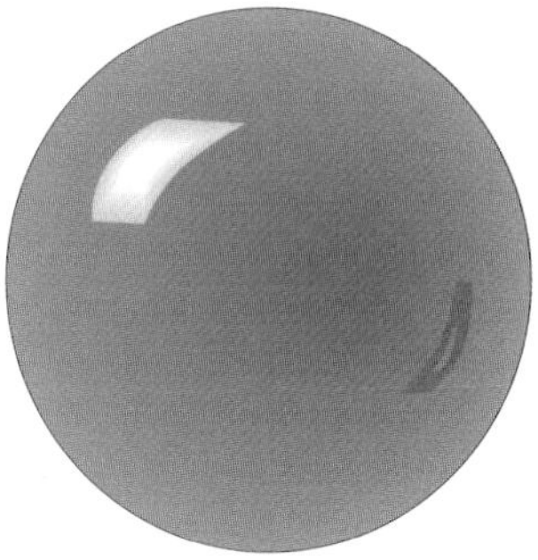

sphere

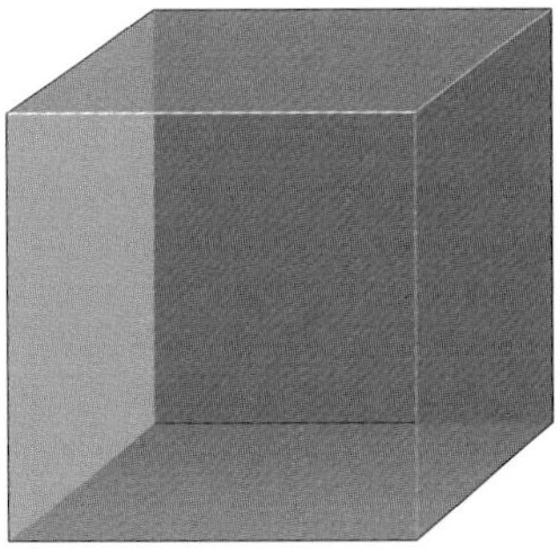

cube

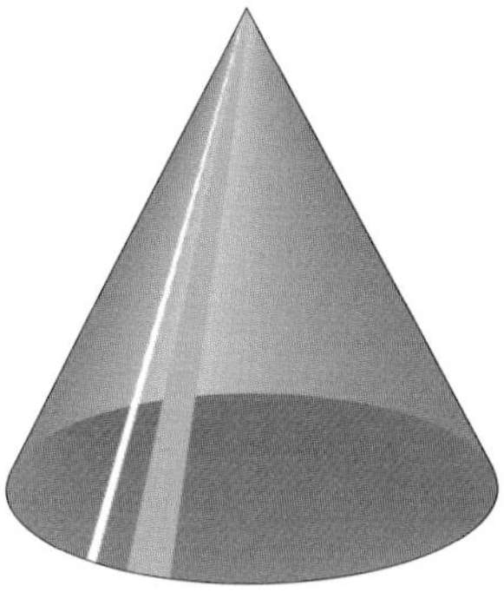

cone

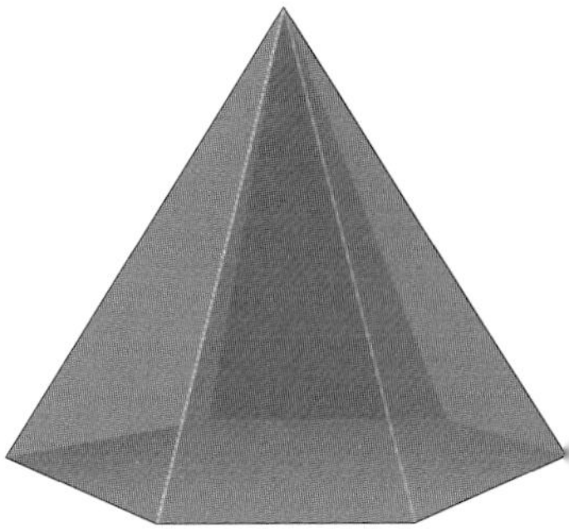

pyramid

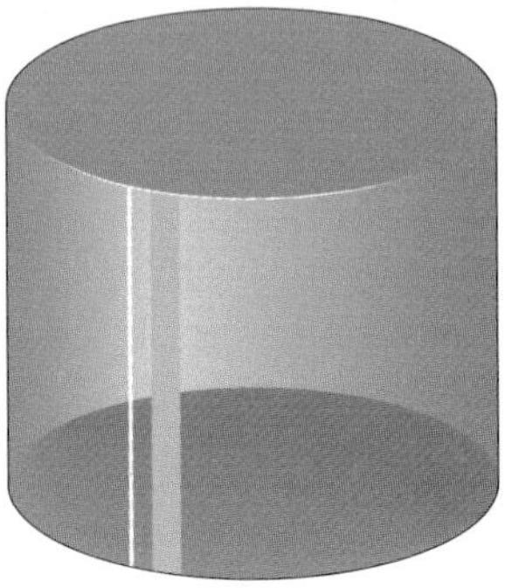

cylinder

parallelepiped

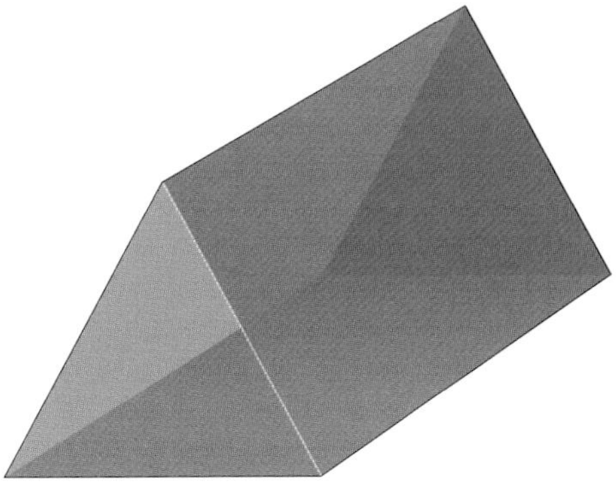

prism

DRAWING

COLOUR CIRCLE

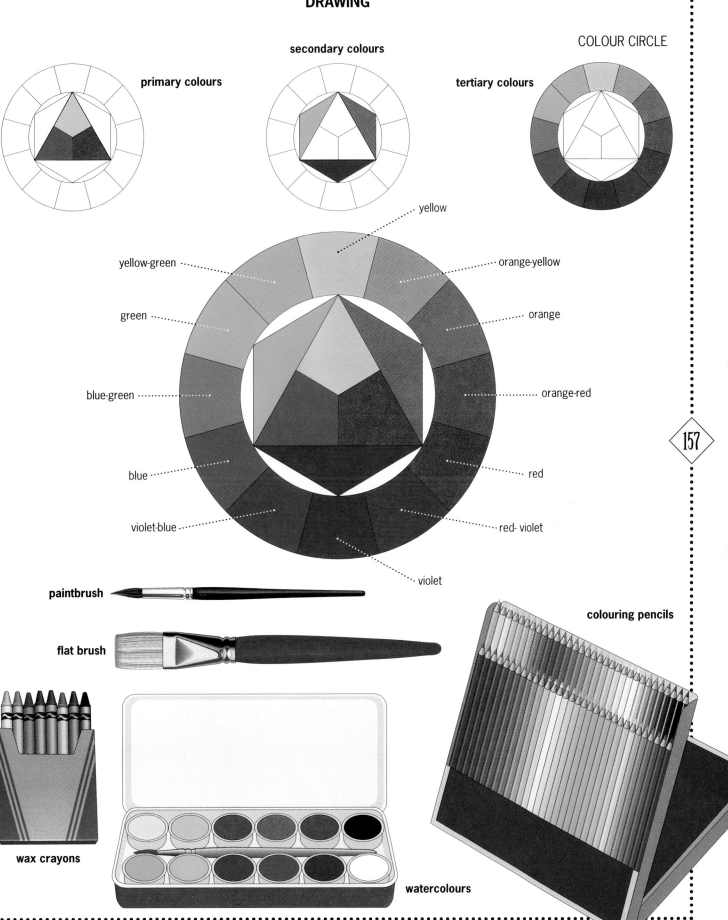

primary colours

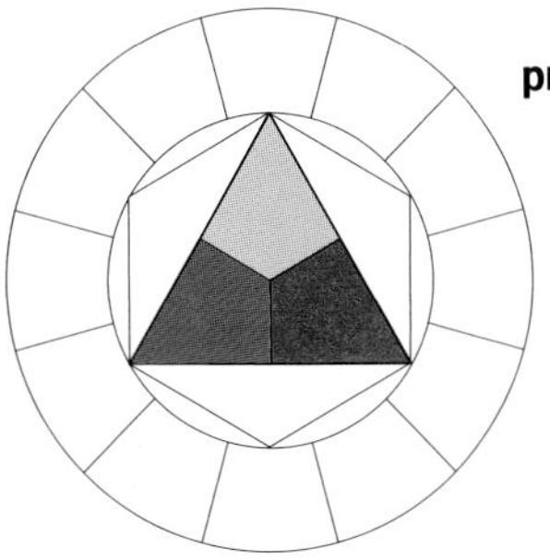

secondary colours

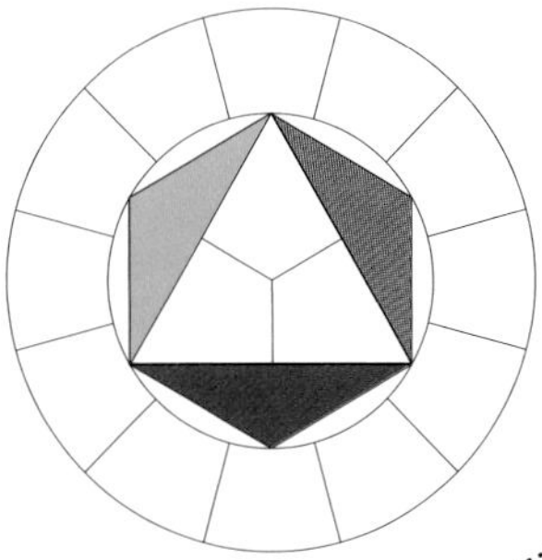

tertiary colours

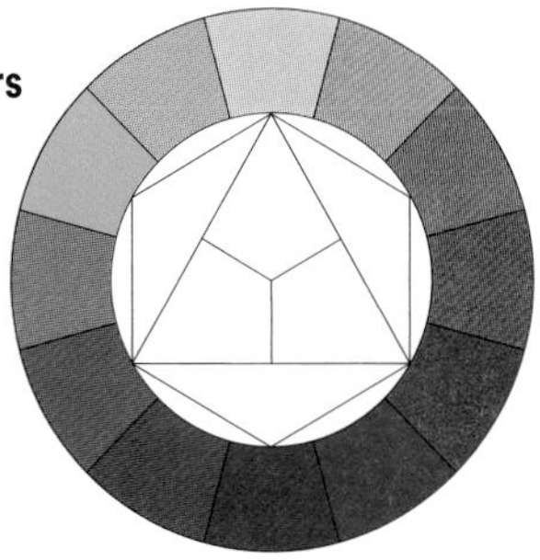

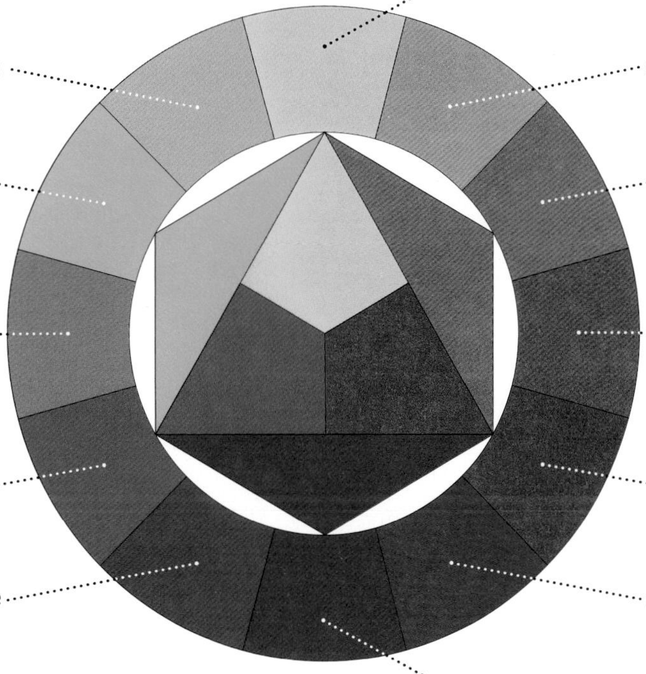
yellow
orange-yellow
orange
orange-red
red
red- violet
violet
violet-blue
blue
blue-green
green
yellow-green

paintbrush

flat brush

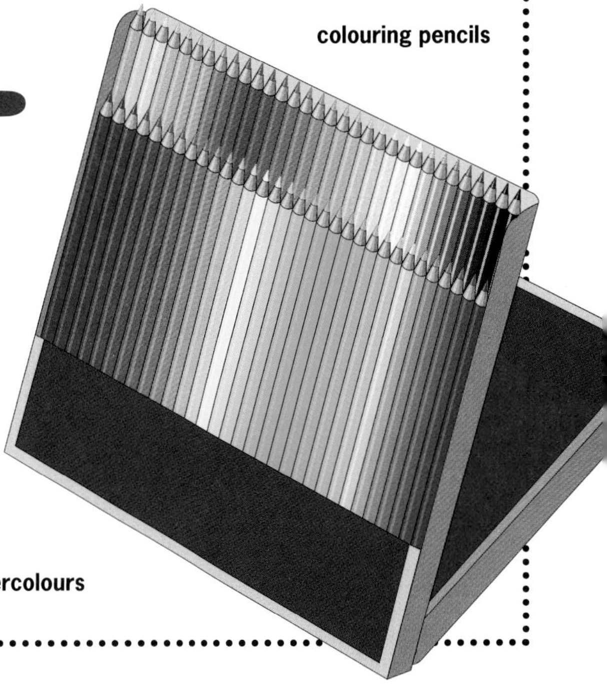

colouring pencils

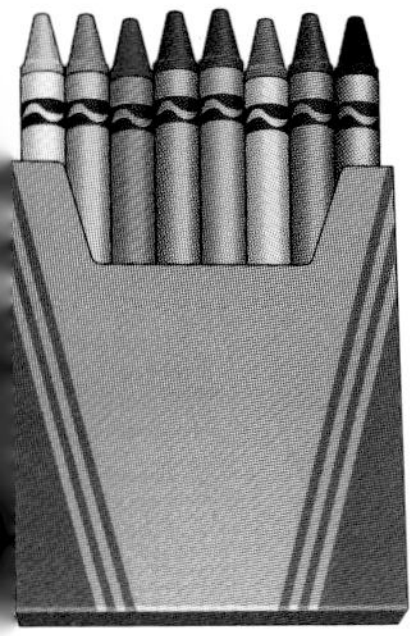

wax crayons

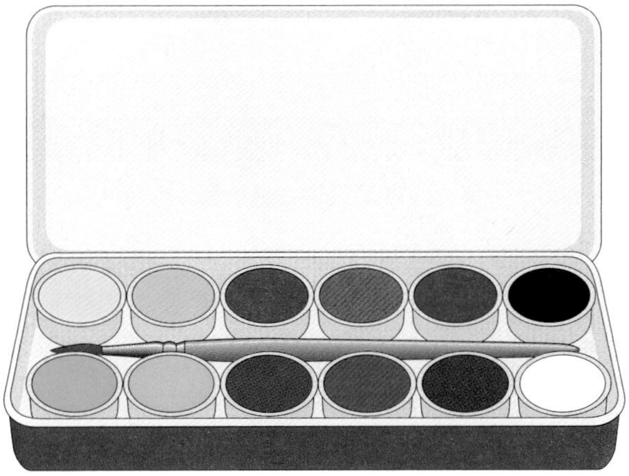

watercolours

TRADITIONAL MUSICAL INSTRUMENTS

balalaika

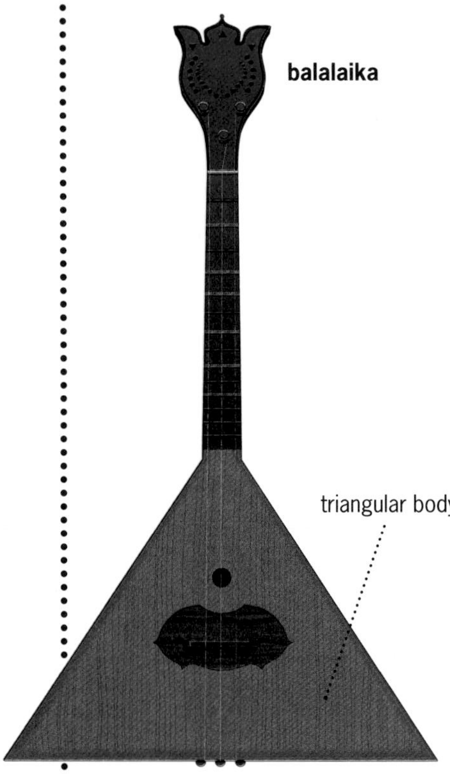
triangular body

mandolin

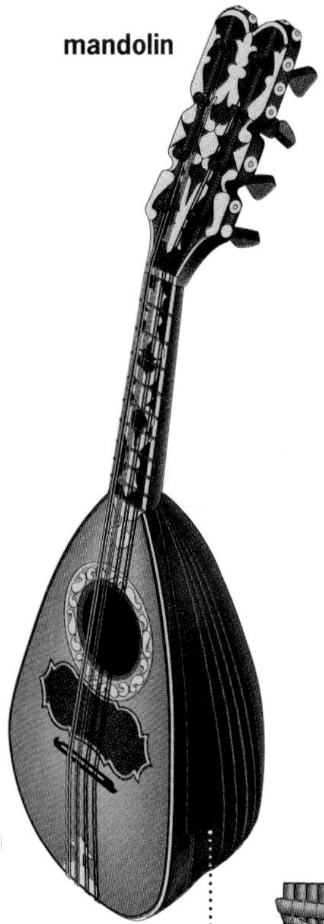
pear-shaped body

zither

soundboard
open strings
melody strings

lyre

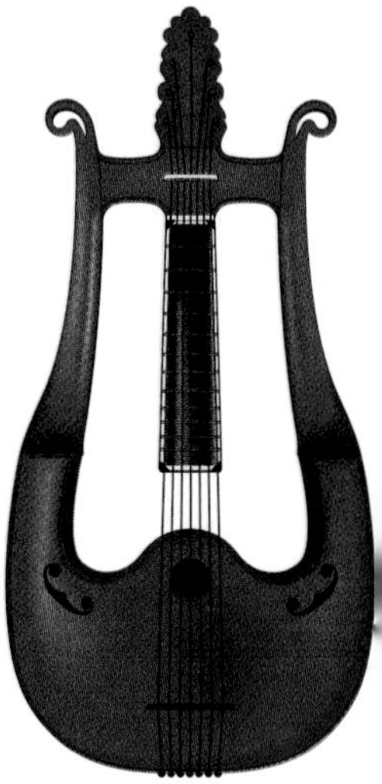

banjo

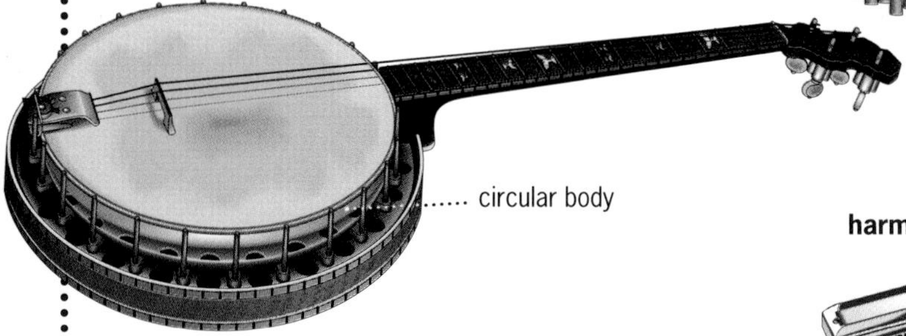
circular body

panpipes

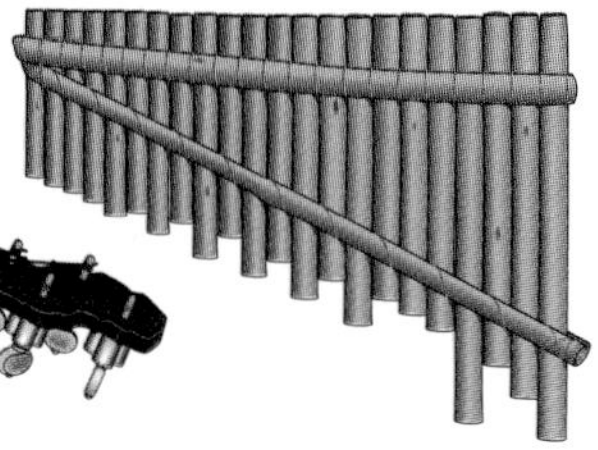

harmonica

bagpipes

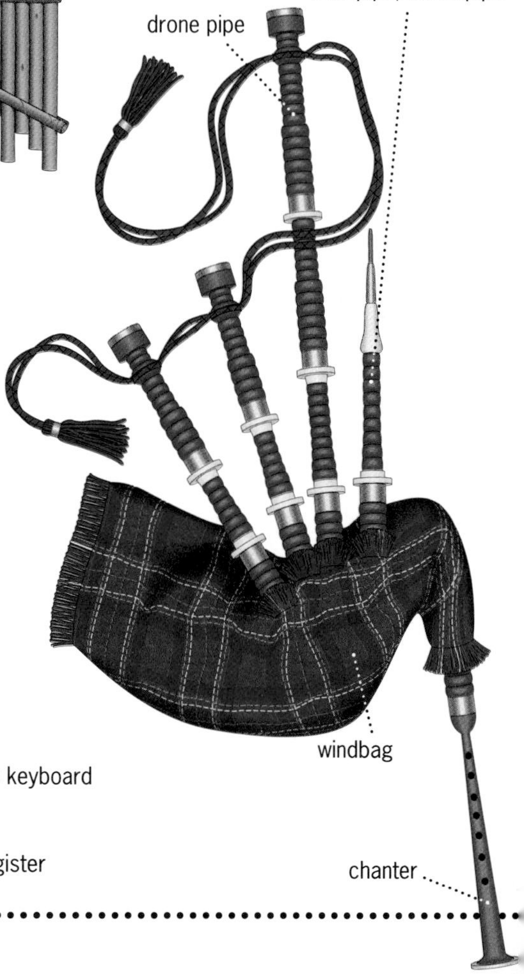
blowpipe; mouthpipe
drone pipe
windbag
chanter

accordion

bellows
treble keyboard
treble register
bass keyboard
bass register

KEYBOARD INSTRUMENTS

upright piano

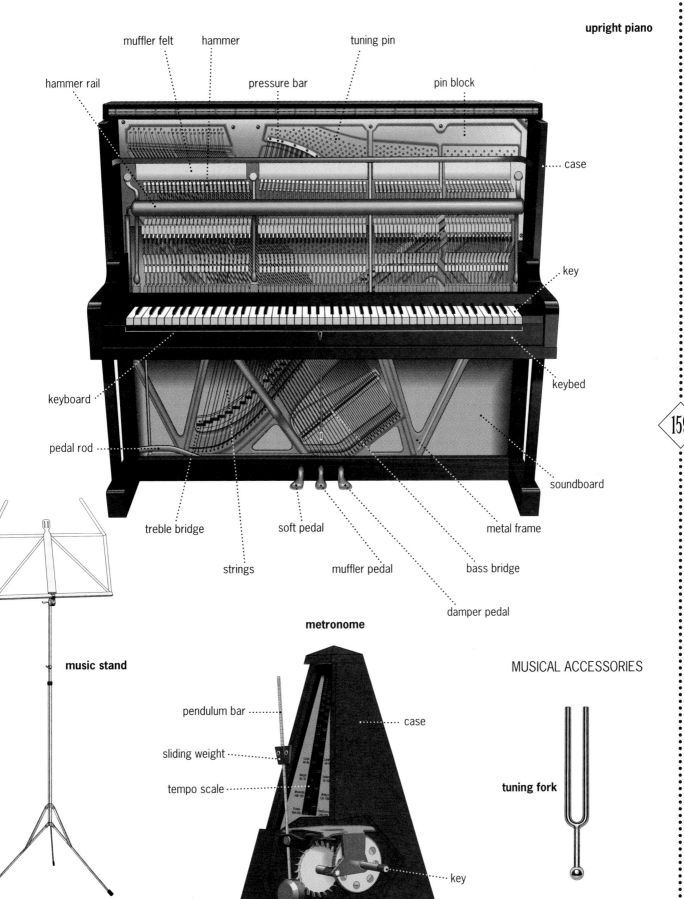

muffler felt
hammer
tuning pin
hammer rail
pressure bar
pin block
case
key
keybed
keyboard
pedal rod
soundboard
treble bridge
soft pedal
metal frame
strings
muffler pedal
bass bridge
damper pedal

MUSICAL ACCESSORIES

metronome

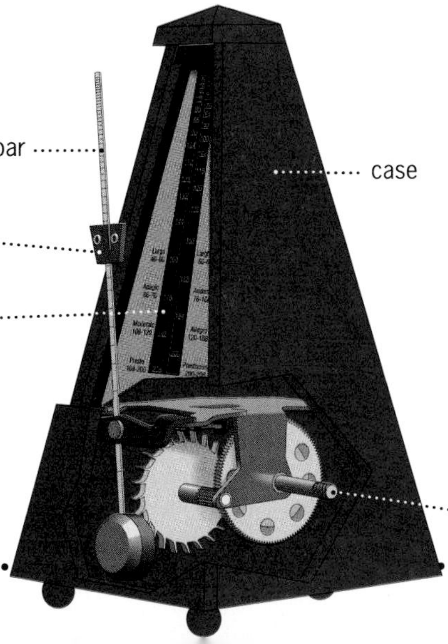
pendulum bar
sliding weight
tempo scale
case
key

music stand

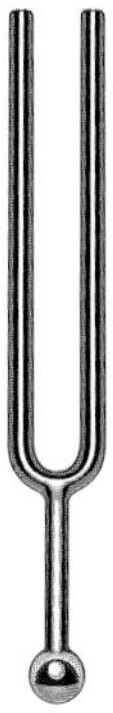

tuning fork

MUSICAL NOTATION

staff

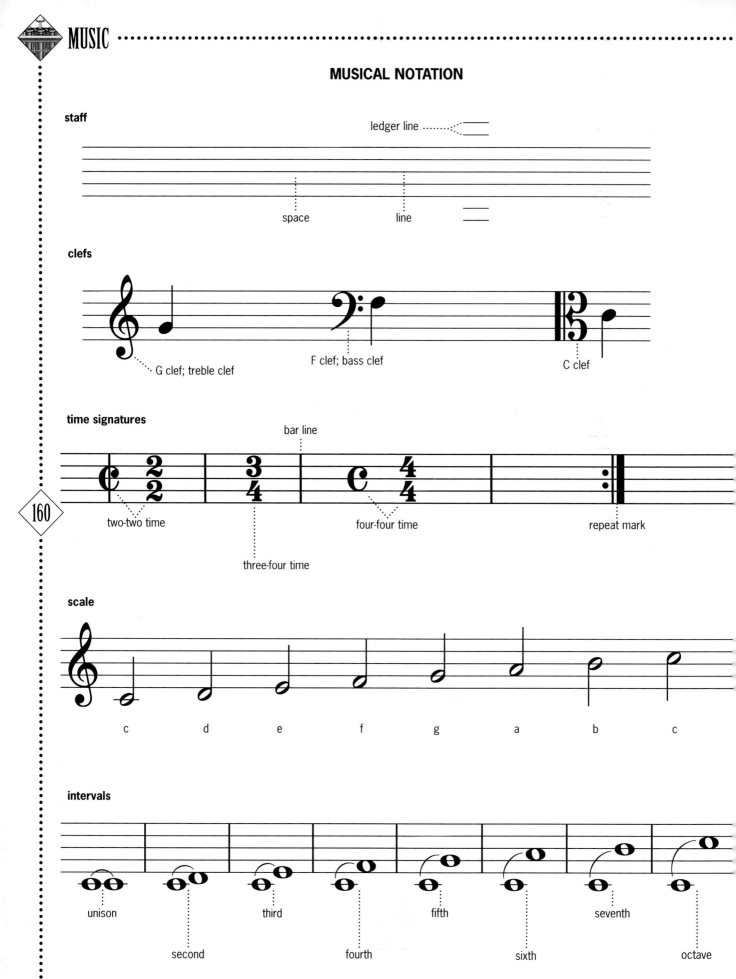

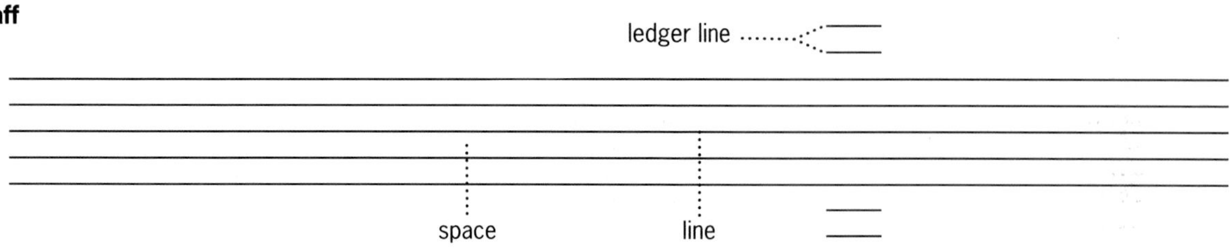
ledger line
space
line

clefs

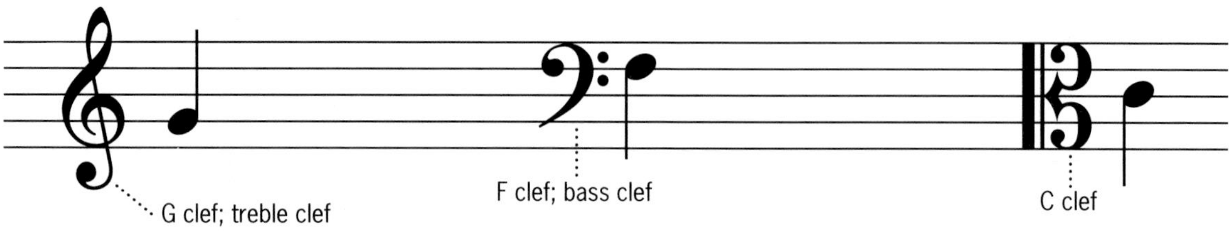
G clef; treble clef
F clef; bass clef
C clef

time signatures

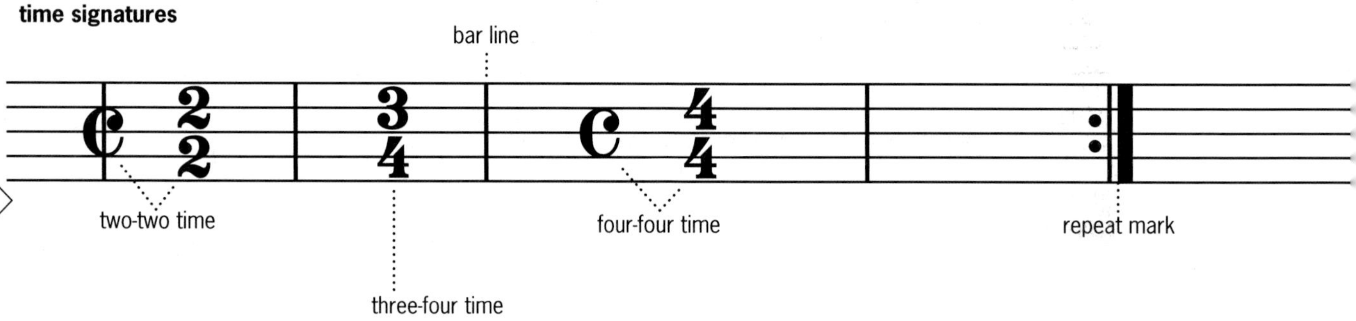
bar line
two-two time
three-four time
four-four time
repeat mark

scale

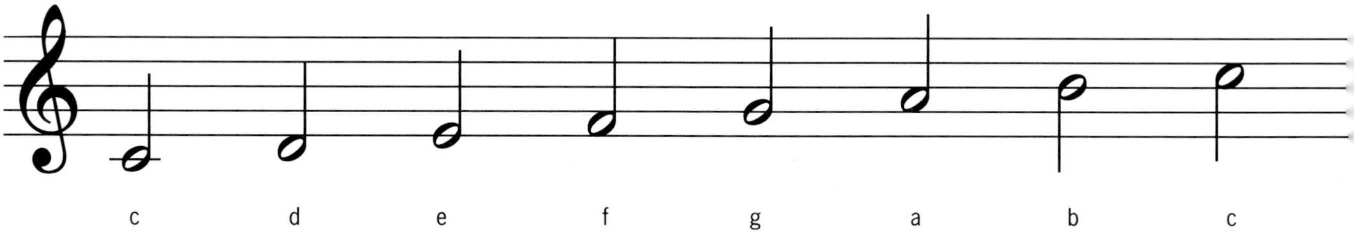
c
d
e
f
g
a
b
c

intervals

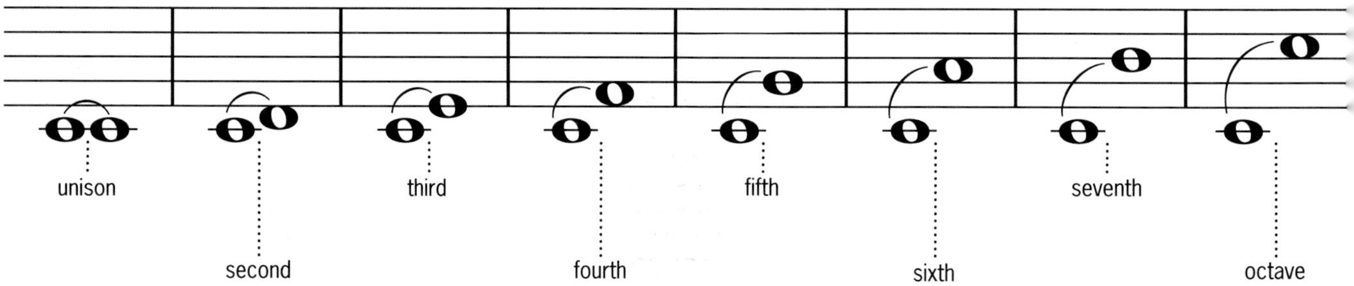
unison
second
third
fourth
fifth
sixth
seventh
octave

note symbols

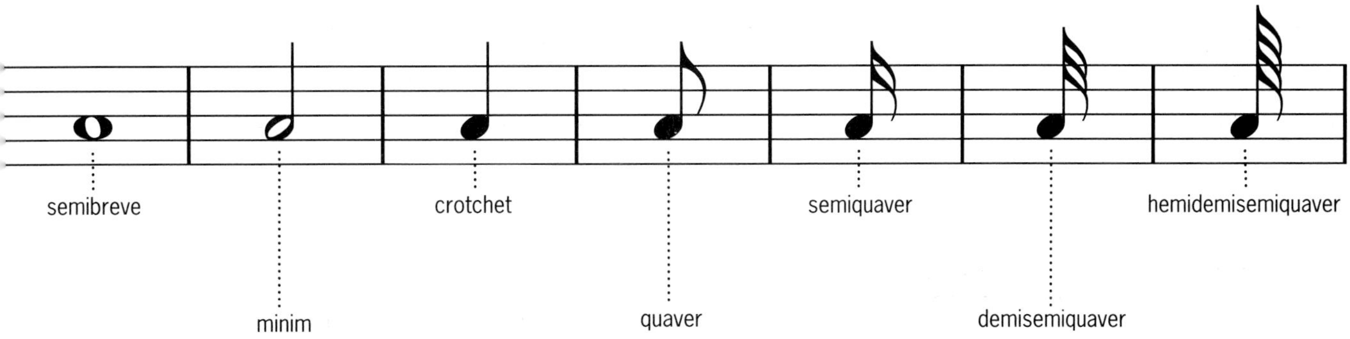
semibreve
minim
crotchet
quaver
semiquaver
demisemiquaver
hemidemisemiquaver

rest symbols

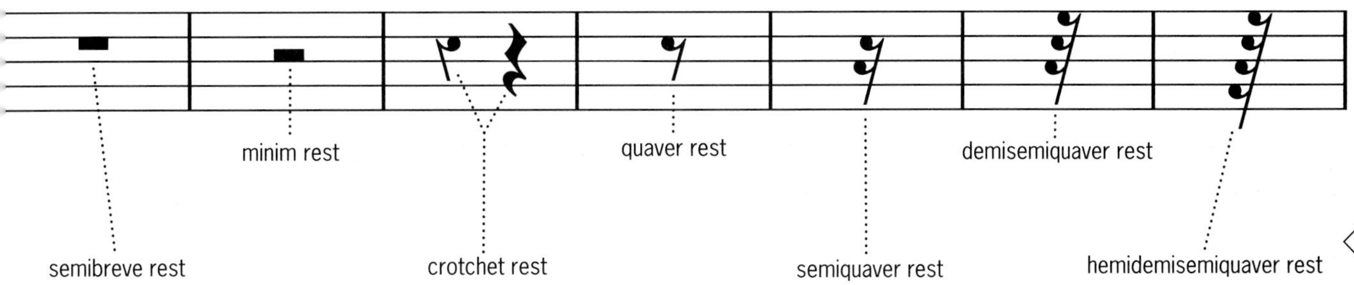
semibreve rest
minim rest
crotchet rest
quaver rest
semiquaver rest
demisemiquaver rest
hemidemisemiquaver rest

accidentals

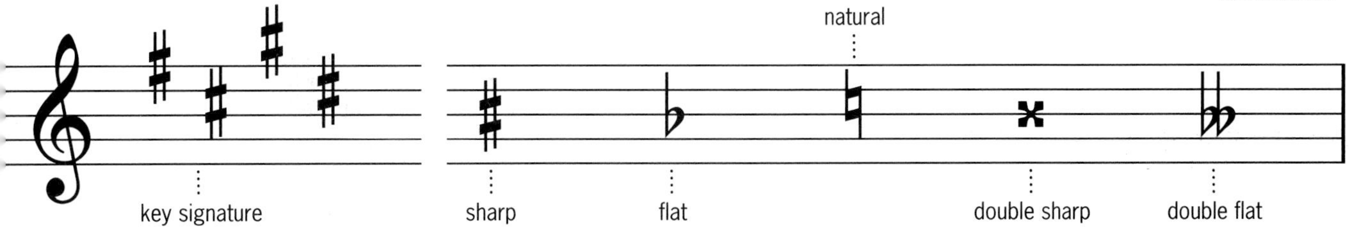
key signature
sharp
flat
natural
double sharp
double flat

ornaments

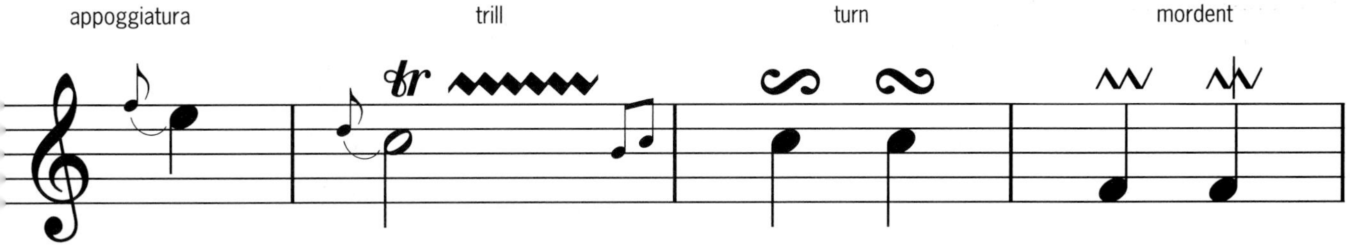
appoggiatura
trill
tr
turn
mordent

STRINGED INSTRUMENTS

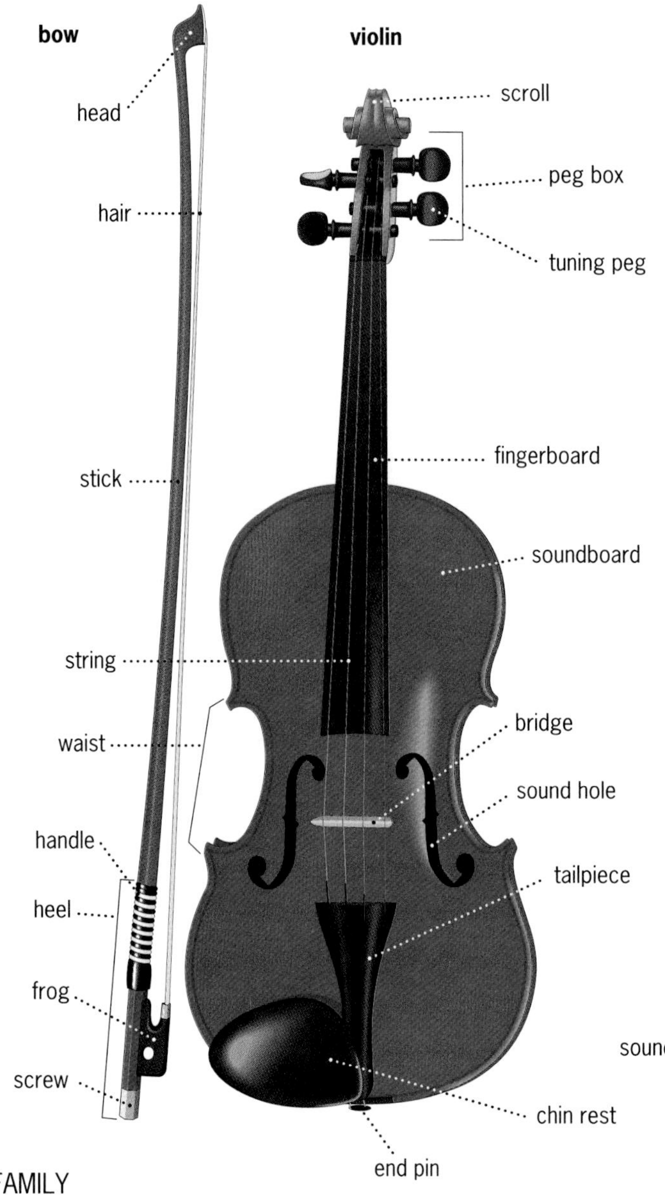
bow
head
hair
stick
string
waist
handle
heel
frog
screw
violin
scroll
peg box
tuning peg
fingerboard
soundboard
bridge
sound hole
tailpiece
chin rest
end pin

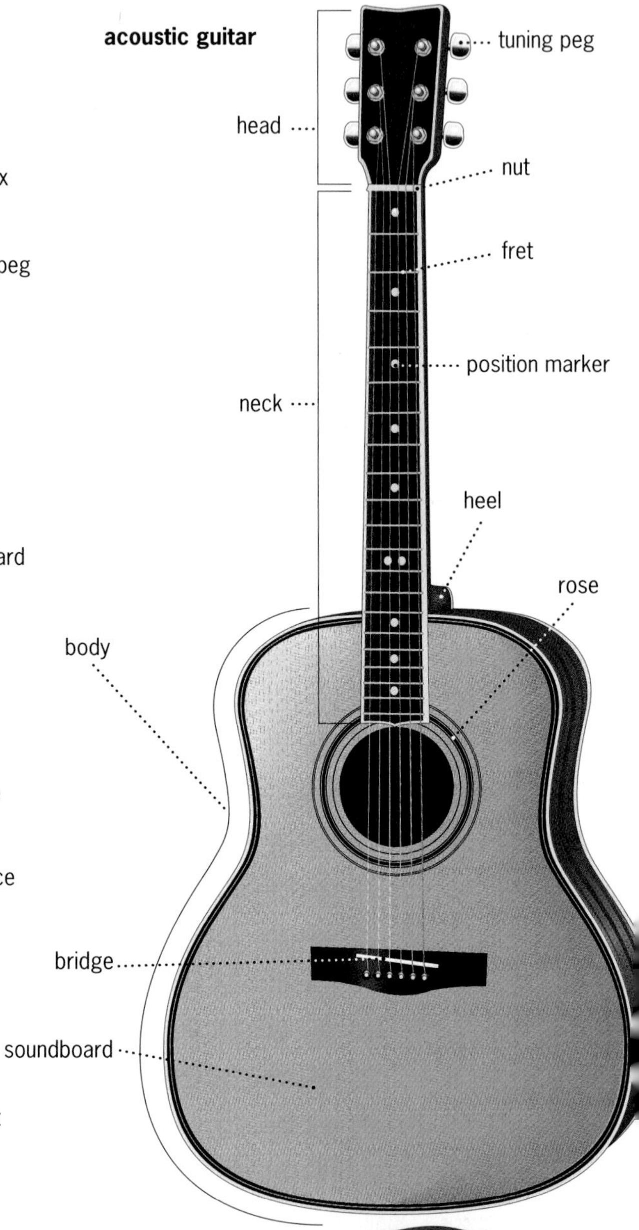
acoustic guitar
tuning peg
head
nut
fret
position marker
neck
heel
rose
body
bridge
soundboard

VIOLIN FAMILY

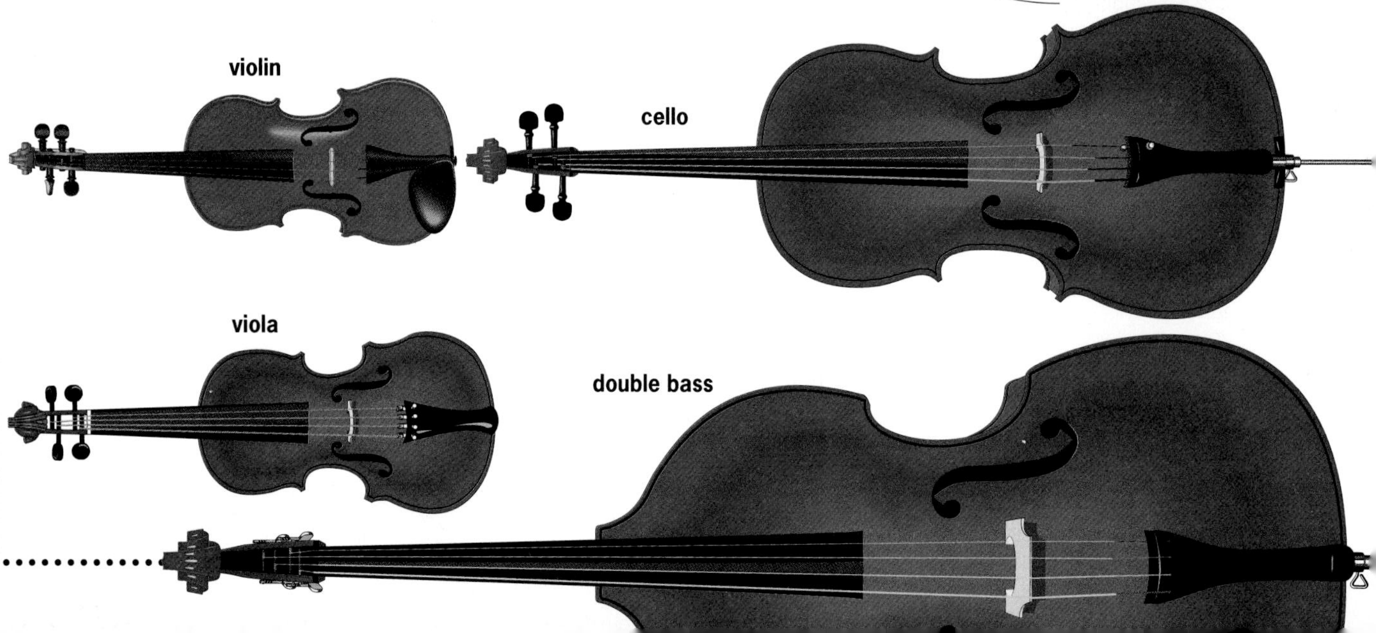
violin
cello
viola
double bass

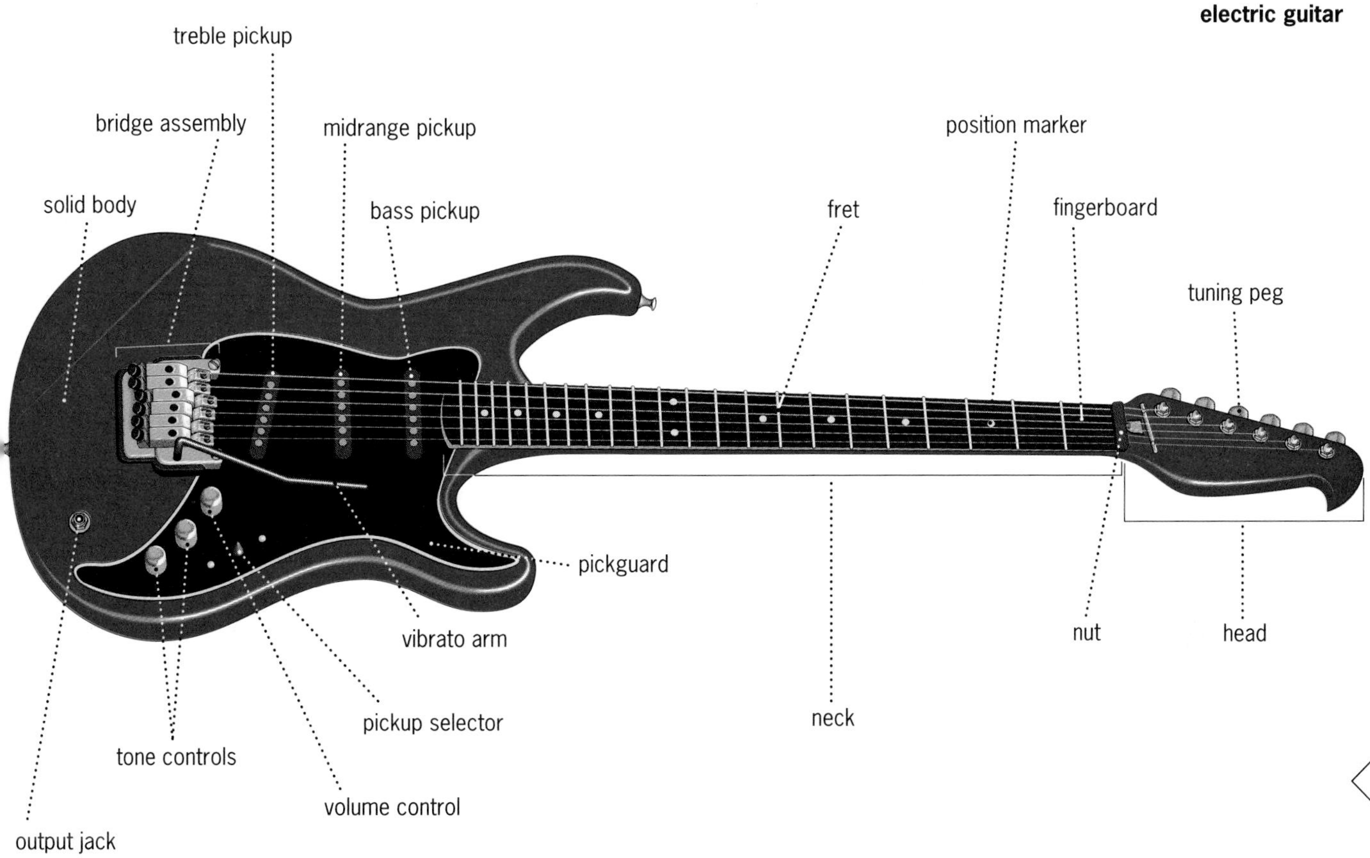
electric guitar
treble pickup
bridge assembly
midrange pickup
position marker
solid body
bass pickup
fret
fingerboard
tuning peg
pickguard
vibrato arm
nut
head
neck
pickup selector
tone controls
volume control
output jack

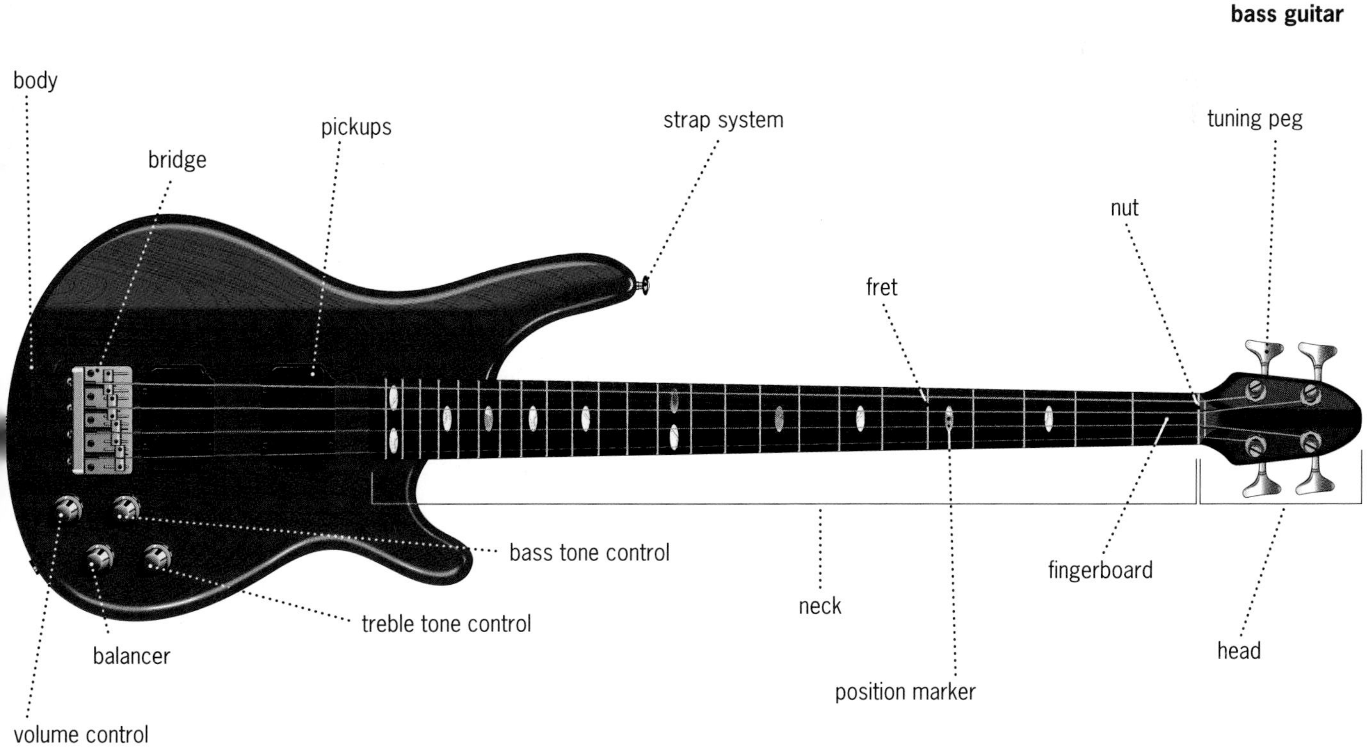
bass guitar
body
pickups
strap system
tuning peg
bridge
nut
fret
bass tone control
fingerboard
neck
treble tone control
balancer
head
position marker
volume control

WIND INSTRUMENTS

trumpet

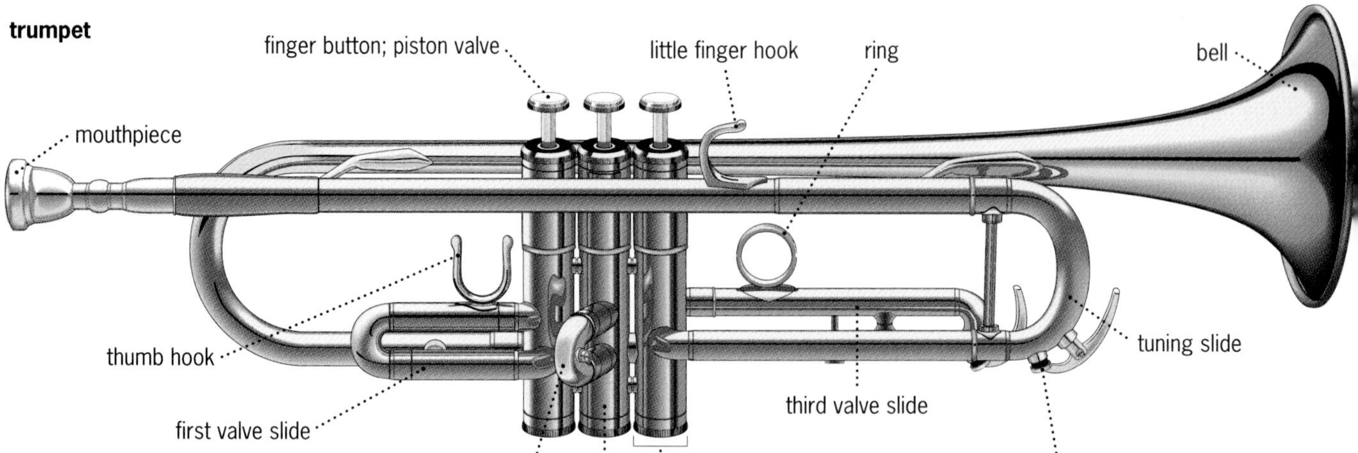
finger button; piston valve
little finger hook
ring
bell
mouthpiece
thumb hook
first valve slide
second valve slide
valve
valve casing
third valve slide
tuning slide
water key

mute

BRASS FAMILY

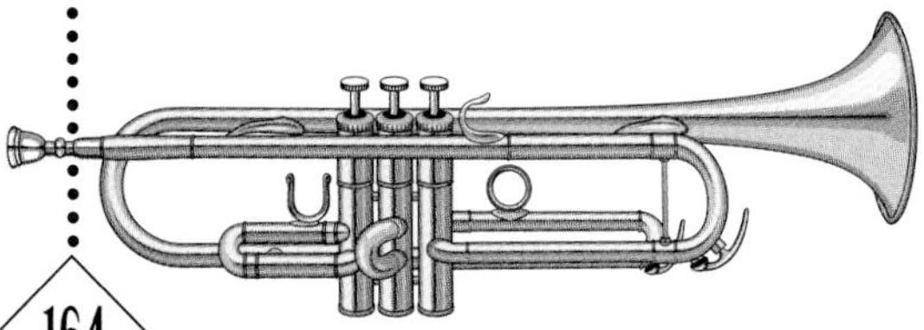

trumpet

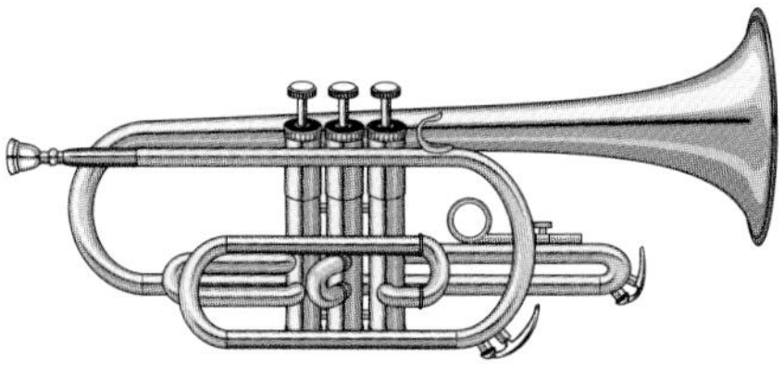

cornet

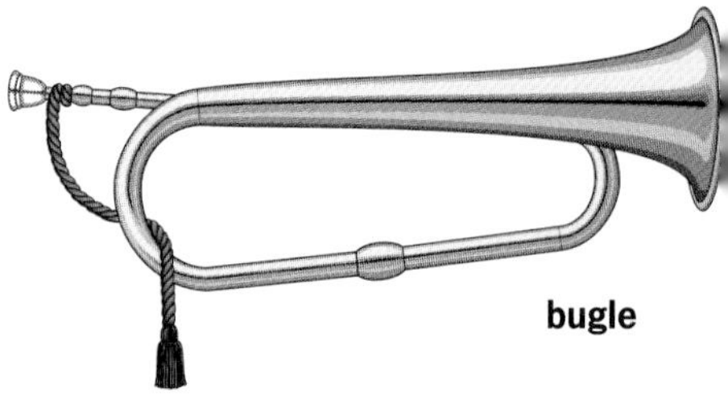

bugle

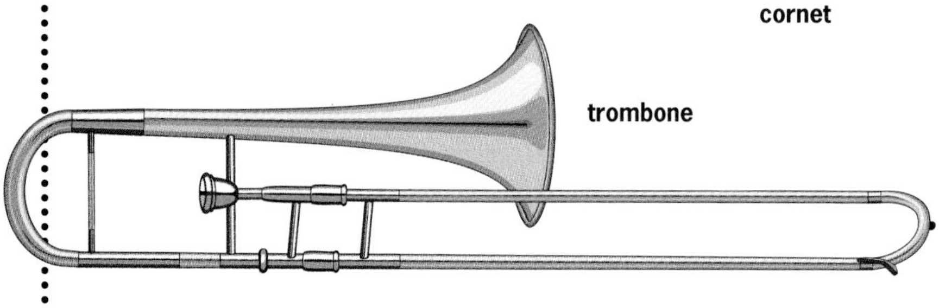

trombone

tuba

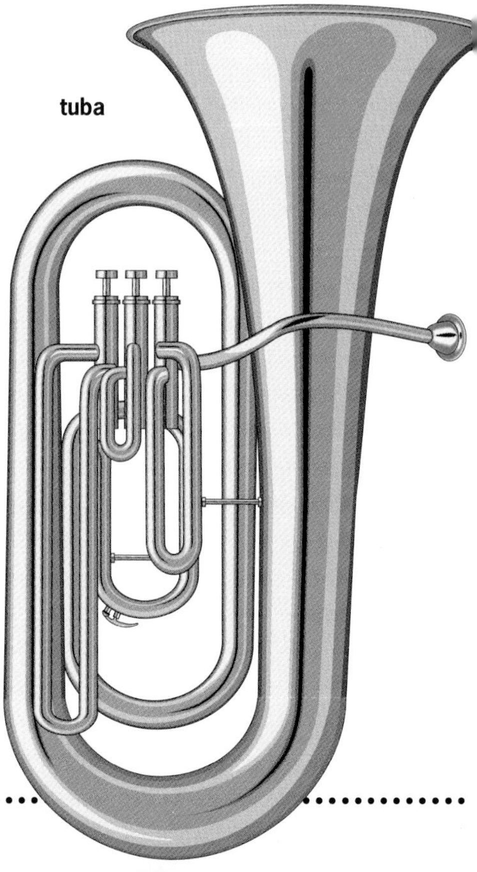

saxhorn

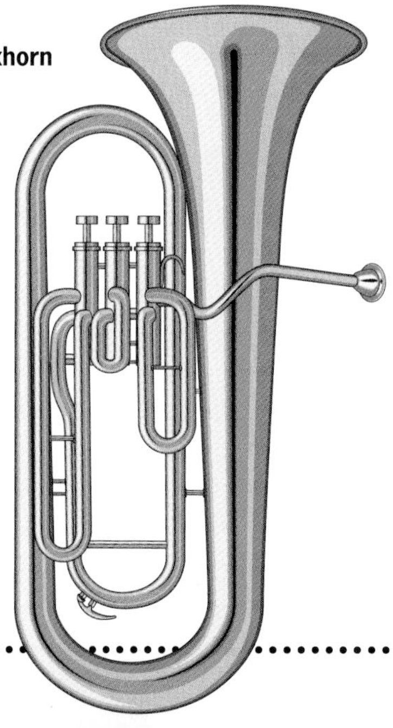

French horn

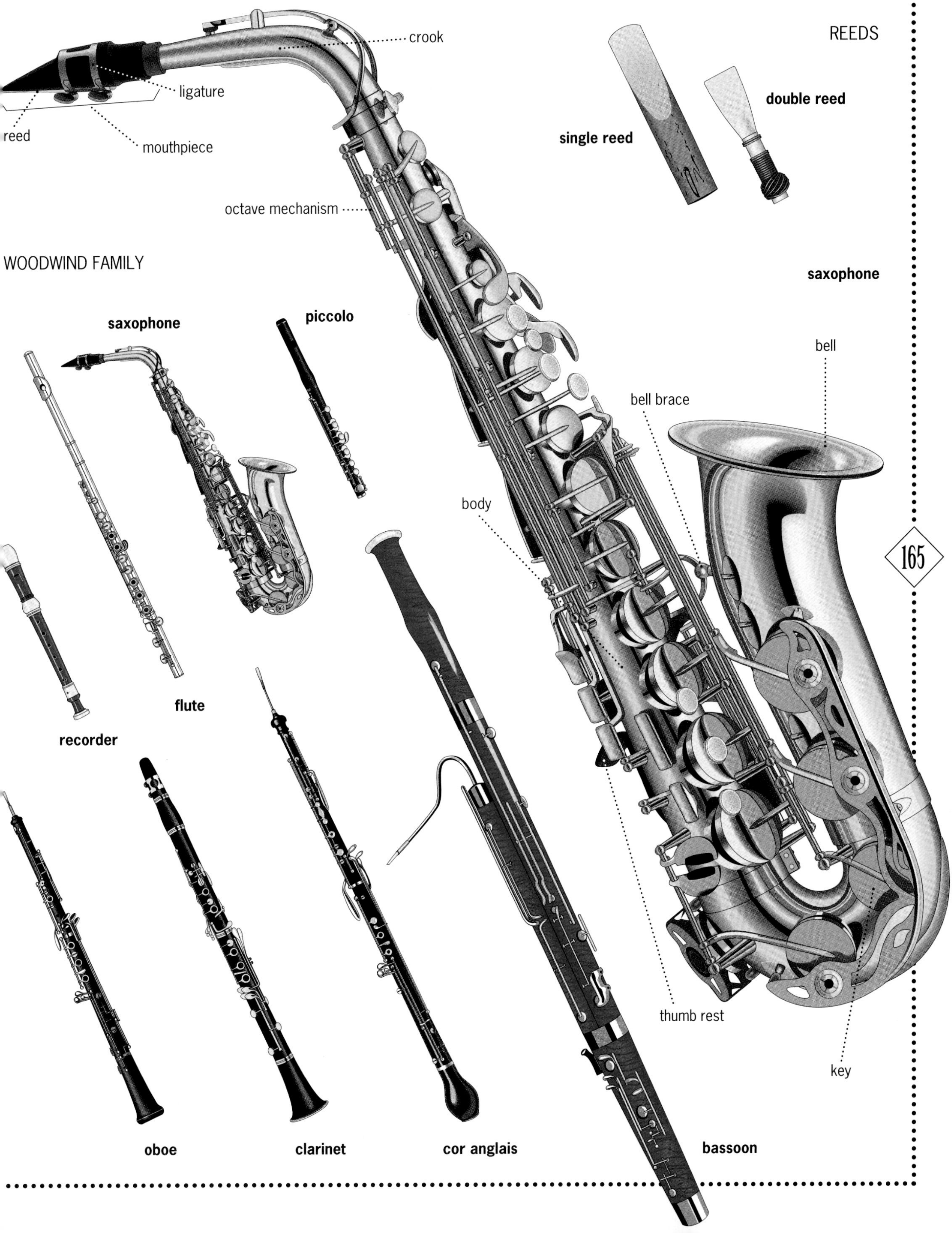
crook
ligature
reed
mouthpiece
octave mechanism
REEDS
double reed
single reed
WOODWIND FAMILY
saxophone
saxophone
piccolo
bell
bell brace
body
flute
recorder
thumb rest
key
oboe
clarinet
cor anglais
bassoon

PERCUSSION INSTRUMENTS

drums

cymbal
tom-toms
Charleston cymbal;
hi-hat cymbal
batter head
snare drum
tripod stand
bass drum
stand
pedal
mallet
tenor drum

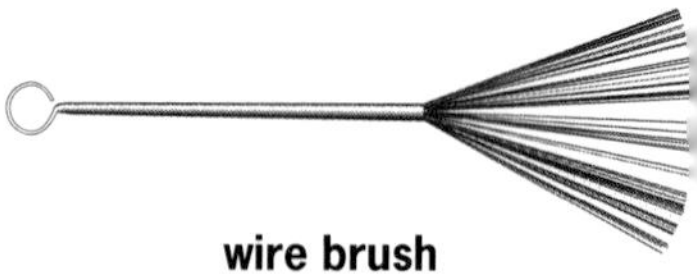

wire brush

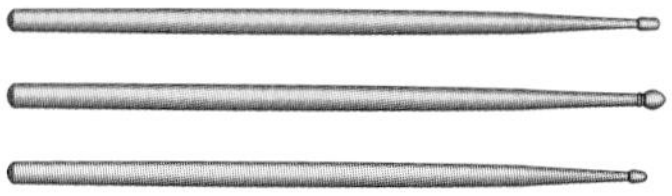

sticks

mallets

triangle

sistrum

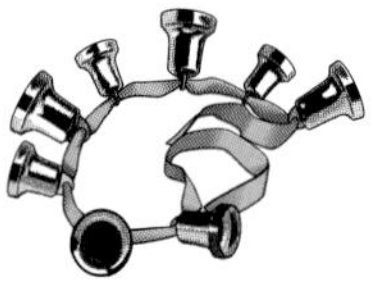

set of bells

sleigh bells

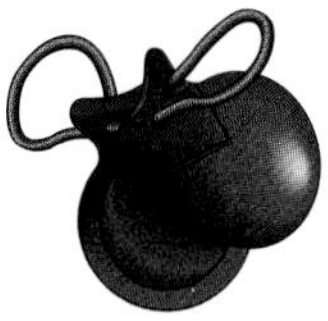

castanets

bongos

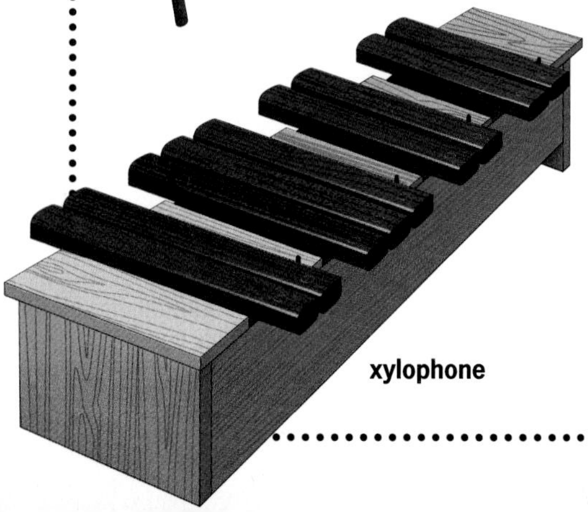

xylophone

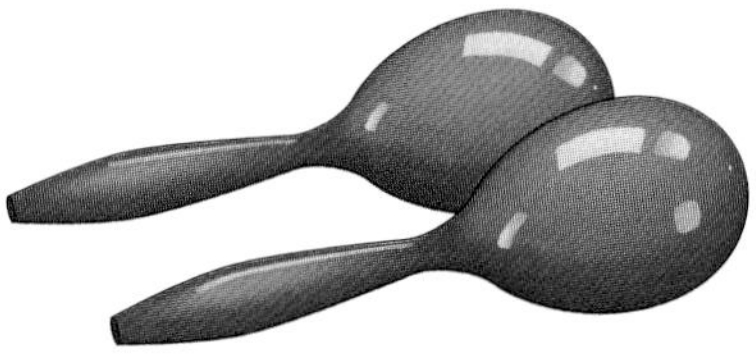

maracas

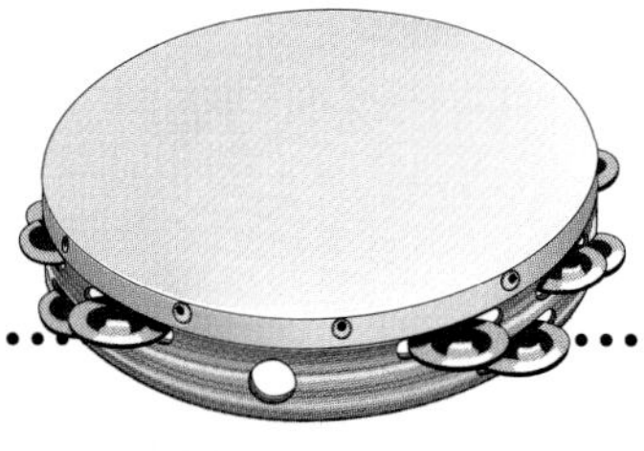

tambourine

SYMPHONY ORCHESTRA

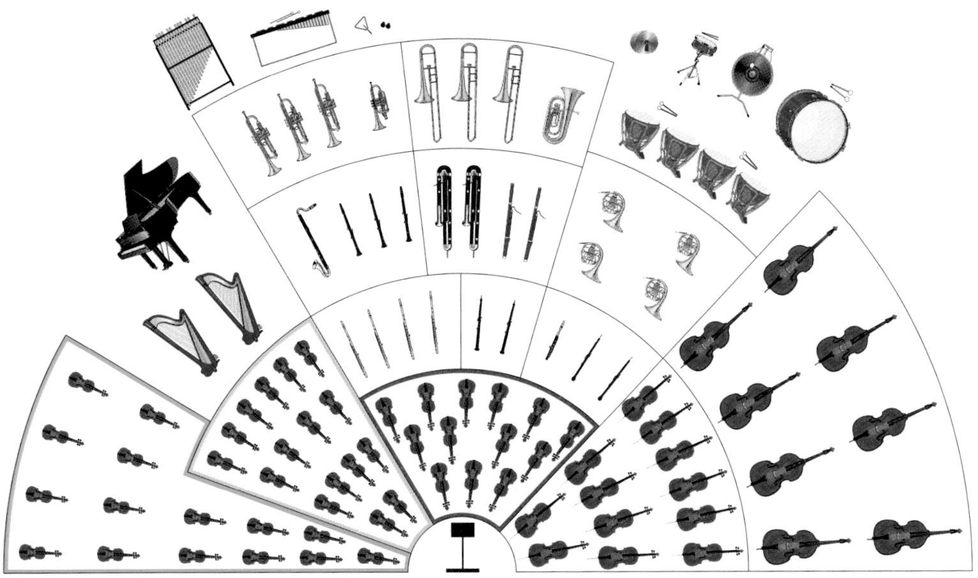

conductor's podium

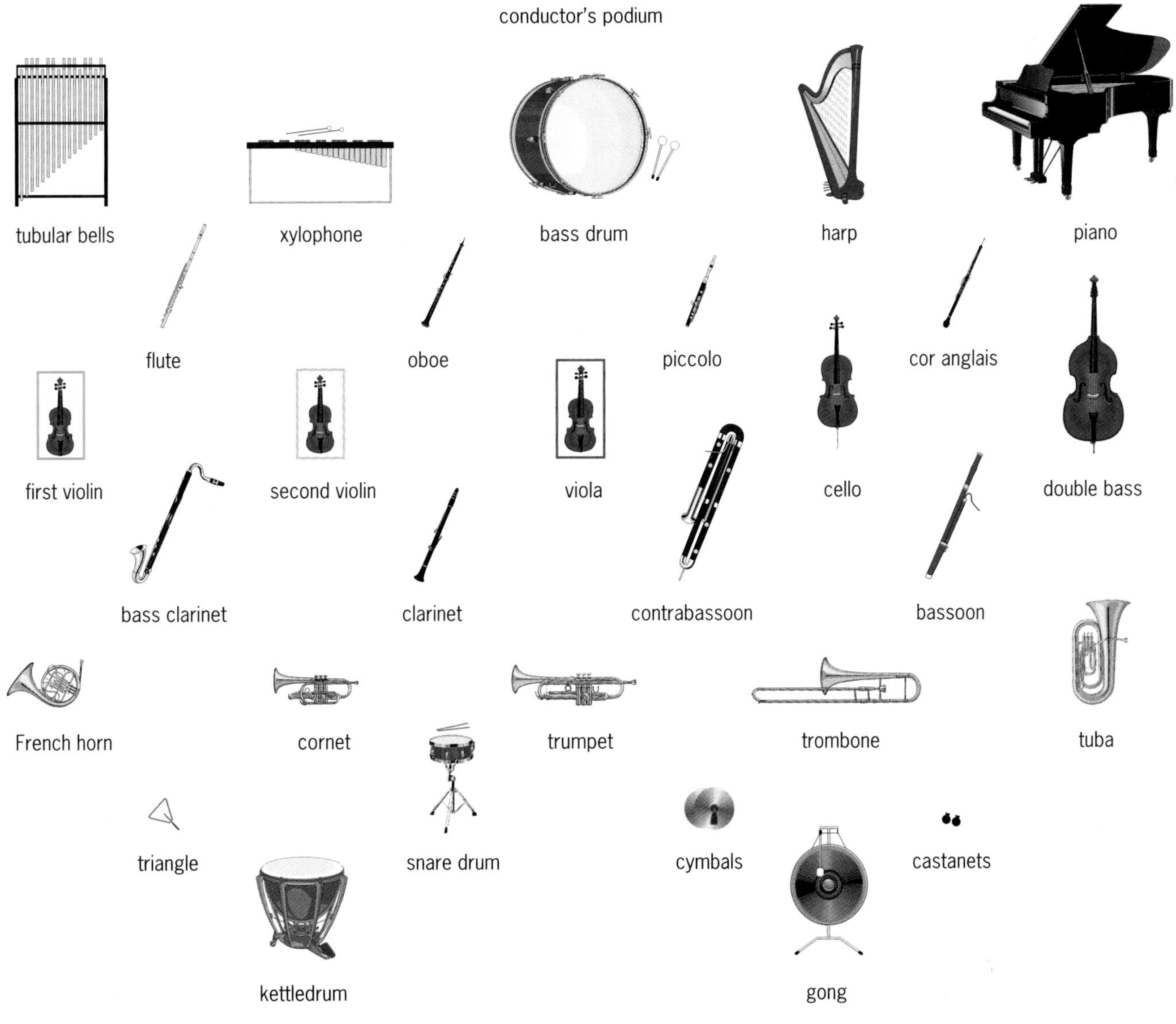
tubular bells
xylophone
bass drum
harp
piano
flute
oboe
piccolo
cor anglais
first violin
second violin
viola
cello
double bass
bass clarinet
clarinet
contrabassoon
bassoon
French horn
cornet
trumpet
trombone
tuba
triangle
snare drum
cymbals
castanets
kettledrum
gong

BASEBALL

fielder's glove

web
strap
thumb
finger
palm
heel
lace

bat

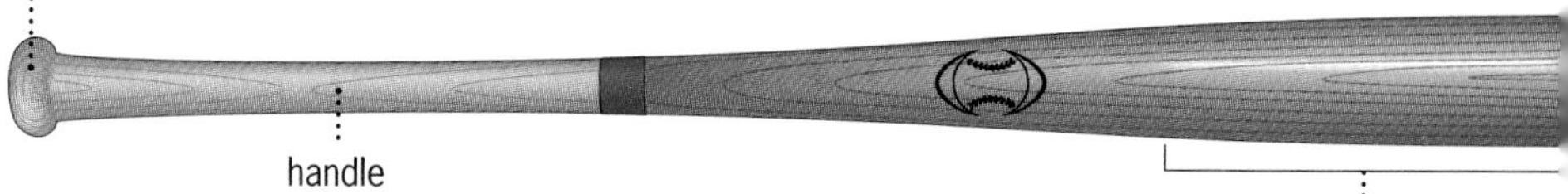
knob
handle
hitting area

baseball

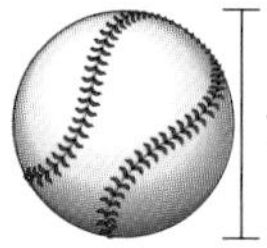
71 – 74 mm

batter

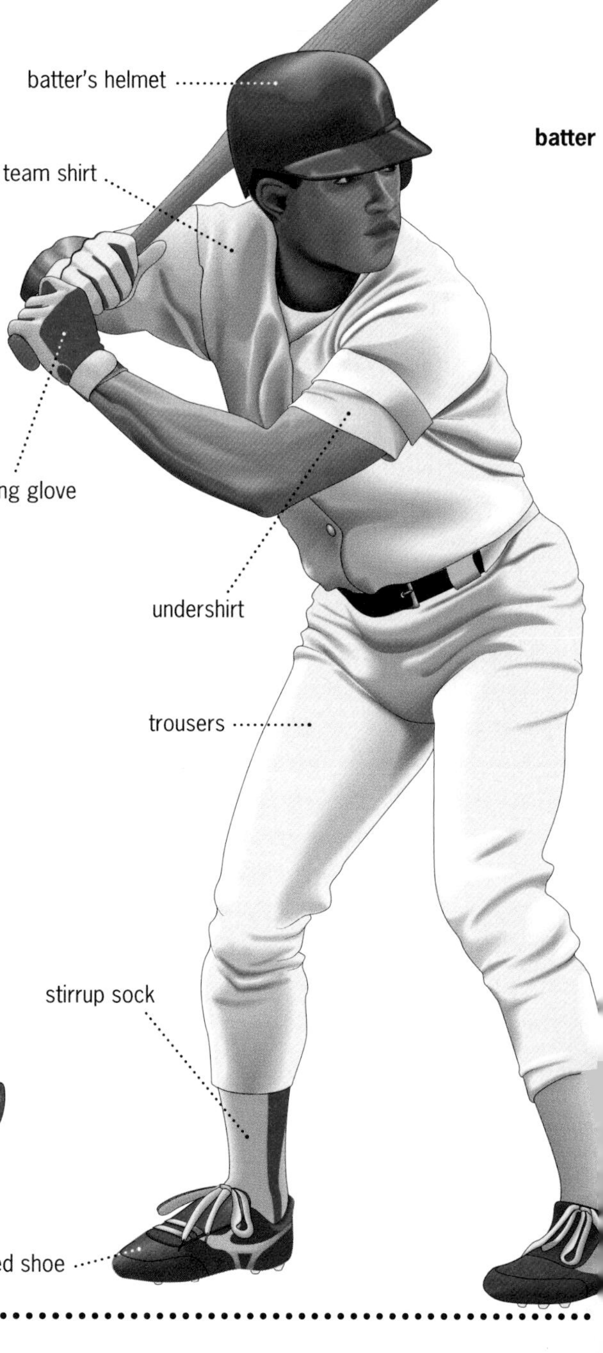
batter's helmet
team shirt
batting glove
undershirt
trousers
stirrup sock
spiked shoe

catcher

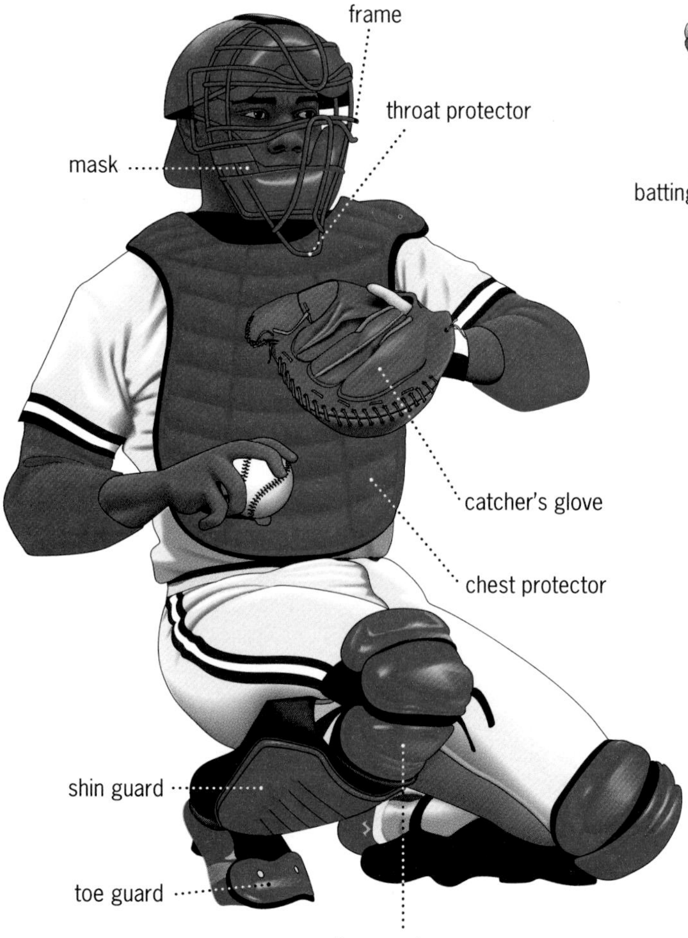
frame
throat protector
mask
catcher's glove
chest protector
shin guard
toe guard
knee pad

field

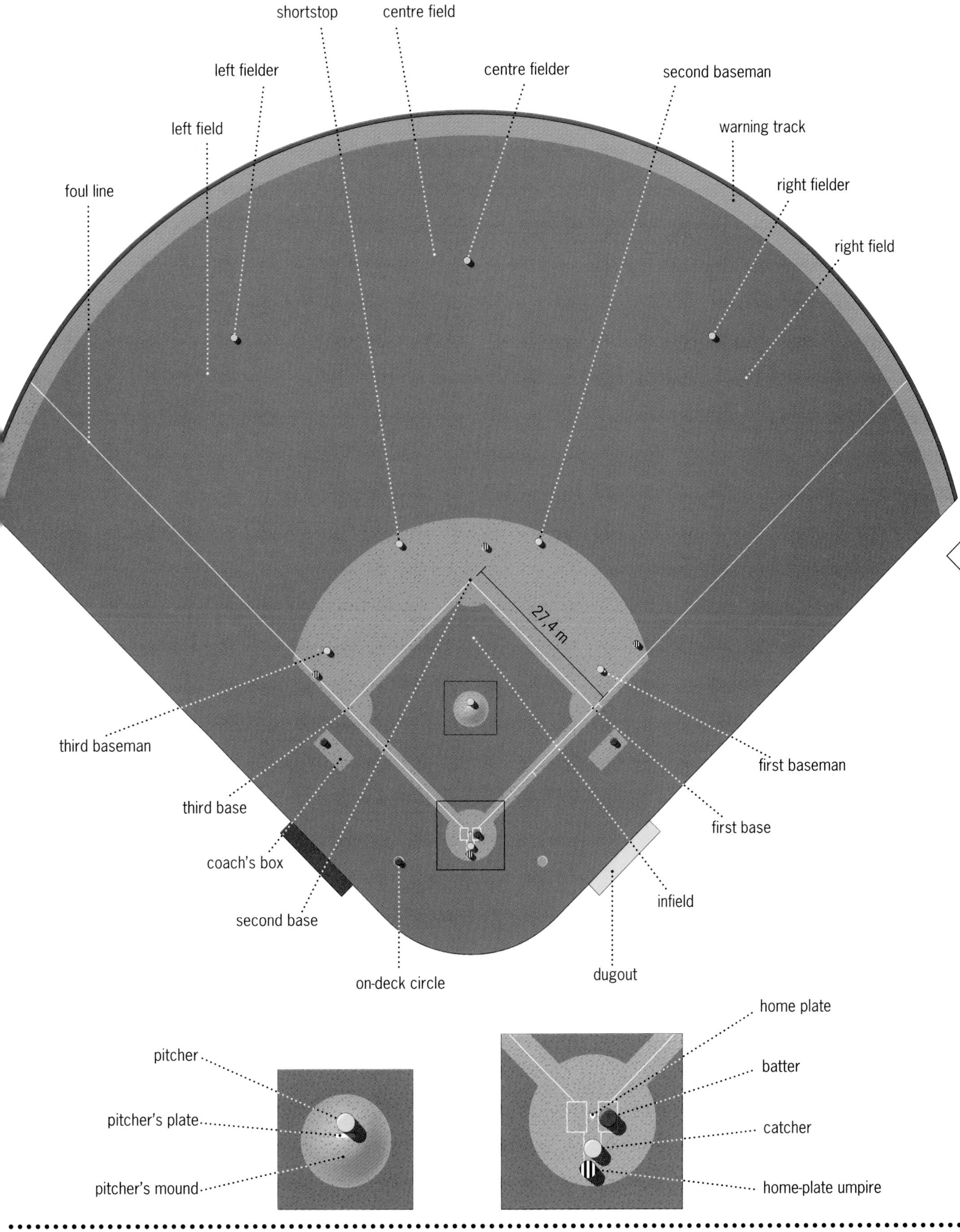
shortstop
centre field
left fielder
centre fielder
second baseman
left field
warning track
foul line
right fielder
right field
27,4 m
third baseman
first baseman
third base
first base
coach's box
infield
second base
on-deck circle
dugout
home plate
pitcher
batter
pitcher's plate
catcher
pitcher's mound
home-plate umpire

AMERICAN FOOTBALL

American football player

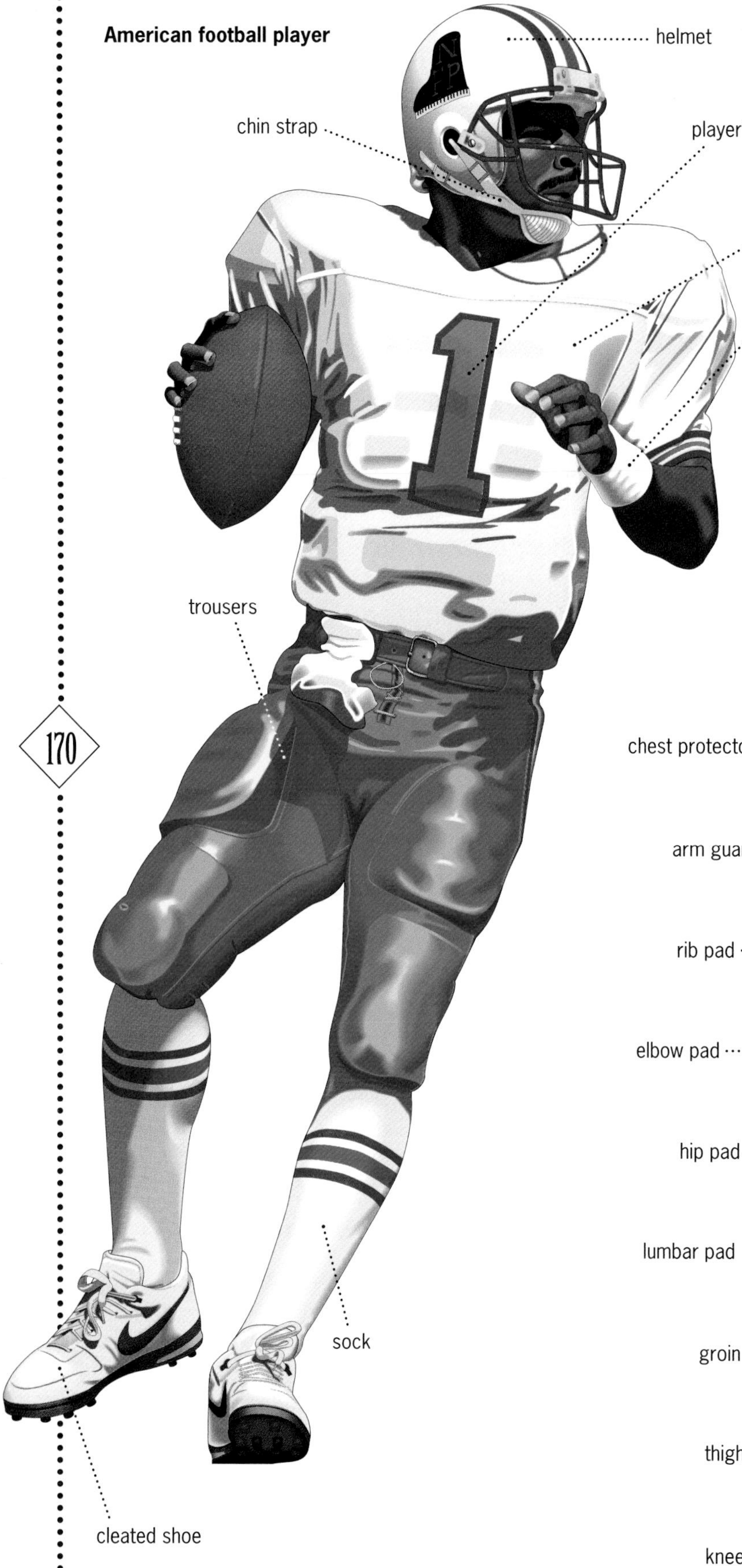
helmet
chin strap
player's number
team shirt
wristband
trousers
sock
cleated shoe

football

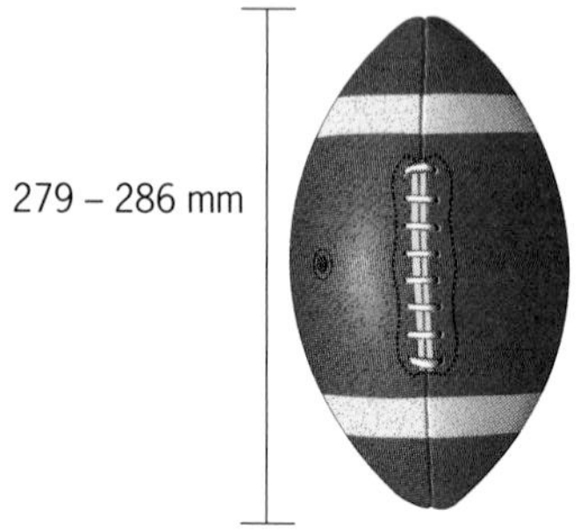
279 – 286 mm

protective equipment

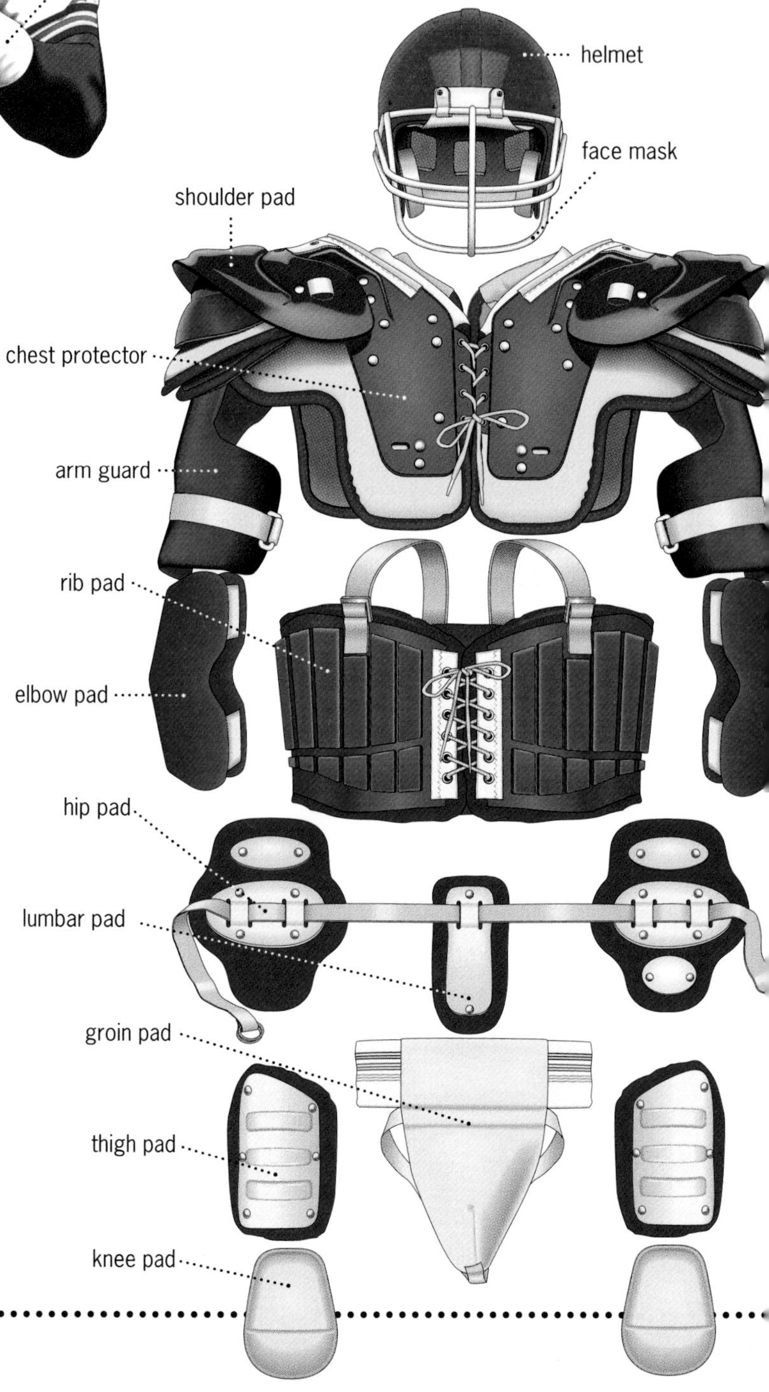
helmet
face mask
shoulder pad
chest protector
arm guard
rib pad
elbow pad
hip pad
lumbar pad
groin pad
thigh pad
knee pad

scrimmage

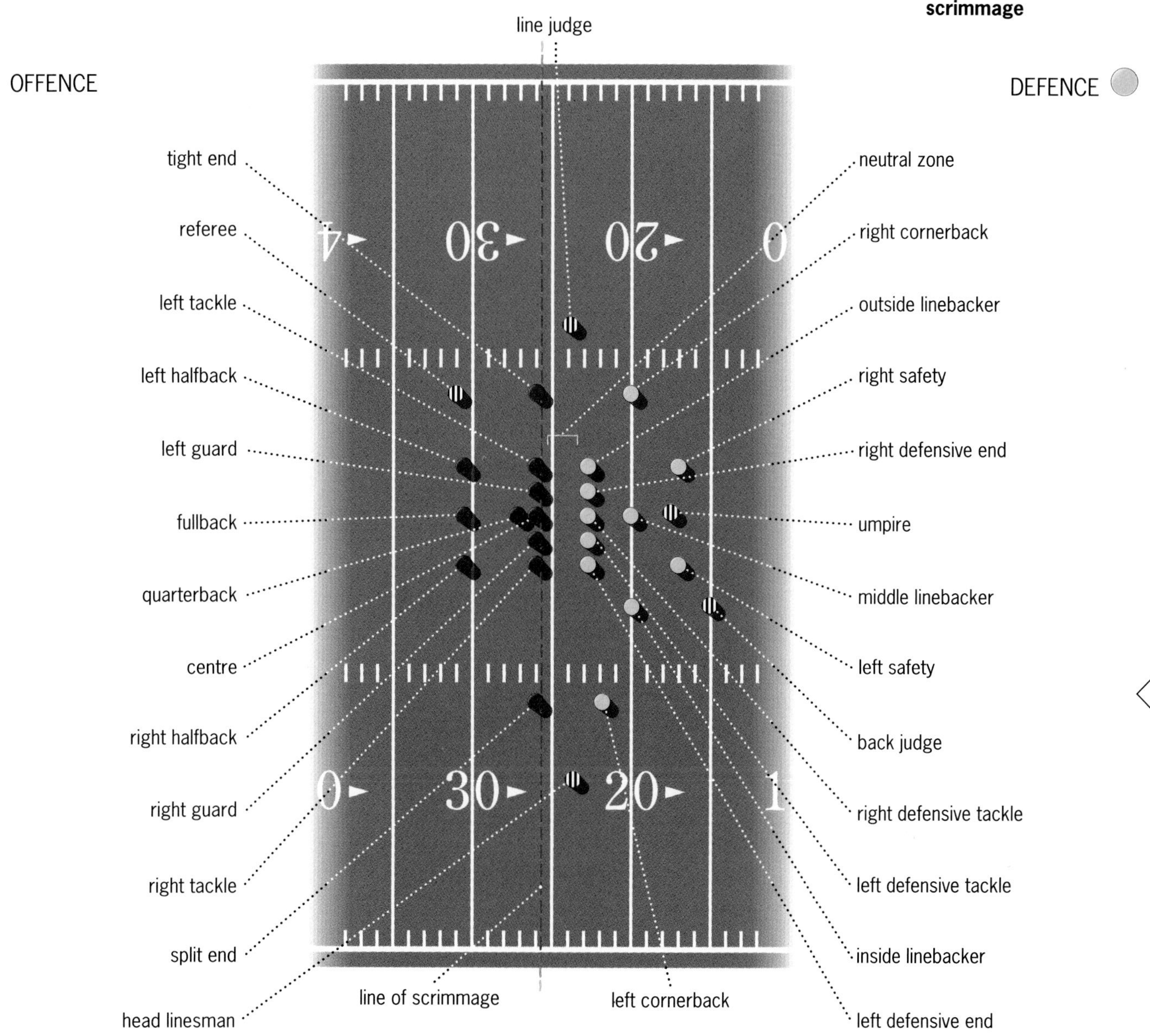
line judge
OFFENCE
DEFENCE
tight end
referee
left tackle
left halfback
left guard
fullback
quarterback
centre
right halfback
right guard
right tackle
split end
head linesman
line of scrimmage
left cornerback
neutral zone
right cornerback
outside linebacker
right safety
right defensive end
umpire
middle linebacker
left safety
back judge
right defensive tackle
left defensive tackle
inside linebacker
left defensive end
30
20

playing field for American football

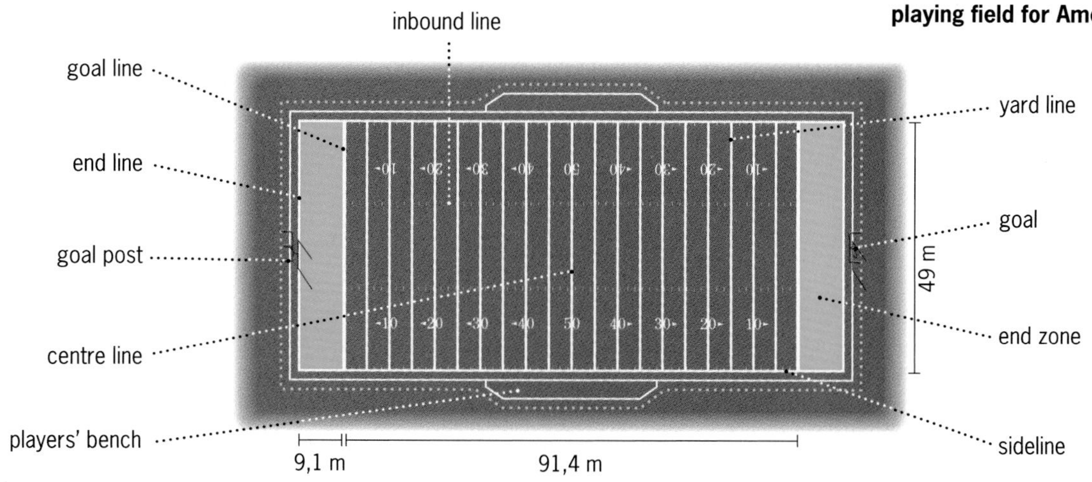
inbound line
goal line
end line
goal post
centre line
players' bench
yard line
goal
end zone
sideline
49 m
9,1 m
91,4 m

SOCCER

soccer player

team shirt
shorts
shin guard
football boot
interchangeable studs

soccer ball

218 mm

playing field

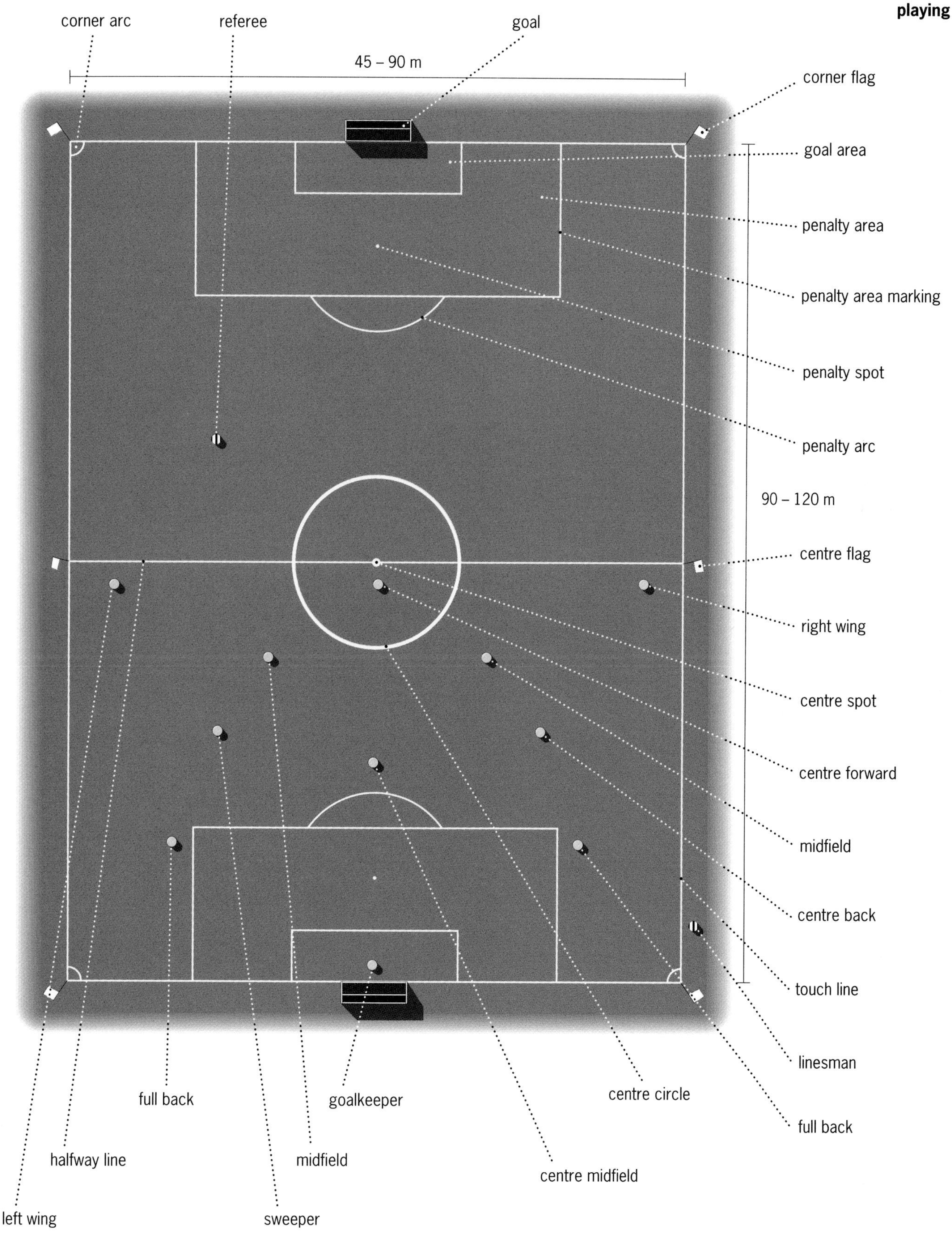
corner arc
referee
goal
45 – 90 m
corner flag
goal area
penalty area
penalty area marking
penalty spot
penalty arc
90 – 120 m
centre flag
right wing
centre spot
centre forward
midfield
centre back
touch line
linesman
full back
centre circle
centre midfield
goalkeeper
full back
midfield
halfway line
sweeper
left wing

CRICKET

cricket player

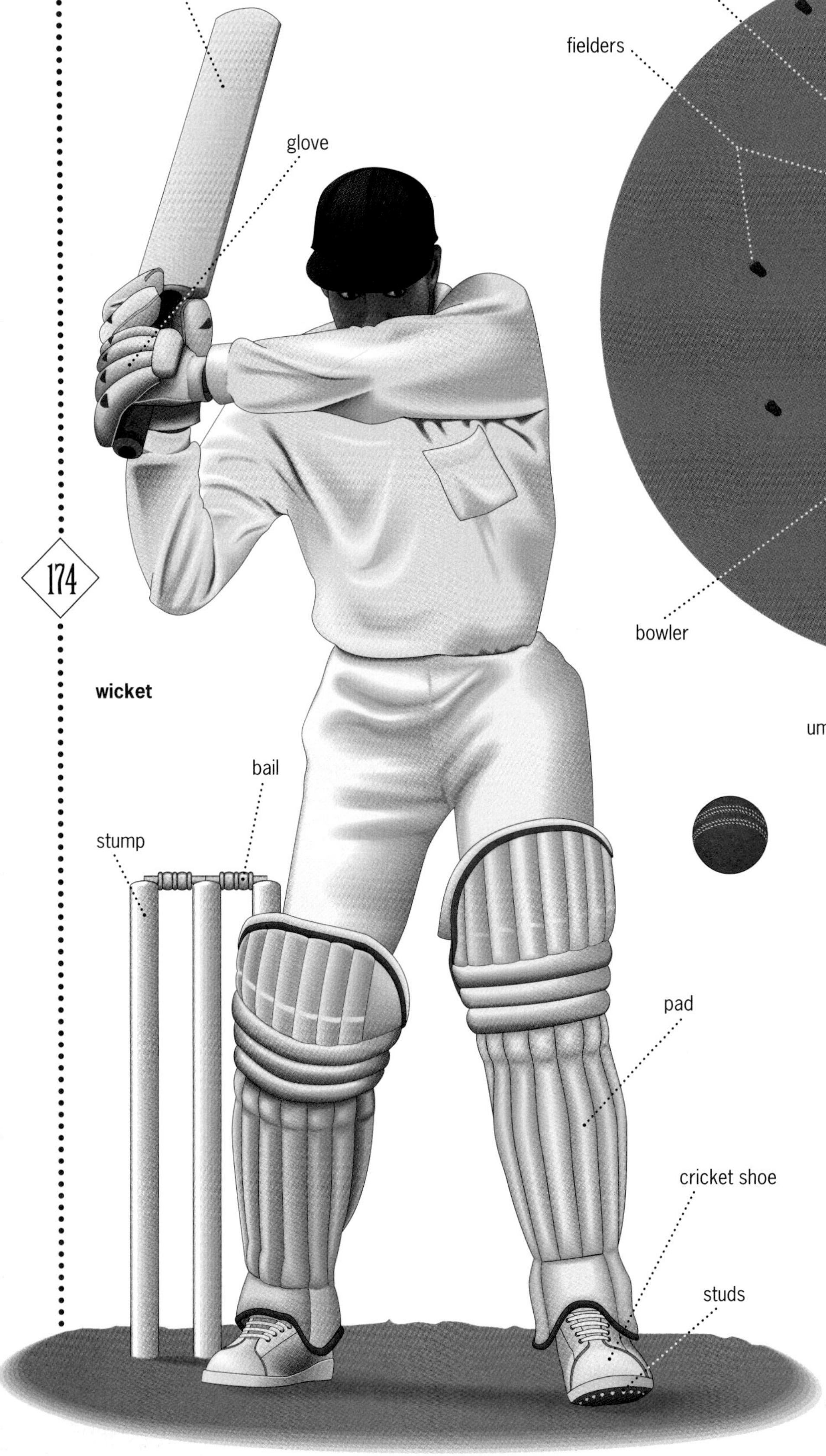
bat
glove
bail
stump
pad
cricket shoe
studs

wicket

field

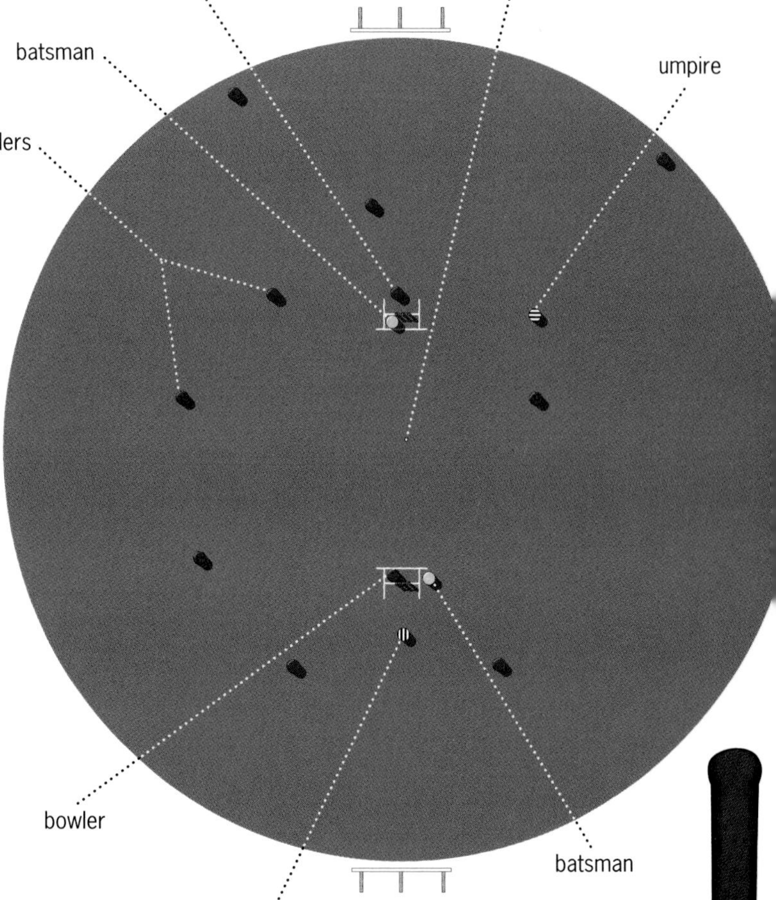
wicket-keeper
pitch
batsman
umpire
fielders
bowler
batsman
umpire

cricket ball

70 – 73 mm

bat

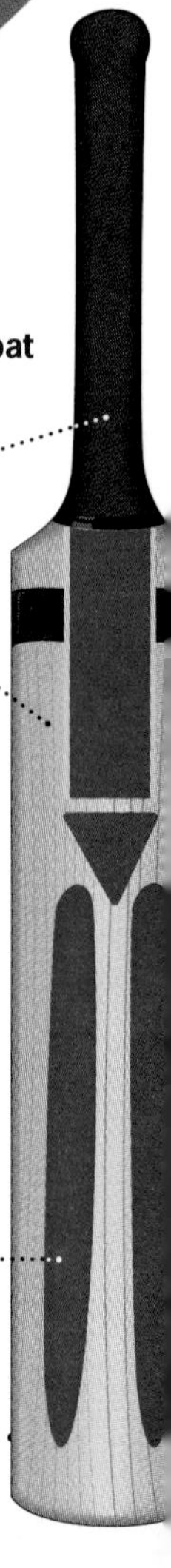
handle
willow
groove

FIELD HOCKEY

playing field

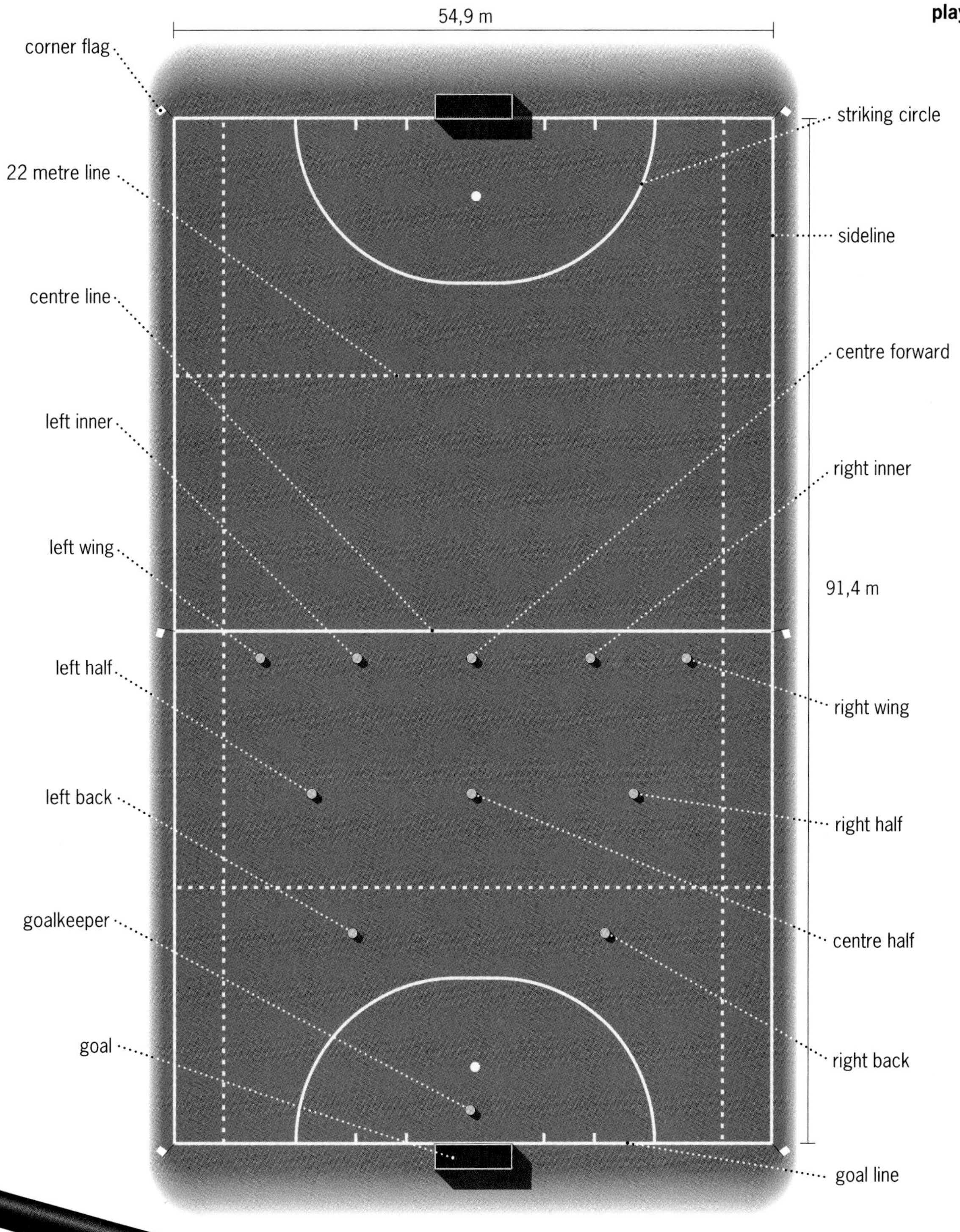
54,9 m
corner flag
22 metre line
centre line
left inner
left wing
left half
left back
goalkeeper
goal
striking circle
sideline
centre forward
right inner
91,4 m
right wing
right half
centre half
right back
goal line

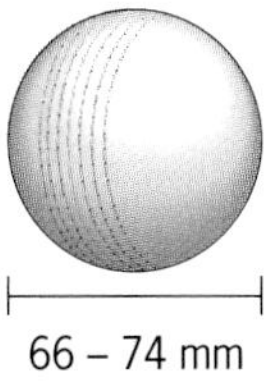
66 – 74 mm

hockey ball

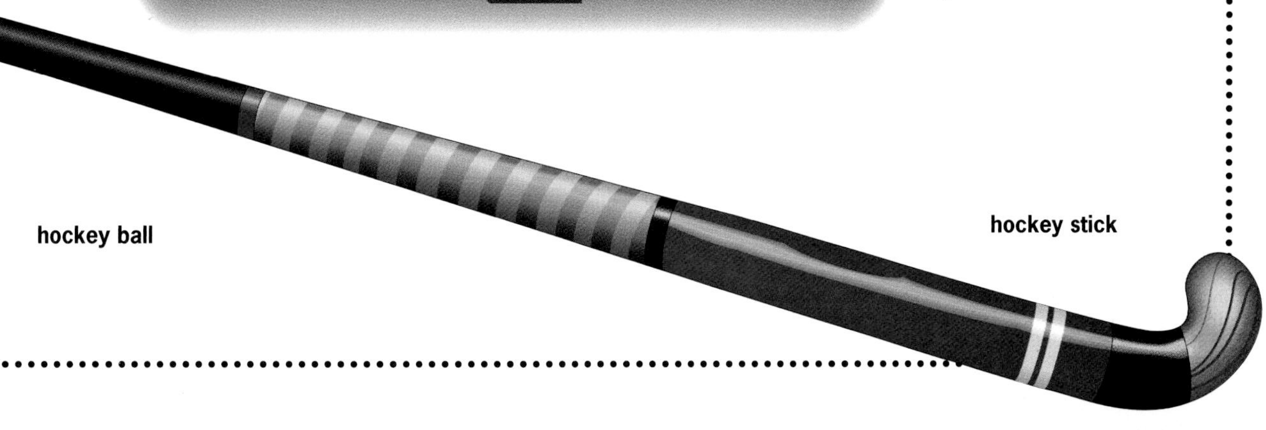

hockey stick

ICE HOCKEY

rink

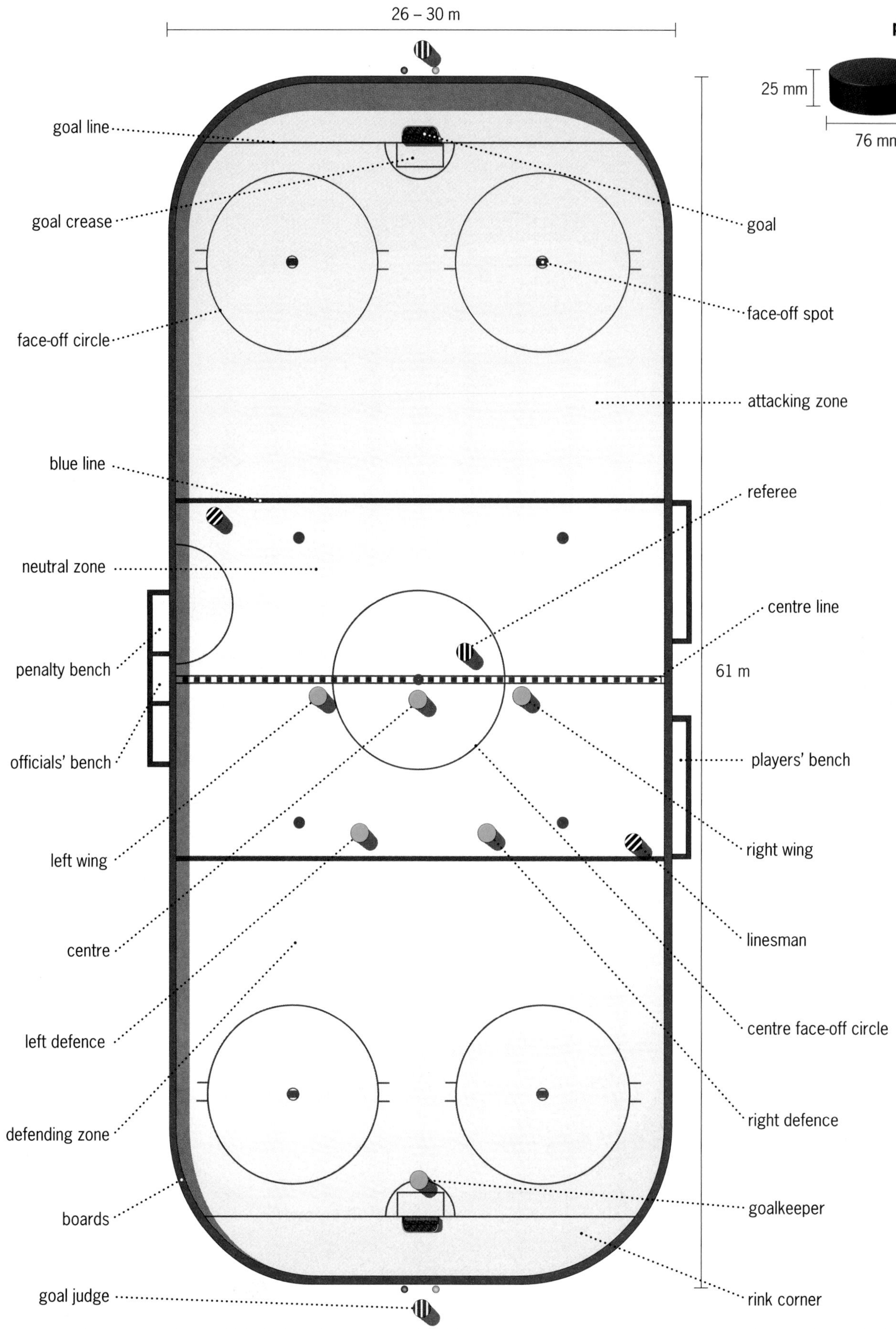
26 – 30 m
goal line
goal crease
face-off circle
blue line
neutral zone
penalty bench
officials' bench
left wing
centre
left defence
defending zone
boards
goal judge
goal
face-off spot
attacking zone
referee
centre line
61 m
players' bench
right wing
linesman
centre face-off circle
right defence
goalkeeper
rink corner

puck

25 mm
76 mm

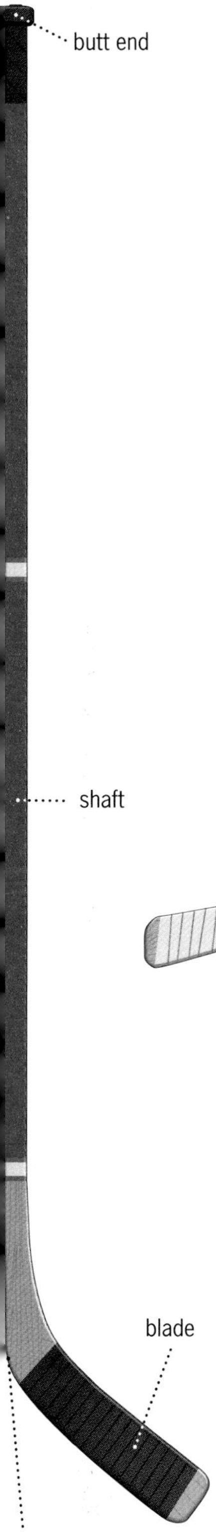
player's stick
butt end
shaft
blade
heel

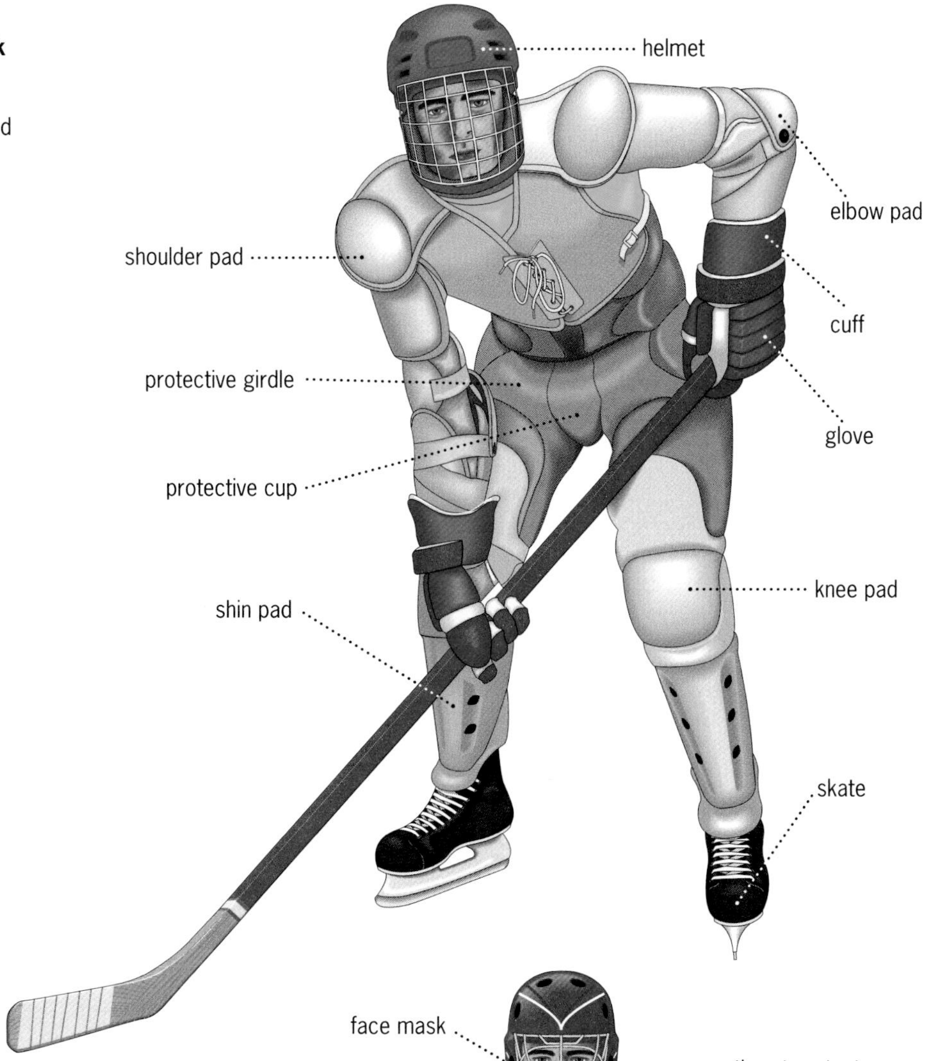
ice hockey player
helmet
elbow pad
shoulder pad
cuff
protective girdle
glove
protective cup
knee pad
shin pad
skate

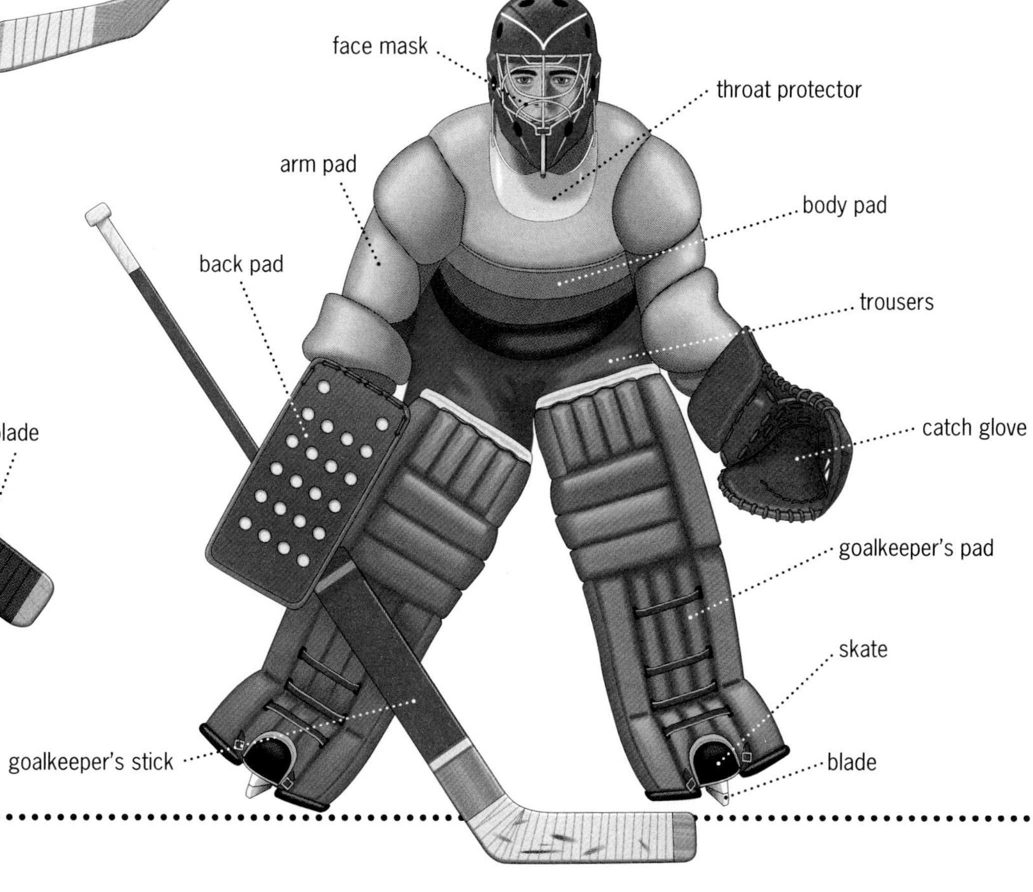
goalkeeper
face mask
throat protector
arm pad
body pad
back pad
trousers
catch glove
goalkeeper's pad
skate
goalkeeper's stick
blade

BASKETBALL

court

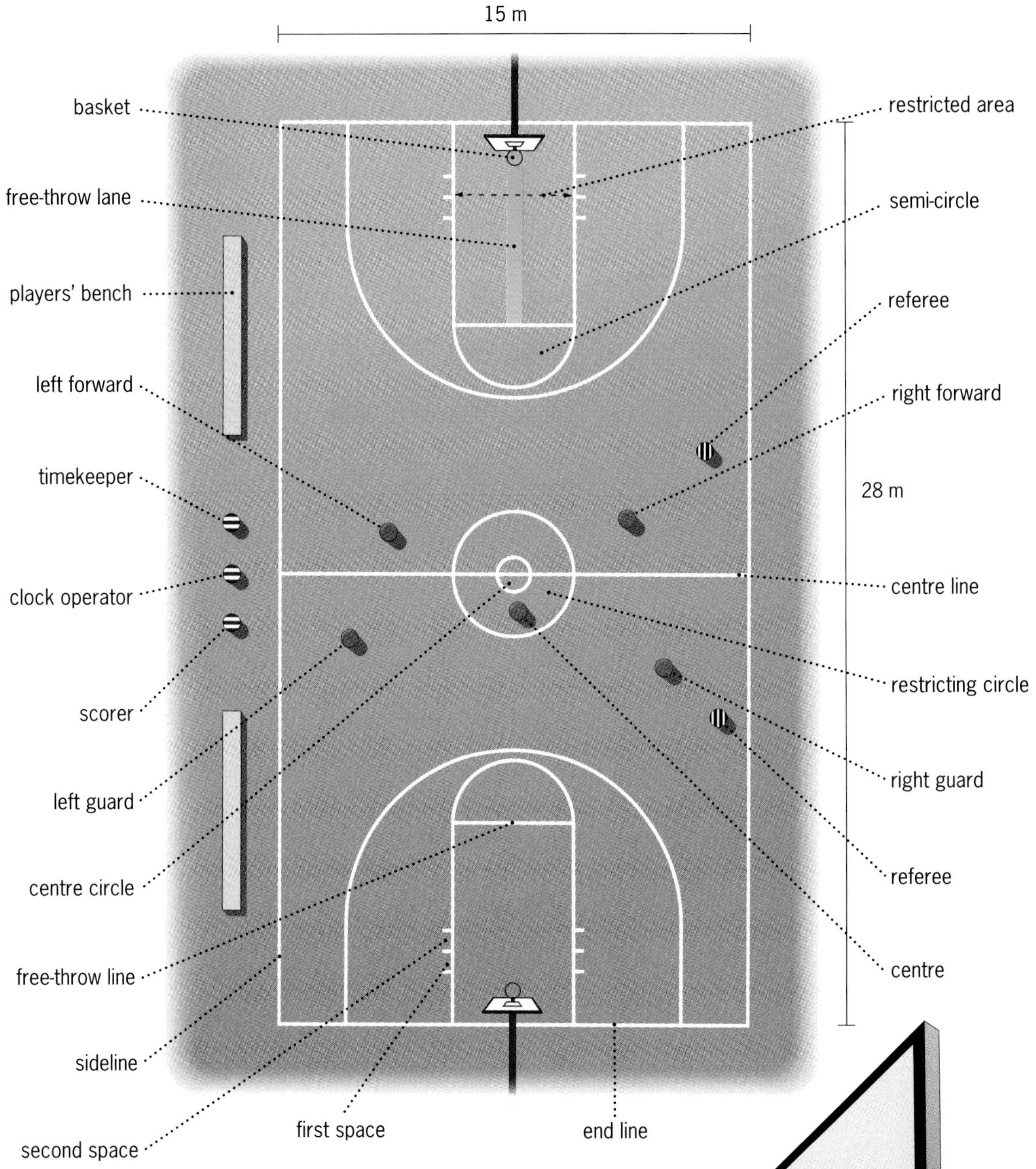
15 m
basket
free-throw lane
players' bench
left forward
timekeeper
clock operator
scorer
left guard
centre circle
free-throw line
sideline
second space
first space
end line
restricted area
semi-circle
referee
right forward
28 m
centre line
restricting circle
right guard
referee
centre

basketball

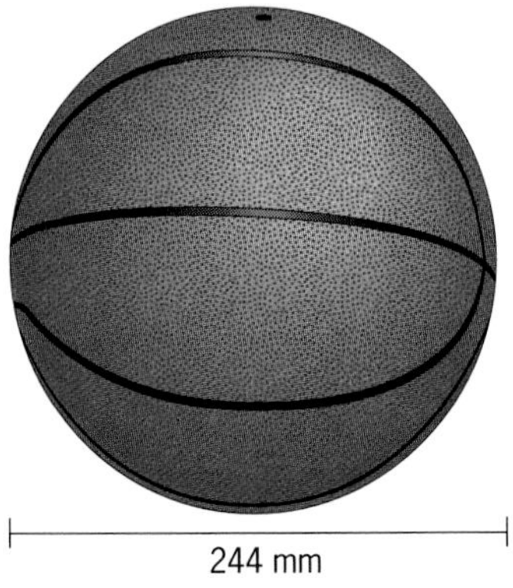
244 mm

basket

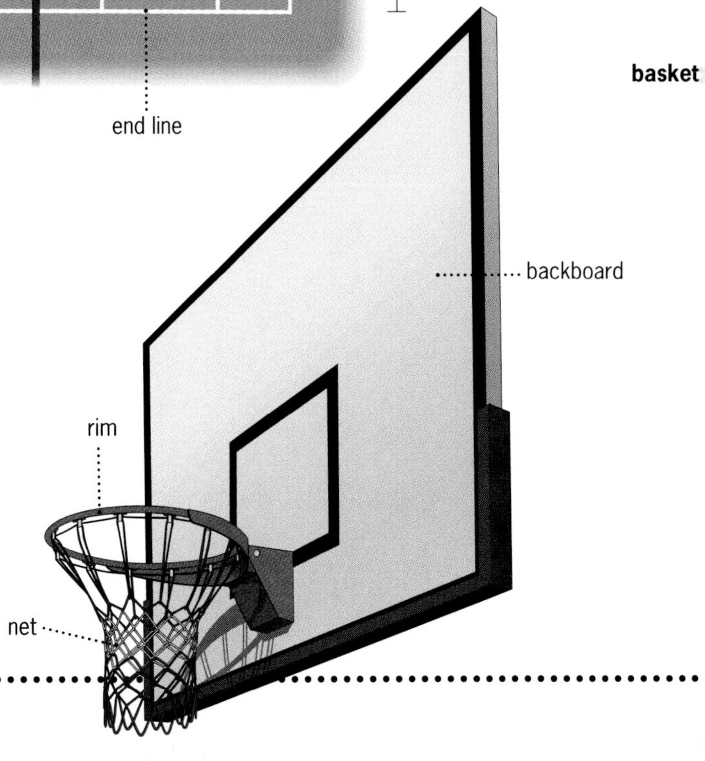
backboard
rim
net

VOLLEYBALL

court

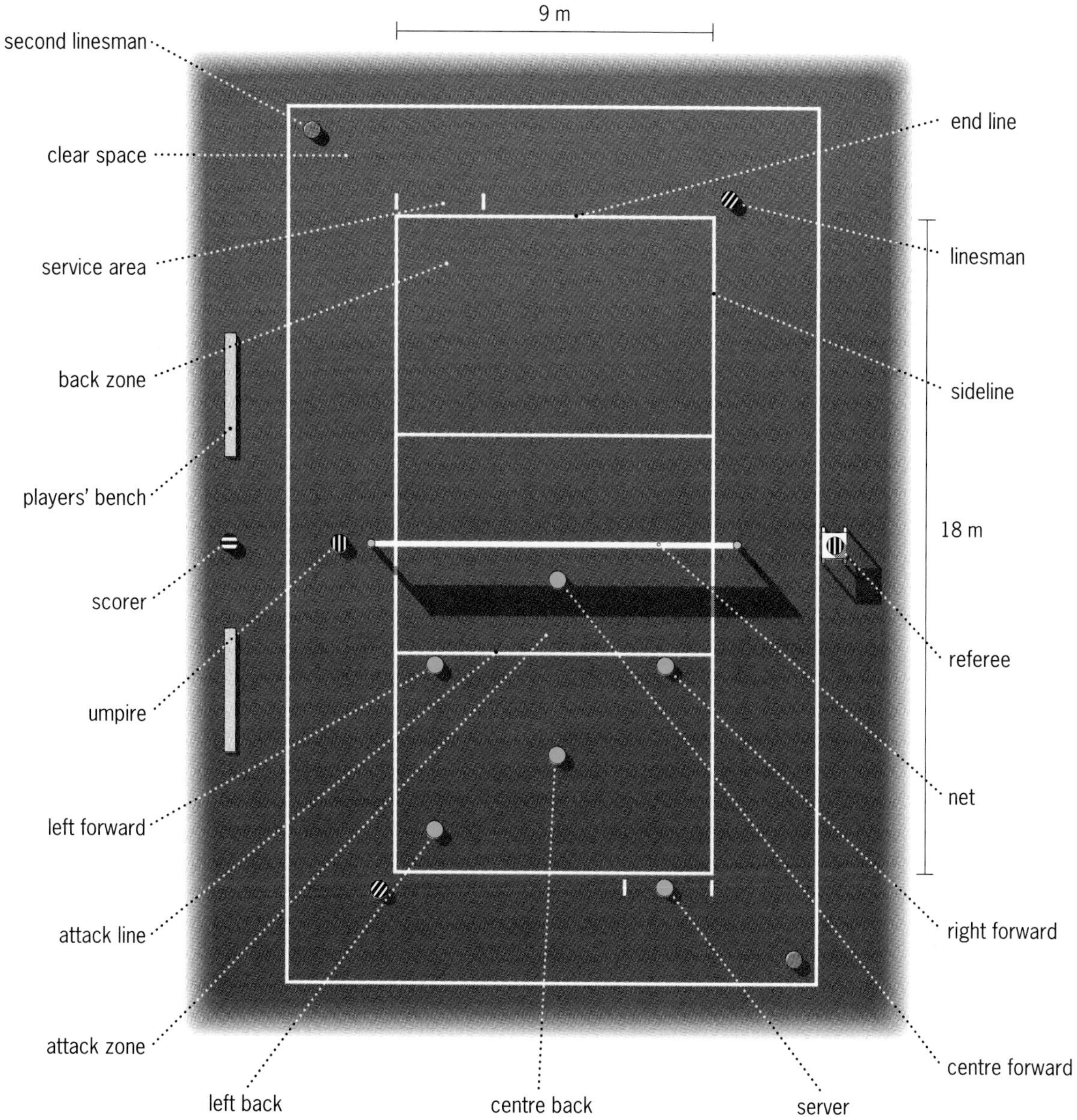
9 m
second linesman
clear space
service area
back zone
players' bench
scorer
umpire
left forward
attack line
attack zone
left back
centre back
server
centre forward
right forward
net
referee
18 m
sideline
linesman
end line

volleyball

206 – 213 mm

net

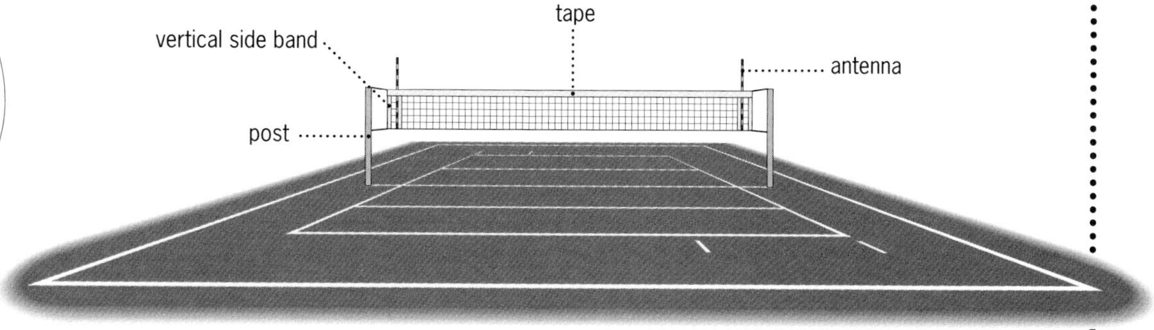
tape
vertical side band
antenna
post

TENNIS

court

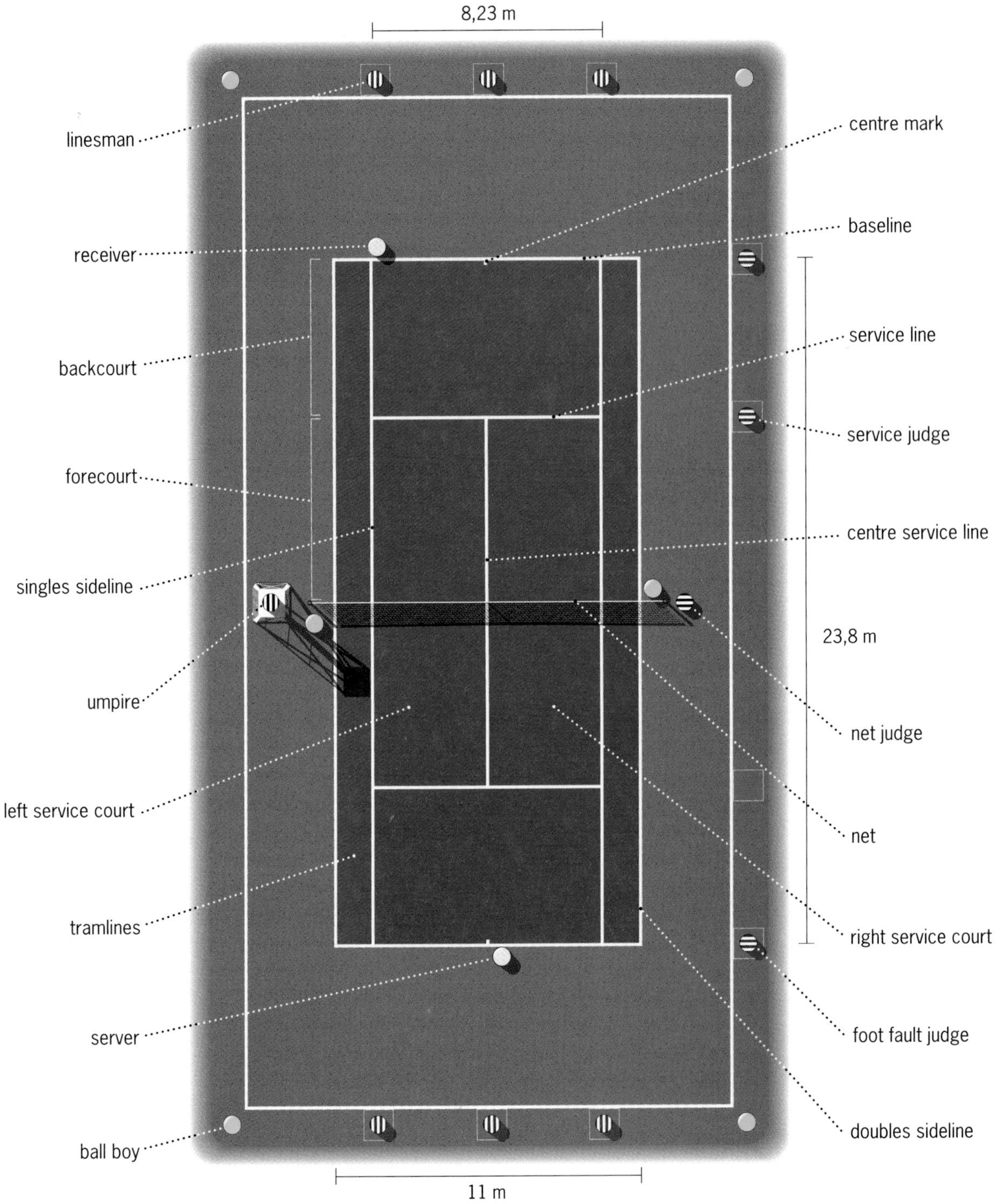
8,23 m
linesman
centre mark
receiver
baseline
backcourt
service line
service judge
forecourt
centre service line
singles sideline
23,8 m
umpire
net judge
left service court
net
tramlines
right service court
server
foot fault judge
ball boy
doubles sideline
11 m

net

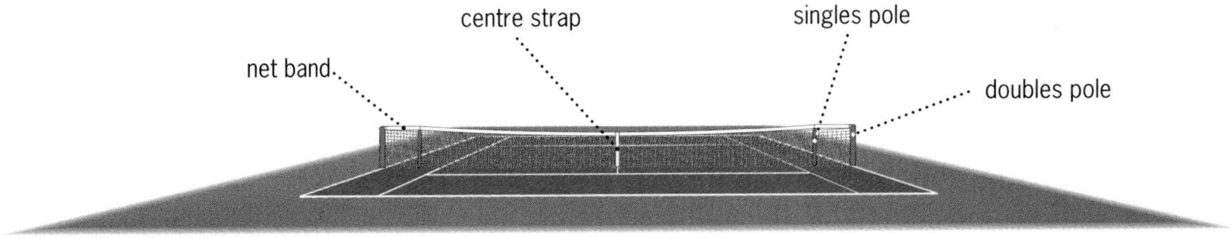
centre strap
singles pole
net band
doubles pole

tennis ball
64 – 68 mm

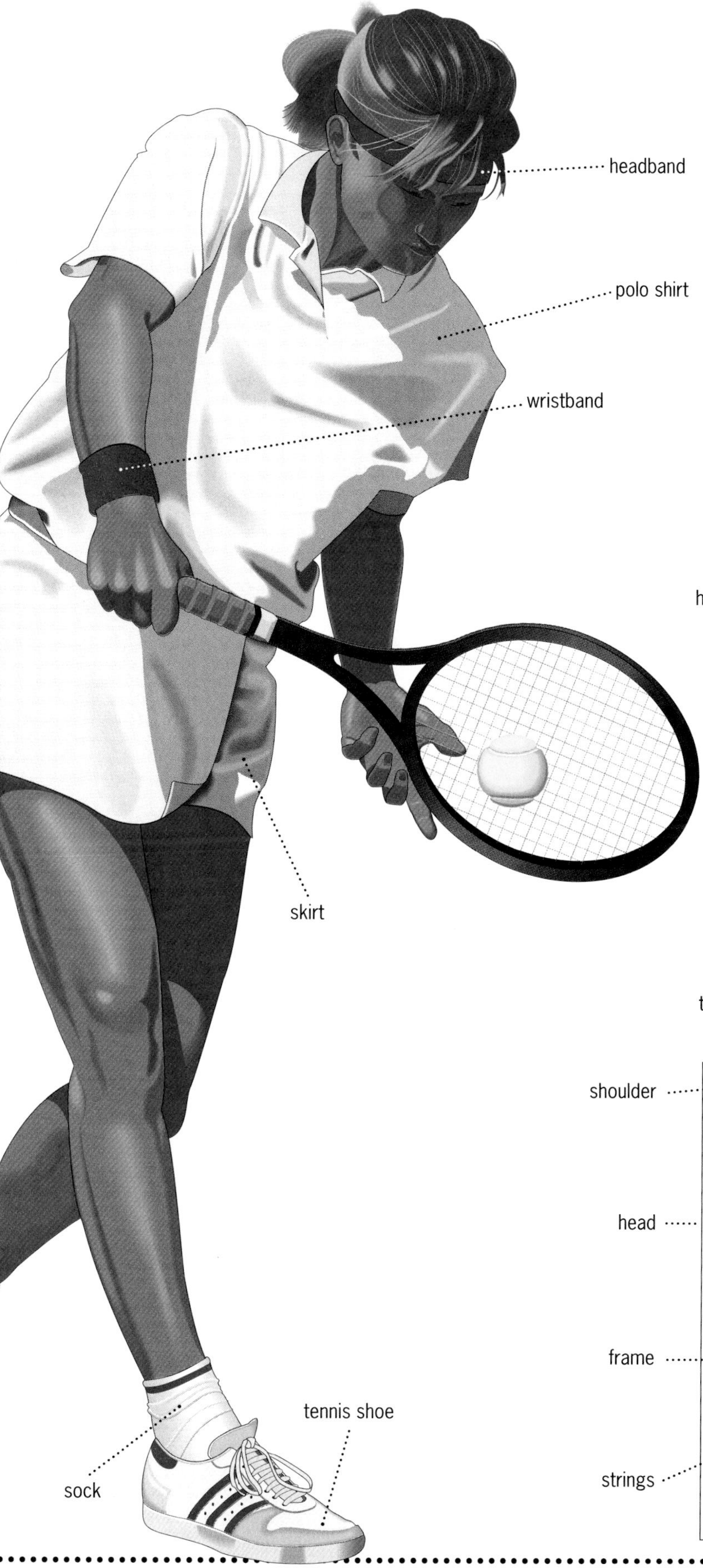
tennis player
headband
polo shirt
wristband
skirt
tennis shoe
sock

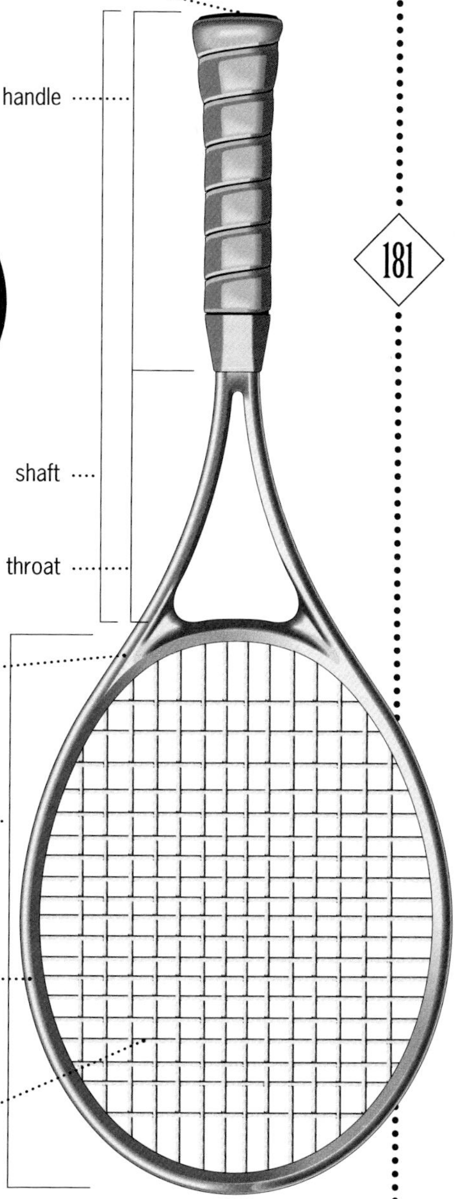
tennis racquet;
tennis racket
butt
handle
shaft
throat
shoulder
head
frame
strings

SWIMMING

competitive course

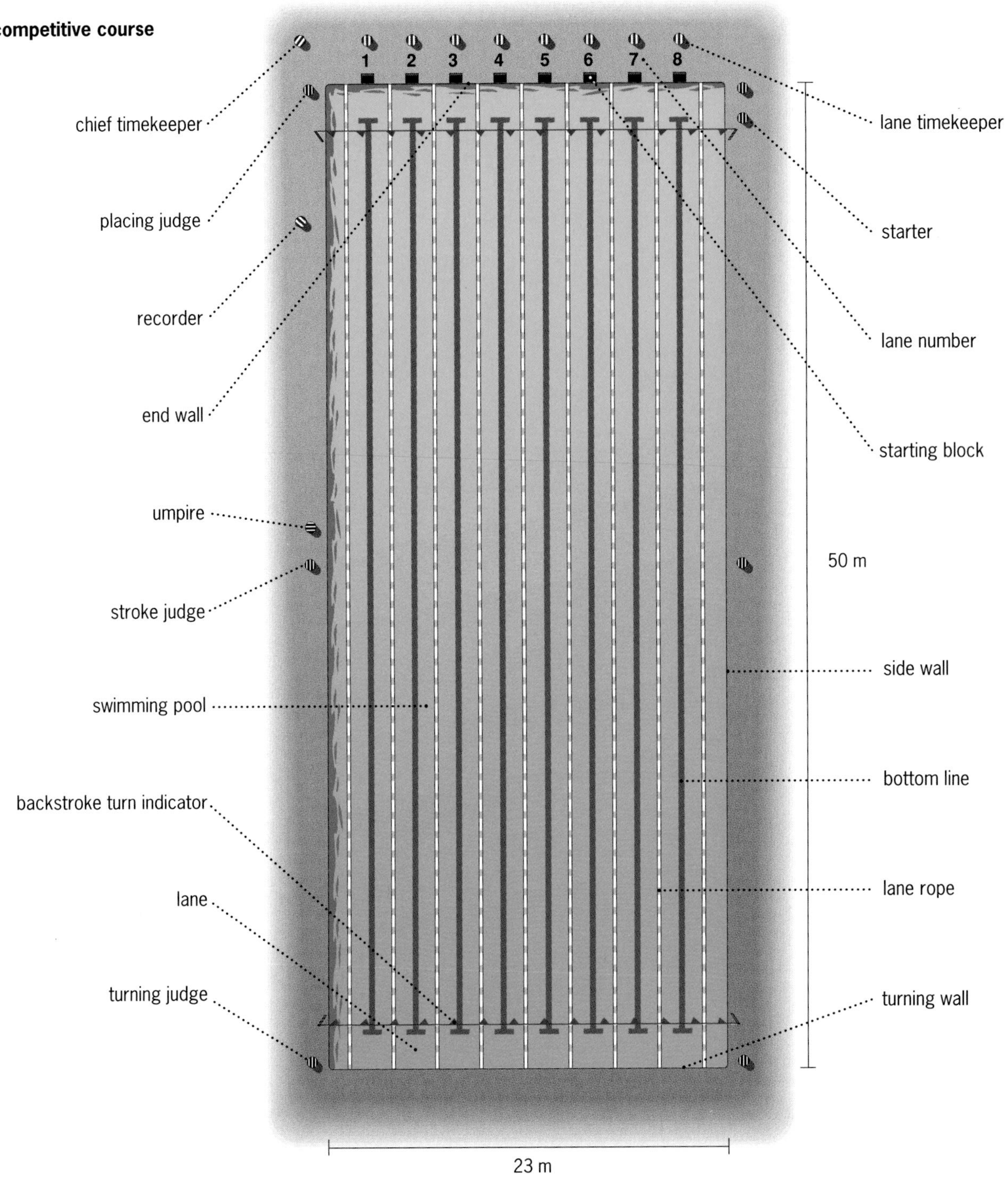
1
2
3
4
5
6
7
8
chief timekeeper
placing judge
recorder
end wall
umpire
stroke judge
swimming pool
backstroke turn indicator
lane
turning judge
lane timekeeper
starter
lane number
starting block
50 m
side wall
bottom line
lane rope
turning wall
23 m

starting block

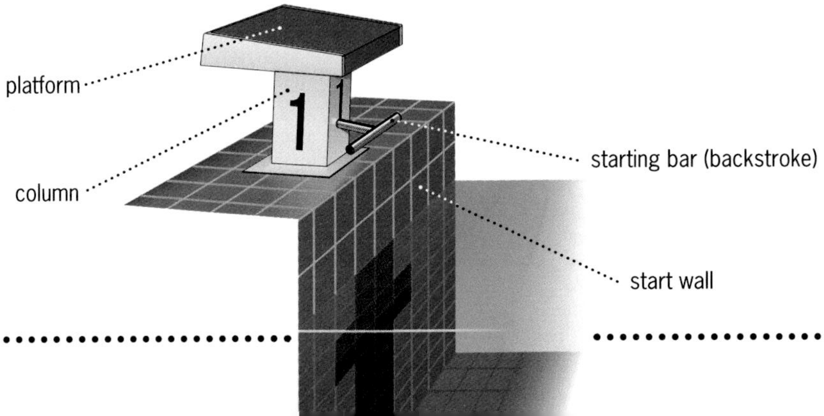
platform
column
1
starting bar (backstroke)
start wall

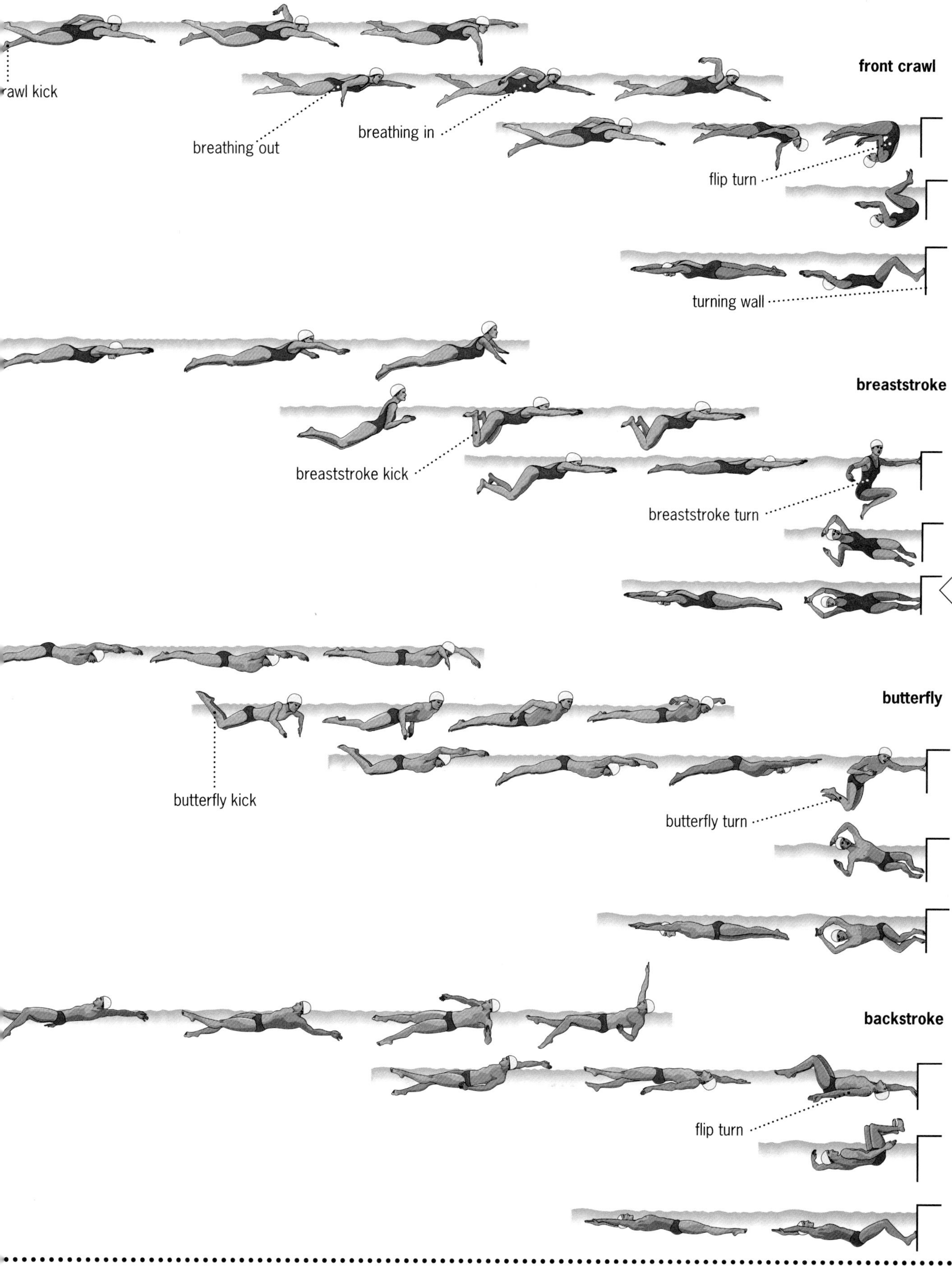
awl kick
front crawl
breathing out
breathing in
flip turn
turning wall
breaststroke
breaststroke kick
breaststroke turn
butterfly
butterfly kick
butterfly turn
backstroke
flip turn

SAILBOARD

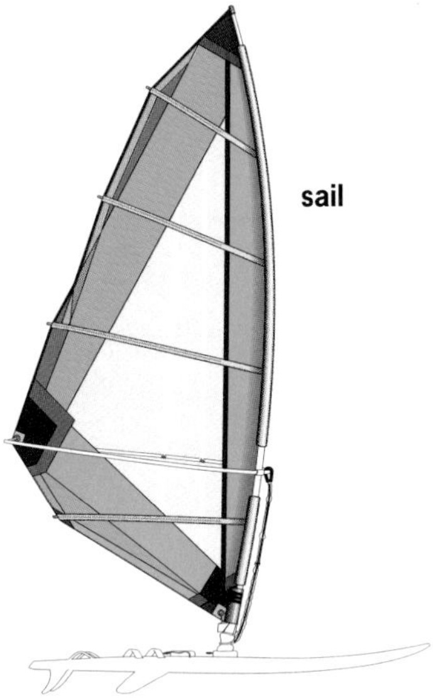
sail

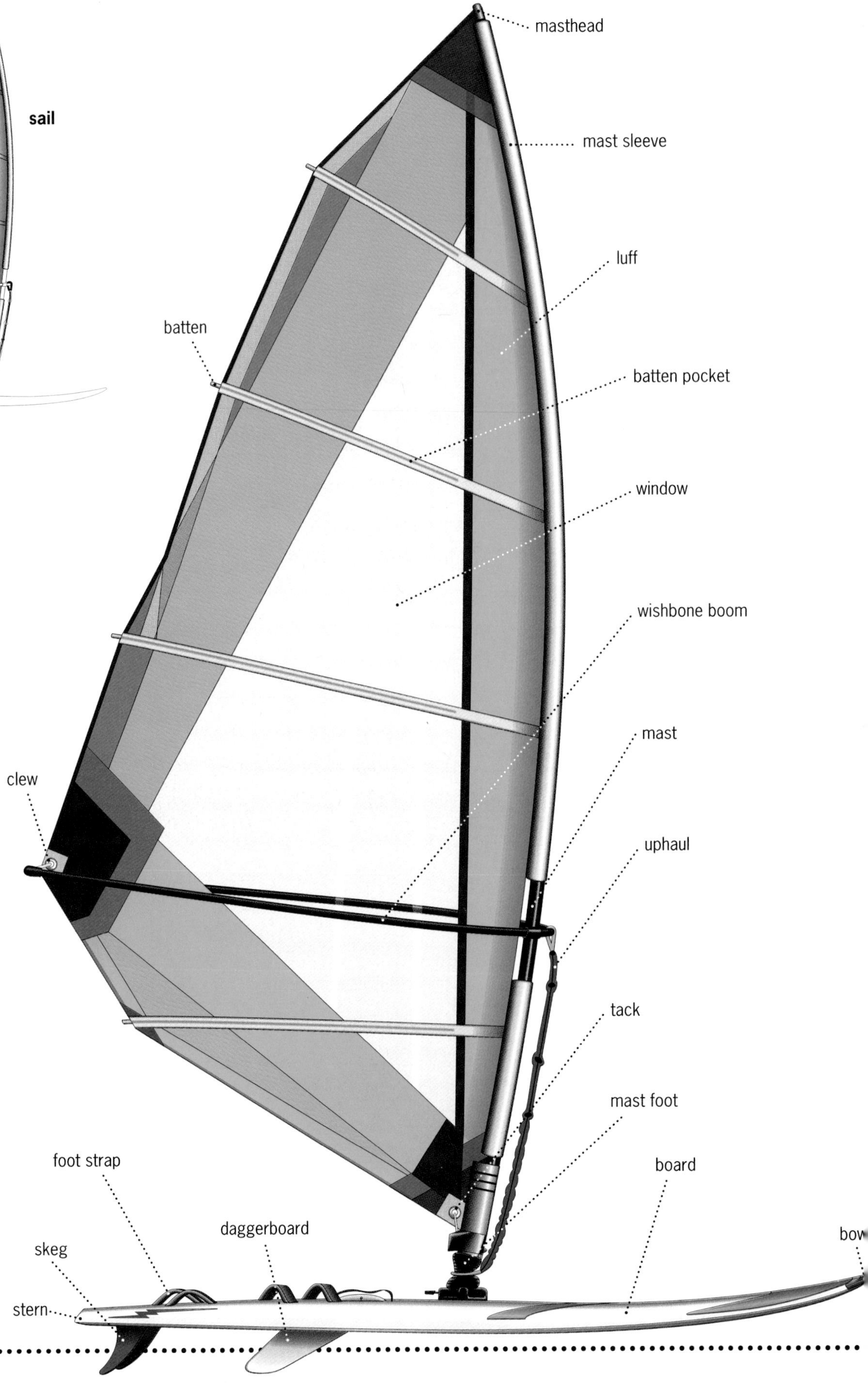
masthead
mast sleeve
luff
batten
batten pocket
window
wishbone boom
mast
clew
uphaul
tack
mast foot
foot strap
board
daggerboard
skeg
bow
stern

SKATING

oller-skate

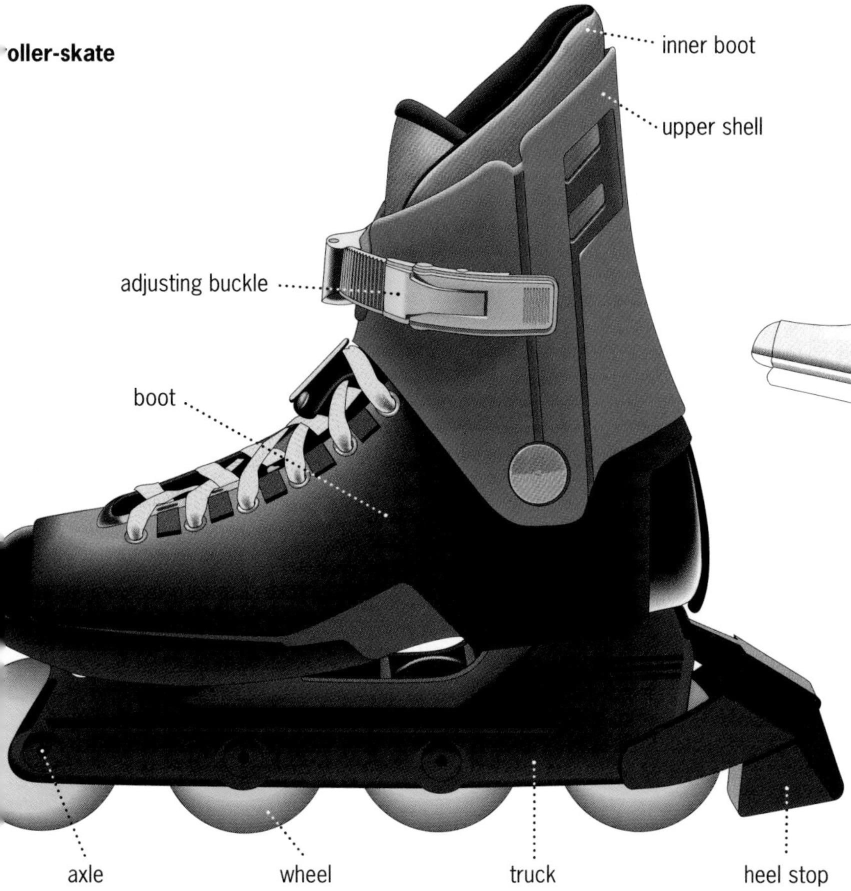
inner boot
upper shell
adjusting buckle
boot
axle
wheel
truck
heel stop

speed skate

hockey skate

tendon guard
boot
toe box
point
blade

figure skate

tongue
hook
backstay
eyelet
boot
lace
stanchion
sole
edge
blade
toe pick

skate guard

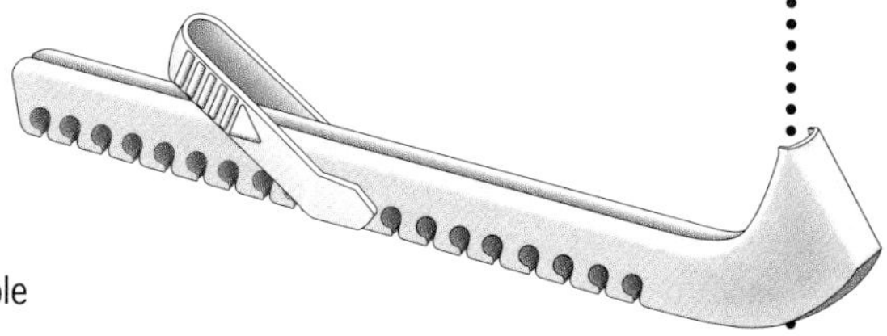

SKIING

alpine skier

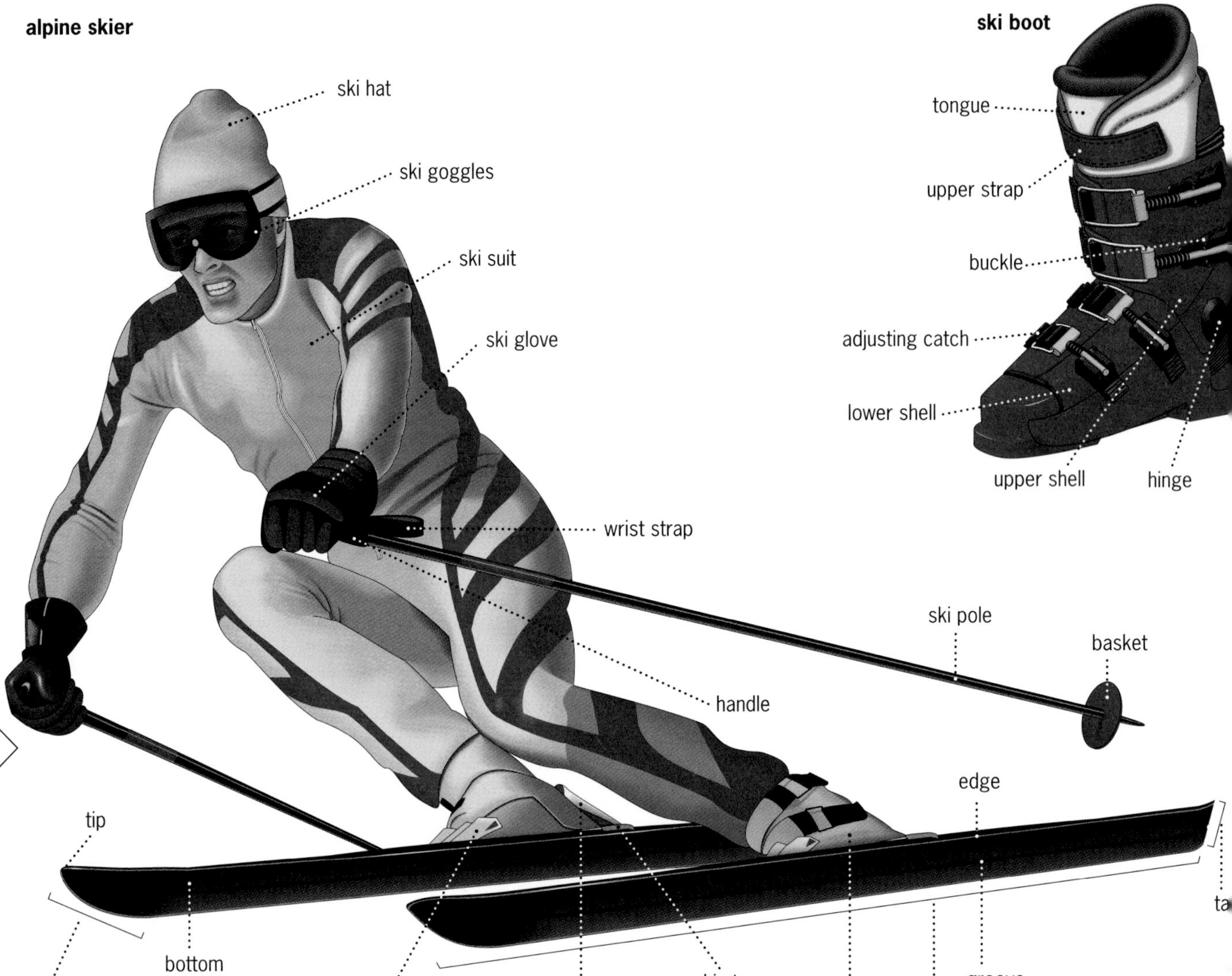
ski hat
ski goggles
ski suit
ski glove
wrist strap
ski pole
basket
handle
edge
tip
bottom
shovel
toe piece
ski stop
groove
ski boot
ski
heel piece
ski boot
tongue
upper strap
buckle
adjusting catch
lower shell
upper shell
hinge

cross-country ski

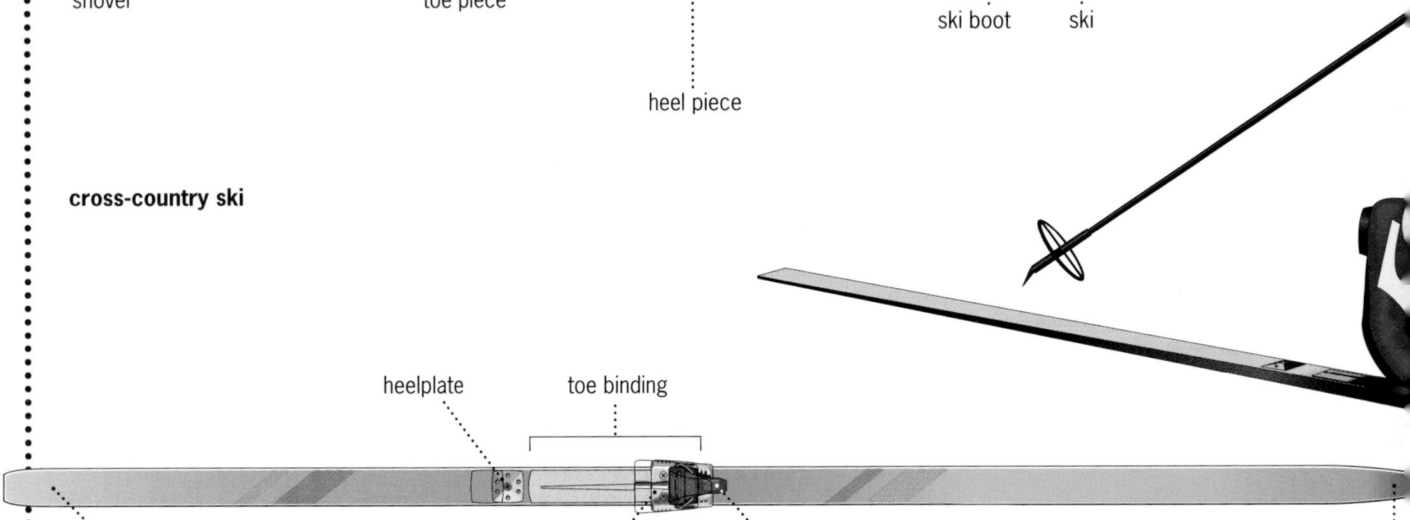
heelplate
toe binding
tail
toeplate
clamp

safety binding

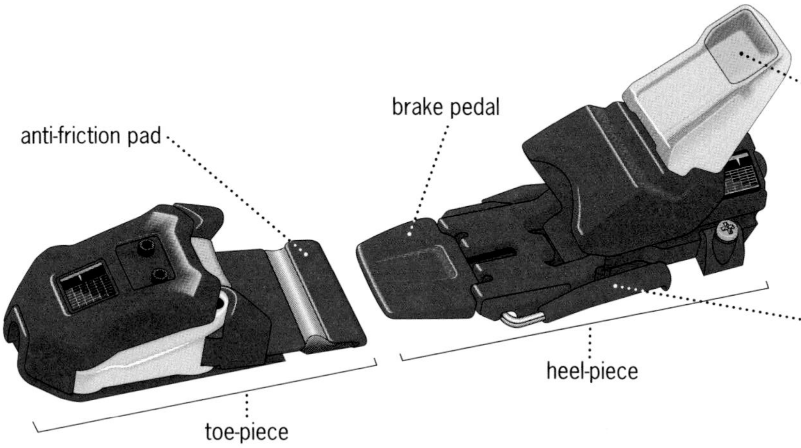
anti-friction pad
brake pedal
manual release
ski stop
heel-piece
toe-piece

cross-country skier

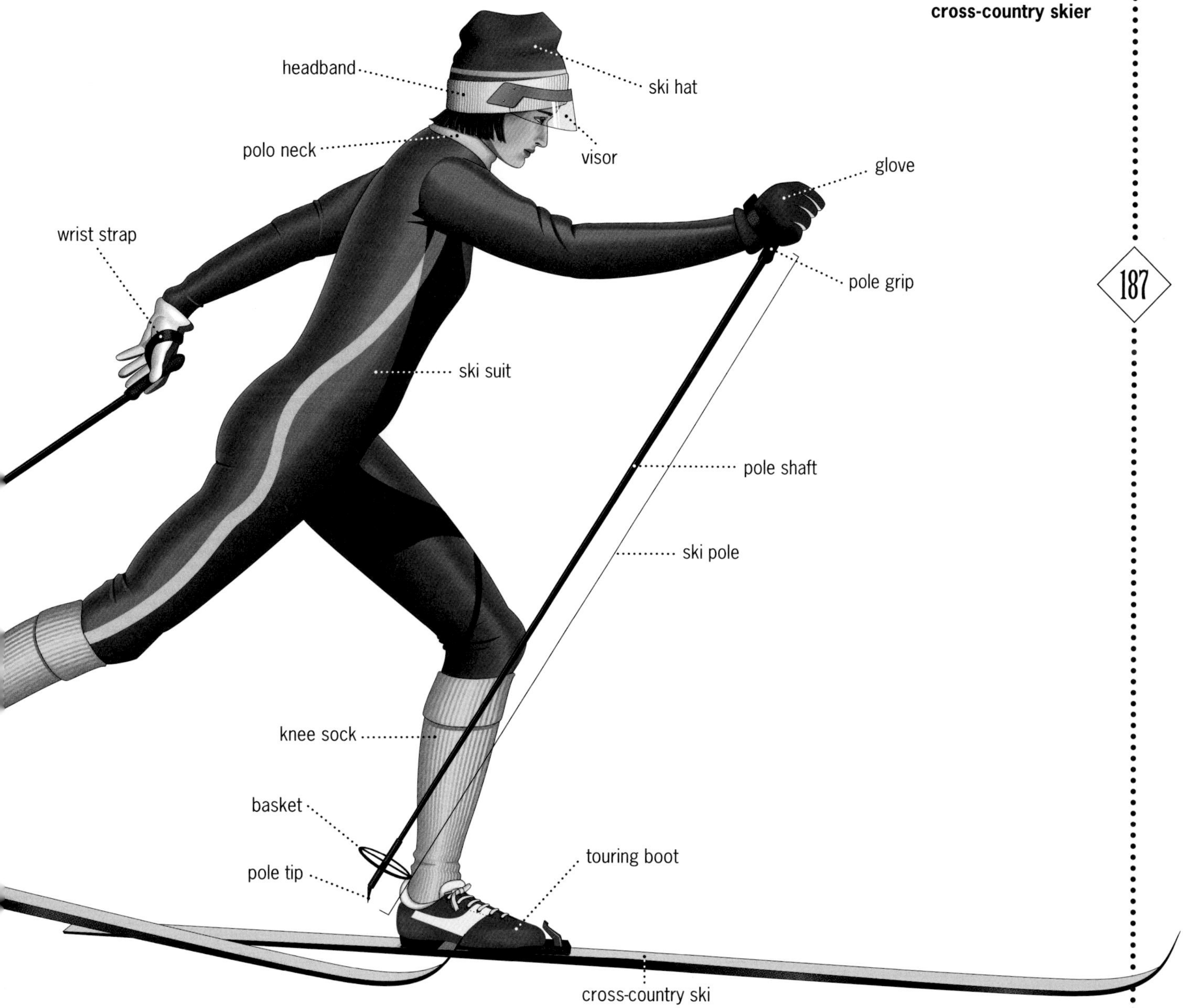
headband
ski hat
polo neck
visor
glove
wrist strap
pole grip
ski suit
pole shaft
ski pole
knee sock
basket
pole tip
touring boot
cross-country ski

GYMNASTICS

pommel horse

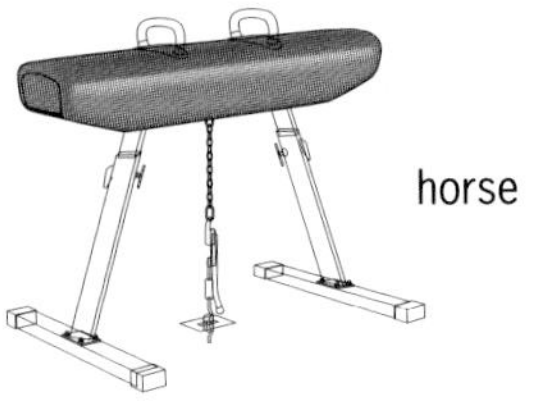
horse

base

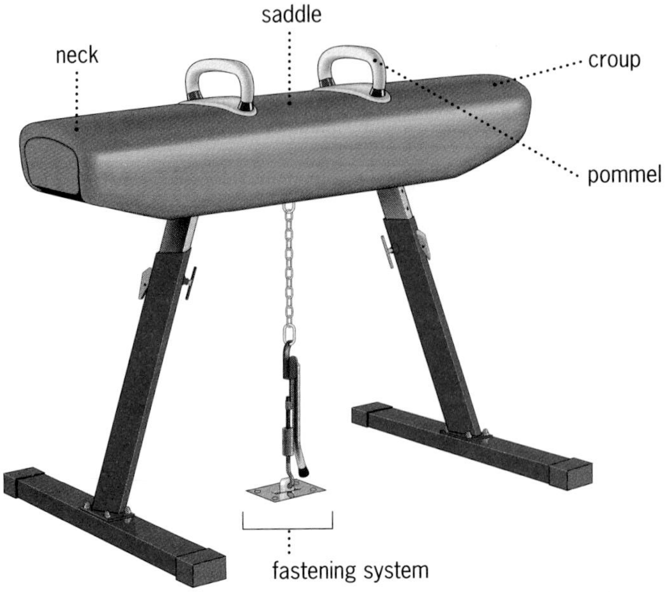
saddle
neck
croup
pommel
fastening system

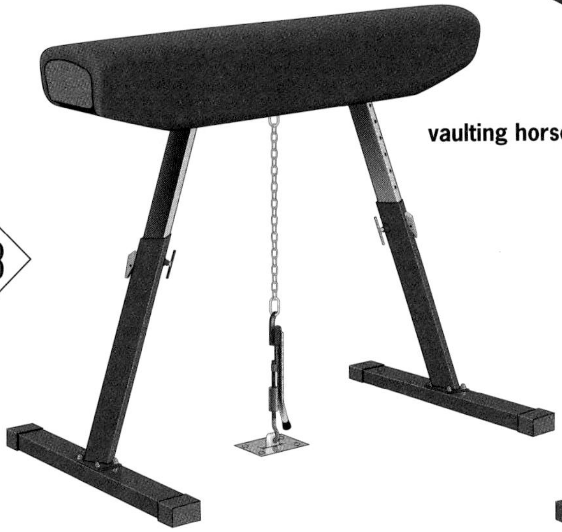

vaulting horse

balance beam

springboard

trampoline

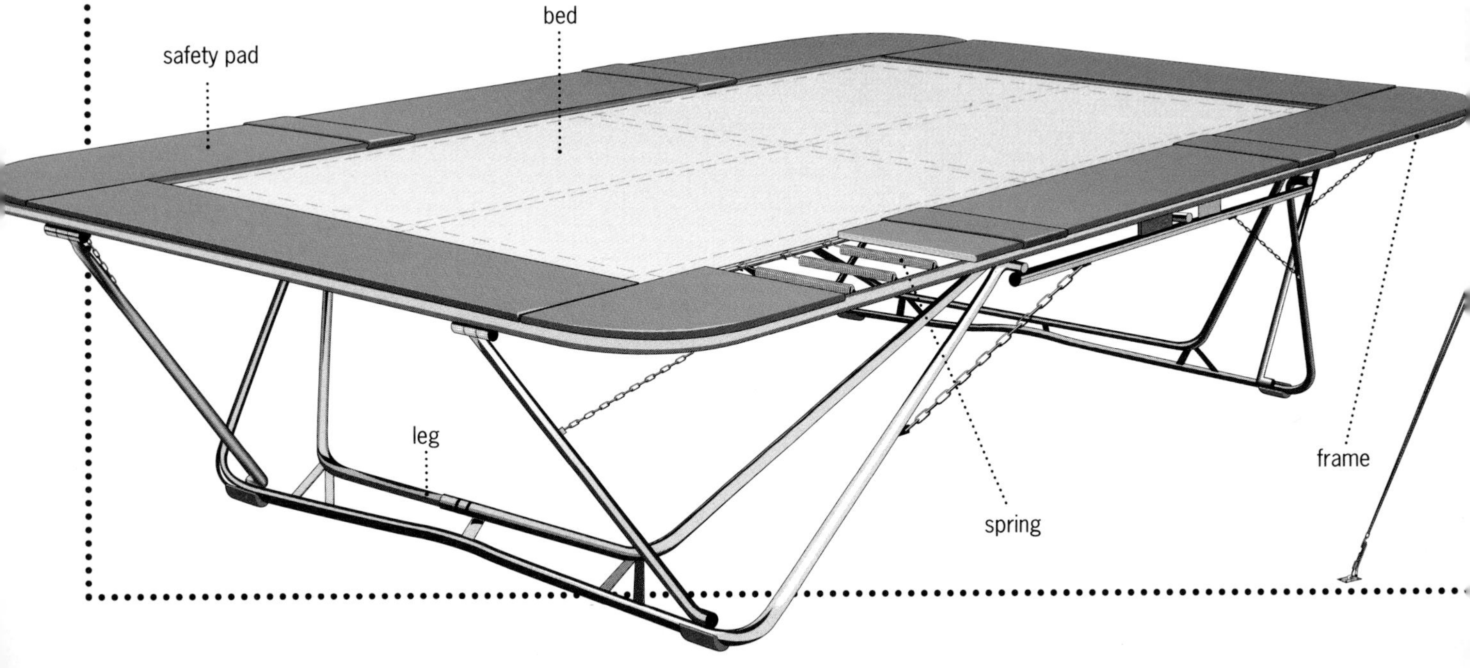
bed
safety pad
leg
spring
frame

symmetrical bars

horizontal bar; high bar

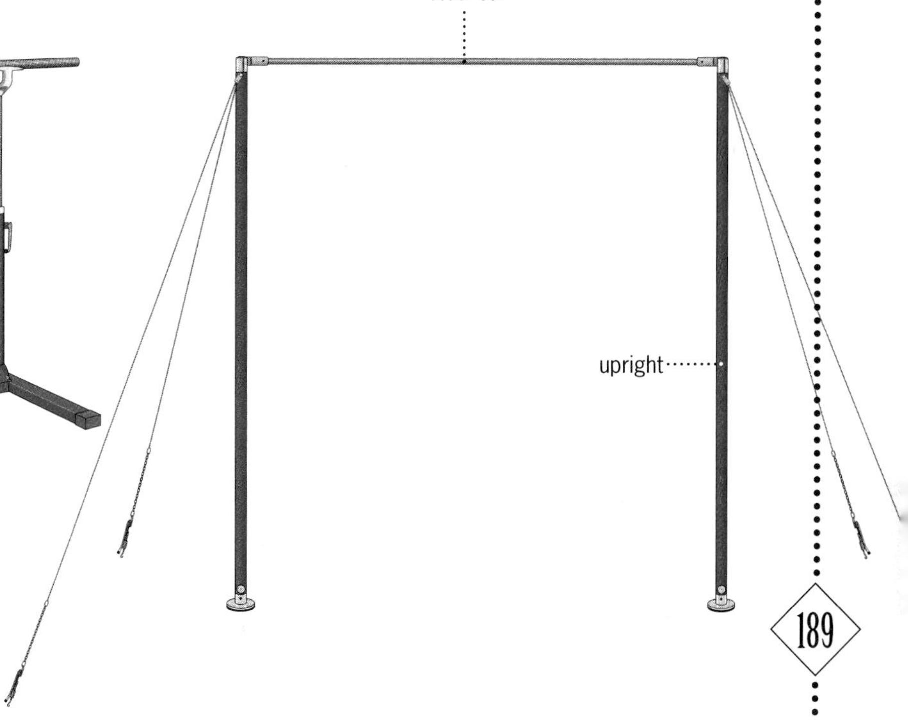
steel bar
upright

ngs

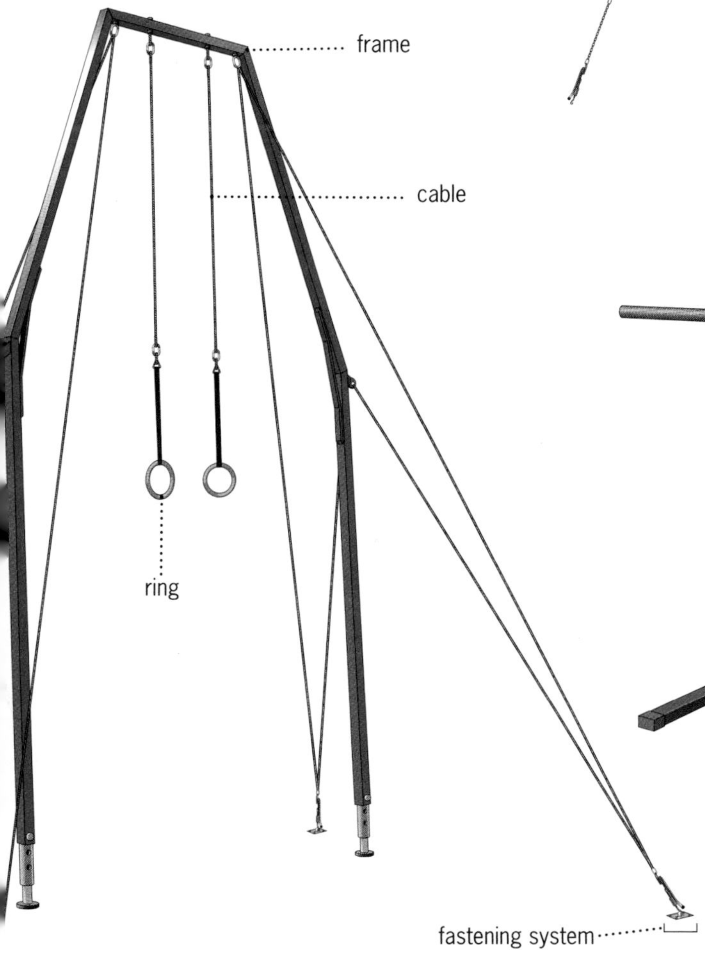
frame
cable
ring
fastening system

parallel bars

TENTS

two-person tent

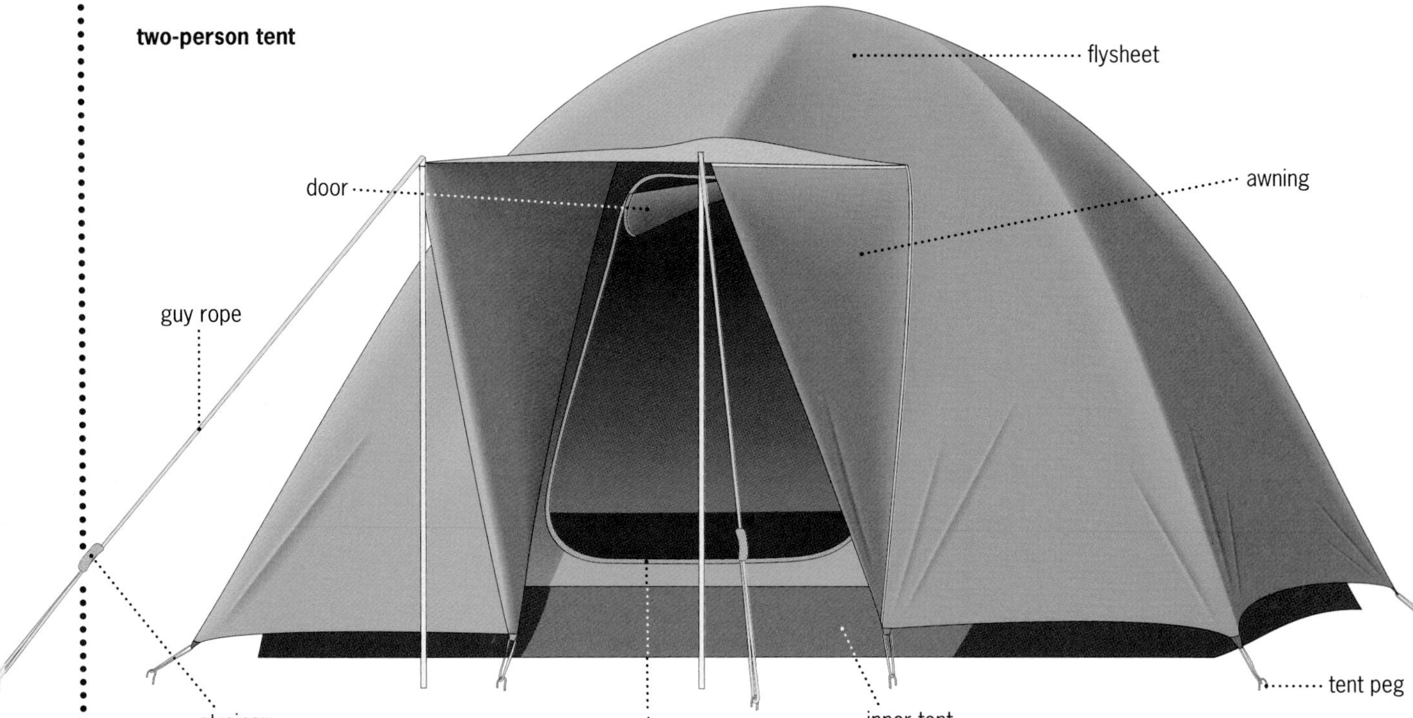
flysheet
awning
door
guy rope
strainer
zip
inner tent
tent peg

MAJOR TYPES OF TENTS

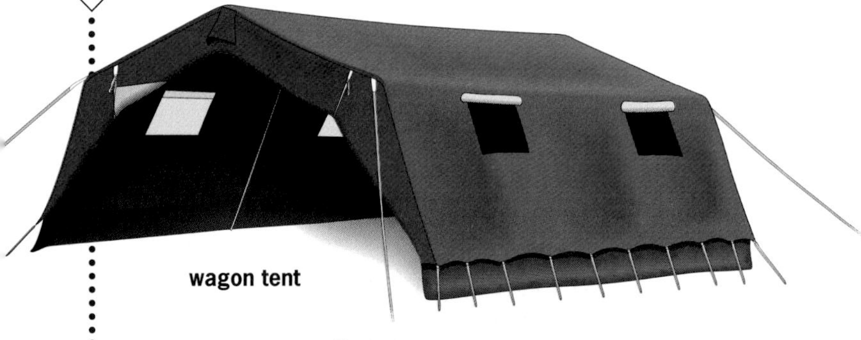

wagon tent

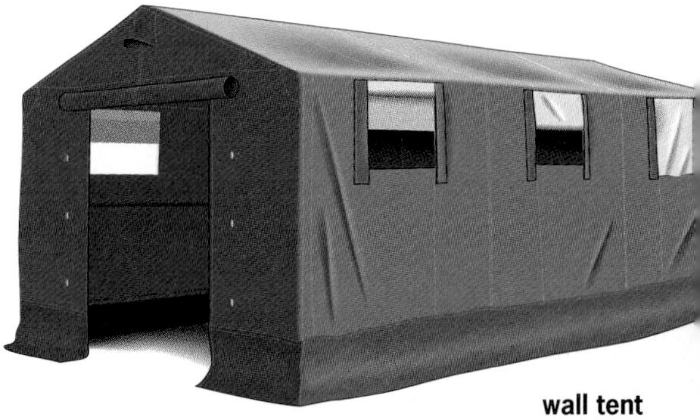

wall tent

ridge tent

dome tent

pop-up tent

family tent

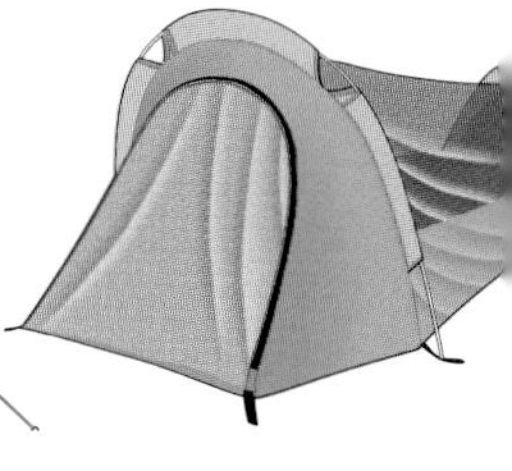

one-person tent

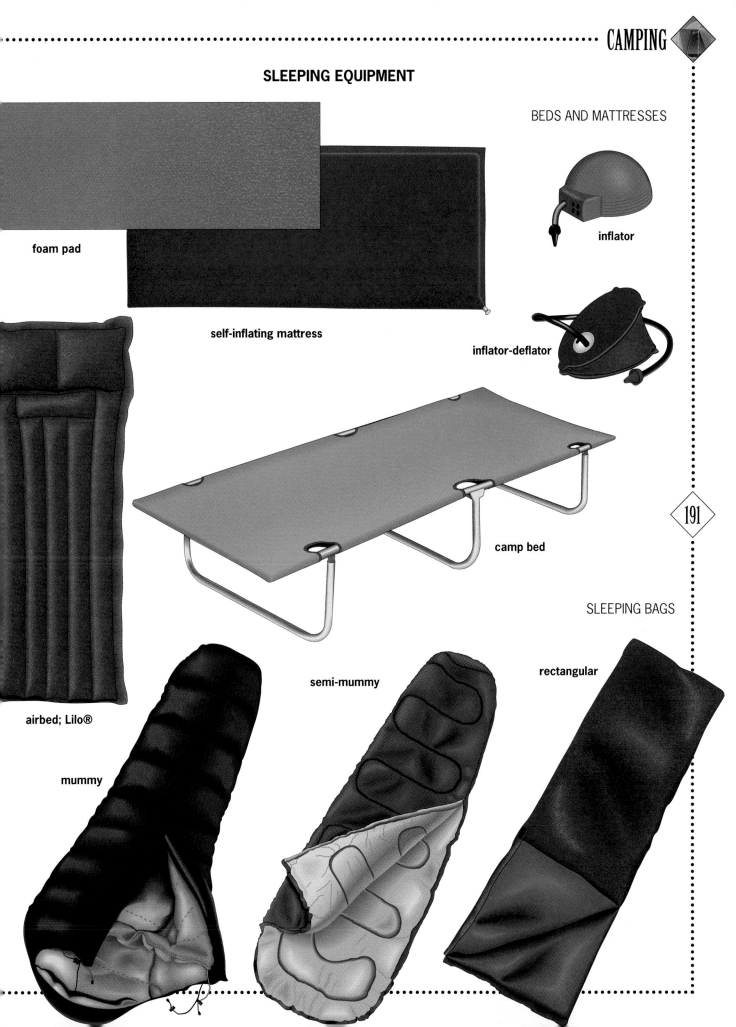

SLEEPING EQUIPMENT

BEDS AND MATTRESSES

foam pad

self-inflating mattress

inflator

inflator-deflator

airbed; Lilo®

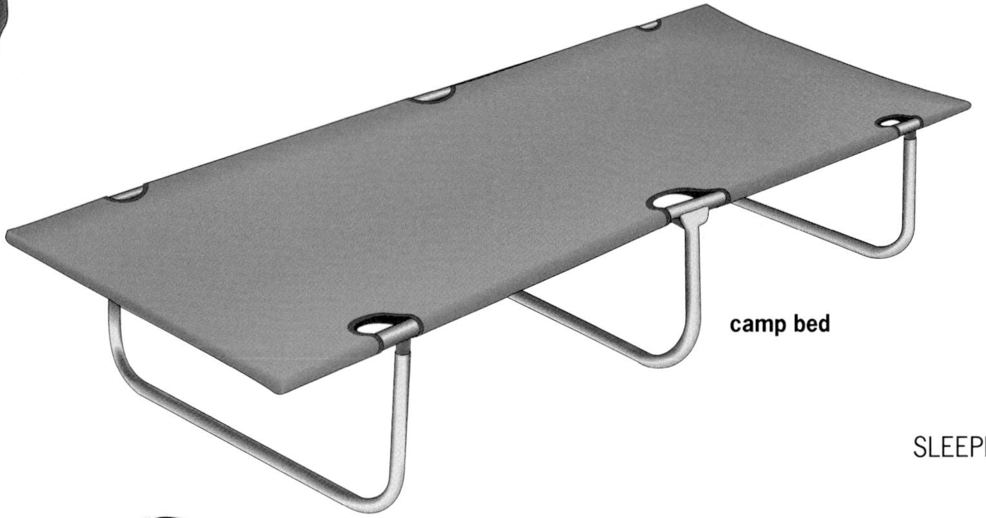

camp bed

SLEEPING BAGS

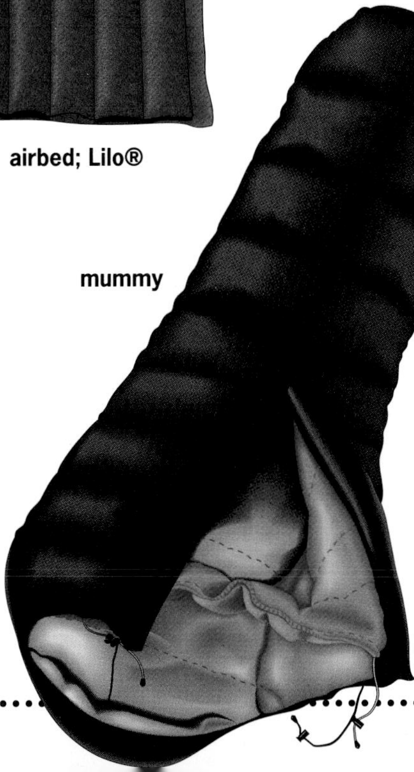

mummy

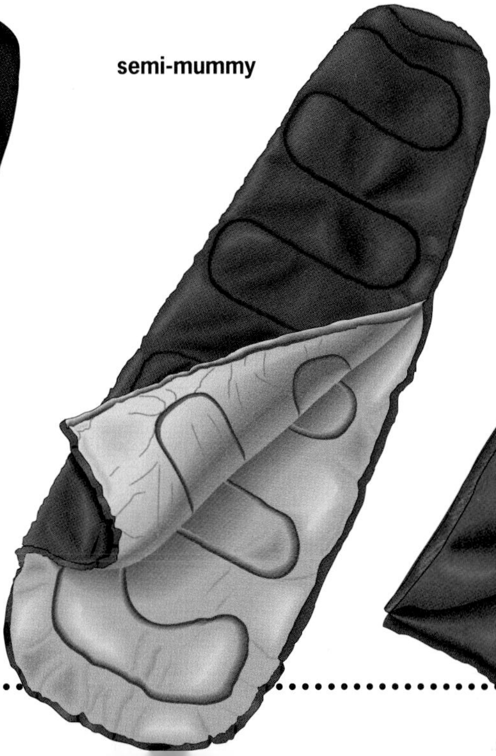

semi-mummy

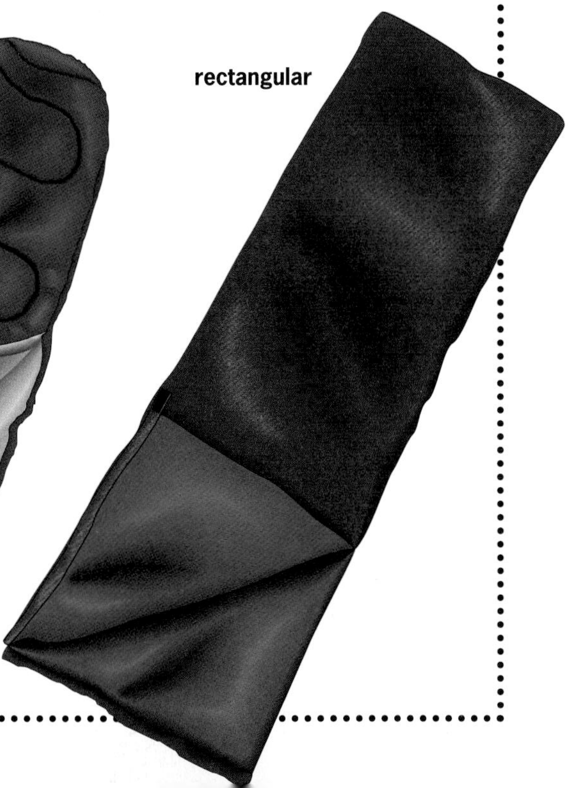

rectangular

CAMPING EQUIPMENT

Swiss army knife

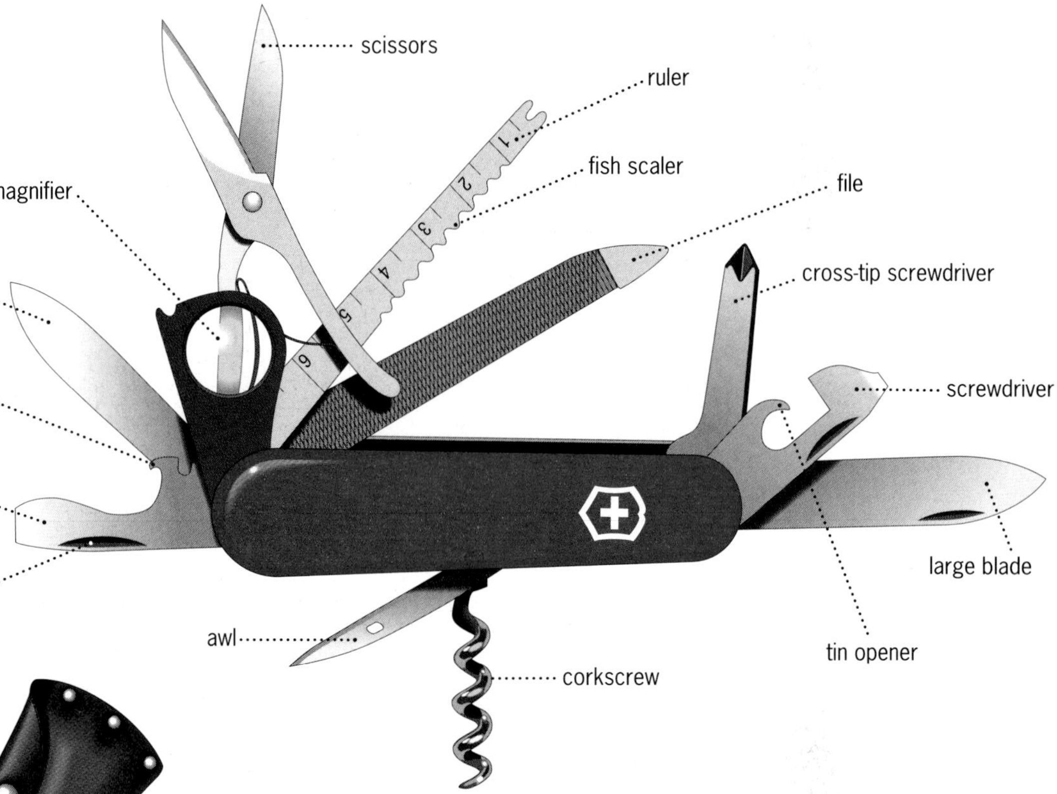
scissors
ruler
fish scaler
file
magnifier
small blade
cross-tip screwdriver
bottle opener
screwdriver
screwdriver
large blade
nail nick
awl
corkscrew
tin opener

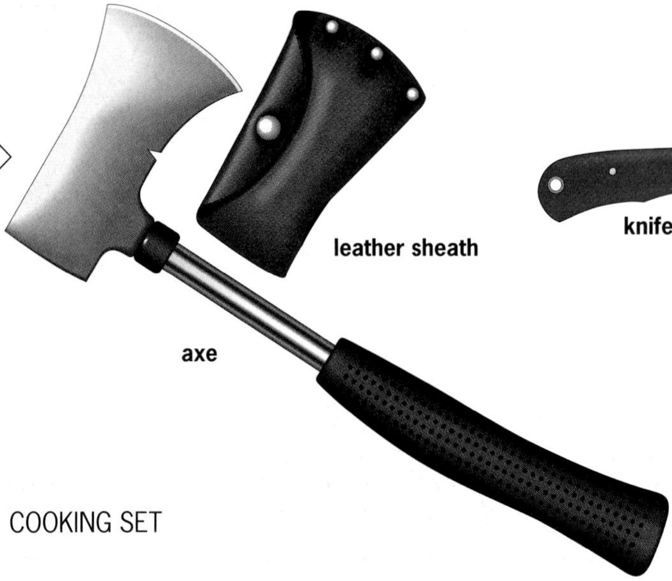

leather sheath

axe

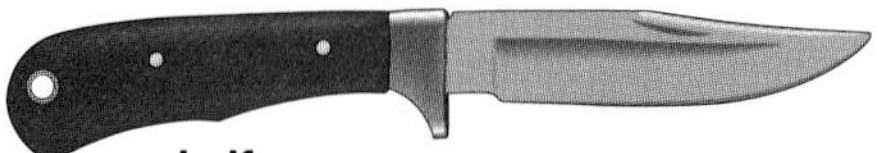

knife

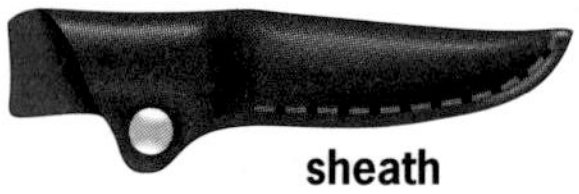

sheath

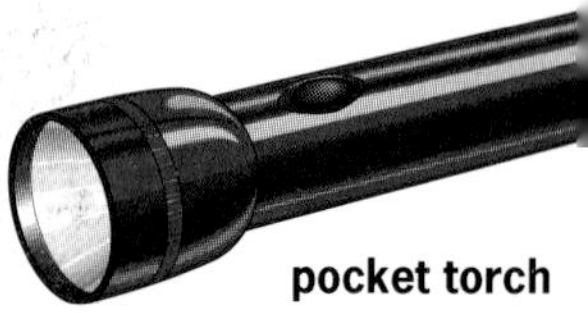

pocket torch

COOKING SET

coffee pot

plate

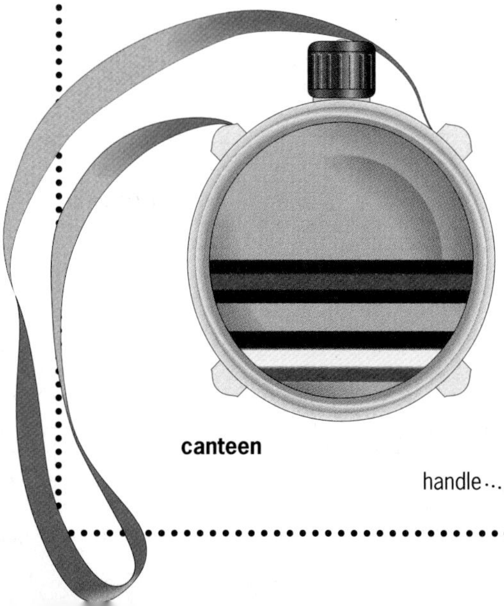

canteen

handle

frying pan

cup

saucepan

rucksack

top flap
shoulder strap
side compression strap
internal frame
waist belt
tightening buckle
strap loop
front compression strap

first aid kit

magnetic compass

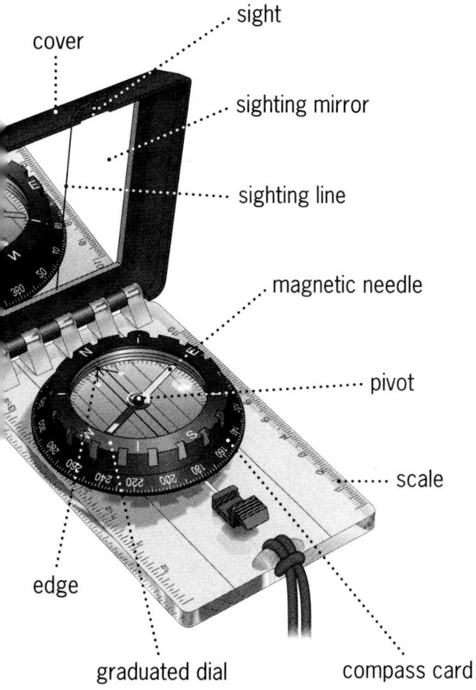
cover
sight
sighting mirror
sighting line
magnetic needle
pivot
scale
edge
graduated dial
compass card

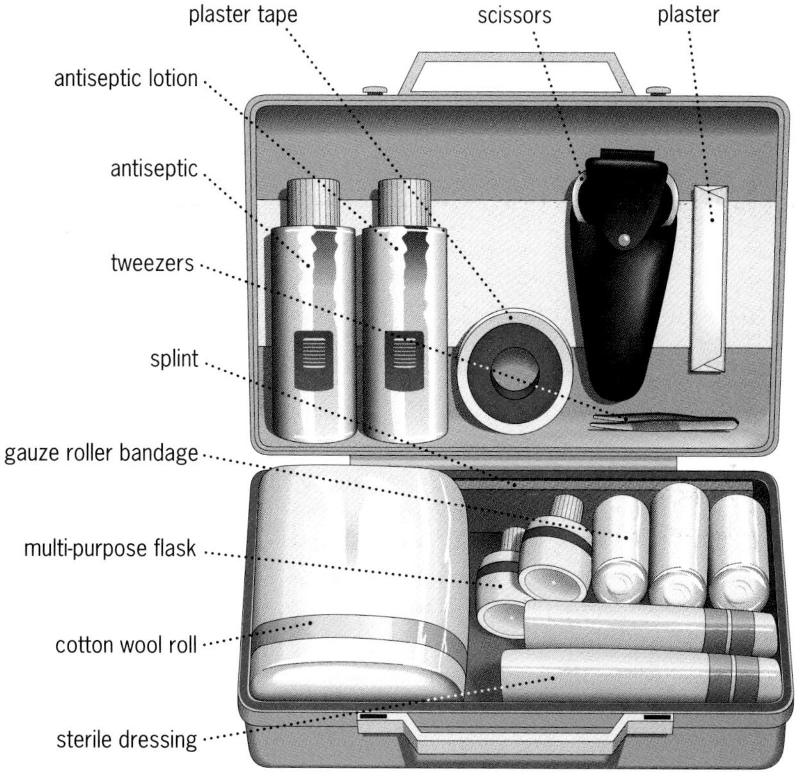
plaster tape
scissors
plaster
antiseptic lotion
antiseptic
tweezers
splint
gauze roller bandage
multi-purpose flask
cotton wool roll
sterile dressing

CARD GAMES

heart

diamond

club

spade

Joker
A
K
Q
J
Joker
Ace
King
Queen
Jack

DICE

poker die

ordinary die

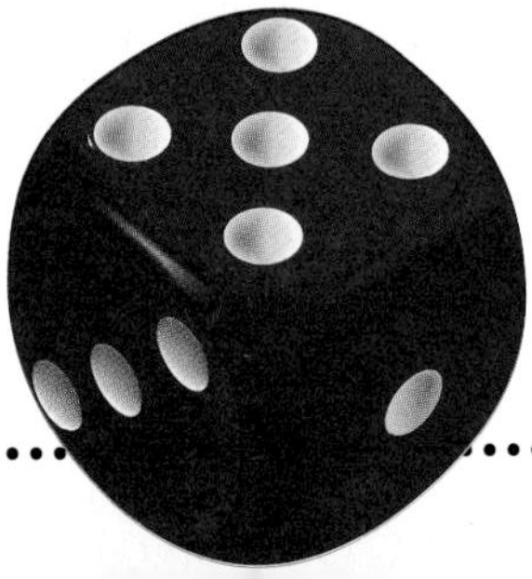

DOMINOES

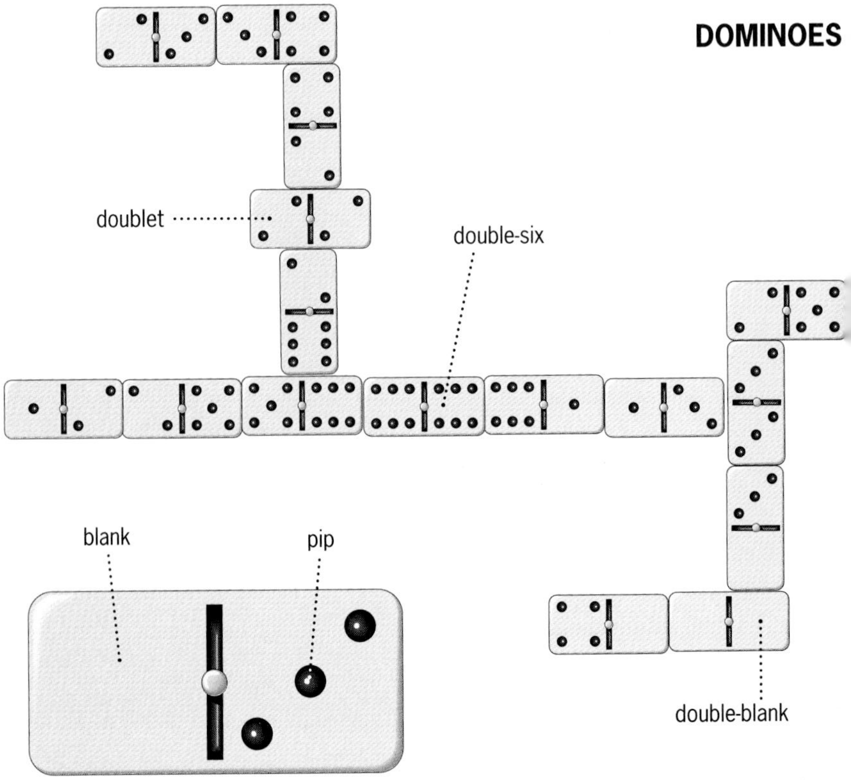
doublet
double-six
blank
pip
double-blank

CHESS

chessboard

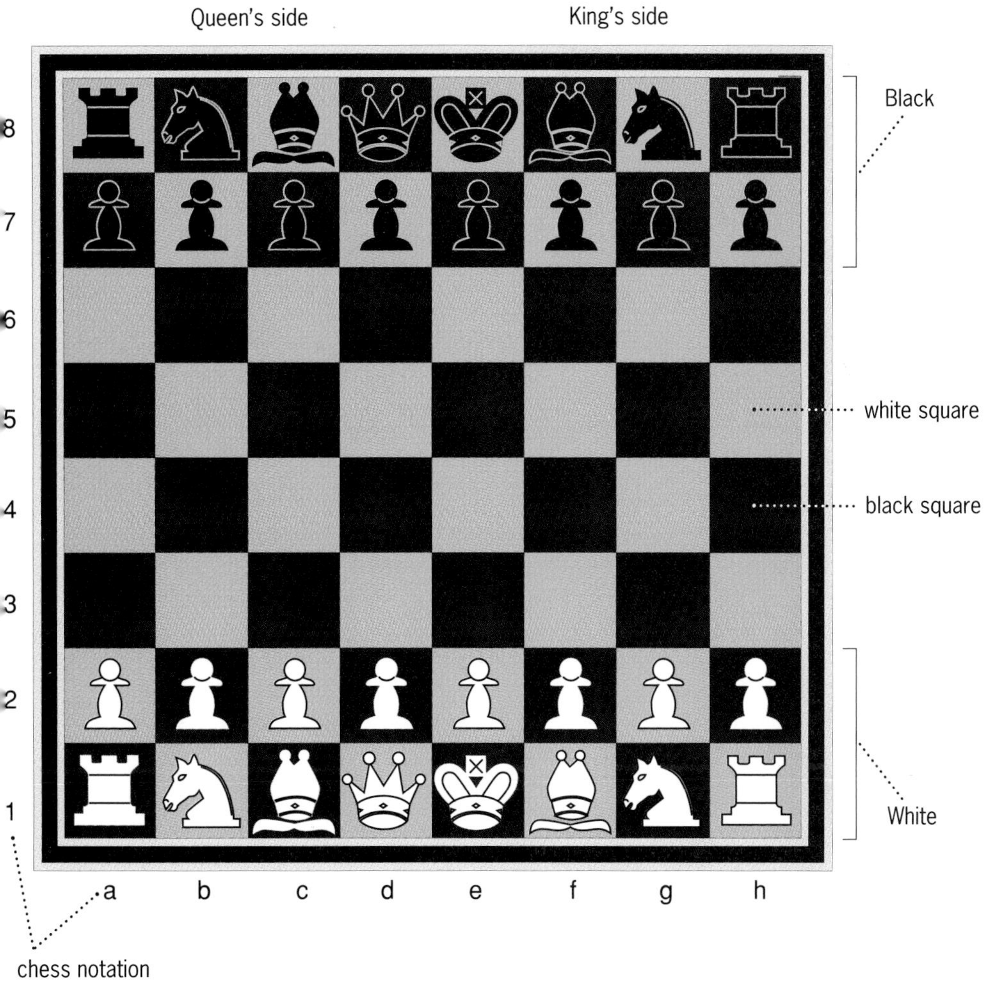
Queen's side
King's side
Black
white square
black square
White
8
7
6
5
4
3
2
1
a
b
c
d
e
f
g
h
chess notation

MEN

Pawn
Knight
Bishop
Castle
Queen
King

types of movements

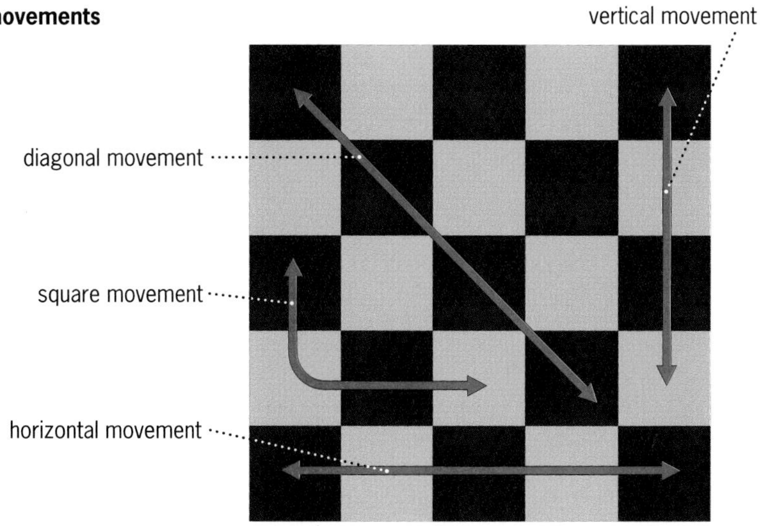
vertical movement
diagonal movement
square movement
horizontal movement

BACKGAMMON

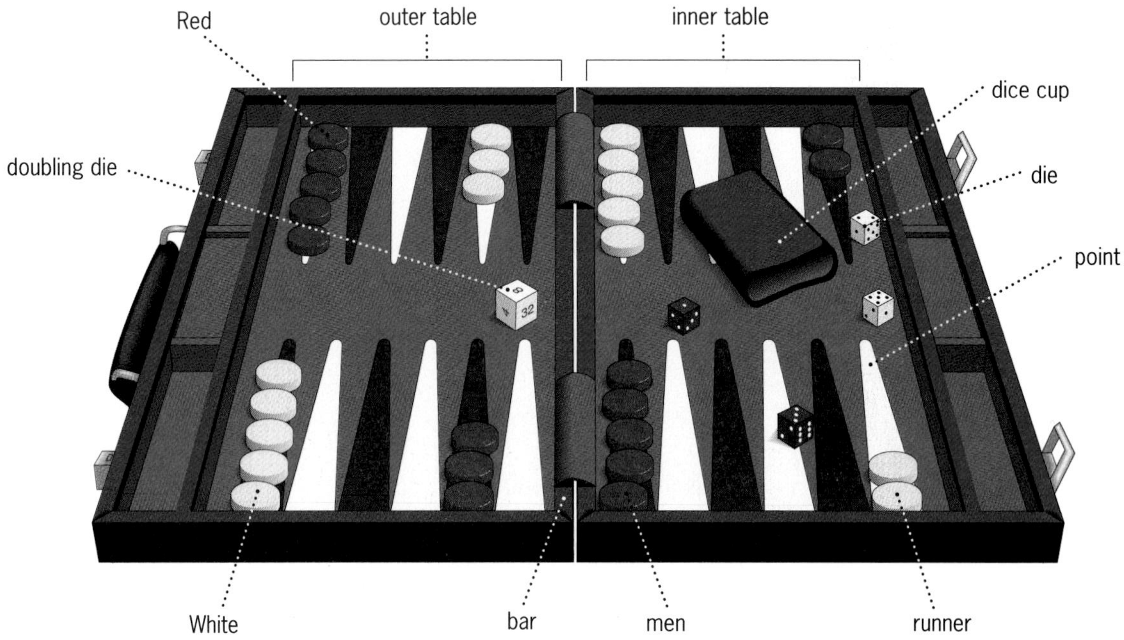
Red
outer table
inner table
dice cup
doubling die
die
point
White
bar
men
runner

DRAUGHTS

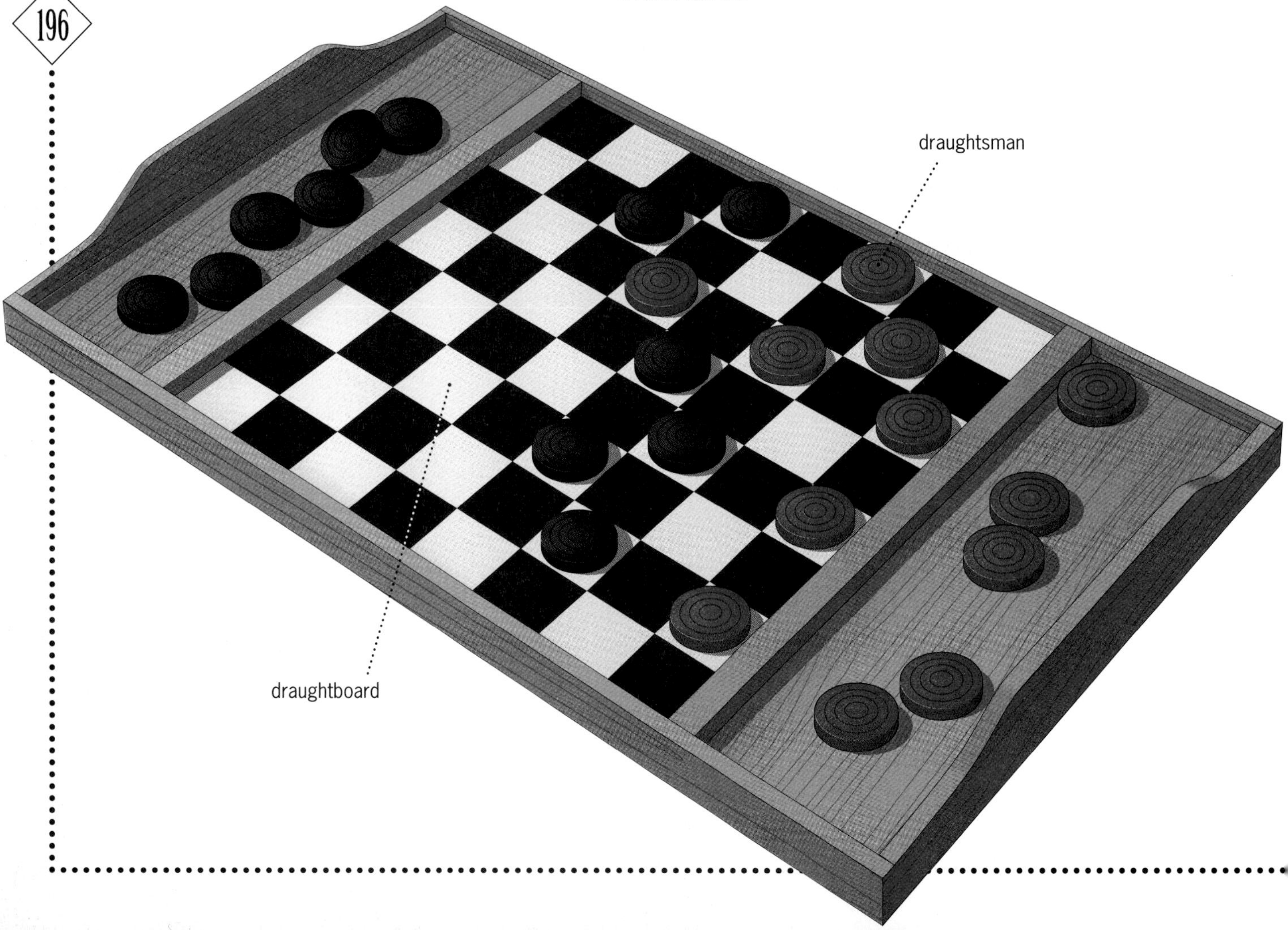
draughtsman
draughtboard

VIDEO ENTERTAINMENT SYSTEM

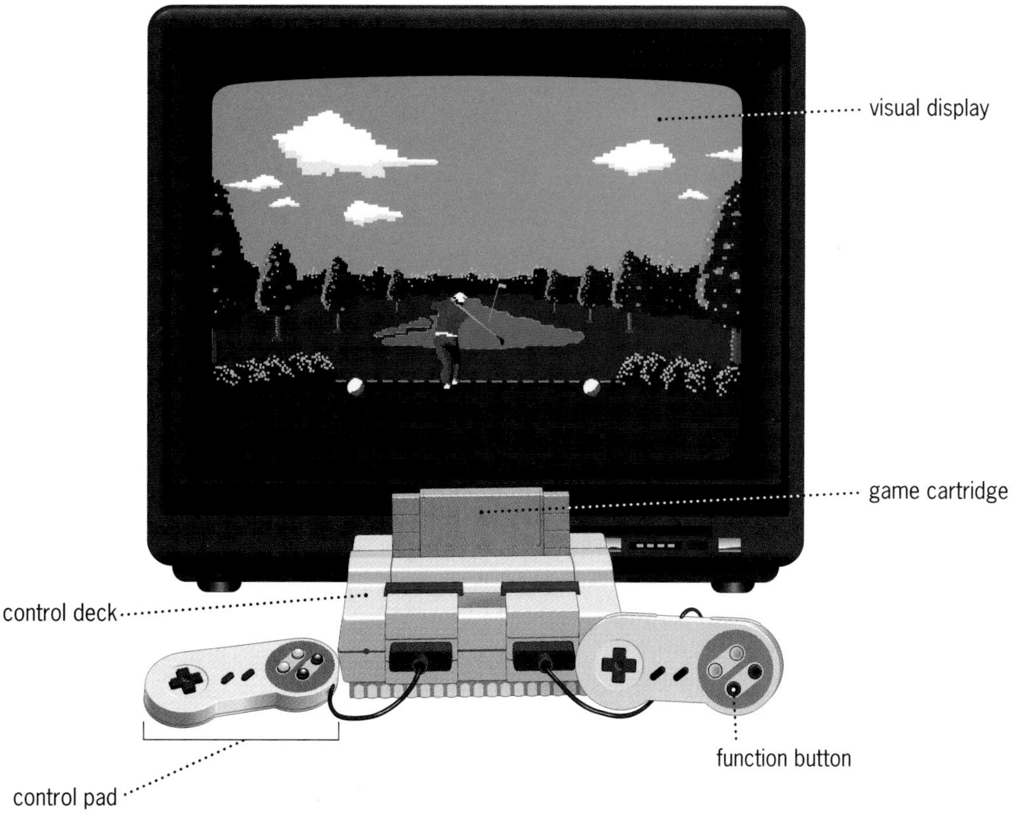
visual display
game cartridge
control deck
control pad
function button

GAME OF DARTS

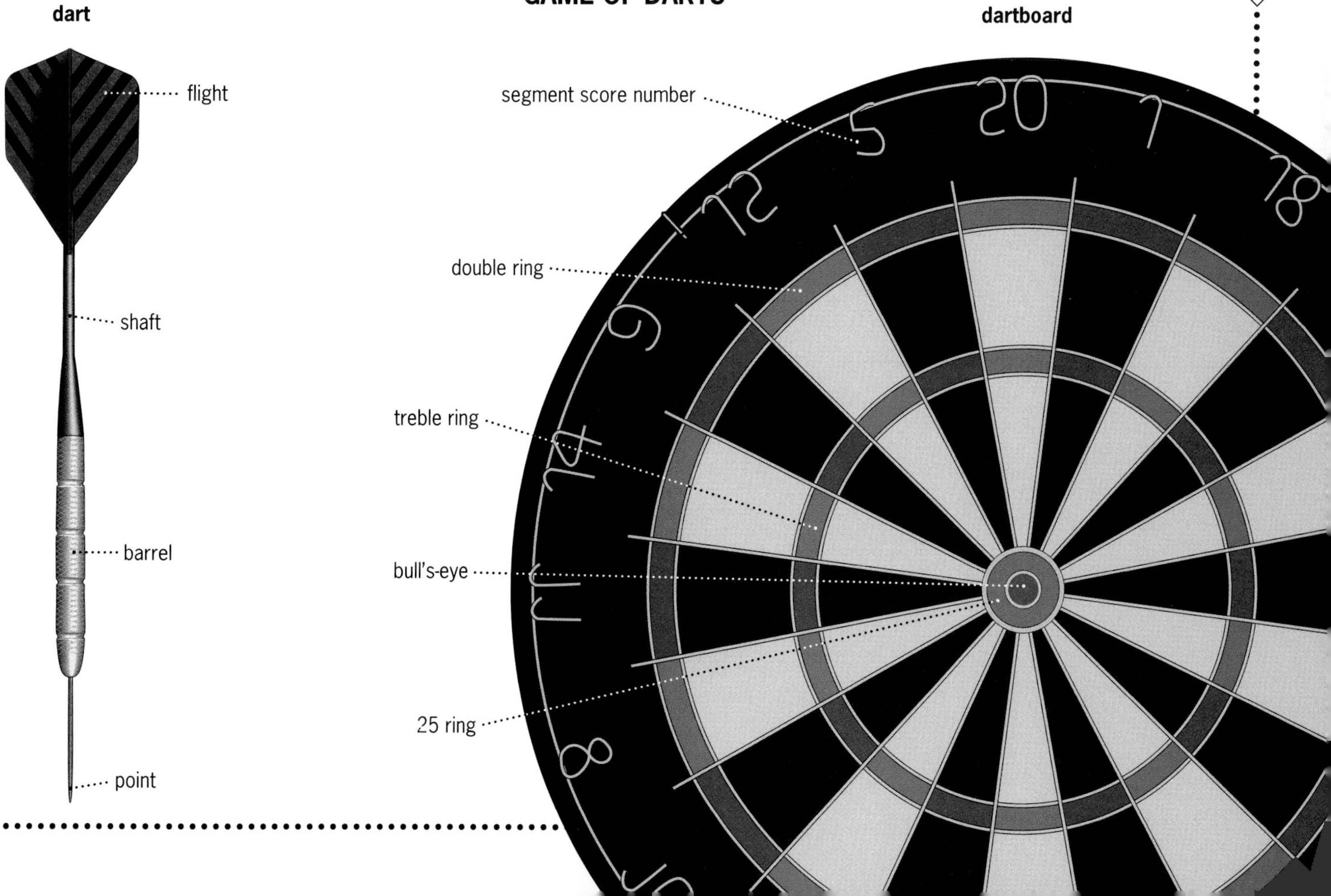
dart
flight
shaft
barrel
point
dartboard
segment score number
double ring
treble ring
bull's-eye
25 ring
5
20
1
18
12
9
14
11
8

MEASURE OF TIME

stopwatch

ring
start button
reset button
stop button
second hand
minute hand
1/10th second hand
case

analogue watch

dial

kitchen timer

egg timer

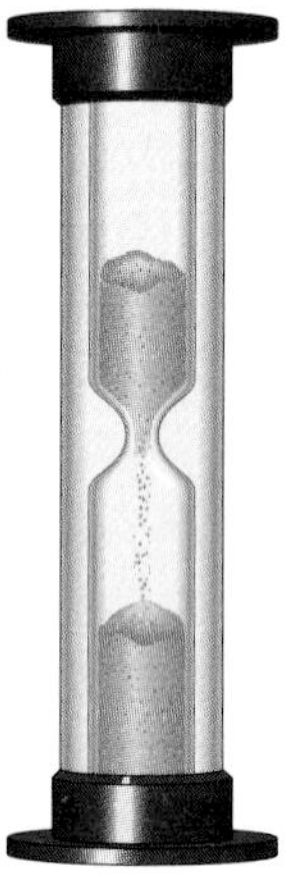

digital watch

liquid crystal display

sundial

gnomon
shadow
dial

MEASURE OF TEMPERATURE

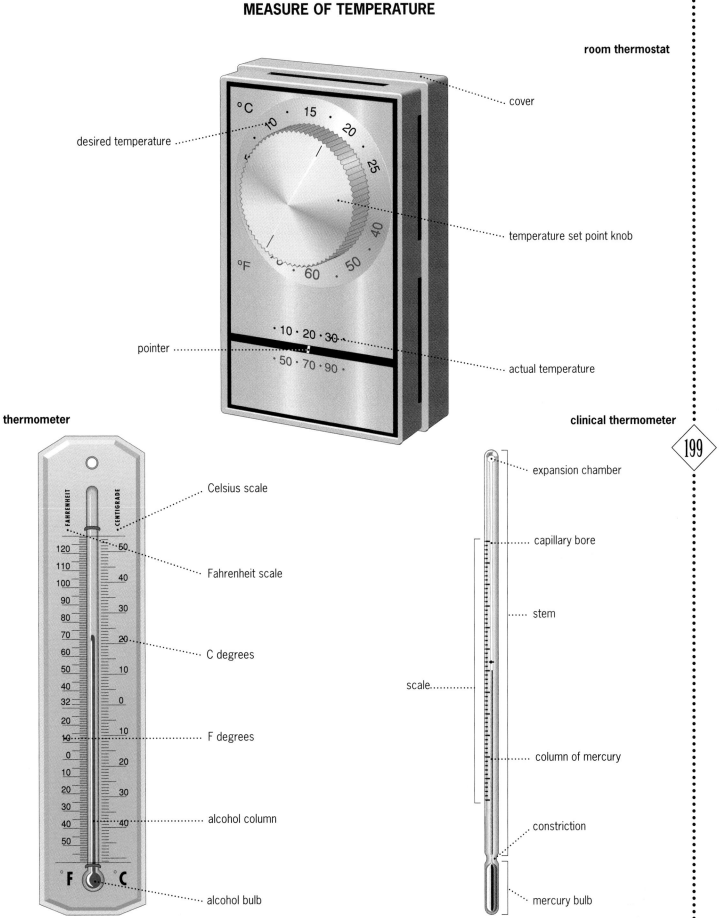

room thermostat

cover
desired temperature
temperature set point knob
pointer
actual temperature
°C
15
20
25
40
50
60
°F
10 · 20 · 30
50 · 70 · 90

thermometer

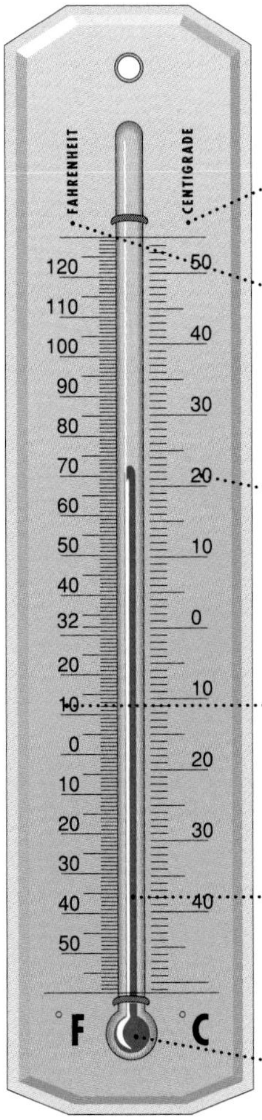
Celsius scale
Fahrenheit scale
C degrees
F degrees
alcohol column
alcohol bulb
FAHRENHEIT
CENTIGRADE
120
110
100
90
80
70
60
50
40
32
20
10
0
10
20
30
40
50
50
40
30
20
10
0
10
20
30
40
°F
°C

clinical thermometer

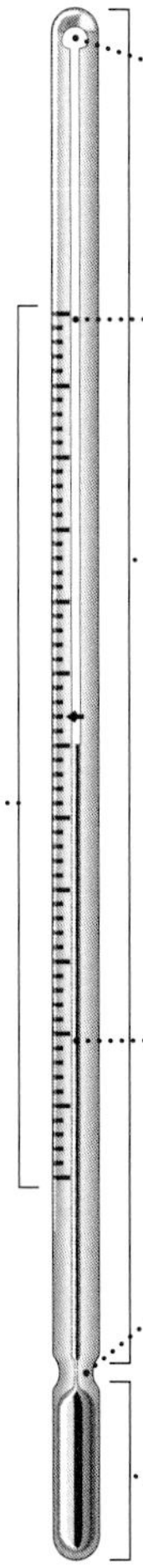
expansion chamber
capillary bore
stem
scale
column of mercury
constriction
mercury bulb

MEASURE OF WEIGHT

balance

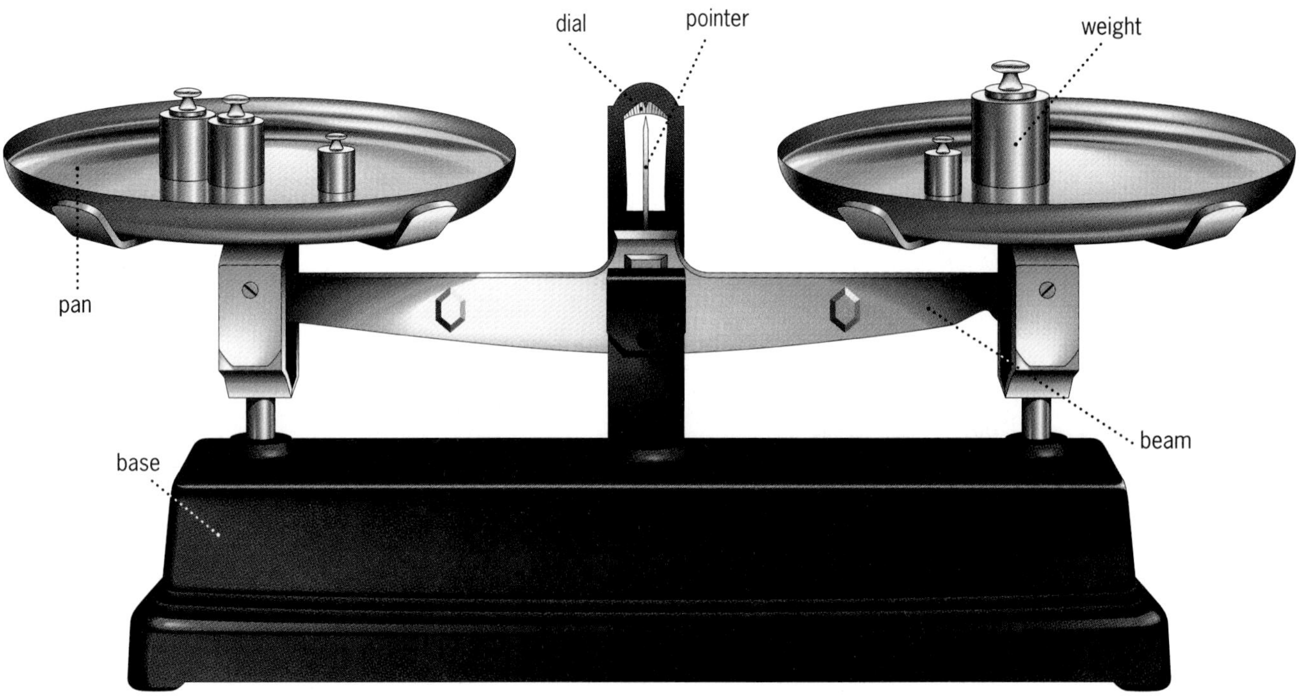
dial
pointer
weight
pan
beam
base

steelyard

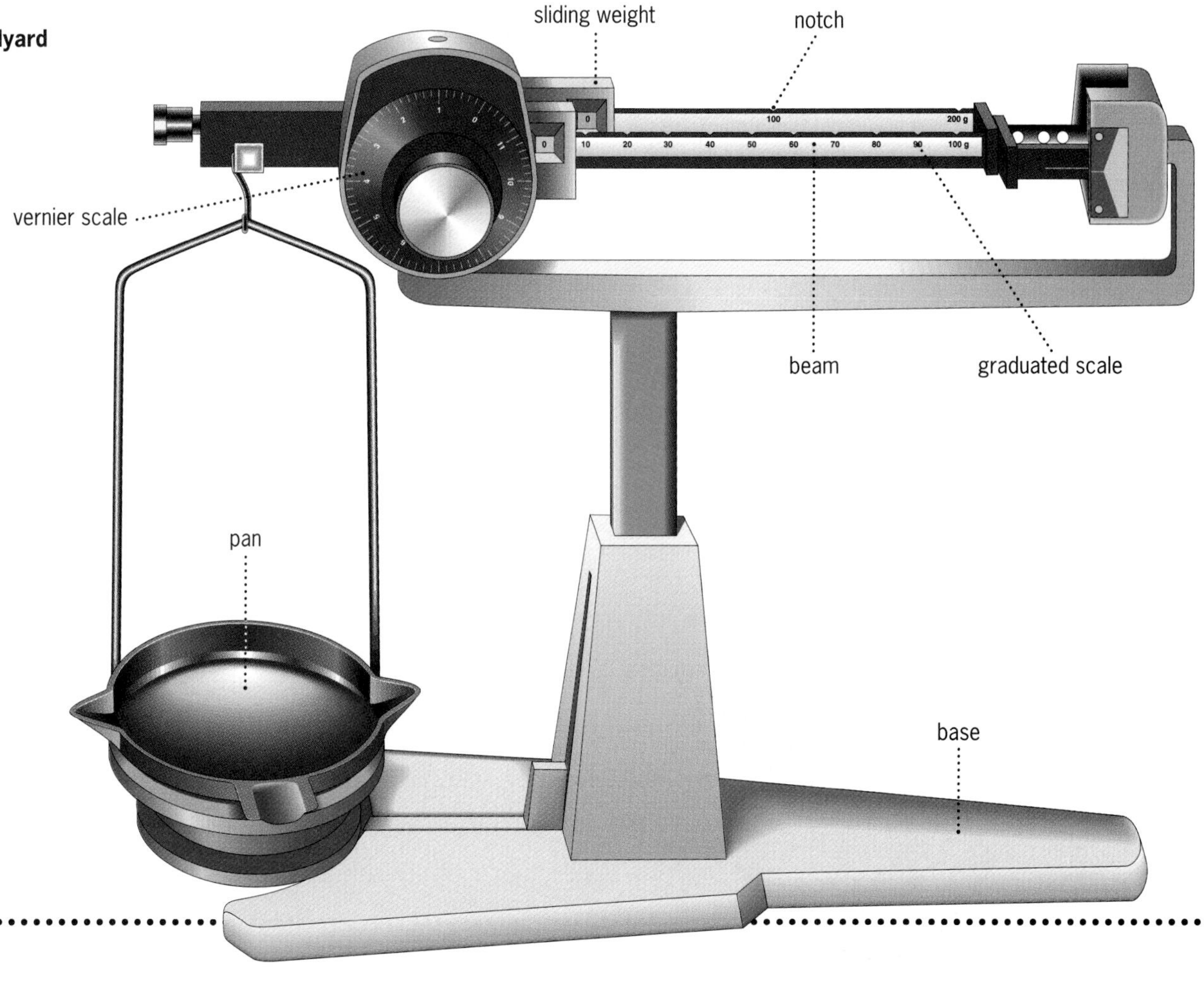
sliding weight
notch
vernier scale
beam
graduated scale
pan
base

spring balance

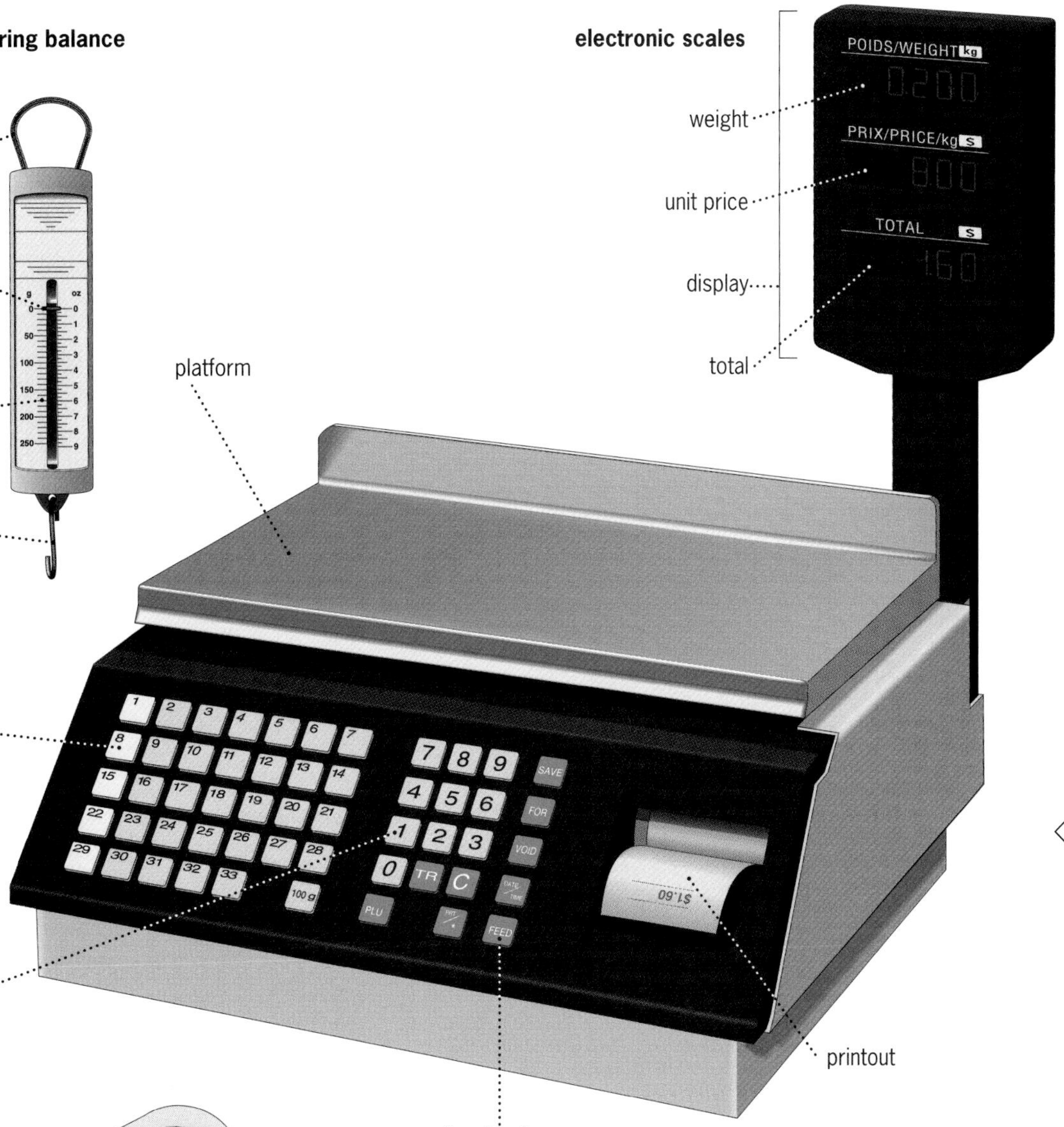
ring
pointer
graduated scale
hook
electronic scales
POIDS/WEIGHT kg
PRIX/PRICE/kg $
TOTAL $
weight
unit price
display
total
platform
product code
numeric keyboard
printout
function keys

bathroom scales

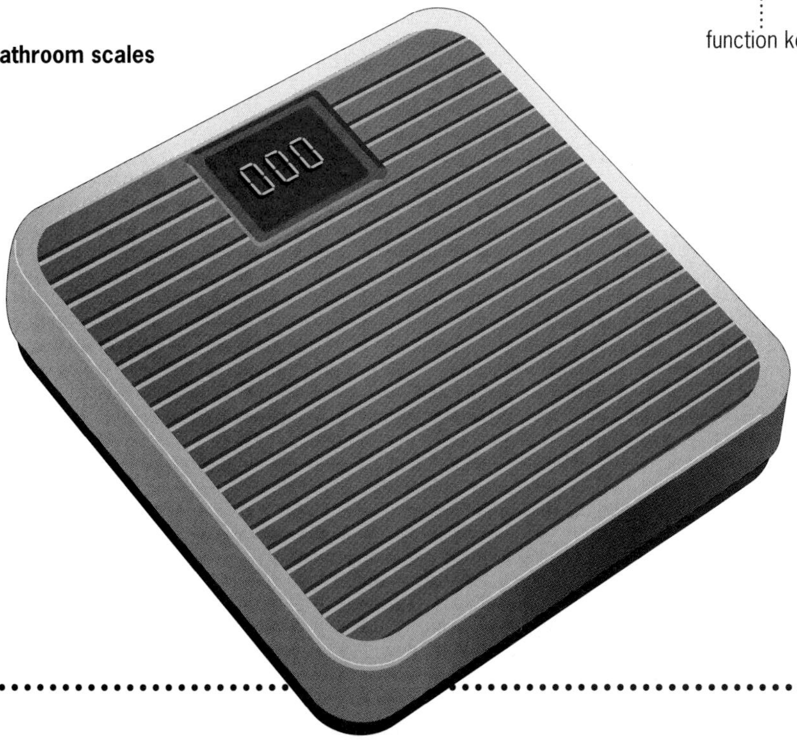

kitchen scales

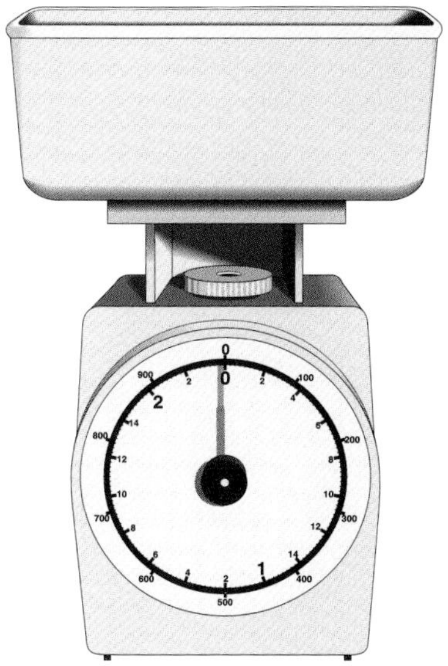

OIL

GROUND TRANSPORT

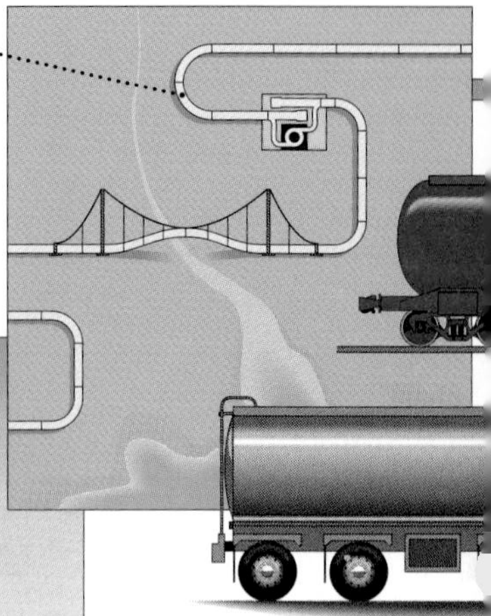
pipeline
road tanker

PROSPECTING

surface prospecting

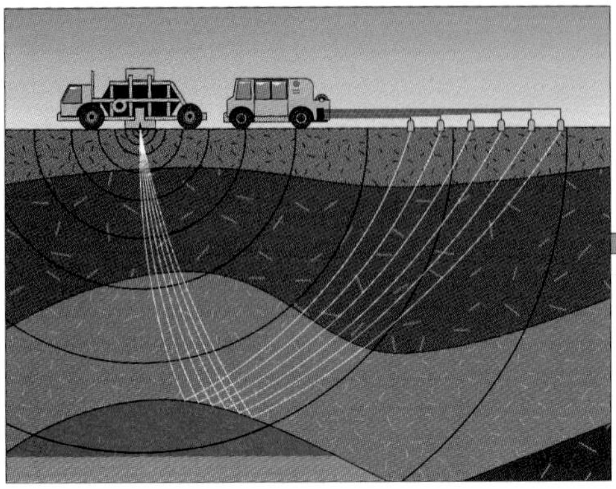

DRILLING

drilling rig

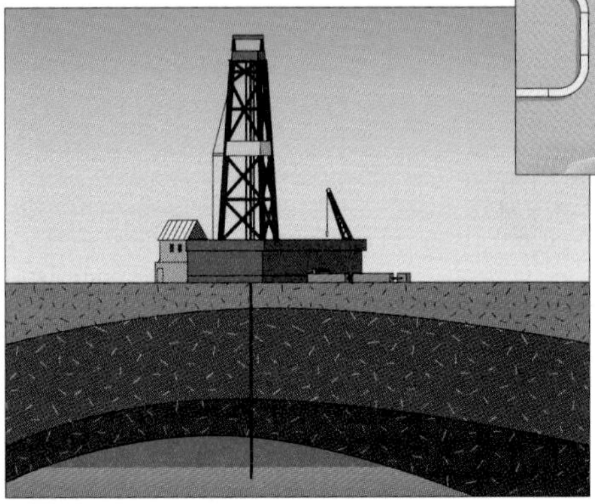

offshore drilling

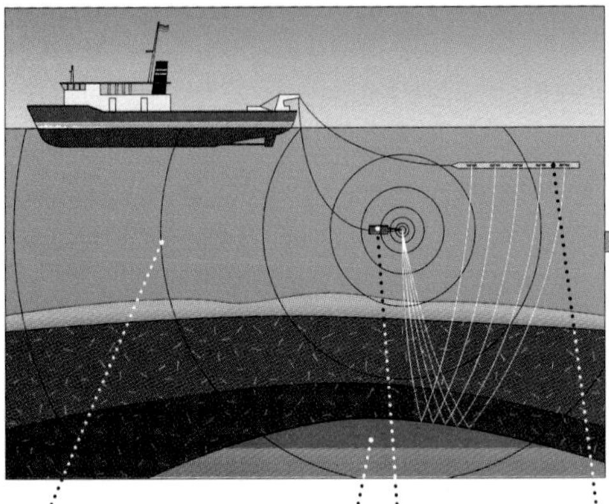
shock wave
seismographic recording
petroleum trap
blasting charge

production platform

MARITIME TRANSPORT

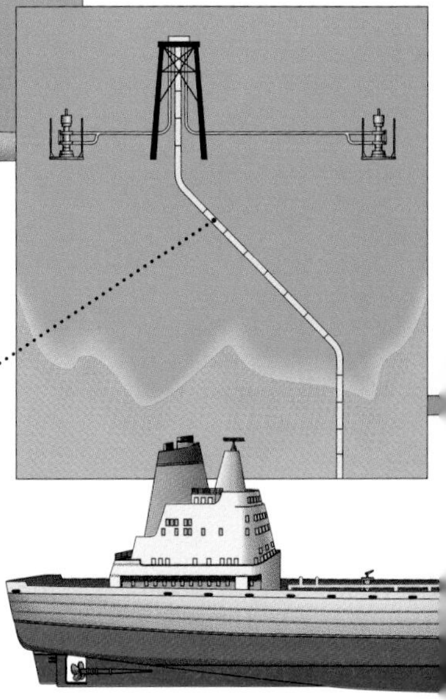
submarine pipeline

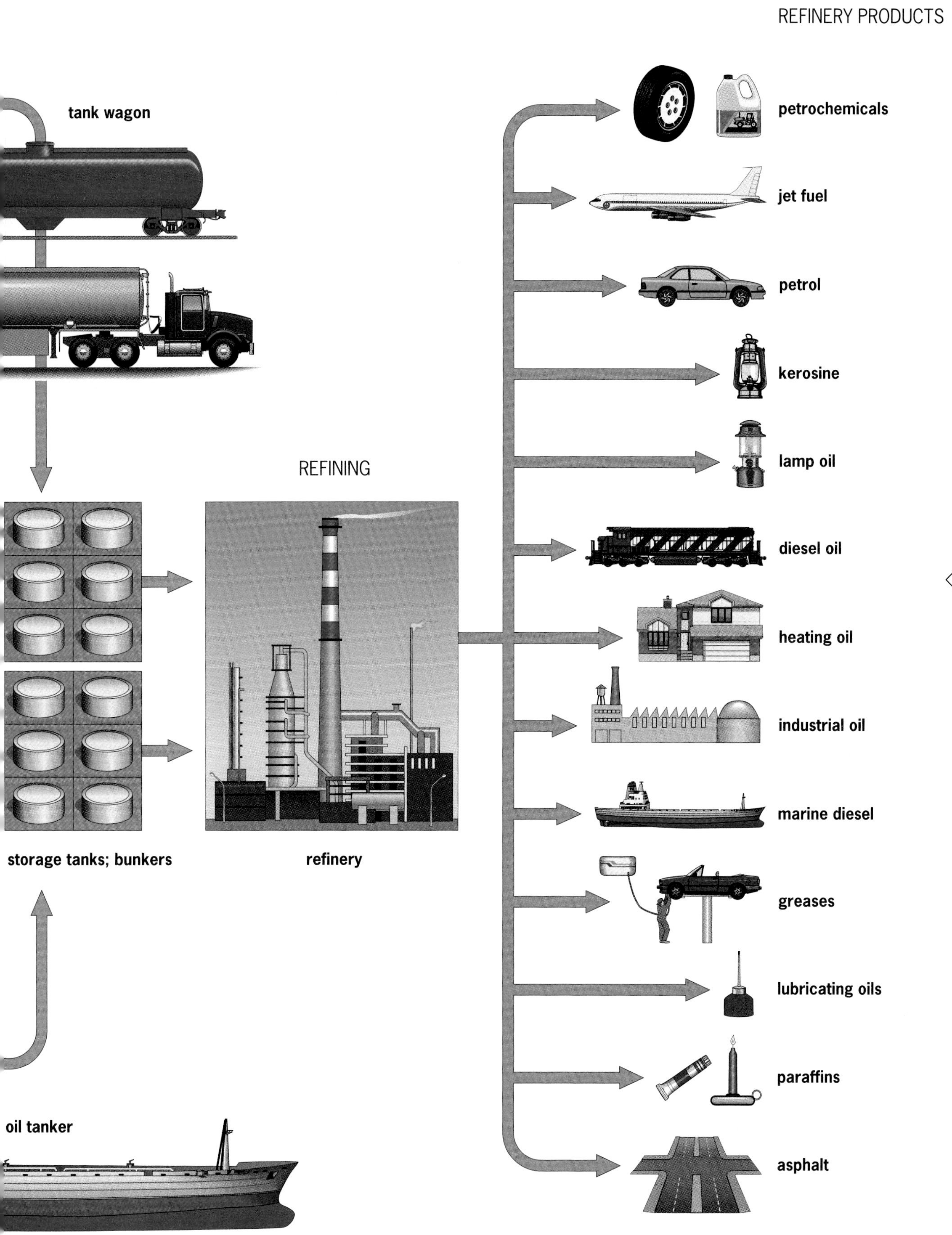
REFINERY PRODUCTS
tank wagon
petrochemicals
jet fuel
petrol
kerosine
REFINING
lamp oil
diesel oil
heating oil
industrial oil
marine diesel
storage tanks; bunkers
refinery
greases
lubricating oils
paraffins
oil tanker
asphalt

HYDROELECTRIC ENERGY

hydroelectric complex

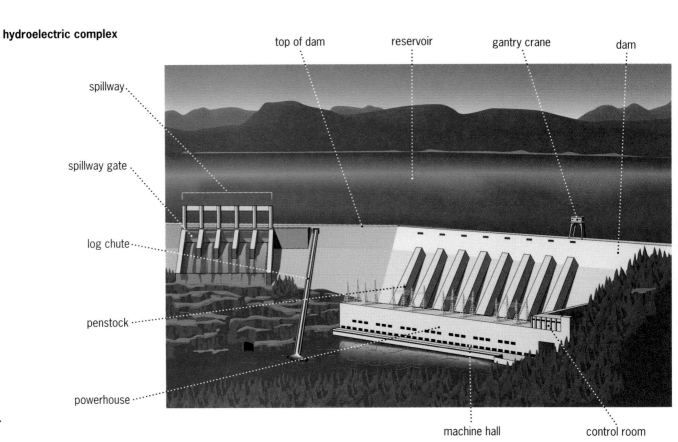

top of dam
reservoir
gantry crane
dam
spillway
spillway gate
log chute
penstock
powerhouse
machine hall
control room

cross section of hydroelectric power station

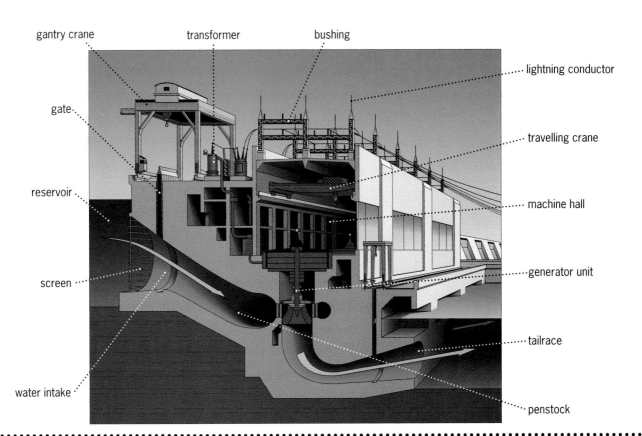

gantry crane
transformer
bushing
lightning conductor
gate
travelling crane
reservoir
machine hall
screen
generator unit
tailrace
water intake
penstock

electric circuit

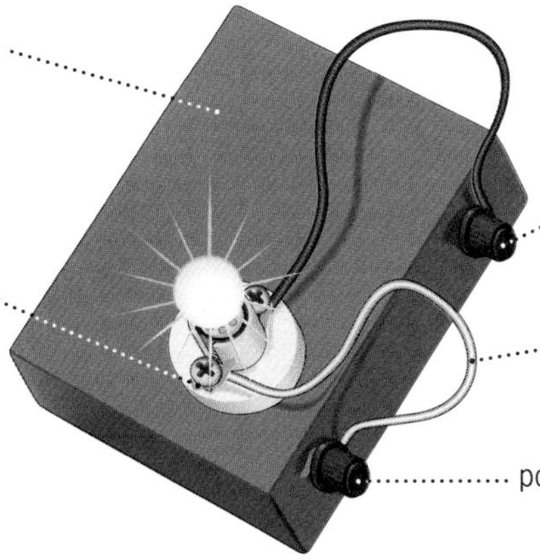
battery
connection
negative pole
electric wire
positive pole

steps in production of electricity

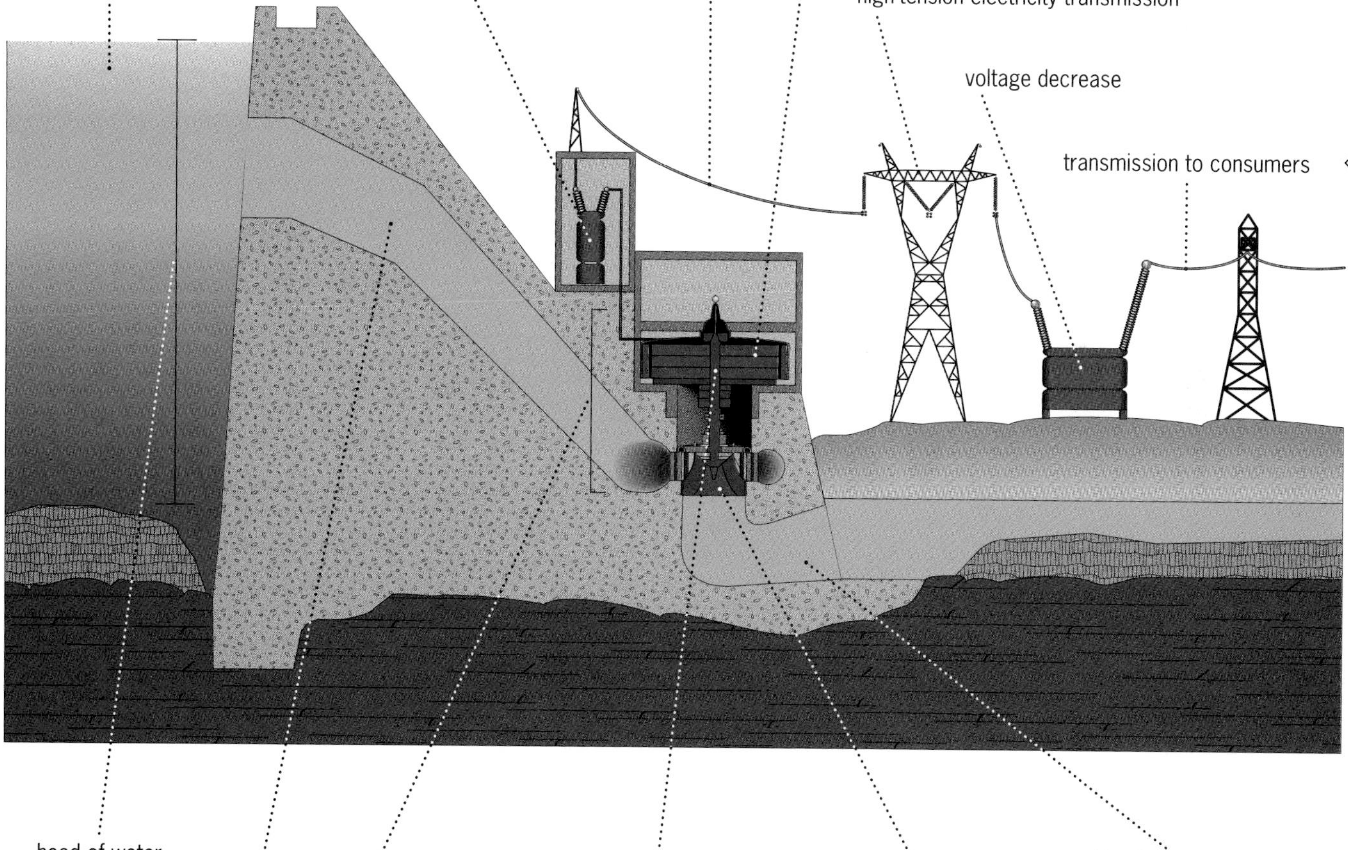
energy integration to the transmission network
production of electricity by the generator
supply of water
voltage increase
high-tension electricity transmission
voltage decrease
transmission to consumers
head of water
turbined water draining
water under pressure
transmission of the rotative movement to the rotor
transformation of mechanical work into electricity
rotation of the turbine

NUCLEAR ENERGY

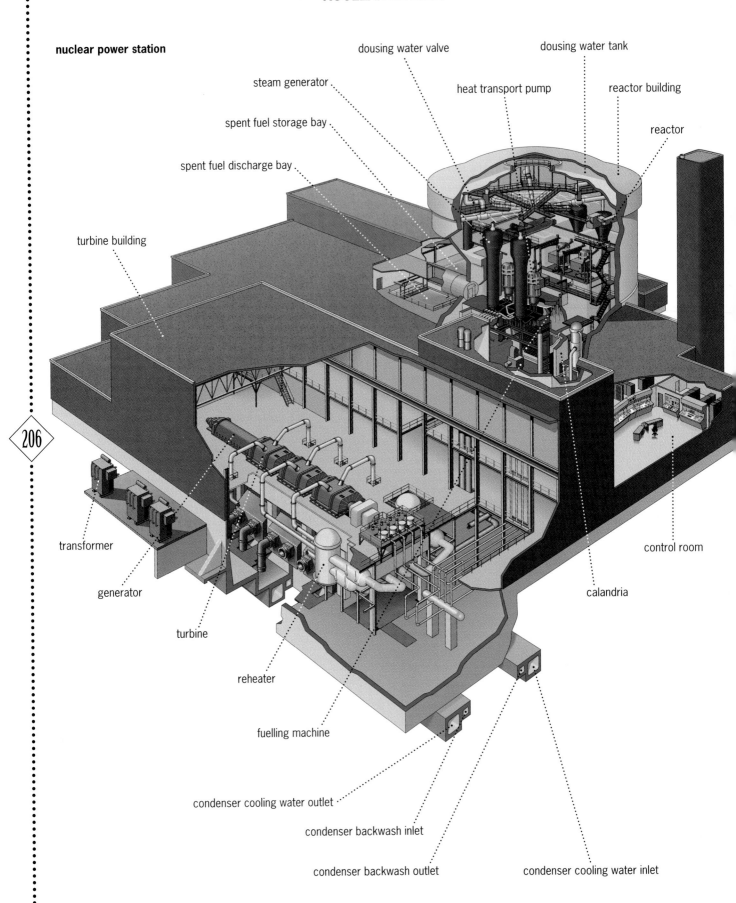

nuclear power station

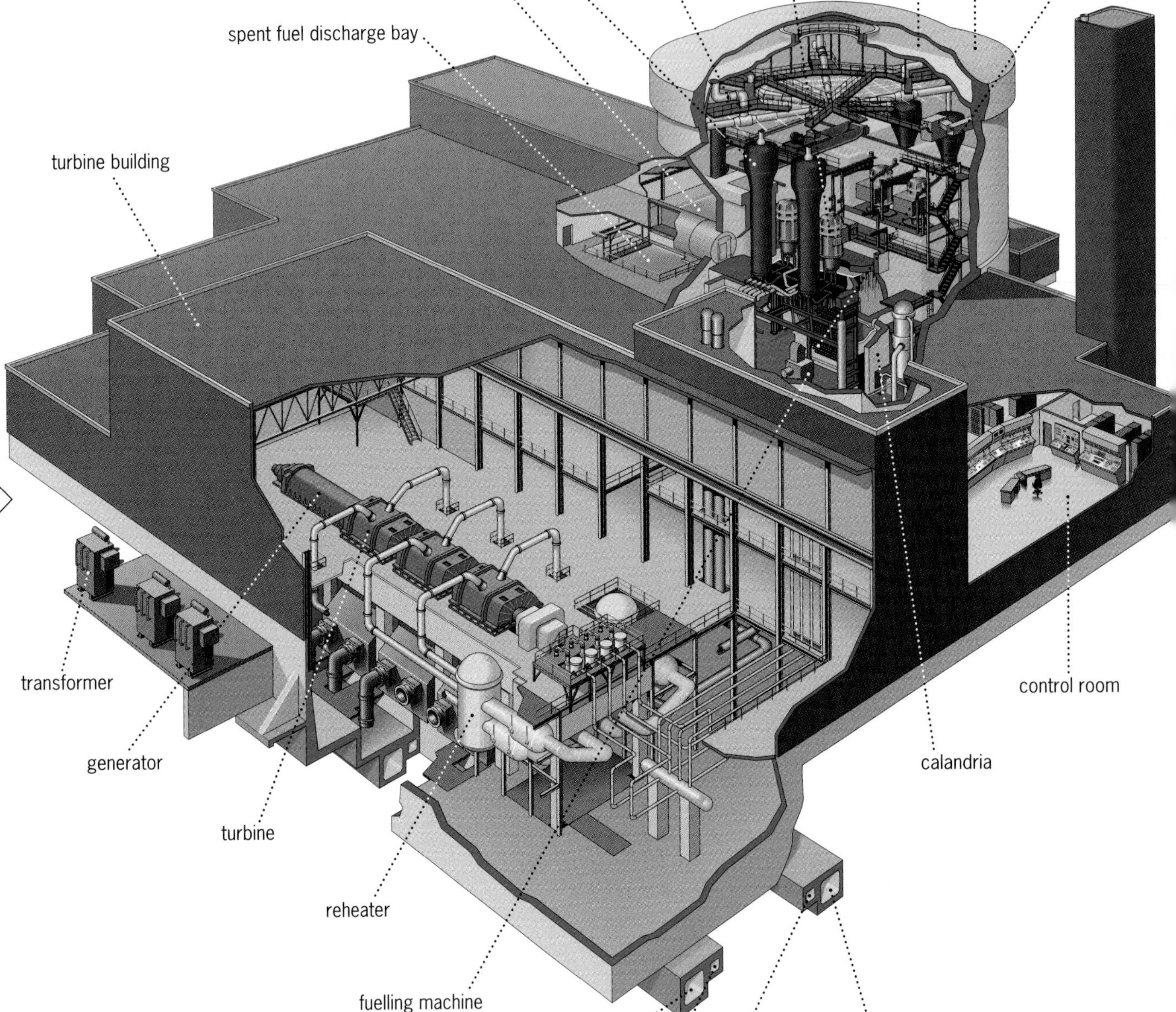
dousing water valve
dousing water tank
steam generator
heat transport pump
reactor building
spent fuel storage bay
reactor
spent fuel discharge bay
turbine building
transformer
generator
turbine
reheater
fuelling machine
control room
calandria
condenser cooling water outlet
condenser backwash inlet
condenser backwash outlet
condenser cooling water inlet

production of electricity from nuclear energy

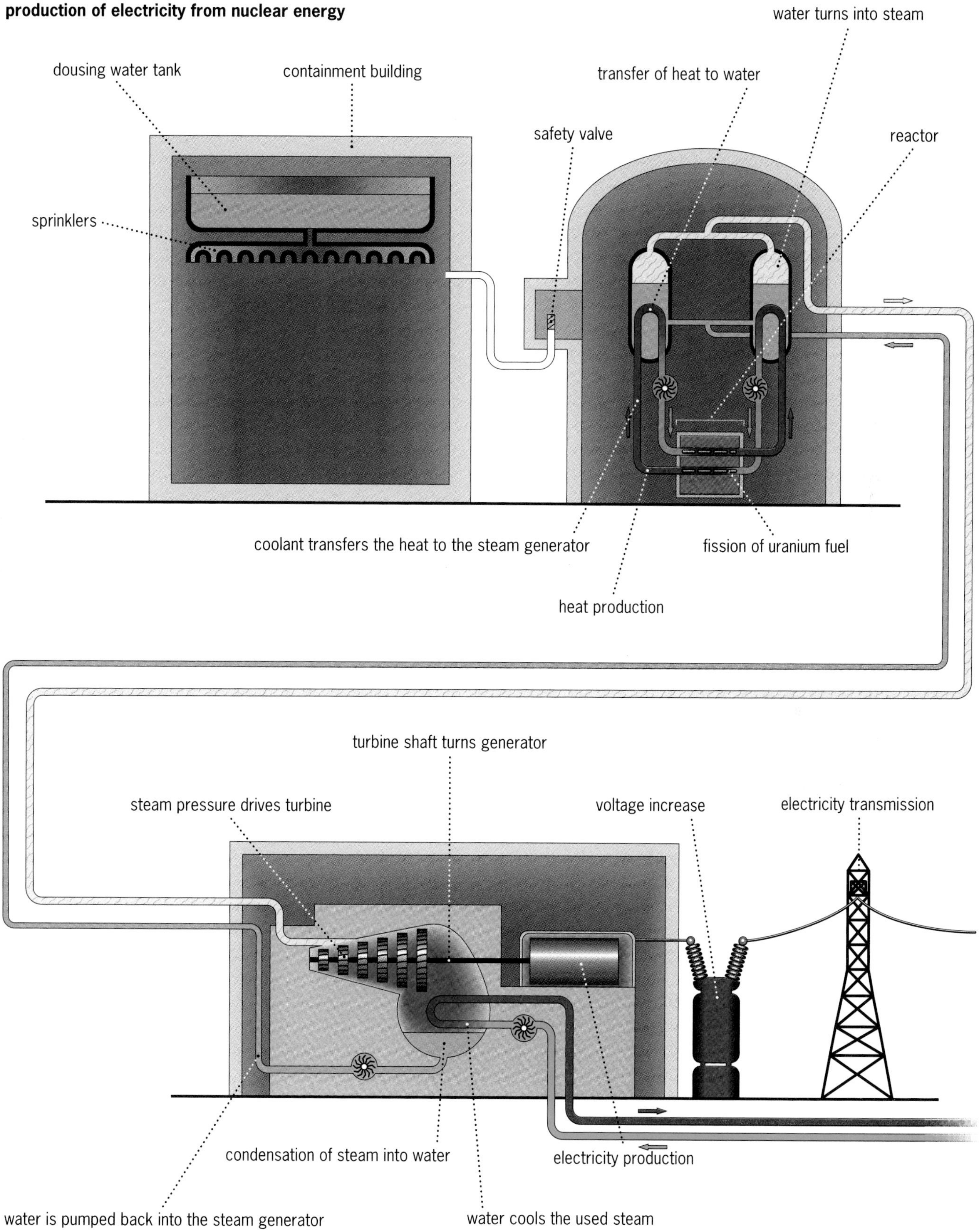
water turns into steam
dousing water tank
containment building
transfer of heat to water
safety valve
reactor
sprinklers
coolant transfers the heat to the steam generator
fission of uranium fuel
heat production
turbine shaft turns generator
steam pressure drives turbine
voltage increase
electricity transmission
condensation of steam into water
electricity production
water is pumped back into the steam generator
water cools the used steam

SOLAR ENERGY

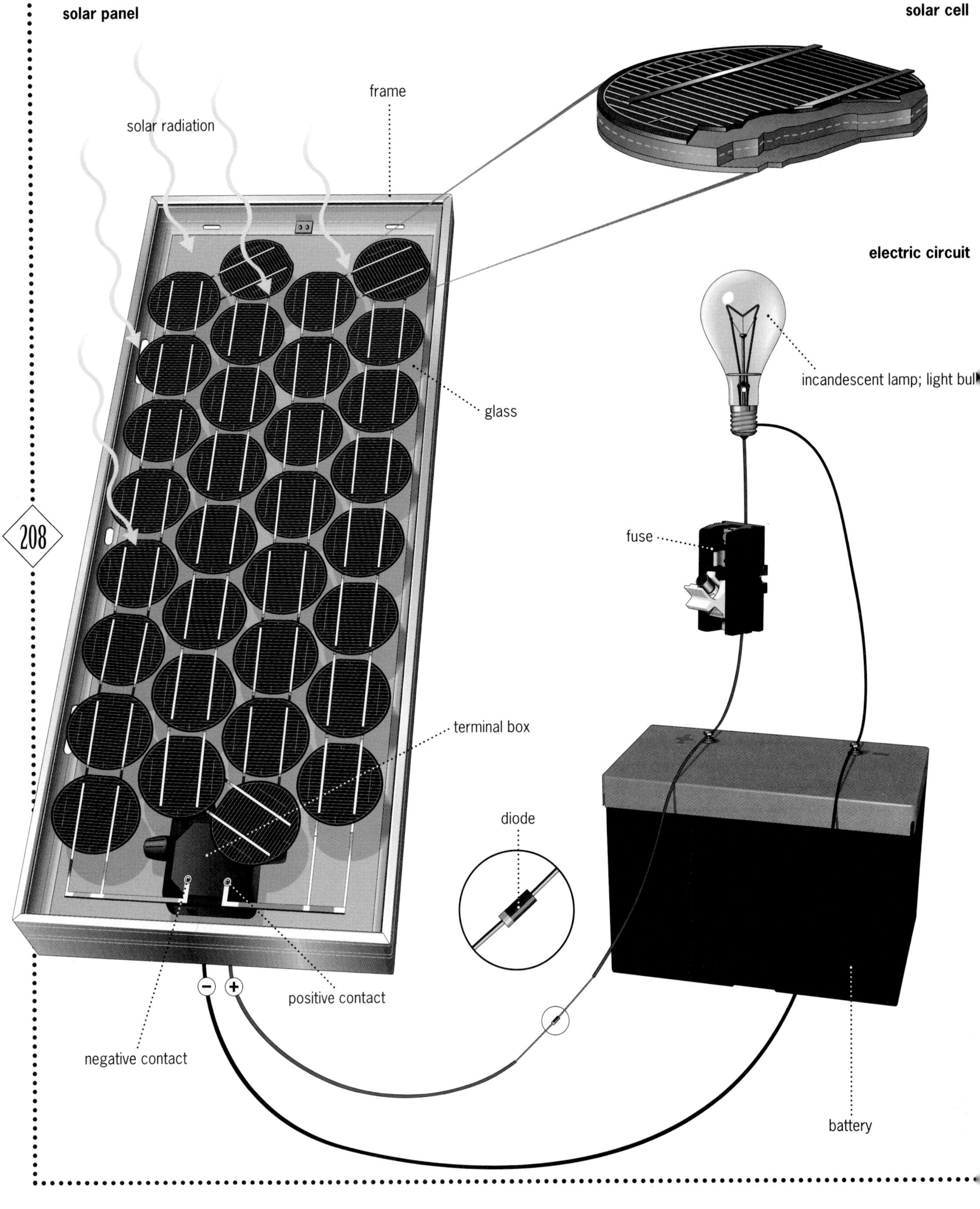

solar panel
solar cell
frame
solar radiation
electric circuit
incandescent lamp; light bul
glass
fuse
terminal box
diode
positive contact
negative contact
battery

WIND ENERGY

horizontal-axis wind turbine

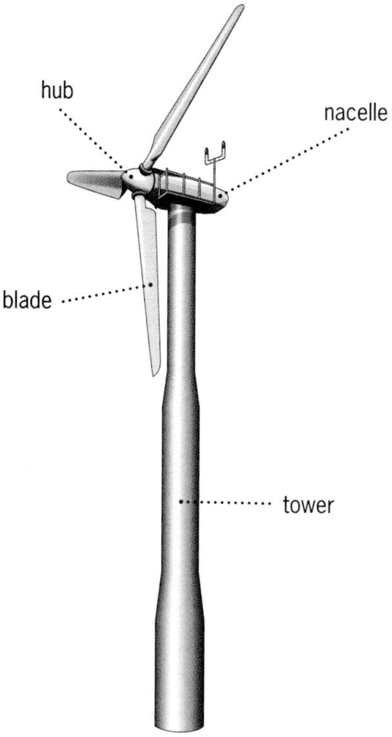
hub
nacelle
blade
tower

vertical-axis wind turbine

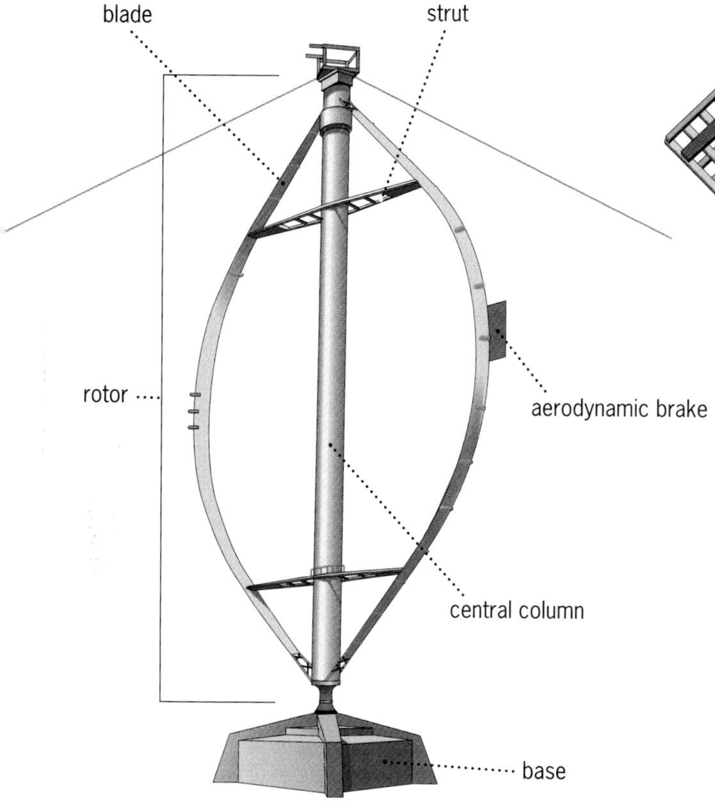
blade
strut
rotor
aerodynamic brake
central column
base

windmill

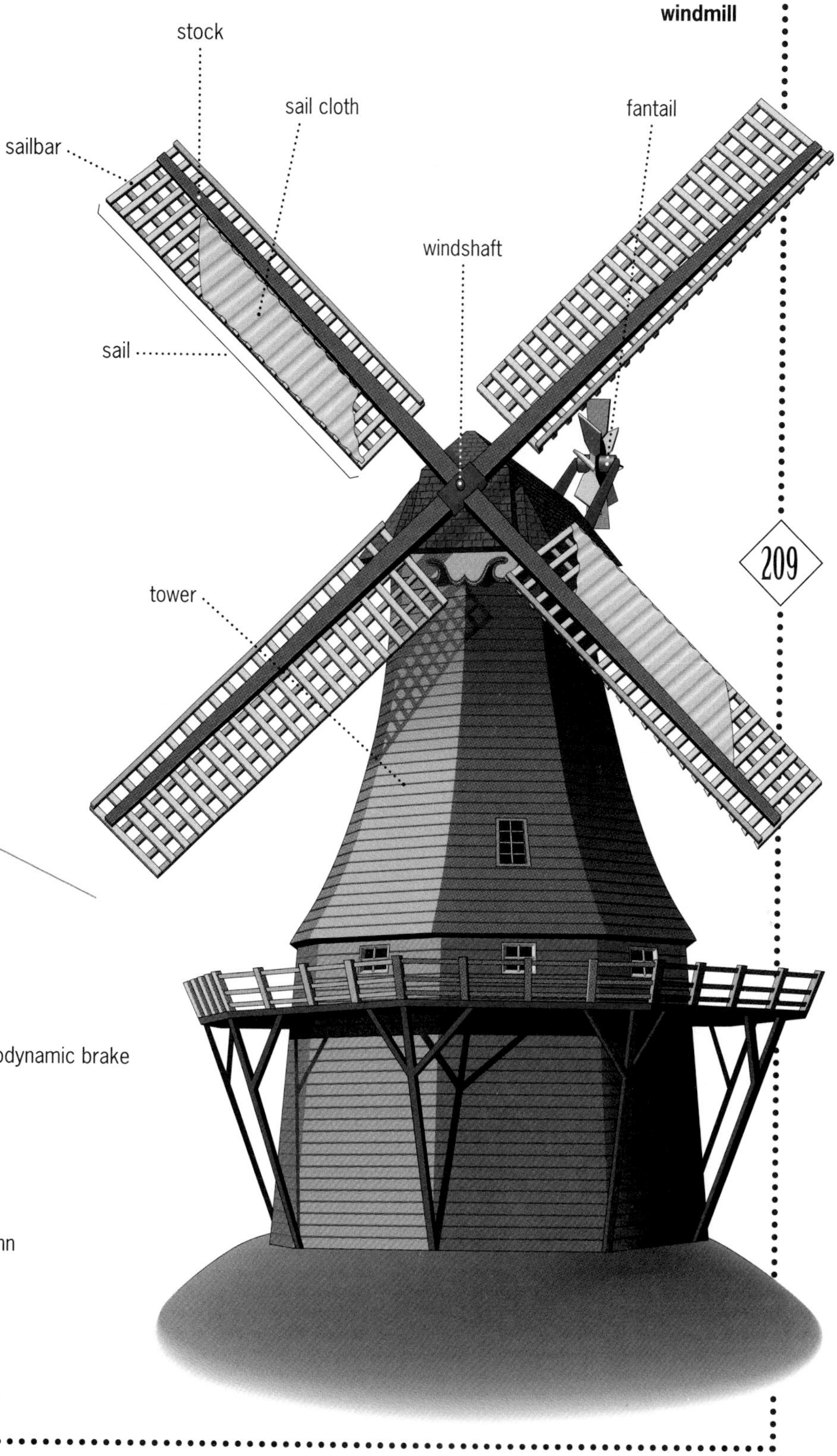
stock
sail cloth
fantail
sailbar
windshaft
sail
tower

FIRE PREVENTION

fire hose

portable fire extinguisher

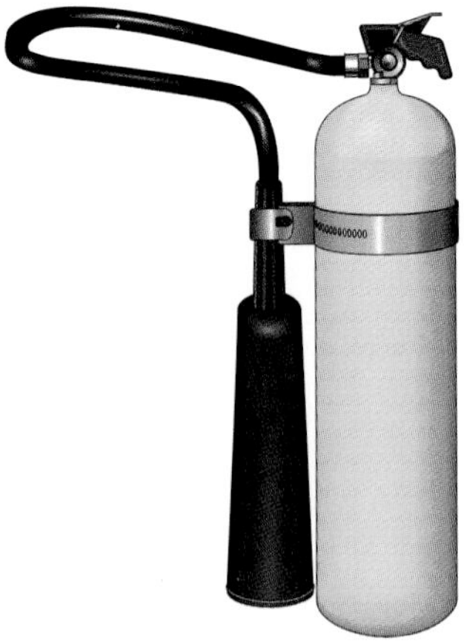

fire hydrant

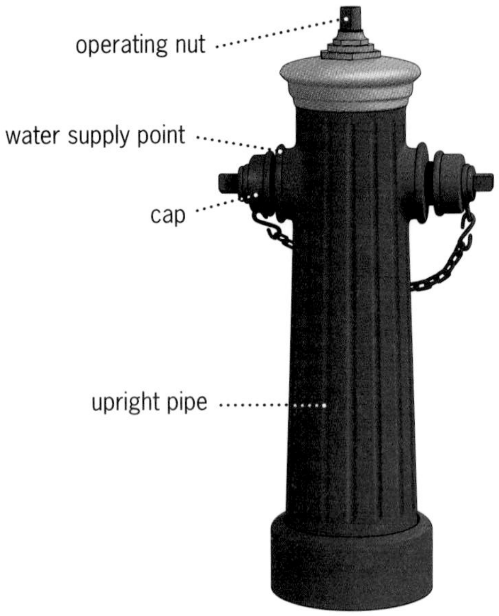
operating nut
water supply point
cap
upright pipe

fire engine

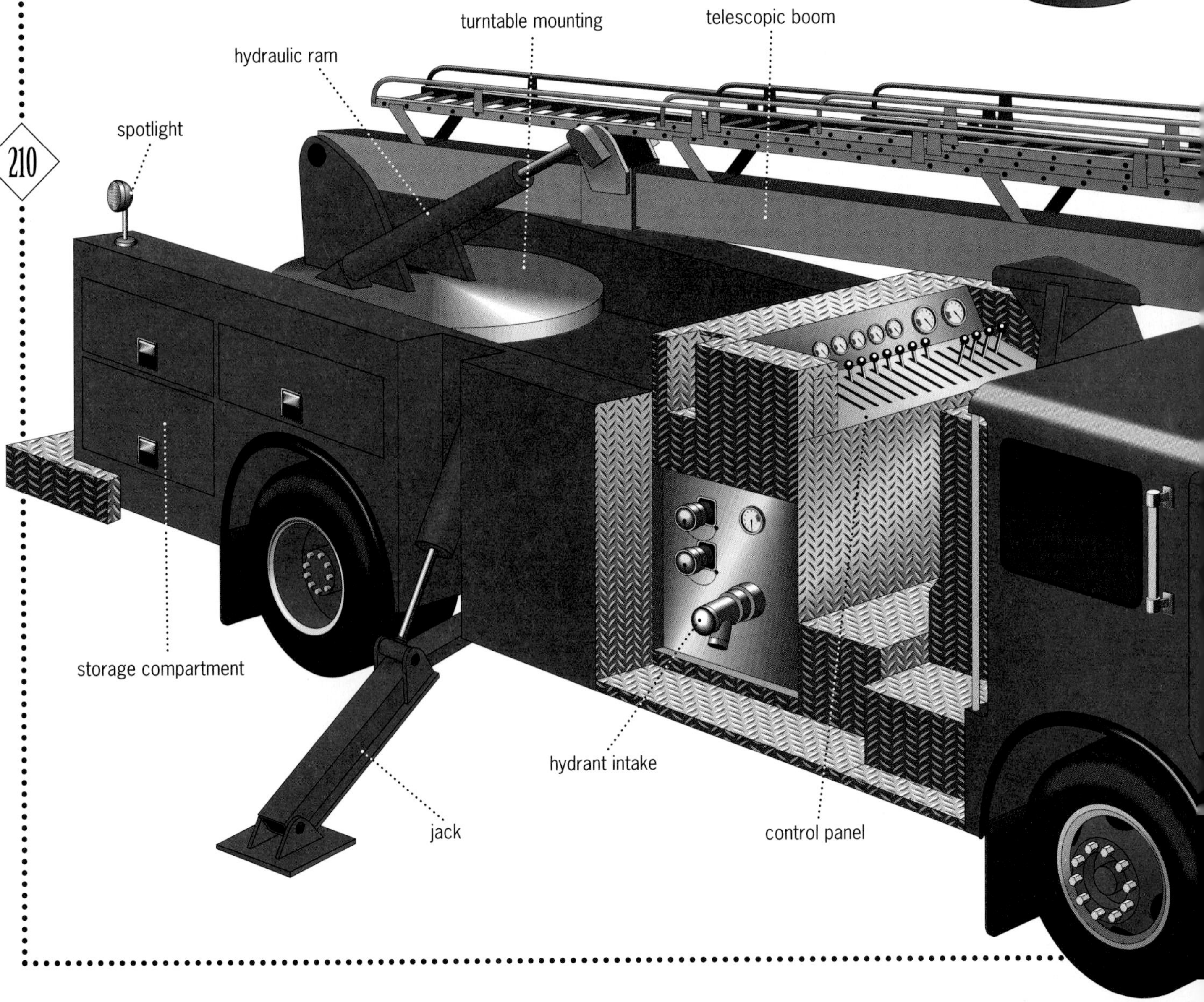
turntable mounting
telescopic boom
hydraulic ram
spotlight
storage compartment
hydrant intake
jack
control panel

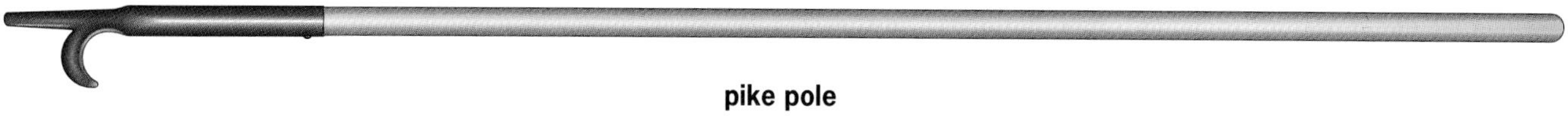

pike pole

fire-fighter

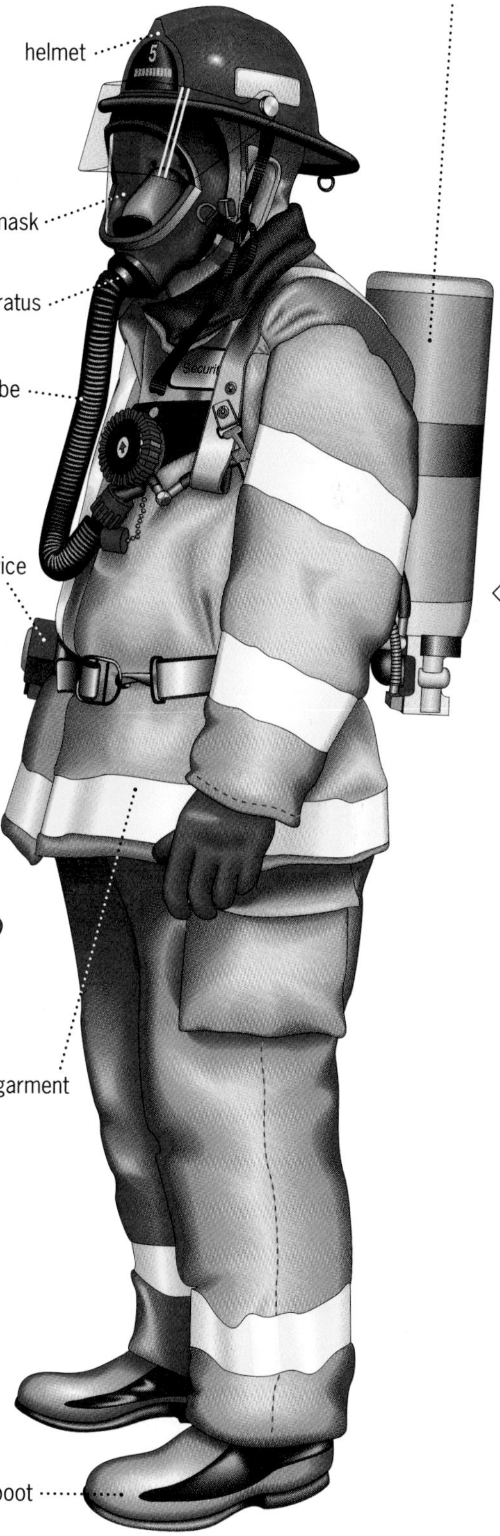
compressed-air cylinder
helmet
full face mask
self-contained breathing apparatus
air-supply tube
warning device
fireproof and waterproof garment
rubber boot

fireman's axe

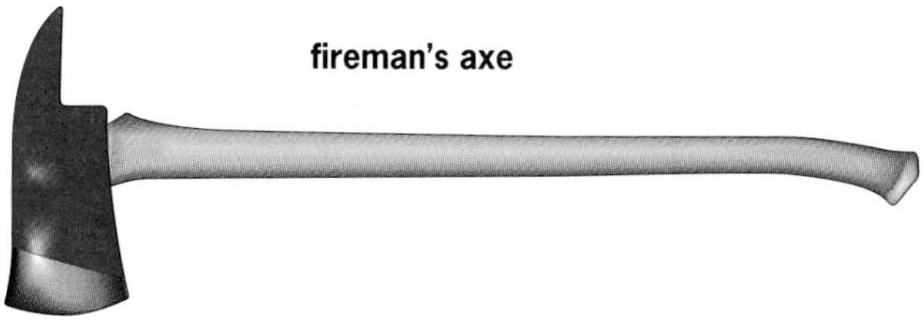

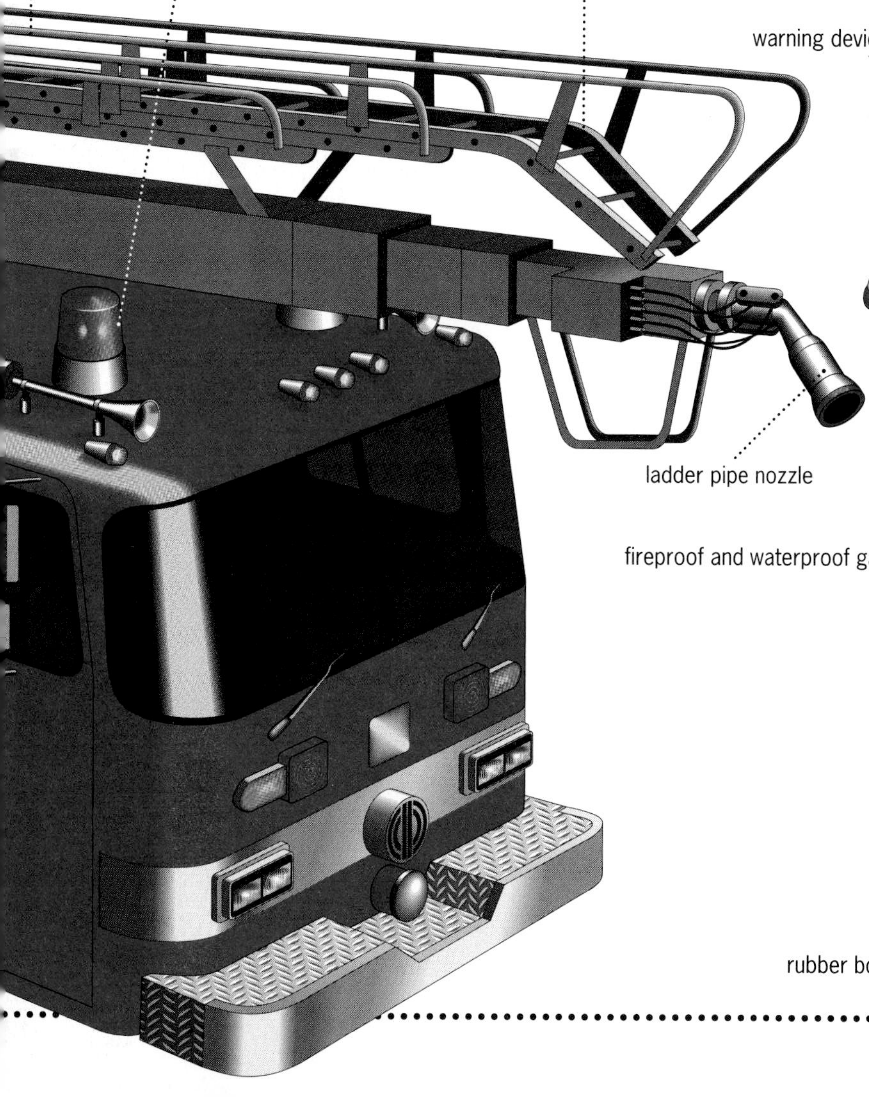
tower ladder
flashing light
top ladder
ladder pipe nozzle

HEAVY VEHICLES

loader

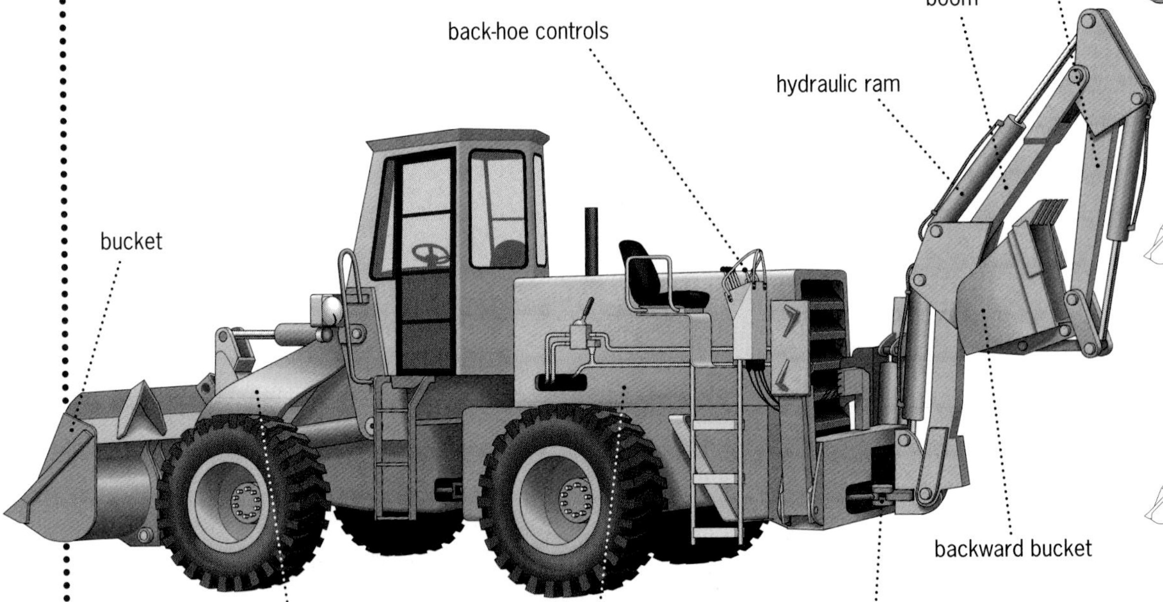
arm
boom
back-hoe controls
hydraulic ram
bucket
backward bucket
lift arm
diesel engine
bucket hinge pin

front-end loader

wheel tractor

back-hoe

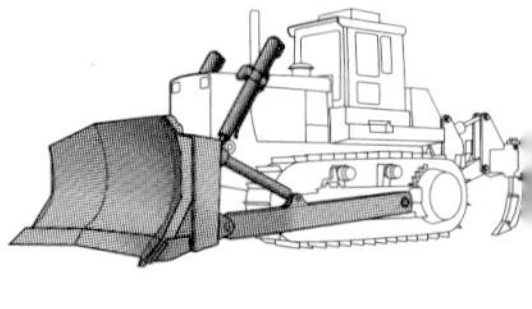

blade

bulldozer

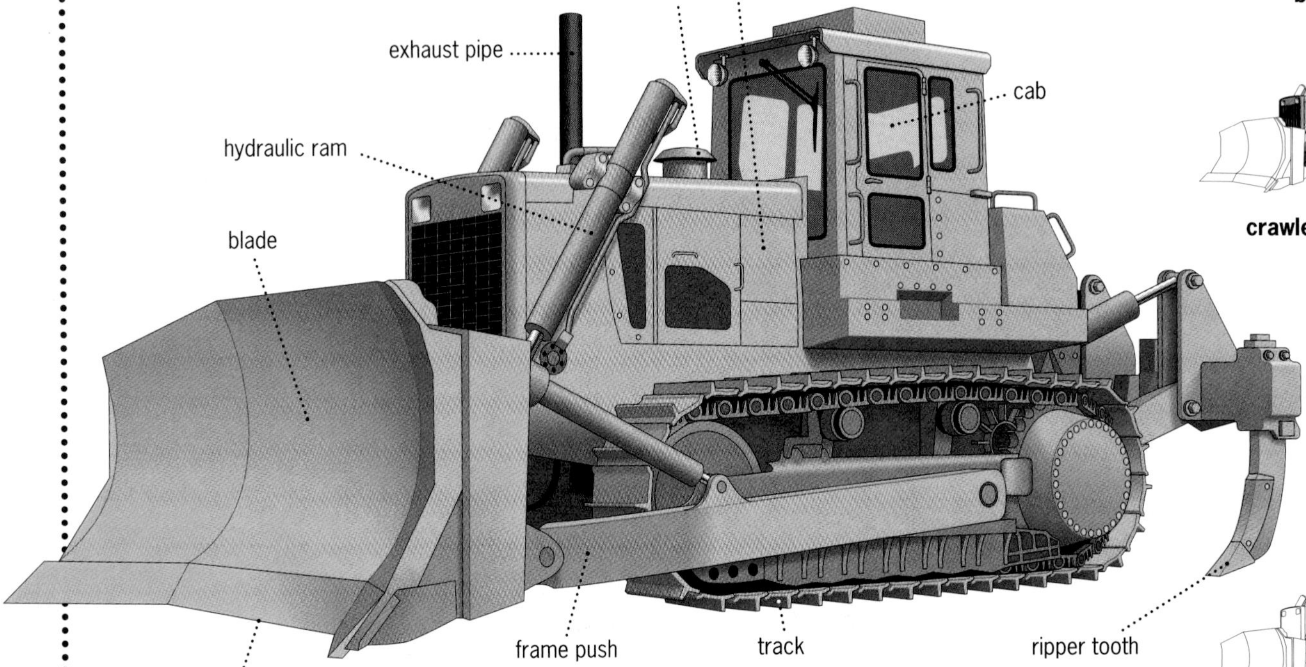
air filter
diesel engine
exhaust pipe
cab
hydraulic ram
blade
frame push
track
ripper tooth
cutting edge

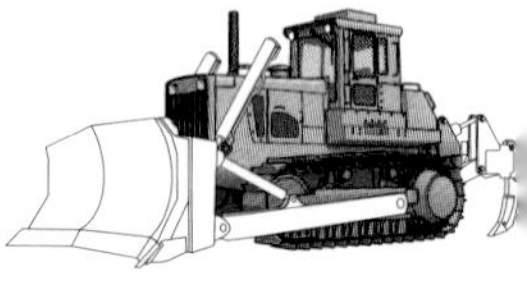

crawler tractor

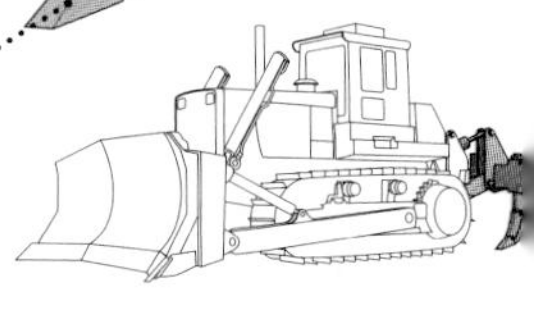

ripper

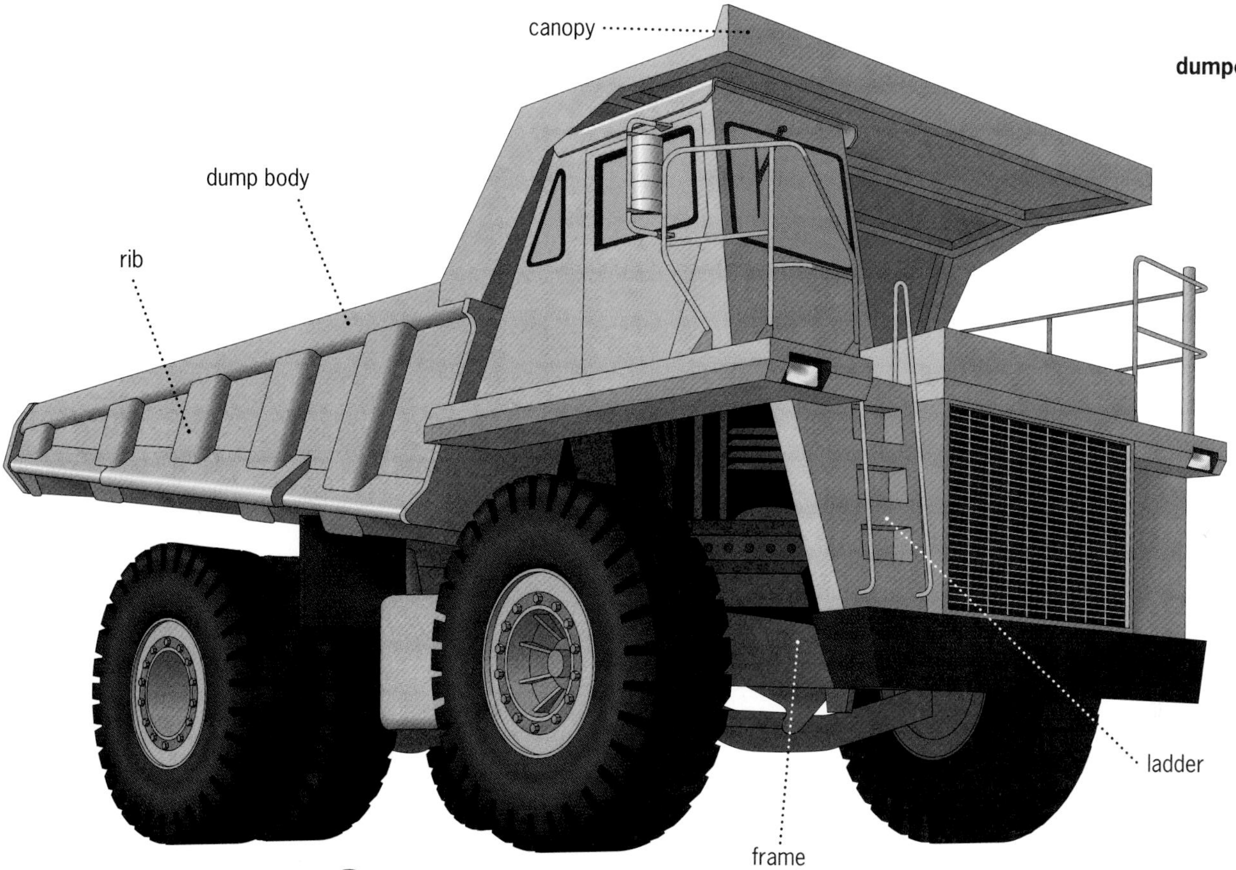
canopy
dumper truck
dump body
rib
ladder
frame

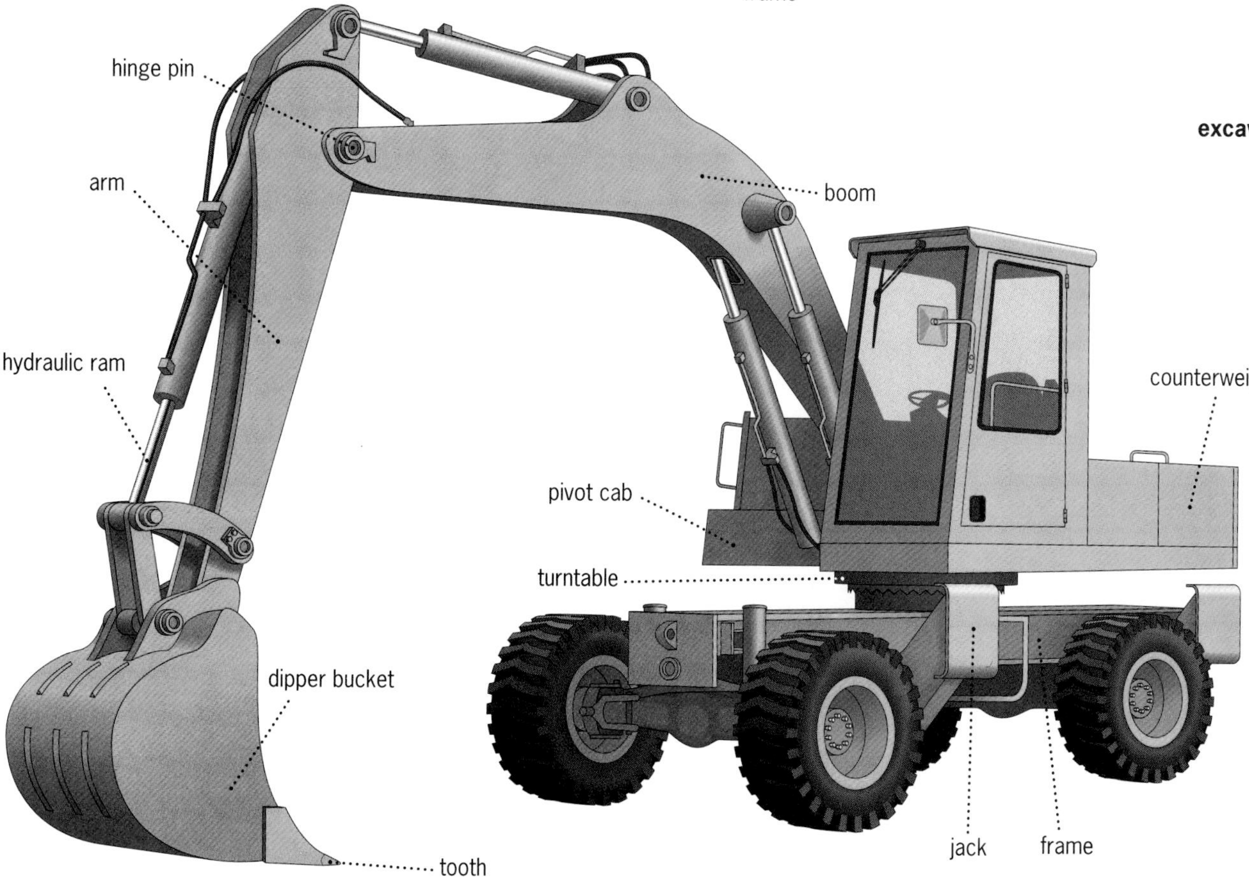
hinge pin
excavator
arm
boom
hydraulic ram
counterweight
pivot cab
turntable
dipper bucket
jack
frame
tooth

HEAVY MACHINERY

tower crane

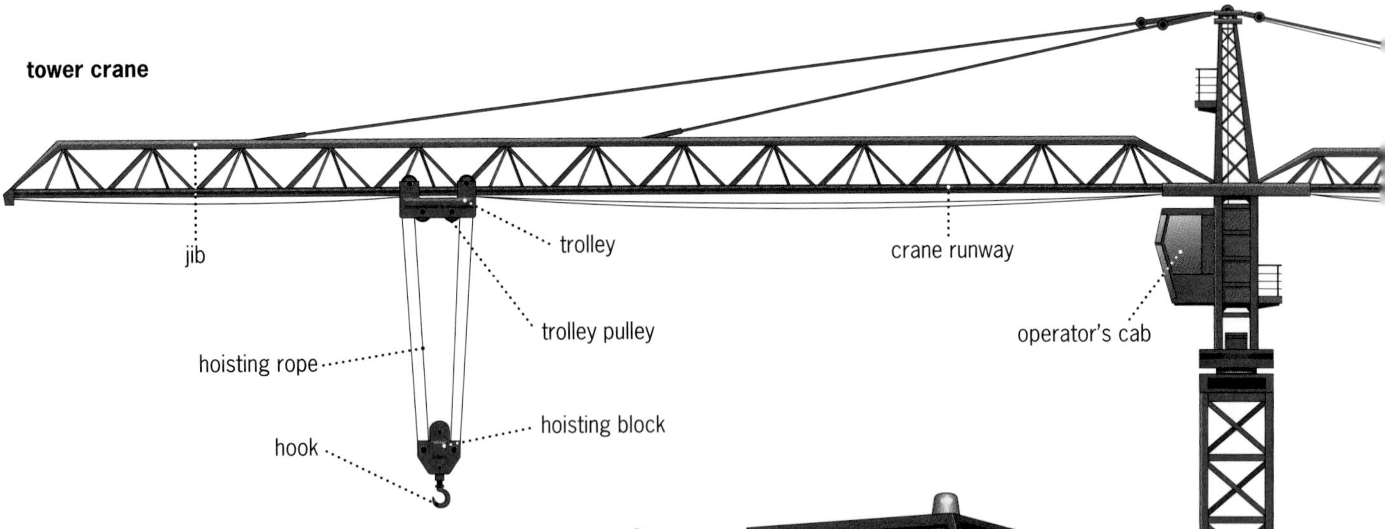
jib
trolley
crane runway
trolley pulley
operator's cab
hoisting rope
hoisting block
hook

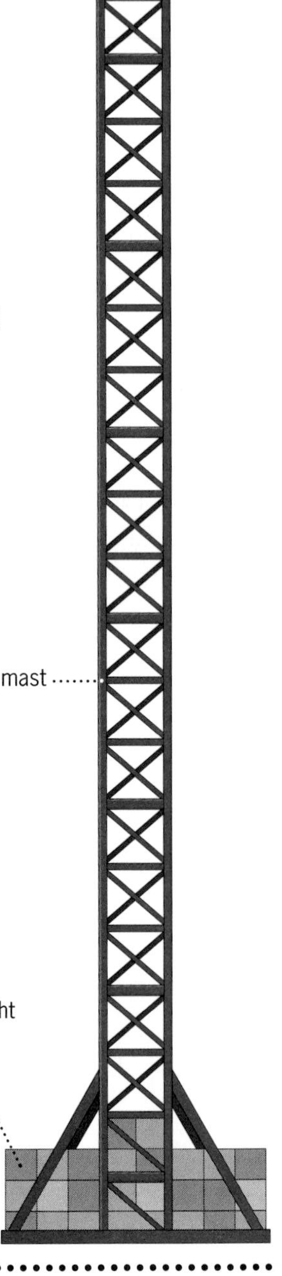
tower mast
counterweight

road sweeper

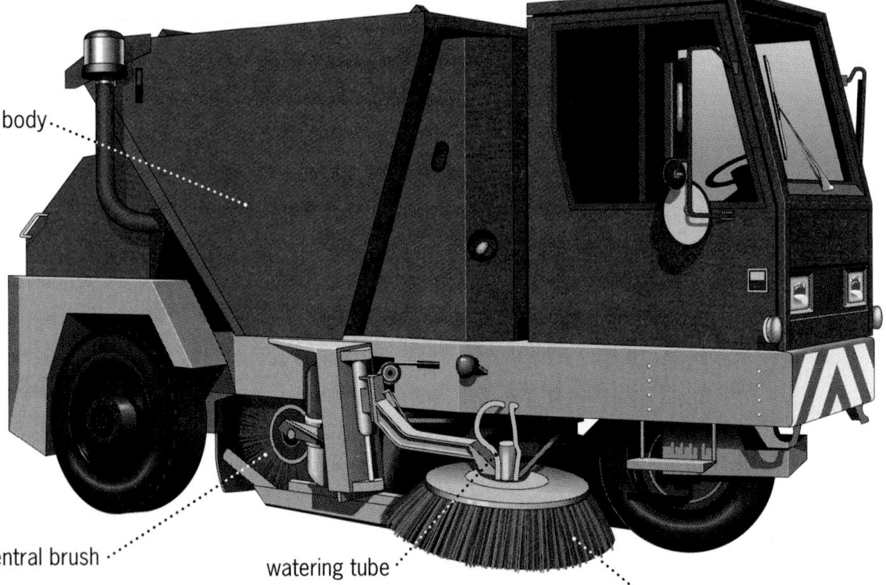
collection body
central brush
watering tube
lateral brush

snowblower

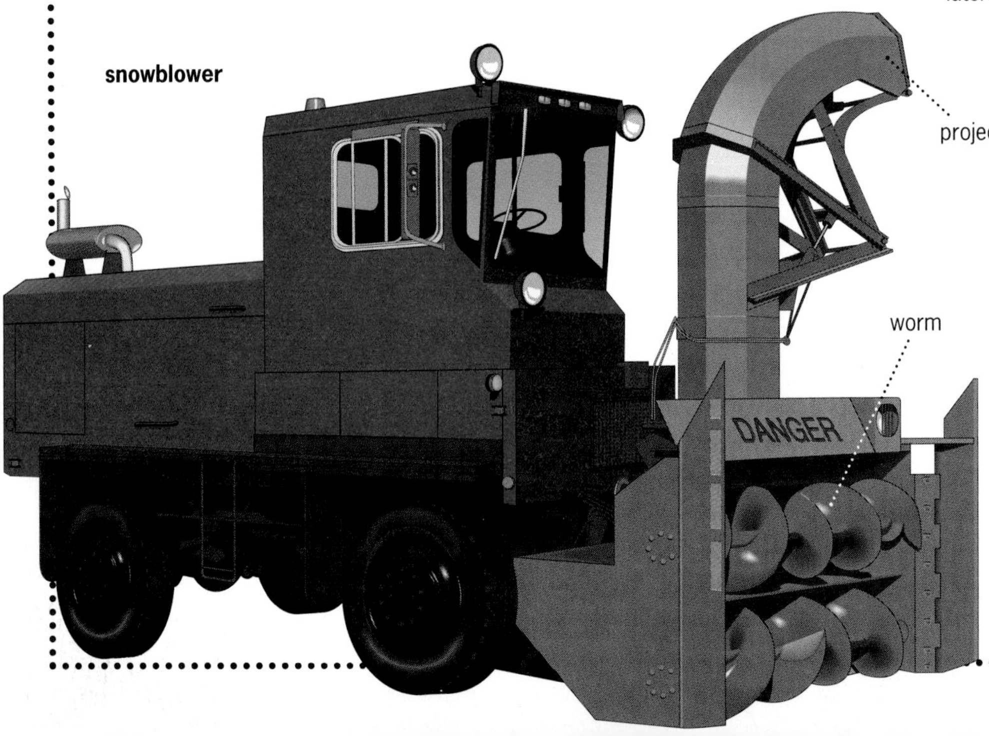
projection device
worm
DANGER

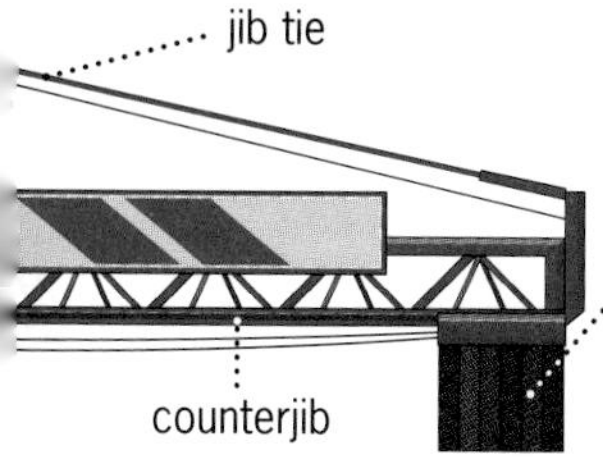
jib tie
counterjib ballast
counterjib

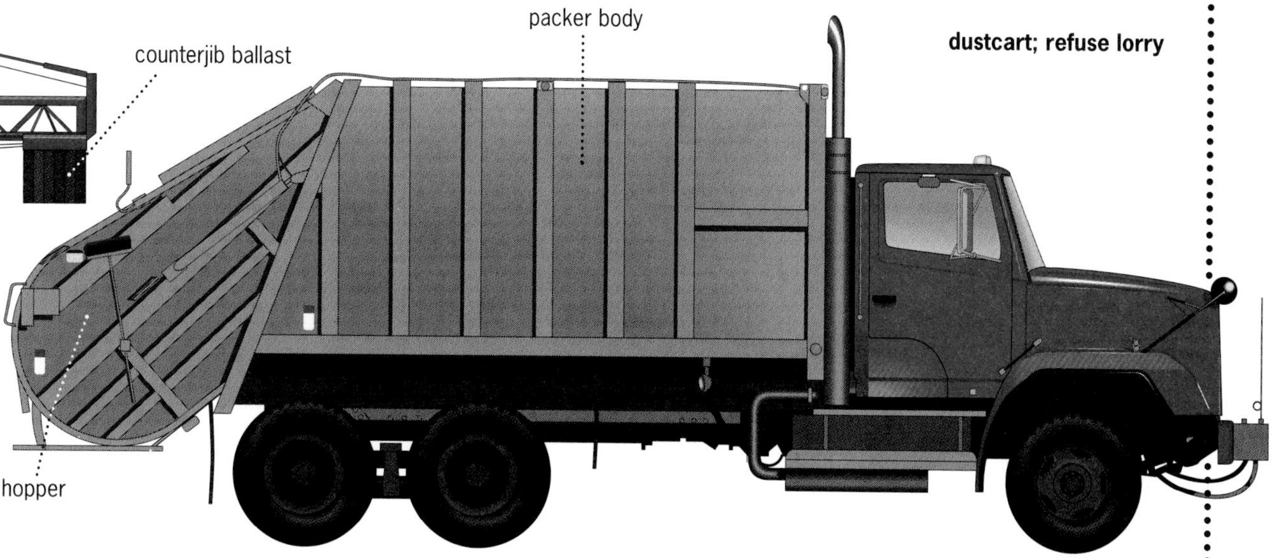
packer body
loading hopper

dustcart; refuse lorry

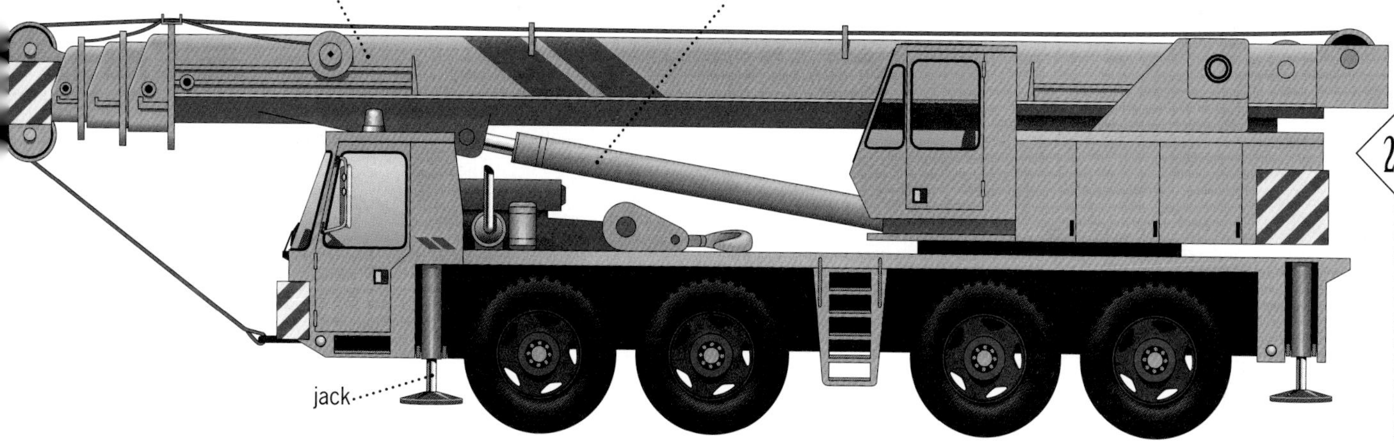
telescopic boom
hydraulic ram
jack

mobile crane

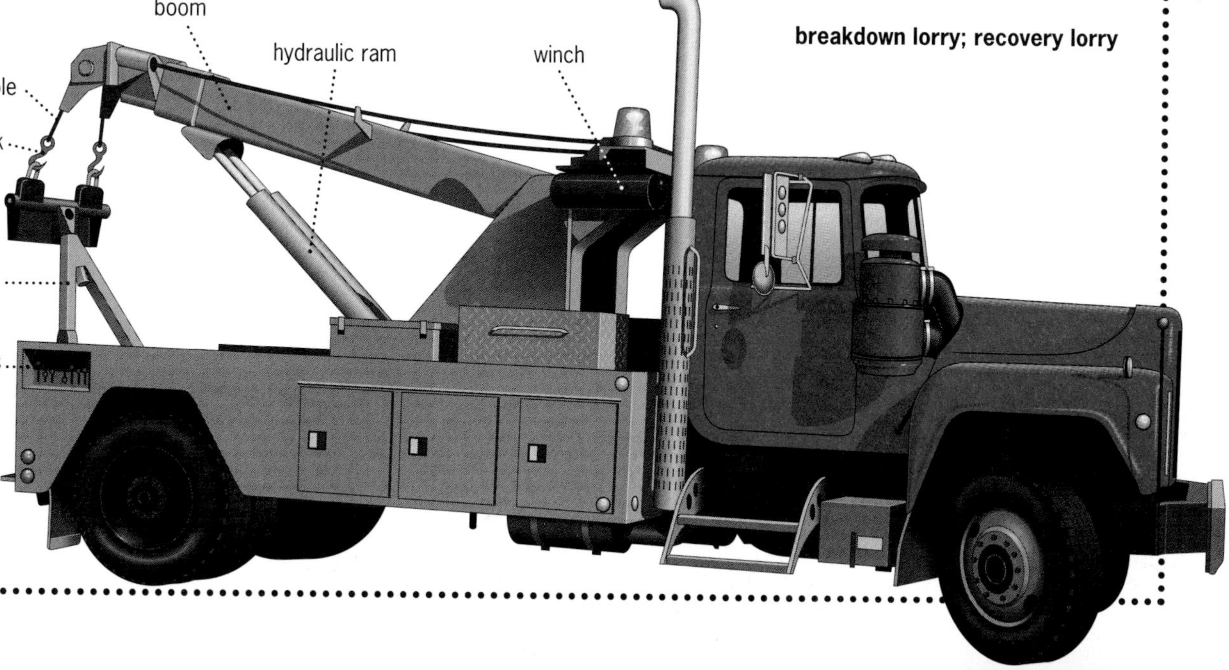
boom
hydraulic ram
winch
cable
hook
towing device
winch controls

breakdown lorry; recovery lorry

COMMON SYMBOLS

women's toilet

men's toilet

access for physically handicapped

hospital

telephone

no smoking

camping (tent)

camping prohibited

stop at intersection

SAFETY SYMBOLS

corrosive

electrical hazard

explosive

flammable

radioactive

poisonous

PROTECTION

eye protection

ear protection

head protection

hand protection

foot protection

respiratory system protection

The terms in **bold type** correspond to an illustration; those in CAPITALS indicate a title.

D

The terms in **bold type** correspond to an illustration; those in CAPITALS indicate a title.

The terms in **bold type** correspond to an illustration; those in CAPITALS indicate a title.

The terms in **bold type** correspond to an illustration; those in CAPITALS indicate a title.

The terms in **bold type** correspond to an illustration; those in CAPITALS indicate a title.

Q

R

S

The terms in **bold type** correspond to an illustration; those in CAPITALS indicate a title.

T

The terms in **bold type** correspond to an illustration; those in CAPITALS indicate a title.

INDEX

U

V

W

X

Y

Z

The terms in **bold type** correspond to an illustration; those in CAPITALS indicate a title.